Third Edition

Introduction to Recreation and Leisure

Tyler Tapps, PhD, CPRP
Northwest Missouri State University

Mary Sara Wells, PhD
University of Utah

Editors

HUMAN KINETICS

Library of Congress Cataloging-in-Publication Data

Names: Tapps, Tyler Nicholas, editor. | Wells, Mary Sara, editor. | Human
    Kinetics (Organization)
Title: Introduction to recreation and leisure / Tyler Tapps, Mary Sara Wells,
    editors.
Description: Third edition. | Champaign, Illinois : Human Kinetics, [2019] |
    Previous edition: 2013. | Includes bibliographical references and index.
Identifiers: LCCN 2017038343 (print) | LCCN 2017041136 (ebook) | ISBN
    1492543136 (e-book) | ISBN 9781492543121 (print)
Subjects: LCSH: Recreation. | Leisure.
Classification: LCC GV14 (print) | LCC GV14 .I68 2018 (ebook) | DDC
    790.1--dc23
LC record available at https://lccn.loc.gov/2017038343

ISBN: 978-1-4925-4312-1 (print)

The web addresses cited in this text were current as of September 2017, unless otherwise noted.

Acquisitions Editor: Gayle Kassing, PhD; **Senior Acquisitions Editor:** Amy N. Tocco; **Senior Developmental Editor:** Melissa Feld; **Managing Editor:** Kirsten E. Keller; **Indexer:** Nan N. Badgett; **Permissions Manager:** Dalene Reeder; **Graphic Designer:** Whitney Milburn; **Cover Designer:** Keri Evans; **Cover Design Associate:** Susan Rothermel Allen; **Photograph (cover):** Getty Images/Juice Images RF/Echo; **Photographs (interior):** © Human Kinetics, unless otherwise noted; **Photo Asset Manager:** Laura Fitch; **Photo Production Manager:** Jason Allen; **Senior Art Manager:** Kelly Hendren; **Illustrations:** © Human Kinetics, unless otherwise noted; **Printer:** Sheridan Books

Printed in the United States of America   10 9 8 7 6 5

The paper in this book is certified under a sustainable forestry program.

Human Kinetics
1607 N. Market Street
Champaign, IL 61820
USA

United States and International
Website: **US.HumanKinetics.com**
Email: info@hkusa.com
Phone: 1-800-747-4457

Canada
Website: **Canada.HumanKinetics.com**
Email: info@hkcanada.com

E6919

Tell us what you think!
Human Kinetics would love to hear what we
can do to improve the customer experience.
Use this QR code to take our brief survey.

Contents

Preface   xi

Worksite Recreation and Health Promotion **239**

Janet M. Bartnik and Jeffrey Ferguson

Recreation in the Armed Forces **246**

Ryan Cane and Diane Blankenship

Chapter 12   Leisure and Recreation Across . . . . .**257** the Life Span

Tyler Tapps and Timothy Baghurst

Chapter 17   Arts and Culture 341
Julie Voelker-Morris

Chapter 18   The Nature of Recreation and Leisure as a Profession. 361
Denise M. Anderson and Tracy L. Mainieri

Chapter 19   International Perspectives on Recreation and Leisure 383

International Perspectives: Sustainability and Ecotourism 384
Richard R. Jurin and Diane Gaede

Recreation and Leisure in Brazil 390
Arianne C. Reis and Alcyane Marinho

Preface

Welcome to recreation and leisure studies. This introductory course textbook provides you with a current view on the foundations of one of the top industries for the 21st century. Recreation and leisure programs serve people 24/7/365 and are part of a global economy. The expectation is that between the years of 2012 and 2022, recreation job growth is expected to be approximately 14 percent, which is about the average for all occupations. These rising opportunities are vital in creating unique and critical experiences for the lives of individuals, families, and communities and can provide you with a challenging, yet rewarding, career path.

This textbook invites you to take an amazing journey as you explore the world of recreation and leisure. Your escorts are 45 professors and professionals in the field from across the globe including the United States, Canada, Europe, Brazil, China, and Nigeria. Their careers and passions mirror the various aspects of this profession. As rising stars, experts, leading thinkers, and icons in the field, the contributing authors serve as your personal guides as you begin your undergraduate studies of this exciting field. Their unique viewpoints provide a foundation for understanding the industry on which your undergraduate studies will build.

Introduction to Recreation and Leisure, Third Edition, showcases a number of authors who are considered eminent and emerging scholars as well as some of the leading professionals in recreation and leisure education, all of whom present underlying theories, concepts, and their practical applications within the various sectors and segments of the recreation and leisure industry. The goal of this textbook is to illustrate the wealth of opportunities within this diverse profession and discuss a number of current issues in the world that impact the field. This third edition delves into themes such as conservation, health and wellness, social equity, and quality of life. These global themes are connected to updated foundational content as they relate to the current directions the field of recreation and leisure is headed. Furthermore, this textbook employs a robust list of ancillaries in order to enhance learning opportunities for the students and instructors who use it in their classes. These should help students to extend their learning from the chapter content into community connections and engagement, thus making them better prepared when they become recreation and leisure professionals.

For students pursuing a career in recreation and leisure or those who are considering the field as a career choice, this book offers vital information that will help in making informed choices. We want to provide you with a big picture of this diverse profession so that in your later studies you can explore specific areas in depth to gain an understanding of recreation and leisure as the following:

- A profession that offers lifetime career satisfaction or perhaps an entry-level start on a career path with many options
- A contemporary industry that provides employment opportunities in a wide variety of fields and associated fields
- A worldwide phenomenon that drives most of the world's economies

ORGANIZATION

Introduction to Recreation and Leisure is divided into three parts. **Part I, Foundations of Recreation and Leisure,** provides the foundation of this industry, including an introduction, history, and philosophical concepts. **Part II, Leisure and Recreation as a Multifaceted Delivery System,** introduces you to various sectors and areas of the field. **Part III, Delivering Recreation and Leisure Services,** presents the different types of programming found in recreation and leisure services. These interest areas include recreational sport; health, wellness, and quality of life; outdoor and adventure recreation; and culture and the arts. This part ends with a chapter that addresses the nature of the profession and what it takes to become a professional and another chapter that provides international perspectives on recreation and leisure.

FEATURES

Several unique and useful features are included in the book.

Learning outcomes. Each chapter lists the many important concepts that you will learn and understand.

Outstanding graduates. Students who have graduated from recreation and leisure programs and gone on to successful careers have been highlighted. They share insights and advice on recreation and leisure as a career.

Glossary. Important terms are printed in boldface in the text, and a glossary is included at the end of the book.

WEB STUDY GUIDE

Students may access the web study guide by following the instructions on the key code page at the front of the book. Students will find chapter summaries, a glossary, on-the-job learning activities, research prompts, and websites to explore more. It has been updated to support today's students' learning through entry-level learning experiences with connections to learning about the field.

INSTRUCTOR RESOURCES

Instructors have access to a full array of ancillary materials supplement the information presented in the textbook. They are available at www.HumanKinetics.com/IntroductionToRecreationandLeisure.

Instructor guide. The instructor guide includes updated chapter overviews, learning outcomes, learning experiences, chapter presentation packages, and a new reading list from current industry resources on the Internet. This update is intended to support today's students and bridge the gap between foundations presented in the book and the changing landscape of the recreation and leisure industry.

Test package. The test package includes a variety of questions: true–false, multiple-choice, and fill-in-the-blank. Instructors can create their own tests.

Chapter quizzes. These ready-made quizzes allow instructors to test students' understanding of the most important chapter concepts.

Presentation package. A Microsoft PowerPoint presentation package covers the major topics and key points from the chapters. Instructors may use the presentation package to supplement their lectures. The presentation package may be adapted to suit each instructor's lecture content and style.

FINAL THOUGHTS

Introduction to Recreation and Leisure, Third Edition, presents a comprehensive view of the multifaceted, expansive field of recreation and leisure. Enjoy learning about recreation and leisure, reading what the principal thinkers and leaders have to say about the field, and meeting outstanding graduates from universities across the United States, Canada, and the world who share their career experiences. Let's enter the world of recreation and leisure.

PART I

Foundations of Recreation and Leisure

CHAPTER 1

Power, Promise, Potential, and Possibilities of Parks, Recreation, and Leisure

Ellen O'Sullivan

SolStock/Getty Images

> " Play for adults is recreation—the renewal of life; for children it is growth—the gaining of life. "
>
> Joseph Lee, father of the American playground movement

LEARNING OUTCOMES

After reading this chapter, you should be able to do the following:

> Describe the role that parks, recreation, and leisure plays in all facets of life for all people
> Define the terms play, recreation, leisure, and flow, and cite subtle differences among the terms
> Recall the four basic benefit categories associated with parks, recreation, and leisure
> Identify ways in which changes in the world influence trends in parks and recreation
> List the unique qualities and opportunities afforded by this professional field

WHAT IF?

What if there were an aspect of life with promise and potential to empower people to grow and thrive; provide communities with facilities and services that enhance quality of life; connect people both locally and globally; preserve and protect our natural, historic, and cultural heritage; and contribute to a prosperous economy? What if there were an aspect of life so central to human existence that people spent more time engaged in it than working or attending school combined? What if there were a category of the economy that accounted for substantial expenditures and appeared to be an ever-growing economic force? What if there were various careers associated with this essential aspect of behavior and major component of the economy that created opportunities for personal growth, professional flexibility, sense of purpose, and resourcefulness for the professionals in that field?

WELCOME TO THE WORLD OF RECREATION AND LEISURE

Welcome to the opportunities, options, pursuits, and possibilities of recreation and leisure. The shortened term for this profession is often cited as either recreation and leisure or parks and recreation, but there are myriad pursuits and passions such as sports, events, tourism, health and wellness, adventure recreation, and environmental preservation and management that can be used with recreation and leisure.

The challenge in learning more about this field as a personal pursuit, a professional career, or a combination of both is to grasp its size and significance. This field is powerful because its activities and pursuits are everywhere, touch the lives of all human beings, and occur 24 hours a day, every day. The potential and promise of parks, recreation, and leisure are challenging for the general public to grasp while at the same time are critical to the well-being of individuals, communities, societies, and the world. The benefits of this field ensure that we have sufficient clean air and water to sustain life, opportunities to live purposeful and pleasurable lives, memories of happy times with friends and family, and options and opportunities for health and well-being throughout our lives.

DEFINITIONS OF PLAY, RECREATION, LEISURE, AND FLOW

Flow is a well-accepted term, whereas *play, recreation,* and *leisure* seem to mean different things to different people and are often used interchangeably with little regard for the subtle differences between them. Even within the field of parks, recreation, and leisure, there are no agreed-on definitions for these terms. As far back as early Greece, Aristotle spoke of his philosophy related to these terms, and those discussions continue as psychologists, sociologists, philosophers, and others discuss the true definitions and specific characteristics of each. There are books devoted entirely to these four topics. What follows are definitions and characteristics of these terms that convey their essence but do not attempt to incorporate all the available literature.

Play

Definitions for **play** date back to previous centuries. These descriptions cite a number of related purposes including biological, physical, cognitive, and social development of children. Theories abound around play; self-expression, surplus energy, arousal, and recapitulation are some of the desired outcomes cited.

By the late 20th century, people understood that a better and more comprehensive definition of play included a set of circumstances rather than one specific definition. A true play experience must be voluntary, spontaneous, intrinsically rewarding, and absorbing.

At the beginning of the 21st century, there was a renewed interest in and attention focused on play and the effect of the lack of unstructured play on the development of children. Contemporary psychologists have addressed the critical need for children to play, and parents and professionals in the field have been listening. Health officials have suggested that growing levels of childhood obesity and the epidemic of adult-onset diabetes could be related to lack of play in contemporary life.

Recreation

Another relevant term is **recreation**. Aren't play and recreation the same thing? Not if we adhere to the more accepted definitions of the two terms. It is widely accepted that recreation refers to activity, as in participation in recreation or a recreation activity. Although participation in a recreation activity can be play, not all recreation is play. A recreation activity that has a structured time frame or lacks true voluntary participation may or may not be play. For example, if someone belongs to a team with a set time and rules for practice, that is more likely to be recreation than play, as would a drop-in craft workshop where the focus is on completing a specific project.

Leisure

The term **leisure** has myriad meanings, and the exact meaning remains a topic of discussion. The Greeks believed that people worked to have leisure, and they viewed leisure as self-development. Leisure is often referred to as unobligated time—time that is not devoted to work or life-sustaining activities. Still others refer to leisure as a state of being in which the mind feels free and unencumbered. Another view of leisure is that it is an antidote to working life.

Flow

For much of his academic career, Mihaly Csikszentmihalyi studied flow. **Flow** is a state of being in which a person is fully engaged in an activity that results in feelings of energy, focus, and success. Engagement in such an activity often turns out to be an optimal life experience for the person. Csikszentmihalyi (1991) considered flow to be the optimal human experience.

Through his studies, Csikszentmihalyi identified eight conditions needed to reach flow. For flow to occur, the undertaking must

1. require skill,
2. merge action and awareness,
3. provide clear goals and feedback,
4. require concentration and absorption of attention,
5. provide an individual with personal control over the act,
6. create a loss of self-consciousness,
7. cause a person to lose all track of time, and
8. provide intrinsic rewards.

Why Do These Differences Matter?

Although the variations among the definitions of these terms might seem relatively small or inconsequential, that assessment is not accurate. A person working in the field of parks and recreation will be called on to implement many activities and provide various experiences for people. At that point, the variations between these terms become clearer. An organized soccer league for 10- and 11-year-olds is definitely recreation, but it is not likely to be a play experience. A soccer league is structured, which lends itself to being recreation, while a small group of children just throwing and kicking would be considered play. Even among adults, differences between the terms can be recognized. Adults may have time available for leisure, but they don't necessarily pursue recreation, an organized activity during that time. Since people often use similar words interchangeably such as play and recreation, there are differences between other terms as well. Consider the differences between a tourist and a traveler: Tourists are generally interested in going to new places, whereas travelers most often seek to become immersed in a culture through travel.

RECREATION AND LEISURE: EVERYWHERE, EVERYONE, ALL THE TIME

Well-worn soccer balls skirt the streets of villages around the world whether the villages are wracked with strife or disaster or have manicured fields and youth and adult teams in matching uniforms. The five rings of the Olympic Games burn brightly every four years as tens of thousands of athletes representing hundreds of countries from around the world gather in the spirit of competition and unity. Street merchants in Bangkok play a checkers-like board game that is hastily constructed of cardboard and discarded bottle caps. Visitors from around the world marvel at the migration of wildlife across the plains of the Serengeti, and others admire the exceptional beauty and unique geological features of Gros Morne National Park in Newfoundland. People travel great distances to snorkel in Belize, fish in New Zealand, explore the Louvre, or observe the changing of the guard in Ottawa or at the Tomb of the Unknown Soldier in Washington, DC. Historic sites and natural areas around the world are preserved and protected so people can engage firsthand in natural, cultural, or historic awareness and appreciation.

It's Everywhere

Parks, recreation, and leisure is everywhere—all the places and spaces in which people gather to play, enjoy, and relax. It is in the far reaches of the Sahara, the crowded seashores of California, the Broadway theaters and museums of New York City, the Hell's Gate Airtram, and the Classic Chinese Garden of Vancouver. Leisure pursuits take place in cities and towns, small villages, the countryside, and mega-urban centers. Leisure experiences occur inside buildings and in outdoor spaces. The array of places is extensive and includes auditoriums, zoos, churches, and casinos. There are health clubs and spas located in airports, rock-climbing walls in retail establishments, and play areas at some fast-food restaurants and retail stores.

Another dimension of the everywhere quality of parks and recreation is illustrated in the fact that all types of organizations and businesses provide parks, recreation, and leisure services. The delivery of services is not limited to only one type of organization. For example, one golf course might be under the governance of a city or state, another similar course might be a private country club for members only, and a third course might be managed by a corporation. Organizations that offer adventure pursuits can run the gamut from local nonprofits, such as a YMCA, that offer outdoor leadership training to travel companies that design and offer adventure experiences around the globe.

It's for Everyone

Consider the ways that parks, recreation, and leisure touches the lives of people of all ages, life stages, cultures, social classes, and genders. Think about personal experiences or observations, and identify the people who participate in a recreation activity or spend time in a natural setting. These might include the following:

- College students playing coed volleyball in the school's intramural league
- A 10-year-old taking beginning drawing lessons at the community center
- A parent and toddler enrolled in a movement class at the local YMCA
- Friends spending time together at a day spa
- Families picnicking while enjoying an outdoor band concert
- A 12-year-old going away to camp for the first time
- People playing pickup basketball at the local park
- An adolescent testing self-sufficiency on an Outward Bound trip
- Grandparents taking grandchildren on a trip to the Grand Canyon
- A teen group teaching retirees how to surf the net
- A stressed-out adult watching the sunset

Recreation can take place indoors or outdoors, at home or in a park, and at any time of day.

- Employees attending the annual company outing to a theme park
- Special Olympics athletes crossing the finish line with elation that brings smiles to the faces of participants and spectators alike
- The over-60 softball team exhibiting a desire to win similar to that of the youth soccer league players
- Fledgling and gifted artists displaying work in the same community art show

An adage often used by parks and recreation professionals employed in the community sector is that parks and recreation takes people "from the cradle to the grave." Although that is not the most appealing description, it does reinforce the presence of parks and recreation in everyone's lives.

All the Time

Although the pursuits of open space, physical activity, and social outings happen all the time (any month of the year, any day of the week, and throughout all the life stages of human existence), some recreation activities are associated mainly with the summer or the winter, and holidays sometimes serve as an impetus. For example, the new year and its emphasis on resolutions motivates people to become more physically active or to seek out new experiences. Independence Day celebrations are commonly accompanied by picnics, concerts, fireworks, trips, and other outings, and Halloween brings out the childlike spirit in young and old alike with parties and parades.

The characteristics of different seasons provide opportunities for year-round activity. The first thaw finds people tending lawns and starting gardens. Summer draws people to mountains, lakes, streams, or seashores. Winter gives way to skiing, skating, curling, and snowboarding. People's passions for certain activities have influenced the all-the-time approach to parks and recreation. It used to be that tennis and soccer could only be played in warm weather, and ice-skating and hockey required cold weather. Indoor facilities, lit playing fields, and trails expand the opportunities to engage in parks and recreation services.

People also pursue recreation at all hours of the day. Ski areas that open at first light give would-be lift-ticket purchasers the chance to check out snow conditions. Health clubs that open at 4:30 a.m. enable early risers to work out before heading to work. Heavily industrialized communities offer adult leagues and activities to accommodate the traditional three shifts of factory work. The city of Las Vegas, with its "Beyond the Neon" slogan, offers unusual times for programs and activities because many residents work shifts in the casinos that operate around the clock. YMCAs and community centers offer sleepovers that provide not only fun and excitement for children but also leisure time for parents. Midnight basketball facilitates recreation participation late at night.

Recreation and leisure also occur throughout the life cycle. Play is essential for children, and from infancy and through adolescence they acquire important life skills through recreation and leisure activities and experiences. The peekaboo games so popular with babies and the duck, duck, goose game so common in early childhood teach important social connections and interactions. At the other end of the spectrum, recreation provides stress reduction for overworked adults and social support for older people who live alone.

Recreation and Leisure Takes Up One-Third of Our Time

People sometimes discount the role and the importance of unobligated, discretionary time and the role it plays in quality of life. They focus on attending school, getting a good night's sleep, and going to work, but those activities don't take up all of their time.

If people living in industrialized nations sleep between six and eight hours every day and work or go to school for another eight hours a day during the week, how much unobligated time do they have? Although the number of hours consumed by sleep, work, and the requirements of daily living, such as housework, commuting, and so on, vary from person to person, one thing is certain: Unobligated time accounts for well over one-third of most people's lives. To see how this is true, consider the following:

- **Life span.** People born today in the United States or Canada can expect to live to approximately 80 years, and school attendance and work do not occur during all of those years.
- **Sleep.** Approximately one-third, or eight hours, of every day is spent sleeping.

- **Play.** Children from birth to 4 years old spend a minimum of six hours per day exploring, learning, and growing through play.
- **School.** The amount of time children and young adults spend in school varies based upon whether they pursue education beyond secondary school. The amount of time remaining for leisure is likely different based upon individual conditions. A sixth grader with three hours of homework every night probably doesn't get a full eight hours of leisure time just as a community college student working to pay for college expenses would not have the eight hours per day either.
- **Work.** Most people work full time for 40 hours per week for 30 to 50 years. Many people have at least two weeks of vacation per year and don't work on select holidays.
- **Third age.** Retirement, or third age, typically lasts at least five years and can be longer depending on longevity. Nearly 30 percent of people who have already reached the age of 65 (or will in the near future) will likely live even longer than 80 years. This suggests that there will be many years that are unencumbered by schooling and full-time employment.

Play around with the years and hours cited in the previous list to see how much time is available after you account for sleeping, eating, schooling, and working. The unobligated time remaining might surprise you.

Beyond Everywhere and Everyone

Although parks, recreation, and leisure facilities and services are everywhere and are available to everyone most of the time, their presence alone isn't enough to prove their value to individuals, families, work groups, neighborhoods, communities, and society. Just being everywhere all the time is not necessarily a valuable or positive attribute. For example, cable television operates 24 hours a day, 365 days a year, but that does not mean that the programs or offerings are positive or of value or interest to the viewer. We need to explore the depth of values and benefits that lie beneath the surface of parks and recreation. Consider the following values of parks and recreation to different individuals:

OUTSTANDING GRADUATE

Background Information

Name: Sarah Martsolf-Brooks

Education: MS in parks, recreation, and tourism from the University of Utah

Credentials: AFO

Awards: Colorado Starburst Award (2016) for her Palisade Bike Skills Park

Affiliations: National Recreation and Park Association (NRPA), Colorado Parks and Recreation Association (CPRA)

Career Information

Position: Palisade Parks and Recreation (Town of Palisade, Colorado)

Organization: Upon completing my master's degree at the University of Utah, I was hired by the town of Palisade in Colorado as the recreation director. Palisade is a small agricultural community of 3,000 people, known for abundant peach orchards, charming wineries, and plenty of outdoor recreation. Palisade also plays host to several special events, which draw in more than 40,000 tourists throughout the year. Town employees often find themselves navigating multiple jobs, with only 30 full-time employees spread out over five departments. The recreation department consists of one full-time employee, three seasonal college interns, and specialty instructors who are hired on as contractors.

Job description: Working in Palisade was most attractive because it gave me the opportunity to build a new recreation department from the ground up. The first programs I started in 2011 included basic fitness classes, DIY activities, family game nights, and outdoor activities such as day trips and hikes. My job is rarely the same from day to day, with job duties that include marketing, program and event planning, program facilitation, grant writing, park projects, supervising interns, aquatics, attending outreach committees, merchandising for events, and coordinating volunteers. What I like most are leading outdoor adventures, bringing my dogs to work, watching new friendships grow, planning park projects, and coaching the summer swim team. However, with limited staff time, it is difficult to expand program offerings without taking away from already-successful programs.

> *When given the choice to take a shorter path or one less traveled, the one less traveled may pose more challenges, but the views from the top are spectacular.*

Career path: I got my start in parks and recreation as a lifeguard with the City of Fruita. Soon after, I progressed into pool management, worked on special events, and taught fitness classes. After completing a bachelor's degree in sports and exercise science, I worked as a personal trainer and coached rugby. I also have experience in campus recreation from both Northern Colorado and the University of Utah.

Advice for Undergraduates

The subject field of public parks and recreation offers a rewarding career because there are many opportunities to make an impact; through trails and open spaces, people of all economic levels can be encouraged to stay active, children can be inspired to become stewards of the environment through after-school programs, and older adults can challenge age stereotypes through outdoor adventure. My advice to students is to search for jobs of interest, not pick based on salary range; find something that you will love getting out of bed for each day—a career that will offer challenges and opportunities to achieve new goals.

- A university student might choose to join the intramural coed volleyball team to be physically active, hang out with friends, meet new people, or have a change of pace from classes and study time (or a combination of these).

- A 12-year-old might look forward to attending a residential camp for one month to acquire new skills, practice being independent, make new friends, or exhibit self-reliance.

- A single mother with a very long day ahead of her might rise at 5:30 a.m. to sit with a cup of tea and watch the sun rise to help her relax, reflect, and regroup before the nonstop demands of her day.

The values and benefits that people derive from the park setting, recreation activity, or leisure experience imbue parks and recreation with its inherent value. The unusual list of questions titled "Guess

Who I Am" (figure 1.1) from an issue of *Parks & Recreation* can serve as a springboard for the various ways parks and recreation can be viewed and the diverse roles it can play (Corwin, 2001).

VALUES AND BENEFITS OF RECREATION AND LEISURE

Developing a list of the benefits that can be attributed to state and provincial parks, community centers, historic sites, and fitness clubs, just to cite a few options within the parks and recreation family, can be cumbersome. A more organized way to consider the benefits is to categorize them into one of the following three types identified by Bev Driver (1998), an early proponent of this approach:

1. **Improved condition.** If a human, natural, or economic factor is not functioning at full capacity or is functioning in a deleterious manner, the benefit of recreation is to ameliorate this condition.

2. **Prevention of a worse condition.** Not every instance of poor performance or threatening condition can be improved; in this case, the value of parks and recreation would be to stem further deterioration of a human, natural, or economic condition.

GUESS WHO I AM

1. I keep you in good health and prevent you from heart disease, but I'm not a doctor or cardiologist.
2. I host parties and events of all sizes, but I'm not a meeting planner.
3. I put a smile on your face, but I'm not a dentist or orthodontist.
4. I often raise lots of money for charity, but I'm not a professional fund-raiser.
5. I provide an outstanding forum for you to learn about many things, but I'm not a teacher or professor.
6. I have often introduced couples who meet and begin long-term relationships, but I'm not a matchmaker.
7. I often bring music to your ears, but I'm not a musician or singer.
8. I have lots of friends in the animal world, but I'm not a veterinarian.
9. I have tons of friends in the insect world, but I'm not an entomologist.
10. I am often surrounded by birds of many types, but I'm not an ornithologist.
11. I enjoy the company of trees and shrubs, but I'm not a nursery manager.
12. I am very photogenic, but I'm not a fashion model.
13. My brethren and I have been in many movies, but I'm not a movie star.
14. I'm often on your local television news, but I'm not a news anchor.
15. I often appear in your local newspaper, but I'm not a reporter or photographer.
16. I work around lots of sneakers, but I'm not an athletic shoe salesperson.
17. I'm a good friend to many of you on the Fourth of July, but I'm not a fireworks technician.
18. I make the value of your house as great as possible, but I'm not a real estate agent.
19. I often entertain children, but I'm not a babysitter.
20. I often prevent crime, but I'm not a police officer.

OK, that's 20 clues. Can you guess who I am?

The answer, of course, is parks and recreation.

Figure 1.1 This list of questions illustrates the diversity of parks and recreation.

Reprinted courtesy of *Parks & Recreation*, National Recreation and Park Association.

3. **Realization of a psychological experience.** This category was added when it became apparent that gains could be made in internal and less tangible ways, such as through awareness, appreciation, and sense of self. This category represents the leisure pursuits that people select for the intrinsic values they gain through the experience. Stress reduction, sense of control, and spirituality are examples of these benefits.

Values and benefits can be further divided into four categories: individual and personal, social and community, environmental, and economic. These categories have been widely accepted since they were first introduced by Canadian parks and recreation professionals and later adopted by the National Recreation and Park Association. The National Recreation and Park Association (NRPA) recently conducted research to ascertain how the general public perceives the benefits of parks and recreation. As a result, the NRPA identified the three pillars of parks and recreation: health and wellness, conservation, and social equity. These pillars help shape the service delivery and help more people understand the roles and benefits of public parks and recreation.

Individual and Personal Benefits of Parks and Recreation

This category encompasses the many different ways a person's life can be enriched, enhanced, or even extended through various leisure pursuits. The various individual benefits and the outcomes associated with these benefits are extraordinary, as is the potential impact they have on one's life (see figure 1.2).

INDIVIDUAL AND PERSONAL BENEFITS OF PARKS AND RECREATION

BROAD BENEFITS

- Full and meaningful life
- Balance between work and play
- Life satisfaction
- Life skills
- Quality of life

SPECIFIC BENEFITS

Physical health

- Muscle strength
- Flexibility
- Cardiovascular conditioning
- Weight control

Emotional well-being

- Sense of self
- Sense of control
- Problem-solving ability

Lifelong learning

- Independent living
- Personal growth
- Adaptation to change

Quality of life

- Awareness and appreciation of the arts, history, and nature

Life skills

- Enhanced creativity
- Improved job performance
- Emotional intelligence

Figure 1.2 There are many benefits of parks and recreation, and the outcomes associated with these benefits are extraordinary.

The benefits of parks and recreation can be observed in people at play and in pursuits such as the following:

- An overstressed adult sits on a beach quietly enjoying the serenity of the sunset.
- A child rides a bicycle without external support for the first time.
- A 78-year-old learns to use the Internet at the community center as a way of keeping pace with the changes in the world.

In recent years, parks and recreation professionals have collected data that better document the roles their services play in well-being and have conducted specific studies. Some of the studies that reveal the benefits of parks and recreation include the following:

- Physical activity for children can improve health, but Active Living Research (2015) found that regular participation in physical activity can also have academic performance benefits. One study of fourth and fifth graders in British Columbia who were underperforming at grade level based upon standardized testing increased their scores after participation in a teacher-led physical activity program.
- Physical activity is especially critical among aging adults. Chronic diseases and years of inactivity can contribute to lack of mobility and problems with independent living. In a study by the Saint Louis University Medical Center (2014), older adults who participated in dance experienced less hip and knee pain and were able to walk faster. Older adults who walk too slowly are more likely to fall, become hospitalized, or require care from others. The study included mostly women whose average age was 80. It compared participants who danced for 45 minutes twice a week to those who carried out their regular physical activities. The dance group reported taking 39 percent less pain medication and the nondance group reported taking 21 percent more medication during that same time period.
- Job candidates often include recreation activities and hobbies on their resumes to provide greater insight into their qualities. A study at San Francisco State University examined the correlation between hobbies and job performance and found that hobbies can improve people's mood, increase their confidence, reduce stress, provide networking opportunities, and help them work better with others, and they make individuals more appealing to potential employers (Association for Psychological Science, 2014).

- According to one study, children who live within 1 kilometer (0.6 mi) of a park playground are almost five times more likely to be of healthy weight (rather than at risk or overweight) compared to children who do not have playgrounds nearby (Potwarka, Kaczynski, & Flack, 2008).
- Participants in green (i.e., outdoor) exercise activities showed significantly greater improvement in self-esteem than those who participated in nongreen exercise activities. The combination of exercise, nature, and social activities could play an important role in mental health treatment (Barton, Griffin, & Pretty, 2011).
- One study showed that people who exercised regularly had lower risk factors related to cardiovascular disease and type 2 diabetes than those who did not exercise (Buchholz et al., 2009).

Social and Community Benefits of Parks and Recreation

Social and community benefits of parks and recreation (see figure 1.3) are characterized by the many opportunities for success and enjoyment that come from interacting with others. These encounters can be positive and enriching for people and for society overall.

The social and community benefits of parks and recreation can be observed in the following scenarios:

- A newly widowed person receives a hot meal and social support during a daily visit to the senior center.
- A young Latino child experiences firsthand the art, food, and songs of his parents' homeland at the community Latino festival.
- A sense of belonging and community envelopes the crowd gathered at the annual Fourth of July picnic and fireworks display.

Similar to the individual benefits of parks, recreation, and leisure, there is evidence of the value of human contact and group interactions for social and community well-being. Some of the commu-

---

SOCIAL AND COMMUNITY BENEFITS OF PARKS AND RECREATION

BROAD BENEFITS
- Social bonds and sense of belonging
- Strong, vitally involved groups and communities
- Ethnic and cultural understanding and goodwill
- Community viability and desirability

SPECIFIC BENEFITS

Sense of community
- Community pride
- Community cohesiveness
- Reduced alienation
- Involvement in issues

Awareness and appreciation
- Tolerance and understanding of differences among people.
- Outlet for conflict resolution
- Cooperation

Social support
- Lifeline for the elderly
- Support for youth
- Cultural identity

Community viability and desirability
- Attractive to millennials and empty nesters
- Desirable location for businesses

Figure 1.3 Parks and recreation offers many social and community benefits that bring about opportunities for success and enjoyment with others.

---

nity benefits of parks and recreation include the following:

- The World Happiness Report (Helliwell, Layard, & Sachs, 2016) determined countries' happiness to augment the more traditional gross domestic product (GDP). Recreation and leisure activities were important components in a country's happiness. The report indicates that Denmark, Switzerland, and Iceland are the three happiest countries. In these countries, physical activity (as opposed to exercise), appreciation of nature and green space, and time with friends are the leading indicators of happiness. In the report, Canada ranks 6th and the United States ranks 13th of the 156 countries included in this study (Helliwell et al., 2016).

- Some communities are more desirable because they are high quality places for people to live, work, learn, and play. For several years Southwest Airlines has recognized the value of community spaces through its Heart of the Community Program, which helps residents feel a sense of ownership in the places they share. This community-driven program supports the activation of public spaces in cities across the country. This project has brought new life to vacant or underutilized areas and has shown that placemaking is a powerful tool for transforming public spaces into vital places that highlight local assets, spur rejuvenation, and serve common needs.

- Good relationships and strong social ties could help people live longer. A review of 48 studies involving more than 300,000 people discovered that those with the strongest social relationships are 50 percent more likely to live longer lives compared with others who are the least socially integrated. According to the report, social support results in improved health benefits for an individual—most specifically, extended life span—as compared to those individuals who smoke and usually experience a shortened life expectancy due to that behavior (Chartered Accountants Benevolent Association, n.d.).

Environmental Benefits of Parks and Recreation

These benefits of parks and recreation address the wide-ranging and critical role of the environment in quality of life (see figure 1.4). An interesting difference between this category and the others is that the environmental benefits sustain human life by

Recreation and leisure bring social and community benefits. Seniors can play bingo and enjoy a meal together at a community center.

protecting the ecosystem in addition to providing other pleasurable benefits.

Some of the environmental benefits of parks and recreation can be observed in the following examples:

- Public lands that are set aside as natural watersheds for preservation allow local residents to pay less for drinking water and provide them with access to hiking trails.
- Urban dwellers flock to city parks to reconnect with nature.
- Fourth graders calculate the speed of the water in a streambed during outdoor classroom sessions.

Some of the studies that reveal the benefits of environmental activities conducted through parks and recreation include the following:

- Having clean air and water does not always mean building dams and filtration plants. A

ENVIRONMENTAL BENEFITS OF PARKS AND RECREATION

BROAD BENEFITS
- Clean air and water
- Environmental protection
- Preservation of natural and historic areas

SPECIFIC BENEFITS
Health and well-being
- Reduced stress
- Venues for physical activity

Education
- Improved science and math skills
- Natural life cycle knowledge
- Environmental ethic

Figure 1.4 The environmental benefits of parks and recreation sustain human life by protecting the ecosystem.

study in *Scientific Reports* compared greenspace metrics and health on a block-by-block level in Toronto. After controlling for income, education, and age, the study indicated that an additional 10 trees per block resulted in a 1 percent increase in how healthy nearby residents felt. The lead researcher concluded that to achieve an equivalent increase in perceived health, each household would need to receive $10,000 or individuals would need to be made seven years younger (Kardan et al., 2015).

• At one time, oil was considered the most critical resource. Although oil is still important, especially economically, water is about to become the most scarce and highly desirable resource. A recent study developed by the Nature Conservancy projects that 1 billion city dwellers globally will be living on less than 100 liters (26 gal) of water per day by 2050. That's about two-thirds of a bathtub of water. The study says an additional 100 million people in cities could experience some sort of water shortages due to climate change and up to 3 billion could experience water shortages at least one month out of the year (The Nature Conservancy, n.d.).

• Some individuals and communities favor removing long-standing buildings and replacing them with modern alternatives; however, rehabilitating historic properties can be a critical part of promoting energy efficiency because it preserves the energy already used (the *embodied energy*) rather than expending additional energy for new construction. It takes approximately 65 years to recover the energy lost in demolishing an existing building when constructing a new, green, energy-efficient office building that includes as much as 40 percent recycled materials (United States Environmental Protection Agency, n.d.).

Economic Benefits of Parks and Recreation

While other values and benefits are often underrecognized, economic benefits (see figure 1.5) tend to be more visible and seemingly more important. The adage "money talks" certainly applies.

By setting aside land for recreation, governments benefit individuals and the environment.

Doug Olson/fotolia.com

ECONOMIC BENEFITS OF PARKS AND RECREATION

BROAD BENEFITS

- Funds generation
- Catalyst for development
- Ongoing community success and viability

SPECIFIC BENEFITS

Cost reduction

- Health care
- Utilities
- Decreased vandalism and crime
- Decreased stress

Increased financial resources

- Enhanced land values
- Neighborhood revitalization
- Increased worker productivity

Economic growth

- Favorable business climate
- Increased tourism
- Attracting and retaining residents

Figure 1.5 The economic benefits of parks and recreation are both numerous and diverse.

Some of the economic benefits of parks and recreation can be seen in the following examples:

- Owners of small stores and restaurants adjacent to national parks make a living providing services to park visitors.
- Corporations increase productivity through fewer sick days by implementing recreation and wellness programs.
- Older adults lower their cholesterol levels by taking daily walks.

Some of the studies that reveal the economic benefits of parks and recreation include the following:

• What could be better than a weekend trip to a park or a camping trip? These pleasurable activities also favorably affect the economy; for example, 89 of the state parks in Texas yielded $774 million in sales, $568 million in outputs, $351 million in value added, and $202 million in improved residents' income as well as 5,871 jobs with an average salary of $34,000 per year (Texas Parks and Wildlife Department, 2014).

• As mentioned previously, quality communities and public spaces are important, and these can translate to tourism dollars. In 2014, Montreal attracted 9.2 million tourists who spent $2.7 billion. Many of these visitors came to participate in the city's numerous events and festivals (Tourisme Montréal, 2014).

RECREATION AND LEISURE: THE LESS DESIRABLE SIDE

Although the benefits and values garnered through play, park visits, recreation activities, travel, and constructive use of leisure time are nearly limitless, some less desirable experiences can also be categorized as recreation and leisure. The vast array of actions and activities that fall within this category have been called *purple leisure, immoral leisure,* or *taboo leisure.* The reality is that numerous activities that may be pleasurable and exciting for some people are not beneficial to them or positive for society overall.

Jay B. Nash, an early American theorist on recreation and leisure, is well-known for his pyramid model of recreation that features levels ranging from detrimental to positive. The lowest levels of his pyramid include activities that are detrimental to self or society, such as recreational drug use or gang membership. Most people accept that drug usage and gang membership are deleterious for the individual and erode societal well-being.

The next level on Nash's pyramid includes passive forms of recreation in which the participant is a spectator, as would be the case with amusement and entertainment. Higher up are those recreation pursuits deemed more positive for the individual participant or society overall. These may inspire greater involvement and participation. Involvement at physical or emotional levels is considered good recreation, and the pinnacle, great recreation, is designated by Nash as creative participation.

What are some of the actions and activities that fall within the less-than-desirable category of recreation? The list includes horse and dog racing, recreational drug use, binge drinking, pornography, prostitution,

What Recreators Can Do

It costs approximately $30,000 to incarcerate a juvenile offender for one year. If that money were available to Parks and Recreation, we could do the following:

- Take him swimming twice a week for 24 weeks,
- And give him four tours of the zoo, plus lunch,
- And enroll him in 50 community center programs,
- And visit the nature center twice,
- And let him play league softball for a season,
- And tour the gardens at the park twice,

- And give him two weeks of tennis lessons,
- And enroll him in two weeks of day camp,
- And let him play three rounds of golf,
- And act in one play,
- And participate in one fishing clinic,
- And take a four-week pottery class,
- And play basketball eight hours a week for 40 weeks,
- After which we could return to you: $29,125 and one much happier kid.

Reprinted, by permission, from E. O'Sullivan, 1999, *Setting a course for change* (National Recreation and Park Association).

vandalism, and the sex tourism trade to countries outside North America, just to name a few. Some of forms of less desirable recreation are legal, and some are illegal. For example, many people gamble, and some gambling is legal through the auspices of government. Others are defined by the norms of society and by various religious groups; for example, physical contact among single people is sometimes considered taboo.

To determine whether a form of recreation falls into this category, ask the following questions:

1. Is the action or activity detrimental to the people involved?
2. Is the action or activity demeaning or harmful to others (i.e., human beings or animals)?
3. Does the action or activity harm the overall well-being of society?

Admittedly these lines are blurring as government and society provide greater leeway for pursuits such as gambling and tobacco smoking, among others, often in return for increased tax revenues.

TRENDS IN RECREATION AND LEISURE

Many people think that the popularity of Pilates, paddleboarding, and pickle ball and increased interest in travel to Cuba by Americans (a place Canadians have long enjoyed) are **trends** in recreation and leisure. In fact, such trends are a result of overall changes in society. For instance, increased participation in women's volleyball and softball represents an overarching trend of increased participation of women in team sports.

True trend tracking in parks, recreation, leisure, and travel requires close attention to factors through an environmental scan. In this case, the term *environmental* refers to conditions outside the control of individuals and organizations. Awareness of these factors is useful in staying ahead of changing behaviors and preferences related to recreation and leisure. Many factors specifically influence trends and emerging directions in parks, recreation, and leisure alternatives. Included among those factors are economics, demographics, legal issues, politics, science and technology, environmental factors, and competition. Another layer that could be added to these factors is whether elements within them have global, national, regional, or local effects.

Rather than create a list of activities that may or may not be popular at any given time, the following list reflects the more general, overarching changes that can be referred to as trends:

Blurring of Life Stages

- Older adults consider themselves young and don't let the number of candles on a birthday cake dictate appropriate recreation and leisure pursuits.

- Children are encouraged to participate in activities at earlier ages than ever before as evidenced by soccer for 3- and 4-year-olds and beauty pageants for tots.
- Young adults are taking longer to finish formal education, marrying later, and becoming independent at later ages, thus blurring the life stages of teenager and adulthood.

Disparities

- Growing inequality in the United States will result in the growth of expensive recreation experiences for an ever-decreasing group of participants.
- Third-tier economies with close ties to tourism may risk damage to or erosion of their natural and cultural environments.

Increased Ethnic Diversity

- As white majorities give way to greater ethnic diversity, which brings with it cultural shifts, the variations and popularity of recreational activities such as sports, music, dancing, and dining will continue to change.
- Common interests in play and recreation pursuits can bring about greater understanding and appreciation of people across the globe.

Health Concerns

- The occurrence of chronic diseases at ever-younger ages and the aging of the population will take a significant toll on resources and influence quality of life.
- The wellness industry will continue to grow as people place increasing emphasis on health outside of physical activity and nutrition and pursue greater quality of life through relaxation or self-improvement.
- The threat of diseases around the world may lead to an increase in virtual travel to avoid illness.

Work Redefined

- The increasing pursuit of employment that requires little or no physical activity will con-

tinue to drive need for and interest in enjoyable physical activity.

- The amount of leisure time available may decrease because people work more than one job or retire at later ages than previous generations.
- The rise of the *gig economy*, in which temporary assignments for specific projects are the norm, is likely to have a mixed impact on leisure time. People might have more flexibility and availability but less money to spend.

Widespread Touch of Technology

- The expansion of affordable technology, especially as it relates to communication and interaction, may lead to increased contact with friends and family and interactions with people from around the world.
- This same technology will reduce human contact.
- Technological advances might enable people with chronic conditions to more fully participate in recreation and leisure experiences.
- Virtual reality (VR) will enable global travel in areas of unrest, but it will also create more alternatives for social contact and emotional intelligence.

Going Green

- Love of the outdoors could result in legal and political ramifications related to preserving open space.
- The popularity and overuse of open space may result in the destruction of valuable natural assets around the globe.
- The ongoing controversy around factors such as global warming will likely keep environmental issues at the forefront of public discourse.

This list is illustrative of what the future might hold. If you pay careful attention to the changes around you, you will not be shocked if the following occur:

- Both Yosemite National Park in California and Mauricie National Park in Quebec close to the public for a minimum of 20 years.

- People with traumatic brain injuries from motorcycle accidents snowboard with joy and abandon.
- People with and without passports sit around a table and discuss their trip to India. The insights and experiences of those who physically made the trip and those who toured the country virtually are difficult to distinguish.
- More than 400 members of the Alberta Skydiving Club are over the age of 85 years.
- Laughing clubs held in public parks are the number one recommendation of physicians for their patients who suffer from complications of serious stress.

A world of surprises lies ahead, and those surprises will not exempt parks, recreation, leisure, and tourism from their effects. In fact, the ongoing evolution of change factors serves as both a challenge and a sense of excitement for this field.

RECREATION AND LEISURE: A PASSION, A PURSUIT, A PROFESSION

For the thousands of people who never pass up an opportunity to collect mineral specimens, plan vacations around the Major League Baseball schedule, or have bumper stickers that read "backstrokers keep their faces dry," recreation and leisure is indeed a passion. For those who continue to play golf every couple of weeks, try to catch new exhibits at the local art gallery, or look forward to planning their various weekend adventures throughout the entirety of their lives, recreation and leisure is a life pursuit.

You may recall the following question from the beginning of this chapter:

What if there were various careers associated with this essential aspect of behavior and major component of the economy that created opportunities for personal growth, professional flexibility, sense of purpose, and resourcefulness for the professionals in that field?

There are! The everywhere, everyone, all the time characteristics of this field and the values and the benefits previously discussed make recreation and leisure a profession with the potential for both making a living and being personally enriched by the many different associated careers. These career options enable people to work in the following situations:

- Work with almost any segment of society—people of all age groups, socioeconomic statuses, ability levels, and everything in between
- Work in diverse areas such as art, music, dance, drama, sports, games, nature, environmental protection, therapeutic settings, fitness, wellness, arts, culture, travel, tourism, and others, which are discussed in later chapters
- Work in a variety of settings, such as parks, nature centers, hospitals, correctional facilities, resorts, college campuses, military installations, corporations, hotels, and communities that are public, nonprofit, private, commercial, or corporate entities or independent contractors

A Professional Career Choice

Because there are so many career options and opportunities, it is challenging to share information and insight into the diverse and dynamic field of parks and recreation. One way you can secure greater insight into this field is by engaging in conversations with people employed in the profession. Throughout the book you will find Outstanding Graduates features that profile graduates of recreation and leisure programs and discuss their career paths.

These interviews are a great introduction to this field, but you can also seek additional insight. If you have extra time and are in the company of professionals working in parks and recreation, ask them how they found this career. The majority will share personal stories about becoming parks and recreation professionals. It could be that a passion for swimming, golf, gymnastics, ceramics, the outdoors, or some other leisure activity set them down this path. Or maybe the positive influence of a coach, camp counselor, theater director, park ranger, or recreation therapist spurred the career choice. Naturally, some professionals are drawn to the field because they want to work with a certain group, such as children, dancers, or active adults.

Qualities and Characteristics of the Profession

Try to discover the characteristics of the work world that these parks and recreation professionals find worthwhile. It is virtually impossible to identify every characteristic of such a diverse field; after all, spas and stadiums don't appear to have a great deal in common. Some of the attributes and characteristics of the working world of parks and recreation include the following:

• **Various settings.** Parks and recreation activities take place indoors, in the woods, on the sea, close to home, and around the globe; therefore, this profession provides the opportunity to accommodate shifts in your career goals. Some activities, programs, and services also take place in less formal settings.

• **Burnout prevention.** Often, professionals who work with people tend to burn out from the continual challenges of one group or another. Human diversity provides ample opportunities to use your skills and knowledge with a different population.

• **Creative approaches.** Although parks and recreation professionals must adopt specific practices, consider safety issues, and meet focused goals, the flexibility to creatively meet these requirements helps many practitioners pursue their own growth and development.

• **Continual change.** Another asset of the parks and recreation field is that often no two days are the same. The rain changes the forest, a child learns to float, and a new exhibit opens at the museum. Part of the attraction of this profession is the continual change that keeps professionals alert and retooled.

• **Responsibility.** Many of the entry-level positions in parks and recreation come with the opportunity to assume responsibility from the start. Whether it be responsibility for a park area, tour group, or swimming pool, new parks and recreation professionals often are in charge.

• **Resourcefulness.** The less formal nature of the programs and settings combined with the challenges of working with a variety of participants with individual goals and abilities means parks and recreation professionals need to be resourceful. One of the many things professionals comment on is the ongoing challenges of their positions.

Making a Difference

When you ask parks and recreation professionals who have spent several years working in this field why they stayed in the profession, you will hear a variety of responses. A common theme, however, is making a difference. Professionals might talk about making a difference in the life of one person or a group, their contributions to the vitality and viability of a community, or the far-reaching difference that results from their efforts to protect nature or preserve cultural or historic sites.

A quote attributed to Socrates perhaps sums up the essence of a career in parks and recreation: "Leisure is the best of all professions." Socrates was most likely suggesting that being at leisure is the best way to occupy time, but based on some of the attributes and characteristics of the field, it can be applied to the professions within parks, recreation, and leisure as well.

Unique Quality of Participating in Parks and Recreation

Aristotle believed that a good life is predicated on engaging in activities that are intrinsically valuable. Recreation activities and leisure pursuits generally fall within this parameter. Other disciplines can create and support activities that are intrinsically valuable, and other employment areas involve working with children or adults or in the outdoors or in the nonprofit sector. What makes parks and recreation unique in its own right?

The qualities that make parks and recreation valuable and unique from other endeavors are the voluntary nature of participation and the potential for fun and enjoyment. Our bodies compel us to eat and sleep, and there are societal norms that contribute to time spent in schooling and work.

Participation in recreation and leisure activities, however, is voluntary. The common elements that draw people to choose a particular leisure activity are the power, promise, potential, and possibility that those choices hold for fun, pleasure, or meaning. That statement may seem a bit misleading when we consider the teenagers who submit to family vacations under duress, people training to run marathons, or even those involved in less-than-positive activities such as vandalism and gang activity, but even those activities hold such possibilities.

Fun is fundamental to attracting people to activities and options that will be valuable to them and to their friends, families, neighborhoods, and communities and to society overall. There are numerous instances when the concept of fun is dismissed as having no value, but it is the element of fun that attracts people to activities and motivates them to remain committed and involved. Fun is fundamental to valuable life experiences because it attracts attention, sparks an interest, engages participation, creates motivation, fuels repeated involvement, and supports results. Fun creates positive results for individuals and society.

MOVING ON

This chapter introduces the profession, but it barely scratches the surface of the unique qualities and characteristics and values and benefits that recreation and leisure holds for individuals, groups, communities, the environment, and the economy. The rest of the book serves as a road map to guide your journey. We explore the history and background of this field and identify the various organizations that provide leisure-related services. We also provide an overview of the variety of settings and populations that make up this unique profession. This book offers in-depth of information about the various career choices in recreation and leisure.

CHAPTER 2

History of Recreation

M. Rebecca Genoe, Douglas Kennedy, Jerome F. Singleton,
Tristan Hopper, and Jill Sturts

Library of Congress, Prints & Photographs Division, LC-B2- 2956-6

" Those who cannot remember the past are condemned to repeat it. "

George Santayana,
Spanish and American
philosopher

LEARNING OUTCOMES

After reading this chapter, you should be able to do the following:

> Identify and explain the historical development of recreation and leisure in prehistoric societies
> Describe the historical development of recreation and leisure in ancient Rome and Greece, Europe, the United States, and Canada
> Explain and describe how government and professional organizations influenced the development of recreation and leisure in Canada and the United States

History shapes what we understand today. To appreciate how recreation and leisure services are now delivered in the United States and Canada, you must understand the historical periods and societal expectations that have influenced the development of these services. North American societies have been affected by the generations of immigrants that have landed, settled, and influenced recreation and leisure. By understanding how leisure has emerged, it is possible to see how history often repeats itself. What we see today is similar to what happened long ago. Whether lessons can be learned from the past undoubtedly requires an appreciation and understanding of our history.

TRACING THE ROOTS OF LEISURE

Past definitions of leisure influence our understanding of leisure today, so we will trace the development of leisure from prehistoric societies to the Protestant Reformation.

Prehistoric Societies

People in prehistoric societies were primarily concerned with survival (Shivers & deLisle, 1997). Hunting and gathering were the primary activities and provided resources to maintain life. There was little free time as we know it today. Work, survival, and rest melded to become one life-sustaining activity. Once prehistoric people could create tools and were able to store information in a larger brain, more free time became available. This free time was used for ritualization or ceremonial acts (Ibrahim, 1991). These acts often focused on celebrations of successful hunts, offerings for bountiful harvests, and beseeching the gods for their favor. It is believed that play-like activities were also critical to the needs of emerging tribes. These activities depicted historical events, transportation practices, war games, and the use of farm tools. Play prepared children for their responsibilities as youth and adults and became a way of achieving solidarity and morality. It also became a healing experience and a means of communication, and it provided pleasure and entertainment. As societies emerged, play-like activities were also a means to relax, recover, and replenish strength after working (Kraus, 1971). These emerging societies also developed structures that allowed people to focus on specific work roles: One person could focus on being a hunter, and another could be a builder. Once such roles were established, more resources were available for activities that did not relate to sustaining life. Thus, for the first time, people had greater opportunities for leisure. We still see this pattern today: People specialize in a vocation needed by society and rely on the specialties of others for their own well-being.

Ancient Greece

Ancient Greece (1200-500 BC) is an excellent example of how societal structure influenced the development of leisure. Greek citizens, who could vote and participate in state affairs, sought to become the well-rounded ideal of that era. They embraced what was known as the **Athenian ideal**, which was a combination of soldier, athlete, artist, statesman, and philosopher. They valued developing in all areas rather than focusing on one area of expertise as is valued today. This was only possible because the tasks of everyday living were provided by laborers or slaves (Shivers & deLisle, 1997) who outnumbered the citizens approximately three to one. Those who were freed from everyday activities had the opportunity to pursue the range of activities necessary to become the Athenian ideal.

Leisure was very important in Greek society. The Greek philosopher Plato and his student, Aristotle, supported this in their beliefs that virtuous and constructive leisure activities were the route to happiness and fulfillment. **Contemplation**, which involved the pursuit of truth and understanding, was thought to be the highest form of leisure (Dare, Welton, & Coe, 1987). Athenian philosophers strongly believed in the unity of mind and body and valued each. Play was perceived to be essential to the healthy growth of children from both a physical and social perspective (Ibrahim, 1979). Citizens regarded leisure as an opportunity for intellectual cultivation, music, theater, and poetry as well as political and philosophical discussions. The concept *schole* meant to have quiet or peace. It meant having time for oneself and being occupied in something for its own sake, such as music, poetry, the company of friends, or the exercise of speculative faculties (Ibrahim, 1991). Schole embraced the experience and not the outcome. This is different from today, when the pursuit of an activity is often valued only if something tangible, such as a victory, mastery of a skill, or a specific expectation, is gained.

An important part of ancient Greek culture, and perhaps at odds with the notion of schole, was passion for games. Athletic games were held to celebrate religious rites and heroes, for entertainment, and for pleasure. Only men played the games; women were often excluded from public life (Shivers & deLisle, 1997). Four Panhellenic games were very popular among the spectators and athletes. These included the Olympic Games, the Pythian Games, the Nemian Games, and the Isthmian Games. These were thought to be held in honor of the gods, although others suggest that they commemorated the death of mythic mortals and monsters (Ibrahim, 1979; Mendelsohn, 2004). When athletic games were held, wars often ceased so participants could compete (Poliakoff, 1993). The early Olympic Games, which honored Zeus, included chariot races, combat events, boxing, wrestling, footraces, and the pentathlon, which was a five-sport event that embraced the Athenian ideal. Athletes also competed individually rather than on teams and represented their home villages (Ibrahim, 1991). This is similar to the modern Olympic Games in which participants represent their countries. The early Olympics were extremely serious events. It was not uncommon for participants in aggressive sports such as *pankration* (a combination of boxing and wrestling) to be encouraged to fight to the death. This fate was seen as especially noble because it would immortalize the competitor in story for generations to come as having sacrificed his life in the pursuit of victory. So important were the Olympics that Athenians would place an olive wreath on their door when a boy was born, thus signaling the hope that he would become an Olympian (Mendelsohn, 2004). This seriousness of purpose and the use of leisure time to develop sport-specific skills are still found today. We work at getting better so we can play a sport well. Like the ancient Greeks, we claim to value well-rounded people, yet parents increasingly encourage their children to specialize in one sport, which is often played all year round, so they have the greatest opportunity to become better than their peers. Success in sports now rivals that of the adulation shown to the earliest Olympic victors, so it should be no surprise that the world finds itself facing an epidemic of competitors turning to illegal performance-enhancing drugs to ensure victory.

Ancient Rome

The emergence of Rome as a dominant society influenced how leisure was perceived at that time. Rome conquered the majority of Europe and Asia after about 265 BC and emerged as a dominant power in the Mediterranean (Shivers & deLisle, 1997). The Roman Empire influenced the judicial systems and societies it conquered by attempting to overwrite with its own culture what had come before. The Roman government was based on distinct classifications of citizens. These included senators, who were the richest, owned most of the land, and had most of the power; curiales, who owned 25 or more acres (10 ha) of land and were office holders or tax collectors; plebes, or free common men, who owned small properties or were tradesmen or artisans; coloni, who were lower-class tenants on land; and, finally, indentured slaves. Early Roman slaves were captured in war and served as agricultural laborers. Much later, large numbers of captives from Asia, Greece, and central Europe became slaves and were exploited by their owners (Shivers & deLisle, 1997). As in societies that came before it, the opportunity to participate in leisure during the Roman era was limited to those who had the appropriate resources. The greater a person's standing was, the greater their opportunity for freedom from the daily requirements necessary to live a comfortable life. Senators enjoyed almost unlimited leisure, while coloni struggled to make a comfortable life. This is not unlike the present day, in which distinct economic classes enjoy varying degrees and types of leisure.

Different from the ancient Greeks, who saw leisure as an opportunity for well-rounded development, Romans perceived leisure to be primarily rest from work. Considering that the Romans were on an almost constant crusade to dominate foreign cultures, this viewpoint was necessary and allowed recuperation before the next crusade. Play then, in the case of the Romans, served utilitarian rather than aesthetic or spiritual purposes (Horna, 1994). As the Roman Empire grew and the increasing availability of slaves decreased the amount of daily work people were required to do, leisure time increased and was increasingly used

to control the masses. During Emperor Claudius' reign (41-54 AD), Rome had 59 public holidays and 95 game days, and by 354 AD, there were more than 200 public holidays and 175 game days. The reason for this was simple: As Romans became less occupied with work, they became increasingly bored and critical of the government. The government then attempted to pacify unrest by providing pleasurable experiences through spectacle and celebrations of holidays. What they called *bread and circuses,* which consisted of free food and entertainment, provided the framework for Roman society (Horna, 1994).

To hold people's attention, leisure activities became increasingly hedonistic and shocking. When battles between gladiators became less interesting, animals from foreign lands were brought in to become part of the savagery seen in the great coliseums. When the scale of those battles became ordinary, artificial lakes were created by

Leisure in ancient Rome focused on spectacle and entertainment for the masses instead of participation. Today, some sporting events such as boxing also take on the appearance of spectacle, and sometimes the participants are even called gladiators.

slaves who were then used to recreate bloody sea battles depicting successful conquests. This focus on the entertainment of the masses, instead of their participation, has led some historians to argue that one of the reasons for the fall of the Roman Empire was its inability to deal with mass leisure (McLean, Hurd, & Rogers, 2005). This concern is often heard today regarding current leisure habits. Increasingly, it appears that people are more content to be spectators than participants. Some sporting events, such as football and boxing, look similar to spectacles seen in ancient Rome. In fact, it isn't uncommon to hear the participants in these events referred to as gladiators. Should this be a concern? Well, with the rate of obesity greatly increasing in Canada and the United States, it is worth considering whether the focus on mass leisure seen during the Roman era (and perhaps the eventual outcome) is being repeated.

Middle Ages

With the collapse of the Roman Empire, the Catholic Church became the dominant structure in Europe (Shivers & deLisle, 1997). The Catholic Church rejected the activities that the Roman Empire had accepted, including its hedonistic ways (Horna, 1994). One example of this was the fact that people involved in theater could not be baptized. The concept of idleness as the great enemy of the soul emerged, and doing nothing was thought to be evil. The church wielded great influence during this time over the social order, which consisted of nobility and peasants. The clergy dictated societal values whose adoption would lead to saving souls, and this was the highest goal at the time. Although the Catholic Church influenced what were acceptable and unacceptable leisure activities, many rules were so strict that at the end of this period the church went through a renaissance in which individuals within the church developed different perspectives. This renaissance saw a renewed appreciation for a variety of leisure activities.

Renaissance

Spreading from the 14th century in Italy to the 16th century in northern Europe, this era saw power shift from the church to the nobility. Previously ostracized by the church, artists were now supported and encouraged by the nobility to express their art (Horna, 1994). Play was perceived to be an important part of education. During the 16th century, Francois Rabelais (1490-1553) emphasized the need for physical exercise and games. Michel Eyquem de Montaigne (1533-1592) supported the concept of unity of mind, body, and spirit, which opposed the medieval ideal of separation, or dualism, of the mind and body. John Locke (1632-1704) was so concerned with play as a medium of learning that he made the distinction between play and recreation: Recreation was not being idle; it provided a specific benefit by easing and helping to recover the people wearied by their work. Jean-Jacques Rousseau (1712-1778) advocated for the full freedom of physical activity rather than constraint. It was during the Renaissance that an increased interest in play, both as a form of popular entertainment and as a medium of education, developed.

The following three types of parks emerged during the late Renaissance:

1. Royal hunting preserves that provided wild-game hunting

2. Formal garden parks in which participants viewed their surroundings much as you would experience a museum

3. English garden parks that emphasized interacting with the environment through activities such as picnics and other restful pursuits

These parks, developed by the nobility for their own use, were often seen as status symbols. People caught hunting in a royal hunting preserve who were not nobility were often killed. Still, the growth of parks within the nobility provided other classes with an understanding of what was possible and led to the first thoughts of parks for the masses.

Protestant Reformation

During the Protestant Reformation (16th century), Martin Luther and others questioned the accepted practices of the Catholic Church and split off into other Protestant religions. Each religious group governed the perception of what was acceptable as leisure. Play was frowned on as evil by certain churches during this transition. John Calvin believed that success on earth determined your place in heaven. With that in mind, extraordinarily hard work and lack of leisure time were signs of great success. The influence of the Protestant and Catholic churches in Europe was critical to the earliest development of leisure in Canada and the United States because settlers came primarily from Europe and brought these values and social structures to the New World. Today we also see that immigrant groups in Canada and the United States participate in different recreation activities, have different perspectives on leisure, and expose others to different beliefs.

DEVELOPMENT OF RECREATION IN THE UNITED STATES

Recreation developed over time in the United States and Canada. Exploration in Canada began in the 11th century and in the United States in the 15th century. It continued to develop as the populations in both colonies grew. By the late 19th century, governments in both countries began to play a role in providing recreation and leisure services. This role changed and developed throughout the early part of the 20th century. Never static, recreation and leisure in the United States evolved through wars and the depression, longer and shorter workweeks,

and other periods. In Canada, the post–World War II era brought renewed interest in recreation services, but later declines in resources meant a lack of funding for recreation. One consequence of this ever-changing face of recreation and leisure was the emergence of **professional organizations** that addressed the needs of both countries' citizens. In the 21st century, challenges such as lack of funding for recreation continue, and demographic changes, such as population aging, affect service provision.

Early Settlement

To fully understand leisure during the settlement period, it is important to recognize the purpose of the earliest inhabitants and visitors. Christopher Columbus opened up the Americas when exploration for the purposes of trade, profit, and control resulted in circumnavigation of the world (Shivers & deLisle, 1997). Europeans seeking adventure, wealth, or freedom from persecution arrived in the United States and brought their traditions and beliefs. Two early colonies founded in the United States were in Virginia and New England (Shivers & deLisle, 1997). Before this, Native Americans had developed their own forms of recreation. Although their activities often celebrated great religious rituals, they were also often highly competitive. One

"Ball Players." Artist: George Catlin

Men of the Choctaw tribe playing lacrosse, which continues to grow in popularity today.

of the well-known recreation activities that is still growing in popularity is lacrosse. Given its common name by French settlers, this activity was common throughout Native American tribes in the east, the Great Lakes region, and the south; each area had variations of the same activity. The game was often filled with great traditions and ceremony, was used to release aggression or settle disputes, and often included wagering (Vennum, n.d.). Specific Native American tribes developed their own unique activities. For example, the Illinois developed a straw game in which wagering revolved around who could guess the correct number of straws after a large pile was divided. Although this was often a male-dominated game, women were known to participate in their own game involving plum stones that were used like modern dice (Illinois State Museum, 2000).

Virginia

The settlement in Virginia, established in Jamestown in the 17th century, was composed of aristocracy, adventurers, and traders. These people loved sports games, theater, books, music, and exercise and continued to pursue these activities once they arrived. However, with little free time available as they tried to survive, the governors banned recreational activities (Shivers & deLisle, 1997). One of the primary reasons for the strict control over these activities was the harsh conditions the colonists faced and the need for diligence to ensure survival. The conditions were so difficult that of the 8,000 colonists who arrived in Virginia by 1625, only 1,200 survived an additional 10 years (Edgington, Jordan, DeGraff, & Edgington, 1998). The Virginia Assembly enforced observance of the Sabbath, prohibited gambling, and regulated drinking (Ibrahim, 1991). Penalties for partaking in Sunday amusements or failure to attend church services included imprisonment. Activities common to the weekend, including dancing, fishing, hunting, and cardplaying, were among those strictly prohibited (Kraus, 2001). These restrictions were lifted once survival became easier and a leisure class began to emerge through the benefit of indentured servants and slaves. This societal arrangement mirrored those discussed previously in which the absence of a significant and identifiable middle class suggested the development of a leisure class. With laws

and social mores relaxing in response to a social class seeking new ways to take advantage of its free time, activities such as cockfighting, dice games, football, forms of bowling, and tennis (all of which were illegal) became more common among the privileged but were still unavailable to the working class (Kraus, 2001).

New England

Although the settlement in New England also had to fight for its survival, its settlers were Calvinists escaping persecution in Europe. All forms of recreation were illegal, and the Puritan ethic restricted social activities. This philosophy valued frugality, hard work, self-discipline, and observance of civil and religious codes. Pleasure was considered to be the devil's work, and time not spent in worship or productive labor was considered wasteful (Shivers & deLisle, 1997). People were expected to behave religiously all the time, and thus work became a holy task. If daily activities belonged to God, then God's time should not be wasted in trivial pursuits. This Protestant work ethic often removed pleasure from lives. Leisure was considered a lure to sin and a threat to godliness. Puritans believed that they should avoid pleasures in their own lives and struggle against pleasure in the community (Cross, 1990). New England Puritans banned labor, travel, and recreation on Sundays. Recreation was tolerated, however, if it could help with work, such as quilting bees and barn raisings (Cross, 1990).

Eventually, the strict control over the masses could not be sustained. Towns saw construction of meeting houses and taverns. The love of games and sports was rediscovered in these taverns. Hunting became a popular leisure activity among the men because game was abundant. Training days, where young men learned how to serve in the militia, were held in Boston, and these were celebrated at the local tavern. Taverns were also used for cockfighting, animal baiting, dances, and orchestras. The church during this period of the 18th century, while increasingly concerned with these activities, was content to allow their participation in the relatively controlled setting of public facilities. Acceptable leisure activities included public readings and moral lectures. Amateur musical performances were occasionally tolerated. Plays were eventually accepted in Boston and Philadelphia. New York City had its own theater. The mercantile class enjoyed many leisure activities including sleigh rides, horse races, balls, and card parties (Ibrahim, 1991). The trend of allowing questionable activities to occur behind closed doors and encouraging acceptable activities to be held in public is still seen today. Blue laws restrict the sale of items such as liquor on Sundays. Laws often prohibit activities such as drinking in public, and taxes might support community events such as picnics and parades that are seen as more wholesome.

Early Park Development

An important development during the early colonial period was the realization that open space was important to growing communities. The Boston Common, a 48-acre (19-ha) oasis of nature in the middle of the city, was established in 1634 and is viewed as the first municipal park (Kraus, 2001). This influenced the creation of laws in Massachusetts requiring that bodies of water larger than 10 acres (4 ha) be open to the public for fishing and hunting (Edgington et al., 1998). As communities grew and the first organized urban planning efforts took shape, further efforts were undertaken to ensure open space was provided. The center of Phil-

adelphia is a prime example. Several north–south streets are intersected by streets named after species of trees. Within each of the resulting quadrants is a park area that provides a touch of nature within the metropolis. The creation of Central Park in New York City is probably the best-known example of early urban open-space provision.

Frederick Law Olmsted, who is considered the founder of American landscape architecture, was hired to design New York's Central Park in 1858 and to design municipal parks in Brooklyn, Philadelphia, Detroit, Chicago, and other areas in the late 19th century. He adapted the English style of a natural park to the rectangular restrictions of American parks (Ibrahim, 1991). He also established the initial purpose for city parks throughout the United States: to provide a space for contemplative leisure (Ibrahim, 1991). Organized and structured sports that are common in parks today were not permitted. Instead, the parks were initially intended to soothe the minds of newcomers to North America who were facing an increasingly industrial age and limited amounts of open space (Kraus, 2001). Olmsted felt that parks should be large enough to shut out the city and that green spaces could inspire courtesy, self-control, and temperance. Olmsted's parks involved walkways, natural vistas,

Library of Congress/Detroit Publishing Co.

The sheep meadow in New York City's Central Park in the early 20th century. As you can see, the park's designer, Frederick Law Olmsted, was successful in bringing the countryside to the city.

and landscaping to create a feeling of nature in the middle of the city (Cross, 1990). Parks developed by Olmsted were an attempt to regain the countryside in the city. They had artificial lakes, regularly mowed grass, and pathways for carriages. Although the parks existed for passive use, they were full of people enjoying activities such as baseball, cycling, skating, and horseback riding. Refreshment stands and restrooms were included for people spending the day at the park (Goodale & Godbey, 1988).

The Playground Movement

The **playground movement** was first adopted by New York City when land was allocated for Central Park in 1855 (Ibrahim, 1991). Its purpose was to provide passive rest and aesthetics. In Chicago, however, Washington Park was opened in 1876 for more active sport. In Boston, Dr. Maria Zakrzewska promoted the concept of a sand garden that would eventually shape the idea of playgrounds for generations to come. In 1868, city leaders determined that an ever-increasing number of children without constructive free-time pursuits needed more constructive outlets, so they developed the first organized playground program. It grew until 1886, when the addition of a pile of sand changed the notion of playgrounds. Started by school leaders and well-meaning citizens, a sand garden was created in Boston solely for use by children. Although this may seem commonplace today, for most children it was the first time they had ever played in sand or experienced a space designed for the active use of children only. It was so successful that city leaders produced 21 more playgrounds of the type by 1889. The popularity of this effort grew until many more playgrounds were created in New York City, Chicago, and other areas (Edgington et al., 1998; Kraus, 2001).

Government Involvement

As the United States' population grew, the government became increasingly concerned with the national quality of life. In 1880, President James Garfield stated: "We may divide the whole struggle of the human race into two chapters: first, the fight to get leisure; and then the second fight of civilization—what shall we do with our recreation when we get it" (Kraus, 1990, p. 154). One major issue confronting government leaders was the amount of natural resources that would be available for future generations. Forests were being eliminated at breakneck speed to support massive amounts of construction. The conservation movement was born out of this concern and was intended to protect the national heritage of America, not to influence specific leisure behavior of Americans (Ibrahim, 1991). Mindful of what many thought was a perilous decline in available natural resources, the Forest Service was created in 1906 and the National Park Service was created in 1916. Yosemite Valley and the Mariposa Grove were granted to California to protect and preserve for future generations. Yellowstone National Park in Wyoming was the first national park, and Yosemite was taken back by the federal government and became the second (Ibrahim, 1991).

While the conservation movement sought to preserve natural resources that were typically far from the centers of the population, recreation participation within urban areas steadily increased. Perhaps no era of American history so embraced the free-spirited notion of leisure than the Roaring '20s. This era saw the widespread increase of commercial recreation and disposable income and the use of recreation as a sign of status. However, the economic pendulum swung back quickly and in a shocking reversal of fortune: The stock market crash and the ensuing Great Depression quickly ended the lifestyle of the Roaring '20s. The stock market crash led to never-before-seen levels of unemployment, poverty, and inadequate housing. With local governments struggling, the federal government assumed a larger role in the provision of parks and recreation (Goodale & Godbey, 1988). Massive unemployment stimulated a growing concern for the mass leisure that was now thrust on the unemployed. This sparked a new discussion of how people defined free time. Studies showed that people were humiliated by unemployment and that leisure was meaningless without a job (Cross, 1990).

During this period, the U.S. federal government tried a variety of actions to combat the economic peril that befell many. One effort included an attempt to spread jobs by implementing a 34-hour workweek (Ibrahim, 1991). The creation of the Works Progress Administration (WPA) had the biggest effect on the following generations.

This massive organization sought to put citizens back to work through a variety of methods. One of the most important to parks and recreation was the branch of the WPA known as the Civilian Conservation Corps (CCC). The CCC was responsible for countless construction projects that provided a variety of recreation areas, many of which are still in use today. To get an idea of the scale of the CCC's work, consider that it employed enough workers to complete the following: the building of 800 state parks, 46,854 bridges, 28,087 miles (45,200 km) of trails, 46,000 campground facilities, and 204 lodges and museums and the planting of more than 3 billion trees (Edgington et al., 1998).

The increase in facilities provided by the federal government spurred state and local governments to establish and enhance their own agencies responsible for recreation. After six CCC camps were created in Virginia in 1933, the state created its first state parks from the camps and opened them all on the same day in 1936 (Virginia State Parks, n.d.). In Missouri, after 4,000 men were employed by the CCC to construct facilities, the state developed an independent state park board in 1937 (Missouri State Parks and Historic Sites, n.d.). Other states, such as Delaware, Florida, and Georgia, also created state park systems during this time to address the increasing popularity of the new sites provided by the federal government.

Professional Organizations

Professional organizations emerged early in the United States. In 1906, Jane Addams, Joseph Lee, Luther Gulick, and others organized the Playground Association of America. In 1911, the name was changed to the Playground and Recreation Association of America. In 1926, the name was changed again to the National Recreation Association. As employment in leisure-related agencies grew and professional preparation and competence continued to be of interest, additional professional organizations were formed. Initially acting independently, the National Recreation Association, the American Institute of Park Executives, the National Conference on State Parks, the American Association of Zoological Parks and Aquariums, and the American Recreation Society merged in 1965 to become the National Recreation and Park Association (NRPA).

Shortly thereafter, the National Association of Recreation Therapists and the Armed Forces Section of the American Recreation Society were added. Even after the American Association of Zoological Parks and Aquariums left to form its own organization, the NRPA was the largest organization in the United States to serve the needs of the general public and professionals in the promotion of parks, recreation, and leisure-related opportunities (Ibrahim, 1991). The mission of the NRPA is "to advance parks, recreation and environmental conservation efforts that enhance the quality of life for all people" (NRPA, n.d., para. 3). Affiliate parks and recreation associations within each state further address this mission. These affiliates, such as the Virginia Recreation and Park Society, the Florida Recreation and Park Association, and the Texas Recreation and Park Society, serve their members through local outreach that meets the demands of professionals who serve unique populations.

The American Alliance for Health, Physical Education, Recreation and Dance (AAHPERD) was founded in 1885 when William Gilbert Anderson invited a group of people who were working in the gymnastics field to discuss their profession (AAHPERD, n.d.). In 2014, AAHPERD changed its name to SHAPE America (Society of Health and Physical Educators). The name change was initiated to provide a more inclusive and visible approach for health and physical educators and for parents, school administrators, and the media. The professional organization's mission is to advance professional practice and promote research related to health and physical education, physical activity, dance, and sport. The organization is committed to ensuring that all children can lead healthy, physically active lives (SHAPE America, n.d.).

Post–World War II Growth

After World War II, recreation and leisure saw changes, challenges, and growth in several areas. Among these were the following:

• **Therapeutic recreation.** The extraordinary increase in the number of citizens who faced disabling injuries from their wartime fighting provided a challenge. The use of recreation as therapy and the birth of therapeutic recreation as a distinct discipline occurred largely from its provision in government-sponsored Department of Veteran's Affairs (VA) hospitals. As recreation therapy grew and expanded from VA facilities to services provided in the community, a growing need for training and education evolved. Colleges and universities filled this need by creating a distinct body of knowledge. Professional organizations such as the National Therapeutic Recreation Society (NTRS) and the American Association for Therapeutic Recreation were formed (in 1966 and 1984, respectively), although the NTRS recently disbanded. Professional certification of recreation therapists was provided by the National Council for Therapeutic Recreation Certification in 1981.

• **Concern for youth fitness.** A critical development in recreation and leisure came about in 1956. A battery of physical fitness tests comparing U.S. youth to their peers in Europe produced shocking results that showed European children to be in much better condition. Having been involved in two world wars within the last half-century, the government, under President Eisenhower, created the President's Council on Youth Fitness in 1956. Eventually changing its name in 1966 to the President's Council on Physical Fitness and Sports, this initiative promotes health and wellness for all ages by first introducing physical skill testing and awards in schools and offering active lifestyle awards for all ages. In 1983, Congress declared May National Physical Fitness and Sports Month. These initiatives mirrored a growth in mandatory physical education classes throughout the school year. Unfortunately, as time passed, the concern for youth fitness and the need for physical education were eclipsed by the concern for academic achievement in other areas. Perhaps it is worth considering whether this decreased emphasis on physical education in schools is just one factor in the sedentary lifestyle that many see as contributing to a growing obesity epidemic in the United States.

• **Concern for youth sports.** In addition to an increased concern for youth fitness, youth sports have evolved and grown. The National Alliance for Youth Sport (NAYS), a nonprofit organization that promotes the value of sports and physical activity as part of the emotional, physical, social, and mental development of children, provides support for youth sports administrators, coaches, parents, and officials. Increased parental involvement and single-sport specialization have surfaced as two trends in youth sports (NAYS, n.d.).

DEVELOPMENT OF RECREATION IN CANADA

How did recreation emerge in Canada? The following sections provide insights into the development of recreation in Canada.

Early Settlement

Canada, a frontier settlement, consisted of a few homesteads and resource-dependent rural communities (Harrington, 1996). The economic well-being of these communities was based on natural resources such as fishing, logging, and agriculture. The first European explorers arrived in Canada in the 11th century. The first permanent European settlements were founded in the 1600s (Francis, Jones, & Smith, 1988). However, before the Europeans began to explore and settle, there were many different nations and languages among Canada's Indigenous peoples (LaPierre, 1992). The origin of Canada's first people is uncertain. Some argue that the Indigenous peoples emerged on the continent, and others argue that they migrated from Siberia. Regardless of their origin, Indigenous peoples were living in North America at least 10,000 years before the arrival of the Europeans (Francis et al., 1988). The Indigenous peoples in southern Canada enjoyed games, music, and storytelling for entertainment. Games were often based on hunting and fishing skills (Karlis, 2004). The Inuit, who lived in the Arctic, played many games including *nalukatook,* which involved bouncing on a walrus hide held by others, and *ipirautaqurnia,* which involved flipping a whip accurately. *Baggataway,* which was played by the Algonquins and Iroquois and involved a curved, netted stick, is now called lacrosse (Karlis, 2016).

Between 1604 and 1607, the first Acadian settlement was formed when the Frenchman Samuel de Champlain and his men explored the coastline of the Maritimes and wintered at Port Royal, the first agricultural settlement in Canada. In 1606, Champlain's men took part in Canada's first theatrical production, and in 1607, Champlain founded the Order of Good Cheer, which was the first social club in Canada. However, the colony was abandoned in

1607 due to lack of money (Francis et al., 1988). In 1608, Champlain constructed a habitation, or wooden buildings forming a quadrangle, which became the center of the first permanent French settlement. The French colony existed only for trading fur, and it grew very slowly. By 1620, there were only 60 people in New France. However, by the 1650s, the French colony began growing steadily, and by the late 1700s, the language was altered by settlers to reflect traditions of the emerging country; thus, the identity of Canadians emerged.

While the French were settling New France, the British were settling colonies in Newfoundland, Virginia, New York, and Massachusetts. They also sponsored expeditions north of New France, and in 1610 and 1611, Henry Hudson discovered the Hudson Bay. Fifty years later, British fur-trading posts were established around the bay (Francis et al., 1988).

Because early settlement in Canada focused on the fur trade and farming in Canada required a great deal of hard labor and preparation for winter, recreation opportunities were limited for the early settlers (Harrington, 1996). Men and women enjoyed activities such as curling, skating, ice hockey, snowshoeing, and tobogganing in the winter. Drama and music were also popular leisure activities at that time (McFarland, 1970).

Park Development

The first park in Canada, the Halifax Common, was established in 1763. Two hundred forty acres (97 ha) were designated for exercise for the militia in the early years (McFarland, 1970). Later the park was used for skating, lawn tennis, croquet, and archery (Wright, 1983). Municipal parks and public squares were established throughout the 19th century (McFarland, 1970; Searle & Brayley, 1993). For example, 14.9 acres (6 ha) of land in London, Ontario, were deeded from the federal government for Victoria Park in 1869. In 1875, 200 acres (81 ha) of land on the Halifax peninsula were leased from the federal government for 999 years for Point Pleasant Park, where all members of the community could enjoy exercise and recreation. Much like in the United States, however, games were often prohibited in the parks, as was walking or lying on the grass. Parks were largely used for walking, sitting,

horse-drawn carriage driving, bird watching, and enjoying the plant life (McFarland, 1970).

As transportation improved in Canada and the railway was built, it became possible to travel for pleasure. This led to the formation of national parks. In 1885, the Canadian Pacific Railway suggested the establishment of Rocky Mountain Park in Banff (Wetherell & Kmet, 1990). Although the difficult work required of the early settlers to build the country meant that there was little time for leisure, recreation eventually became a part of the lives of Canadians.

The Playground Movement

In Canada, the playground movement developed supervised playgrounds for children. Similar to its development in the United States, the playground movement in Canada was born from an increasing sense that recreation and leisure were important in bettering citizens' quality of life. In the 1800s, municipal parks were used by the upper classes, and the lower classes did not have access to open areas. However, concern for those who lived in overcrowded areas with high crime and disease led to the creation of safe places for play (McFarland, 1970). This movement was based on the notion that play was the only appropriate method for physical development for children and was necessary for their health, strength, and moral character (Searle & Brayley, 1993). There was a belief that children required encouragement to play and that the playground could be used to teach health and social customs in a play environment (McFarland, 1970). In 1893, the National Council of Women was formed, and the council and its local groups played a major role in initiating the playground movement (McFarland, 1970).

According to McFarland (1970), there were two different justifications for the playground movement. The first was the prevention of delinquency and drunkenness, and the second was the belief that all people had the right to opportunities for leisure. However, the emphasis on preventing delinquency and drunkenness was necessary for receiving funding and to justify giving time to the playground movement. School grounds were selected for the playgrounds, and in 1908, the Toronto school board was the first to develop summer playground programs. In general, playground programs were initiated by local branches of the National Women's Council. Later, a playground association and a civic department responsible for playgrounds and recreation programming were established. In the beginning, teachers were chosen for playground supervisors, and programs included games, stories, reading, sewing, and music. Eventually, summer and winter programs merged and indoor programs were developed, which led to the hiring of full-time supervisors for public playgrounds. The playground movement led to the concept of a comprehensive parks system (McFarland, 1970).

Government Involvement

Federal, provincial, and municipal governments have long been involved in providing recreation opportunities for Canadians. The land for the first parks in Canada was often deeded or leased to municipalities from the federal or provincial governments. For example, the Canadian government authorized the Saint John, New Brunswick, horticultural society to establish gardens, a park, and a pleasure resort with 1,700 acres (688 ha) for Rockwood Park (McFarland, 1970). Also, the city of Vancouver received permission from the federal government to establish Stanley Park on part of the local harbor peninsula. In 1865, a Montreal city bylaw designated 13 open spaces for citizens to enjoy (McFarland, 1970).

In 1883, the province of Ontario passed the first legislation that affected the development of provincial parks. The Public Parks Act established parks in cities and towns with the consent or petition of the electors. The local government could appoint park management boards that included the mayor of the municipality and six board members. These park boards could purchase land for parks—up to 1,000 acres (405 ha) in cities and 500 acres (202 ha) in towns. In 1892, the province of Manitoba passed a similar act (McFarland, 1970); thus, the provincial governments played an important role in the development of parks in Canada.

In the 1940s, the federal and provincial governments, under the National Physical Fitness Act, provided recreation services that influenced municipal recreation (McFarland, 1970). In Ontario in 1945, 18 municipalities passed recreation bylaws,

iStockphoto/Bart Broek

Emerald Lake is located in Yoho National Park in the Canadian Rocky Mountains, which is one of many Canadian National Parks established by the federal government.

and within one year an additional 70 had passed bylaws (Markham, 1992). The governments focused on leadership development in schools and the community and increased awareness of the possibilities of public recreation programs. The act was repealed in 1954 (Westland, 1979). The Ontario provincial government gave grants to municipalities and encouraged the local provision of recreation opportunities for all. In the 1950s, British Columbia and Alberta supported local governments in developing municipal grant structures suitable for social and economic situations (McFarland, 1970).

All three levels of government continue to be involved in providing recreation services. The Interprovincial Sport and Recreation Council (ISRC) developed the National Recreation Statement in 1987. The statement defines the roles of each level of government. In 1978, the provinces and territories agreed that recreation was within their jurisdiction; thus, their role in recreation became significant. Once local volunteers make decisions about recreation services, provincial governments are responsible for providing the assistance, leadership, and recognition necessary to deliver these services. They provide support to community volunteers who manage recreation clubs and societies and provide leadership and instruction, raise money, and coordinate programs. The interprovincial council agreed that it is the role of the provincial governments to state policy outlining the goals and objectives and stress the importance of recreation as a social service. Some of their other roles include observing and analyzing trends and issues to update policy; providing municipal governments with resources to enhance the quality of life of a community through grants for conferences and training; providing programs and services to build a delivery system that links the three levels of government and voluntary, private, and commercial sectors; and planning and supporting recreation research.

The role of the municipality in providing recreation services is to ensure a wide range of opportunities for all community members. Municipalities are responsible for establishing a recreation authority to provide opportunities, be aware of resources and opportunities and ensure that information is available to the public, provide incentives and services to develop opportunities based on needs, conduct regular assessments of needs and interests that are not being met, and develop a council to determine the best use of community resources (ISRC, 1987).

Finally, the Interprovincial Sport and Recreation Council outlined the federal government's role in providing recreation services. The council agreed that the federal government must act to influence the scope of recreation and work closely with all recreation agents in implementing programs that affect recreation services. The federal government should provide recreation through national organizations and ensure Canadian representation in activities that serve a national purpose. The federal government should contribute to the development of recreation services through provision of resources to support public, voluntary, and commercial sectors. And finally, the federal government should provide promotional materials to encourage recreation participation (ISRC, 1987).

Parks Canada is one federal agency that provides recreation opportunities for Canadians. The mandate of Parks Canada is to "protect and present examples of Canada's natural and cultural heritage and foster understanding, appreciation, and enjoyment in ways that ensure their ecological and commemorative integrity for present and future generations" (Parks Canada, n.d., para. 1). The agency serves as the guardian of parks, historic sites, and national marine conservation. The agency guides visitors to national parks and serves as a partner in building on the traditions of Indigenous peoples, diverse cultures, and international commitments. Parks Canada recounts the history of the land and people and is committed to protecting heritage, presenting the beauty and significance of the natural world, and serving Canadians (Parks Canada, n.d.).

Professional Organizations

Professional recreation groups began to emerge in Canada in the first half of the 20th century. Both national and provincial associations serve recreation professionals and volunteers. The Canadian Parks and Recreation Association (CPRA) developed from the expanding mission and influence of the Ontario Parks Association in the later years of the war. During postwar discussions, the Ontario Parks Association called on the government to consider parks, playgrounds, and recreation a separate reconstruction project after the war. On July 11, 1944, in Windsor, Ontario, the CPRA started as a means of broadening the mandate of the Ontario Parks Association for Ontario and Quebec. Formal creation of CPRA occurred one year later (Markham, 1995). At that time, it was known as the Parks and Recreation Association of Canada. Its purpose was to deal with changes that occurred after World War II, including the need to provide parks and recreation services. Today, the society responds to social, economic, and political changes within the country (CPRA, n.d.). The mission of CPRA is to build healthy communities and enhance the quality of life and the environment. The association serves as a national voice for parks and recreation, and it advocates on behalf of parks and recreation as essential for the health and well-being of Canadians. CPRA communicates and promotes the values and benefits of parks and recreation, responds to diverse and changing needs, and provides educational opportunities (CPRA, n.d.). In 2015, CPRA

OUTSTANDING GRADUATE

Background Information

Name: Emilie McIntosh

Education: BA in recreation and leisure studies from Virginia Wesleyan College

Credentials: Certified Park and Recreation Professional (CPRP)

Awards: Spring 2014 Outstanding Major Award

Affiliations: Rho Phi Lambda

Career Information

Position: Park General Manager

Organization: I work for Outdoor Venture Group as a designer and operator of aerial adventure courses. The adventure parks of Outdoor Venture Group provide active, enjoyable outdoor activities involving a personal interaction with nature. Outdoor Venture Group owns nine aerial adventure parks in the United States and employs over 400 people. The adventure parks serve over 350,000 climbers every year.

Job description: I am responsible for all aspects of The Adventure Park at Sandy Spring Friends School (SSFS). I oversee a team of managers who are responsible for group sales and marketing, retail sales and customer experience, course maintenance, training, and staff development. I coordinate the activities of all the departments so that they all can work together to meet the park goals.

© Emilie McIntosh

Career path: I began my career working at summer camp and quickly realized that I had a passion for outdoor recreation. After working as a camp director, I decided to return to school to earn my degree in recreation and leisure studies so I could go further with my career. After graduation I took a job as a park supervisor at The Adventure Park at Virginia Aquarium because I loved the opportunities that the park offers guests. I was promoted to course manager there, and then I was offered the position of park general manager at The Adventure Park at SSFS.

Likes and dislikes about the job: I love seeing guests overcome their fears and finding that they can do things that they never thought they could do. This job is my dream job and what I have worked toward throughout my career.

Advice for Undergraduates

I encourage students to find a job doing what you love. If you are passionate about what you do, then it doesn't ever feel like work. Working somewhere people come because they want to (versus have to) gives you the responsibility to make every moment with them the best it can be.

---

released the Framework for Recreation in Canada, which outlines five goals for achieving well-being of Canadians through recreation. These goals include active living, inclusion and access, connecting with nature, supportive environments, and development of recreation capacity (CPRA, 2015).

Another national organization for recreation professionals is Physical Health Education Canada (PHE Canada), which promotes physical activity among young children and youth (PHE Canada, n.d.-b). This organization started as the Canadian Physical Education Association in 1933. It changed to the Canadian Association for Health, Physical Education, and Recreation in 1948, added dance in 1994, and in 2008 adopted its current title Physical & Health Education Canada (PHE Canada, n.d.-a).

Provinces also have recreation associations. For example, the Saskatchewan Parks and Recreation Association (SPRA) aims to "promote, develop, and facilitate parks and recreation opportunities throughout the province" (SPRA, n.d., para.1). Recreation Nova Scotia, another provincial organization, promotes the values and benefits of recreation toward a healthier future. Recreation Nova Scotia came into existence in 1998 with the merger of three organizations: Recreation Association of Nova Scotia, the Recreation Council on Disabilities in Nova Scotia, and Volunteer Nova Scotia (Recreation Nova Scotia, n.d.). A third provincial organization, Parks and Recreation Ontario (PRO), is a not-for-profit group that formed in 1995 (PRO, n.d.). The aim of PRO is to promote and develop benefits of recreation through education, collaboration, and research (PRO, n.d.).

Post–World War II Growth in Canada

Canada also experienced a host of challenges related to recreation and leisure after World War II; some were similar to and some were different from those experienced in the United States. Among those challenges were the following:

• **Concern for fitness.** The 1960s were characterized by renewed concern for physical fitness (Searle & Brayley, 1993). The Fitness and Amateur Sport Act, which was passed in 1961, redefined the role of government in sport, recreation, and leisure. In the 1960s, all levels of government became involved in financial assistance to promote recreation development. Much of this money was dedicated to building facilities (Searle & Brayley, 1993). ParticipACTION began in 1971 with the aim of increasing awareness of physical fitness (The ParticipACTION Archive Project, n.d.-a). ParticipACTION's 1973 media campaign suggested to Canadians that a 60-year-old Swede was as fit as, or more fit than, a 30-year-old Canadian (The ParticipACTION, Archive Project, n.d.-a.). ParticipACTION continued until 2001, when board members decided to close the program (The ParticipACTION Archive Project, n.d.-b.). However, ParticipACTION reemerged several years later with the mandate of increasing physical activity and decreasing the amount of time spent sitting (ParticipACTION, n.d.).

• **Economic challenges.** In 1973, the Arab oil embargo ended the rapid development of recreation resources and opportunities. High energy costs led to empty arenas and poorly maintained parks. The oil embargo also affected pleasure travel when gas was rationed and higher jet fuel costs made flying expensive. Provincial and municipal governments were forced to limit the growth of recreation. They needed to adopt a new style of leadership. Municipal recreation agencies became less involved in directly providing services and started playing a facilitative role instead (Searle & Brayley, 1993).

• **Changing demographic trends.** The changing nature of the family throughout the 1980s and 1990s influenced recreation service delivery and caused service providers to respond to different needs, opportunities, and constraints. Various family structures had to be considered, including blended families, single-parent families, childless families, multiple generation families, and traditional nuclear families, to name a few (Searle & Brayley, 1993). The majority of single-parent families were headed by women in the 1980s; and these families had lower incomes than two-parent families (Harrington, 1996). Common-law relationships became more common throughout the 1980s and 1990s, and marriage rates were lower. The age of first marriage rose during the 80s and 90s, divorce rates rose, and fertility rates declined (Harrington, 1996). All these trends affected leisure services delivery.

• **Poverty.** People living in poverty also posed a new challenge for service providers. The new poor were of particular concern and included children living in poverty, the working poor, and frail elderly community members. Leisure services were needed to help build self-esteem, develop social support networks, and teach self-reliance skills. Focus was on satisfying needs and delivering programs in the most appropriate way for clients (Searle & Brayley, 1993).

• **Multiculturalism.** This is another consideration that arose in the 1980s and 1990s, and it continues today. Canadian public policy defends the idea that differences in a nation are good for it, and the government protects the cultures of new Canadians. As a result, recreation services must provide relevant and meaningful recreation opportunities for new Canadians.

CURRENT TRENDS AFFECTING RECREATION AND LEISURE

The following emerging trends influence recreation and leisure service provision today, and they will continue to do so in the future:

• **Immigration and diverse populations.** As individuals migrate to North America, their perceptions of recreation and leisure may change the dynamics of service delivery models. Individuals who migrate from developing nations often do so for two common reasons: They leave voluntarily for a better life in a developed nation, or they are refugees who are forced to leave their country due to oppression or war (Kim, Compton, & McCormick, 2013). According to the United Nations (UN, 2015), there were 244 million international immigrants in 2015. Of these, 54 million are living in North America. Because these numbers are sure to increase with time, recreation and leisure practitioners need to be cognizant of the different experiences immigrants have had compared to those who did not migrate (Kim & Van Puymbroecke, 2011). The need for recreation and leisure programming designed for these newcomers is a must, particularly programs that are provided by public parks and recreation agencies. These agencies serve the broad population within a community and must be responsive to the needs of newcomers and long-term residents alike. The increase in diversity has resulted in changes to populations served, programs offered, facilities, hiring practices, and policies. In an effort to be more inclusive and to target individuals who were not being reached, recreation and leisure programming has been expanded to meet needs of individuals of different ages, genders, ethnicities, and ability levels. Communities have diversified programming efforts to include opportunities for increasingly diverse racial and ethnic populations. For example, the city of Seattle offers female-only swim times to accommodate women of Islamic descent who cannot wear bathing suits in the presence of men. As a result of the program, women who ordinarily would not participate in swimming have the opportunity to do so. In addition, city parks and recreation departments are diversifying their staff to mirror populations served; specifically, they are hiring employees who are fluent in languages other than English. The Washington, DC, parks department initiated a Black History Invitational Swim Meet in an effort to increase African American participation.

• **Technology.** Rates of childhood obesity and screen time have increased in correlation with reduced time spent in physical education classes and recess. Many attribute increases in obesity rates to sedentary lifestyles associated with screen time. In response, recreation and leisure programs have been diversified to include various platforms for engagement through apps, online gaming that encourages movement, and wearable devices. These technological components provide opportunities for competition, exploration, and information and can track progress.

• **Economic challenges.** Recreation and leisure services have had to rely on fees and charges due to decreased government funding during tough times. The funds collected offset program costs and produce profits that support other programs. These fees and charges have subsidized many programs, but they have been criticized for potentially excluding those with less income.

• **Shopping as recreation.** An additional emerging trend is the notion of shopping as recreation. The term "shopping fever" was introduced to incorporate concepts such as mall mania, home shopping, online shopping, and shopping as therapy, all of which related to the "dogged pursuit of more" and a condition known as "affluenza" (DeGraff, Wann, & Naylor, 2001, p. 2). Shopping then, both online and in person, provides not only a recreation activity to occupy leisure time but also a way to purchase those things that demonstrate one's economic level.

• **Population aging.** In North America, population aging has been evident for several decades as older adults comprise a larger proportion of the population (MacNeil & Gould, 2012). Increased life expectancy and declining fertility rates contribute to population aging. Baby boomers (those born between 1946 and 1965) make up a large percentage of this aging population. Pruchno (2012) argued that baby boomers are transforming what it means to be an older adult; they view retirement differently than their predecessors and seek work–leisure balance in this life phase. They tend to be more physically active and interested in outdoor pursuits than previous generations of older adults (Sperazza

& Banerjee, 2010). Baby boomers are affecting how leisure services are offered to older adults because they require a broader range of options.

SIMILARITIES BETWEEN CANADA AND THE UNITED STATES

Recreation has developed similarly in the United States and Canada. For example, both countries developed playgrounds in similar ways at about the same time. The following are among the trends that have been identified in Canada and the United States:

- Expansion of activities for children to activities for people of all ages
- Expansion of summer programs to yearlong programs
- Provision of indoor and outdoor activities
- Expansion of playgrounds into rural areas
- Shift from philanthropic to community financial support of playground programs
- Increased importance of organized play over unorganized play
- Shifting philosophy to include use of leisure and not just provision of facilities by communities
- Increased importance of community and group activities over individual interests (Rainwater, 1992)
- Creation of play spaces
- More opportunities for child development through play
- Growing belief in the importance of outdoor play for young people
- Increased opportunities for public recreation
- Quest for a better balance between work and play
- Appreciation of the value of play in children's lives

At the end of the 19th century the playground movement in Canada and the United States continued the trend of increased appreciation for recreation and leisure. Economic class separation in Canada and the United States was a growing reality (as it was in ancient Greece), and class structure in Western society after the industrial revolution was structured along the lines of economic wealth. The upper classes demonstrated a growing concern for those in the lower classes. Recreation and leisure were no longer seen as privileges but were rather seen as an important part of life and a way for those who were well off to help those who were less so. This sense of obligation encouraged the use of recreation and leisure as a way to address life's challenges and facilitated the playground movement.

Government has played an important role in providing recreation and leisure opportunities in both the United States and Canada. In the United States, the government began to play a role in providing social services during the Great Depression when the lack of jobs increased the amount of time available to pursue leisure activities. The federal government also developed organizations to protect natural resources and preserve them for future generations. This continued a trend of governments tackling societal problems through concern for the leisure-related issues facing their citizens.

SUMMARY

Leisure in the United States and Canada has been influenced by past definitions of leisure. Primitive societies had little time for leisure as they fought for survival. However, as their tools became more sophisticated, they gained more free time. Play was used to teach children about their roles as adults and as an opportunity for ritualization, rest, and relaxation. Among the ancient Greeks, contemplation, education, philosophy, and athletics were important leisure activities that helped people reach the Athenian ideal. However, only full Greek citizens had opportunities for leisure. In ancient Rome, leisure was time away from work, and recuperation was of great importance. Leisure was also used as a method of social control. After the fall of the Roman Empire, the Catholic Church, which restricted leisure participation, controlled what people perceived to be leisure by placing values on activities. Further restrictions were placed on leisure and social activity during the Protestant Reformation as new churches emerged. These strict rules were relaxed during the Renaissance when artists were supported and play was considered important for education.

Early settlers in the United States and Canada brought these perceptions of what was acceptable leisure to their new countries. These views and the environmental conditions they faced have influenced leisure today. The first colonies in the United States restricted leisure because settlers were fighting for survival and had time for little else. However, as restrictions were lifted, working bees, hunting, and going to the tavern became popular pastimes. As time passed, exploration and settlement resulted in increasing recreation opportunities for European settlers. As governments established parks as early as the 1700s, participation started to grow and a concern for the appropriate use of leisure time emerged.

The playground movement in both the United States and Canada began in the late 1800s and early 1900s. The first sand garden was founded in Boston, and more playgrounds followed in New York and Chicago following Boston's success. The movement was started in Canada by the National Council of Women to give children opportunities for supervised play to prevent delinquency and promote healthy development.

All levels of government in both countries are involved in recreation. Governments provide facilities, funding, support, policy, information, and training for recreation services. The growth of organizations concerned with recreation program provision and the workers responsible for it emerged in the United States at the same time as the playground movement. These organizations evolved to become the two main national organizations today: the National Recreation and Park Association and SHAPE America. In Canada, professional organizations emerged on the national level with the Canadian Parks and Recreation Association and at the provincial level in the 1940s with Recreation Nova Scotia. As in the United States, these agencies provide support for recreation programs and promote the importance of recreation and leisure for health and well-being. In the United States, the President's Council on Physical Fitness and Sports was formed in the 1960s to address fitness, and in the 1970s the ParticipACTION program was developed in Canada to encourage citizens to become fit. As the new millennium unfolded, it became clear that many themes of the past, including how best to serve a changing society, the appropriate use of mass leisure, the government's role, and the importance of professional organizations, were as important as ever. Nearly two decades after the turn of the century, recreation and leisure service providers continue to experience changing trends that influence service delivery. From the economic challenges with providing services to changing population, to activities that increase and decrease in popularity, these trends and more have made recreation and leisure ever-changing and history suggests that will always be true.

CHAPTER 3

Philosophy and Leisure

Donald J. McLean

Christopher Futcher/Getty Images

" Happiness is thought to depend on leisure; for we are busy that we may have leisure, and make war that we may live in peace. "

Aristotle, Greek philosopher

LEARNING OUTCOMES

After reading this chapter, you should be able to do the following:

> Explain the five branches of philosophy, the relevance of each to leisure research, and the effect of each on leisure services delivery

> Compare and evaluate the concepts of leisure as a state of mind and a state of being and apply these two conceptions of leisure to the provision of recreation services

> Demonstrate a comprehensive understanding of the leisure research literature by comparing theories of leisure based on empirical research and philosophic analysis

> Describe the importance of being able to justify conclusions and decisions logically in leisure services

> Discuss why aesthetics is important to our understanding of leisure and how considerations of aesthetics influence the provision of leisure services

> Apply ethical reasoning to evaluate the worthiness of leisure services

The methods of philosophy can be put to good use in the study of recreation and leisure phenomena and the delivery of leisure services. Contrary to the popular belief that philosophy provides obscure answers to theoretical issues, philosophical inquiry has many practical implications for and is important to leisure research and service delivery because it helps focus our attention on important questions and issues related to recreation and leisure. Perhaps the best way to summarize the usefulness of philosophy to the field of recreation and leisure studies and services is that it provides us with guidance in *how* to think rather than *what* to think about issues and problems related to leisure and recreation.

WHY DOES PHILOSOPHY MATTER?

For many people, the subject of philosophy appears to have little relevance to recreation and leisure. Our stereotype of philosophers suggests that they are deep thinkers who are uninterested in practical matters relating to relaxation, pleasure, or fun. This highbrow image of philosophy is spoofed in the old Monty Python skit of the philosophers' soccer game: Aristotle, Kant, Hegel, and other great thinkers from the past stand like statues deep in thought on a soccer field. The ball just sits there for the whole match until Archimedes suddenly has a revelation and kicks the ball to Socrates who then fires it into the net while the other players look on in bewilderment.

Like the immobilized philosophers in the skit, many recreation students become frozen in their seats, their eyes glazed over, when their instructor announces that the week's topic is the philosophy of leisure. Typically, students have chosen recreation and leisure studies because they prefer active, hands-on experiences to abstract thinking. What use, students ask, is there in learning what some dead white guy from long ago thought about leisure and recreation? Wouldn't their time be better spent learning how to program activities, create budgets, and market events?

Because the philosophy of leisure is often taught as a history lesson or as part of the intellectual foundations of leisure and recreation, it is understandable that students are doubtful that philosophy has any real application to leisure services. Yet philosophy affects both the study of leisure phenomena and the delivery of recreation services in fundamental ways. It is just that we tend not to recognize the importance of philosophy to recreation and leisure studies because it typically functions in the background of our thinking and practices. But when we understand what philosophical inquiry is, it is not difficult to see the contribution that it makes to the theory and practice of leisure and recreation. To learn why philosophy does matter to people interested in recreation and leisure, let's begin by first examining why philosophy has gained a reputation for being irrelevant.

The term *philosophy* translates from ancient Greek as "lover of wisdom," and originally it referred to all scholarly inquiry. Over the last several hundred years, however, the evolution of modern-day universities has seen the rise of many separate disciplines such as physics, chemistry, sociology, and anthropology as knowledge and methods of inquiry have become increasingly complex. In fact, the discipline of leisure studies follows this pattern of the increasing specialization of knowledge because most recreation curricula and departments did not exist before the 1960s.

The division of knowledge into a variety of specialized fields is an important explanation for why philosophy appears to have lost much of its relevancy. As discipline-based knowledge has grown, the scope of philosophic inquiry has been whittled away. But despite the loss of academic ownership to other disciplines, philosophy is primarily associated with five branches of inquiry: metaphysics, epistemology, logic, aesthetics, and ethics. Each of the five types of philosophical inquiry has relevance to recreation and leisure studies, but as will be explained later, the first two, metaphysics and epistemology, have more importance to leisure researchers, whereas ethics is more relevant to leisure practitioners. The fourth branch of philosophical inquiry, logic, has important implications for leisure researchers and leisure practitioners, whereas the fifth branch, aesthetics, has received relatively little attention from either practitioners or researchers. To advance our understanding of the relevance of philosophical inquiry, let's now examine the ways in which each of the branches of philosophy has influenced thinking and practice in recreation and leisure.

METAPHYSICS AND LEISURE

Metaphysics concerns questions about the fundamental nature of reality. It is the branch of philosophic inquiry that is most likely to generate amusement and derision from nonphilosophers. Questions such as "Does a tree make a sound when it falls in the forest if no one is around?" or "Is the cup really on the table?" or "Does God exist?" are classic examples of metaphysical inquiries that can seem pointless to more practically minded people. (I remember being in a philosophy seminar in which we really did discuss whether the professor's coffee cup was on the table!) Many people have argued that metaphysical inquiry into the ultimate nature of reality is too speculative to be of any practical use. Even famous philosophers such as David Hume dismissed metaphysics as so much gibberish about nothing.

Although most contemporary philosophers do not subscribe to the view that metaphysical inquiry is meaningless, ironically, it was advanced physics that popularized speculation about the nature of reality. Scientist–media personalities such as Carl Sagan and Stephen Hawking have done much to fuel the public's imagination about such topics as the ultimate nature of the universe and our place in it. Many people today are fascinated by theories of alternate realities as predicted by quantum mechanics, the origins of the universe, and other metaphysical speculations that stretch beyond the boundaries of empirical science.

In recreation and leisure studies, metaphysical inquiry has mainly revolved around more down-to-earth questions of how leisure should be defined. Although the average person might believe that everyone knows what leisure is, scholars and researchers have gone to great lengths debating the essential qualities of leisure. And, as many researchers have noted, the term *leisure* is difficult to define. Unlike phenomena studied in the natural sciences, in which the subject matter stays the same no matter the time or place (e.g., water has the same physical properties that it did 1,000 years ago and does not vary from one society to another), socially constructed phenomena such as leisure are continually in flux (e.g., ideas about leisure vary from culture to culture and at different periods in time). The variability of leisure as a socially evolving phenomenon of human existence makes it much more difficult to determine what its essential qualities are. Nonetheless, intellectual debates concerning the essence of leisure have historically fallen into two opposing theses about the fundamental nature of leisure. The traditional view is that leisure is a public, objective state of being. The modern view is that leisure is essentially a private, subjective state of mind. Let's first examine the traditional view of leisure and then compare it with the modern definition of leisure.

The idea that leisure is a state of being—that is, a set of life circumstances—is attributable to the ancient Greeks. According to Aristotle, having leisure meant being free of the burden of work so that one could engage in more ennobling activities such as music and philosophy. For the ancient Greeks, an essential element of leisure was to possess sufficient material resources so that one could have time for leisure. Thus, if you were a slave in ancient Athens, you were incapable of having leisure because you did not have the resources to engage in it.

The idea that leisure is a state of being is also reflected in contemporary conceptualizations of leisure as unobligated time. Modern economic systems, which formalized the division between work time and leisure time, have helped reinforce the idea that the most fundamental feature of leisure is that it is a time when we are free from work and other obligations of life. As well, the ancient Greek ideal that leisure time should be used to engage in worthwhile activities still resonates with many people, although research indicates that most of us do not devote much of our free time to uplifting activities. Sebastin de Grazia's book *Of Time, Work and Leisure* provides a modern-day justification for the idea that people should use their leisure time to perform worthwhile activities. For both ancient and contemporary thinkers who see leisure as a state of being, the critical point is that leisure is defined by the circumstances and actions of people that can be observed by others. Leisure, therefore, is not a private experience, but instead it occurs in a public, social context where others can judge whether we are at leisure or whether the activities that we are engaging in qualify as leisurely. Leisure as a state of being thus depends on a social consensus as to what activities and living conditions qualify as leisure.

In contrast to the notion that leisure is a state of being, many leisure researchers have argued that leisure is primarily a private state of mind. John Neulinger, for example, theorizes that leisure is a psychological state in which the experience of leisure depends on how a person perceives a situation. Neulinger's theory of leisure is based on two variables: perceived freedom and motivation (Neulinger, 1974). According to his theory, perceived freedom means that a person thinks he or she is free in a particular instance. With Neulinger's theory, perception of freedom does not depend on the individual's actual circumstances. Even for people who are desperately poor or repressed, so long as they

think that they have freedom, a necessary condition for leisure is satisfied. The other psychological component necessary to having leisure is whether the person perceives that his or her motivation is intrinsic or extrinsic, in other words, whether motivation is generated internally (e.g., one plays music because it is pleasing to oneself) or externally (e.g., one plays music to make money). Thus, when people perceive that they are free to choose to engage in a leisure activity that they find intrinsically motivating, then the resulting outcome is a state of mind whereby they experience pure leisure. According to many modern-day leisure researchers, leisure is therefore a private, subjective state of mind rather than a public, objective state of being.

Although it may seem fine and well that leisure researchers investigate and debate the fundamental characteristics of leisure, students and practitioners may wonder how such discussions could have any relevance to delivery of leisure services. But the choice between thinking that leisure is a state of being or a state of mind can have a profound influence on leisure services delivery choices (Sylvester, 1991). Sylvester states that viewing leisure as a state of mind may encourage practitioners to provide leisure experiences that are inauthentic, illusory, and even immoral:

> Regardless of the actual content, context or consequences, *anything* counts as leisure as long as the individual avows a subjective experience of freedom. Applying to illusions as well as real events, the potential for leisure is virtually boundless. If you experience leisure, then leisure it is, for there is no disputing the truth of subjective states of mind (1991, p. 441).

Sylvester argues that viewing leisure as a private state of mind opens the door to all sorts of horrid and depraved activities that qualify as leisure. Less shocking, but still worrisome, he says, is the possibility that leisure services practitioners may choose to provide clients who live in inequitable and repressive circumstances with leisure experiences that encourage them to accept their disadvantaged situations. And, even for well-to-do clients, he questions whether practitioners should "engineer" pleasant subjective leisure experiences. Rather than providing impetus for true personal growth,

OUTSTANDING GRADUATE

Background Information

Name: Nicki L. Ellis

Education: BS in recreation, park, and tourism administration from Western Illinois University at Moline

Credentials: Certified Nonprofit Professional (CNP)

Awards: 2014 Anita H. Magafas Nontraditional Student Award, 2014 departmental nominee for the Lincoln Academy of Illinois' Student Laureate Award

Career Information

Position: Sales Manager

Organization: The Quad Cities Convention and Visitors Bureau (QCCVB) is the tourism marketing and management organization for the Quad Cities region of Illinois and Iowa. We increase visitor expenditures and overnight stays through strategic sales, marketing, and services to our customers, members, and communities. The QCCVB is a 501(c)(6) nonprofit organization operated by a board of directors and has just under 20 full-time and part-time employees.

Job description: I am responsible for prospecting accounts that have potential for bringing meetings, group tours, conventions, tradeshows, and sporting events to the Quad Cities. I coordinate leads, develop proposals and bid packages, track progress, and assist in closing sales while working with several levels of partnerships.

> " *Be the change you wish to see in the world.*
> —Mahatma Gandhi "

Career path: After graduating from Western Illinois University, I taught at a nonprofit preschool where I had previously interned (in their marketing department). Through networking and volunteering in the community, I kept in touch with the QCCVB.

Likes and dislikes about the job: What I like most about my job is the formation of lasting relationships that benefit my community. The least favorite part is the uncertainty that is associated with working with a nonprofit organization's budget.

Advice for Undergraduates

My advice to undergraduate students is that change is the new constant! You can't be afraid to embrace change and try something new. Also, network, network, and network some more!

©Nicki Ellis

---

development, and achievement, subjective leisure may deceive people into thinking that their leisure lives are fulfilling and meaningful when, in fact, the leisure activities that they are engaged in lack ennobling qualities.

Although the concerns that Sylvester raises about subjective leisure are well-founded, regarding leisure as a state of mind may be beneficial in many situations. For example, some adventure recreation programming, such as high-ropes courses, deliberately uses the perception of risk to facilitate participants' personal growth. Being suspended 40 feet (12 m) off the ground can result in a perception of adventure and risk, but participants are safe because they are harnessed and belayed. Exposing participants to real danger in this situation would be not only unnecessary for achieving the benefits of the recreation experience but also irresponsible and unethical.

We can readily think of other examples in which approaching leisure as a state of mind is the proper approach. We would be unwise and insensitive to tell an enthusiastic young child that his or her piano playing is not very good. Nor should we disparage those who sometimes seek out artificial leisure environments such as Disney or engage in virtual reality experiences. And what of harmless, idiosyncratic types of leisure such as eccentric hobbies that few people other than those engaged find enjoyable? Should these activities not be classified as leisure because other people do not appreciate their merit?

Even though treating leisure as a state of mind is desirable in many situations, it is equally true in other instances that it is reasonable to conceptualize leisure as an objective state of being. For example, we make the effort to visit a significant natural or cultural resource because we want to experience the authentic object or environment. No replica or simulation will suffice. We join a competitive sports program because we want to see how our skills match up with the skills of others. We set challenging goals to exercise, become fit, and lose weight. In these instances, the leisure experience is guided by the ability to achieve a particular objectively recognized state of being.

Therefore, in some situations and contexts, it is helpful to think of leisure as a state of being, and at other times it would be best to treat leisure as a state of mind. Perhaps the lesson here is not that we must define leisure in one way to the exclusion of the other but instead that we must be aware of the fundamentally different ways that leisure can be conceptualized and understand how our presuppositions about the nature of leisure can influence our assumptions about the kinds of leisure experiences that will be beneficial to people. Thinking about the essential nature of leisure, therefore, is not simply an academic exercise for researchers. Let's now consider the next branch of philosophic inquiry, epistemology, and its influence on the field of recreation and leisure.

EPISTEMOLOGY AND LEISURE

Epistemology is the study of knowledge itself. The term is derived from the Greek words *episteme* (knowledge) and *logos* (explanation); hence, epistemology is the branch of philosophy that explains knowledge or provides theories about how it is we know what we know. Epistemology concerns questions of how we can acquire knowledge, what types of things we are capable of knowing (the scope of our knowledge), and how trustworthy the knowledge that we possess is (how certain we can be of what it is we know).

Traditionally, epistemological debate about the source of knowledge divides into two camps: those who think that knowledge is derived from sense perceptions (**empiricists**) and those who believe that knowledge comes from ideas generated by our minds (**rationalists**). Empiricists believe that ultimately knowledge must be based on evidence. Thus, empiricists place a great deal of importance on how observations are collected.

Whether we are leisure researchers or practitioners, we want to have the best information possible for advancing knowledge and making decisions. In

North America, the study of leisure has predominately been data driven, but debate has been ongoing about whether observations should be collected to produce quantitative or qualitative data. Many leisure researchers believe that the investigation of leisure phenomena should use methods conducive to producing quantitative data; that is, observations of leisure should primarily take the form of numeric scores. Examples of quantitative data include the numbers generated from questionnaires that use Likert scales or the tallies from observational checklists. Researchers can then use such data to perform statistical analyses and test hypotheses about factors that are thought to influence people's leisure experiences. Often, the collection of quantitative data has a narrow focus so that the amassing of information concerning a few variables can be carefully controlled.

Other researchers take the position that observations of leisure should be gathered primarily by interpreting the meaning and significance that people associate with their leisure experiences. To understand the meaning that people attribute to leisure, researchers collect and analyze the words and statements of subjects from interviews or create field notes based on the their interpretations of subjects' behavior and actions. Qualitative analysis emphasizes explaining and understanding the lived leisure experiences of the subjects being studied and tends to have a broader focus than quantitative analysis.

The fact that there are two schools of thought about how observations should be collected has, not surprisingly, created an epistemological debate between the adherents who favor quantitative data collection and those who favor qualitative data collection. Although we need not trouble ourselves with the details of this lively controversy, supporters of research that produces quantitative data maintain that it is more trustworthy than qualitative data, whereas those who support the collecting of qualitative data argue that it provides a more comprehensive understanding of people's leisure experiences. The debate is thus largely a disagreement between which epistemic qualities of knowledge are more important: the certainty and trust that arise from knowledge derived from observations (quantitative) or the scope and relevancy of the knowledge derived from gathering data about people's lived leisure experiences (qualitative). But despite these disagreements about the strengths and weaknesses of quantitative and qualitative data, note that both sides agree substantially on one fundamental point: Knowledge about leisure is based on the collection of evidence. Both believe that the source for new knowledge about leisure comes from the ability to collect observations of leisure phenomena. Thus, the debate about quantitative and qualitative data is essentially a quarrel between empiricists.

In contrast to the empiricist belief that knowledge of leisure must derive from observation, rationalist epistemology says that our minds are the primary source for our knowledge about leisure. To those of us who have been trained in empirical research techniques, it might seem inconceivable that any new knowledge about leisure could be produced by simply thinking about it. Yet many of our fundamental ideas about leisure have not been derived from empirical research. It would be absurd to believe that the classical conception of leisure was the result of data collected by questionnaires, interviews, or field notes. Although Aristotle is thought of as an empiricist philosopher for his copious observations of the natural world, his methodology when examining leisure is better classified as philosophic analysis. Similarly, many modern scholars, such as Josef Pieper, have greatly advanced our understanding of leisure without employing empirical research methodologies. The method of inquiry that these nonempiricist leisure scholars use is often referred to as *theoretical research*. Rather than looking to external sources for knowledge of leisure by collecting observations from research subjects, theoretical research generates knowledge by the internal thought processes of the leisure researcher who applies reason and logic in the form of philosophic analysis of leisure concepts and issues.

Theoretical research is particularly helpful when we are trying to come to conclusions about matters of values rather than matters of fact, as the following example illustrates. Gambling is a popular but controversial leisure activity that has been the subject of considerable empirical research, particularly since the relaxation of gambling restrictions in the latter third of the 20th century. Yet the collection and analysis of data on gambling can provide only partial answers to the practical question of whether it is a desirable leisure activity. Statistics on tax revenues generated, employment and economic multipliers, gambling addiction rates, and so on

Photodisc/Getty Images

Theoretical research can help us come to conclusions about matters of value as opposed to matters of fact. For example, is it right to try to restrict and control people's access to gaming?

cannot fully answer the question of whether the vast expansion of the gaming industry has been beneficial. To conclude that the expansion in gambling opportunities has improved people's quality of life requires us to employ nonempirically based reasons as well. Does, for example, the enjoyment that many people gain from visiting casinos outweigh the pain experienced by the relatively few who are addicted to gambling? Should gambling opportunities be expanded because governments find themselves needing more tax revenues? Is it right to try to restrict and control people's access to gaming? Answers to these and other questions about gaming surely help enrich our understanding of gambling as a leisure activity and cannot be wholly determined simply by collecting information. Rather, we also need to employ our ability to reason abstractly, analyze various value issues relating to gambling, and construct arguments to justify the conclusions that we draw.

So, our understanding of leisure seems to depend on both empirical data and theoretical or philosophic analysis. Given that leisure is a complex social phenomenon, perhaps we should not be surprised that it cannot be adequately comprehended by a single method of knowing. Although we naturally have our preferred method of comprehending leisure—whether by quantitative or qualitative research or by theoretical or philosophic analysis—we should be wary of excluding other ways of knowing. Simply being aware that there are multiple ways to gain knowledge and understanding of leisure can help us avoid thinking that our preferred way of understanding leisure is the only way.

LOGIC AND LEISURE

We have learned from our examination of the epistemology of leisure research that both empirical and theoretical or philosophic analysis is needed for comprehensive understanding of complex social phenomena such as leisure. The generation of new knowledge by empirical and theoretical or philosophic analysis is based, in part, on accepted rules of logic. **Logic** is the branch of philosophy concerned with principles and structure of reasoning. It is the study of the rules of inference that we can use to determine whether our reasons (premises) properly support conclusions that we make. Infer-

ences (reasoning from premises to conclusions) can be either deductive or inductive. Deductive inferences are constructed so that if our premises are true, then our conclusion *has* to be true as well. In contrast, the premises of inductive inferences are structured so that if our premises are true, then it is *likely* that our conclusion is true. Because research aims at finding out new things that we think are true, logic plays an important role in our inquiries by making sure that the conclusions we draw are properly supported. Both empirical research and theoretical or philosophical analysis place a high premium on conformity to accepted rules of logical inference. Leisure research that is deductively invalid or inductively weak is likely to be judged as fatally flawed and be rejected.

Although the rules of logical inference are important to leisure researchers, logic is also important to leisure services practitioners. While many day-to-day work tasks of leisure services practitioners can be implemented in a routine manner, other important management functions such as strategic planning, budgeting, policy creation, and evaluation and action research involve systematic processes whereby decisions must be supported by reasons and rationales. Leisure services practitioners can use inductive and deductive reasoning in these formal management processes to help structure and guide their decision-making.

Besides using logic to aid their decision-making, practitioners often need to be able to justify their decisions to a variety of stakeholder groups. To be effective managers and providers of leisure services, practitioners must have some understanding of the formal rules of logic for their own decision-making purposes and knowledge of rules and principles of informal logic that relate to everyday conversation. Informal logic—also referred to as **critical thinking**—assesses how people use reasoning and language to try to persuade others to accept conclusions. It focuses not only on detecting fallacies of reasoning but also on understanding nonlogical aspects of communication that may influence the acceptance of a conclusion. Thus, we use informal logic to assess both the structure of inferences and the context in which they are made (e.g., who is making the argument, in what situation is it being made, and who is the audience to which it is being directed). As philosopher Leo Groarke (2017) notes, informal logic is intended to "improve thinking, reasoning, and argument as they occur in real life contexts: in public discussion and debate; in education and intellectual exchange; in interpersonal relations; and in law, medicine and other professions." Whether leisure services providers work in the public, nonprofit, or commercial sectors, being skilled in the application of informal logic helps them effectively justify their decisions and actions to the many constituencies they serve and to whom they are accountable.

AESTHETICS AND LEISURE

Up to this point, we have primarily considered how philosophy relates to leisure in terms of generating scientific knowledge about leisure, but we have not examined our understanding of the art of leisure. **Aesthetics** is the branch of philosophy that deals with questions of the nature of beauty and the value that we associate with art and the natural environment. Our love of beauty is a primary motivation for our interests in the arts, whether we delight in dance, music, theater, painting, sculpture, or other aesthetically oriented leisure activities.

The aesthetic value of the arts has influenced public leisure policy and the development of modern cultural institutions. For example, the 19th century Victorian era gave rise to the **rational recreation movement**, which attempted to use aesthetic appreciation as a method for elevating the character of the working class and instill in them middle-class values. It was thought that the burgeoning masses of immigrants from abroad and migrants from the farms would be a socially disruptive force in quickly growing industrial cities. Recreation reformers believed that these newcomers to urban life needed to refine their leisure so they would not resort to unsavory recreation activities such as drinking and prostitution (Cross, 1990). While restrictions were imposed on what was deemed morally objectionable leisure, it was also thought that exposure to high culture would encourage the working classes to become more productive, responsible citizens. Thus, there was growing public support for cultivating the aesthetic sensibilities of the lower classes by encouraging attendance at cultural institutions such as museums. Art museums, in particular, were seen as well-suited to refining the character of common people by elevating their tastes.

Photo courtesy of Western Illinois University Visual Production Center.

The aesthetic value of the arts and the belief that exposure to high culture would encourage the working class to become more responsible citizens has influenced the development of present-day museums.

As noted by Alexander and Alexander (2008), "European art museums following the French revolution served the public through their displays of beauty to 'inspire and uplift' the lower classes," and for American art museums, "the contemplation of art was sometimes considered as a means of fighting vice and crime" (p. 41).

Of course, whether the Victorians were correct in believing that the aesthetic value of fine art actually elevated character and reduced criminal behavior of the working class is an open question. And the agenda of raising the aesthetic taste of the lower classes to that of their "betters" is a form of **paternalism** that most people today would find offensive. Furthermore, as has been argued by leisure studies theorist Chris Rojek (1995), we now live in a **postmodern** age where "the divisions between high and low art, elite and popular culture, have collapsed" (p. 165). This dissolving of the barriers between high and low culture has resulted in the "aestheticization" of everyday life (Featherstone, 1991), in which the regard for beauty takes on a heightened importance in the decisions of ordinary people in their day-to-day doings. Expert opinion on what constitutes the fine and beautiful is not as important as it once was. Today, people are more at ease with determining how to individually style the way they live their lives. Therefore, the idea of using aesthetic appreciation to "improve" certain classes of people has much less currency now than in the past. As a result, while cultural institutions such as museums still conserve and interpret rare and beautiful objects for the public's edification, there is now more emphasis on encouraging visitors to create their own personal sense of appreciation and meaning (Falk & Dierking, 2000; Hein, 1998). This shift toward catering to the various aesthetic interests and tastes of visitors is also reflected in the adoption of new types of leisure opportunities and programming that even a generation ago would be unimaginable. It is now typical for cultural institutions to host a variety of events and activities, such as child–parent sleepovers, community festivals, themed dinners, fundraising events, and amateur night performances, that would have previously be considered kitschy or low brow.

The blurring of the distinction between high and low culture has fundamentally altered the role that aesthetics plays in culturally based leisure and recreation. While some are critical of this leveling of the field of aesthetic judgment (e.g., Cuno, 2004), it also presents the prospect for greater participation of students trained in leisure services delivery to work in cultural institutions. Prime opportunities include not only the creation and delivery of innovative, alternative forms of recreational and interpretative programming but also the possibility of becoming involved in the growing field of **visitor studies,** which examines and evaluates the leisure motivations, behaviors, and informal learning experiences of attendees at cultural venues.

Influencing cultural leisure and recreation, aesthetics is also an important factor in outdoor recreation, particularly for those who are attracted to wilderness. Issues concerning the aesthetic values of wilderness constitute a significant part of the outdoor recreation literature. For example, Roderick Nash, an environmental historian, argues that the aesthetic values that Western society has associated with wilderness have run the gamut from seeing nature as repugnantly ugly to sublimely beautiful. In his book *Wilderness and the American Mind*, he argues that wilderness is not a physical place so much as a "mood or feeling in a given individual" (1982, p. 1). Nash notes that ancient Greek, Western pagan, and Judeo-Christian value systems traditionally regarded wilderness as an alien, threatening environment that was repulsive rather than attractive. The ancient Greeks regarded the wild heath as fit only for barbarians and found beauty instead in the city and rural countryside. The ancient Hebrews saw wilderness as a harsh, forbidding wasteland that was the antithesis of the beautiful, idyllic Garden of Eden. The medieval people of northern Europe thought of wilderness as dark, sinister forests inhabited by pagan beings such as trolls and wood-sprites. When the pioneers came to North America, they brought with them these negative images of wilderness. Combined with the fact that these pioneers were faced with the very real need for survival, wilderness was seen as a forbidding environment to be subdued and civilized.

But Nash notes that as life in North America became more "civilized" by settlement and urban development, people had less reason to see wilderness as an imminent threat to survival. In addition, in the 18th and 19th centuries, a new aesthetic judgment arose toward wilderness based on a philosophic movement called *romanticism*. Rather than seeing nature as ugly and evil, the romantics took the opposite view that wildlands represented the height of divine beauty.

The idea that nature could be aesthetically pleasing was also taken up by the 19th century transcendentalist philosophers and essayists such as Ralph Waldo Emerson and Henry David Thoreau. The New England transcendentalists believed that profound spiritual truths must be discerned using intuition and imagination rather than rational thought, and they believed that the sublime beauty of nature was a primary pathway to understanding reality. For writers like Thoreau, who retreated to his cabin at Walden Pond, civilization rather than nature was what threatened the well-being of humankind.

Interest in the aesthetics of the natural environment waned for the better part of the 20th century as the field of philosophical aesthetics focused primarily on art, which is, of course, the creation of humans rather than nature. But issues concerning aesthetics and the natural environment have been revived recently with the rise of the new field of environmental aesthetics. This renewed interest in the aesthetics of the natural environment has been driven by the growth of environmentalism and environmental legislation that can be traced back to the National Environmental Policy Act of 1969, which requires that consideration of aesthetic values be included in environmental impact assessments. Our aesthetic values and judgments concerning nature thus have some practical implications for the management of wilderness. Do we, for example, manage wildlands so that the aesthetic values of the landscape are not altered, much in the way that we try to preserve a fine artwork? Should we determine the aesthetic value of a natural environment by collecting data concerning the aesthetic experiences of visitors? Do we try to optimize the aesthetic appeal of natural environments by introducing nonnative species, for example, if visitors judge them to be more beautiful than the indigenous ones? Should ecosystems that are aesthetically pleasing receive more management resources and attention than those that are unremarkable in their beauty (or perhaps even ugly) but are ecologically more important? Should we alter the natural environment in ways that make it less aesthetically attractive so that disabled recreationists can have access, say by paving a trail to make it wheelchair accessible? In these and in other instances, we find ourselves in situations where we must judge the importance of aesthetic values against other important nonaesthetic values to make practical managerial and policy decisions. Given that society is becoming more sensitive to environmental issues, we can expect that environmental aesthetics will play an increasingly important role in decision-making for natural resource management. An awareness and understanding of aesthetics is therefore not an abstract exercise in philosophizing; instead, it can help us make better-informed decisions about our roles as stewards of nature and providers of meaningful leisure experiences.

ETHICS AND LEISURE

Of the five branches of philosophy, **ethics** is the one most closely allied with leisure. We often do not think of ethics being that relevant to leisure and recreation. After all, leisure services provide nice things in life such as fun, pleasure, and enjoyment. Why would people working in recreation need to worry about ethical issues? (In fact, it has been suggested that both leisure researchers and practitioners themselves tend to associate recreation and leisure activities with the notion that they are intrinsically good.) But leisure services providers are likely to encounter many vexing ethical issues and dilemmas during their careers to which they must devise acceptable solutions. Consider the context in which leisure services occur. Leisure services are people oriented, and when people interact things can go awry. Leisure services providers are often put in positions of trust. Park rangers are charged with protecting both the natural environment and the safety of park visitors. Therapeutic recreation specialists are often entrusted with the care of vulnerable populations. Supervisors and program leaders of youth programs are expected to exercise a high degree of responsibility and provide healthful activities for their young charges. And the list goes on. Clearly, the provision of organized leisure services is not simply fun and games; it is a serious undertaking that imposes significant ethical responsibilities on service providers.

Ethics, the philosophical study of morality, is closely allied historically to the Western conception of leisure. The ancient Greeks, whose writings form the basis of the study of morality in Western culture, framed ethical inquiry in terms of how people could find happiness and how society should be organized to facilitate living a good life. For philosophers such as Plato and Aristotle, leisure played a critical role in living an optimal style of life.

Let's first see how Plato handled the question of how ethical behavior relates to living a good life. Then we can compare it to how his student Aristotle refined his master's teachings on the value and ethics of leisure.

Plato's Philosophy of Leisure

Plato wrote several dialogues to answer the practical question of how people should best live their lives. His dialogues read like the script of a play. In them, various characters debate with each other about a question or issue. Plato's greatest dialogue, *The Republic,* lays out his vision of a utopian society. He reasons that a perfectly ordered society would maximize the happiness of its citizens. To achieve such an ideal state, Plato argues that people's thoughts and actions must be strictly controlled. He proposes a harsh censorship of playful leisure activities that he believes would disrupt the order of a perfect society:

> We must begin, then it seems, by a censorship over our story makers, and what they do well we must pass and what not, reject. And the stories on the accepted list we will induce nurses and mothers to tell their children and so shape their souls by these stories.

Plato is taking aim at the telling of various Greek myths and the epics of the poet Homer. Anyone familiar with Greek mythology knows that the residents of Mount Olympus were hardly good role models. Their chief god, Zeus, is depicted as a philandering husband who is taken with the seduction of both mortal and divine females. His jilted wife, Hera, hatches various plots for revenge on her hapless rivals. The rest of the Olympian gods are no more admirable and are portrayed with all sorts of human failings, vices, and weaknesses. Plato believed that telling these stories of debauched and corrupt gods would harm individuals and society, so he wanted them banned.

In addition to controlling storytelling, Plato believed that other types of leisure activities should be censored. He thought some musical instruments, such as flutes, should not be allowed in his ideal society because their sound would stir the passions of listeners. Similarly, he thought music that was either dirge-like or effeminate should be prohibited because it would make people sad or weak.

Plato carefully separated good leisure activities from bad ones based on his theory of what an ideal society should be like. According to his political philosophy, leisure activities are tools to be used to shape the character of citizens of his utopian society. Only those types of leisure activities that he judged to be virtuous were allowed. He saw many forms of leisure and recreation as threats to his perfectly ordered society. He was most fearful of playful forms of recreation that excited the emotions. Plato thought an ideal society should be ruled by reason alone. The citizens of his ideal Republic were expected to behave as somber, sober rationalists. Perhaps the metaphor of an anthill would best describe his vision of how society should be structured. The workers, soldiers, and rulers who were the citizens of Plato's utopia would all go about doing their assigned **work** with the greatest seriousness. Leisure, recreation, and play would only be encouraged if they had educational or developmental value (Hunnicutt, 1990).

We can still see a legacy of Plato's political philosophy in present-day leisure services. For example, a lot of recreational programming for youth is based on the notion that activities should contribute to positive character development (Johnson & McLean, 1994). And, like Plato, many adults are concerned about the influence of music and stories on children. Even though modern-day democracies permit many freedoms, V-chips are used in televisions, sales of "adult" books and magazines are restricted, and filters are used on computers to try to prevent young minds from being exposed to the images and ideas that parents and community leaders believe are harmful.

Plato's philosophy makes it clear that leisure and recreation are important tools for influencing individuals and society. He does not regard leisure and recreation as mere fun and games, but instead treats them as critical components of a properly functioning society. Yet his vision of leisure emphasizes repression and control. Who would really want to live in his dreary, regimented utopia? Where is the notion that freedom is an integral part of experiencing leisure? To put the freedom back into leisure, we need to turn to Plato's student, Aristotle.

Aristotle's Philosophy of Leisure

In many ways Aristotle followed Plato's political teachings. Aristotle was willing to advocate the repression of most people living in his society. Women and slaves were not allowed the luxury of leisure; that privilege was reserved for the male citizenry. But Aristotle did not picture this leisured class as the idle rich. Rather, the leisured elite was expected to strive for self-perfection. For Aristotle, living the ideal lifestyle was a practical matter. It required following those habits of living that were virtuous and avoiding those that were vices (Hemingway, 1988).

In *Nicomachean Ethics,* Aristotle defined *virtue* as a midpoint between the vices of excess and deficiency. Take, for example, the virtue of courage. It is an excellence of character that results from being neither cowardly (a deficiency) nor foolhardy (an excess). He recognized that every person's situation varies according to personal circumstances. However, each should live his or her life to maximize virtue—in other words, each person should try to be his or her very best. To excel in one's life requires a continual commitment to self-improvement. Aristotle therefore argues that one needs to develop habits of living that lead to excellence. It is instructive that the Greek word for ethics is derived from the word *ethos,* which means "habit"—a behavior or practice we continually engage in throughout our lifetime.

But what is the ultimate purpose of developing virtuous habits? Aristotle says that happiness results from being the best we can be. The sort of happiness that Aristotle is thinking of should not be equated with simple pleasure. Amusing ourselves can be pleasant, but he says it is childish and has the potential to cause us harm. **Amusement** for sheer pleasure degrades rather than improves us. Aristotle admits that amusement is helpful if it refreshes us from work. But amusement is never as good as true leisure, which provides a life of deep fulfillment rather than fleeting bodily pleasures.

By using leisure to become our best, Aristotle is not simply thinking of moral goodness but also those characteristics that make us uniquely human. And what did he think was our most noble quality? Aristotle says that it is our capacity for rational thought that distinguishes us from all other forms of life. He argues that the employment of reason in intellectual contemplation leads to perfect happiness. Therefore, he concludes that the person who has the most rewarding lifestyle is the philosopher who is at leisure to develop his intellect to its highest capacity.

We may disagree with Aristotle that being an intellectual is the most rewarding life people can live. It could be plausibly argued that excelling at other human activities, such as food preparation, athletics, or art, could produce equally satisfying lifestyles. But perhaps it is not important to quibble over which human activity is best. Instead, the important feature of Aristotle's theory of happiness is that it is based on the idea that human fulfillment

Ludovisi Collection

Aristotle began his philosophic inquiry by asking himself what an ideal lifestyle for human beings should be like. What do you think?

results from achieving excellence from things we choose to do when we use our leisure appropriately.

Aristotle's philosophy of leisure, which emphasizes discipline and commitment rather than the freedom and choice we associate with our modern-day leisure experiences, may seem demanding. Nonetheless, freedom is an important element of Aristotle's concept of virtuous leisure. First, we need freedom from material wants so that we can have time for leisure. This means that we cannot be enslaved to our work. We need a sufficient level of material comfort (food, shelter, clothing, and so on) so that at least during part of our day we can have time for leisure. Second, we need intellectual freedom to understand why virtuous leisure activities are good. When we are children, we can be trained to practice virtuous habits without knowing why those things are desirable. For example, we learn at a very young age not to lie. But it is only when we are older that we fully understand why lying is wrong (e.g., it is hurtful to others). So it is with the practice of virtuous leisure activities. If you are an ancient Greek freeman, you choose certain activities to excel at not because someone has trained you to do them, but because you understand and appreciate that these activities are noble. Third, freedom is the essential characteristic of any virtuous leisure activity. These activities are simply worthy in themselves; we do not do them because they will bring fame, wealth, or other extrinsic rewards. In other words, virtuous leisure activities are intrinsically good.

CONTEMPORARY PHILOSOPHY OF LEISURE

We might ask whether Aristotle's elitist definition of leisure has much relevance to our modern lifestyles. Perhaps we can relate to Aristotle's refined version of leisure when we think of the high level of accomplishment of professional athletes, cordon bleu chefs, and concert pianists. These people live lives devoted to perfecting their talents. But these examples are not leisure activities. Instead, they are occupations—ways of making a living. It is difficult for us to think of excellence apart from working. Typically, when we are very good at something, we want to turn it into a career. We tend to value activities that can be made productive. We are very

work oriented, whereas the ancient Greeks were work averse. It was not that the Greeks thought that work was something evil, but rather they regarded it only as a necessity of life. They worked so that they could enjoy life. According to their value system, it was leisure that gave meaning and purpose to their life, not work (de Grazia, 1963).

For most of us, it is typically our work, our career, and our occupation that give us our sense of self-worth. If you do not believe this is true, think back to the last time you met someone at a social occasion. When making new acquaintances, was it your leisure activities or your work that you primarily used to describe yourself to others? In our modern culture, the question "So what do you do?" implicitly assumes that you will respond by describing your occupation and workplace. Extolling the virtues of work would seem very odd to the ancient Greeks. We appear to have reversed that equation.

Weber's Analysis of the Work Ethic

Have you ever heard someone being praised for having a strong work ethic? The term is derived from Max Weber's influential book *The Protestant Ethic and the Spirit of Capitalism* (Weber, 1930/1958). The **Protestant work ethic** refers to a cultural ideal that regards work as the most important activity in an individual's life. Weber believed that a new reverence for work arose from the Protestant Reformation, when Christian religious leaders such as Martin Luther and John Calvin rebelled against the Catholic Church. Both Luther and Calvin saw the medieval church as a corrupt institution in which the upper echelons of the clergy lived a life of wealth and leisure. Up until the time of the Reformation, the church had followed Aristotle's teachings concerning leisure and the good life. The clergy and the nobility comprised the leisured class; both were educated and wealthy enough to have the free time to engage in refined intellectual and cultural activities. The many ordinary, uneducated peasants were little more than slaves who provided brute labor for the upper classes. In their radical break from the church, Luther and Calvin turned Aristotle's conception of the good life on its head, making work—not leisure—the foundation of a worthy life. Both Luther and Calvin believed in

dinostock/fotolia.com

Weber's work ethic changed our view of the good life to one that valued hard work over leisure.

the notion of a *calling*, whereby everyone had been assigned by God a certain task or occupation to perform throughout life. Answering one's calling in life was considered a virtue because you would be doing the work God intended for you. Conversely, ignoring your calling was a vice and would lead to an empty, directionless life. Thus, since the time of the Reformation, it has been work rather than leisure that culturally defines our conception of the good life.

Russell's Critique of the Work Ethic

Some modern philosophers have taken great exception to the notion that work can make our lives truly happy. Bertram Russell penned a tongue-in-cheek essay in the early 1930s titled "In Praise of Idleness" in which he criticizes the idea that work is virtuous. Russell argues that preindustrial societies were based on a "slave morality" used to justify the subjugation of large numbers of manual laborers so that a privileged aristocracy would have leisure to

pursue spiritual, cultural, and intellectual activities. However, with the coming of the industrial revolution, modern technology created such an abundance of goods that it was possible for everyone to have sufficient resources for a leisured lifestyle. But rather than using technology to give everyone adequate leisure, Russell says we continue to support the idea that leisure should be reserved for the upper crust of society and denied to the working class.

Russell argues that it would be more rational to replace the traditional, but outmoded, slave morality with a leisure ethic that distributes work evenly. Rather than having a leisure class that does no work at all and a working class that is either overworked or unemployed, Russell proposes a work-sharing arrangement that would reduce people's working time to four hours per day and still provide the "necessaries and elementary comforts" of life (Russell, 1960, p. 17). Russell believes that with these greatly reduced work hours, humanity would enter a new golden age of leisure, giving people the freedom to pursue cultural and intellectual interests. Perhaps Russell is naive to think that everyone would use their liberation from work for ennobling leisure activities. Would not many people choose to waste their free time engaged in frivolous amusements? Nonetheless, even if many people would not use their leisure wisely, we can still ask if that is a good enough justification for keeping people busy with work. Maybe what is really needed is not only sufficient free time but also attractive and meaningful leisure opportunities that professionalized leisure services can provide.

Pieper's Critique of the Work Ethic

Josef Pieper, a Catholic philosopher, also strongly criticizes allegiance to the work ethic in his book *Leisure: The Basis of Culture* (1998). Pieper, who is writing of Europe in the aftermath of World War II, says that we no longer know what leisure is because we live in a totally work-oriented culture. Pieper argues that our fixation on work is so complete that even liberal arts disciplines such as philosophy are now treated as a type of "intellectual labor" and are only valued for their usefulness for solving practical problems. (And isn't this why many people ridicule philosophy and leisure studies, because these disciplines are thought to be useless?) According to Pieper, knowledge for knowledge's sake is devalued by our culture of work, and our leisure time is only thought to be useful if it refreshes us so that we can then resume our work with renewed vigor. Ironically, Pieper observes, our worship of work produces a meaningless, unsatisfying lifestyle. We live to work well rather than working so that we can live well.

Rojek's Critique of the Work Ethic

As the title of his book *The Labour of Leisure* (2010) suggests, Chris Rojek also argues that leisure has become a form of work. But whereas Pieper thought that modern Western society is marked by a shift from leisure to a work ethic, Rojek believes that present day postmodern culture has blurred the traditional boundaries between work and leisure. Work, he says, now contains elements of play, whereas leisure can be a type of work. According to Rojek, leisure no longer functions as a respite from work but instead is the setting in which we learn the skills for living a successful life. He identifies **emotional intelligence** and **emotional labor** as the two key abilities that "competent, relevant and credible" people seek to develop during leisure (Rojek, 2010, p. 3). The changes in our economic means of production from manufacturing to services means that personal interactions are now much more central to success in life. Emotional intelligence primarily refers to the capacity to accurately perceive and understand one's own emotions and the emotions of others. The closely related concept of emotional labor focuses on the ability to manage one's emotional responses when confronting work situations that are emotionally challenging, such as maintaining an appropriately professional demeanor with a rude, agitated customer. People who capably understand and regulate their emotions are, therefore, at a competitive advantage in their work and leisure lives in comparison to people who bludgeon their way through life lacking the ability to control their own emotions or are unable to respond appropriately to the emotions of others. Rojek concludes that leisure is not about freedom (which he says is for the birds), but rather it is where we school ourselves in emotional intelligence and

emotional labor. If Rojek's analysis is correct, then the implication for leisure services practitioners is that emotional intelligence and emotional labor are critical competencies that they should be ready to deploy when providing leisure services and strive to build up when engaging in their own leisure.

Veblen's Critique of Consumption

Although many people believe that being a success entails working hard to achieve enough financial independence to be able to retire to a life of luxury, could our worship of work sabotage our leisure lives? Many critics argue that our economic system works against our aspirations for a truly leisured lifestyle.

Modern economies encourage ever-expanding growth in the production and consumption of products and services. As individuals, we live in a consumer culture where our success is measured by how much we can purchase. The more luxurious and expensive the goods we can own, the higher our social status. The American economist Thorstein Veblen termed the ostentatious displays of wealth "conspicuous consumption" (Veblen, 1899/1998). Veblen criticized the superrich of his era—the Vanderbilts, Carnegies, and Rockefellers—as status seekers who used the great wealth they had amassed from their 19th-century business empires to give themselves an air of nobility. Their mansions, yachts, and lavish parties were symbols that these American industrialists "had arrived" at the good life.

Of course, most of us are not billionaires. We cannot hope to own executive jets, hand-built sports cars, or vacation homes on private Caribbean islands. Yet compared to the standard of living of ancient Greek freemen, the lifestyle of the average person living in postindustrial societies is opulent. We have at our disposal a vast array of consumer products and services that Aristotle and his compatriots could not have imagined.

Other Critiques of Consumption

Unfortunately, being able to afford these products and services means that most of us must devote a huge portion of our adult lives to work. The flip side of a highly consumptive lifestyle is that we must also be highly productive to pay for it. During our working lives, many of us find our time for leisure is limited. Our careers require us to put in long days at work, leaving little time or energy for family and friends.

The consumerist lifestyle that most of us have adopted encourages us to think of leisure as a basket of commodities from which we pick and choose. Instead of being participants in unique and personal recreation activities, we are consumers of leisure experiences designed and mass produced by others (Hemingway, 1996). In this market-driven context, the concept of freedom is inextricably tied to the act of purchasing: When there are many leisure products and services for sale, we have greater freedom to choose.

This free-market model of leisure services and products is undeniably attractive to most people. The leisure industry is one of the biggest and fastest growing sectors of the economy. Yet this apparent success masks several drawbacks to our commercialized leisure. As social economist Juliet Schor (1998) argues in her aptly titled book *The Overspent American*, the most obvious problem with the idea that we can buy happiness is that many of us spend more on our leisure than we can afford. Indications of overspending can be found in the level of household debt, which provides a reasonable measure of the level of stress on consumer finances. The post–World War II period has witnessed continually rising household debt levels, except for the period of the financial crisis and Great Recession that led to a one-time reduction of debt from 2008 to 2013. However, since mid-2013, debt levels have resumed their upward trajectory and are now equal to the pre-recessionary levels of 2008. While credit delinquencies significantly fell during the Great Recession, credit card, auto, and, in particular, student loans defaults are again growing. So, the reduction in debt triggered by the financial crisis has been a one-time event (Haughwout, Lee, Scally, and van der Klaauw, 2017). The use of borrowing to finance the consumption of goods and services has returned us to our "normal" state of affairs where we use debt accumulation to help finance our current standard of living that we may not be able to afford in long run. Evidence of this overspending can be gleaned from the fact that even higher income earners may find their retirement savings insufficient to maintain lifestyles they were accustomed to while working.

Aside from the question of the long-term viability of consumerist lifestyles, the commodification of leisure may discourage personal growth by making our recreation experiences too convenient.

Getty Images/Caiaimage/Dan Dalton

The consumerist lifestyle demands that we work more to afford more goods. These shoppers hope to find happiness from the products they purchase.

Commercial providers of leisure services typically want to make their offerings as attractive as possible to their potential clientele. Competitive advantage can be gained by making the consumption of leisure services and products as effortless as possible. The examples are many: Golf manufacturers advertise that their clubs alone will lower your handicap and you don't have to improve your swing; resort operators provide familiar fast-food items at exotic destinations so that guests will not have to adjust to the local cuisine; movie and television producers "dumb down" the content of popular entertainment lest audiences be made to think; and the list goes on.

Although our modern leisure services and products may be convenient, we might ask whether most of them are worthy of our time, not to mention our money. Aristotelian leisure is based on the idea that we should devote our free time to being the best we can be. The ancient view of leisure emphasized commitment and accomplishment. In contrast, as philosopher Albert Borgmann notes, commodified leisure appeals to our desire for comfort (Borgmann, 1984). Often, our modern leisure practices do not result in self-improvement. In fact, many of our recreational activities may cause us harm. Watching television, our most popular leisure pastime, has been linked to several modern maladies including obesity, depression, and paranoia (Gerbner, 1999; Kubey & Csikzentmihalyi, 1990). But it is attractive because of its easy access—you simply turn on the TV and then sit back and enjoy. But even our more active forms of recreation tend to cater to our desire for creature comforts. When practical and affordable, we often choose to motorize outdoor recreation activities. Why climb up a slope when you can use a chairlift? Why paddle or row when you can simply twist the throttle on an outboard engine? Why carry your clubs when you can ride in a cart? These uses of machines are said to enhance our leisure experiences, but they may also disengage us from our environment and each other. Harvard sociologist Robert Putnam (2000) argues in his book *Bowling Alone* that Americans are becoming increasingly socially isolated. He cites a wealth of statistics showing that membership in community organizations dropped dramatically at the end of the 20th century. As a result, Putnam believes that Americans have become less satisfied with their lives because they have experienced a decline in

their **social capital**—the social connections that support people in times of difficulty and make life more enjoyable in times of leisure. He attributes diminishing social capital to the changes in society that alter our work and leisure values:

> Over the last three decades a variety of social, economic and technological changes have rendered obsolete a significant stock of America's social capital. Television, two-career families, suburban sprawl, generational changes in values—these and other changes in American society have meant that fewer and fewer of us find that the League of Women Voters, or the United Way, or the Shriners, or the monthly bridge club, or even a Sunday picnic with friends fits the way we have come to live. (Putnam, 2000, p. 365)

A similar decline in social capital may be happening in Canadian society, although the data are more mixed. For example, a study of social cohesion found that Canadians perceived themselves as having a high level of personal social support ("someone they can confide in, count on in a crisis situation, obtain advice from when making important decisions, and someone who makes them feel loved and cared for") but a low level of social involvement ("frequency of participation in associations or voluntary organizations and frequency of attendance at religious services") (Jackson et al., 2000, pp. 66, 68).

Putnam compares the malaise in community involvement to the problems that faced American society at the end of the 19th century when rapid industrialization created a host of social problems in large cities. He notes that people responded to these social ills by becoming more involved in civic activities and voluntary organizations, and he argues that we need to find ways to use our leisure time to be more civically engaged.

Perhaps it is because we are at least subconsciously aware that many of our leisure activities are unworthy experiences that we devise various rationales to justify our modern leisure lifestyles. We see shopping as an exciting recreational activity rather than a mundane necessity of life. We tell our employees that we value wellness, but what we are really worried about are rising absenteeism and medical expenses. We take mini-vacations that cause the least disruption of our work schedules and take along our laptops and handheld devices to avoid falling behind. At home, rather than spending unstructured, spontaneous time with our kids, we plan infrequent special activities and call it *quality time*. Unfortunately, this list goes on.

What we seem to lack is a sense that our leisure activities can be self-justifying. Our view of leisure as a commodity is based on the implicit premise that our leisure activities are a means to achieving some other goal. Perhaps that is not a surprising mind-set given that we live in a commercialized culture in which we are constantly bombarded with messages about products and services that promise this or that benefit. But this lifestyle is ultimately unsatisfying for many of us because it keeps us focused on our leisure as a means to something else rather than a worthy end in itself. The ancient Greeks understood very well that leisure should be reserved for activities that were good in and of themselves. Aristotle did not recommend philosophic inquiry as the best leisure activity because it made him more productive at work. Rather, he simply argued that it was the most intrinsically worthy activity that human beings could do.

Aristotle, it must be acknowledged, did not face the challenges to leisure that we do today. His social environment was far less complex than what we must deal with as leisure services providers. Of course, it may seem that there is little we can do to influence the quality of people's lives given the strong cultural and economic forces that encourage people to be workers and consumers. But we are not completely powerless. As leisure services providers, we can make a difference in the lives of the people and communities that we serve. It all begins with a clear understanding of our own leisure values. For example, if we know that people are stressed by a culture that overvalues work, then we have an obligation as leisure services providers to advocate for the value of leisure. If we see that people are stressed by an economic system that encourages the overconsumption of products, then we can offer alternative leisure activities that encourage social interaction and community building. Surely if we think of ourselves as quality-of-life specialists, then we need a philosophical understanding of some of the major problems that people and communities face; otherwise we may unwittingly become part of the problem rather than part of the solution.

SOLVING ETHICAL DILEMMAS IN LEISURE SERVICES

So far, we have used ethical analysis to help us evaluate our leisure lifestyles. In our roles as socially responsible leisure services providers, we need this macro, or big-picture, understanding of the broad social and political issues that affect the quality of people's leisure lives. Essentially, we are using ethical analysis to continue the ancient Greeks' project of determining the role of leisure in a worthwhile life. This sort of analysis is prescriptive rather than descriptive, because it aims not simply to describe our past or current lifestyles but instead to determine how we should live our lives. But we can also use ethical analysis in a micro, or small-picture, way to help us solve problems relating to the delivery of leisure services. Consider the Philosophical Analysis: Tanning-Bed Case sidebar, which presents an **ethical dilemma** that narrowly focuses on a situation and set of individuals at a public recreation center.

Dealing effectively with the tanning-bed problem mentioned in the sidebar requires more than having a big-picture understanding of the situation. After all, the big picture tells us that skin cancer is a serious health problem, and as socially responsible leisure services providers we shouldn't provide equipment or services that are potentially dangerous. Yet, many of the people we serve don't agree with our point of view; therefore, we are left in an uncomfortable position in which a lot of people may be angry or unhappy. What we need is a way to resolve these ethical dilemmas that are common in leisure services. Fortunately, ethical analysis can help us decide the proper course of action in cases where we are confronted with a moral conflict involving specific people at a particular time and place.

To deal effectively with ethical dilemmas, we need an ethical decision-making method we can use to justify our decisions. And as responsible leisure services providers, we are obligated to provide the people who are affected by our decisions with reasonable explanations for our actions. Not everyone will agree with our decisions, but we need to demonstrate that our decisions are not made arbitrarily. Skepticism about the wisdom of our decisions is likely to be stronger when we are dealing with ethical dilemmas, and emotions tend

Philosophical Analysis: Tanning-Bed Case

You are the recreation supervisor at a multipurpose community recreation center. The mission of the center is to promote the well-being of the citizens in the local community by providing a wide variety of high-quality recreation activities. Since the center opened, the fitness area has played an important role in satisfying the recreation center's mission. The fitness equipment and programs are popular, and they benefit participants' physical health and well-being. Recently, however, some of the patrons have asked the recreation center to install tanning beds. Many of these requests are from teenagers and young adults who say they like to work out at the center, but they also want to be able to get a deep tan. You have never wanted to install tanning beds, because you have read research that indicates that the exposure to UV rays that these

beds produce increases the likelihood of skin cancer, including the deadliest form of the disease, malignant melanoma. You announce that the center will not purchase the beds because of the possible negative health effects. Unfortunately, your decision is met with dismay and even outright hostility. Many of the young people who want the beds installed say they are not worried about cancer. Some say they will drop their memberships and join a nearby private health club that has the beds. Several of the middle-aged members have contacted their representatives on the city council (to whom you report) to lobby for purchasing the beds. And a few have threatened to go to the local media and "raise a stink" about how adults should be allowed to choose whether they can tan and should not be treated like children by the recreation center staff.

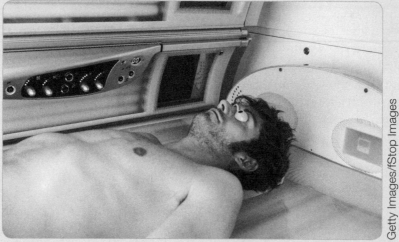

Getty Images/fStop Images

Philosophical analysis can help solve the problem of whether tanning beds should be used at a recreation center.

Ethical Analysis: Three Approaches

Let's consider how you might apply ethical theory to decide what to do in the tanning-bed case. Three basic ethical theories can help you decide whether to install the beds: (1) **consequence-based ethics,** (2) **duty-based ethics,** and (3) **virtue-based ethics**. Using the first approach, you weigh the consequences of installing or not installing the tanning beds. If you install the beds, you will make many people who use the recreation center happy. You will also not lose members to the private health club because you lack tanning beds. You also will not have to deal with client complaints to the city council or the newspapers. From a consequence-

based ethics perspective, the only downsides would be the initial cost of the equipment and the possibility that some recreation center clients might eventually develop skin cancer. Because there seems to be several definite, immediate benefits to installing the beds, it would be reasonable to conclude that you should go ahead and spend the money on the tanning beds.

The second way you can determine the most ethical course of action is to use a duty-based ethics perspective to evaluate your duties and obligations. One important duty you have is to carry out the mission of the recreation center. You are there

Philosophical Analysis

to serve the public, so you have an obligation to provide services that people want. But you also have an obligation to provide services that benefit people's well-being. Given that public recreation organizations receive tax monies to provide leisure services that serve the public good, it is reasonable to assume that protecting the community's well-being is a more important duty than simply providing services that people want. Therefore, from a duty-based ethics perspective, you should not install the tanning beds because that would betray your obligation to provide healthy leisure services.

At this point in the moral deliberations, you have come to opposing conclusions. Analysis from consequences-based ethics indicates that you should install the tanning beds, and duty-based ethics argues that we should not install them. How do you break this moral deadlock? You might want to turn to the third way of analyzing ethical dilemmas: virtue-based ethics. With virtue-based ethics, moral decisions are made by reflecting upon your character. Instead of comparing outcomes or weighing duties, virtue-based ethics resolves ethical dilemmas using your personal integrity. For example, will you diminish yourself and become a less noble person if you install the tanning beds in the fitness center? If the users of the beds are mature adults aware of the dangers of UV exposure, then possibly not. These adults have simply made a choice to engage in an activity that endangers their health. But what about the teenagers who also want to use the beds? Will you find it hard to look at yourself in the mirror before you go to work knowing you have helped expose teenagers to health risks that they might not be willing to take if they were mature adults? Therefore, from a virtue-ethics perspective, you might install the tanning beds only if you have an effective way to prohibit teens from using the beds and if you can ensure that the adults at the center are well-educated about the risks of UV exposure.

to run high when moral points of view come into conflict. Although it is a common belief that ethical issues are based on opinion rather than fact, we can nonetheless apply ethical theories to help us create a rationale for our actions.

We can see from the application of the three ethical theories to the tanning-bed scenario that solutions to ethical dilemmas are not always obvious. Some might think that tanning beds should be installed, while others might be opposed to placing this type of equipment in a community recreation facility. Furthermore, we might disagree on which ethical theory is best for solving the dilemma. Some people may think consequences should decide the issue, others might believe duties are paramount, and a third group might believe that considerations of our character should dictate what to do. The important point is not that we might disagree about the proper solution to the ethical dilemma, but instead that our moral deliberations help us justify and explain our decision to people who disagree with us. For example, suppose the people who want the tanning beds are thinking in terms of the consequences. They want the beds because they are after certain outcomes such as what they believe to be a healthy look or a sexier body. Now we can talk to them on their wavelength by pointing out negative outcomes such as skin cancer and premature aging. If they still insist that the benefits outweigh the costs, then we can also explain that we have a duty to uphold the mission of the agency to provide healthy recreation, and that according to our own professional standards, we would not feel right about providing equipment that could cause serious health problems. Of course, it is completely possible that people still will not be persuaded that we are making the right decision, but at least we have provided them with a reasonable, well-thought-out explanation for the decision. And we have accomplished this very practical task by using ethical analysis to justify it.

Serious social and ethical issues are bound to arise as we work to help people improve their leisure lifestyles. If we are unable to assess the worthiness of various leisure activities, then we run the risk of providing leisure opportunities that may not enhance the quality of people's lives. Ethical analysis can give us a macro understanding to judge the worthiness of the various leisure and recreation activities that we might choose to provide. We have seen that most of our current leisure experiences seem to be geared toward the worlds of work and commerce rather than with the provision of opportunities to engage in intrinsically satisfying activities and personal growth. But besides providing us with a big picture of some of the social issues facing leisure services, ethical analysis can also help us deal with micro issues arising from the ethical dilemmas that we will inevitably encounter during our careers as leisure services providers. Without an awareness and understanding of the ethical issues arising from leisure and recreation activities, we run the risk of causing unintended harm to the people we serve and the resources that we have been entrusted with. Rather than having to rely solely on our intuition, we can use methods of ethical analysis to help us justify and explain our solutions to difficult moral dilemmas.

SUMMARY

We hope that our examination of the five branches of philosophy—metaphysics, epistemology, logic, aesthetics, and ethics—has persuaded you that philosophic analysis plays a fundamental role in leisure research and the provision of leisure services. Philosophy and leisure are often misperceived as being frivolous and of little practical consequence. Yet our examination of the relevance of philosophy to leisure illustrates that neither is trivial. Leisure and recreation, both as an academic discipline and as a service practice, has tremendous potential to affect the quality of people's lives and the natural environment. Leisure and recreation are complex social phenomena and are essential to living a worthwhile life. Philosophical inquiry helps us understand leisure and recreation and guide service practices in many ways. Metaphysics emphasizes understanding of the essential qualities of leisure. Epistemology teaches us that knowledge of leisure needs to be generated by empirical and rationalist methods. Logic helps leisure services decision-makers not only avoid making faulty inferences but also persuasively defend and justify their positions to others. Aesthetics reveals to us the significance of beauty to our leisure experiences and the need to find a proper balance between aesthetic and nonaesthetic values. Finally, ethics helps us deal with larger questions of what constitutes worthwhile, fulfilling leisure and provides us with theories to analyze moral dilemmas that practitioners inevitably face.

Contrary to popular opinion, leisure services is not a matter of fun and games, and philosophy is not idle speculation. Far from being either impractical or inconsequential, the study of leisure and philosophy is fundamental to helping us think and act in ways that improve the quality of people's lives and protect the natural environment.

CHAPTER 4

Leisure and Recreation for Individuals in Society

Juan Tortosa Martínez and Daniel G. Yoder

Pavel Losevsky/fotolia.com

“ The person and the group are not separable phenomena, but are simply the individual and collective aspects of the same thing. ”

Loran David Osborn and
M.H. Neumeyer, sociologists

LEARNING OUTCOMES

After reading this chapter, you should be able to do the following:

> ❯ Show how leisure and recreation are complex human endeavors that take place within society.
> ❯ Describe how leisure and recreation, whether as solitary activities or undertaken with friends, family, or larger groups, affect and are affected by society
> ❯ Describe how gender, ethnicity and race, religion, and socioeconomic class affect leisure and recreation and how leisure and recreation in turn affect those factors
> ❯ Demonstrate that the values of goodness or badness can be applied to leisure and recreation
> ❯ Explain the implications of a social perspective for leisure and recreation professionals

Consider the leisure of the individual *in* society, not the leisure of the individual *and* society. Although this distinction may seem trivial, it is important. Individuals and societies do exist as separate entities in concept, but on a practical level, neither can exist independent of the other. Societies are composed of men, women, and children of various ages, races, classes, and so on. Without these essential parts, there could be no whole. Nor do individuals exist isolated from society; human beings are social animals by nature. All human existence (including leisure and recreation) takes place at the intersection of the individual and the diverse social structures that make up our world. Even the act of thinking, which is seemingly the quintessential individual activity, is impossible without the use of mental cultural symbols. These mental images are possible only within the borders of a common cultural context.

It's worth noting again that leisure and recreation are often used interchangeably, as if they are two words for the same phenomenon. While they certainly are related, they are not the same. The term leisure has often been referred to as nebulous. It can be conceived as time, various activities, or even a state of mind. On the other hand, recreation is much more concrete or definable. Recreation is activity consciously undertaken with anticipated outcomes. Those who recreate do so with some purpose or expectation of a certain outcome. Recreation is a type of leisure, but leisure is not a kind of recreation. Thus, it is appropriate to use the phrase "leisure and recreation" and not be redundant.

We begin this chapter with a general discussion of how leisure and recreation activities take place against a social backdrop. Even when people are physically alone in their activities, **society** influences them, and their activities may in turn influence society. We also discuss the relationships between leisure and primary groups of family and close friends, secondary groups, and four social institutions: gender, ethnicity, religion, and social class. Because the moral value of a leisure activity (its goodness or badness) is determined by both leisure participants and the world in which they live, we consider good and bad leisure. Finally, we discuss the implications of leisure and recreation in society for the professional practitioner.

LEISURE AS A COMPLEX SOCIAL PHENOMENON

Leisure is a wonderfully complex social phenomenon that is affected by many social institutions including economics, politics, work, technology, and war. But we must be careful in thinking that leisure and recreation are trivial pastimes that are influenced and even dictated by these social structures. In fact, leisure and recreation significantly affect the social forces just listed. Consider, for example, Las Vegas, Nevada. Without the leisure and tourism industries that pour billions of dollars into Las Vegas each year, the town would be much different (or perhaps nonexistent). Examples like this, although perhaps not as obvious, play out every day in thousands of communities across North America and around the globe.

Solitary Leisure and Society

A few leisure activities are entirely solitary, some are purely social, and most can be either private or communal. Reading is almost always undertaken alone, and playing a game of tennis always requires interaction with others. Playing cards is an example of an activity that can be either solitary or social, and most leisure activities fall into this category. Some people spend hours playing the classic solo card game solitaire, but you cannot play bridge without other players to compete against.

Although we might be inclined to think that our **solitary leisure** is ours and ours alone, it does not take place in a social vacuum. Indeed, other people and groups of people profoundly affect our solitary leisure activities. Furthermore, the leisure activities we undertake while we are alone have an influence—sometimes significant and sometimes not so significant—on the people and the world around us. The world around us affects our private leisure in many ways: It might support leisure, infringe on it, prohibit it, or even force us into it.

Let's consider one single act of solitary leisure and its influences. Even if you don't recognize the name, nearly everyone is familiar with the story of Aron Ralston, the young climber who was forced to cut off his arm after it became trapped between two boulders in the Utah backcountry. Thousands of dollars were spent by state and county agencies in an effort to find and save Ralston. Hundreds of volunteers sacrificed days for the search. The tragedy could have been averted if Ralston had hiked with a companion. But Ralston chose to go it alone on this adventure. However, this story has been a tremendous inspiration to many people—not just outdoor enthusiasts. It is impossible to measure the positive consequences of this single act of courage on a solo hike in the Utah desert.

Leisure and Primary Groups

When other people are involved in a leisure activity, they are not merely bystanders but essential components of the activity. Kelly (1987) has noted that "in general, people are more important in leisure than the form of the activity" (p. 158). Especially significant are those who are part of the participant's **primary group**. Sociologists have defined primary groups as "small groups in which there are face-to-face relations of a fairly intimate and personal nature. Primary groups are of two basic types, families and cliques. In other words, they are organized around ties of either kinship or friendship" (Lenski, Nolan, & Lenski, 1995, p. 48). We examine leisure activities with family and close

friends only briefly here because this topic is more thoroughly considered in chapter 12.

Social customs and societal expectations profoundly affect leisure when activities are undertaken with family members and close friends. Defining the term *family* is not as simple as it may seem at first glance. Because different cultures use various forms of kinship groupings and even the same culture may change its notion of family over time, a definition that all can agree on has been elusive. But no matter how it is defined, the family profoundly influences leisure.

The leisure lifestyle of adolescence clearly shows the effect of two occasionally competing forces: family and friends. Let's consider electronic gaming as an example. Kelsey is a 16-year-old from Montreal. Like many teenagers, she considers her parents to be out of touch, especially regarding her leisure activities. She is off for a night of gaming at a local teen hangout. Several of her friends play the same or similar electronic games on computers for several hours each Friday night. Her parents do not understand the fascination with the computer games Kelsey and her friends play and talk about.

Families typically move through a series of somewhat predictable stages. Not all families go through every stage, but most do or aspire to. These stages are not distinct; instead, each stage merges with those around it. Each phase of a family's development includes typical leisure activities, roles, and patterns. For example, many new families without children have a great deal of flexibility. Leisure activities can be spontaneous. Couples might be able to throw a few items together and get away for a weekend vacation in an hour or so. This is not the case for a family with children. Work and school schedules must be coordinated. Considerably more clothing and equipment must be organized. Child safety must be considered. If the children are not going away with the parents, child care must be considered. Even the destination of the vacation is affected. A quick trip to Las Vegas is more common for a family without children, whereas a trip to visit grandparents is common for families with children.

A clear example of familial influence is found in sport. Clark (2008) used data from the General Social Surveys of 1992 and 2005 to study children's participation in sport. He found that the family affects not only children's choices of a sport but also

A person may participate in various athletic pursuits throughout his life because of childhood experiences skiing with his mother.

choices through adolescence and early adulthood. Other studies support his contention that "sporty parents have sporty kids" (p. 55).

Leisure and Secondary Groups

Secondary groups affect a person's leisure activities, and a person's leisure activities have the potential to affect the secondary group. Henslin (1993) defines a **secondary group**, compared with a primary group, as "a larger, relatively temporary, more anonymous, formal and impersonal group based on some interest or activity, whose members are likely to interact on the basis of specific roles" (p. 150). Some secondary groups, such as a college classroom, a political party, or a labor union, are not related to leisure, but many are. The following examples show the obvious influence a secondary group can have on its members:

- Jane dedicates Wednesday evenings to attending a pottery class at the local park district. Instead of returning home after work on Wednesdays to spend time with her family, Jane grabs a quick bite to eat and heads straight to the pottery class.

- Nick is a member of the National Rifle Association (NRA), and with a particularly contentious national election coming up, he receives promotional material from this organization nearly every week. Instead of watching his favorite TV shows on Wednesday night, Nick attends NRA meetings each week. Nick decides to vote for a candidate who supports the NRA and opposes gun control.

- Jim and Margaret, who are recently retired and fairly affluent, love to travel. They have joined a local group that organizes trips for its members. They benefit from the reduced group rates and the opportunity to interact with people with similar travel interests.

- Rusty has been involved with a poker league that plays Texas Hold 'Em every Friday night. Not only does he enjoy playing, but he also sees a great deal of potential for this activity as a fund-raiser. When the board of the local food pantry (of which Rusty is a member) discusses fund-raisers, Rusty volunteers to organize a poker tournament for the community.

Although we can see how a secondary group influences the actions of individuals, the influence an individual may have on the group is not quite so obvious. It is nevertheless very real, as these examples show:

- Jane, the fledgling potter, has had a very bad week. When she attends the week's pottery session, she gets into an argument with the instructor about the schedule for firing her pottery pieces. Their heated conversation is overheard by several other class members, and it casts a pall on the evening's class.

- Although Nick believes in most of the positions taken by the NRA, he cannot support the right of Americans to own assault rifles. It is one thing to have a rifle or a shotgun for hunting, but he believes assault rifles are just too dangerous. Thus, he begins to encourage other members to write letters to the NRA to put pressure on it to change its stance on this issue.

- Jim and Margaret believe that the local travel club has been a little too conservative in planning trips. At a meeting, they ask why the club cannot plan a trip to an exotic location such as Tahiti. Although some of the members balk at the idea, some become convinced that this is a good idea, and they assign a subcommittee to look into the possibility of such a trip.

- Rusty has convinced the food pantry's board to take on the poker tournament as its primary fund-raiser. The organization needs to discontinue two other fund-raising events to have enough volunteers for this activity. Moreover, one of the board members has to resign from the board because he has been convicted of a felony and the state will not issue a license for the poker tournament as long as a convicted felon is on the board of directors.

The possibility of significantly affecting the group is more likely if the secondary group is local, such as the pottery class. Although it is difficult for an

Getty Images/DAJ

A member of a pottery class may have as much influence on the group as the group influences the individual. One student in the pottery class may subtly but effectively change this period of time from a social event set against the backdrop of fun pottery-making to a serious, individual creative activity. If most take that student's lead, fewer people will feel free to spend much time talking and laughing with their classmates.

individual to change a national organization such as the NRA, it is possible.

Social categories also affect leisure activities. Lenski and Lenski (1987) note that people can be grouped into a variety of societal classifications. We become members of some of these groups voluntarily, and we are born into others. For instance, we can choose to become a member of a cooking and dining club, but our gender is largely predetermined.

SIMILARITY AND DIVERSITY IN RECREATION AND LEISURE

The human race possesses a unique dynamic balance among all the fascinating characteristics that make us different and all the equally fascinating characteristics that make us similar. Over the last three decades, it has become popular to focus on the richness of our differences. Diversity is an incredibly important physiological and social phenomenon, but we dare not forget or minimize our sameness. We are much more alike than we are different. In a commencement speech at Howard University, President Bill Clinton (2013) said:

> We are all 99.5% the same. But, we spend 99.5% of our time thinking about the half percent of us that is different.

Such may be the case in leisure. A huge majority of people socialize as a leisure activity, but only a relative few go on wilderness excursions. Unfortunately more attention is devoted to the difference in rates of outdoor recreation according to race than to the commonality of socializing as leisure activity. Let's look at four examples.

Nigata is an 18-year-old female member of the Tarahumara tribe in the interior of Mexico. She is looking forward to the upcoming *tesguinado*, a festival that will celebrate the good news that the men of the tribe have won a running race against another tribe of Native Americans. There will be food and much drinking of *tesguino*, a beer made from corn. But to Nigata, what is important is not the food or the alcoholic beverage but the chance to spend time with a Juriuaco, a young man from her tribe. Young men and women customarily begin lives together at ceremonies like this (Beauregard, 1996).

Hameed is a 73-year-old Islamic man who lives in Pakistan. Tomorrow he will go to a large community gathering to celebrate the national team's victory in an international cricket match. The huge crowd will consist of men and women of all ages from his village. Hameed is often called on to supply trained horses for the event. One of the most popular parts of the celebration is a feast of lamb and rice. In contrast to several celebrations in other cultural feasts, the consumption of alcoholic beverages in this gathering is strictly prohibited. Few would even contemplate drinking wine or beer during this activity. For Hameed, however, the best thing about this celebration is the opportunity to gather his extended family around him. Nearly 40 of his children, grandchildren, and great grandchildren will gather. Although the year has been difficult because of violence and a terrible drought that has devastated the local crops, Hameed will be able to forget those issues for a couple of days (Countries and Their Cultures, n.d.).

No one has more reason to complain than Mable Johnson. The 36-year-old Pointe-aux-Chenes, Louisiana, native suffered through hurricane Katrina and a serious economic downturn that resulted in the loss of her job. Although it did not seem things could get worse, the Gulf oil spill devastated the beaches in her community. For a few days, however, she can forget her troubles and celebrate Mardi Gras. Many of her friends who moved to Texas after the hurricane will return, and they will have a huge Gulf seafood feast. Her brother was just recently able to begin harvesting shrimp again. He will not only supply fresh seafood from his boat but also help pay for the party that will go on for a week. Mable is looking forward to reliving the excitement that her entire family felt when her beloved New Orleans Saints football team won the Super Bowl a few months ago.

On July 6 at noon in Pamplona, Spain, the *chupinazo* (firework) indicates the start of the famous festival of Sanfermines, which honors Saint Fermin. Pablo is excited because he will be attending this large, well-known celebration for the first time. The festival lasts through July 14. Thousands of people will gather around the city hall for the *chupinazo*. There will be events all day and all night, and most of them will involve plenty of food and drinks. During this week, people will set aside work and personal problems to have a good time with family and friends. The most famous event of the week is the running of the bulls, which occurs at eight o'clock every morning. Pablo has decided to run tomorrow morning, but he is already drinking wine and it seems that he is going to party hard. The running of the bulls is dangerous, and in some years people die. Maybe Pablo will change his mind.

On the surface, these four scenarios may seem quite different. The key characters are different in terms of age, race, religion, nationality, gender, ability, and economic status. In one celebration alcohol is strictly forbidden, but in others it is common. In one setting the game of cricket occupies an important place, whereas in others it does not. Closer examination, however, reveals that the similarities are profound. Each situation involves a person who is attending a community gathering that involves friends, family, and others and serves to create and maintain a shared culture. Each activity involves food, although the food differs markedly. All four

events include or allude to some type of sport or physical activity. Moreover, each scenario demonstrates that recreation and leisure can provide a break from the routine of life. In the next few sections we will examine how gender, sexual orientation, ethnicity and race, religion, and socioeconomic status influence recreation and leisure.

GENDER

It is important to first discuss the difference between gender and sex. *Sex* refers to the biological component of being either male or female. *Gender* is a social category that includes attitudes, expectations, and expressions of masculinity and femininity. Gender is one of the most defining characteristics people possess. Because of that, it is linked to leisure in many complex relationships.

Historically, men have enjoyed a privileged position in all Western cultures. Although patriarchy has been most evident in politics, industry, the arts, and many professions, male superiority has

Getty Images/Pablo Blazquez Dominguez

Community gatherings serve to create and maintain a shared culture through recreation and leisure. Here, the chupinazo indicates the start of the famous running of the bulls in Spain.

also been expressed and fortified in leisure and recreation. In the 1800s, many recreation activities were reserved for men only. At that time, no self-respecting woman would have gone to a tavern. In addition, segregation of the genders for no apparent reason was common; for example, men rode bicycles and women rode tricycles in the early years of cycling in the United States. It simply was not proper to do otherwise.

The traditional roles within the family also affected the leisure activities and recreation of men and women. Men were breadwinners who earned the family's financial resources, and women cared for their children and husbands and maintained the home. Thus, many recreation activities for women took place in the home and included a domestic component such as cooking, decorating, or supervising activities for children.

The roles and expectations of men and women in Western society have changed significantly over the past century. Robinson and Godbey (1997) noted that "perhaps the most important ongoing social revolution in the United States is the change in women's roles" (p. 13). However, many authors and researchers caution that although change has been made, androgyny (the balance of both male and female characteristics) has not yet fully arrived. Sociologists have pointed out that one of the barriers to a more androgynous society is that parents and teachers tend to treat children differently based on their gender. For example, a father invites his son to go hunting but never considers that his daughter might want to go as well, or a mother teaches her daughter to bake without considering that her son might like to participate. Teachers might discourage young boys from playing with dolls and little girls from playing with toy trucks because it is not acceptable in their eyes. Such behaviors, although not meant to harm children, have the long-term effect of denying rewarding and self-enhancing activities to millions of Americans (Eshleman, Cashion, & Basirico, 1993).

Today, although men are responsible for more housework than they were in the past, women still take on far more of the housework and child care responsibilities (Roberts, 2010). This circumstance limits the time available for leisure. The apparent imbalance in leisure time between men and women is somewhat offset by the fact that men, on average, work more hours outside the home than women do. Women have lower unemployment rates than men, but they are twice as likely to have part-time jobs. Furthermore, although the gap is slowly closing, employed women earn less than men do (U.S. Department of Labor, 2010). Thus, regarding income, women are still disadvantaged. This condition affects the choices that they make about leisure time (Roberts, 2010).

Historically, sport has been male dominated, but progress has been made. It is no longer true that only boys perform and only girls cheer. One of the most important steps toward this end was the adoption of **Title IX** in the United States in 1972. This legislation directed educational institutions to develop parity between men's and women's sports. As evidence of its effectiveness, in 1971, 300,000 females took part in high school sports in the United States; by 2011, that number had risen to over 3.17 million (National Federation of State High School Association, 2011). This increase in participation by girls and women shows that the gap in sport participation rates is narrowing.

In Canada, progress has also been made toward gender equity in sport. Canadian Interuniversity Sport, the leading national organization to control sport at the university level, developed a policy statement that included 12 goals to achieve gender equity (Beaubier, 2004). Some in Canada believe that the policy is incomplete and encourage Canadian sport organizations to look to the Title IX legislation in the United States for further development on this issue.

Russell (2002) offers the following five conclusions about gender, recreation, and leisure:

1. Although the disparity has decreased over the past century, men continue to experience more breadth and depth of leisure. More diverse recreation activities are available to men and boys, and it is easier for males to devote more time and effort to activities that are especially important to them. (These activities are often referred to as **serious leisure**.)

2. Long-entrenched roles for the different genders significantly affect recreation. Especially in older and more traditional families, women typically assume the complex and time-intensive task of caring for others. It is not uncommon for the woman in the family to plan, purchase, prepare, and

serve the food and then clean up after an evening barbecue with neighbors. The values and benefits of this leisure activity will likely be different for the woman than for the man in this family. The woman values her ability to provide a meal and an enjoyable evening to her neighbors despite the amount of work involved, and the man values spending time with the neighbors in a relaxing atmosphere.

3. Because men tend not to be the primary caregivers in the family, their recreation more often takes place outside the home. Women, on the other hand, more often spend leisure time in the home. Often their leisure activity is blended with, or at least compatible with, caring for the home.

4. The burden of family care has a greater effect on women; thus, women's leisure and recreation are often quite fragmented. Men, as a result, may have more opportunities to block out an entire afternoon or even a few days exclusively for leisure. Although a woman may plan an afternoon of relaxing reading, she may be interrupted by children who need clothes washed or a husband that needs her help.

5. Older women especially might labor under the false belief that leisure must be earned or that they are not entitled to leisure at all. If they do not do work outside the home, they may not feel like they are worthy of leisure.

SEXUAL ORIENTATION

People of all sexual orientations have diverse recreation and leisure preferences. Although the situation has improved significantly over the last decades, people who identify as lesbian, gay, bisexual, or transgender (LGBT) and who acknowledge their sexual identity in public are still at risk of being marginalized, isolated, insulted, harassed, and, in some cases, victimized by homophobic attacks. In some countries, LGBT people are punished severely, and in Saudi Arabia and Nigeria, they are subject to the death penalty. Unsurprisingly, therefore, **sexual identity discrimination** in leisure and recreation exists in most of the world, including in the United States and Canada. LGBT people experience constraints on opportunities to freely choose leisure activities and whom they spend their leisure time with based on prejudices regarding their sexuality.

LGBT young people are especially at risk of harassment. As a coping mechanism against bullying,

they may avoid leisure activities with heterosexual people or hide their sexual identities in public (Kivel & Kleiber, 2000). Considering that leisure and recreation activities may represent the primary means by which people start forming relationships and eventually opportunities for sexual expression, these strategies may protect them from bullying but also may deny them opportunities for self-expression, belonging, or even sexual or love expression.

LGBT older adults are certainly an understudied group despite the fact they have been identified in the U.S. national health priorities (Fredriksen-Goldsen, Kim, Shui, Goldsen, & Emlet, 2015). Although leisure participation by LGBT older adults seems to be positively correlated to physical and mental health quality of life, this group often has to face additional barriers due to social and historical contexts such as experiencing victimization and discrimination (Fredriksen-Goldsen et al., 2015) or coming out at an older age after living a heterosexual life for many years.

Gay-friendly spaces have emerged in some hotels, resorts, and restaurants that are designed to provide a safe environment and eliminate the need to adopt self-protection strategies. LGBT people represent a business opportunity for leisure and recreation companies and agencies, which explains the significant increase in the delivery of specific recreation activities for LGBT people. On the one hand, these activities may allow LGBT people to act freely without feeling questioned, observed, or judged and promote a sense of belonging. On the other hand, some argue that places or activities should not be labeled according to sexual orientation and should be accessible to everyone regardless of sexual identity.

Unique leisure activities of this social group are the gay or LGBT pride celebrations in many places around the world. These have important economic effects in cities such as San Francisco, London, and Madrid. This initiative started in the United States to honor the 1969 Stonewall riots in Manhattan and is designed to defend the rights and dignity of LGBT people.

Equal rights for LGBT people must be the goal in the entire world, and leisure and recreation should play a crucial role in this. Leisure and recreation professionals should be aware of the types of discrimination that LGBT people experience and send the message that any form of discrimination against them is simply unacceptable.

ETHNICITY AND RACE

Race and *ethnicity* are sometimes used interchangeably, but there are important differences: **Race** refers to biological characteristics, whereas **ethnicity** refers to cultural characteristics. Henslin (1993) notes that people of the same ethnicity "identify with one another on the basis of common ancestry and cultural heritage. Their sense of belonging centers on country of origin, distinctive foods, dress, family names and relationships, language, music, religion and other customs" (p. 311). Leisure and recreation are part and parcel of these various cultural qualities. Some social scientists and politicians argue that more equity exists among racial and ethnic groups today, whereas others contend that stereotyping, prejudice, discrimination, and racial inequality are every bit as prevalent as they ever were, but they are more difficult to detect. Others operate under the assumption that even if race and ethnicity are issues that must be attended to, they have little relation to leisure. Phillip (2000), however, disputes this line of thinking: "Perhaps, nowhere else does race matter as much as during leisure. While schools and workplaces have been integrated over the past three decades by force of law, no similar laws have been enacted to secure the racial integration of leisure spaces" (p. 121).

Slightly more than 308 million people lived in the United States in 2010 (U.S. Census Bureau, 2010). The diversity of the population in terms of race and ethnicity has been increasing exponentially. For instance, the state of California has a population of over 37 million people, including 14 million Hispanics or Latinos (U.S. Census Bureau, 2010). These are still considered minority groups, although in California this may need to be reconsidered. Minority groups on average still have lower socioeconomic statuses (U.S. Census Bureau, 2010) and are at greater risk of social exclusion. Not surprisingly, therefore, leisure participation rates vary according to race and ethnicity (Bell & Hurd, 2006). For example, park usage varies significantly among various ethnic groups. Most park users are Caucasian (Byrne, 2007). People from minority ethnic groups or races may feel uncomfortable or even unwelcome in some leisure settings in which their ethnic group is underrepresented. For example, some Hispanics might not participate in programs because of a perception of discrimination, fear of not being liked, absence of other Hispanics, and language difficulties (McChesney, Gerken, & McDonald, 2005). Besides variations in participation rates, usage patterns vary among races and ethnic groups. For example, African Americans may choose not to participate in activities that are stereotypically Caucasian. Instead, they may choose activities that adhere more to their cultural norms (Shinew Floyd, & Parry, 2004).

Beyond recognizing differences, attention has been devoted recently to the issue of *why* leisure is different for racial and ethnic groups. Two general explanations have come to the forefront: the marginality hypothesis and the ethnicity explanation. The marginality hypothesis explains lower participation in some activities as the consequence of a history of discrimination that has resulted in fewer socioeconomic resources. To explain why fewer African American children than white children join swim teams, this theory holds that African American children were historically denied access to quality aquatic facilities and coaches. On the other hand, the ethnicity explanation suggests that different rates and patterns of participation are the result of different norms, beliefs, and social organizations. According to this theory, African Americans would be more inclined to participate in track and field events rather than swimming because black role models are common in track and field and are relatively rare in swimming. Floyd (1998) argues that these two approaches to accounting for differences in leisure and recreation may be only a beginning. He suggests that each has serious weaknesses and that leisure researchers must continue to conduct research in this area. Although research in sport seems to be continuing, little research has been done recently in other types of recreation and leisure activities.

RELIGION

Although religion is fundamentally related to ethnicity, it warrants further attention. For our purposes, we must differentiate between two related concepts. *Spirituality* is a personal belief system that may, but most often does not, have a strong social component. *Religion*, on the other hand, is a thoroughly and universally social institution. According to Eshleman et al., "religion has always been the anchor of identity for human beings. Religious beliefs give meaning to life, and the experiences associated with them provide personal gratification, as well as release from the frustrations and anxieties of daily life" (1993, p. 344). In all its wonderfully diverse forms, religion pervades nearly every human endeavor such as presidential elections, child-rearing, marriages and funerals, hairstyles, and clothing choices. Even the recreation activities of those who do not consider themselves to be religious are affected by religion. For example, Norman and Arlene are a middle-aged couple who haven't attended church for the past 20 years. One of their favorite leisure activities since their oldest daughter started high school is watching her participate in athletic events. Because of Arlene's work schedule, she has had difficulty getting time off on Saturdays for her daughter's volleyball games. It would be much easier for her if some of them were played on Sunday afternoons. That's not likely, however, because their community, like many others, does not hold school events on Sundays to avoid conflicts with church services. In addition, the mascot for the sports teams was changed a few years ago as a result of vocal and influential Christian parents. Norman and Arlene no longer cheer for the Fighting Blue Devils; now they cheer for the Lightning. One of the biggest tournaments of the season is held at the local YMCA. The Young Men's Christian Association, an international organization with its roots in the Christian faith, was one of the pioneers in developing volleyball; therefore, it is possible that the games they now enjoy watching would not exist if it were not for this faith-based organization.

We must be careful not to portray religion as simply a constraint on leisure and recreation. In fact, churches use recreation to maintain a sense of community, attract new members, and keep members from activity they perceive as harmful. For example, instead of promoting traditional Halloween events such as trick-or-treating, churches across the country offer parties that emphasize other types of fun and worship. Many churches and synagogues have athletic teams that participate either in community leagues or in leagues with other churches and synagogues. Moreover, many children attend summer camps operated by faith-based organizations.

Nowhere is the relationship with religion in the United States and Canada more complex and intriguing than in the special arena of sport. This should come as no surprise given that these countries not only have the greatest diversity of sports but also have the greatest diversity of religions. Many athletes have had to struggle with the demands of their faith and their desire to participate in sport. One of the classic examples of this struggle is depicted in the 1981 movie *Chariots of Fire*, in which devout Christian Eric Liddell must choose between the biggest race of his life and honoring his faith's admonition about running on the Sabbath. More recent examples include a girl who could not compete in a state gymnastics event because of her Orthodox Jewish family's observance of the Sabbath on Saturday and an Iowa high school wrestler's refusal to wrestle a female competitor because of his Pentecostal religion's prohibition against contact sports between males and females.

Much attention has been given to the theory that sport has replaced religion in the lives of many North Americans. Edwards' seminal work on the topic of sport as religion continues to influence sport sociologists. According to Edwards (1973), sport and religion have 13 important similarities. Four of them follow:

1. Just like religion, sports have their saints. These are the great athletes of previous eras that serve as examples for current athletes and fans.
2. The world of sports has its "gods": those superstars that transcend time and culture and dominate the lives of individuals and even countries.
3. Sports have their hallowed shrines. These range from the widely recognized hall of fame sites to the trophy rooms of colleges and high schools.
4. Sports have powerful symbols of faith. The bat that Babe Ruth hit his record home run

Getty Images/Al Messerschmidt

One of the similarities between sport and religion can be seen in the hall of fame gallery at the Pro Football Hall of Fame in Canton, Ohio, where former players are enshrined each year.

with and the ball that Dwight Clark caught to win the 1982 National Football League playoffs are examples. And who can argue that there is not a certain sacred quality of an Olympic gold medal?

In writing about the similarity between religion and sport, Prebish noted that "religion is the raft that ferries from profane reality to the realm of the sacred, that enables us to transcend ordinary reality and directly apprehend the extraordinary" (1993, p. 3). He goes on to make the case that, for some people, sport does the same thing. When we watch the Super Bowl, we make a mental and emotional journey from everyday life to a world of fantasy.

SOCIOECONOMIC STATUS

People in nearly all societies are categorized according to some combination of wealth, power, party affiliation, life chances, and prestige. Some systems, like the **caste system** in India, are very rigid. The boundaries are distinct and movement between the different categories is nearly impossible. A **class system**, like that in many developed countries including the United States and Canada, is much more fluid, and there is overlap between classes and the possibility of movement among the classes. In many countries, classes are designated according to a combination of income, education, and occupation. This classification system is referred to as *socioeconomic status* (SES).

Contemporary industrialized societies comprise four classes (Newman, 1999). The upper class consists of owners of vast property and wealth. The middle class is made up of managers, small-business owners, and professionals. The working class is made up predominantly of laborers who earn modest wages and own little property. Finally, the people of the lower class are those who either work for minimum wages, are periodically unemployed, or are unemployable.

Socioeconomic inequalities around the world are significant and have recently increased in many countries. Inequalities in the United States are relatively high, and they too have increased over the last several years. According to the Central Intelligence Agency's *World Factbook* (2013), the United States ranks 43rd on the world's inequality scale of average income as measured by the Gini index, which measures the degree of inequality in the distribution of family income in each country. On this scale, African countries such as Namibia and South Africa rank as most unequal followed by most South and Central American countries. On the other end of the spectrum are countries of northern and eastern Europe such as Sweden, Hungary, Norway, and the Czech Republic, which have less difference in average family income.

There is general agreement that SES affects leisure. There is, however, less agreement on exactly *how* it affects it. Addressing a particular leisure category, Gruneau wrote: "Recent research on sports and social equality in the United States demonstrates a general pattern of under-representation of people from the lowest income levels among active participants in organized sports and physical recreation" (1999, pp. 52-53). Recognizing some of the disagreement about the relationship between socioeconomic status and leisure, Kelly noted that "economic stratification is at least a filter, with low incomes simply eliminating the majority of the population from cost-intensive activity" (2012, p. 78).

Research supports the notion that class affects travel and tourism. Mill (1986) determined that economic standing, one of the key elements of SES, affected several aspects of tourism. Not surprisingly, people in the upper and middle classes traveled more often through commercial providers, whereas the working class tended to travel by some form of public transportation. The destinations for travel were also different. The upper classes tended to travel internationally more often than other classes. The higher on the SES scale, the longer the time spent at a destination. And, as might be expected, the upper and middle classes spent more money when they traveled for leisure purposes.

We should not overlook the fact that although class affects leisure, the reverse may also be true. Thorstein Veblen, in his classic 1899 treatise *The Theory of the Leisure Class*, argued that the upper class, which he called the *leisure class,* used leisure to display and maintain their prized position in society (1899/1998). Elegant and exclusive social gatherings and highly consumptive activities sent a clear message to those in lower social positions that class mattered. At the same time, many of the lower classes emulated the upper classes and tried to match their leisure styles. When a sufficiently large group from the middle class was able to participate in activities that resembled those of the rich, the upper class found even more expensive and elaborate leisure activities to maintain their status.

BENEFITS AND CONSTRAINTS OF LEISURE

Most leisure activities offer some benefit. Leisure is a voluntarily chosen activity; therefore, if nothing else, leisure activities provide participants with opportunities to express free will. However, leisure activities do have some constraints. For example, few activities (leisure or otherwise) are without cost. The following example of Nicole, an active 21-year-old college student at a Midwestern university, illustrates the mixed nature of leisure:

I am mostly into leisure activities with my friends. Like during last spring break my best friend and I went to Panama City in Florida. Lying on the beach for three days and doing pretty much nothing was pretty nice. I seriously needed a break from school and work. I just wish my boyfriend could have gone with us, but he had to work. I probably should not have gone because I really didn't have the money. But I decided that I could do it if we traveled by car and stayed in a cheaper motel a few blocks from the beach. One of the things I have always wanted to do was parasail, but on the day I was going to do it, the wind came up. The people who ran the company said they could not do it if the wind was over 20 miles per hour. It was the last day, and I couldn't go. I was disappointed, but then I saw some people surfing. I rented a board and spent the rest of the day surfing. I had a great time and a wonderful workout.

One night my best friend and I wanted to go to a really great bar, but she got a little sick and could not go. I really wanted to go but didn't want to go alone. I had heard the place was a little bit wilder than I am used to. It would have been fun, but my parents always told me to be careful when I am by myself in a strange place, so I just stayed in our room that night. All in all, it was a really wonderful time, and

I hope to have another spring break trip but with my boyfriend.

Nicole obviously got more out of her spring break trip than a nice tan. She mentioned that she got to relax on the beach and got some exercise while surfing. She was also able to share these experiences with her best friend. The individual benefits of recreation and leisure are easy to observe, but there were other less obvious leisure and recreation contributions as well. Nicole and her friend spent money on transportation, lodging, and food. This spending contributed to the economies in communities along the way and in Florida. The beaches are a main attraction to the area; thus, a great deal of effort is made to keep the beaches clean, partially as a means of attracting locals and tourists to the area, which can have a positive impact on the local economy. Finally, Nicole alluded to the trip being recuperative. After a week of fun and sun, she was revitalized and ready to go back to school and her part-time job. In turn, her increased productivity at work was valuable to her, her community, and her employer.

The National Recreation and Park Association (NRPA) recognizes that many people take recreation for granted and do not understand the contribution of this field. Thus, they developed a program called Parks and Recreation: The Benefits Are Endless to promote the role of recreation and parks to the public. Even if the benefits are not truly endless, they are certainly numerous and varied. The benefits are classified as individual and social (Henderson, 2010). Within the individual benefits category are physiological benefits and psychological benefits. Subcategories of the social value of recreation include economic and environmental benefits and recuperation from other activities such as productive work.

Let's also consider what this tells us about leisure and its inherent constraints. Although Nicole had a generally good time on her spring break, she is certainly not operating without constraints on what she wanted to do for leisure. She was limited by

- whom she could travel with,
- how much money she could spend,
- the weather,
- a company's unwillingness to provide an activity,

- her parents' values of appropriate leisure activity, and
- her apprehension about going to a bar alone.

Another lesson that we can learn from this scenario is that most of these constraints did not prevent Nicole from participating. She negotiated most of them and had an enjoyable time regardless.

The great variety of possible constraints poses a challenge for categorizing; therefore, researchers have developed several models for grouping them. Structural constraints include time, money, health, and equipment; intrapersonal constraints include fear, low self-esteem, and attitudes; and interpersonal constraints include family responsibilities and a lack of people to share the leisure activity with (Crawford, Jackson, & Godbey, 1991). Henderson (1997) grouped constraints as antecedent limitations such as attitudes and lack of skill and intervening constraints such as weather and resources.

GOOD AND BAD LEISURE AND RECREATION

If we're not careful, we may assume that leisure and recreation are unequivocally good. Who can argue that an exercise program for seniors or making parks available for picnics are not admirable and decent efforts? Certainly no one could be opposed to arts and crafts classes and family vacations. But some activities are not wholesome, and some seem to be just downright wrong. We could list the bad activities, but that wouldn't be especially helpful because the list would be in a constant state of flux. It might be more productive for us to consider how to determine the goodness or badness of an activity.

Participation in recreation cannot be forced on us. We decide to participate because we think it will be fun and possibly rewarding. In fact, the defining quality of recreation is the freedom to participate. But the same freedom in leisure and recreation can be problematic when considering the moral value of an activity. We might think that our leisure is just that—entirely and completely *our* leisure. How dare anyone tell us that our chosen activity is wrong and then try to stop us from doing it? Although that may be our initial reaction to placing moral value on recreation and leisure, we must go beyond that if we are to truly understand our society and ourselves.

OUTSTANDING GRADUATE

Background Information

Name: Michael D. Lukkarinen

Education: PhD in leisure behavior (emphasis in sport management) from University of Illinois at Urbana-Champaign; MS in recreation, park, and tourism administration from Western Illinois University; BS in recreation, park, and tourism administration from Western Illinois University

Affiliations: Academy of Leisure Sciences, National Alliance for Youth Sports, National Federation of State High School Associations, National Wrestling Coaches Association

Career Information

Position: Associate Professor

Organization: Western Illinois University (WIU): The department offers outstanding and nationally accredited master's and bachelor's degrees in recreation, park, and tourism administration (RPTA). Students and faculty are engaged in service learning, research, and grant writing aimed at preparing the professionals of tomorrow. The faculty is committed to providing the tools needed to be successful in the field and in life. A career in RPTA enables students to make a positive difference in their communities.

Job description: As an associate professor, I am directly engaged in preparing students to be difference makers, both during their time at WIU and when they enter the field upon graduation. I also currently serve as the department internship coordinator. This is a position that connects our students as future professionals with their counterparts already in the field. I am both a gatekeeper and a relationship maker. I involve my passion with sport in my classes, my research, and my life. I also serve as chair for the Western Illinois Senior Olympic Games and volunteer my time as a wrestling coach at Macomb High School and as a women's golf coach at WIU.

Career path: Like many in the field, I stumbled upon my career focus. After trying many other things, I kept coming back to my roots—as a kid who hung out at the local YMCA, ballfields, and gym. Once RPTA became my major, I was able to shine and enjoy my classes thoroughly. I have never forgotten that, and I try to share this with my students who may be unsure of themselves.

Academia wasn't on my mind until after I graduated with my master's degree and left the field briefly. Realizing my mistake, I came back and again felt at home. I enjoy the interaction with students, colleagues, and other members of the university community. It is a great responsibility to educate others, and this is something I take very seriously.

Likes and dislikes about the job: I truly enjoy meeting students every year and seeing the world through their eyes. This can be a challenge. Bridging the gap between theory, practice, and the students of today is simultaneously a challenge and a reward. Seeing them blossom as people and become successful professionals who then go on to give internships to our students is very gratifying.

Advice for Undergraduates

Be involved in as many activities as possible. Travel down many roads. These roads will help you zero in on the road where you belong. You may want to take the first exit ramp because the road is not for you, but that puts you on another road, getting you closer to where you are supposed to be. Once you find that road, you will know, and you will not want to exit anymore.

Let's take a moment to consider how we determine good and bad in contemporary culture.

Goodness has been discussed by every culture since the ancient Greeks. Today we have several different and competing theories about what is good and bad or right and wrong. Although there are a lot of diverse ideas, nearly all agree that goodness is not a concept simply left up to the individual to determine. Even proponents of **hedonism**, a philosophy in which individual pleasure is the chief good, recognizes that our consequences have actions that affect our pleasure seeking; thus, we have to consider our behaviors in light of those around us. Other ethical theories place concerns for others at the middle of the debate about good and evil. The point is that people and the various societies of which they are a part jointly determine goodness in all things, including leisure and recreation.

Let's briefly consider a couple of contemporary theories about good and bad leisure. Nash (1953) was one of the first to tackle the issue. His model of good and bad recreation resembled a pyramid with the very best activities at the peak. These activities not only provided satisfaction to the actor but also contributed to making a better society. In the middle of the pyramid were activities that were merely entertaining to the participants. They were not harmful to anyone, but they did not affect society either. Near the bottom were activities that, although freely chosen, were harmful to the individual. Finally, at the bottom of the diagram, were activities that not only hurt the participant but also damaged society. Curtis (1979) devised an even simpler continuum with good recreation activities on one end and bad recreation activities on the other end. Curtis labeled bad activities as **purple leisure** and defined them as activities that might bring pleasure to the individual but would cause harm to society.

Let's look at various recreation activities in light of this discussion of goodness and badness. Activities at the top and bottom of Nash's model and at either end of Curtis' continuum are easy to understand. Most of us would agree that writing and performing a beautiful song is good and vandalizing a playground is bad. But it is much more difficult to reach consensus on the goodness of many other activities. Where would we put hunting? How about alcohol use? Marijuana use? Cocaine? Television viewing? Playing violent video games? Ultimate fighting? Going to a strip club?

Then there is the thorny issue of gambling. At one time in the United States, almost every type of gambling was banned. Then it became available only in certain states and locations such as Nevada and American Indian reservations. Now, some form of gambling is available in almost every state and county. Many states have horse and dog races to bet on. Casinos are floating on almost every major body of water in the United States, and there are only three or four states that do not have a legal lottery. In Canada, gambling is legal to anyone over the age of 18. Options include scratch tickets (similar to the lotteries in the United States), horse races, bingo, betting on sport events, and gambling at one of the 106 casinos scattered across Canada. So, is gambling good or bad? It's legal and widespread, provides jobs, provides resources for schools (and whatever else governments do with the money), and provides entertainment for many. But it is also associated with addiction, corruption, and other negative aspects such as the possible diminution of work ethic. As you can see, determining whether a leisure activity is good or bad is not easy. But as a society, we must attempt to because leisure activities affect us all.

IMPLICATIONS FOR PROFESSIONALS

Charged with the task of providing leisure and recreation opportunities, leisure and recreation professionals must first understand how leisure and recreation take place. Who participates? How do they participate? What are their motivations? What are their constraints and limitations? What are the benefits of recreation? Are there direct consequences or indirect consequences that will not be evident for years? Armed with the answers to these questions, we can design programs, facilities, and open spaces that make it possible for people to flourish.

For example, knowing the demands and limitations placed on single mothers, recreation and parks professionals must offer programs that allow them to participate. Perhaps that means that some fitness programs take place in the middle of the morning and the agency offers a toddler play period at the same time. Given that money is often in short supply for this population, the agency must also subsidize the program so the mothers do not have to choose between their own physical fitness and paying the utility bills. This must all be accomplished without perpetuating the stigma that single-parent households are inferior and a societal burden that must be dealt with as conveniently as possible.

But even these efforts, as challenging as they are, are not enough. On another level, leisure and recreation professionals must be educators. They must continue to drive home the point that leisure and recreation are essential; they are so important that all people, regardless of their lot in life, color, age, ethnicity, gender, religion, or class, have a right to participate. Showing the current benefits and extolling the future benefits of leisure and recreation for all will strengthen the case. The world really can be better today and tomorrow for all of us through equal leisure and recreation opportunities.

SUMMARY

As we have seen, leisure is a wonderfully complex human phenomenon that is never undertaken in a social vacuum; it is absolutely inseparable from society. A multitude of social institutions, including stratification, religion, ethnicity, gender, family, and friendships, thoroughly influence leisure. But the causation arrow goes both ways. Leisure often profoundly affects the society in which it takes place. Thus, contrary to the thinking of previous eras, leisure is not a trivial pursuit relegated to the realm of leftover time and energy. Rather, it is an essential ingredient of the lives of individuals, communities, nations, and humankind. Leisure and recreation professionals venture into this rich boiling stew of the human experience.

PART II

Leisure and Recreation as a Multifaceted Delivery System

CHAPTER 5

Leisure Service Delivery Systems

David N. Emanuelson

" Just call me Bond, Municipal Bond. "

Ben Wyatt, character from the television show *Parks and Recreation*

LEARNING OUTCOMES

After reading this chapter, you should be able to do the following:

> ❭ Identify the three sectors that deliver leisure services to the public and the ways they operate
> ❭ Compare the challenges facing leisure service professionals in the three sectors
> ❭ Explain how various challenges require leisure service professionals to possess diverse technical skills
> ❭ Describe the educational courses that leisure service professionals should take to prepare for the opportunities that await them

Thank goodness for popular culture such as the television show *Parks and Recreation,* which provided the public with a look at how municipal governments deliver leisure services. Unfortunately, that view, although humorous, is not always accurate. What is most misleading is that there are many levels of government and sectors of the economy that provide leisure services.

Leisure is a human need, which makes it inevitable that different sectors of the economy will be developed to meet that need. According to the U.S. Department of Labor and the Canadian government, in 2010, Americans and Canadians spent about 38.5 hours per week working. Because a week is 168 hours, the average time that most people spent working was less than 25 percent of that total, suggesting that Americans and Canadians have nearly 130 hours of week to do things other than work.

If the average person sleeps eight hours, 56 hours a week are spent sleeping, which leaves 74 hours for other things. Estimates indicate that people use half of the remaining time in a week to do things essential for existence, such as cooking, cleaning, and personal maintenance, which leaves about 30 hours a week for recreation. (In this chapter, we use the term *recreation* interchangeably with the *leisure service industry.*)

It should be no surprise that major portions of the national economies of Canada and the United States are dedicated to satisfying their citizens' desires for recreation. In fact, leisure services are the largest segment of the **gross domestic national product** in both countries. Gross domestic national product is the sum of total goods and services manufactured or provided by all businesses, nonprofit organizations, and government entities in a country.

The leisure service industry is a vast marketplace that includes travel and tourism, amusement and theme park operations, hospitality and restaurant management, sport and entertainment, and community parks and recreation—practically anything that people do when they are not working. Because it is a diverse field, leisure service professionals need to be trained in more than one discipline.

This chapter reviews the leisure service field and the delivery systems and sectors in which it exists. The discussion identifies technical skills common to all sectors, determines which ones are specific to a sector, and suggests a course of education that will prepare professionals for success in the leisure service industry.

This chapter considers leisure service delivery systems in Canada and the United States largely because they are similar, but also because they have important differences. The differences between governmental units are important. Canada is a **constitutional monarchy**, part of the British Commonwealth with allegiance to the queen of England. In Canada, the Crown is the foundation of the executive and judicial branches of government. By contrast, the United States is a **constitutional republic**, in which the executive branch is elected and the judicial branch is appointed by the chief executive. While many of the same leisure service delivery systems exist under the two forms of government, the differences are important.

In the United States, leisure services provided by the National Park System in the Department of the Interior are considered both administrative and legislative functions of the national government. The department head is a cabinet-level position and is appointed by the president, but the department was created through legislative action and its funding comes from Congress. Understanding the distinctions is important.

The United States also differs from Canada because it has a different form of federalism. In the U.S. federal system, states have substantial power. States charter businesses, nonprofit organizations, and local governmental units. A **governmental unit** is a generic term that describes a government group at any level: national, state, county, city, or other local unit. The term can be used to refer to one large unit, such as the state, or subdivisions within the unit, such as departments. In Canada, chartering of these entities is done at the national level. Yet by most other appearances, businesses, nonprofits, and local governments deliver leisure services in a similar way in Canada and the United States.

Leisure services are provided by three sectors of the economy: the private, or commercial, sector; the nonprofit sector; and the public, or government, sector. The private sector was the first to provide leisure services—primarily recreation services—which is why this chapter begins with an overview of private-sector delivery systems and how they function. Discussion then moves to the nonprofit sector, which also primarily provides recreation services, because it was the second to deliver leisure services. Last discussed is the public sector, which provides a unique array of services that businesses and nonprofit organizations are not able to offer, such as parks, which were initially offered for everyone with no fee. Since the creation of government-owned and -operated parks, fees have sometimes become necessary. For example, municipal governments provide parks and open space, which the public can enjoy without paying fees. This free use of parks and open space is possible because governments collect taxes to support these services. State and federal parks, however, sometimes charge fees for admission and for specific services. The chapter touches on these services and explains why these fees and charges are necessary.

PRIVATE SECTOR

The commercial recreation sector is the largest of the three sectors. It is about 100 times larger than the public sector, and it provides students with the greatest career opportunities. In 2010, there were more than 22.5 million businesses operating in the United States and 2 million in Canada. The U.S. leisure service sector comprises more than 8 percent of the gross domestic product of the United States and nearly 2 million commercial recreation businesses. In Canada, it comprises more than 12 percent of the gross domestic product and more than 200,000 businesses.

Leisure services are part of the service industry segment of national economies, which is called the *soft sector*. Although the service industry contains other subparts including insurance, banking, retail, education, and health care, its largest segment in the United States and Canada is the leisure service industry. The service industry is not thought to produce any "hard" products such as appliances or furniture. For the most part, the leisure service industry buys and sells hard products, but it doesn't produce them. Exceptions are the sports retail, recreational vehicle, and souvenir industries, which manufacture hard products and sell them in retail outlets. This means the leisure service industry is not limited to the service industry; it can include the manufacturing of leisure service products as well as the delivery of those products.

The leisure service industry is composed of many industries, including the following:

- Travel and tourism
- Hospitality
- Resorts
- Gaming
- Amusement parks
- Restaurants
- Professional sport
- Sporting goods manufacturers and retailers
- Movie and entertainment industry
- Camping and outdoor recreation
- Video games

In March 2017, there were about 15.8 million Americans employed in the leisure service industry who earned an average of $15.33 per hour, and their pay was growing monthly at a rate of about 5 cents per hour (Bureau of Labor Statistics, 2017). The leisure service industry generated $117.5 billion in annual national and state tax revenue in 2016. Economists have estimated that $1 of every $12 in the U.S. economy is from leisure service industry spending. The total gross national product of the United States is estimated to exceed $14 trillion, so the amount of money spent on leisure services exceeds $1.17 trillion annually (Bureau of Labor Statistics, 2017).

What makes the leisure service industry unique, and therefore makes leisure service delivery systems unique, is its diversity. Other than health care, a sector in which hospitals can be operated for profit, not for profit, or by governmental units, no other profession spans all three sectors. And no other profession requires the diversity of management skills required in the leisure service profession.

The leisure service industry can offer a broad array of services, even within a single industry. As an example, the cruise industry, a subcomponent of the travel and tourism industry, provides voyages to the four corners of the world. For as little as $500 per person, cruisers can live on a ship for a week, be fed gourmet meals, see Las Vegas–quality shows, purchase jewelry and other retail goods, and visit exotic ports of call that often offer adventure excursions. Each of these individual services are subsets of the cruise industry, and provided individually, each could stand alone as components outside of the cruise industry.

As a growing industry that seeks to keep up with the need of Canadians and Americans to travel in comfort at an affordable cost, the cruise ship industry serves as an example of what has been taking place in the leisure service industry worldwide. Since 2000, the cruise industry has been growing by leaps and bounds. Cruise lines are introducing new ships on an annual basis, and some cost more than $1 billion to build. According to Cruisecritic. com, in 2016, Royal Caribbean Cruises launched its newest ship, which cost more than $1.2 billion and had 2,747 staterooms and a maximum capacity of 6,780 passengers. In 2017, Norwegian Cruise Line launched its newest ship, which had 1,925 staterooms. These ships employ and house almost one crew member for every stateroom; this makes the ships small cities that serve the needs of customers willing to pay for the pleasure of traveling on the high seas and visiting exotic places.

Innovation has become the hallmark of the private-sector leisure service industry. Las Vegas, founded as a place where gamblers could make

wagers with no fear of breaking the law, is now a major convention center and family vacation destination. Las Vegas now has amusement parks, restaurants, entertainment venues, luxury resorts, and, of course, casinos. New hotels are regularly added to the market, and there are more than 90,000 hotel rooms available in the city.

It is easy to see why the private-sector leisure service industry keeps getting bigger: People love to play. Economists predict that leisure services will continue to grow as the middle classes grow worldwide. Because the burgeoning international middle class with disposable income seeks leisure services at every life stage, the leisure service industry has the potential to be a growth industry worldwide over the long haul, just as it has been in Canada and the United States.

PRIVATE-SECTOR LEISURE SERVICE DELIVERY SYSTEMS

Private-sector delivery systems are called *businesses*. In the United States and Canada, **businesses** are organizations created to provide a service or product. They charge a higher price than the cost of producing the product or service, and the difference between the cost and the price is the profit. Businesses can be as small as a single person who sharpens and waxes skis near a ski resort or as large as the resort operation itself, which provides lift services, food, accommodations, and transportation.

Making a profit changes the power dynamic of leisure service businesses. To make a profit, managers of leisure service businesses must possess a level of power that exceeds that of government and nonprofit managers. All leisure service managers need some power; it's just that leisure service private sector managers need more than their counterparts do. The additional power that leisure service private sector managers need is the power to focus on their customers without interference from their bosses or employees, meaning that customers become more important than the employees in the private sector.

Because leisure service businesses are always looking for ways to make a profit, they are motivated to identify unmet customer needs and meet them—for a fair price, of course. In some ways, that challenge makes the private sector more exciting than the nonprofit or government sectors. Those

Getty Images/Corbis/George Hammerstein

Innovation is key in the private-sector leisure service industry. Las Vegas has become a family vacation destination that includes amusement parks.

who work for businesses always have something to do because there is always more money to be made. People who find that type of career exciting tend to gravitate to the private sector. Leisure service students need to decide whether that type of life is for them.

All leisure service organizations focus on their customers at some level. But leisure service businesses are different from delivery systems in other sectors because they focus on customers who are willing and able to pay for services. If they didn't, the businesses wouldn't profit. Being focused on profitability means that businesses cannot afford to waste their time on people who will not pay them for services. Nonprofit organizations are often established to serve those who cannot pay, and government leisure service delivery systems cannot ignore those who cannot pay.

Business authors have developed a theory of the firm that suggests that everyone working for the business will act in the best interest of the business, focus on the customer, and help the business make a profit; this is in their own best interest. The economic reality is that if the business prospers, employees will retain their jobs or even share in the profits. Therefore, managers need not worry about being overbearing in their attempts to motivate employees to work hard. Employees will work hard on their own because it's in their own best interest to do so.

Challenges of Managing Leisure Service Businesses

Managing a leisure service, regardless of the sector, requires understanding the formal and information rules for management. Each sector has its own traditions, rules, and standard operating procedures that make it different from the others and from other services in their sector.

Businesses operate in the private sector. They focus on the customer because the transaction between the business and the customer provides the business its lifeblood. This is called taking a **marketing approach**. University-level marketing programs tend to teach the five Ps of marketing: product, price, place, promotion, and position. Often the emphasis is on promotion, suggesting that marketing is all about advertising. More modern marketing approaches acknowledge the importance of promotion but primarily focus on creating products or services that meet peoples' needs. As the adage goes, if you build a better mousetrap, the world will beat a path to your door.

The singular focus on the customer provides private sector managers with a challenge that doesn't exist in the public and nonprofit sectors of the leisure service industry. With no taxes or donations to sustain them, private sector leisure service managers have no safety net. Private leisure service managers walk a tightrope, particularly those who manage start-up businesses. Because of their dependence on revenues, commercial recreation managers confront challenges that managers in the other two sectors don't face. Businesses are susceptible to economic downturns and must comply with government regulations. Stockholders and owners expect a return on their capital. Lenders need to be repaid with interest. Customers need change, and competition is a constant threat.

Leisure service managers in the commercial sector also have advantages compared with their counterparts in nonprofit and government organizations. The level of transparency required of businesses is not as great as that required of government and nonprofit agencies. The media has no access to financial records of privately owned companies and limited access to those of publicly traded companies.

Another advantage is that private-sector employees have fewer rights than public-sector employees, allowing private sector labor costs to be lower than public and nonprofit labor costs. The salaries and wages of business employees can be kept secret, and in some cases, business employees can be terminated for divulging their pay. Managers can use pay as a motivational tool.

Unlike governmental units, privately held businesses do not have public board meetings. Businesses are not required to make their decisions public; doing so would provide competitors with strategic information. Setting prices for services is not open to debate in the private sector as it is in the public sector. And board members of companies in the private sector, unlike their counterparts in the public sector, can be paid substantial sums of money for attending meetings.

Corporate board members in privately held companies are themselves the owners. Any discussion about corporate strategy occurs within that group.

For publicly traded companies, corporate board members can be appointed by senior management, which is tantamount to allowing the senior executive to select his or her own bosses, or they can be elected by the stockholders, although the major stockholders control most of the votes.

Capital financing in the private sector is also an important difference. Leisure service managers in the nonprofit sector can solicit funds from donations to make capital improvements, and these never need to be repaid from operating funds. In the public sector, tax monies are levied to repay municipal, state, and federal bonds, but the monies are generally not repaid from operating funds.

In the private sector, almost no one makes donations to businesses. Customers pay for services. To finance capital expenses, commercial recreation managers can borrow money from banks and other lenders, but these loans are repaid from operating revenues. In addition, before lending institutions make loans to businesses, these enterprises need to demonstrate they can generate sufficient revenues to service the debt. That's why leisure service business managers as entrepreneurs face capital finance challenges that don't exist in the nonprofit or public sectors.

Skills Required for Managing Leisure Service Businesses

The most important skills that business managers need are economics, business accounting, finance, marketing, and organizational leadership. These skills are taught as academic courses in leisure studies and business programs at the university level. Traditionally, business schools have taught these subjects as having principles and formulae for success. In leisure service commercial recreation courses, some of these principles are taught as well, with the most advanced leisure service academic programs focusing on teaching them to students intending to have a career in the public sector.

NONPROFIT SECTOR

The nonprofit sector of the leisure service industry consists of organizations chartered or otherwise permitted by the national government in Canada and state and federal governments in the United

States. In the United States, most nonprofits are chartered by individual states, but some are nationally chartered, such as the Boy Scouts of America. All U.S. nonprofits must follow the codes of the Internal Revenue Service (IRS). In Canada, the national government takes a more vigilant approach, making sure nonprofit organizations do charitable work.

In the United States, nonprofit organizations are exempt from paying federal taxes under section 501(c) of the Internal Revenue Code, and they file annual reports with the IRS to substantiate their tax exemption. Numerous categories are identified under this section, but the most pertinent for leisure services are social and recreational clubs allowed under IRS code 501(c)(7) and charitable organizations allowed under IRS code 501(c)(3).

According to the Internal Revenue Code, to receive exempt status, a social club must be organized for pleasure, recreation, and other similar purposes and cannot discriminate against any person based on race, color, or religion. "A club may, however, in good faith, limit its membership to members of a particular religion in order to further the teachings or principles of that religion and not to exclude individuals of a particular race or color." The other category, charitable organizations, is for religious, educational, scientific, literary, public safety testing, national or international amateur sport competition, and animal and child cruelty prevention organizations.

The tax code defines *charitable* as including

> relief of the poor, the distressed, or the underprivileged; advancement of religion; advancement of education or science; erecting or maintaining public buildings, monuments, or works; lessening the burdens of government; lessening neighborhood tensions; eliminating prejudice and discrimination; defending human and civil rights secured by law; and combating community deterioration and juvenile delinquency (IRS, n.d.).

In the nonprofit sector, although meeting the needs of clients is important, doing it for a price to cover operating expenses, let alone to make a profit, is not always important. Whereas business organizations exist to earn and distribute taxable wealth to owners and shareholders, nonprofit

corporations cannot distribute excess revenues to shareholders because there are no shareholders. Businesses retain profits and use those profits for the capital expansion of the businesses. Nonprofits strive for excess revenue over expenditures so they can reinvest into their organizations, but they can use donations to cover operating expenses and capital improvements.

In the nonprofit sector, if donations and operating revenues fall short of covering expenses, organizations face survival issues. Nonprofit organizations are like businesses in that way, as are governmental units. In none of the sectors can organizations lose money and expect to be in existence in the long run. Nonprofits can solicit donations to pay for operating expenses, and governmental units can subsidize them with taxes.

As mentioned, the IRS allows various kinds of nonprofit leisure service organizations. Some nonprofit leisure service providers do charitable work, such as Boys and Girls Clubs of America, and they rely on donations rather than fees for existence. Other nonprofit leisure service organizations, such as country clubs, don't do charitable work and charge substantial fees for their leisure services. Both organizations have nonprofit status approved by the Internal Revenue Service that permits them to exist with the understanding that they will stay true to their purpose and reinvest excess revenue into the organization. Their profitability is closely monitored by the IRS because nonprofit organizations have to file tax reports just like private corporations do. Nonprofit organizations walk a tightrope between generating too much in revenues and donations and generating too little.

In the U.S. leisure service sector today, tens of thousands of youth sport organizations are organized as nonprofits. They are organized to avoid paying taxes on surplus revenues in good years and to be permitted to solicit donations and not be taxed for them. Nonprofits are organized so that their governing boards have the flexibility of providing services without having the IRS to look over their shoulders.

It has been a complaint that nonprofit organizations often compete against businesses and governmental units for clients. For instance, a local YMCA might compete with a private fitness club or the local parks and recreation department by selling memberships to their fitness club. A local youth club athletic team might compete with the local park district for youth baseball players. Because they are not taxed on their short-term profits and they are permitted to solicit donations to cover operating expenses, a YMCA fitness club will likely survive an economic downturn, whereas a private fitness club might not.

On the other hand, nonprofit leisure service providers often exist in many communities to fill a void because a governmental or private leisure service provider is not available. A charitable organization may be needed to meet the needs of children or adults who have low incomes or are disabled. People may not be able to pay fees for services, and by being able to solicit donations to cover these services, nonprofit leisure service organizations can provide services that businesses or governmental units cannot. Even where a governmental provider is available, some nonprofits exist because people want their leisure service needs met in different ways or want them met in private rather than among the public. Country clubs, tennis clubs, swimming clubs, and other athletic clubs exist because of their exclusiveness, but to maintain their tax-exempt status, they cannot discriminate by race, color, or religion.

Leisure service nonprofit organizations face a unique challenge from other nonprofits. The primary management responsibility of the charitable ones is to seek donations so that they can continue to exist because fees from clients, who mostly have low incomes, do not generate sufficient operating revenues. The primary management responsibility of less charitable ones, such as country clubs, is to ensure the happiness of their members so that they will continue to pay membership fees.

NONPROFIT-SECTOR LEISURE SERVICE DELIVERY SYSTEMS

Like the business sector, the nonprofit sector of the field offers many opportunities for leisure service professionals. Among the 1.8 million nonprofit organizations in the United States today, approximately 20 percent deliver leisure services, so almost 360,000 nonprofit leisure service organizations are delivering services to Americans.

These nonprofit organizations range from such well-known organizations as the YMCA and the

Nonprofit leisure service providers, such as a private swim club, exist because either those services aren't available in the community or they meet users' leisure needs in other ways.

Boys and Girls Clubs of America to nonprofit resident and day camps, local youth baseball and softball programs, and hospitals that provide wellness centers. Not every nonprofit provider employs full-time staff. For example, local youth baseball programs don't, but Boys and Girls Clubs and YMCAs employ full-time leisure service professionals.

Nonprofit leisure service delivery systems differ from leisure service businesses in that the nonprofit leisure service sector has boundaries that businesses do not. For instance, in search of revenue, businesses can venture into markets that are off limits to nonprofit organizations. For example, state governments will not issue charters for nonprofit organizations to provide services such as cruising, hospitality, and gaming. Businesses are permitted in these industries because state governments recognize that these industries are profitable but are not appropriate for nonprofit leisure service organizations.

Nonprofit leisure service delivery systems are, therefore, more limited in the range of services that they can provide. Athletics and fitness programs and residential and day camps are within the scope of nonprofit leisure service organization services. Bowling, amusement parks, hotels, resorts, retail outlets, and other products or services that can make a profit are not within those boundaries, as determined by the IRS when they issue nonprofit status to new organizations.

Challenges of Managing Nonprofit Leisure Service Agencies

Because fees and donations are their primary sources of revenue, nonprofit organizations need to focus on their revenues to remain financially viable. Like businesses, nonprofits must be creative in the services that they provide to their clients, but setting fees that clients can afford and raising donation revenues are skills that nonprofit managers need to have.

Transparency is another way that nonprofits are similar to businesses. Like businesses, the records of nonprofit organizations are not readily available to the media or public, although they are required to submit reports to the IRS, but few citizens read these reports. Faking financial reports has crimi-

nal consequences in the private sector, but in the nonprofit sector, financial reports are available for donors to discern the necessity of their donations.

The boards of directors for nonprofits are similar to those of private-sector companies. When an opening on a board of directors occurs, the remaining board members select the replacement. Also, board meetings are not open to the public or regulated by state open meetings acts, so replacing board members can be done without public scrutiny. Nonprofit board members are rarely compensated for their service to the organization. In fact, their primary responsibility is to bring money into the agency through their fund-raising efforts.

Managing a nonprofit organization can be different as well. Because employees are generally not rewarded by profit sharing, managing nonprofit employees is similar to managing public employees. Management is generally done on a group basis using sociological principles of group motivation, whereas business management of employees is more psychological and uses business leadership and organizational management techniques taught in business schools.

Nonprofit managers do not share in the surplus revenues of the organization. Big salaries or other perks are supposed to be absent. Nonprofit managers are supposed to focus on how much revenue the agency generates from services, which clients receive free services, how judiciously the agency spends its money, and how the agency can maintain an environment in which clients can be donors and employees will say complimentary things about the organization. There has been negative publicity about large salaries and perks for executives within nonprofit organizations. There are measurements of the percentage of donations that go to administrative costs; some nonprofits spend as little as 10 percent for administration and others spend as much as 50 percent. Those comparisons are now available on the Internet, which allows donors to decide what organizations will spend their donations the most judiciously (e.g., see www.givewell.org).

The good news is that nonprofit organizations usually succeed in their missions of servicing public needs that would have otherwise gone unserved. Of the new nonprofit organizations created each year, less than 20 percent fail, partly because a safety net is present. When nonprofits are chartered by states, the people who charter them usually have established a need for their services and sources of revenue for their operations. Initially, these organizations have volunteers performing the work, and eventually donors provide a stable base of revenue. Therefore, the risk that the agency will fail is smaller, although the financial reward to management is also less.

Skills Required for Managing Nonprofit Leisure Service Agencies

Nonprofit leisure service managers need to have a blend of skills in business and public administration. Managers need to understand economics, business accounting, finance, marketing, business leadership, fund accounting, organizational theory, and fund-raising. Several universities have emerging academic programs in public service that focus on nonprofit agency management. These programs blend business and public administration classes.

It is often said that people who pursue careers in nonprofit leisure service are not necessarily doing it for personal enrichment. They are typically intrinsically motivated people who want the security of a stable environment as they perform a service for the community. Like for-profit managers, they need financial skills, but they must have a certain level of human compassion that is not required of business managers. They need to identify what unmet human needs their organization can meet.

PUBLIC SECTOR

Government spending in the leisure service industry makes up about 1 percent of all money spent. Even so, leisure service governmental services are a cornerstone of employment in the leisure service field. Many graduates from academic programs in leisure service are drawn to the public sector, particularly at the county and municipal levels. State and federal leisure service professionals attain their positions by political appointment or competitive testing.

Federal and State Agencies

The U.S. government is primarily in the business of maintaining national forests, parks, and recreation areas. Most recreation services are park and nature conservation oriented, and most of the user fees charged are for admissions, parking, and use of camping, food, and accommodation facilities. The federal government provides outdoor services through many agencies in various departments. The Canadian government also provides national and provincial parks and recreation services.

The 50 state governments in the United States provide services similar to those of the National Park Service. State departments of natural resources primarily manage their state park systems, some of which have restaurants, hotels, campgrounds, boat rentals, and other supplemental services. Some parks charge fees for admission and parking, whereas others are free of charge.

For the most part, federal, state, and county agencies are not considered entrepreneurial. They exist to conserve land and, in some cases, to block public access and maintain land in its natural state.

State governments have created special taxing districts that own athletic stadiums and convention centers. The construction and maintenance of these facilities can be funded by property, sales, excise, and hotel room taxes. These facilities can be rented to professional and university sports programs and generate millions of dollars in revenue.

MUNICIPAL PUBLIC-SECTOR LEISURE SERVICE DELIVERY SYSTEMS

At the local level, the United States has more than 25,000 municipalities. At the municipal level, many structures of government provide parks and recreation services. The most common are parks and recreation departments of cities, villages, and towns. Canadian municipalities are organized similarly. Municipal departments of parks and recreation are nearly identical in Canada and the United States.

At the local level in the United States, special districts are another way of delivering public parks and recreation services. Some states have provisions within state law to create park districts at the local level (e.g., Illinois, Ohio, Colorado, Utah, California, Oregon, Washington, North Dakota). Of the states that provide park districts, the option of providing parks and recreation services as municipal departments is still available. Only in Illinois and North Dakota do park districts outnumber parks and

Felix Mizioznikov/fotolia.com

A park district, a public-sector leisure delivery provider, has many duties including maintaining and providing playground equipment for children.

recreation departments. Although California has more than 175 park districts, in the other states that permit park districts, municipalities and voters have been reluctant to create them.

Challenges of Managing Government Leisure Service Agencies

It has been said that public administration is like managing in a fishbowl because nothing is private, and managing public employees is like herding cats who each have a lawyer. The public has the right to review all public documents and meeting notes under the Freedom of Information Act, and public employees have rights under the 1965 Civil Rights Act. The main reason for public scrutiny of government is the relationship between taxation and responsibility. Unlike businesses or nonprofit organizations in which revenues are exchanged through transactions that both parties agree on, taxation is not voluntary. Because the public is required to pay taxes, government officials bear a greater burden to explain how the taxes are spent. This principle is called **transparency,** which means being clear and open. To ensure that government dealings are transparent, laws adopted at the federal, state, and local levels require that all information, with a few exceptions, be public; that meetings be announced and take place in public; and that individuals or companies doing business with governmental units bid competitively for that business.

Public employees have greater rights than do business and nonprofit employees. In most states, public employees cannot be hired and fired by managers without consent of the elected board. Thus, every employee who is terminated has the right to a board hearing before termination. As in the private sector, the public sector might have employee unions to deal with, which means another set of rules for hiring and firing employees and giving pay increases. Except for public administrators, who usually have employment contracts, public employees are not at-will employees like private and nonprofit sector employees are. *At will* means employees serve at the will of the administration (i.e., can be dismissed by the employer for any reason). Public employees serve at the will of the public who, in a republican form of government, elect representatives to make decisions.

Boards in the public sector are different, too. The governing boards that levy taxes and approve budget expenditures must be elected. Appointed parks and recreation department boards may have advisory authority with leisure service managers, but only the elected boards have the power to decide. Directors of parks and recreation departments therefore have two boards as their bosses—the city council and their appointed advisory boards. Sometimes leisure service managers have three bosses (city council, park board, and city manager), depending on whether the municipality has a strong mayor–council system or a council–manager system. This arrangement can make managing a public leisure service agency an extremely difficult assignment.

Working for an elected board in an environment where everything that a leisure service manager does is public information adds a dimension of politics to the management process. Although nonprofit leisure service managers might worry about offending potential donors, a governmental leisure service manager who offends a member of the public may find the offended party seeking election to the manager's governing board. Disgruntled employees can run for election as well, and many of each group do.

Another challenge of managing a governmental leisure service agency is that managers need two types of financial management skills. One is the management of tax-supported services, typically the parks, which usually do not have admission fees and are supported entirely by tax revenues. The other is the operation of recreation programs and facilities, which usually generate self-sustaining revenues from user fees. Public-sector managers are therefore running governmental units that provide both tax-supported and fee-supported services in a transparent arena in which disgruntled employees or members of the public can run for their boards, which is more difficult than running a business that needs to make a profit.

Skills Required for Managing Government Leisure Service Agencies

The skills required of leisure service public administrators are somewhat different from those required of business or nonprofit managers. Leisure service public administrators have less need to understand economics because governmental units rely heavily on relatively stable tax revenues. Financial management is less important because state governments are stringent about how governmental units handle public funds. That is not to say that economics and finance are unimportant. Working in an economic environment has political consequences, and capital funding through the issuance of tax repaid bonds requires an understanding of finance.

Government accounting is different from business or nonprofit accounting. To maintain the required levels of transparency, governmental units have much more complex accounting rules than do business and nonprofit agencies, which report to the IRS and state departments of revenue and are not required to produce detailed reports. Governmental units report directly to the people, so their reports are more detailed. Such is not always the case in Canada, where public officials often report directly to the Crown or representatives of the Crown.

The skills required of public leisure service managers need to include government accounting, organizational theory, political science, economics, and finance. If a leisure service manager oversees the operation of parks only, it could be argued his or her skills need to include those related to park maintenance and conservation. If the leisure service manager manages recreation programs or facilities, it could also be argued the skills need to be more diverse, including marketing and financial management and skills related to the recreation facility or program.

If managing a leisure service agency in the public sector can be more difficult than managing in the other sectors, why would someone choose to do it? The answer is that working in the public sector is just as rewarding as working for a nonprofit organization. Serving the public has its intrinsic rewards.

PROFESSIONAL PREPARATION FOR LEISURE SERVICE DELIVERY

Regardless of whether a student seeks a career in the private, nonprofit, or public sector of the leisure service industry, all students should pursue proficiency in certain areas. Previous discussion of the challenges facing leisure service professionals

OUTSTANDING GRADUATE

Background Information

Name: Brittany Fischer

Education: BS in corporate recreation and wellness from Northwest Missouri State University

Career Information

Position: Health and Wellness Supervisor

Organization: City of Liberty, Missouri

Job description: In my job, I manage the fitness center. I provide leadership to wellness employees: group exercise instructors, personal trainers, and wellness coaches. I create and implement corporate wellness programs and design and implement a variety of wellness programs that fit the needs of the community. My job has provided me an opportunity to network with others in the recreation field as well as in public health.

> *If you want to go fast, go alone. If you want to go far, go together. Collaboration is key.*

Career path: My career path began with my internship in Sioux City, Iowa, with their parks and recreation department. I then became employed with the YMCA of Greater Kansas City as a wellness specialist. I stayed with the YMCA in a variety of roles (trainer, instructor, healthy living director, youth development) until the spring of 2015, when I joined the Liberty Parks and Recreation team. I'm always striving to learn more and grow so that I can continue to move up the career ladder.

Likes and dislikes about the job: I dislike roadblocks and people who are resistant to change. I like the opportunity to have an impact on citizens while expanding the role of health and wellness in the community.

Advice for Undergraduates

My advice to undergraduates is to get as much hands-on experience as possible, because that will prepare you for the field more than any textbook or lecture.

and the skills required of them suggest that every leisure service professional needs to understand how to manage money and people and how government works.

Understanding how to manage money means that leisure service professionals need to understand accounting so they can read financial reports. They need to understand financial management so they can take appropriate action when their financial reports are not in order. Students seeking to prepare themselves to manage finances should take courses in financial accounting if they seek careers in business or nonprofit leisure service management or governmental accounting if they seek careers in governmental leisure service management. And all students need to take courses in finance to understand how to manage their budgets.

To prepare for leisure service delivery in all three sectors, students need to take courses in marketing. Marketing teaches how focusing on product (service), price, place, and promotion leads to understanding what the customer needs, how much the customer is willing to pay, where and how the service ought to be provided, and how to communicate its availability to the customer. Understanding these essentials of marketing is crucial for managers in all sectors.

Political science and public administration courses are essential to students pursuing careers in public-sector leisure service delivery and are useful to those seeking careers in nonprofit and business leisure service delivery. Public-sector managers need to understand how government works if they intend to be successful working in government. But because the government creates and regulates business and nonprofit entities, managers in those sectors need to understand what they will face. The government taxes businesses and forces some nonprofit organizations to provide a certain portion of their services as charitable work, suggesting that business and nonprofit leisure service managers would benefit from understanding what makes government tick.

PROFESSIONAL ACCREDITATION

All leisure service professionals need to consider professional accreditation not only because many agencies require it but also because accreditation teaches some of the skills required for successful careers in the field. The National Recreation and Park Association (NRPA) in the United States, in conjunction with state associations, has developed an accreditation program called the certified park and recreation professional (CPRP) program. Undergraduate students who complete an accredited NRPA curriculum with the NRPA-prescribed learning outcomes are eligible to take the accreditation test.

The NRPA also has an accreditation program for agencies provided by the Commission for Accreditation of Park and Recreation Agencies (CAPRA). The CAPRA process is based on 144 standards for national accreditation, which can be determined only after CAPRA members make an onsite visit to verify eligibility.

If an undergraduate student completes a program that is not NRPA accredited, he or she is required to take continuing education units (CEUs) before taking the exam. After a leisure service professional has obtained CPRP accreditation, he or she is required to take CEUs on a regular basis to maintain accreditation. Continuing education units need to be approved by the NRPA.

SUMMARY

Leisure service delivery systems exist in the private, nonprofit, and governmental sectors of the economy, and they account for a substantial proportion of the national economies of Canada and the United States. As subunits of the leisure service industry, the private sector operates businesses that serve the leisure needs of people by charging fees for services that exceed the costs, nonprofit organizations provide services for fees to some people and waive fees to others, and governmental units levy taxes for services where it is not practical to charge fees and charge fees for leisure services where doing so is practical.

The private leisure service business sector is characterized by innovation. In pursuit of profits, entrepreneurs are alert to new and changing leisure service needs of their customers. Nonprofit sector organizations have other challenges, including fund-raising, because they seek donations to support operations that in many cases serve low-income people who cannot afford to pay fees or make donations. Governmental units provide leisure services that are necessary but cannot be provided by the private and nonprofit sectors, such as parks and open space.

Students who want to prepare themselves for a leisure service professional career in any of the three sectors need to consider taking business courses such as accounting, finance, economics, and marketing. They also need to understand government and should study political science and public administration. NRPA-accredited undergrad curricula that teach these learning outcomes allow students to become CPRPs without meeting postgraduate continuing education requirements.

CHAPTER 6

Parks and Protected Areas in Canada and the United States

Paul F.J. Eagles and Jeffrey C. Hallo

©Paul F.J. Eagles.

❝ There is nothing so American as our national parks. . . . The fundamental idea behind the parks . . . is that the country belongs to the people, that it is in process of making for the enrichment of the lives of all of us. ❞

Franklin D. Roosevelt, U.S. president, 1933-1945

❝ The day will come when the population of Canada will be ten times as great as it is now but the national parks ensure that every Canadian . . . will still have free access to vast areas possessing some of the finest scenery in Canada, in which the beauty of the landscape is protected from profanation, the natural wild animals, plants and forests preserved, and the peace and solitude of primeval nature retained. ❞

James Harkin, Dominion Parks Commission for Canada, director of the first national park agency in the world, 1911-1936

LEARNING OUTCOMES

After reading this chapter, you should be able to do the following:

❯ Describe the history and development of Canadian and American park systems as well as their similarities and differences

❯ Differentiate and discuss various types of parks and other protected areas

❯ Name and describe the accomplishments of a few of the most prominent people who promoted and created parks

❯ Summarize current issues and trends in park resources management

❯ Define the terms *preservation*, *wilderness*, *conservation*, *multiple use*, and *wise use of natural resources and parks*

❯ Explain a few career opportunities in park settings

Parks and other protected areas are important parts of the cultures of Canada and the United States. Just mentioning a national park, **wildlife refuge**, or wilderness evokes strong feelings among many citizens and foreign tourists. This chapter presents the history and a current description of the major park systems and other protected areas in Canada and the United States.

The term *park* is derived from the Old French and Middle English term *parc*, which means "an enclosed piece of ground stocked with beasts of the chase, held by prescription or by the king's grant" (Runte, 2010). One of the first parklike areas was the Greek *agora*, which were plazas established and used for public assembly. Today, however, parks and other protected areas may be defined as places set aside to protect and provide for the use and enjoyment of natural, cultural, historic, or recreational resources. The movement to create parks and protected areas that emerged in the late 1800s and continues strongly to this day was driven by society's need to reconnect with nature after having been removed from it because of industrialization and technological advancement.

Modern parks in the United States and Canada reflect our ideals of democracy and are managed for public use and enjoyment. Parks are places for the public to escape the stresses of life, rejuvenate, and connect with nature and history. Parks in one form or another exist in every country in the world, which indicates their critical role in society. Their purpose may be particularly crucial in the United States and Canada, where well over a billion visits occur annually to local, state, provincial, and national parks. A substantial body of research has shown that parks and other protected areas aid considerably in child development, public health, economic growth, and quality of life. Parks also serve a critical function in protecting and ensuring the long-term sustainability of plants, wildlife, fish, historic or cultural sites, geology, and natural processes (e.g., bird migration routes and the filtration of water).

This chapter contains two major discussions. First is an outline of the situation in Canada. Second is a similar outline for the United States. Those sections are followed by a summary and comparison of the two countries.

HISTORY OF PARKS IN CANADA

Canada is a large country composed of 10 provinces and 3 territories. The nation was created when four British colonies came together to form a country through confederation in 1867. Over time, other colonies joined as new provinces, and other provinces were created from territories. In 1885, the national government started to create a national park system in Canada with the creation of Banff National Park in the Rocky Mountains, which became Canada's most famous national park. Also starting in 1885, Ontario, Canada's most populous province, purchased private land near Niagara Falls for the creation of a park and tourist destination. This site was the first major park created by a province in Canada. These two parks were the start of the development of the national and **provincial park** systems in Canada.

As the country grew, the provinces retained considerable land management responsibilities. One important power was the ownership and management of all Crown land, or public land as it is called in the United States. Because the provinces owned the Crown land within the provincial boundaries, creating parks was relatively easy for them. Conversely, the federal government could not easily create parks within provinces because provincial cooperation was required. Therefore, some of the provincial park systems in Canada are as large and prominent as the **national park** systems in many other countries.

First Parks in Canada

The first parks created in Canada were in cities. The movement to form city parks was strongly influenced by parks existing in England. The large, green, central parks of London were well known to the early populace of Canada and became a model for park creation in British North America. For example, Hyde Park, now in downtown London, was created in 1536 by Henry VIII for hunting. Over the next centuries, it was increasingly opened for public use.

In 1763, the lieutenant governor of the British Colony of Nova Scotia granted the Halifax Common, former military land, to the City of Halifax. It was first used as community pasture and for military exercises. The Halifax Common later became city parkland and is now located in the heart of the city. It is recognized as the first park created in Canada.

Toronto was the first city in British North America to formally create a public agency to manage those parks. After eight years of operation, Toronto's Committee on Public Walks and Gardens, Canada's first park management agency, took political action and asked the city council to lobby the provincial government to change the law and give cities an explicit power to create parks. The chairman of the committee spoke at a Toronto City Council meeting in 1859 and said the following:

> In the first place, they furnish to the wealthy places of agreeable resort, either for driving or walking, and free from exposure to the heat and dust of an ordinary road . . . thus enabling them to enjoy the inestimable blessing of the free open air of the Country—so conducive to the promotion of health and morality.

©Paul F.J. Eagles.

The creation of Banff National Park, the first national park in Canada, was influenced by the Canadian Pacific Railway, which saw the promise of tourism.

In the second place, to the mechanic and working classes, Public Grounds are of incalculable advantage. How much better it is for the families of such to have these places of recreation and healthful exercise, than to have them exposed on the crowded streets of the city? (as cited in McFarland, 1982, p. 258)

As seen in this speech, the committee assumed the responsibility for providing public grounds for all classes of society, especially for the working class who badly needed access to "places of agreeable resort" free of charge. This public-spirited and socialistic approach to parks—public use subsidized by community taxes—became a fundamental aspect of park management in Canada. Over the next 150 years, virtually every city and town in Canada created parks for the welfare, use, and health of its citizens. The municipalities fund these parks from income earned by **land taxes** and provide most of the parks and their facilities free to local citizens who want to use them.

In the initial days, city parks were managed by volunteers working on parks boards. Starting in the early decades of the 20th century, staff members were hired to manage special facilities, such as agricultural fairs and sport grounds. Many of the first park managers were gardeners. Not until the 1960s did universities and colleges in Canada start to train people specifically for working in parks and recreation in cities. The first program of this type in Canada was the Department of Recreation at the University of Waterloo, which first took in students in 1968.

Provincial and National Parks

The origin of provincial and national parks in Canada can be traced to the 1880s and occurred simultaneously in Niagara Falls in Ontario and on the remote mountain pass of the Bow Valley in the Northwest Territories of western Canada now in the Province of Alberta.

From the beginning of European settlement, Niagara Falls attracted tourists. Because the Niagara River and Niagara Falls are in the United States (New York) and Canada (Ontario), cross-border discussions determined how to manage this rapidly developing tourist attraction. The Canadian side of the river had the best view of the falls, and by 1885,

every possible view was privately owned. Entrepreneurs charged fees for visitors to enter their premises to look out windows at the magnificent waterfalls and cataracts. One planning idea proposed by people in New York State in the early 1880s was to create reserves and organize tourism management institutions to develop public parks and foster cooperation between the two countries. Ontario adopted the idea and asked the Canadian government to fund and operate the Canadian portion as a park and tourism reserve. The idea was to create a national park on the Canadian side of the river by buying out all the private properties and replacing them with a properly designed park and tourism facility. The vast expense of the proposed land purchase and park development incited opposition from members of the Canadian Parliament from Quebec and the Maritime provinces. They objected to large amounts of federal money being spent in Ontario on this development and effectively stopped federal involvement. In 1885, Ontario moved alone to create a major park and tourism facility along the Niagara River and Niagara Falls. This action involved the purchase and removal of thousands of buildings on the lip of the falls and the gorge and the creation of a green parkway available for all to use. The Ontario Parliament also passed legislation for the creation of the Niagara Parks Commission, a park and tourism management body (Seibel, 1995).

The Ontario actions at Niagara set precedents in three important areas. First, Niagara was the first park created by a provincial government in Canada and had the first stand-alone park management agency with its own legislation and mandate. Second, the park stimulated the creation of future parks in Ontario by the provincial government, not the national government. It also set a tone of American–Canadian cooperation in park management. All three movements continued and strengthened in subsequent years. This book is an example of the ongoing sharing of ideas and cooperation in park management between the United States and Canada.

Simultaneous to the debates over Niagara in Ontario, the Canadian government pushed the first national cross-country railway through the Rocky Mountains to link Eastern Canada to the Province of British Columbia in the West. When hot springs were discovered near the railway tracks

Niagara Falls parks in Ontario were created in 1885 to manage a major international tourism activity.

©Paul F.J. Eagles.

in the Bow Valley in the eastern Rocky Mountains, the potential for tourism was quickly recognized. The national government acted through a cabinet order in 1885 to reserve the hot springs for public use and to stop private tourism development. This action was followed in 1887 by federal legislation to create Rocky Mountain Park, Canada's first national park, which was later renamed Banff National Park. This national government activity started the federal government of Canada in the parks business. Many historians state that Rocky Mountain Park was the third national park in the world after Yellowstone National Park in the United States, created in 1872, and Royal National Park in the British Colony of New South Wales, now a state of Australia, created in 1879 (Marty, 1984). However, all three followed much earlier and older park developments in England such as the New Forest created in England in 1079.

In 1887, Canada's federal government created North America's first wildlife conservation reserve at Last Mountain Lake in the Northwest Territories (now in Saskatchewan). This small reserve was established to protect the nesting and migration habitat of wildlife in the Canadian prairies (Foster, 1978). This reserve became the first of many national wildlife areas and migratory bird sanctuaries created by the national government in Canada.

In 1893, Ontario made the next important move by creating Algonquin National Park. This huge area of forested and rocky hills, lakes, and rivers in Southern Ontario became a forest conservation area and park. The government wanted to manage the logging industry in this area, protect the headwaters of five important rivers, and stop farmers from clearing the forests. This creation of a large conservation park along the American national park model by a provincial government was a first for Canada. It set a precedent for Ontario and other provinces (Killan, 1993; Saunders, 1998). The name was changed to Algonquin Provincial Park in 1913, giving notice that the parks operated by provinces were unique and separate from those operated by the national government, which were called national parks. Henceforth, the federal government moved forward in creating national parks and each province created provincial parks.

By 1900, the die was cast in Canada. The initial debates and decisions coalesced into precedents that would guide future park creation and management across the country. After this date, cities and towns throughout the country saw park creation as a normal and expected activity. Provincial parks were increasingly created for **conservation** and tourism purposes. Provincial governments also created regional parks for specific tourism and resource management concerns in regional geographical areas. Two types of federal reserves were established: national parks and national wildlife areas. The signing of the Migratory Bird Treaty with the United States in 1916 gave the federal government a powerful tool to regulate waterfowl and bird hunting in cooperation with the U.S. government. This action also gave this federal government the power to deal with wildlife management all over the country. This treaty was an early recognition of the international nature of ecology; that is, birds move widely across countries during their yearly life cycles. Therefore, international cooperation is needed for ecological conservation to be effective.

Over the next century, these emerging approaches strengthened and deepened. Many more parks and reserves were created. Management institutions were created. Canadians increasingly used and appreciated these areas in growing numbers. During the 20th century, parks were a major part of the culture of the country. After World War II,

a massive expansion in personal auto ownership and increasing prosperity led to a vast increase in outdoor recreation, which spurred increased park creation across the country.

Long-Distance Hiking Trails

Canada has many long-distance hiking trails, all of which are operated by nongovernmental organizations called *trail clubs*. Provincial governments do not have a formal role in the creation or management of long-distance hiking trails. The oldest trail is the Bruce Trail in southern Ontario, which runs along the Niagara Escarpment from Niagara Falls in the south to Tobermory in the north on the Bruce Peninsula. This trail was opened in 1967, Canada's centennial. Initially, the trail was almost entirely on private land, but over time many landowners removed permission for public use of their land, so the trail is now on a combination of private land, parkland, and land owned by trail clubs. The Canadian long-distance trail movement was heavily influenced by earlier trail activities in the United States, especially the Appalachian Trail.

The most ambitious trail effort in Canada is the Trans Canada Trail. The creation of this trail

©Paul F.J. Eagles.

Algonquin Provincial Park in Ontario became a model for provincial park creation across Canada.

is ongoing, and the goal is a national trail from Newfoundland in the east across Canada to the West Coast including a branch north to the Yukon, for a total length of 22,500 kilometers (14,000 mi). The trail also involves a water route from central Alberta to the Arctic Ocean. By 2017 it was 93 percent complete (Trans Canada Trail, 2017). The Bruce Trail in southern Ontario is one of Canada's oldest—it first opened in 1967—and best-known trails. It has no government funding, operating entirely through a nongovernmental organization, volunteers, and donations.

National Heritage Rivers System

Canada has a national heritage rivers system that is cooperatively managed by the provinces and the federal government. The system contains 42 rivers covering 12,000 kilometers (7,456 mi) of waterway. The goal of the system is to promote, protect, and enhance Canada's river heritage and ensure that Canada's leading rivers are managed in a sustainable manner (Leduc, 2009). The system has no legal mandate and is entirely cooperative among governments.

Wilderness in Canada (1600-2005)

In Canada, the concept of establishing large areas of uninhabited lands as designated wilderness is largely restricted to lands within national and provincial parks. This situation is markedly different from that in the United States, and reasons for the differences are important. In Canada, aboriginal land rights have long been respected, meaning that the creation of parks or wilderness sites involves negotiation with aboriginal peoples who have land rights according to the Canadian constitution. In Canada, land is influenced by the rights of aboriginal people. Very little land is considered vacant. A summary of the history of this situation follows.

After the American Revolution, the British government formed alliances for political and military reasons with many of the aboriginal groups that lived in the area that is now Canada. One of the major reasons for these alliances was the shared concern of the British government and the aboriginal peoples of the expansionist nature of the aggressive United States to the south. Shared actions were in both their interests to preserve independence. Because the British needed the military prowess of the many aboriginal people, their land rights were recognized and supported.

Therefore, the wilderness in Canada contains aboriginal people. It was a living landscape composed of forests, rivers, wildlife, and native people. In the United States, the situation was much different; native people were killed or persecuted, removed from the land and placed into reservations, or driven into Canada, thereby creating the mythology that the area was wilderness—land without people. Widespread support never arose in Canada for the classical American view of wilderness as large expanses of land without people; Canada's wilderness contains people. These are the substantive reasons why the American wilderness concept, outside of national parks, has never gained traction in Canada.

Important People in Canadian Parks

During the 1870s and 1880s, Sir Sandford Fleming was the engineer in charge of the construction of the Canadian Pacific Railway, which was built to link the industrial eastern provinces through the open prairies to the west coast Province of British Columbia. In an attempt to increase the use of his developing railway, Fleming proposed a series of national parks across Canada to create tourism demand and railway use. The discovery of thermal springs in the Bow Valley in the Rocky Mountains in 1883 provided an opportunity for the national government of Prime Minister John A. Macdonald to create the first of Fleming's proposed parks. Fleming and Macdonald were central figures in the creation of Canada's first national park in 1885, which is now known as Banff National Park.

In 1887, the federal government of Canada created the first bird sanctuary in North America. Areas around Last Mountain Lake in the Northwest Territories, now Saskatchewan, were withdrawn from settlement and set aside for the breeding of waterfowl. The creation of this reserve was the work of Edgar Dewdney, then the lieutenant governor of the Northwest Territories. He feared that the extension of the railway into this area would destroy the wildlife habitat. The creation of this wildlife reserve set the precedent for the national government to set aside areas for wildlife conservation. This reserve was designated as a National Historic Site of Canada in 1987.

Starting in 1885, Alexander Kirkwood, a clerk in the Ontario Department of Crown Lands, lobbied for the creation of a national forest and park in the Algonquin Highlands of southern Ontario. Over the next eight years, his idea slowly gained the support of other government officials, influential members of the community, and ultimately elected officials. In 1893, the Government of Ontario created Algonquin National Park, which was later renamed Algonquin Provincial Park. This action created the first large provincial park in Canada based on the emerging American model of large, uninhabited wilderness reserves. The Algonquin Indian people retained hunting rights in the park, but they never lived there because of its inhospitable environment in winter. This action set in motion events that resulted in the creation of thousands of provincial parks in all Canadian provinces.

In 1911, the Canadian government created the Dominion Parks Branch, which was the first national park management agency in the world. James Harkin was appointed as the commissioner and was the first national park director in the world. Harkin was an aggressive supporter of park creation and management. He was a strong supporter of parks, wilderness values, and tourism. He set out to attract Canadians to national parks and to ensure that national parks became cultural icons that rivaled the historic sites and art in Europe. He was famously successful in his goals, and as a result, he is recognized as the person who started the movement to make national parks the cultural icons that they are today.

These five people, Fleming, Macdonald, Dewdney, Kirkwood, and Harkin, set in motion ideas that resulted in Canada's national and provincial park systems. Although many of their ideas can be traced to England and the United States, they adapted them to the Canadian reality. Note the influence of politicians and government employees in this movement, which reflects that the Canadian style of government, largely borrowed from Britain, involves a powerful professional civil service reporting to elected politicians. Notably absent from the Canadian experience (unlike the American park movement described later) are writers, artists, and scholars. A possible exception to this rule is Sir Sandford Fleming, the railroad engineer who was also a planner, author, and civil servant.

PARK SYSTEMS OF CANADA

By 1900, there were five types of parks in Canada: city parks, regional parks, provincial parks, federal national parks, and federal wildlife areas. All over the country, towns and cities made park creation and management a normal role of government. In some provinces, special regional park agencies were set up to manage parks, usually around geographical features such as rivers or lakes. An example in Ontario is the St. Lawrence Parks Commission, which has a series of parks along the Canadian side of the St. Lawrence River and Seaway. All provincial governments moved forward in creating provincial park systems, often in active competition with the emerging national park system. Over the years, successive Canadian governments worked slowly but diligently to add to the two major federal systems: the national parks and the national wildlife areas.

City Parks

Parks are located in virtually every village, town, and city in Canada. They fulfill many functions; sport, recreation, and health are particularly important among them. In the 1980s, some cities added conservation of natural lands to these functions, such as those in river valleys and wetlands. Today, city parks are a mixture of recreation areas, parks, and green spaces.

Most city parks are managed by a parks and recreation department that is part of the municipal government. This department is responsible for facility construction, park maintenance, and recreation programs. Advisory groups, sport organizations, and volunteers are hallmarks of municipal parks and recreation management. Park management at the municipal level is operated by a combination of professional managers, specialized part-time employees, and many volunteers. Land taxes pay for most municipal park management. Some recreation service fees are used for special-purpose activities, such as renting a community hall or paying for sport lessons.

No national inventory of the number and size of municipal parks exists in Canada. The amount of land used for parks in cities varies from a small percentage of the city land area to nearly 40 percent. Examples of city parks include Stanley Park in Vancouver, a large natural park on the ocean near the downtown; Victoria Park in Kitchener, a traditional city park of trees, lawns, gardens, and statues located downtown; and Point Pleasant Park in Halifax, a park with impressive lawns and gardens.

Regional Parks

In Canada, provincial governments often create regional park agencies to fulfill both conservation and recreation mandates. The Province of Ontario has the most extensive system of regional parks in the country. Over many decades, the Parliament of Ontario passed legislation to create regional park agencies to establish and manage park systems in specific areas of the province. For example, the Niagara Parks Commission manages parks in the Niagara River and Falls area. The Niagara Parks have one of the highest park visitation rates in the world with as many as 16 million visitors per year. The Ontario Parliament also passed legislation to create regional planning bodies that coordinate the conservation and management of specific landscape features. The best example is the Niagara Escarpment Commission, which coordinates planning and conservation over the Niagara Escarpment that runs through southern Ontario from Niagara Falls to the Bruce Peninsula in the mid-north. The creation of this commission was strongly influenced by the recreational users of the Bruce Hiking Trail that weaves throughout the Niagara Escarpment lands.

Unique in Canada, Ontario provincial legislation encourages and provides for the creation of 36 conservation authorities that manage watersheds in the populated areas of the province. Each of these local government authorities oversees a park system that is largely composed of water management projects such as dams, river valley protection areas, and wetlands. Many of these conservation areas are close to large cities and are therefore important for providing outdoor recreation near urban areas. Each year, Ontario conservation authorities serve about 5 million **visitor days** of outdoor recreation on 250 conservation areas. These parks are typically located close to urban areas and serve a valuable near-urban outdoor recreation function. They also have a major role in providing environmental education sites for local schools.

Provincial Parks

Every province and territory in Canada has a provincial or territorial park system, but the size and use of the systems vary considerably. Some provinces, such as British Columbia, Alberta, and Ontario, have developed large and well-used provincial park systems. Other provinces, such as New Brunswick, Newfoundland, and Prince Edward Island, oversee small systems. These differences result from the history and political cultures of each province.

The wealthier and more heavily populated provinces created large provincial park systems predominantly for the middle- and upper-middle-class members of their societies while concurrently discouraging federal efforts to create parks in their provinces. The poorer provinces encouraged the national government to meet the demand for parks through federal funding, creation, and management of national parks in their provinces. This approach ensured that federal tax dollars rather than provincial tax dollars were spent on parks in these provinces.

National Parks and Wildlife Areas

The national park system in Canada is large, popular, well-funded, and growing. Because most Canadians grew up visiting Canada's national parks (or at least heard about them or saw them in the media), national parks in Canada are national cultural icons. In the 1930s and 1940s, the mountain parks were backdrops for many popular Hollywood movies. This exposure created a positive profile in the minds of both Canadians and Americans that helped create a boom in tourism that continues today. The national parks are one of Canada's premier international tourism destinations.

As of 2017, Canada had 38 national parks, nine national park reserves, and four national marine parks managed by Parks Canada. More national parks have been proposed and are under land-claim discussions with aboriginal groups; therefore, more parks will be created in the coming years (Parks Canada, n.d.). Parks Canada, the federal park management agency, is responsible for four park and reserve systems: national parks and reserves, national historic parks and sites, national canals, and national marine conservation areas. The Canadian Wildlife Service with Environment Canada is responsible for two park and reserve systems: national wildlife areas and migratory bird sanctuaries.

National parks in Canada are created according to a system plan that calls for at least one national park in each major biogeographic region of the country (see figure 6.1). This plan divides the entire country into 39 easily recognizable biogeographic regions, such as the Pacific Coast Mountains, the Prairie Grasslands, and the Hudson-James Bay Lowlands. This approach is ecologically sound in that the park creation is based on the existing biogeography of the country. This approach ensures that national parks are created in all regions of the country. Parks Canada was one of the first park agencies in the world to develop such a system plan, and the system plan idea subsequently spread all over the world. The weakness of this approach is that it does not consider outdoor recreation demand, so many of the newer parks are in very remote parts of the country that have low levels of visitor use.

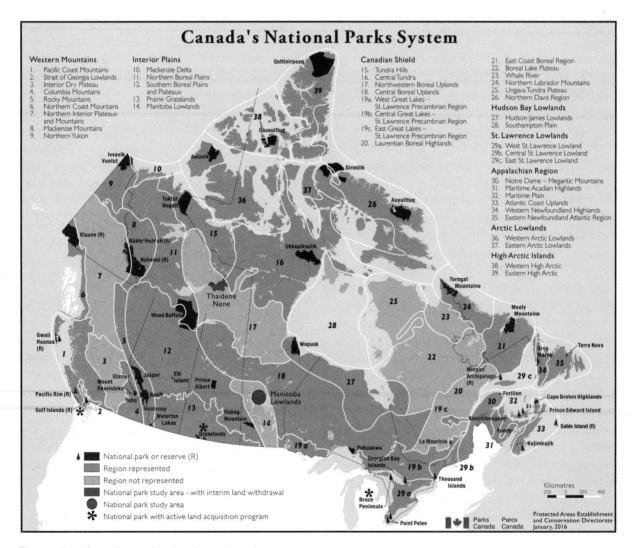

Figure 6.1   Canadian national parks system plan.

Reprinted, by permission, from Parks Canada, 2017, *National parks: Map of completing the parks system* (Gatineau, Quebec: Parks Canada National). Available: www.pc.gc.ca/en/pn-np/cnpn-cnnp/carte-map

The number of national parks continues to increase in Canada as the demands of the system plan are fulfilled. Most of these new national parks are in the arctic and subarctic, but substantial new parks have recently been created in the populated areas of British Columbia and Ontario. For example, the Rouge National Urban Park was recently created on the eastern edge of Toronto, which is Canada's largest city.

The national parks attract approximately 26 million **person visits** per year. Because national park visitors tend to stay for more than two days each visit, the total number of visitor days is more than 50 million per year. The highly popular mountain parks of Banff, Jasper, Kootenay, and Yoho attract the most visitors. Those four parks combined serve approximately 7 million person visits per year or more than 15 million visitor days. Some of the remote northern parks receive fewer than 1,000 visitors per year.

Canada also has an extensive system of national historic parks and sites. Historic sites are chosen according to a national historic sites system plan. The goal of this plan is to represent the country's important historic and cultural themes within the park and site system. The plan has five themes:

1. Peopling the land
2. Developing economies
3. Building social and community life
4. Expressing intellectual and cultural life
5. Governing Canada

All historic sites and parks are commemorated within one of those broad themes. To be recommended for designation, a site, person, or event must have had a nationally significant effect on or illustrate a nationally important aspect of the history of Canada. Places designated as national historic sites are occasionally acquired by the federal government for protection and interpretation. Of the 956 national historic sites, Parks Canada administers 168 and contributes money to others managed by other governments or organizations. Parks Canada serves approximately 10 million visitors per year at the 168 historic sites that it manages. The number of yearly visitors to the individual sites varies dramatically from 3.6 million person visits to the historic fortifications of Quebec City to a few hundred person visits to historic sites in the far north of the country.

Parks Canada also manages a series of historic canals. These canals were originally built for military purposes but are now used for recreation and are extremely popular with boaters. The Trent-Severn Waterway in southern Ontario serves approximately 1.5 million person visits per year.

Parks Canada has the responsibility, shared with the Fisheries and Oceans Canada and the Canadian Wildlife Service, to create a system of national marine conservation areas. These areas are found off the Atlantic, Arctic, and Pacific coasts of Canada. Major reserves are also planned in the Great Lakes area. As of 2016, Parks Canada has created only four such reserves, but many more are planned. Canada has committed to place 10 percent of its marine areas in some form of protected area by the year 2020. Given that it now has only 0.98 percent of its waters in such designations, a massive establishment effort is underway.

The Canadian Wildlife Service manages two large national systems: national wildlife areas and national migratory bird sanctuaries. The national wildlife area system in Canada is large, poorly funded, and not well known by the Canadian public. Fifty-four national wildlife areas are scattered across Canada (Environment and Climate Change Canada, n.d.). These sites are important for migratory birds both for nesting and migratory stopover. The national wildlife areas have just 100,000 visitor days per year. The visitation rates at the 92 sites in Canada's national migratory bird sanctuary system are not documented and therefore cannot be reported. The very low visitation and tourism profile of these wildlife areas leads to a low political profile in Canada.

The differences between the Parks Canada systems and the Canadian Wildlife Service systems are vast. The national parks, national historic parks, and heritage canals focus on conservation and tourism. Canadians are encouraged to visit through excellent information sources, tourism facilities, and programs. As a result, visitation is high, the public profile is high, and the government responds with substantial funds. The wildlife areas focus on wildlife conservation. Recreation is not encouraged, with the exception of some hunting and fishing. Hunting is a rapidly declining activity in Canada with fewer participants every year. As a result, the public profile is low, visitation is low, and the government provides limited management funds. This shows that for a park system to obtain sufficient government funding for effective management, it must have a positive public profile and a clientele that is mobilized to politically support the parks. Many people argue that a park or reserve with low visitation has fewer management stresses and therefore has more effective conservation. This position ignores the many stresses that occur in such a reserve besides recreation, including poaching, resource extraction, illegal logging, destructive farming, all-terrain vehicle use, and many other resource-damaging activities. Such stresses can be effectively curtailed only if the reserve has sufficient funds, staff, and political support. This example from Canada shows that without tourism, political support does not exist and therefore government funds are not allocated, resulting in little or no management staff. For a park to be successful, it must have users who are vocal in their support. Tourism and recreation are the mechanisms by which this use and support are created.

Budgets and Finance

Park budget allocations can be very political depending upon the philosophy of the government in power. Park funding varies by jurisdiction; for example, major reductions occurred in provincial parks budgets in British Columbia, but increases occurred in Alberta. The large park system in Ontario saw budget increases as it became dependent upon tourist fees and charges (Eagles, 2014). The national parks saw major increases in budget along with substantial growth in the numbers of national parks over the 1980s and 1990s, then a massive budget reduction under the Harper government in 2012, and a major increase under the Trudeau government elected in 2015. In all jurisdictions, the trend was toward increased use of tourism fees and charges to fund parkland management.

Different Approaches to Park Management

Canada has a tremendous range of diversity in the approaches used in park management. The institutions used include a government agency that is largely funded from taxes (e.g., Parks Canada); a stand-alone government agency that functions like a private corporation (e.g., the Niagara Parks Commission); a government agency that has a few supervisory staff but uses private corporations to provide most of the public services (e.g., British Columbia Provincial Parks); a nonprofit organization that functions like a private corporation and provides all park services (two national historic parks and some provincial parks in Ontario are operated using this approach); and a mixture of public agencies and private operations that use public funding and tourism fees and charges. This wide range of management approaches is an important area of park management that needs further investigation by scholars in the parks and recreation field. It is important to understand if the different management approaches affect the overall management effectiveness of parks. Is one model better than another in delivering conservation and recreation services? This diversity of activity reveals that future park managers in Canada need to have a broad background in business as well as cultural and natural resource management.

One important aspect of the management of parks in Canada at all levels is the adoption of the British model of civil service. This means that the systems are meritocracies with all positions, from the field ranger up through to the agency director, assigned according to educational attainment and work experience. None of the appointments are political, that is hiring according to political experience or political party membership. At municipal, provincial, and federal levels, politicians make the overall policy decisions, but not hiring decisions.

Parks, reserves, and other types of protected areas exist because of the acceptance and approval of society and therefore of government. For the sites to exist and be effectively managed, political support must be sufficient to counter the many societal forces that would see these lands used for other purposes. Parks need to be used and appreciated by substantial numbers of citizens.

HISTORY OF PARKS IN THE UNITED STATES

The history of parks in the United States illustrates a combination of concern for the social and psychological well-being of children and adults, the conservation and **preservation** of natural areas as the country developed and resource extraction and urbanization accelerated, and the evolution of natural areas as attractions that spurred tourism business opportunities. Improvements in transportation, the rise of the middle class, the recognition of the need for workers to renew and refresh themselves, and the fascination with the natural world increased the demand for parks and protected natural areas (Sears, 1980).

City Parks and Playgrounds

Boston Common, which was created by the British colonial government in 1634 and is now in downtown Boston, is recognized as the first park-like area created in the United States. As early American cities began to grow due to an influx of immigrants and prosperity brought on by the industrial movement, awareness grew of a need for public parks in bustling, increasingly congested, and hygienically challenged cities such as New York, Chicago, and Philadelphia. Thus began a period from about 1850 through the 1930s when city parks and playgrounds were built for the public (Cavallo, 1981; Young, 2004). Most notable among these was Frederick Law Olmsted and Calvin Vaux's 1858 plan to landscape Central Park in New York City. Olmsted felt strongly about the concept of park access for people as a demonstration of democratic principles. Olmsted believed that parks could serve as meeting grounds for people of different backgrounds and classes, unlike other developed spaces in cities that were highly stratified by social class. He also believed that great parks and open space in cities were evidence of the progressiveness of American democracy (Rybczynski, 1999). Olmsted went on to play a role in designing, planning, and building major city parks in or around Boston, Atlanta, Chicago, Buffalo, and Niagara Falls.

Federal Conservation Initiatives

Early federal protection of natural areas dates from 1832 when the federal government created the Hot Springs Reservation in Arkansas as a protected area for the use of Native Americans, people traveling through on their way west, and local residents. The site was later redesignated as a national park in 1921. The first national park in the world, Yellowstone, designated by President Ulysses S. Grant in 1872 in the territories of Montana and Wyoming, was clearly an idea ahead of its time that was made possible by the incredible confluence of natural features present at Yellowstone and the prescience of prominent citizens and scientists who led expeditions into the area in 1869 through 1871 and proposed the creation of a park. The idea also received considerable support from the corporate leaders of the Northern Pacific Railroad, who understood the potential of the park to attract tourists (Runte, 2010). It is interesting that in both Canada and the United States, railway leaders encouraged the creation of the earliest national parks to stimulate tourist use of the emerging cross-country railways. Progress in creating federal parks and protected areas was slow at first; by the turn of the century, only five national parks had been designated and three of those were related to California redwood or sequoia forests. Among them was Yosemite National Park, which was designated by the U.S. Congress in 1890. The seed of the idea for national parks had been sown in the 1800s but needed time and leadership to grow.

Despite the presence of national parks, there was no federal park agency in place to lead the charge for preservation of parklands or outdoor recreation. After years of advocating for such an agency by people such as Frederick Law Olmsted, Horace McFarland, Henry Barker, and Stephen Mather, Congress passed the law creating the National Park Service (NPS) on August 25, 1916 (National Park Service, 2003). Stephen Mather, a Chicago businessman, was named the first director of the NPS. Congress transferred the management of historic sites, army forts, battlefields, cemeteries, and monuments to the newly created NPS as well as the existing national parks and national monuments. Immediately after establishment of the NPS there

OUTSTANDING GRADUATE

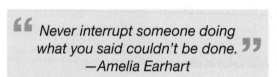

Courtesy of Kristine Roblin.

Background Information

Name: Emily B. Martin

Education: MS in parks, recreation, and tourism management from Clemson University

Awards: 2010 Phi Kappa Phi Certificate of Merit

Career Information

Position: Interpretive Ranger

Organization: The National Park Service is the federal agency that manages all the national park units across the country. I have spent time as a ranger in both Yellowstone National Park (Wyoming) and Great Smoky Mountains National Park (North Carolina). The mission of the NPS is to "preserve unimpaired the natural and cultural resources and values of the National Park System for the enjoyment, education, and inspiration of this and future generations." There are 417 national park units, 58 of which are national parks (the others being battlefields, monuments, historic sites, etc.). Millions of people visit the parks every year, with over 330 million recorded in 2016. The number of employees fluctuates on a seasonal basis, with part-time rangers like myself largely working during the summer. Altogether there are around 22,000 permanent and seasonal employees. At Yellowstone I worked directly with around 25 other rangers, and at the Smokies I work directly with 7 or 8.

Job description: There are three main parts to my job as an interpretive ranger:

1. *Visitor services.* I staff the visitor center to provide frontline orientation to the park, helping visitors plan their trip, distributing material, and dealing with incidents as they arise.

2. *Education.* I research, develop, and deliver engaging educational programs to the visiting public. These programs include talks, guided hikes, activities, children's programs, and special events. This is called *interpretation*, and the goal is to facilitate a meaningful connection between the visitor and the park resources.

3. *Roving.* I act as an informal presence in the park to interact with visitors who might not go into a visitor center or attend a program. I help monitor safety and renegade behavior. But more importantly, I interact casually with visitors to give them a friendly, helpful point of contact.

There are many other things I take care of as they arise, such as keeping up facilities, managing visitor–wildlife interactions, swearing in junior rangers, and helping with emergency response.

Career path: I followed my love of the outdoors into the subject field of parks and protected area management during my undergraduate career. Early on, I was captivated by the narrative and mission of the National Park Service. When Fran Mainella, the 16th director of the NPS, came to Clemson as a visiting scholar for several years, I was chosen to be her office assistant. She became an invaluable mentor and friend. Near the end of my undergraduate experience, I interned at Great Smoky Mountains National Park for a summer. After earning my bachelor's degree, I transitioned into doing graduate research on interpretive programs with the NPS. I traveled to many national parks to collect my data, which was used for developing better training tools for rangers. After earning my master's degree and taking a short hiatus to have children, I then started as a seasonal ranger in Yellowstone.

Although a permanent job would be nice, I enjoy the seasonal life and the travel and flexibility it brings. Because I have an extensive off-season, it has allowed me to spend time on my other passion: fiction writing and illustration. After a lot of hard work and rejection, I now have two novels published through a major publishing house, with a third releasing in 2018. My freelance illustration work has grown to include a children's book and many book covers. So at the moment, if I can be a ranger during the summer and an author and illustrator in the off-season, that's about as close to a dream career as I can imagine.

> *Never interrupt someone doing what you said couldn't be done.*
> —Amelia Earhart

Like and dislikes about the job: I love the opportunity to work in these great, storied places and be part of the tapestry of the NPS. I love the goal of facilitating an emotional connection between the visitor and the park. I feel privileged to work with incredibly dedicated, hardworking, fun-loving rangers. I also love the seasonal nature of the work because it gives my family flexibility. I get to bring along my children so they can spend their summers in some of the greatest places in our country—that's pretty special.

I dislike how difficult it can be to have a family and still work these jobs—many parks simply don't have enough housing to support a married ranger with children. I have also disliked how some professionals and academic mentors wrote me off once I had my first child, as if my degrees and career aspirations were null and void because I now had a family.

Advice for Undergraduates

People will view these professions as "fun" or "not serious" careers. The difference is that *you* make it serious. If you care about what you do and believe in the benefits you're providing for people, that makes it important and valuable.

My job isn't so much a matter of education, but of provocation and enrichment. If I can help one person develop a deeper connection to our national parks, or one child believe they have a place in the story of our national parks—whether it's as a ranger or as an author and illustrator—that is success for me.

was substantial growth in the number of national park sites, but their use waned during the Great Depression (1929-1939) and the U.S. involvement in World War II (1941-1945). However, during the Great Depression, the Civilian Conservation Corps (CCC) (1933-1941) was created as a separate program of the federal government to employ about 3 million young men in public works projects, which benefited many national park sites. The CCC was instrumental in building hundreds of roads, trails, campgrounds, visitor centers, and water systems that exist today in national and state parks.

Strong leadership for national government involvement in conservation came from President Theodore Roosevelt. In fewer than eight years as president he created six national parks and supported the passage of the Antiquities Act of 1906, which created an initial 16 national monuments (including the Grand Canyon). Over the years, U.S. presidents used this act to take bold and often controversial conservation action by creating national monuments without congressional approval. National monuments are often transformed into national parks through congressional legislative actions. Two major figures in land protection were advisors to President Roosevelt: Gifford Pinchot, scientific conservationist and head of what became the U.S. Department of Agriculture (USDA) Forest Service and founder of the Society of American Foresters, and John Muir, ardent preservationist, Sierra Club founder, writer, and lobbyist for wilderness and parks (Ehrlich, 2000; Keene, 1994; Miller, 2004; Zaslowsky & Watkins, 1994). The use of the Antiquities Act to protect land, and the controversy surrounding the unilateral authority it provides to the president to preserve vast tracks of land, continues today. By the end of his second term, President Barack Obama had created more national monuments than any U.S. president in history.

Two other realms of conservation, wildlife and forests, also benefited from federal action during Roosevelt's time. President Roosevelt used executive orders to create 51 bird reservations during his presidency, and he established the Pelican Island National Wildlife Refuge in 1903. This was the beginning of a system of national wildlife refuges.

©Paul F.J. Eagles.

Yellowstone National Park in Wyoming contains significant geothermal features that are viewed by millions of people each year.

Their primary function is to preserve habitat and migration routes for wildlife (particularly waterfowl), but they also allow wildlife-related recreation such as hunting, fishing, and bird watching. Roosevelt also created the U.S. Forest Service in 1905 and set aside 148 million acres (60 million ha) as national forests. Although national forests were at the time primarily viewed as a place to manage timber resources, they are now heavily used and managed for outdoor recreation.

All these efforts at creating protected natural areas—along with the increasing urbanization of the country and the increasing popularity of automobiles and the expansion of the roads associated with them starting in about 1910—gradually increased the pressure on national park and national forest managers to provide access, accommodations, campgrounds, and information for an increasing number of visitors (Belasco, 1979). The See America First patriotic movement generated public interest in America's natural wonders (Shaffer, 2001), and rangers began to expand their focus from protecting resources to accommodating and educating larger numbers of recreationists and visitors. This activity foreshadowed a massive expansion in travel and outdoor recreation that took place following the end of World War II. This era might be considered the golden age of parks and outdoor recreation in the United States.

State Park Initiatives

Several states initiated efforts to protect natural areas for public use, such as Massachusetts' Great Pond Act (1641); Georgia's Indian Springs (1825); New York's off-and-on attempts to protect the scenic attributes of Niagara Falls culminating in state acquisition in 1885; and California's failed attempt to support Yosemite State Park starting in 1864. According to Landrum (2004), in addition to Niagara Falls, other early **state parks** that have remained successful include Texas' San Jacinto Battleground State Historic Site (1883), Minnehaha Falls Park (1885) and Itasca State Park in Minnesota (1891), Miller State Park in New Hampshire (1891), and New York's Adirondack State Park (1892). Each park's story typically involved local proponents who were persistent and creative in garnering support. Stephen Mather, as the new director of the National Park Service in 1916, saw one of his challenges to be maintaining the quality of the national park system.

©Paul F.J. Eagles.

Adirondack State Park in New York, one of the oldest state parks in the United States, contains a mixture of public and private land.

He was concerned about attempts to designate parks of little national significance as national parks, and he became a prime sponsor of a national conference in 1921 that promoted the idea of a system of parks that would come under the domain of each state. Although it is unclear who proposed it, the idea arose of creating a park every 100 miles (160 km) (the distance that automobiles at that time typically traveled in a day) for the public to enjoy and camp in, and it was suggested it was more appropriate for state parks to fulfill this (Landrum, 2004). The idea developed that state parks should preserve representative environments, preferably scenic or historical and cultural sites, that were typical of each state to provide outdoor recreation areas for residents and for tourists.

Trail Initiatives

In 1921, Benton MacKaye, a forester and planner, proposed a foot trail along the Appalachian ridges from the highest mountain in the north, Mount Katahdin in Maine, to the highest peak in the south, Springer Mountain in Georgia, that passed through 12 other states along the way. The approximately 2,150-mile (3,460 km) Appalachian Trail was completed in 1937. The National Trails Systems Act of 1968 gave the NPS the responsibility of overseeing the Appalachian Trail and provided funds to start the process of purchasing the entire trail and buffering it where possible with federal land. The act also designated three types of trails: national recreation trails; national scenic trails; and connecting, or side, trails. The act designated the Appalachian Trail and the Pacific Crest Trail (stretching from the Mexican border to the Canadian border along the mountain ranges of the Pacific Coast states) as national scenic trails. As of 2016, amendments to the act have created 11 national scenic trails, 19 national historic trails, and more than 1,200 national recreation trails in all 50 states, most of which are in or near urban areas. National Park Service maps of these trails can be viewed at www.nps.gov/nts/maps.html.

Another form of trail park is located along rivers. In 1968, the Wild and Scenic Rivers Act was passed to protect free-flowing (not dammed) rivers, thereby assuring that white-water recreational opportunities such as kayaking and rafting could be protected.

Three categories of rivers were established: wild rivers, scenic rivers, and recreational rivers. The differences were based on different levels of access, primitiveness, and shoreline development; wild rivers were the most pristine. As of December 2014, 12,709 miles (20,453 km) of 208 rivers in 40 states and Puerto Rico were protected (National Wild and Scenic Rivers System, n.d.). Most rivers are managed by the agency that manages the land through which the river flows, usually the USDA Forest Service, NPS, Bureau of Land Management, or U.S. Fish and Wildlife Service (National Park Service, n.d.-c).

Wilderness

In the 1930s, forward-thinking preservationists saw that the American **wilderness** was a rapidly diminishing resource. A paradox was becoming apparent. Protecting an area by declaring it a national park virtually assured that roads would be built to and within that park. Eventually thousands of people would visit it, and the characteristics of wilderness would be diminished or lost. In the 1960s, an oft-repeated phrase was that "Americans were loving their parks to death" as congested roads and campgrounds became the norm, at least in the summer vacation season or the autumn leaf-color season. This helped solidify the movement to protect vast roadless areas that were largely absent of both people and signs of human presence. Early proponents of creating protected wilderness areas included Aldo Leopold, U.S. Forest Service scientist and the father of wildlife ecology; Robert Marshall, an environmental lawyer; Howard Zahniser, president of the Wilderness Society; and Hubert Humphrey, a senator from Minnesota who sponsored four versions of the Wilderness Act over eight years. The fourth amended version eventually passed Congress and was signed into law by President Lyndon Johnson in 1964 (Nash, 1982).

Because wilderness designation would permanently prohibit development, roads, timber removal, and motorized activities, this bill caused considerable concern among lumber interests, some outdoor recreationists, and real estate developers. But Congress passed the Wilderness Act anyway. The process of designating new wilderness areas provided some of the most heated environmental battles in the second half of the 20th century and the first decade of the 21st century. Especially controversial were the USDA Forest Service Roadless Area Review and Evaluation (RARE) process, the Endangered American Wilderness Act of 1978, and the 1980 Alaska National Interest Lands Conservation Act. The two acts were signed and engineered by President Jimmy Carter and doubled the size of the NPS and National Wildlife Refuge lands and tripled the size of designated wilderness. Recently, in the greatest expansion of wilderness areas in 15 years, President Barack Obama signed the Omnibus Public Lands Management Act of 2009 that protected 2 million acres (800,000 ha) of wilderness. In 2016, there were about 765 wilderness areas. Designated federal wilderness comprises about 110 million acres (45 million ha); 57 million of those acres (23 million ha) are in Alaska. California, Arizona, Idaho, and Washington have the next largest wilderness areas.

Era of Fiscal Restraint

Starting in the 1970s, after the rapid growth in participation in outdoor recreation and the expansion of federal programs to accommodate this growth, a series of developments led to a leveling off and even decline of federal actions. A few initiatives were associated with the nation's bicentennial celebration in 1976: the creation of bicentennial parks around the country and the Urban Park and Recreation Recovery (UPARR) program, which provided federal assistance to counteract the decline in many urban areas by rehabilitating critically needed recreation and park facilities. Recreation use in parks is closely tied to the costs of transportation. If fuel prices are high, people tend to use parks closer to home. If fuel prices are low, long-distance travel increases. In 2015 and 2016, several U.S. national parks set visitation records as low fuel prices encouraged long-distance travel. For example, Yellowstone National Park, which is remote from most large cities, set a visitation records in 2015 and 2016 of 4,097,710 and 4,257,177 visitor days, respectively (National Park Service., n.d.-b).

Parks are successful when competent, dedicated, and innovative employees manage them. There is an ongoing debate on the use of private companies to provide services to the visitors. The very first NPS

director, Stephen Mather, introduced concessions into the national parks. These private companies provided services such as accommodations, food, and transportation. Much later, nongovernment groups, usually called *friends groups,* became active in many parks and concentrated on providing educational services to the visitors. It has been estimated that about 75 percent of all people working in parks in the United States are employed by concessionaires and only 25 percent are government employees.

In the 1980s, the practice of hiring private companies to perform some park jobs once done by park employees (privatizing) became popular in an effort to lower the operating costs of parks. Privatization of jobs such as trash collection, vehicle maintenance, lawn care, and even staffing visitor centers or gift shops, were considered. To further reduce expenditures and generate revenue, President Ronald Reagan's Secretary of the Interior James Watt eliminated the Bureau of Outdoor Recreation, reduced the rate at which new federal lands were purchased for parks, instituted staff reductions in the land agencies, and supported natural resource extraction through mining and drilling for oil on federal lands. During this time, and in a response to these types of threats to land protection, a grassroots backlash, the Sagebrush Rebellion, began. In this, local proponents of private land rights and public access performed actions of civil (and occasionally criminal) disobedience in opposition to various threats to conservation.

In the late 20th and early 21st centuries, few federal conservation initiatives were launched and new park acquisitions were limited because federal budgets were tight. One bright spot was the Transportation Efficiency Act of 1991 and its successors, the Transportation Equity Act for the 21st Century (1998) and the Safe, Accountable, Flexible, Efficient Transportation Equity Act of 2005, which designated that 10 percent of the allocations for highway construction be set aside for alternative transportation options such as mass transit and walking, biking, and horse trails. Many localities used these funds for rails-to-trails initiatives to develop corridor park trail systems. In the 1990s, many federal agencies became better connected to and appreciated by local and state tourism promoters, and now partnerships abound between what used to be separate entities. Local tourism businesses began to better understand how livelihood in ecotourism was based on quality parks (because they attracted tourists and their money), and they became partners in supporting parks in Congress or state legislatures and in volunteering labor and services to assist parks. Congress authorized the Recreation Fee Demonstration Program in 1996 and the Recreation Enhancement Act in 2004 to allow federal lands that charged entrance fees to increase their fees and retain funds from fees collected to improve their recreation facilities and services.

After the September 11, 2001, terrorist attacks in New York City, most federal parks had to divert a segment of their tight budgets to homeland security efforts, especially the National Park Service, which manages many high-profile monuments that could present symbolic targets for possible future attacks. The cost of extra security patrols and the addition of law enforcement officers and metal detectors to the entrances of many park buildings put a strain on other operations. Another area of concern is parks on national borders, such as Big Bend National Park in Texas and Organ Pipe Cactus National Monument in Arizona. Some believe that illegal immigrants or terrorists could sneak into the country through these areas. Because of these concerns, some visitors stay away, park rangers are trained in law enforcement and border patrol strategies for 24-hour guarding, and more time and money are spent on security and less on visitor services or programs (Lovgren, 2004). By 2005, with federal budget deficits growing and gasoline prices remaining higher than in the past, funding for park agencies and programs had decreased or remained level. President George W. Bush proposed not providing grants from the Land and Water Conservation Fund to individual states. These funds have been used since 1965 to purchase parklands and develop facilities such as campgrounds, playgrounds, trails, and visitor centers (National Park Service, n.d.-c).

From 2007 to 2009, a national and global recession occurred—termed the Great Recession. This recession, followed by several years of slow economic recovery, further strained parks. Many local, state, and national parks saw additional cuts to funding for their operation and maintenance. Some parks, such as state parks in New York and California, reduced their services or were closed as cost-savings strategies. A long history of underfunding parks that created a backlog of needed maintenance, facility upgrades, and staff even before the recession hit made this problem worse. The national parks have a maintenance backlog of approximately $12 billion, which is more than three times their annual budget (National Park Service, n.d.-a). Currently, park leaders and managers are attempting to address these funding issues by reducing costs, partnering with private industries and nongovernmental organizations, and turning toward a more revenue-focused business model. Many parks use volunteers and friends groups (advocacy groups affiliated with a park that raise funds through donations) to ease constraints related to funding.

In 2006, the National Park Centennial Initiative was undertaken that created a matching fund for government and philanthropic contributions to benefit parks in the years approaching the system's centennial in 2016. In 2009, the NPS invested $750 million in nearly 800 projects to stimulate the economy through the American Recovery and Reinvestment Act. Both programs created the promise of a positive boost in funding for the national parks. Continued economic struggles from 2010 to 2012, however, resulted in declines in national budgets. In 2013, more than $150 million in budget cuts affected the NPS through a process called *sequestration*, which caused park closures and reductions in visitor services and substantial public controversy. Some states took action to reopen closed national parks, which led to a renewed debate about the importance of parks and their funding. In 2016, the 100th anniversary of the National Park Service was celebrated with a national marketing campaign called Find Your Park, and there were events in parks, substantial public attention among news and media outlets, and partnerships with corporations. In addition, the Katahdin Woods and Waters National Monument in Maine was established. This new national monument, like many past parks, was the result of a private land donation by a wealthy philanthropist. This land donation came with a $40 million endowment for developing and operating the national monument. This monetary gift seemed to symbolize and solidify the place of private funding in the second century of national parks.

PARK SYSTEMS OF THE UNITED STATES

Most parks have been created on undeveloped lands and waters and reserved for public use and enjoyment; therefore, most publicly owned parks are managed by some level of the government. Similar to schools, public water supplies, and airports, parks are services that local, state, and federal governments provide their citizens for their benefit and enjoyment. Most parks have **front country** areas with facilities, roads, and primary visitor attractions, but many parks also have **backcountry** areas where nature predominates.

City Parks

Historically, city parks were created to address social needs by providing safe areas for children to play and soothing islands of green in which to escape from urban crowding, congestion, and concrete. Most city parks are smaller, closer to home, and more sport-oriented than other kinds of parks. City parks, by definition, are owned, managed, and staffed by city governments. City parks are used in more varied ways than traditional resource-based state or federal parks. For example, city parks often provide swimming pools, concerts, and food stands. Some even have small zoos, botanical gardens, or carnival rides. City parks usually are less concerned with maintaining natural resources in an undisturbed state; in most cases, the natural environment has already been heavily altered and the area artificially landscaped or designed. Therefore, the grounds are often heavily modified to provide amenities such as tennis courts, golf courses, swimming pools, fountains, paved walkways, ice-skating rinks, skateboard ramps, soccer fields, and playgrounds. Despite the less-than-pristine environment, city parks often provide inner-city children with their first taste of a natural area (American Planning Association, 2007; Harnick, 2000; Taylor, Kuo, & Sullivan, 2001; Wals, 1994).

City parks vary greatly depending on the size of the city. Some New England towns, such as Burlington, Vermont, and New Haven, Connecticut, have classic "greens" of a few acres or less. Larger and more well-known or unique city parks are Central Park in New York City; Boston Common; Jackson Square in New Orleans; the Riverwalk in San Antonio, Texas; the town square of Savannah, Georgia; Grant Park in Chicago; Phoenix's unusual mountain parks (including the largest city park in the United States, South Mountain Park and Reserve); and Water Gardens Park in Fort Worth, Texas. It has been said that there are no great cities without great parks, and when you think of these large cities, this does seem to be true (Tate, 2001). But even the smallest cities and towns in the United States have parks that are often centerpieces of local pride.

County Parks

County parks are usually larger, more natural, less congested, and quieter. They are typically oriented to activities such as swimming, hiking, boating, fishing, and camping that require a more natural setting than city parks can provide. They are owned and managed by county governments and are usually operated by county employees, although there is a recent trend to subcontract park operations to private operators or groups such as the YMCA. County parks are larger and less oriented to urban uses than city parks, but they are often not as environmentally sensitive, as usage restricted, or as large as most state parks. Some county parks have larger facilities than those found in city parks, such as multiple playing fields or arenas for sports tournaments and sport events. Local school systems often conduct lessons in environmental education at county parks because they are typically close and easily accessible and have parking. Fishing, sailing, canoeing, or water safety lessons are also conducted in county parks. In coastal states, many beach parks, especially the more developed ones, are county parks.

State Parks

State parks are typically more focused on preserving the natural or historic characteristics of an area and providing compatible outdoor recreation. Usually, they are more distant from urban population centers than most city or county parks, although in a few cases, population centers have grown around state parks. In general, state parks are larger than most city or county parks. In 2017, there were 10,336 state parks in the United States (America's State Parks, n.d.). Often state parks are associated with water bodies, have substantial wildlife populations, and are representative of key environmental ecosystems that characterize the state, such as beaches in Florida, deserts in Arizona, prairie in Illinois and Kansas, and mountains in California, Colorado, and New Hampshire. Most state parks are not unique enough, scenic enough, large enough, or filled with enough features to warrant being designated national parks. Besides highlighting natural areas, many state parks promote the state's important historical figures or events.

The character of state parks varies substantially. Some are similar to large city parks in a more natural setting, and others are as wild or wilder than some national parks or forests. Adirondack State Park and Forest Preserve in New York is the largest park in the lower 48 states (6 million acres [2.4 million ha]) (Adirondack State Park Agency, n.d.). Most state parks are of modest size, usually ranging from a hundred to a few thousand acres, and they provide basic facilities such as campgrounds, picnic areas, trails, visitor centers, and environmental education programs. Some are more like city parks, however,

such as Eugene T. Mahoney State Park in a rural area south of Omaha, Nebraska. It has an outdoor swimming pool with water slides, a large playground area with play equipment, and an ice-skating rink (Nebraska Game and Parks Commission, n.d.).

Several states have created resort state parks to increase visitation and self-generated revenues. These parks provide resort-like services, but they are located on state parklands and are managed and funded by the state park service or a corollary association, often with subcontracts to concessionaires. Lake Barkley State Resort Park in Kentucky has a golf course, aerobic fitness center, swimming pool, tennis courts, small airport, cabins, lodge hotel, restaurant, and marina (Kentucky State Parks, n.d.). Seyon Lodge State Park in Vermont provides overnight stays in bed-and-breakfast-style accommodations and guided fishing. The resort state park idea has expanded to at least 12 states, many of which are in the South (e.g., www.alapark.com/resorts, www.pipestemresort.com).

Besides having state parks, most states, especially those in the East, also have state forests. Many of the forest areas have camping areas, hiking trails, and hunting areas. Many states, mostly in the Mid-

Point Lobos State Park in California protects valuable shoreline habitat and provides opportunities for nature-based recreation.

west and West, operate state fish and game or state wildlife management areas that are usually available for various forms of outdoor recreation.

Federal Parks, Forests, and Refuges

Before 1700, most of what became the United States was the domain of millions of Native Americans who were later largely exterminated by war, killed by disease, evicted from their natural territories and moved onto reservations, or forced to seek refuge in Canada (Brown, 1970; Nash, 1982). Their lands became available to European immigrants who had to apply for ownership from the federal General Land Office, which claimed to have the original title to the land. Tracts of land not delegated to the states or claimed by private owners were retained in federal ownership after the creation of the U.S. government in 1776. Much of this land was not suitable for agriculture or residential development or was eventually recognized as land that the public should have access to (public domain land). Growing societal needs for recreation and the preservation of dwindling natural resources prompted Congress to establish national parks, national forests, national wildlife refuges, and other federal protected areas. A variety of agencies were created to manage these places (Zaslowsky & Watkins, 1994; Zinser, 1995). Although most of these areas were initially conserved for reasons other than recreation, recreational opportunities were often a side benefit.

National Parks

The National Park Service (NPS) has been a world leader in establishing and managing national parks. The NPS operates under a principle of preservation and is funded by the U.S. Department of the Interior. Its mission is to "conserve the scenery and the natural and historic objects and the wildlife therein and to provide for the enjoyment of the same in such manner and by such means as will leave them unimpaired for the enjoyment of future generations." Maintaining a balance between allowing use and protecting and preserving resources is a constant challenge. Providing recreational opportunities that do little or no permanent harm to the park or its wildlife is one of NPS's prime missions. Many believe that the national park idea is one of the best ideas that the United States has contributed to the world (Sellars, 1999). With 417 National Park Service units, the national park system encompasses approximately 84 million acres (34 million ha) and manages many categories of parks (see table 6.1). In 2016, a record number of 330,971,689 recreation visits were recorded by the National Park Service (National Park Service, n.d.-b).

With such diversity of areas, many forms of outdoor recreation occur in the national park system. Activities include mountain climbing, horseback riding, boating, camping, history reenactments, hiking, white-water rafting, and driving and sightseeing, especially during spring wildflower or fall leaf-changing seasons. The more than 300 million annual visitor days to the national parks make a significant contribution to the economy of the nation and especially to rural areas that depend on the tourism that the national parks attract. Considerable adaptability and creativity are needed to manage these diverse areas, and expertise from many disciplines is needed across the system of parks. These disciplines include ecology, geology, archaeology, military history, national history, fisheries, wildlife and resource management, forestry, outdoor recreation management, interpretation, business management, marketing, public relations, urban recreation programming, environmental education, alternative energy, public works, transportation management, tourism, law, and political science. The NPS also coordinates the Land and Water Conservation Fund, which is a program in which federal funds are distributed to the states and federal agencies for new or continuing park or conservation projects.

National Forests and Grasslands

The Forest Service was created in 1905 and is an agency of the USDA. The Forest Service manages large forests and grasslands and follows a basic conservation and **wise-use philosophy**. The agency's mission is to achieve quality land management under the sustainable multiple-use concept to meet the diverse needs of people. Gifford Pinchot, the first chief of the Forest Service, described conservation and wise use as providing "the greatest good to the greatest number for the longest time." **Multiple-use management** means that Forest Service areas can be used for outdoor

Table 6.1 U.S. National Park Service Categories and Examples

Categories	Total number	Examples
National parks	59	Yellowstone, Grand Teton, Yosemite, Smoky Mountains, Grand Canyon, Rocky Mountain, Shenandoah
National monuments	87	Grand Portage, Bandelier, Craters of the Moon, Coronado, Fort Sumter
National preserves	19	Big Thicket, Big Cypress, Timucuan, Gates of the Arctic
National historic sites	78	First Ladies, Fort Davis, McLoughlin House, Carl Sandburg Home, Lincoln Home
National historical parks	51	Minute Man, Women's Rights, Valley Forge, Chaco Culture, Cumberland Gap
National memorials	30	Chamizal, African American Civil War, *USS Arizona,* Mount Rushmore, World War II, Flight 93
National military parks	9	Shiloh, Gettysburg, Horseshoe Bend, Pea Ridge
National battlefields	16	Manassas, Fort Donelson, Cowpens, Antietam
National recreation areas	18	Gateway, Santa Monica Mountains, Golden Gate
National reserves	2	New Jersey Pinelands, City of Rocks
National seashores	10	Gulf Islands, Padre Island, Cape Canaveral, Cape Cod, Point Reyes
National lakeshores	4	Pictured Rocks, Sleeping Bear, Apostle Islands, Indiana Dunes
National rivers	5	Buffalo, Big South Fork, New River Gorge, Mississippi
Wild and scenic rivers	10	Obed, Ozark, Rio Grande, Farmington, Salmon
National parkways	4	Baltimore–Washington, George Washington
National scenic trails	3	Natchez Trace, Potomac Heritage, Appalachian
International historic site	1	Saint Croix Island
Other designation	11	National Mall, Rock Creek Park, Catoctin Mountain, Wolf Trap National Park for the Performing Arts

National Park Service, n.d.-a

recreation, livestock grazing, timber production, watershed management, and wildlife and fish habitat. Providing recreational opportunities, which the agency tries to balance with the other uses, is a major focus of the Forest Service. The 174 Forest Service units (154 national forests and 20 national grasslands) cover 193 million acres (78 million ha) in 44 states (USDA Forest Service, 2017). National forests constitute 98 percent of Forest Service lands. These lands contain designated wilderness areas, recreation areas, national monuments and preserves, and national scenic areas. The Forest Service also manages scenic byways, wild and scenic rivers, campgrounds, alpine ski areas, boating areas, picnic areas, and over 158,000 miles (254,000 km) of trails (USDA Forest Service, 2017; Zinser, 1995).

Historically, the Forest Service gave priority to timber management, but it was induced, especially since the 1960s, through court cases, political pressure, and debates on wilderness to increase the outdoor recreation opportunities in the forests. Today recreation is a primary focus and use of the national forests. From 2011 to 2015, an average of 149 million visits occurred to Forest Service lands, waters, and recreation sites per year (USDA Forest Service, 2016). Common recreation activities on national forests and grasslands include hiking, camping, wildlife watching, hunting, fishing, mountain biking, horse trail riding, skiing, and **off-highway vehicle** (OHV; e.g., all-terrain vehicle, snowmobile) use. In general, more consumptive, higher-impact forms of recreation are permitted and deemed appropriate in national forests and other federal lands compared with state and national parks.

Wildlife Refuges

The U.S. Fish and Wildlife Service (USFWS) is part of the U.S. Department of the Interior. Its mission is to work with others to conserve, protect, and enhance fish, wildlife, and plants and their habitats for the continuing benefit of the American people.

Its programs (including administering the U.S. Endangered Species Act and other federal wildlife laws) are among the oldest in the world dedicated to scientific wildlife conservation, although Canada created a wildlife conservation reserve in 1887. As of 2013, the USFWS manages a 150-million-acre (60-million-ha) national system of more than 560 national wildlife refuges and thousands of small wetlands and other special management areas. Under the fisheries program, it operates national fish hatcheries, fishery resource offices, and ecological services field stations (U.S. Fish and Wildlife Service, 2013).

Most wildlife refuge areas are water related, either freshwater or saltwater, and therefore are often found along rivers, lakes, marshlands, or coastal areas. The primary focus of refuges and fish hatcheries is wildlife and fish habitat protection, promotion of breeding, and provision of safe refuge to animals. Refuges permit secondary recreational activity as long as it is compatible with the primary purpose of the refuge and funds are available to administer it. The primary recreational uses in wildlife refuges are hunting, fishing, wildlife observation, nature photography, environmental education and interpretation, hiking, and motorized and nonmotorized boating. Hunting and fishing are permitted in wildlife refuges because much of the funding and support of wildlife refuges came from hunters and anglers when Congress expressed little interest in spending money on wildlife, birds, and fish. The hunting and fishing is regulated and in some areas controls the populations of animals whose natural predators have been long removed. About 30 percent of refuges are not open to recreation; these are mostly in Alaska.

Other Areas Managed by Federal Agencies

Several other federal protected areas exist that are not as well-known, but many are found only in certain regions of the United States and they usually provide fewer recreation programs and facilities. The Bureau of Land Management, the U.S. Army Corps of Engineers, the Tennessee Valley Authority, the Bureau of Reclamation, and American Indian reservations manage these areas. In addition, wil-

©Paul F.J. Eagles.

Aransas National Wildlife Refuge in Texas provides winter habitat for the endangered whooping crane.

derness areas are specially designated lands owned by the federal government.

National Resource Lands

The Bureau of Land Management (BLM) manages 245 million acres (99 million ha) of land (about one-eighth of the land in the United States), which is more than any other federal agency (Bureau of Land Management, n.d.-a). Most of the lands that the BLM manages are in the western United States, including Alaska, which contains about one-third of the BLM-managed land. Most BLM lands are dominated by extensive grasslands, forests, high mountains, arctic tundra, and deserts. The BLM manages a variety of resources and uses, including energy and mineral mining; timber; grazing; wild horse and burro habitats; fish and wildlife habitats; wilderness areas; and archaeological, paleontological, and historical sites.

BLM recreation management areas include backcountry areas with minimal development of recreation facilities and special areas that provide recreation facilities such as campgrounds, boat launch ramps, cabins, and environmental education centers. BLM reports about 59 million visits per year (Bureau of Land Management, n.d.-b). Most of the land managed by BLM is desert and barren, but some of the land contains lakes, rivers, and mountains, and some of it is extremely scenic. BLM lands contain trails, campgrounds, picnic areas, boating areas, visitor centers, horse-riding trails, and OHV sites to sustain a variety of recreational pursuits.

Wilderness Areas

Areas designated under the 1964 Wilderness Act and the 1973 Eastern Wilderness Act are managed by the Bureau of Land Management, the U.S. Fish and Wildlife Service, the Forest Service, and the National Park Service. The Wilderness Act defined wilderness "as an area where the earth and its community of life are untrammeled by man, where man himself is a visitor who does not remain." Wilderness areas are generally open to the public for nonmotorized and nonmechanized (i.e., no bikes) recreation. Road, buildings, and other manmade structures are typically not found in wilderness areas. Permits are often required. These areas are truly wild and contain only a minimum of facilities. Following is a summary of the 765 federal wilder-

ness areas that cover 109.5 million acres (44.3 million hectares):

- National Park Service—61 sites, 44.4 million acres (18.0 million ha) and many other areas managed as wilderness but awaiting formal designation
- Forest Service—445 sites, 36.7 million acres (14.9 million ha)
- U.S. Fish and Wildlife Service—71 sites, 20.7 million acres (8.4 million ha)
- Bureau of Land Management—224 sites, 8.8 million acres (3.6 million ha)
- Total national wilderness—765 sites, approximately 109 million acres (44.5 million ha) (www.wilderness.net)

These national wilderness areas are subareas designated from existing national parks, monuments, preserves, forests, grasslands, resource lands, and fish and wildlife refuges. For example, 86 percent of the Everglades National Park is designated wilderness. Some states have state-designated wilderness areas that are smaller than federal wilderness areas and tend to follow the same principles of no development or motorized access.

U.S. Army Corps of Engineers Waterways and Sites

The Army Corps of Engineers is the steward of the lands and waters at thousands of federal water resource sites like dams, reservoirs, and flood-control projects. This agency is part of the Department of Defense, but most of its employees are civilians. Its natural resources management mission is to manage and conserve natural resources consistent with principles of ecosystem management while providing public outdoor recreation experiences to serve the needs of current and future generations (U.S. Army Corps of Engineers, n.d.).

The Army Corps of Engineers is the nation's largest provider of outdoor recreation. It manages thousands of recreation areas at 403 projects (mostly lakes and reservoirs). A substantial number of these recreation areas are leased to state or local park and recreation authorities or private interests. The Corps hosts about 370 million visitors a year at its lakes, beaches, and other areas, and estimates that 1 in 10 Americans visits a Corps project at least once a year. Recreationally, the Corps manages campgrounds, boat launch ramps, fishing piers, marinas, bathrooms, and swimming areas. In total, the Corps manages 12 million acres (5 million ha) of land and water for recreation, including 33 percent of all freshwater fishing opportunities in the United States. The Corps also manages the intracoastal waterway and reservoirs that provide substantial boating opportunities in many states (U.S. Army Corps of Engineers, n.d.).

Tennessee River Valley

The Tennessee Valley Authority (TVA) is a federal agency that operates in a limited service area encompassing seven states: Tennessee, Alabama, Georgia, Kentucky, Mississippi, North Carolina, and Virginia. President Franklin Roosevelt created the TVA during the Great Depression in 1933 to create electricity, flood control, and economic development in an underdeveloped region. TVA is the largest U.S. public power company, and because it manages a major river (650 miles [1,050 km] long), many recreation opportunities are available on TVA-managed areas. Millions of people enjoy recreational activities on TVA reservoirs or rivers and adjacent land each year. The reservoirs and the 290,000 acres (117,000 ha) of land surrounding them offer opportunities for recreational activities including waterskiing, canoeing, sailing, windsurfing, fishing, swimming, hiking, nature photography, picnicking, bird watching, and camping. Recreation management has not been a priority of TVA, and recently it has begun minimizing the amount of active recreation management that it does (Tennessee Valley Authority, n.d.). But because of its water-related resources, millions of people still engage in recreational activities on areas managed by TVA.

Large Western Reservoirs

Across the arid western states, water management became a critical focus as the population in those areas grew. In 1902, Teddy Roosevelt established the Bureau of Reclamation (BOR). This agency is part of the U.S. Department of the Interior and is best known for the dams, power plants, and canals that it has constructed in 17 western states. These water projects led to homesteading and promoted the economic development of the West. The mission of

BOR is to manage water and water-related resources in the western United States in an economically and environmentally sound manner for the American people. As a recreation provider, BOR serves a major role in providing water recreation opportunities to the rapidly growing western states. In otherwise dry western states, BOR reservoirs make possible water-based recreational activities such as boating, waterskiing, bird watching, fishing, waterside camping, and swimming in natural areas. Over 90 million visitors make use of 7.1 million acres (2.9 million ha) of BOR recreational land and waters each year (Bureau of Reclamation, n.d.).

American Indian Reservations

The Bureau of Indian Affairs (BIA) is responsible for administering and managing 55.7 million acres (22.5 million ha) of land held in trust by the United States for American Indians, Indian tribes, and Alaska natives. Most of the land is in Arizona, New Mexico, Montana, and South Dakota, although 31 states have some Native American lands. The BIA is an agency within the U.S. Department of the Interior. Developing forestlands, leasing assets on those lands, directing agricultural programs, protecting water and land rights, developing and maintaining infrastructure, and promoting economic development are among the agency's responsibilities. As part of their economic development efforts, many tribes attract tourists to their lands by offering guided tours, camping, hunting, fishing, museums, lodges, and alpine skiing. Since the passage of the Indian Gaming Act (1988), many tribes have opened casinos and associated resorts, hotels, shopping areas, and restaurants that attract visitors to American Indian lands (U.S. Department of the Interior, n.d.).

National Marine Sanctuaries

Two federal agencies that are part of the U.S. Department of Commerce's National Oceanic and Atmospheric Administration (NOAA) manage ocean area parks: the National Marine Sanctuary Program and the National Marine Fisheries Service. During the 1970s, when many environmental acts were passed, the Marine Protection, Research, and Sanctuaries Act of 1972 created the sanctuaries program, partially in response to oil spills and reports of toxic dumping in the ocean. Today, 13 national marine sanctuaries as well as the Papahanaumokuakea and Rose Atoll Marine National Monuments protect 170,000 square miles (440,298 sq km) of ocean and coasts (http://sanctuaries.noaa.gov).

The act to create these underwater sanctuaries was passed 100 years after the legislation to create the first national park on land. The primary purpose of the sanctuaries is to conserve natural and cultural marine features. These sanctuaries also provide underwater environmental education and opportunities for snorkeling and scuba sightseeing, fish and coral watching, and photography. In recent years, major new marine sanctuaries were created especially in American waters around Hawaii and off the New England coast.

INTERNATIONAL TREATIES AND PROTECTED AREA DESIGNATIONS AND PARKS

Protected natural areas that transcend national borders are known as *transboundary protected areas*. Because the world's natural resources and parks are best managed on an ecosystem scale, some believe that the programs should be developed so that national borders do not interfere with good conservation practices.

Transboundary protected areas have been created around the world. Typically, these areas were created to facilitate conservation of biological diversity across national boundaries. By 2007 there were 227 transboundary complexes involving 3,043 individual parks or protected areas in many countries (Lysenko, Besançon, & Savy, 2007). North America's first international transboundary cooperation was founded in 1932 and involved the Waterton–Glacier International Peace Park World Heritage site in Alberta and Montana. Another major U.S.–Canadian transboundary protected area includes a vast complex in the northwestern Yukon and northeastern Alaska involving the Ivvavik and Vuntut National Parks in Canada and the Arctic National Wildlife Refuge in the United States. A world-renowned wilderness canoeing area is also a transboundary unit. This area comprises Quetico Provincial Park in Ontario and the Boundary Waters Canoe Area in Minnesota. In total, Canada and the United States have nine transboundary protected-

area complexes. Canada also has a transboundary area with Greenland (Denmark), and the United States has two with Mexico (Lysenko et al., 2007).

In addition, the United Nations Educational, Scientific and Cultural Organization (UNESCO) designates international **biosphere reserves**, which are terrestrial and coastal areas representing the main ecosystems of the planet in which plants and animals are to be protected and where research, monitoring, and training on ecosystems are carried out. These reserves are designed to operate as examples of sustainable land use. Many of the larger national parks and adjacent areas in the United States and Canada have been designated as international biosphere reserves. Canada has 18 biosphere reserves and the United States has 47 (UNESCO, 2017a-b). However, the Trump Administration removed 17 of these biosphere reserves in mid-2017 (Smith and Greshko, 2017). Examples of biosphere reserves in Canada are Long Point in Ontario and Waterton in Alberta. Examples in the United States are the Mammoth Cave Area in Kentucky and the California Coast Ranges.

Similarly, UNESCO designates **World Heritage sites** to encourage countries to protect natural and cultural heritage sites that are of universal significance. Many of the nature sites are major national parks. In 2016, 1,031 World Heritage sites were designated globally. Canada contains 18 World Heritage sites (Parks Canada, 2017), and the United States contains 23 sites (UNESCO, n.d.). Some sites were designated for world-class natural features, such as Dinosaur Provincial Park in Alberta, the Rocky Mountain Parks in Alberta and British Columbia, Nahanni National Park in the Northwest Territories, Redwood National Park in California, and Everglades National Park in Florida. Other sites were designated for world-class cultural and historic values, such as L'Anse aux Meadows National Historic Site in Newfoundland, the Old Town of Lunenburg in Nova Scotia, the Statue of Liberty in New York, and Independence Hall in Philadelphia.

Another international designation for wetland areas is the **Ramsar Convention**, which designates internationally important wetlands for conservation (Wetlands International, 2005). In 2016, there were 2,241 Ramsar wetlands designated worldwide within 169 countries. Canada had 37 sites, and the United States had 38 sites (Ramsar, 2017).

©Paul F.J. Eagles.

Dinosaur Provincial Park in Alberta is a World Heritage site that protects significant dinosaur fossils.

The World Heritage sites and the Ramsar wetlands are designated through international conventions. Once designated, each site must be managed according to international law as outlined in the convention. The biosphere reserve designation is simply a cooperative arrangement among countries that has no international legal structure and thus requires much less conservation commitment.

COMPARING CANADA AND THE UNITED STATES

Table 6.2 shows the status, as of 2017, of the parks and protected areas in Canada and the United States according to the United Nations List of Protected Areas (Chape, Blyth, Fish, Fox, & Spalding, 2003). Urban parks are not included in the list because of their small size, and historic parks are not included because of their cultural focus.

Similarities Between Canada and the United States

The park systems in the countries are similar and often designate the same types of lands for protec-

tion. This resemblance is not surprising because both countries developed their park systems with constant communication and friendly competition over 200 years. The United States and Canada are similar in geographic size, so directly comparing the area dedicated to various types of parks and protected areas is possible (see table 6.2). Both countries have similar amounts of area designated as nature reserves and habitat and species management areas. Canada has much more national parkland in part because the large provincial parks are of national-park stature and size and are recognized as such in the international classification of parks. The data in table 6.2 are presented according to the **International Union for Conservation of Nature and Natural Resources (IUCN)** categories of protected areas, not according to the official titles of the parks. For example, many provincial parks in Canada are classified in the UN list as category II parks or national parks. Therefore, table 6.2 shows 1,725 national parks in Canada, although only 38 of them are owned and operated by the national government; provincial governments own and manage the rest. Additionally, neither national historic sites nor historic canals are included in the database used

Table 6.2   Parks and Protected Areas in Canada and the United States

IUCN category	Number in Canada	Number in the United States
Ia: Nature reserve	495	607
Ib: Wilderness	269	1,325
II: National park	1,725	41
III: Natural monument	575	1,804
IV: Habitat & species management area	2,983	755
V: Protected landscape	142	28,414
VI: Managed-resource protected area	1,187	418
Unclassified	266	711
Total number of sites	7,642	34,075
Total area in km²	964,194	1,230,734
Total number of marine protected area	817	1,484
Total area in km²	49,681	3,527,430

All data are from the United Nations Environment Programme's World Conservation Monitoring Centre's (UNEP-WCMC, 2017) World Database of Protected Areas and were up-to-date as of September 2017 (www.protectedplanet.net).

for the table. The IUCN does not recognize cultural or historic sites in its classification system, and historic sites are discussed only briefly in this chapter.

The similarity in the form and function of parks in Canada and the United States is caused by several factors. The government structures are similar and include cities, towns, counties, provinces or states, and a federal government. Each of these levels of government develops and manages parks. Both countries have cultural roots in England, which transferred to North America the English love of nature, outdoor recreation, and the use of specialized reserves for conservation and recreation (Glendening 1997; Hudson, 2001; Jones & Wills, 2005; Ritvo, 2003). The green parks in the central areas of English cities were widely emulated across the various British colonies in North America (Sheail, 2010). As the park movement in Canada and the United States deepened and strengthened through increasing activities by cities, provinces or states, and national governments, communication of ideas between the two countries was ongoing. Many government precedents, numerous management details, and much wording in legislation moved back and forth between agencies in the two

countries over a 200-year period. Therefore, both countries have national parks, national historic sites and parks, national wildlife reserves and areas, provincial and state parks, regional parks, and municipal parks. And it is not surprising that parks in both countries have been created for everyone's use and are funded primarily by taxes.

After the parks were established, their management was done first by volunteers and later by hired professionals. Starting in the United States in the 1930s and followed by Canada in the 1960s, specialized college and university programs were developed to provide training for leisure, parks, recreation, and resource management professionals. Park managers in both countries are now viewed as professionals who have received training appropriate to the challenging tasks of conservation and recreation.

Canada and the United States both played a large role in park management internationally. Both countries have influenced the types and forms of park management that have developed around the world. U.S. government officials and academic scholars were particularly influential in spreading the U.S. model of national parks worldwide.

The U.S. model is typically seen as consisting of extremely large areas from which aboriginal people have been removed. Management is by a government agency that concentrates on conservation and outdoor recreation. Canadian officials have been influential in international activities such as creating biosphere reserves and management of the World Heritage Convention. Scholars in both countries have written abundant literature that has widely disseminated the concepts of park planning and management and outdoor recreation planning and management. The United States and Canada have consistently shown international leadership in park planning and management.

Differences Between Canada and the United States

Although the park systems in both countries are similar, there are important differences (Eagles, McLean, & Stabler, 2000). The wilderness concept is more popular in the United States than in Canada; therefore, the United States has much more designated wilderness. Through the power of the use of the Antiquities Act, the United States has a national monument designation that is not used in Canadian park law. But the biggest differences occur in the amount of land making up protected landscape and managed resource-protected areas. In the United States, the federal government manages these lands and has designated large areas as national forests and Bureau of Land Management protected areas. In Canada, however, the provinces manage the forest lands, and Canada does not include all undesignated Crown lands managed by the provinces, territories, and the national government in its tabulation of protected areas. Therefore, formal lists of protected areas create the impression that the United States has much more protected land. This conclusion is misleading because massive amounts of Crown and aboriginal land in Canada are available for outdoor recreation but are not formally designated as some form of protected area.

One major difference between Canada and the United States is the constitutional structure of land ownership. In the United States, the federal government owns most of the public land, especially in states that came into the union after the Civil War. Therefore, the U.S. government has the capacity to create parks and reserves on this land. As a result, many land management agencies have been created to manage the variety of reserves created on federal land. The United States has more diverse management institutions and reserves than Canada does. For example, the following systems exist in the United States but not in Canada: national forests, national parkways, national scenic rivers, national wilderness areas, U.S. Army Corps of Engineer waterways, and BLM national resource lands.

Another difference between the two countries is that in Canada the provincial parks are much larger than most state parks in the United States. For example, the provincial park system in Ontario is larger in land area than all 50 of the U.S. state park systems combined. In essence, many provincial park systems in Canada are of national park stature largely because the provincial governments control most of the Crown land within their borders. Therefore, the provincial governments found it relatively easy to create provincial parks on land that they already owned and managed. Some of the richer provinces, such as Ontario, British Columbia, and Quebec, blocked national park creation while putting the best lands into their own provincial park systems. A few provinces, however, have gone a different direction. Poorer provinces, such as New Brunswick, Nova Scotia, and Prince Edward Island, welcomed national park creation because the federal government would then pay the cost of land management. In these provinces, the national parks are prominent and the provincial park systems are smaller and less developed.

Within the territories in Canada, the federal government holds Crown land and takes into account aboriginal land rights. Therefore, national parks and wildlife areas were most easily created by the national government in territories. For that reason, the major concentration of national parks occurs in the western mountains and in the High North. In the Canadian West, the national parks were created before the provinces had been created. In the North, park creation is ongoing. Canadian parks have been managed more as a system of parks with national planning, whereas in the United States, although there have been several attempts at national plans, they rarely last long, often because of changes in presidential or congressional priorities and the difficulties in coordinating 50 states.

Canada is a signatory to the Convention on Biological Diversity. Under that convention, all countries have agreed that 17 percent of their land surface and 10 percent of their marine areas will be protected areas by 2020. Canada currently has 10.36 percent of the terrestrial area of the country in some form of protected area and 0.98 percent of the marine area in protected areas (CCEA, 2016). To reach the 17 percent and 10 percent targets, the current federal government headed by Prime Minister Justin Trudeau has promised to create substantial amounts of new parkland by 2020. If successful, this will be the largest area of park creation in Canada's history.

The United States is not a signatory to the Convention on Biological Diversity because the Senate refuses to approve this convention. On March 10, 2016, however, President Obama and Prime Minister Trudeau issued a joint statement that said "Canada and the US re-affirm our national goals of protecting at least 17% of land areas and 10% of marine areas by 2020. We will take concrete steps to achieve and substantially surpass these national goals in coming areas" (Trudeau & Obama, 2016). This is a dramatic example of the cooperation of the United States and Canada in park management at the highest levels possible.

CAREER OPPORTUNITIES

Traditionally, the operation of most public natural areas occurs within the federal, state or provincial, or municipal levels of government. City parks and recreation departments offer countless opportunities to parks and recreation specialists. Thus, employment opportunities are available with agencies such as the national park agencies, the national wildlife agencies, the forest services, and the many regional, local, and municipal parks and recreation agencies. In the United States, opportunities are also available with the AmeriCorps program, the Student Conservation Corps (SCA), and many state and local nonprofit groups such as the Vermont Youth Conservation Corps. Many different job positions are available at parks, forests, and refuges (administrative, financial, clerical, secretarial, maintenance, law enforcement, biologists, historians, lifeguards, and so on).

Park rangers carry out various tasks associated with the following:

- Forest or structural fire control
- Protection of property
- Gathering and dissemination of natural, historical, or scientific information
- Development of interpretive material for the natural, historical, or cultural features of an era
- Demonstration of folk art and crafts
- Enforcement of laws and regulations
- Investigation of violations, complaints, trespassing and encroachment, and accidents
- Search and rescue
- Management of historical, cultural, and natural resources such as wildlife, forests, lakeshores, seashores, historic buildings, battlefields, archaeological properties, and recreation areas

They also operate campgrounds, including such tasks as assigning sites, replenishing firewood, performing safety inspections, providing information to visitors, and leading guided tours. Differences in the exact nature of duties depend on the grade of the position, the size of the site, and specific needs (National Park Service, n.d.-d).

Educational requirements vary depending on the position, but a university degree is preferred for most permanent positions. Seasonal employment is available in most areas to gain experience when the employee is in college or has recently graduated. Educational training should relate to the position sought (e.g., history degree for historians; parks, recreation, and tourism degree for visitor management; biology, ecology, forestry, geology, or wildlife management degree for natural resource management positions). Except for some maintenance positions (electricians, plumbers, and so on), law enforcement jobs, or lifeguard positions, certifications are generally not required, although for some positions preference might be given to candidates who have certified park and recreation professional (CPRP) status. Information on obtaining that certification is available from the National Recreation and Park Association in Ashburn, Virginia, United States. Canada does not have a national recreation accreditation system. However, in the United States the most senior positions in park agencies are political appointees, chosen partly because of their affiliation with the political party in power.

In Canada and the United States there is a positive relationship between universities and park managers. Many parks rely heavily on student employees for many activities ranging for biological inventories to campground management and from visitor management to environmental education. Most senior park managers and planners are university graduates. Maintenance and construction employees have appropriate technical training. Law enforcement staff have specialized policing training.

Many professional organizations are relevant to those interested in a park-related career. Most have student membership rates and hold annual conferences that offer good opportunities to network and find out about internship or employment opportunities. Some of the better-known ones include the National Recreation and Park Association, the Canadian Parks and Recreation Association, the National Parks and Conservation Association, the Society of American Foresters, Society of Outdoor Recreation Professionals, the National Association for Interpretation, state and provincial park and recreation associations, the George Wright Society, and the Wilderness Society. The best way for a young student to become permanently employed in a park is to obtain temporary seasonal work to gain experience and become known to managers.

There are also recreation employment opportunities in the private sector, both the profit-making sector and the nonprofit sector. A range of jobs is available including program planning, direct program delivery, resort-park concessionaire or lodging operations, and the sale of specialized recreation merchandise. Growing opportunities in small businesses are available for people interested in providing outdoor programs and services for activities such as rafting, birding, bicycling, and kayaking. Some resorts recognize the need for a staff naturalist or recreation employee to answer guests' questions and offer tours and sightseeing trips. Summer camps, ski resorts, tour boat companies, bed and breakfasts, park and beach concessionaires, park lodges, watercraft and bicycle rental companies, water parks, marinas, and outdoor equipment stores are a few more examples of potential job

sites. Increasingly, nongovernment organizations that assist with park management, such as friends groups, have become important sources of employment for parks and recreation graduates.

A glance at websites such as Cool Works, Eco-Jobs, the NRPA careers webpage, state parks job pages, and federal job pages will show that the number and diversity of career opportunities related to parks and protected areas are immense. Perhaps the best part of these careers is the intangible benefits that a person receives from living and working in a place and often doing things that others pay to see and experience.

CHALLENGES AND TRENDS FOR THE 21ST CENTURY

Parks are a product and reflection of our society, its needs, and its culture. Most citizens use, know about, and support the creation and management of parks. Over time, public demand has resulted in increasing amounts of land being reserved for parks and removed from other types of land use. Park usage is increasing in some regions but decreasing in others. Park tourism leads to two complicated problems. First, how can the cultural and ecological values of the parks be conserved and interpreted while at the same time be actively used by large numbers of tourists? Second, how can the management of all this parkland and visitor use be financed? We are fortunate to have thousands of park resources available because of the farsightedness, willingness to sacrifice, and preservation ethos of previous generations. But those resources face challenges and trends that current generations must respond to.

Carrying Capacity

This is a primary issue associated with parks because of the inherent conflict between providing parks for public use and enjoyment while protecting the resources that make them special. This dual mandate requires that a balance be achieved among the number and types of users allowed and the effects of their use. The point at which this balance is made is the **carrying capacity** of a park. Carrying capacity is inherently a subjective decision, but it can be informed by strong empirical science. For example, social scientists have determined public opinion regarding the acceptable level of crowds, traffic, noise, or environmental effects caused by park visitors (Manning, 2007). Likewise, experts can evaluate visitor-created effects on resources such as wildlife or plants. These opinions (both public and expert) can help inform standards for managing parks within a carrying capacity; if standards are violated, then the carrying capacity of a park has been reached and park managers should take action. These actions could include redistributing visitors to lesser used areas of the park, reducing visitor impacts, or limiting the number of visitors. The concept of carrying capacity can help ensure the sustainability of parks and their resources for future generations.

International Tourism

In both countries, the impact of international tourists is becoming increasingly important as large numbers of people from other countries, especially Europe, Japan, China, and other Asian countries, visit high-profile parks. The increase in visits to national parks by international tourists can be attributed to greater awareness of environmental concerns, scarcity of natural land at home, and higher levels of travel. As international tourism increases, so does the demand for a higher quality of service management and park staff with advanced education in tourism management, cultural sensitivity, and language skills.

Funding

Over the years, government funding for public parks has become increasingly limited, and the number of park agencies that compete for these funds has grown. Some of the causes of the funding shortage include rising land prices and energy and fuel costs and a trend toward reducing taxes. Insufficient funding hinders the provision of environmental and historical interpretation programs and the retention of sufficient park rangers or staff to maintain facilities, manage resources, and serve the public. Parks not only compete with each other for funding but they also compete with other large and popular public institutions such as education and health care for these limited public funds.

Innovative responses to funding shortfalls include increasing the use of tourism fees and charges, relying more on volunteer efforts such as friends groups, and encouraging park agencies to function like businesses by tapping all possible streams of income. Many park agencies are aggressively moving into a business model of management in which they can set prices, retain funds, hire staff, and operate programs with flexibility similar to that of a private business. Traditional income sources continue to include government appropriations and grants, campsite rentals, and day-use fees. Innovative income sources used include souvenir sales, grocery sales, recreation equipment rental, specialized clothing and equipment sales, specialized accommodation rental, fees for using parks as movie-filming sites, art sales, interpretive program charges, corporate sponsorships, leases to private companies, and corporate advertising. Friends groups are also entrepreneurial. Examples of fundraising activities include providing specialized festivals; developing aboriginal-themed activities; encouraging film, art, and cultural development; and staffing book or gift stores and donating a portion of sales income to the park and encouraging donations of time and money. A complete review of Ontario's experience in tourism funding for parks was outlined by Eagles (2014). Advanced training in the business of leisure and tourism is now needed in all park agencies.

Major park management debates revolve around the types of activities that should be encouraged and allowed, the management structures used, and the source of the funding. The proportion of funding that should come from taxes or from user fees also produces heated debate. In recent years, a trend has developed toward increasing the use of various types of fees and charges to fund park management, especially in state and provincial parks. There is an urgent need for park managers with specialized training in finance and business management. Many universities train resource managers, but only a few train business managers for parks.

Market Specialization

Over the years, various park agencies have increasingly specialized in providing services to a segment of the population. For example, youth and people without much discretionary income heavily use city parks. Conversely, well-educated and wealthy older people who have the time and money to travel heavily use national parks. The baby boom generation is now a key target market. Today's park managers must plan and manage for the needs of the largest, healthiest, and wealthiest cadre of retirees in world history. For example, the picturesque landscapes of North American parks attract older travelers, but the services and facilities are usually more appropriate for young, physically active visitors. Aging baby boomers seem to prefer what has been labeled *soft ecotourism* in which they hike and sightsee in the parks in the daytime but retire to nearby lodges, bed and breakfasts, restaurants, and cabins at night. The boom in the development of ecolodges near parks is based on this trend of visiting parks for a nature experience but spending the evenings with good food and innovative accommodations. Resolving this competition poses a challenge to parks.

Changing Demand

The national park agencies of Canada and the United States saw a slight but steady decline in national park use until 2014, when a major increase occurred (Balmford et al., 2009; National Park Service, n.d.-b; Parks Canada, n.d.; Pergams, Czech, Haney, & Nyberg, 2004). There were several key reasons for declines in park use, such as the increased cost of fuel, the global economic recession, information technology and social media increasingly taking more time (a phenomenon called *videophilia* by Pergams & Zaradic, 2006), and immigration of people to both countries who do not have a cultural backgrounds in nature-based outdoor recreation. Adapting to these challenges that reduce visitation remains one of the biggest problems on the horizon for parks. However, more fuel-efficient vehicles, decreased gasoline prices, emergence from the economic recession, and marketing and programming efforts to get more adults, diverse visitors, and children outdoors seem to have helped increase demand to visit parks of all kinds. For example, in 2015, the NPS launched an initiative to allow fourth-grade children and their families into parks for free as part of a program called Every Kid in a Park. In 2015 and 2016, the NPS set new records for the number of visitors.

Encroachment

As private-land development encroaches on park borders, wildlife loses some of its ability to move across natural areas. Development of power plants, housing, and large retail stores adjacent to parks threatens aesthetics and air quality. Development pressures also increase the temptation for government to use public parklands for public services such as roads, power lines, cell phone towers, and pipelines. A major management focus of many agencies is to stop illegal encroachments by adjacent landowners on parklands, such as homeowners who extend their activities into parkland (McWilliam, Eagles, Seasons, & Brown, 2010).

Environmental Threats From Outside the Park

Problems originating elsewhere can affect park resources. For example, polluted river water originates in a populated area but flows through a park, or air pollution from outside a park can spoil the fresh air and views within the park. Exotic plant species seeds are dispersed by wildlife or wind and cause nonnative plants to flourish inside park boundaries, which possibly crowds out native species. Historically, park management focused on factors within a park's boundaries. Many park managers (particularly at the regional and national levels) are beginning to recognize, plan for, and respond to these transboundary issues through partnerships and collaboration with governmental officials, nonprofit organizations, scientists, and other stakeholders.

Climate Change

All global environments are facing increasing threats from a climate that is affected by human forces. While once debated, climate change is now widely recognized among leaders and managers as a primary influence in the future of parks and protected areas. In fact, both the NPS and the Forest Service have made understanding and responding to climate change a primary focus of their efforts. This threat is of great concern because it is pervasive and has the potential to cause significant alterations in current parks and protected areas.

For example, climate change threatens glaciers that are a centerpiece of several U.S. national parks (e.g., Kenai Fjords National Park, Glacier Bay National Park, Glacier National Park), and it may cause the loss of Joshua trees from Joshua Tree National Park. Within the western United States and Canada, a warming climate has resulted in a population explosion of native bark beetles that have damaged and killed millions of trees. These dying trees have created a major forest fire threat. Alberta and British Columbia saw record levels of forest fires in recent years, including the destruction of all or parts of two cities in northern Alberta. This change is an example of the types of ecosystem transformations now underway.

Illicit and Illegal Behavior

Vandalism, drug use, public sexual behavior, crime, and gang activity have made many people afraid to visit urban parks. Approaches to addressing these problems include establishing zero-tolerance zones for crimes committed within 100 yards (91 m) of a park, adding special fines or sentences for doing so, and monitoring parks with cameras. Another strategy is national night-out events to encourage large numbers of people to use the parks, which usually discourages crime. In state parks, national parks, and other protected areas, the growing of drugs (particularly marijuana) in remote regions has been an increasing concern for managers and visitors. Likewise, illegal immigration, border security, and related human trafficking at parks that share an international border (particularly with Mexico) are an increasing problem. Law enforcement is an important activity in all parks. No conservation or recreation programs can be successful if the laws underpinning these programs are not enforced.

Motorized Vehicles

OHV use is one of the most prevalent and fastest growing leisure activities on public lands in the United States. From 1999 to 2005, the estimated number of OHV users in the United States grew from 36 to 51 million (Cordell, Betz, Green, & Owens, 2005). This figure indicates that nearly one in every five U.S. residents uses an OHV. National forests and BLM lands are frequently used as places to ride OHVs, and many of these places have trails that cater to OHV recreationists. But OHV use, particularly when not intensively managed, may lead to substantial resource impacts and controversy in these places. In 2006, the Forest Service labeled unmanaged OHV use as one of the four leading threats to the health of the nation's forests and grasslands in the 21st century. Also, inappropriate and illegal use of motorized vehicles in parks and protected areas is a concern for managers.

Coastal Development

On many coastlines, condominiums and high-rise buildings with thousands of residents are being built, which greatly increases the use of nearby coastal parks. Coastal lands have become so expensive that existing coastal parks cannot be expanded. In addition, the high density creates large human-use pressure in the parks.

Natural Darkness and Quiet

A broadened consideration of park resources has led to both noise and light pollution becoming concerns in national and state parks (Manning et al., in press). Some parks are now actively working to protect the important, yet previously unmanaged, ability to enjoy the stars in the night sky or natural sounds like birds singing or water flowing. Lightscapes and soundscapes are now recognized and managed resources in some parks. A few parks have sought and received designations as International Dark Sky Parks to certify the exceptional quality of their night sky and night environment. Other parks, like Muir Woods National Monument, have created quiet zones where people can enjoy the park without being disturbed by human-caused noise.

Multiethnic Cultural Changes

Projections are that an amalgam of minorities will make up more than 50 percent of the U.S. population by 2050. Because of immigration from a diverse set of countries, the Canadian and American populations are becoming more diverse in cultures and ideas. This transformation creates concern for park managers because some cultures have little experience visiting parks or participating in traditional outdoor recreational activities (Chavez, 2002;

Johnson, Bowker, English, & Worthen, 1997; Virden & Walker, 1999). As the ethnic balance in North America shifts, park, forest, and refuge agencies at all levels must understand the preferences and outdoor recreational behaviors of minority groups and work to introduce them to activities that they may have little experience with or adapt facilities or programs to their cultures. This approach will be necessary to continue the legacy of public service that makes park resources available to all citizens and guests in the United States and Canada.

Workforce Changes

Many parks and protected areas are staffed and managed by a large cohort of people who are nearing retirement age. Almost half of all U.S. federal employees are within five years of retirement age, although the recent economic downturn may delay some of those retirements. Having such a large percentage of experienced park staff leaving brings with it challenges of retaining knowledge within the organization, providing adequate training, and finding qualified replacements. This change in the workforce also indicates that substantial opportunities will be available to those looking for careers in parks and protected areas.

Seasonality

Most parks in Canada and the United States deal successfully with large fluctuations in visitation resulting from changes in the seasons. In northern areas, visitation is largely concentrated in the warmer months, so many parks are staffed by short-term employees (often university students). A few parks in northern areas have snow-based recreational activities, typically downhill skiing, that enable year-round employment. But many parks in northern areas are staffed at very low levels or not all in the colder winter months, especially in Canada. In southern Canada, warmer weather in the last decade in September, October, and November has caused a surge in visitation.

SUMMARY

The parks in Canada and the United States contain some of the most significant and attractive natural landscapes in North America. Each year, they illustrate for millions of people the ecological and cultural values of both countries. The parks of Canada and the United States are highly valued not only by their citizens but also by an increasing number of international visitors. These parks have become icons that represent the strong political, social, and cultural ideas that formed each country. Although European countries have many castles and cathedrals that mark centuries of cultural history, in North America the beauty of the wild lands—the mountains, deserts, prairies, rivers, and lakes—celebrates a major aspect of this continent and its people.

Those who work in park settings feel strongly about the value of their role, and many consider their jobs positive lifelong endeavors. In an increasingly urbanized, technology-filled, overstimulated, and fast-paced culture, people seek opportunities to connect with nature. Public parks, forests, rivers, mountains, beaches, lakes, deserts, and oceans can provide inspiration, fascination, and education. These protected natural resources, gifts from earlier generations, can provide escape from work and social challenges, peace and relaxation, and a place to spend quiet time with family and friends or alone. They are living schools for ecology, wildlife, nature, and self-discovery.

Not many places endure unchanged over a lifetime. Over the past 150 years, North America has lost many farms and natural areas to development. Most parks, however, remain more or less unchanged over the years: There are places for children to swing or slide in a local park; for swimming or camping with family; for strolling hand in hand or sharing a kiss on a park bench; for celebrating anniversaries in park lodges; for hiking, fishing, canoeing, or camping; and for watching sunsets and moonrises across a scenic natural landscape. Parks are invaluable for creating personal memories as well as maintaining national heritage and culture. All citizens should visit parks, make memories in them, celebrate natural roots and connections to the animal and plant kingdoms, and play a role in protecting and sharing existing parks and creating new ones.

CHAPTER 7

Public Recreation

Susan Markham-Starr, Mary Sara Wells, and Terry Long

iStockphoto/Edwin Verin

> My friends, love is better than anger. Hope is better than fear. Optimism is better than despair. So let us be loving, hopeful and optimistic. And we'll change the world.
>
> Jack Layton, leader of the opposition of the government of Canada, 2011

LEARNING OUTCOMES

After reading this chapter, you should be able to do the following:

> Identify the groups that helped create public recreation services in Canada and the United States

> Describe the basic types of recreation programs found in Canada and the United States

> Demonstrate an understanding of why partnerships are important in public recreation

> Recognize the trends in the changing profession of public recreation and the leadership skills needed to advance a professional career

> List and describe the various certifications available in public recreation

> Describe the philosophy of community-based recreation approaches

> Identify the role of the ADA in the development of inclusive recreation opportunities in public recreation

> Explain the role of accessibility, accommodation, and adaptation as building blocks to inclusion

> Recognize potential limits to reasonable accommodation

> Differentiate between Special Olympics, disability sport, adapted sport, and Paralympics

> Communicate the value of social inclusion to participants and community members

---

Public Parks and Recreation in the United States and Canada

Susan Markham-Starr and Mary Sara Wells

❝ I am not concerned with our inability to nail down the specifics of what we do in parks and recreation. As I see it, our strength lies in our diversity. We can do anything. More specifically, I believe our job is to help people improve their quality of life through recreation and parks. ❞

Robert F. Toalson, Champaign Park District, Illinois

Public recreation continues to face numerous changes. Many public agencies that provide these valuable services are seeing their budgets cut, their resources shifted, and their priorities redefined. Public recreation is no longer always considered a staple for a high quality of life within a community. Today we need new ideas, new leadership methods, and, most important, a constant dedication to educate people about the benefits of recreation. A paradigm shift has been underway over the past few years regarding the future of public recreation because many of us still feel the effects of the recession of the last decade. But throughout history, one undeniable fact is that public recreation is needed to provide fun and exciting leisure opportunities for people of all ages. The need to embrace 21st-century thinking and advance the future is upon us. The question to our profession now is how to relate to a changing environment in a modern world.

In the past, public recreation has been dependent on costly physical features such as playgrounds, trails, swimming pools, and recreation centers. These types of facilities provide valuable recreation opportunities and tend to be focused on providing something for everyone. But recreation programs are now becoming more specialized for target user groups. Does this approach make sense for the public today? The public in today's world is plugged in to constant information streams that are available on their terms. The use of technology in our everyday lives has quickened our information-based lifestyle. Knowledge is available instantly. Interacting on social technology networks has become a major form of leisure for multiple generations. How we spend our leisure time is changing. New leadership in our field is needed to reach the public in ways not considered just a few years ago.

This section explores the realm of public recreation as a possible career path. The world of public recreation has a different focus from that of our colleagues in the private sector. This section examines the pulse of public recreation and leisure services in Canada and the United States, the social and political environments in which public recreation professionals operate, the primary roles of parks and recreation professionals, and the constantly changing face of public recreation.

HISTORICAL OVERVIEW OF PUBLIC RECREATION IN THE UNITED STATES

Public recreation in the United States originated around the middle of the 19th century in the Midwest and Northeast. Although recreation in general can be found in the United States before explorers from England and other countries arrived, this represents the time when government and other organizations first began providing specific services. A review of how parks and recreation developed up until this point can be found in chapter 2. Public recreation perhaps first began with the development of parks and playgrounds. Although parks and open spaces may not have been uncommon prior to this point, it is generally believed that the Boston Common and New York City's Central Park were early demonstrations of the need for intentional green space planning within urban environments. The construction of playgrounds in the mid- to late 1800s further served the needs of urban residents by providing structures on which children could engage in active and constructive play.

Among the early pioneers in the playground movement was the Massachusetts Emergency and Hygiene Association in Boston, which developed a sand garden in 1885 that led to the development of 21 more similar playgrounds by 1889. The first municipal park in the United States to have a permanent playground was Seward Park in New York City in 1903. The playground movement of this area led to the foundation of the Playground Association of America in 1906, which eventually grew to become the National Recreation and Park Association; this is the preeminent professional organization for the field today.

HISTORICAL OVERVIEW OF PUBLIC RECREATION IN CANADA

In considering the development of public recreation in Canada, people often look at the services that are closest to its citizens at the local level and primarily at the municipal level. In the early 21st century, these municipal services are supported by and driven by provincial and federal programs that operate in a system propelled by professional, community, and political initiatives. Local public recreation began as a set of independent initiatives aimed at solving problems (real or perceived) or creating opportunities for residents. The roots of today's integrated public recreation system come from parks, playgrounds, fitness, and employment initiatives; from those who wanted to reform the "sorry condition of Canada's big cities" (Rutherford, 1974, p. xv); from those who wanted to enhance the physical, mental, and moral health of all; and from those who wanted to enhance investment growth and prosperity in cities. The results were parks established to create civic beauty and promote a healthy environment, playgrounds established to provide wholesome play opportunities for children, and physical activity programs to build the fitness levels of young people so that they would be fit for work or war. The system has been advanced by those who wanted to create a better environment, although each proponent of recreation might define *better* in a different fashion.

Influences on recreation in Canada came from Great Britain, Europe, and the United States. There are readily identifiable links between British proponents of wholesome and uplifting educational and recreational programs such as the Young Men's Christian Association (YMCA) and the

Young Women's Christian Association (YWCA) from England; Scandinavian promoters of physical fitness; and American advocates for supervised playgrounds and urban recreation programs. Each of these groups helped plant ideas and provide information to Canadians, but the version of each idea evolved according to the social, economic, and political influences in Canada. The expansion of eastern Canadian cities in the mid- and late-19th century, the rapid expansion of the West in the early 20th century, the depression of the 1930s, the post–World War II urban growth, and the role of government as the provider of a social safety net all contributed to the Canadian solution.

Playgrounds Came First and Then Recreation

Municipal recreation in Canada can trace its roots to the National Council of Women's (NCW) Committee on Vacation Schools and Supervised Playgrounds in 1901 after lobbying from the Saint John Local Council of Women led by Miss Mabel Peters

(McFarland, 1970). The NCW focused on "'prevention' as its guiding principle" (Strong-Boag, 1976, p. 268), and by 1913 the NCW's committee was able to firmly state its mission and successes using ideas familiar to us today:

> Its work is formative as opposed to reformative. It seeks to eventually dispense with the curfew, the juvenile court, the jail and the reform school for the young of our land. Educationists are now agreed that the public supervised playground and recreational Social Center stimulates and guides a child's life in a way which no other factor of modern living can do. (Peters, 1913, p. 48)

We no longer have reform schools and seldom have curfews, but we now speak of at-risk youth. The ideas of a century ago are still with us.

Although the NCW and its local councils were advocates for playgrounds and the catalysts for their development, they were not committed to their long-term operation. They wanted to hand off responsibility to other groups such as local

John Joseph Kelso / Library and Archives Canada / PA-120557

A local playground association's advocacy work to promote playground development in the early 20th century. The sign reads "Try and secure one for your neighbourhood."

playground associations and municipal governments. The accompanying photo shows the publicity efforts of one playground association as its members urged visitors to try to get a playground in their neighborhood.

Recreation departments became the norm in Canadian cities in the early to mid-20th century, and they often merged with parks departments. In the last decades of the 20th century, further mergers occurred between municipal parks and recreation and other units with similar mandates or client groups. For example, agencies that provided recreation, parks, and other social services and culture or tourism services merged into a local department of community services or community development.

Federal and Provincial Governments

The involvement of provincial governments and the federal government in recreation can be primarily attributed to the search for antidotes to unemployment during the depression in the 1930s. Two intertwined threads were involved. One developed in British Columbia, and the other included the efforts of the federal government.

In British Columbia, the government began its provincial recreation program, Pro-Rec, in 1934 to provide physical recreation for unemployed young men and women as an attempt to deal with "the large number of unemployed youth . . . who are exposed to the demoralizing influences of enforced idleness" (Schrodt, 1979, Appendix A). The first director was Ian Eisenhardt, a Vancouver Parks Board staff member who had been trained in Denmark. When the federal government established the National Employment Commission in 1936 to investigate the needs of the unemployed, it was searching for solutions to address not only employment but also leisure needs. The commission consulted experts such as Eisenhardt and devised programs to alleviate the problems of unemployment, and programs like the British Columbia program emerged. Through the Federal Unemployment and Agricultural Assistance Act of 1938 and the Youth Training Act of 1939, the provinces were given assistance to create training programs that would prepare young people to work in physical training and health education in local communities and to provide recreation opportunities for trainees in other programs such as forestry, agriculture, mining, industrial apprenticeships, and domestic and household work (McFarland, 1970). Responsibility for these training programs, including recreation workers, was delegated to the various provincial governments. Provinces that established training programs frequently relied on expert advice from Eisenhardt and staff from British Columbia.

Federal involvement in recreation had an influence on the municipal level through its programs of assistance in partnerships with most of the provinces. In 1943, the National Physical Fitness Program was established. The objective of this program was to "encourage, develop and correlate all activities related to physical development of the people through sports, athletics, and similar pursuits" (The National Physical Fitness Act, 1943, p. 158). The program ended in 1954. It was succeeded by the Fitness and Amateur Sport Act in 1961 and the Physical Activity and Sport Act in 2003. As the federal government's involvement in recreation and leisure services evolved, various government programs came and went, such as Recreation Canada, which was established in 1971 and dissolved in 1980 (MacIntosh, Bedecki, & Franks, 1988; Westland, 1979). The role of the federal government in recreation in Canada is to support sport governing bodies, health promotion initiatives, indigenous peoples' concerns, the provinces, recreation-related associations, and physical activity strategies including ParticipACTION, a national nonprofit initiative to promote fitness through physical activity.

DELIVERY SYSTEMS IN PUBLIC RECREATION

The public recreation system as we know it today has a variety of delivery systems in place within the various forms of governmental units. Public recreation must provide inclusive recreation and leisure services to all people, including disadvantaged and disabled patrons. This integrated approach reflects the spirit of the Americans with Disabilities Act and the Canadian Charter of Rights and Freedoms. Inclusion addresses the need to provide integration of leisure services for people of all ages, abilities, cultures, ethnicities, genders, races, and religions. This nondiscriminatory approach goes beyond the placement of special needs participants in separate recreation program settings.

In the most basic form, recreation programs found in public recreation fall into two classes of activities. The first is active recreation, which includes all types of sport, swimming, and most physical exercise recreation opportunities. The second is passive recreation, which includes low-impact exercise and creative-based recreation programs such as walking, arts and crafts, and trips and excursions.

American Delivery Systems

Recreation professionals in the United States provide numerous programs and services through numerous delivery systems including municipal, state, and federal governmental agencies. Each type of agency serves a unique purpose or mission.

Municipal Recreation Leisure Services

Municipal recreation departments that serve communities are the primary providers of parks and recreation services. More than 2,100 community parks and recreation providers are registered with the National Recreation and Park Association (NCHPAD, n.d.). These include departments at the city and county levels and through special-use districts. Services provided by these organizations often include structured programs and facilities for drop-in participation. More specifically, many municipal recreation departments have offerings such as classes, aquatic facilities, youth sports, field trips, after-school programs, golf courses, cemeteries, parks and playgrounds, and trails.

State Recreation Leisure Services

Whereas municipal recreation services provide opportunities at a local level, state recreation services tend to focus on the wants and needs of the entire state population and the land. State recreation services typically focus on activities that take place in state forests and state parks. For the most part, there is little specific programming, and more energy is given to providing access to services and opportunities through beaches, marinas, hiking trails, golf courses, campgrounds, and other sites. By doing this, state agencies not only serve residents

Municipal departments offer programs such as sport camps, day camps, and track meets.

but also attract tourists and the economic benefits related to tourism.

Federal Recreation Leisure Services

Similar to the services provided by state agencies, the federal government also tends to focus less on specific programming in favor of providing outdoor resources for numerous activities such as hiking, camping, fishing, education, and interpretive centers. The agencies associated with these opportunities include the USDA Forest Service, the National Park Service, the Bureau of Land Management, U.S. Fish and Wildlife, and the U.S. Army Corp of Engineers.

Canadian Delivery Systems

The issue of the various levels of government jurisdiction over matters of recreation and leisure services has often been a source of debate. As a result, the National Recreation Statement of 1987 jointly signed by the Canadian federal, provincial, and territorial governments laid out the following broad principles to guide the respective responsibilities of the three levels of government:

1. The federal government focuses on national-level programs and programs within the agencies under its jurisdiction (Interprovincial Sport and Recreation Council [ISRC], 1987).

2. The provincial and territorial governments have substantial responsibilities related to recreation such as coordinating programs, providing information and financial resources to program delivery agencies, planning, and supporting research. They are very rarely the direct delivery agents for recreation and leisure services (ISRC, 1987).

3. Municipal governments are the primary suppliers of recreation services because they are close to the recipients and are perceived to be more nimble and able to respond effectively. The basic role of the municipality is to ensure the availability of the broadest range of recreation opportunities for every individual and group consistent with available community resources (ISRC, 1987).

The Canadian Constitution Act (1982) guarantees the following freedoms through the Charter of Rights and Freedoms:

- Freedom of conscience and religion
- Freedom of thought, belief, opinion, and expression, including freedom of the press and other communication media
- Freedom of peaceful assembly
- Freedom of association

Although the Constitution Act does not allocate legislative responsibility for recreation and leisure or state how recreation and leisure services are delivered, it does guarantee the freedoms that are essential elements of leisure. Professionals and the agencies in which they operate must uphold the Charter of Rights and Freedoms.

In keeping with the emphasis on national activities, the federal responsibility for recreation-related matters is governed by the Physical Activity and Sport Act of 2003. This act is under the jurisdiction of two departments. The responsibility for physical activity is allocated to the Minister of Health, and the responsibility for sport is under the Minister of Canadian Heritage (Justice Canada, 2017). That latter assignment is in keeping with that department's mandate for programs that promote "an environment in which all Canadians take advantage of dynamic cultural experiences, celebrating our history and heritage, and participating in building creative communities . . . supporting the arts, our two official languages and our athletes" (Canadian Heritage, n.d.). Several sports programs contribute to Canadian identity through high-performance and international sport. To the Canadian federal government, recreation is a physical activity that enhances health, and international sport solidifies Canada's identity. This focus often seems far removed from the day-to-day responsibilities of recreation professionals.

The various provinces and territories have different views of recreation. All have some type of government unit responsible for recreation, but the labels differ. Over the past half century, provincial governments have committed themselves to assisting recreation and leisure services through various government departments such as education and health and public welfare (McFarland, 1970). The provincial government to establish a department whose sole mandate was recreation was Nova Scotia in 1972. Most provinces carried out similar actions in the 1970s. But just as a province can establish a recreation department, it also can change it. Provincial recreation agencies went through amalgamations and disintegrations with partners that now include departments for community services, health, seniors, sport, tourism, culture, parks, and so on, all in the interest of efficiency, effectiveness, and political expediency. Table 7.1 in the web study guide shows the names of provincial and territorial departments responsible for recreation.

How do government departments carry out their responsibilities? Tim Burton, former University of Alberta professor, created an explanatory model that explains the five roles that governments can take in delivering public services:

1. Direct provider
2. Enabler and coordinator
3. Supporter and patron
4. Arm's-length provider
5. Legislator and regulator (Burton & Glover, 1999)

Many recreation students will be most familiar with the **direct provider** role, which "describes the situation in which a government department or agency develops and maintains leisure facilities, operates programs, and delivers services using public funds and public employees" (Burton & Glover, 1999, p. 373). If you have been a town playground supervisor or a city swimming pool instructor, you have been part of the direct provider role. The municipality that developed the program owned the facility, ran the program, and paid you.

The next three roles involve decreasing amounts of direct involvement by the government. When a government department acts as an **enabler and coordinator**, it identifies "organizations and agencies which produce leisure services for the public and help coordinate their efforts, resources and activities" (Burton & Glover, 1999, p. 374). If you have worked for a local community group that received funds and services, such as leadership training from a recreation department, you have seen a government unit acting as an enabler and

coordinator. When a government department acts as a **supporter and patron**, it "recognizes that existing organizations already produce valuable public leisure services and can be encouraged to do so through specialized support" (Burton & Glover, 1999, p. 374). If your local community festival received a government grant to assist with the production of a special event or to develop a facility, the government acted as a supporter and patron. Furthest away from government's direct influence is the role of **arm's-length provider**, which "requires the creation of a . . . special purpose agency which operates outside the regular apparatus of government" (Burton & Glover, 1999, p. 373). Arts and culture organizations, such as museums or galleries, operate in this relationship. In theory, the government unit does not interfere with the internal operations of these organizations, but theory and practice occasionally conflict when political decision-makers object to an organization's decisions to acquire a controversial piece of art or mount a controversial play using public funds.

The last role of government, **legislator and regulator**, affects many of our actions as providers and consumers of recreation opportunities. This role operates in the background of many parts of our work and leisure lives because we must abide by laws passed by various levels of government. When a government agency requires you to obtain a permit to put on an event or have a fireworks display, it is acting in this role. When you must get a fishing license or be of a certain age to enter a facility that serves alcohol, you are also experiencing these powers of government.

The municipal, provincial and territorial, and federal levels of government do not all engage in each of these five roles to the same degree. Municipal governments have traditionally operated using a direct provider role, but as cities and towns have faced financial stresses, many have shifted to a model in which they have transferred services to community groups while providing financial or in-kind support, thus moving toward an enabler and coordinator or a supporter and patron model. Provincial and federal government departments have historically used the latter two models, arm's-length provider and legislator and regulator. Provincial and federal governments have also created arm's-length

Various delivery systems exist for providing public recreation. This photo shows the direct provider role.

agencies to carry out cultural programs. Many provincial agencies' mandates require that they operate in a legislator and regulator model.

PARTNERSHIPS: CONNECTIONS TO THE COMMUNITY

Forming partnerships, cooperative ventures, and collaborative agreements or alliances has long been practiced by recreation and leisure professionals in the public sector. But today the emphasis on reviewing, revising, and renewing partnering efforts is more critical than ever. No agency or entity can thrive alone. Seeking new, inclusive, innovative, flexible, and commonly focused opportunities is imperative. Why? Because in forming partnerships, recreation and leisure professionals might be able

to reduce the duplication of existing services, save money, and streamline organizations. Inevitably, they will increase the visibility of the organization, gain better networks, and develop more viable resource pools. In addition, personnel will have the opportunity to grow along with the community.

Any governmental unit can form a partnership with another governmental unit, a nonprofit organization, or a private entity. All these organizations can bring useful resources to the table to advance an opportunity, which often produces better results than going it alone. One of the most useful partnerships for a public recreation agency to develop is one with the local school district. A goal for many communities is an indoor pool. This type of facility can be cost prohibitive for most in the public environment. If the school district wanted to upgrade its existing pool but did not have sufficient capital funds and the local parks and recreation agency identified the need for an indoor pool but had limited funds as well, a partnership could be explored. This partnership would allow the parks and recreation agency to use the school's indoor pool in return for the investment of capital dollars, and the school district would get the upgraded pool. In this win–win solution, the community would recognize the benefit of the partnership. These partnerships can work wonders if the parties can produce a win–win outcome.

Most partnerships are intergovernmental agreements that outline the benefits received by the parties involved. Parks and recreation departments work with police and fire departments on safety protocols, camps, and programs such as bicycle or fire safety. Ongoing partnerships with the public works department can address building needs and general maintenance operations.

Local neighborhood groups work with parks departments to provide events, develop facilities, and carry out cleanup programs. These partnerships not only benefit the parks and recreation department but also bring families and friends closer together because they are working toward a common goal. What better way is there to share facilities that are funded by taxpayers?

Every community can provide examples of successful partnerships. Look for examples of the following in your community:

- Programs that strengthen families such as Big Brothers and Big Sisters
- Business relationships, such as public and private partnerships, that develop or operate a facility
- Program development relationships between municipal recreation departments and universities or colleges with available facilities
- Justice departments involved in community crime prevention programs
- Volunteer groups, such as community leagues or neighborhood recreation associations, that are advocates for their communities and deliver programs
- Trails built by governments and citizen groups that link communities

The future of partnerships is bright. As agencies and communities realize the many benefits of working together, more opportunities to develop partnerships will arise.

FACES OF PUBLIC RECREATION

Most people who have chosen a career in public recreation find that they enjoy working with people through providing an essential governmental service. The need to provide recreation programs, facilities, parks, and open space for community enjoyment is a powerful mission that provides direct quality of life benefits. The diversity of activity types, civil servant calling, and the thrill of a variety of work environments leads to a profession that provides self-fulfillment.

Public Recreation Professionals

In the field of public recreation, many career paths include specialized areas of knowledge such as recreation programming, facilities management, parks, outdoor education, therapeutic recreation,

Public recreation departments can cooperate with outside groups to construct playgrounds. As you discover the various aspects of recreation and leisure, community involvement with a variety of interest groups will be one of your most frustrating, and perhaps one of your most rewarding, experiences.

and recreation administration. Professionals within the field of public recreation use a variety of skills obtained from academic study and on-the-job training. The core skills used at any level include

- ability to navigate the political environment;
- effective communication techniques;
- excellent customer service;
- ability to plan and implement programs, events, and activities;
- demonstrated leadership;
- fiscal forecasting and effective budgeting control; and
- conflict resolution.

Because recreation and leisure professionals need to be well-rounded, professional training and preparation are detailed yet practical. Besides taking program development classes, recreation and leisure students take courses in environmental design and planning, leadership, and management.

The opportunity to grow professionally in public recreation is based on a variety of internal and external forces. One topic is diversification in the workplace, which is the ability to develop a wide range of job skills through on-the-job training and advancement. The ability to achieve job satisfaction can be linked to job diversification within an organization. An enhanced skill set will provide value to the organization and professional advancement opportunities for the individual. The variety of jobs within the public recreation realm sets up the opportunity for diversity within the workforce that few other careers can match. Most people still believe that the field of parks and recreation encompasses sport, fun, and games. Although these elements are certainly part of the profession, they do not begin to cover the diverse areas and links to other professions.

Public Recreation Management

Managers and leaders in recreation and leisure services plan, organize, direct, and control various areas of the agency. Managers fall into three categories: top, or executive, managers; middle managers; and frontline, or supervisory, managers. Other positions report to these managers.

Managers must possess three types of skills:

1. Technical skills that require specialized knowledge in operations, techniques, and procedures.
2. Human skills that require understanding people and the ability to motivate and work with employees.
3. Conceptual skills that allow the development and organization of a philosophy, mission, goals, and objectives.

Besides performing organizational and administrative functions within an organization, managers are also involved in strategic planning, which encompasses community involvement and coordination with municipalities and other agencies. Managers need to work with community members to plan the many activities and facilities that are needed. By working with the community, managers help community members buy in to the activities and develop a sense of ownership. Successful collaboration draws on all the skills required of recreation and leisure professionals.

Professionals must ask themselves the following: What do we do as professionals in public recreation? Whom do we serve? Do we serve our career? Do we serve the public? Do we serve the politicians? Whom do the politicians serve? Coming to your own answers to those questions is a major step in your professional career.

American Professional Organizations and Certifications

As in almost any career, professional organizations provide invaluable resources for professionals. Among other benefits, professional organization membership serves public recreation providers by giving them networking opportunities, information on the latest trends and issues in the profession, education on new products and services, and, in some cases, extra services such as access to liability insurance. In the United States, the largest professional organization in the field is the National Recreation and Park Association. In addition, there are a multitude of other state and local organizations that also serve public recreation professionals.

One means of ensuring quality services is through certification of employees and agencies. These certifications demonstrate that the individuals holding them either meet or exceed a specific defined standard. Although certification might not be required for many positions or organizations, it does demonstrate that these employees have met the standards chosen by professionals in the field that are necessary for quality services. In some cases, such as in therapeutic recreation, certification might be required to practice. As you are looking at careers, be sure you are aware of potential certification requirements to ensure that you meet all qualifications for employment.

The following are among the possible certifications for leisure professionals; these are offered through the National Recreation and Park Association:

- **Certified park and recreation professional (CPRP)** certification is granted to people employed in the recreation, park resources, and leisure services profession who meet high standards of performance.

- **Aquatic facility operator (AFO)** is a state-of-the-art certification for pool operators and aquatic facility managers.

- **Certified playground safety inspector (CPSI)** provides the credentials to inspect playgrounds for safety and ensure that each playground meets the current national standards set by the American Society for Testing and Materials (ASTM) and the U.S. Consumer Product Safety Commission (CPSC).

To earn certification, you must demonstrate through examination that you have the basic knowledge and understanding specific to the topic. Once certification is achieved, you can improve your potential for professional advancement through your commitment to the profession and continuing education.

Canadian Professional Organizations

Many recreation and leisure service professionals work within the framework of public and governmental jurisdictions. Just as these professionals have established or worked in organizations to deliver services, they have also joined associations to promote the cause of recreation and leisure services. From the roots of the Ontario Parks Association grew the Parks and Recreation Association of Canada (PRAC) in 1945. PRAC's mandate was "the Dominion-wide stimulation of recreation, [and] the Dominion-wide extension of parks including municipal, provincial and national parks and recreation activities" (Parks and Recreation Association of Canada, 1947). As the organization adapted to changes in the environment in the 1960s, it changed its name first to the Canadian Parks/Recreation Association (CP/RA) in 1969 and later refined it to the Canadian Parks and Recreation Association (CPRA). CPRA promotes itself as "the national voice for a vibrant grassroots network with partnerships that connect people who build healthy, active communities and impact the everyday lives of Canadians" (Canadian Parks and Recreation Association, 2017). Today CPRA provides services through its partnership with provincial or territorial organizations, each of which is autonomous and offers services in keeping with its local requirements. It has also developed partnerships with organizations such as the Canadian Playground Safety Institute (CPSI) and Canadian Sport for Life (CS4L), and it offers the CPRA Professional Development Certification. Other key players and allies in the municipal and recreation arena are the Federation of Canadian Municipalities (FCM), the Canadian Council on Social Development (CCSD), the Canadian Parks Council (CPC), and the Canadian Recreation Facilities Council (CRFD). Table 7.2 in the web study guide lists the national, provincial, and territorial associations.

OUTSTANDING GRADUATE

Background Information

Name: Rachel Bedingfield

Education: BRM (Bachelor of Recreation Management) from Acadia University

Awards: Canadian Association for the Advancement of Women in Sport and Physical Activity 2015 list of Most Influential Women in Canada

Affiliations: Common Wealth Games Canada member, 2004-2016; Recreation Nova Scotia board member (vice president of monitoring), 2012-present; Women Active Nova Scotia board chair, 2016-present

Career Information

Position: Director of Parks and Recreation

Organization: Town of Kentville, Nova Scotia, department of parks and recreation. Kentville is a municipal unit that serves a tax base of $6,500 and a user base of 22,000.

Organization mission: Kentville Parks and Recreation's vision is a healthy, vibrant, integrated, and complete community where citizens can live, work, and play in an environment that supports a high quality of life. Kentville Parks and Recreation fosters a creative, progressive, and inclusive community where everyone belongs and everybody gets to play. We believe that recreation is the experience that results from freely chosen participation in physical, social, intellectual, creative, and spiritual pursuits that enhance individual and community well-being.

Job description: As the director of parks and recreation for the town of Kentville, I am responsible for ensuring that the vision of our department and of the town of Kentville is upheld, the standard of service is maintained, tax dollars are spent responsibly, and all members of our community, regardless of who they are, are able to access the many benefits of recreation. I manage anywhere from 10 to 40 staff daily, depending on the time of year. I report directly to the CAO as well as an advisory committee made up of elected officials and community members. I work to ensure that recreation remains relevant to all citizens of our community and that recreation is used as a way to build our community. As a recreation professional, I also ensure that we are aligning with the provincial shared recreation strategy as well as the National Recreation Framework. On this note, my main focus areas include providing opportunities to engage in active recreation; creating policies that focus on inclusion and access; connecting people with nature and building leadership capacity in this area; building, creating, and maintaining supportive environments; and building recreation capacity by focusing on leisure education principles.

> **"** If you want to make a real difference in the day-to-day lives of folks, working in municipal recreation is definitely the way to go! **"**

Career path: I started my career working in Europe and East Africa in international development. I then worked for Recreation Nova Scotia as the inclusion specialist. I next worked for the Halifax Regional School Board as the sport animator. I then worked for the province of Nova Scotia as the regional physical activity consultant. Finally, I began work as the recreation director for the town of Kentville. I never intended to be a municipal recreation director, but I am challenged daily by this position and can certainly see myself staying here for a very long time.

Likes and dislikes about the job: The things I like most about my job are the ability I have to have a positive impact on my community, and that every day is different. In our department we tackle everything from bike lanes to youth homelessness to facility development to community engagement and diversity training. My role is to also keep a pulse on the community, including their needs and wants. We work hard to build community empathy and provide opportunity for folks to look after one another.

There is not much I don't like about my job, but at times it requires long hours, and hard decisions have to be made. Despite all that, I have never held a position where I have felt more solution oriented, nor have I ever felt more in control of being able to respond to identified needs—it's very empowering.

Advice for Undergraduates

My advice would be to simply keep trying new things. Discovering what you don't like is just as important as discovering what you do like. I graduated with the intent of becoming an inclusion specialist for people with a disability, and immediately I was taken off this track because I jumped at the opportunities that were in front of me—and I have never looked back. Be prepared to work hard, and learn to reflect on yourself as both a professional and as an individual. I have been in the field now for almost 20 years and I am still very much learning from my peers, my colleagues, my community, and myself.

Being a recreation professional is one of the most rewarding and exhausting (not only exhausting physically, but also emotionally) things you will ever do. The longer I am in this field, the more powerful a tool I realize recreation is to have. And the more vulnerable I make myself emotionally, the better the results I get with regard to community development. Do not be afraid to take risks and fail. In fact, failing publicly—though scary—is a great way to endear yourself to others.

CHAMELEON PROFESSION: EVER-CHANGING SOCIETAL ISSUES AND NEEDS

Being a chameleon is often viewed in a negative sense, perhaps as selling out to external influences, but in the case of the public recreation profession, it is positive. We must be adaptable. We must respond to changes in physical, economic, political, or social parts of the environment. But we must not lose sight of our founding roots, our reasons for being, and our desire to contribute to the public good. What is the future of public-sector recreation and leisure? To discover where we are headed, we must understand the current reality.

Demographic Trends

Recent labor, leisure, and longevity trends affect how much unobligated time people have and how they use it. These trends in turn affect recreation and leisure services and professionals who provide them. Our aging, retired population is growing, and people aged 50 years and older have more free time today than they did in previous eras.

As leisure patterns in North America continue to change, one of the best predictors of change is our aging citizens, who are more active than ever before. In addition, urban areas are becoming more diverse. More people are pursuing higher levels of formal education, and women are taking on increasingly diverse roles. The gap between the haves and the have-nots is widening. Citizens expect the government to do more, but they want to pay less. People are obsessed with health, but citizens of the United States and Canada are now more obese than ever, especially the younger age groups. All this means that recreation and leisure service professionals must deal with a wide set of issues when creating programs, making plans, and obtaining resources and funding.

Trends in Canadian Public Recreation

Statistics Canada's 2011 census yields the following insights into the current population and the trends that affect employees of Canadian recreation agencies and the people whom they serve:

Age-related demographics

- The number of seniors (those aged 65 and older) increased 20 percent between 2011 and 2017 to 5.9 million. This rate of growth was higher than that of children aged 14 and younger (4.15 percent) and the overall population (5 percent).

- Seniors accounted for a record high of 16.9 percent of the population in Canada in 2016, up from 14.1 percent five years earlier.

- In 2016, the working-age population (those aged 15 to 64) represented 66.5 percent of the Canadian population, down from 68.5 percent in 2011.

- In 2016, the proportion of seniors was the highest in the Atlantic provinces (Newfoundland and Labrador, Prince Edward Island, Nova Scotia, and New Brunswick), Quebec, and British Columbia.

- In 2016, the proportion of children was highest in the Prairie provinces (Manitoba, Saskatchewan, and Alberta) and the territories (Northwest Territories and Nunavut) (Statistics Canada, 2017, May 3).

Immigration

- One out of five people in Canada's population is foreign born.

- Among the G8 countries, Canada had the highest percentage of foreign-born people (20.6 percent), which was well above the shares in Germany (13 percent in 2010) and the United States (12.9 percent in 2010) (Statistics Canada, 2013b).

- More recent projections indicate that immigration is the main source of population growth in Canada (Statistics Canada, 2017, February 8, p. 3).

Aboriginal people

- In 2011, the aboriginal population (First Nations, Métis, Inuit) in Canada reached 1,400,685—a growth of 20.1 percent since 2006.

- This growth rate is nearly four times greater than the 5.2 percent increase for the nonaboriginal population (Statistics Canada, 2013a).

- There were 392,105 aboriginal children aged 14 and younger in Canada in 2011. These children represented 28 percent of the total aboriginal population and 7 percent of all children in Canada.

- There were more than 254,515 aboriginal youth aged 15 to 24 in Canada in 2011. These youth represented 18.2 percent of the total aboriginal population and 5.9 percent of all the youth in Canada (Statistics Canada, 2013a).

- Fifty-six percent of the aboriginal population lives in urban areas such as Winnipeg, Edmonton, Vancouver, Toronto, Calgary, Saskatoon, and Regina (Indigenous and Northern Affairs Canada, 2016).

Age-related demographics are affecting the recreation service delivery needed to provide opportunities that are innovative and stimulating to all age groups while not stereotyping seniors as a monolithic age group. At the same time as this is an opportunity, the reality is that there is a substantial challenge in many geographic areas as the proportion of the population in their working years declines often due to outmigration to growth centers in other parts of the country and abroad. This has an impact on local and provincial tax bases that support recreation services.

Despite the efforts of many communities to provide recreation services to new immigrants, the diverse mosaic of traditions, needs, interests, and expectations causes challenges. There are many barriers to participation such as high fees and related costs, insufficient funding, difficulties in finding information, and linguistic and cultural barriers (Social Planning Toronto, 2016). There are numerous examples of diverse recreation programs in cities with a substantial multicultural makeup. One example is the Sunset Community Centre in Vancouver, which serves over 36,000 residents with first languages including Panjabi, Chinese, Tagalog, Hindi, Vietnamese, and English (Vancouver, n.d.). The Centre has a vision of being "a healthy community where diverse cultures thrive, everyone belongs, and feels welcome to play, create and succeed in their own way" (Sunset Community Association, 2016, p. 8).

In much of Canada, the life experiences of the aboriginal population are major social and political issues, and agencies and governments struggle to address the issues of a growing, young aboriginal population on reserves and in urban areas. As noted earlier, the aboriginal population is growing faster than the nonaboriginal population. Aboriginal youth are not well served by the traditional urban recreation delivery systems, and new initiatives are being developed, such as the Winnipeg Broadway Community Centre's programs, that serve a large aboriginal population (Broadway Neighbourhood Centre, n.d.). Work must continue not only in delivering services on and off reserves but in training aboriginal leaders and getting them into the recreation profession.

Trends in U.S. Public Recreation

The pace of change in today's world is accelerating, and leisure patterns and recreation needs will continue to change as well. If the public sector does not embrace the changes within recreation, nonprofits and the private sector will become the dominant providers. In some markets, such as fitness, they already are.

The biggest trends facing leisure services in the United States today center on a changing population. The challenge within the profession is to develop new programs that can meet these needs. Much work needs to be done not only in program development but also in operations and facilities to prepare for these challenges. To date, public recreation agencies have identified the need to adjust core thinking, but little real headway has been made.

Public sector agencies need to address the following critical trends in the 21st century:

- The general population is becoming more culturally and racially diverse.

- The population is mobile, and there is substantial internal and economic migration in response to national and global economic fluctuations.

- Seniors are becoming a significant group that needs innovative programming ideas that can provide rewarding leisure experiences.

- Young adults are seeking new ways to recreate.

- Health concerns due to the obesity epidemic continue to make headlines while the population becomes more sedentary.
- Children's programs are geared for active recreation activities to keep them fit.
- Nature-deficit disorder and the need to reconnect with nature are increasingly recognized as issues.
- The discussion about safety versus overprotection and the perception of "bubble-wrapping" children continues.
- Agencies need to embrace private-sector product models and respond quicker to market changes.
- Governments need to invest in replacing deteriorating parks and recreation infrastructure.
- Strategies need to be developed to combat shrinking budgets relative to increasing costs.
- Parks and recreation can become an economic engine through wise investment in increasing tourism and providing a higher quality of life.

Parks and recreation professionals in the United States and Canada need to understand these new demographics. The traditional ways of providing park and leisure services need to change to match the ever-changing public.

Tomorrow's Leadership Skills

The changing profession and the trends facing public recreation require new leadership skills to lead public recreation into the future. What does the new breed of professionals entering the public sector look like? Can they make a difference? New leaders need to innovate as the pioneers of parks and recreation did a century ago. Now is the time for strong leadership to act. Public recreation has grown steadily because advances in technology have given people more free time. The real quest is to use ongoing research to define what public recreation will become. Making tough decisions will be easier when research is used to validate the direction on a given topic.

The ability to grow leisure services offerings by understanding the needs of the population has led many public agencies to find untapped markets. Capital construction costs are generally lower during times of recession and projects are delivered under budget and ahead of schedule. All this is made possible by the valor to act. Now more than ever is the time to build on our ability to deliver quality of life by practicing what we do best.

The Changing Profession

While there is no guarantee of what the future might hold, the future of public leisure and recreation seems to lead to a greater interest in the environment. People now seem to be more interested in the quality of the experience and a sense of place. More diversity of leisure expression is likely to occur because the population is becoming more diverse.

The types of programs needed to meet the demands of the public are becoming more diverse based on several factors. The standard focus on youth and athletics programs is still popular, but senior, adult-only, family, and fitness-based recreation are becoming requested more often. New ideas need to be created to address these growing interests. Communities are becoming more polarized, and recreation services that fall in the middle of the general population are less able to meet all needs.

Because state and federal funding of recreation and leisure services are declining, these services will be more locally focused. Citizens want local assistance in enhancing their quality of life. Providing parks and recreation services for all ages and diverse populations is critical. For example, citizens want the local parks and recreation agency to provide parks, various programs, and facilities. Therefore, recreation agencies need to be flexible and innovative in their work efforts including staff assignments, decision-making, training programs, and the knowledge, skills, and abilities needed to do the job.

Finally, outsourcing may become the norm instead of the exception. Recreation and leisure service agencies may become more enterprising than they have been in the past. The customization of leisure programs in which people are treated appropriately, not equally, will be necessary to retain community consumers. For instance, additional strategic planning will be necessary to place appropriate, applicable facilities and programs in a community based on numbers and needs. This means that the squeaky wheel may not get the

Community Schools

Introduction to and instruction in recreation activities have long been considered essential elements of a well-rounded K-12 curriculum. Recreation activities have been vital not only to nurturing strength, flexibility, and self-esteem in young people but also to furthering educational achievement. **Community education** responds to a need to provide young people with constructive activities. Through participation in community education, such as in after-school and evening classes and activities and programs at schools, students can further enhance their strength, flexibility, self-esteem, and academic performance.

The following six components make up the philosophy of community education. Each component is vital to an effective, comprehensive community school.

1. **Community involvement.** Building a feeling of inclusion among community members by providing encouragement and opportunities for involvement and leadership in the development of community school activities
2. **Facility use.** Making use of existing school facilities that are owned by the taxpayers
3. **Adult programming.** Organizing and implementing classes and activities that are requested and designed by adults in the community and that appeal to their needs
4. **Youth programming.** Organizing and implementing classes and activities that are requested and designed by young people in the community and that appeal to their needs
5. **Classroom enrichment through community resources.** Augmenting and enriching classroom curriculum and lessons by requesting the expertise and passion of knowledgeable speakers who live in the community and scheduling hands-on learning opportunities during the school day through field trips to community sites
6. **Coordination and cooperation in the delivery of community services.** Bringing people to the table who are involved in similar pursuits to benefit the entire community, thus avoiding duplication of effort and resolving issues

The community education concept was originally grounded in involvement and participation, and this has been the hallmark of its extended success. The practice of community education invited a new, collaborative spirit to the old model of program development. It promoted a process in which people could become involved rather than simply attending an event. This application in the development of community school services offered a seat at the table for all members of the community including adults, youth, senior citizens, people with disabilities, males, females, and citizens of all cultural backgrounds and faiths.

Current Conditions of Community Education

Over the years, community education has continued to provide programs and activities that are driven by expressed community needs and has involved community members in meaningful leadership roles that enrich community living. Community school advisory councils and advisory boards have become important components of successful community schools that provide the foundation, voice, and representation for community members and community organizations (individuals, schools, businesses, and public and private organizations) to become partners in addressing community needs.

Community education advisory councils and boards became incubators for site-based leadership, a model used across the country in school reform efforts. And the influence did not end there. Community participation in education issues and school reform has been embraced by school districts from shore to shore and has become part of the institutional culture of those organizations. In the United States, the influence of education reform has been seen in federally funded programs such as Immigration Goals 2000, Education 2000 (see www.ed.gov/G2K/index.html), 21st Century Community Learning Centers, and the No Child Left Behind Act, all of which highlight activities that enhance academic achievement, literacy, and the unique needs of urban and rural communities.

The original community education model was founded on components that provide for the delivery of quality programs, activities, and services; the development of leadership; the shared use of school and community facilities; the integration of resources into the K-12 classroom curriculum; and

(continued)

Community Schools *(continued)*

the conversations necessary to achieve collaborative and inclusive relationships, all of which are driven by the desire to respond to identified needs. When all these components are given equal voice in a community school, the result is a balanced program that invites participation and welcomes diverse activities that meet the comprehensive needs of the community. When attention is cast on just one or two of these elements, a threat to the full capacity of the model arises.

Careers in Community Education

The following skills are needed for professional entry-level positions in community schools: volunteer management; publicity, promotion, and marketing; programming; funding and resource development; demonstrated leadership ability; group-process skills; customer service skills; positive attitude; sense of humor; and ability to build, maintain, and deepen relationships with community members, businesses, and organizations.

The following are some of the types of community education positions available: community college continuing education coordinator or director, community school coordinator or director, community education agent, school business partnership director, service learning coordinator, volunteer manager, facilities scheduling manager, community resources center manager or director, and community school or community learning center grant manager.

grease. In the past, different areas of a community were often treated as though their needs were all the same. This effort created more amenities but was not necessarily a strategic approach that addressed real needs.

As the members of diverse communities request more and different services, recreation and leisure professionals need to address emerging trends and issues to meet the ever-changing needs and expectations of their clientele. As services continue to evolve, parks and recreation professionals will create the future.

The Changing Professional

The profession of public recreation is at a crossroads. As with all careers, the growth of the profession is fueled by economics. Unfortunately, many public recreation agencies have had a hard time keeping budgets in pace with the demand for recreation services in times of recession or low economic growth. The amount of professional skill needed for those within the field is different from in years past. The baseline standard of education within the field is moving past a bachelor's degree into a master's degree. The public is also more sophisticated and is armed with knowledge obtained from the Internet.

The new frontier in public recreation is building an organization that can be adaptable in a changing landscape. This is a contradiction in the public recreation realm. Governments are historically slow to react and are set in a traditional hierarchical operational model. The future professional can monitor the public in ways not thought of in the past and can communicate quickly using new technology applications such as social media. Research will allow professionals to understand the will of the public and produce better decisions. Public recreation professionals need to invest in continuing education to keep skills sharp and learn about new tools that will allow then to work smarter. Organizations such as the Leisure Information Network (LIN) that collect and disseminate research knowledge are essential to the profession. All agencies are being asked to do more with fewer resources. Professionals in the field today face several major issues:

- How to secure financing for major capital initiatives including parks, facilities, and open spaces
- How to set spending priorities with shrinking budgets
- How to make parks safe while maintaining visitor enjoyment

- How public parks and recreation can strengthen its political position by shaping community quality of life

Parks and recreation professionals will need to understand finances and budget better than they did in years past. The ability to execute two critical activities, leading and managing, will be important. The distinction is that management is doing things right, whereas leadership is doing the right things. The ability to provide strong leadership for the organization will be a necessary trait for professional success.

POLITICAL REALITIES: NO PAIN, NO GAIN

To many novices in recreation, the words *politics* and *politicians* are incredibly negative. Why? The reality of public recreation is that the ultimate decision-makers are often elected officials, and it is us who elects them. In the abstract, the challenge and the role of public recreation are to serve all of us. But does this really happen? And who is *us*? Is it realistic to believe that the public recreation system can serve all? Who takes up the challenge to try to serve all? Can they succeed? Is recreation really a public good?

Public recreation is about creating a sense of inclusion. Are you prepared to listen to and assist everyone in your community? You should be. How will you deal with competing interests? Think about a small community park. How many groups with competing interests can you imagine want to use that park? How about young soccer players and their parents, older aggressive soccer players, baseball players of all ages, parents of small children, dog walkers, neighbors who want peace and quiet, neighbors who want a pretty park to enhance their property values, kids who want a place to splash in the hot summer, teenagers who want a place to hang out, musicians who want a place to jam, skateboarders who want a place to practice stunts, pacifists who want a place to protest against a war, a theater group that wants a place to perform, a religious group that wants to perform a religious play, a new immigrant group who wants to commemorate their culture's heritage, a group of indigenous people who want to celebrate a sacred ritual, or homeless people who want a place to hunker down at night?

Balance will always be needed between the requests of communities and the other desires or actions that political powers believe need attention. Somewhere in the middle of the issue are the parks and recreation staff members who will try to resolve the situation or create a win–win scenario. This is what we do.

Leaders in the recreation profession need to realize that political responsiveness becomes more difficult and complex as the size and diversity of the population grow. Problems of political responsiveness are most likely found in one of two types of settings. The first and most widely recognized is the scenario in which a new group either moves into a community or rapidly increases its percentage of community members. One example of this is the growth of youth soccer and parents' desire for more fields and amenities. Difficulties are frequently encountered in accommodating the views and attitudes of the new group in policy-making processes. The second setting is one in which the community experiences rapid population growth that outpaces the ability to provide resources and facilities. This setting further identifies the city with the haves and the have-nots.

What role can interest groups play in obtaining recreation services? Interest groups can be powerful, vocal advocates for recreation services, or they can be adversaries. They can publicly address issues that a recreation staff member cannot. They can provide a public face for those who need services. They can provide the political face for the agency. Recreation professionals must decide how they will work with interest groups. That brings us right back to the question of whom do we serve?

The public recreation profession in the United States began with the advocacy work of Joseph Lee, the father of the playground movement. In the late 1800s, he helped create the first model playground in a dejected Boston neighborhood. Lee was convinced that all young people needed a place to play. He promoted a bill in the Massachusetts state legislature that required towns and cities with populations of more than 10,000 to develop playgrounds. Joseph Lee's actions set the stage for future actions by other state and local governments. This example illustrates how powerful a citizen with a cause can be and the difference a committed person can make.

When we think about developing the work that we do, we must begin with our community members. We work with many members of diverse communities to help them experience, in some form or fashion, a better quality of life. That is why we provide services, activities, and events. That is why we build facilities. That is the very reason that we exist as a profession.

BENEFITS OF RECREATION

Since the foundation work of Joseph Lee in the United States and the National Council of Women in Canada more than a century ago, we have intuitively known that recreation benefits people and their communities. But we must go beyond intuition to research. The Benefits Project collected past research about how parks and recreation helps people, their communities, and the environment. The product of this collection is the online National Benefits Hub (http://benefitshub.ca), which moves the exercise from collecting research studies to packaging them into a form that can be used in the political arena. The National Benefits Hub presents benefits in four main categories and eight subcategories: personal (health, human development, individual quality of life), social (community quality of life, antisocial behavior, families and communities), economic (prevention, economic impact), and environmental benefits of recreation.

The Benefits Project was created to address a substantial political issue: the perception, more real than imagined, that recreation services, although important to our communities, are not considered essential by decision-makers. This is our biggest challenge as we strive to contribute to the public good.

Strong public recreation delivery systems that provide the core benefits of recreation are crucial to helping people lead healthier lives and to protecting natural resources and quality of life in the communities in which we live. As parks and recreation professionals, we must educate the public about why we provide one of the most cost effective and essential quality of life services around. Research is continuing to advance in this area. As noted earlier, the technology available to us is continuing to influ-

ence many facets of our lives. The natural human desire to play outside is still evident even though technology has changed the way we think about recreation. Public recreation allows us to reconnect with the outdoors. In 2007, the Outdoor Recreation Research and Education strategic plan conducted by the USDA Forest Service noted that outdoor recreation has increased in the United States. The opportunities to experience nature are becoming more valued in the 21st century.

Three core components should be noted and continually explored through research and practical practice:

1. Public recreation should provide access to recreation for all.

2. Public recreation should provide opportunities to live a healthy lifestyle through physical activity. Parks and recreation agencies have the parks and facilities to support physical activity.

3. Public recreation is essential to lifelong learning through the inherent nature of its diverse programs.

SUMMARY

Most parks, open spaces, facilities, and recreation activities that people can participate in are from the public sector. Several powerful trends are affecting public recreation. New leadership is needed to meet the future needs of the public. Special interest groups are more vocal than ever and are seeking partnerships that can advance leisure services. The political realm is not to be understated. The challenge in seeking adequate funding in tight budget cycles and severe economic downturns is causing stress in the public recreation system.

Public recreation provides an exhilarating opportunity for public service and offers challenges, benefits, and opportunities to make a difference. The profession can touch many segments of the community and provide quality moments of career satisfaction. Finally, the opportunity to become a pioneer within the industry by trailblazing new frontiers is certainly available. The countless opportunities available to make a difference mean that today is a wonderful time to be in the field of public recreation.

Inclusive Recreation

Terry Long

The importance of inclusive public recreation is a relatively new idea within society; institutionalization was the norm well in to the 1980s. The latter part of the 20th century brought the American civil rights movement, which challenged norms of institutionalization and segregation, but the rights of people with disabilities were the last to be addressed in the battle for equality. Early disability rights legislation included the Rehabilitation Act of 1973 and the Education for all Handicapped Children Act of 1975, but these initial efforts fell short of addressing the concept of **inclusion** or inclusive recreation. The Americans with Disabilities Act (ADA, 1990) was the first meaningful legislation in the United States that guaranteed the right to accessible and inclusive public recreation.

When ADA became law, the immediate focus fell mostly on physical accessibility of built environments. Municipal parks and recreation agencies scrambled to determine the financial impact of updating facilities to meet ADA code. Despite the worry, public parks and recreation agencies were able to withstand the financial impact of the ADA mandates regarding built spaces. Older public facilities were grandfathered in, and most changes came with new construction or remodels. Codes specific to recreation facilities took over a decade to be developed and were gradually implemented. As a result, it was well in to the 21st century before communities began to evolve into navigable environments for people with disabilities. Still, ADA was pivotal in the development of physically accessible recreation facilities and spaces.

The greater challenge for public parks and recreation came with ensuring that the programs delivered within the facilities were accessible. It was no longer acceptable to deny participation to a person with a disability simply because it was an inconvenience. The ADA required public recreation agencies in the United States to provide access to all government programs. Furthermore, the law states that participation should occur in the most integrated setting possible. In essence, ADA mandated that people with disabilities be given the opportunity to participate in the same recreation programs as the general public. As a result, every public recreation facility in the United States has the responsibility of providing inclusive recreation services to all citizens, regardless of disability. As one might expect, there are limitations to the law. The following section will clarify some key terminology and elaborate on the details of what it means to provide inclusive public recreation programs.

BUILDING BLOCKS OF INCLUSION

There are three important concepts that are interrelated but uniquely important to the delivery of inclusive recreation and leisure services: access, accommodation, and adaptation. These do not ensure inclusion, but they are necessary elements of inclusive recreation.

Access

Accessibility is a building block for the provision of inclusive recreation opportunities, and it is relevant to facilities and programs. Accessible facilities allow a person to physically navigate and engage with the environment and all its elements. In the early days of the ADA, it was common to hear people explain the requirements regarding accessibility by saying "if you turned the facility upside down, everything that doesn't fall off has to be accessible." This is an inaccurate statement when it comes to true accessibility. Accessible parking, entryways, bathrooms, and signage are all important, but so are moveable objects such as furniture and fitness equipment and written materials such as brochures. In addition, a facility can be built to be accessible, but simple mistakes such as placing a heavy step stool in front of an accessible water fountain can quickly compromise access. Another common mistake is blocking accessible routes with boxes or other items, which makes it impossible to navigate a wheelchair through the area. Professionals must understand what makes a facility accessible so they do not inadvertently compromise accessibility. Of course, an accessible facility is of little use if the programs taking place inside the facility are inaccessible. The fundamental principle regarding program access is that individuals cannot be turned away simply because they have a disability. Furthermore, specialized (segregated) programming is not an automatically acceptable alternative. Every effort should be made to ensure that programs and services are provided in the most integrated setting possible.

Accommodation

Program access is often best achieved through appropriate **accommodation**, which is the removal of barriers that otherwise might prevent participation. For example, a deaf participant should be provided an interpreter during the recreation programs that he or she takes part in; a child with autism might be accompanied by a buddy during certain activities to facilitate social interactions and behaviors; or a participant is allowed to use crutches or a wheelchair on the field during a youth softball game. The ADA requires that "reasonable" accommodations be provided to patrons of public recreation programs. Typically, accommodation requests are granted, but the following are several circumstances in which accommodations might be denied:

- The accommodation changes the inherent nature of the activity.
- The accommodation presents a safety risk to participants or others.
- The accommodation presents an undue financial hardship.
- The accommodation presents an undue administrative hardship.

Each limitation should be considered closely before declining a requested accommodation, but there are times when an accommodation might not be appropriate. For example, a tackle football league is not required to remove tackling to accommodate an individual who is at high risk of injury from being tackled. This would change the inherent nature of the game. Agencies do, however, have the option of providing accommodations beyond what the law requires. For example, some agencies choose to manage participant medications or provide diapering services during programs, both of which are beyond what public parks and recreation agencies are typically required to provide. In addition, it should be noted that any services provided to the public should also be provided to people with disabilities. For example, if administration of medication or transportation are services provided to all program participants, then the agency must provide equivalent services to a person with a disability. Failure to do so constitutes discrimination and is a violation of ADA.

Adaptation

Adaptation is similar to accommodations, but is typically tied to a specific activity. For example, providing an interpreter is an accommodation, but it does not change the way that the recreational activity is performed. Adaptations usually target an element of an activity that is problematic for the participant. Using a lighter ball to play catch, using a shorter golf club to hit a golf ball from a chair, or making a no strikeout rule during a Wiffle ball game are all examples of adaptations. Adaptations can involve the rules of the game, the equipment used, the surrounding environment, or any other factor that affects the nature of the game.

Adaptations can be counterproductive if they are not actually necessary and if they change the inherent nature of the activity beyond what is acceptable to participants. For example, it is inappropriate to alter the difficulty of a softball game by using a tee for batting if participants are perfectly capable of hitting a ball out of the air. Likewise, moving a water polo game to the shallow end would significantly change the skill set required when playing, which would be concerning to participants in a competitive polo league. Adaptations only should be made to the extent that they are necessary, and they should not compromise the experience of other participants.

DEFINING INCLUSION

On the surface, inclusion is often seen as occurring when persons with and without disabilities participate in an activity together. The ADA's mandate that programs must be provided in the most integrated setting possible affirms this perspective. Most public recreation agencies differentiate inclusive and specialized programs based on the extent to which this integration occurs. This distinction is by no means bad, but it has limitations as too much focus is often placed on physical presence rather than the lived experience of participants. Being present does not ensure true inclusion.

Successful delivery of genuinely inclusive recreation programs requires that the following considerations be kept in mind at all times. First, true inclusion involves genuine relationships that are mutually beneficial. This synergistic relationship between participants is sometimes referred to as **social inclusion**. Simply putting people into a room together will not naturally lead to positive interactions, especially if some members tend to stigmatize others based on disability.

Second, inclusion involves a mutually respectful relationship with the surrounding culture. Hironaka-Juteau and Crawford (2010) describe inclusion as a "cultural characteristic whereby that culture is characterized by attitudes and behaviors that are open and accepting of all people" (p. 4). This cultural inclusion can expand beyond the participants as an activity or event develops a place of status within society. For example, quad rugby has gained a substantial fan following in recent years following the release of the *Murderball* documentary. Musical group the Blind Boys of Alabama started singing in the school chorus at the Alabama Institute for the Negro Blind in 1939; now other world-famous musicians seek to collaborate with this Grammy-winning group that is an inherent part of the music culture that is respected by their peers. Thus, inclusion is beyond a simple distinction between participating together (inclusion) or separately (segregated). As these examples illustrate, even programs that involve primarily participants with disabilities can be part of a broader inclusive culture as others accept the participants and their activity as legitimate and either peripherally or directly engage in associated activities.

SPECIALIZED PROGRAMS

Facilities can be accessible and accommodations can be provided, but the experiences might still occur in segregated environments. As previously noted, specialized programs can exist in the context of a broader inclusive environment. In some cases, segregated activities will be ideal when they are specialized to meet the participant's needs. In fact, specialized programs are very common and are allowed under the ADA when they are preferred by the participant or when accommodations are beyond reasonable limits; however, best practice is to strive for inclusion whenever possible.

It has been noted that the best way to provide recreation services to people with disabilities is through a continuum of opportunities ranging from most restrictive to least restrictive (Stanton, Markham-Starr, & Hodgkinson, 2013). The level of support needed, as well as the appropriateness and desirability of an inclusive program, will vary based on the circumstances of the participant. Ultimately, we want to provide an experience that is as typical as possible without compromising participants' welfare. Knowing this, sometimes specialized programs are necessary or preferred by the participant. Keep in mind that even when participation is specialized, the surrounding culture can be socially inclusive. Competitive sport for people with disabilities is an example. Although athletes may compete in specialized divisions (e.g., wheelchair vs. traditional basketball), the environment surrounding the sport can be socially and culturally inclusive. Athletes and fans respect the accomplishments of athletes in the same manner regardless of what division they compete in. The same can be said for arts programs. Dance, theater, art, and music can all be performed or exhibited within a culture of inclusion. The following sections highlight some of the specialized programs that serve particular groups of participants.

Disability and Adapted Sport

Formal sports programs for people with disabilities exist in a variety of forms, but there are two important perspectives to consider. First, **disability sports** programs are designed specifically for people with disabilities. There is a continuum of participation levels from introductory skills to elite competition that allows an athlete to develop his or her ability (Davis, 2010). Various sport clubs and associations exist for athletes, providing them with opportunities to compete against others with similar competition classifications. An athlete's classification can be based on disability and skill level, depending on the sport. Athletes competing in disability sport at the highest level take part in the Paralympics, which will be discussed later.

In contrast, **adapted sports** programs are more likely to be associated with interscholastic opportunities for participation (Davis, 2010). These programs are analogous to traditional interscholastic competitions and may involve similar rewards such as earning a letter or winning a state championship. Community-based programs in adapted sport also exist through public parks and recreation agencies or nonprofit organizations like the YMCA, which offer developmental or competitive leagues to local residents. Rule adaptations are more likely to occur in adapted sport; this allows the organizers to adjust the level of challenge and competition to meet the abilities of the participants. In disability sports programs it is less likely that formal regulations will be modified, particularly at higher levels of competition.

Special Olympics

Special Olympics provides opportunities for people with intellectual disabilities and autism to participate in sport and fitness activities. The first Special Olympics event was held in Chicago at Soldier Field in 1968 through the collaborative efforts of the Chicago Park District and the Joseph P. Kennedy Jr. Foundation. Today, Special Olympics is an international organization and event that includes more than 4.5 million athletes worldwide.

Participants must be 8 years of age or older to participate, but there is a Junior Special Olympics program for kids ages 2 to 7. Competitors in individual sports play in divisions based on age, gender, and ability level. Traditional sports include track and field, team sports such as basketball and volleyball, swimming, and some wheelchair events.

In addition, Special Olympics has developed the Motor Activity Training Program (MATP), which is a basic skill-development program for individuals whose skills do not allow them to compete in traditional Special Olympics programs. MATP focuses on developing sport-specific skills for individuals with severe or profound intellectual disabilities or significant physical disabilities. Coaches work with athletes to master skills associated with traditional Special Olympics competition. Areas of training include mobility, dexterity, striking, kicking, manual wheelchair, electric wheelchair, and swimming. This expansion of programming offered by Special Olympics is another example of the spectrum of specialized to inclusive recreation.

Special Olympics also offers the Unified Sports program. This program allows teammates with and without intellectual disabilities to compete together against other similar teams. It is the most inclusive of all the Special Olympics programs. Unified Sports has grown out of the societal shift toward inclusion and the recognition of the limitations that exist within specialized recreation programs that do not offer opportunities for inclusive participation. Unified Sports is sometimes delivered as part of interscholastic sport at the junior high and high school level, and it can also be delivered outside of the schools. Resources and training are available through Special Olympics to assist professionals who would like to develop a Unified Sports or MATP programs in their area.

Paralympics

The Paralympics are the highest level of competition for athletes with disabilities. The first Paralympic games were held in Rome in 1960 with about 400 wheelchair athletes taking part. In 2016, more than 4,300 athletes from 160 countries competed in 21 different sports during the summer games held in Rio De Janeiro, Brazil. Athletes are classified in a variety of divisions across six primary disability categories: visual impairment, intellectual disability, cerebral palsy/traumatic brain injury, spinal cord injury, amputation, and les autres. Athletes must join the corresponding sport association associated with their disability to qualify for Paralympic competition and then pursue qualifying competition advancement similar to Olympic athletes.

SUMMARY

Inclusion is an ideal, but it is also a reality in the daily work of thousands of public recreation professionals around the world. We are far from finishing our work to build a fully inclusive society, but good things are happening. Through the efforts of inclusion-minded recreation professionals, participants are being empowered to engage in genuine leisure experiences in social contexts that foster acceptance, belonging, and self-concept. Providing a diverse array of inclusive recreation opportunities will ultimately allow each member of society to experience the benefits that recreation and leisure can provide.

CHAPTER 8

Nonprofit Sector

Robert F. Ashcraft

“ Nonprofit activity is everywhere. It is hard to find a neighborhood without visible nonprofit presence . . . and impossible to find a neighborhood untouched by nonprofit work. ”

Michael O'Neill, professor emeritus of nonprofit management and founder and former director of the Institute for Nonprofit Organization Management, University of San Francisco

LEARNING OUTCOMES

After reading this chapter you should be able to do the following:

> ❯ Clarify the overall role and characteristics of the nonprofit sector in society
> ❯ Identify the types of national and community-based nonprofit recreation organizations
> ❯ Explain the role of the professional in nonprofit organizations
> ❯ Describe challenges and opportunities for the future

An understanding of recreation and leisure services is incomplete without examining the role of **nonprofit sector** organizations. In neighborhoods and communities across North America, millions of people are served by, and give service to, public and **quasi-public entities**.

It is hard to imagine that anyone goes through life without being touched by a **nonprofit organization**. Yet only in recent years have nonprofits received the attention expected for an organizational form with such a large societal impact. Historian and scholar David Mason notes the influence of nonprofits. When he received the Distinguished Lifetime Achievement Award from the Association for Research on Nonprofit Organizations and Voluntary Action, Mason made the following remarks to the luncheon group assembled in his honor:

> My values, attitudes, and behaviors, like most of yours, have been profoundly influenced by nonprofits. . . . My parents met when they were students in a nonprofit. I was born in one. I learned about God in one, my ABCs in another, how to play ball and be a team player in another, and met my first girlfriend in another. I prepared for my career at a nonprofit university, met my wife in a nonprofit church, went on to several nonprofit graduate schools, joined numerous nonprofit professional groups, brought two newly born sons home from nonprofit hospitals, and on and on it goes, including what I read, how I vote and my avocations. It weaves its way like a golden thread through the tapestry of my life. (Mason, 1999)

Similar stories can be told by millions of citizens who have been affected in comparable ways. The nonprofit sector is ubiquitous, so it is often taken for granted. Yet an examination of the sector reveals countless examples of how nonprofit organizations affect human lives. Nonprofits (the social sector) are growing as part of the **three-sector model** of service delivery; they complement recreation and leisure services provided by businesses that include, in part, private, commercial enterprise (the economic/market sector) and by government (the public, political sector). Whether people organize to serve their personal self-interests or to promote a broader public good, nonprofits are one way citizens often operate along with and sometimes outside the government and business sectors to improve the quality of life in communities. In addition, as a growing career field, the nonprofit sector has emerged as a vocational choice for increasing numbers of recreation professionals.

This chapter reveals the characteristics of nonprofit organizations in the United States and Canada, including their goals and functions, size and scope, and resource bases. The significance of the nonprofit sector is considered in ways that differentiate its service delivery approaches from those found within government or business recreation providers. A variety of types of nonprofit organizations are discussed, as are the professional opportunities that exist within such entities. Finally, the factors that influence the future of nonprofit organizations are addressed, which provides insight into collaborative ventures developing among organizations, the impact of the nonprofit sector in the United States and Canada, and the challenges and opportunities ahead for this important dimension of recreation and leisure service delivery systems.

NONPROFIT SECTOR IN THE UNITED STATES AND CANADA

Although examples of nonprofit sector activities exist across all regions and countries in North America, it is difficult to make direct comparisons from one country to another. There are enormous variations in how nonprofit organizations are structured, how they are registered, and how they operate within the cultural, political, civic, and economic contexts of community life. There are also major differences in the terms used to describe entities that comprise the nonprofit sector. Different terms are found in nonprofit literature such as voluntary sector, charitable sector, quasi-public sector, independent sector, third sector, civil society sector, social sector, nongovernmental organization sector, tax-exempt sector, and nonprofit sector. The terms underscore why understanding the nonprofit sector is a challenging task, given the variety of interpretations noted. However, these variations also suggest

a robust and vibrant sector that accommodates diverse forms and expressions. In this chapter, the term *nonprofit* is used.

Nanus and Dobbs (1999) identify three primary sectors of society: economic (commerce, private and publicly held businesses), political (public and government at all levels), and social (nonprofits). As noted in figure 8.1, these sectors are inextricably linked, and together they represent the variety of ways to organize and deliver recreation and leisure services. The sectors exist within a milieu of forces and forms that shape society.

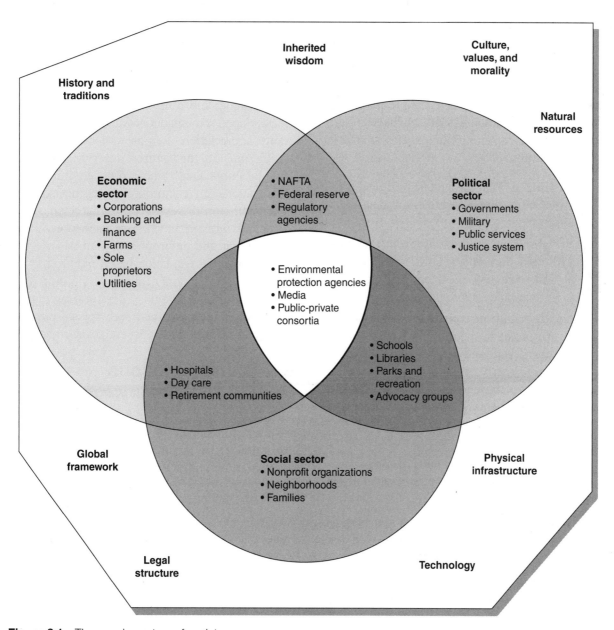

Figure 8.1 Three main sectors of society.

From B. Nanus and S.M. Dobbs, 1999, *Leaders who make a difference: Essential strategies for meeting the nonprofit challenge* (San Francisco: Jossey-Bass). Copyright 1999 John Wiley & Sons, Inc. Reprinted with permission of S.M. Dobbs.

Some nonprofits are widely recognized and provide ready access to their programs, financial statements, governance policies, and so on. However, thousands of small, grassroots, and community-based organizations are lesser known and go largely unexamined. To fully appreciate the nonprofit sector's role, one must consider this segment of recreation and leisure services in all of its vastness and vagueness. One way to understand the range of the nonprofit form is to review what nonprofit organizations hold in common.

Common Characteristics of Nonprofit Organizations

Despite enormous variations, several characteristics apply generally to nonprofit organizations in Canada, the United States, and other countries around the world. According to nonprofit scholars such as Lester Salamon (1999), Michael O'Neill (2002), and others, nonprofit entities share six common features:

1. **Organized**. They have an institutional presence and structure; there is an identifiable entity.

2. **Private**. They are separate from the state. Although they follow laws established by legislative bodies, these entities determine their own policies, programs, and services.

3. **Nondistribution constraint**. They do not return profits to their managers (e.g., board members, staff and directors) or to a set of owners. Whereas publicly traded corporations have shareholders and government entities have voting constituents, nonprofit organizations consider a range of stakeholders when making decisions and providing services.

4. **Self-governing**. They are fundamentally in control of their own affairs.

5. **Voluntary**. Membership in them is not legally required, and they attract some level of voluntary contribution of time and money.

6. **Beneficial to the public**. They contribute to the public purpose and public good.

These characteristics apply to a wide range of recreation and leisure entities found within the nonprofit sector. Therefore, a small running club organized and financed by and for its members in a remote New England community in the United States is as much a part of the nonprofit sector as is the Red Cross, a large, multiservice, social service agency with operating units in Canada and the United States. Nonprofit organizations, therefore, are organized to serve public purposes or mutually beneficial purposes that improve the quality of life in communities.

The nonprofit organizational form is found throughout the recreation field from sport clubs to professional associations to direct service providers. Interestingly, nonprofit organizations and their activities affect people of all ages. Often the introduction to nonprofit organizations occurs through recreation programs such as Boy Scout and Girl Scout programs, YMCAs, Boys and Girls Clubs, Little League, and others. As interests and skills are developed through outlets such as camping programs, appreciation often grows for the outdoors. The Sierra Club, the Nature Conservancy, and the Trust for Public Land, among other environmental organizations, are nonprofit entities that advance specific mission-driven purposes that often appeal to those interested in outdoor recreation. Youth development and environmental entities are just two examples of recreation-based nonprofits that are part of a much larger collection of hundreds of thousands of organizations operating throughout North America to advance both special-purpose and broadly based public benefit goals.

Goals and Functions

Given the vast array of activities and people that comprise the sector, it is not surprising that the goals and functions of nonprofit organizations are also varied. Such organizations often serve widely different needs and, at times, conflicting values. For example, one nonprofit may organize to protect a wilderness area by calling for the elimination of off-road vehicle use and another organizes to open the same area to such activity. Often, however, nonprofit recreation and leisure services organizations share similar values between them and among government and business entities. After-school child care programs, for example, share overall goals regarding the education, safety, and recreation needs of children even though their delivery systems (programs, clientele, fee structure, and so on) are organized in different ways for various reasons.

Despite these variations, Salamon (1999) and others suggest that the following two primary goals frame the orientation of most nonprofits:

1. **Public benefit**. Some nonprofits are organized specifically for social outcomes that appeal to a wide spectrum of population groups. Educational organizations, hospitals, museums, and community recreation centers are examples of public benefit nonprofits.

2. **Mutual benefit**. These nonprofits exist primarily to provide services to a limited number of members with common interests. Examples include business and professional associations, social clubs, and some golf clubs.

Nonprofits, therefore, are organized to serve both individual needs and broader community goals. Some are organized to conserve and preserve historical, cultural, environmental, and other traditions. Others are developed to advance social change with a focus on improving the condition of disadvantaged and disenfranchised people who do not feel a part of mainstream community life. Figure 8.2 shows examples of nonprofit organizations across these various domains.

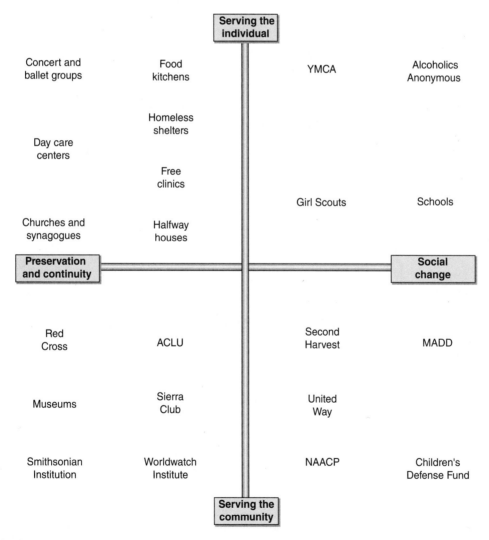

Figure 8.2 Examples of nonprofit organizations.

From B. Nanus and S.M. Dobbs, 1999, *Leaders who make a difference: Essential strategies for meeting the nonprofit challenge* (San Francisco: Jossey-Bass). Copyright 1999 John Wiley & Sons, Inc. Reprinted with permission of S.M. Dobbs.

Organizational Framework

Because the nonprofit sector is so diverse and encompasses such a wide array of types and sizes of organizations, studying its structure and impact can be difficult. A typology known as the International Classification of Nonprofit Organizations (ICNPO), which was developed by researchers at Johns Hopkins University, facilitates understanding of the sector (Salamon & Anheier, 1996). ICNPO divides nonprofits into 12 major activity groups and 24 subgroups according to the primary type of goods or services each one provides (e.g., recreation, environment, health). The following are the major activity groups:

1. **Culture and recreation.** Includes organizations and activities in general and specialized fields of culture and recreation

2. **Education and research.** Includes organizations and activities that administer, provide, promote, conduct, support, and service education and research

3. **Health.** Includes organizations that engage in health-related activities, provide health care (both general and specialized services), administer health care services, and provide health support services

4. **Social services.** Includes organizations and institutions that provide human and social services to a community or target population

5. **Environment.** Includes organizations that promote and provide services in environmental conservation, pollution control and prevention, environmental education and health, and animal protection

6. **Development and housing.** Includes organizations that promote programs and provide services to help improve communities and promote the economic and social well-being of society

7. **Law, advocacy, and politics.** Includes organizations and groups that work to protect and promote civil and other rights, advocate the social and political interests of general or special constituencies, offer legal services, and promote public safety

8. **Philanthropic intermediaries and voluntarism.** Includes philanthropic organizations and those that promote charity and charitable activities including grant-making foundations, voluntarism promotion and support, and fund-raising entities

9. **International.** Includes organizations that promote cultural understanding between peoples of various countries and historical backgrounds and also those that provide relief during emergencies and promote development and welfare abroad

10. **Religion.** Organizations that promote religious beliefs and administer religious services and rituals, including churches, mosques, synagogues, temples, shrines, seminaries, monasteries, and similar religious institutions, in addition to related organizations and auxiliaries of these organizations

11. **Business and professional associations and unions.** Includes organizations that promote, regulate, and safeguard business, professional, and labor interests

12. **Groups not classified elsewhere.**

Size and Scope

As previously noted, determining the size and scope of the nonprofit sector in North America is difficult for several reasons. However, what is known suggests that nonprofits have played a larger role in the United States than in Canada or other countries. This fact in no way minimizes the importance of nonprofits outside the United States. However, given the size and scope of the sector in the United States, it is not surprising that nonprofit literature on recreation and leisure organizations frequently accentuates U.S. examples when examining nonprofit organizations and their purposes and approaches to service delivery.

Distinctive Characteristics of the Nonprofit Sector in Canada

Despite an increasing number of studies on the topic, there is still a great deal that is not known about the nonprofit sector and the role it plays in Canada (Hall & Banting, 2000). Canada has no central registry for nonprofits, so what is known comes from those charities, as a subset of the overall nonprofit sector, that register with Revenue Canada (the government agency similar to the IRS in the United States). According to the 2003 National Survey of Nonprofit and Voluntary Organizations, an estimated 170,000 nonprofit and voluntary organizations operated in Canada, and 85,000 of them were registered as official charities (Hall et al., 2005). According to Revenue Canada, a nonprofit organization (NPO) is "an association [that] must be both organized and operated exclusively for social welfare, civic improvement, pleasure or recreation or for any other purpose except profit" (Revenue Canada, 2001, para. 5). Revenue Canada details these four categories as follows:

1. Social welfare nonprofits assist disadvantaged groups for the common good and for the general welfare of the community.

2. Civic improvement nonprofits are organized to enhance the value or quality of community or civic life.

3. Pleasure or recreation nonprofits are organized to provide a state of gratification or a means of refreshment or diversion.

4. The final category, which can serve any purpose except profit, is a generic grouping of associations that are organized for other noncommercial reasons.

As noted in the previous list, several categories account for the array of Canadian nonprofits that work to advance community life by providing services that address core social needs while advancing overall community well-being. They range from nonprofits that organize parks and museums for general community betterment to sport clubs for special interests such as golf, curling, and badminton that are organized and operated to provide recreational facilities for the enjoyment of members and their families.

One emerging source of information about the Canadian nonprofit sector is Imagine Canada, a nonprofit launched in 2005 from a strategic alliance of the Canadian Centre for Philanthropy and the Coalition of National Voluntary Organizations. Imagine Canada seeks to fill the knowledge gap by working with charities, governments, and corporations to advance the role and interests of the charitable sector for the benefit of Canadian communities. The organization conducts and disseminates research, develops public policy, promotes public awareness, shares tools and standards, and encourages businesses to be more community-minded.

Distinctive Characteristics of the Nonprofit Sector in the United States

As previously noted, the nonprofit sector in the United States is pervasive and robust. According to the National Center for Charitable Statistics (2015), there are approximately 1.41 million nonprofits in the United States. Of those, nearly 1.1 million are public charities and philanthropic organizations (Center for Association Leadership, 2015). The IRS provides 27 types of tax-exempt organizations under Section 501(c) of the federal tax code. The National Center for Charitable Statistics (2015) reveals the major subcategories of the U.S. nonprofit sector as follows:

• **Charitable organizations**. Perhaps the most readily identifiable nonprofits are **charities**. Most nonprofits in the United States (approximately 1 million) are classified as public charities and are exempt under **Section 501(c)(3)** of the IRS tax code. They represent diverse organizations such as those that provide free services to vulnerable populations in soup kitchens and homeless shelters and those that provide wide community development and cultural enhancement activities such as hospitals, museums, and recreation centers. There are many "Friends" organizations in this category to support parks and recreation efforts. For example, the Friends of Buford Park and Mt. Pisgah in Eugene, Oregon, was founded in 1989 to support the ecological integrity of the nearly 2,400 acres (971 ha) that comprise the Howard Buford Recreation Area. Although it works in conjunction with the Lane County Parks Department, this friends group is organized separately. Thousands of such friends groups exist across the United States.

• **Foundations**. One way that individuals, organizations, and communities support causes that benefit society is through private, corporate, operating, or community **foundations**. These also operate as 501(c)(3) nonprofits, and their purposes and operating systems are as varied as those of public charities. Some foundations make grants to a range of community causes. These types of foundations encourage grant proposals from many different areas of the community including recreation and cultural causes. Other types of foundations, however, serve as a conduit for amassing resources to support their own programs and activities. Creating an operating foundation is one way that government parks and recreation programs generate private support for their public goals. There are several other structural variations of this complex nonprofit form.

• **Social welfare organizations**. Some nonprofits advocate for specific issues by lobbying legislators to advance social causes and by actively campaigning for political candidates. These nonprofits, known as *social welfare organizations,* are recognized as Section 501(c)(4) organizations. They are exempt under the tax code, but donations to these causes are not tax deductible. The National Rifle Association and the National Organization for Women are two examples of such organizations.

• **Professional and trade associations**. Nonprofits that promote business or professional interests comprise a collection of nonprofits known as *professional and trade associations*. They usually qualify for tax exemption under Section 501(c)(6) of the tax code, and they focus on the interests of specific industries or professions. They also may have broader community interests such as chambers of commerce or business leagues. Similar to advocacy organizations, donations to these associations are not tax deductible.

Hundreds of thousands of nonprofits are registered as associations in the United States, and depending on their specific mission, they fall within one of the 501(c) categories listed earlier. Nonprofits formed as associations are of interest to the recreation professional and are worthy of expanded discussion in this chapter for two reasons. First, some professional associations, such as the National Recreation and Park Association, benefit the recreation professional by providing training,

certifications, and a network of colleagues that assist in career success and advancement. Second, the association format is one way citizens organize around mutual interests. Frequently, these interests involve recreation, leisure, and sport pursuits.

According to the ASAE Foundation (2012), more than 92,000 trade and professional associations exist in the United States. The following are five of the largest membership associations and the total number of members for each:

• American Automobile Association (56,000,000) (American Automobile Association, n.d.)
• American Association of Retired Persons (40,000,000)
• National Education Association (3,200,000)
• National Rifle Association (4,300,000)
• YMCA of the USA (22,000,000) (YMCA, n.d.)

Several of these associations are directly applicable to recreation, sport, and leisure pursuits.

Resource Base

The resource base of a nonprofit includes all the sources of support that make its programs and services possible. Nonprofits derive their revenue from a combination of one or more sources. The following are the most common sources:

• **Membership fees**. These are fees charged to members, usually annually, in return for programs provided by the nonprofit in service to its members.
• **Program fees**. Participants pay fees for participating in specific programs. Depending on the nonprofit, program participants may or may not be members of the organization.
• **Private philanthropy**. Fund-raising from individuals, corporations, and foundations provides revenue to nonprofit organizations. The skills associated with cultivating donors, developing proposals, and securing gifts from a range of philanthropic stakeholders require increased sophistication because donations have become an essential revenue source for many nonprofits.

- **Government grants**. Many nonprofits compete for and receive government grants from local, state, and federal agencies to provide services based on targeted community needs and priorities.

- **Interest income**. Nonprofits receive income from cash reserves and other unspent monies that are actively managed to maximize earnings until they are used for expenses. Some nonprofits have developed endowment funds that build assets so that the mission of the organization can continue into perpetuity.

- **Earned income**. For nonprofits that own facilities, earned income can occur through rental arrangements, admission fees, and other agreements that turn physical assets into revenue streams.

- **Sales income**. For many youth development organizations, sales from cookies, candy, and other products provide a dual benefit to the organization by providing programs through which young people learn to organize, implement plans, and reach goals and providing revenue for the organization.

- **Social enterprise**. A new and growing trend for some nonprofits is the creation of for-profit companies that channel profits back into their social cause.

Philanthropy in Nonprofit Organizations

Nonprofit organizations often intersect with our lives in deep and abiding ways through philanthropy. **Philanthropy** is the promotion of common good through voluntary action, voluntary association, and voluntary giving (Payton, 1988). Philanthropy is expressed in a variety of forms by people who freely give their money and time to the causes of their choice.

One way sense of belonging and feelings are attached to nonprofit organizations is through acts of philanthropy. Mason (1999) notes that "when people describe their relationship to their employer, they state, 'I work for Exxon. I am with Intel.'" However, he continues, "we reserve the 'belonging'

for our voluntary enterprises" such as the nonprofit organizations that we intersect within our lives. Consider the following statements:

> I *belong* to the YMCA.
>
> I *am* a Boy Scout.
>
> I *belong* to the Camelback Mountain Hiking Club.
>
> I *am* a volunteer at the teen center.

The philanthropic tradition in the United States has been well-documented. According to research by the Corporation for National and Community Service (2015), 62.6 million American adults (24.9 percent of the population) volunteered, giving 7.8 billion hours of service worth $184 billion. According to Giving USA (2017), the amount of money given in 2016 is no less impressive; more than $390.05 billion was contributed through private philanthropy in 2016 by U.S. households when including both individual giving and bequests.

In recent years, the growing philanthropic tradition in Canada has been studied as well. According to a 2013 research report released by Statistics Canada, 12.7 million Canadians (44 percent of the population) volunteered through a charitable or nonprofit organization. This number is the equivalent of almost 1.1 million full-time jobs. Almost 24 million Canadians made direct financial donations to a charitable or other nonprofit organization, representing approximately 82 percent of the population aged 15 and older. The average annual donation amount was nearly C$531.

Contributors of time (volunteers) and money (financial donors) provide important resources that nurture, sustain, and bolster nonprofit recreation organizations. For example, in many nonprofit youth development organizations, volunteers serve as coaches, mentors, teachers, camp counselors, troop leaders, and board members. As financial donors they support cookie sales, donate to annual support campaigns, organize special events, and otherwise contribute income that is a vital part of organizational budgets.

Given the importance of philanthropy to nonprofit organizations, a U.S. recreation professional who is responsible for coordinating volunteer programs or raising funds can benefit from a nationwide network of volunteer action centers. HandsOn Network operates action centers in the United States as part of the Points of Light Institute. The centers help connect interested volunteers with organizations and activities. The nearly 250 action centers across the United States are useful resources to recreation professionals interested in developing or expanding their volunteer program capacity.

In addition, two professional organizations advance competencies for volunteer management and fund-raising. The Council for Certification in Volunteer Administration (CCVA) articulates competencies, advances ethical practice, and promotes professional development and education to support volunteer managers. CCVA sponsored the certificate in volunteer administration (CVA) credential intended for those who lead and direct volunteer engagement in all types of organizations and settings. Similarly, the Association of Fundraising Professionals (AFP) provides training, research, and other support to those involved in fund-raising. Through AFP's credentialing program, qualified fund-raisers can earn the designation of certified fund-raising executive (CFRE), which attests to their knowledge, skill, and achievements.

TYPES OF NATIONAL AND COMMUNITY-BASED NONPROFIT RECREATION ORGANIZATIONS

As previously noted, more than a million organizations—large and small, formal and informal—exist within the U.S. and Canadian nonprofit sectors. Nonprofit organizations play a critical role in the recreational and cultural life of the United States. Salamon notes that

> many of the central recreational institutions of local communities—swimming clubs, tennis clubs, Little Leagues, country clubs—are nonprofit in form. Even more importantly, nonprofit organizations form the backbone of the nation's cultural life, producing most of the live theater, symphonic music, and opera, and providing venues for art and for cultural artifacts. (1999, p. 131)

Interestingly, the nonprofit form is often most potent when it is organized around individual special interests in collaboration with government and business to advance mutually agreed-on goals. Instances of these occurrences in the recreation field abound. One example is that of Kartchner Caverns State Park located outside Benson, Arizona. First discovered in 1974 by Gary Tenen and Randy Tufts, the cave was kept secret for years to protect its natural and fragile beauty. Tenen and Tufts worked with several people and organizations to realize their dream of preserving their unique geological find, including a nonprofit, The Nature Conservancy, and a government entity, the Arizona State Parks Department, along with the private land owner on whose property the caverns were discovered. Following years of study and design, Kartchner Caverns opened in 1999 as a state park. Today, three sectors work together to sustain the caverns including government (Arizona State Parks, which owns the land and administers the park), business (Aramark Sports and Entertainment Services, which holds the contract for concessions at the park), and nonprofit (Friends of Kartchner Caverns State Park, which raises funds to support educational, scientific, and conservation programs). Thousands of examples exist whereby nonprofit organizations help to nurture and sustain recreation settings in collaboration with government agencies and business enterprises.

Whether organized in direct collaboration with government and business or as largely independent entities, various types of national and community-based nonprofit recreation organizations produce significant social benefits. Some of these organizations are identified clearly by their mission, purpose, logo, and other features, and they have a history as a successful entity. Many are part of the essential delivery system of the recreation movement.

Nonprofits that are part of the recreation and leisure services arena can be generally categorized as follows:

- Voluntary youth-serving organizations
- Religious and faith-based organizations
- Social service and relief organizations
- Special populations–serving organizations
- Environmental and conservation organizations

OUTSTANDING GRADUATE

Photo courtesy of Gordon Chaffin

Background Information

Name: Eric Legg

Education: PhD in parks, recreation, and tourism from the University of Utah

Credentials: Certified Park and Recreation Professional (CPRP)

Awards: 2013 Inspirational PhD Student Award

Career Information

Positions: Assistant Professor at Arizona State University and President of Tennis on the Hill

Organization: Arizona State University is a large public research university located in Tempe, Arizona. I am in the School of Community Resources and Development, where I work with students majoring in nonprofit leadership and management, community sports management, and parks and recreation management. Approximately half of my job is devoted to teaching classes in program planning, assessment and evaluation, and sports and recreation for youth development. The other half of my job involves research related to community sports and youth development. In that role, I work with local schools and recreation departments to enhance the youth development outcomes and organizational efficiency of their sports programs.

Organization mission: The mission of Tennis on the Hill is to facilitate the playing and enjoyment of tennis as a means of healthy recreation and lifelong physical fitness for all ages, abilities, income levels, and backgrounds in the community of the greater Capitol Hill area. We do this through six-week clinics in the spring and fall, and we serve approximately 100 youths each year.

Job description: I absolutely love my job and frequently describe it as my dream job. I have the privilege of working with college students who are figuring out life and career paths. Given my own background in both nonprofit management and community sports in a parks and recreation agency, I enjoy working with students in all of these areas, and I am regularly inspired by their energy and passion to make a positive impact on the world. I also get to work directly with community organizations to help them design programs, improve coaches, and improve their own organizational structures to maximize positive youth development outcomes. To top it off, I get to do this all around a topic I love—sports! I also continue to be the president of the nonprofit organization that I founded, and I am heavily involved in volunteer roles with the United States Tennis Association (USTA). For the USTA, I am currently the national volunteer chair of the Training Advisory Group.

Career path: My path to this job took several turns; though many of them may not seem obviously related, I have found that each step has provided me with skills that I use in my job today. I received a bachelor's degree from the College of William and Mary and a master's degree in American religious history from Wake Forest University. After receiving my master's degree, I worked for several years as an editor and then as a consultant on issues related to pay packages for corporate executives (e.g., CEOs, CFOs). This path provided me with valuable analytical, marketing, and management skills. During this time, I also received a master's degree in sports studies from the United States Sports Academy. I then went to work for the parks and recreation department in Arlington, Virginia, where I worked in recreation and sports programming. While working for Arlington, I founded a small community-based nonprofit organization, Tennis on the Hill. Following six years with Arlington Parks and Recreation, I chose to pursue a doctoral degree in parks, recreation, and tourism at the University of Utah. Following completion of my PhD program, I accepted my current position at Arizona State.

Likes and dislikes about the job: Though I love my job, I would not recommend following this career path for the salary. Although I make a comfortable living wage, I actually made more money working in executive pay consulting 13 years ago!

Advice for Undergraduates

My advice to undergraduate students seeking careers in recreation and leisure students is to do this because you love it and are passionate about it, but more than that, because you are passionate about making a positive impact on the world around you through recreation and leisure. On a more practical note, take initiative at every chance you can—volunteer, reach out to people and ask about their careers, do crazy things like start your own nonprofit organization, say yes to opportunities, and don't be discouraged when you receive a no.

- Associations
- Membership or service clubs and fraternal organizations

The mission and programs of some nonprofits cut across more than one category. The Salvation Army, for example, serves youth, is faith based, provides wide-ranging social services, and often serves special populations. In some communities, the local affiliate of the Boys and Girls Clubs of America resides inside a Salvation Army unit. It is helpful to consider these varied categorizations when thinking about the core missions of organizations and their targeted client or customer populations. A sampling of these organizations follows. Descriptions are derived directly from organization websites and materials provided by these organizations.

Voluntary Youth-Serving Organizations

More than 50 leading nonprofit youth and human services organizations across the United States belong to the National Collaboration for Youth, an affinity group of the National Assembly of Health and Human Service Organizations. Collectively, they serve more than 40 million young people. These organizations enlist more than 6 million volunteers to provide services and employ more than 100,000 paid staff. Many of the organizations use sport and recreation activities, community service, youth and adult partnerships, and other programming features to instill core values in their youth members. Some of these organizations are also organized with affiliates in Canada. A sampling of nonprofits with specific youth development goals include the following:

- **Big Brothers Big Sisters of America**. Founded in 1904, Big Brothers Big Sisters of America is the oldest and largest youth-mentoring organization in the United States. The organization serves over 17,000 youth aged 5 through 18 years through a network of over 300 agencies. Big Brothers Big Sisters promotes one-on-one mentoring relationships between capable adult volunteers and youth. Research studies show that mentoring relationships between positive adult role models and youth have lasting effects on children. Big Brothers Big Sisters

of Canada was organized in 1921; similar to its U.S. counterpart, it is organized to provide high-quality volunteer-based mentoring programs to more than 1,000 Canadian communities.

- **Boy Scouts of America**. The Boy Scouts of America was founded in the United States in 1910 with the mission of preparing young people to make ethical and moral choices during their lifetimes by instilling important values. Ranging from 7-year-old Tiger Cubs to teenage Varsity Scouts, Boy Scouts of America strives to build character; foster citizenship; and develop mental, moral, and physical fitness in young people. In 2010, the Boy Scouts of America had more than 2.3 million youth members and approximately 960,000 adult volunteer members. The Boy Scouts organization serves more than 300 councils geographically distributed across the United States. Scouts Canada shares a similar purpose—forming the character of boys and imparting patriotic and civic values among members.

- **Boys and Girls Clubs of America**. Founded in 1906, Boys and Girls Clubs of America annually serves approximately 4 million children, particularly boys and girls from disadvantaged circumstances, encouraging them to realize their full potential as productive, responsible, and caring citizens. In facilities that include game rooms, learning centers, and gymnasiums, trained professionals help young people learn to solve conflicts, develop study skills, and work as part of a team. Boys and Girls Clubs also offers programs aimed at developing leadership, career, health, and overall life skills. The organization planted strong roots in Canada in 1929 and serves nearly 210,000 children and youth in 95 clubs annually.

- **Camp Fire USA**. Founded in 1910, Camp Fire USA is committed to building caring, confident youth and future leaders through its educational programs. The organization serves over 150,000 children and youth annually with the help of volunteers and paid staff. Camp Fire is organized primarily as a club and offers age-appropriate programs for younger children. For older children, Camp Fire offers self-reliance classes aimed at building the skills necessary to resist peer pressure and cultivate healthy relationships. It also offers service-learning courses intended to instill the importance of com-

James Steidl - Fotolia

Boy Scouts of America is an example of a voluntary youth-serving organization.

munity service and offers camping and environmental education programs for children of all ages.

- **Girl Scouts of the USA**. Girl Scouts of the USA was founded in 1912 with the purpose of helping today's girls become tomorrow's leaders. For nearly 100 years, the Girl Scouts program has served girls locally, nationally, and internationally and encouraged them to develop integrity, good conduct, financial literacy, and health so that they can become fulfilled and responsible citizens. Besides emphasizing expression through the arts, Girl Scouts encourages girls to explore their potential in math, science, and technology. Through more than 100 councils throughout the United States, Girl Scouts of the USA has more than 1.9 million youth members and 800,000 adult volunteer members and paid staff. Girl Scouts has a strong North American presence through the Canadian organization Girl Guides.

- **Girls Incorporated**. Girls Incorporated was founded as Girls Clubs of America in 1945. There is formal history and informal history of many of the early affiliates. Technically, the first organization in the United States that was a precursor to

Girls Clubs operated in the 1860s. The organization changed its name to Girls Incorporated in 1990. Its goal is to inspire all girls to be strong, smart, and bold. Local affiliates of Girls Incorporated work to help girls and young women overcome the effects of discrimination and develop their capacity to be self-sufficient, responsible citizens, and they serve as vigorous advocates for girls. The organization also works to build girls' skills and interest in science, math, and technology and to prevent girls from falling victim to peer pressure. Girls Incorporated reaches over 140,000 girls through its affiliates in the United States and Canada and through its website and educational publications. Most Girls Incorporated centers are in low-income areas and provide a weekly average of 30 hours of after-school, weekend, and summer activities.

- **Little League Baseball**. The Little League program was derived from leagues for preteen children that were formed in New York in the 1880s. In the 1920s and 1930s, an organization began to emerge. In 1939, the first Little League game was played. Little League Baseball is the largest organized youth sports program in the world with over 2.4 million children participating in more than 80 countries worldwide each year. Through proper guidance and exemplary leadership, the Little League program assists youth in developing the qualities of citizenship, discipline, teamwork, and physical well-being. By espousing the virtues of character, courage, and loyalty, the Little League Baseball program develops superior citizens rather than superior athletes.

Religious and Faith-Based Organizations

Some nonprofits have grown to become nonsectarian organizations with historical roots in faith-based communities. The YMCA and YWCA are two examples. Other nonprofits are created and administered by faith-based or church communities. The Catholic Youth Organization (CYO), the Young Men's Hebrew Association (YMHA), and the Young Women's Hebrew Association (YWHA) are examples. The largest organizations with historical faith-based roots are as follows:

• **YMCA of the USA (the Y)**. The first Young Men's Christian Association (YMCA) of the USA was established in 1851. Its initial purpose was to meet the spiritual needs of young men. Today, that philosophy has expanded to include multiple services directed toward a much broader cross section of the population with an emphasis on families. The mission statement, "to put Christian principles into practice through programs that build healthy spirit, mind and body for all," reflects the organization's commitment to its Christian roots and its global perspective. YMCA programs are family based. Purchased memberships for individuals and families cover the use of basic services such as gymnasiums, game rooms, swimming pools, locker rooms, and lounges. Members are also eligible for reduced fees on other programs such as resident and day camp programs for children and youth sports. The Y's program offerings are virtually endless and serve members nationwide in 2,700 YMCAs and camps. The YMCA has a strong volunteer program that includes more than 600,000 volunteer program leaders and more than 19,000 full-time staff.

• **YMCA Canada**. YMCA Canada was founded in 1851 and is dedicated to the growth of all people in spirit, mind, and body and in a sense of responsibility to each other and the global community.

The YMCA of the USA is an example of a faith-based organization.

YMCA Canada provides health, fitness, and recreation programs that encourage people of all abilities to pursue healthy lifestyles. Disease prevention and health promotion continue to be mainstays of the YMCA. Program offerings are similar to those in the United States. There are 43 YMCAs and 5 joint YMCA–YWCAs across Canada.

• **YWCA of the USA**. The Young Women's Christian Association (YWCA) of the USA was established in 1858, and it now has 2 million members and more than 225 associations. The program, rooted in Christianity, is a women's membership movement sustained by the richness of many beliefs and values. Strengthened by diversity, the YWCA draws together members who strive to create opportunities for women's growth, leadership, and power to attain a common vision: peace, justice, freedom, and dignity for all people. The YWCA seeks to empower women and eliminate racism. Programs include services for women in crisis, refugee women, single parents, homeless women, women in prison, women coping with substance abuse, and other women in the general population.

• **YWCA Canada**. The YWCA in Canada was established in 1870 with the tagline "a voice for equality—a strong voice for women." The YWCA movement in Canada has provided many of the same services as the YWCA of the USA, emphasizing women's shelters and camping programs. YWCA Canada consists of 32 member associations serving 25,000 women, teen girls, and their families through operations in more than 400 districts and communities across Canada.

Social Service and Relief Organizations

Some of the most recognizable names and logos in the nonprofit sector belong to organizations that provide social and relief services. These organizations are difficult to categorize because some are nonsectarian and others are part of faith-based communities. Each has a mission to improve the quality of individual lives in communities. They intersect in ways that bolster the goals of recreation service providers by providing direct services themselves or by joining forces with other service providers to meet mutual goals. The Red Cross is perhaps one of the best known of any organization in this category.

• **American Red Cross**. The Red Cross was organized internationally in 1863, and the American Red Cross was founded in 1881 as a humanitarian organization to provide relief to victims of disasters and help people prevent, prepare for, and respond to emergencies. Through a network of more than 600 chapters in the United States, the American Red Cross provides numerous services to meet its mission, including disaster relief services; international services; blood, tissue, and plasma services; services to military members and families; community services; and health and safety services. The Red Cross is served by more than 330,000 volunteers and 23,000 paid employees. Local Red Cross chapters assist recreation professionals by providing water safety, CPR, and first aid training and certification.

• **Canadian Red Cross**. The Canadian Red Cross was founded in 1909. Its work is organized into over 300 branches and is supported by more than 20,000 volunteers. Services of the Canadian Red Cross include disaster relief, international services, first aid and water safety education, and home-care services in some communities (e.g., meals and general assistance for seniors).

Inclusive and Special Recreation

Although similar in structure to other types, some nonprofits are organized to meet the needs of specific population groups. For example, the United Service Organization (USO) was created in 1941 to support the needs of enlisted military personnel. Many services provided by the USO are oriented toward the leisure and recreation pursuits of its clientele. Other nonprofits work with people with specific disabilities. The following are two examples:

• **Arc of the United States**. The Arc of the United States works to include all children and adults with intellectual and developmental disabilities in every community through more than 700 chapters nationwide. Founded in 1950, the Arc is the national organization of and for people with intellectual disabilities and related developmental disabilities and their families. It is devoted to promoting and improving support and services for this group. The association also supports research into and education about the prevention of intellectual disabilities in infants and young children.

• **Special Olympics**. Special Olympics was founded in 1968 to provide year-round sport training and athletic competition in 30 Olympic-type sports for children and adults with intellectual disabilities. With the help of its strong volunteer corps, Special Olympics gives athletes ages 8 years and older opportunities to develop physical fitness, demonstrate courage, experience joy, and participate in a sharing of gifts, skills, and friendship with their families, other Special Olympics athletes, and the community. Through the Family Leadership and Support initiative, Special Olympics offers families opportunities for sport, social interaction, and fun and also a much-needed support system. Special Olympics served more than 4.5 million athletes in 2015 worldwide.

Environmental and Conservation Organizations

Environmental organizations are primarily involved in lobbying and education activities for specific concerns such as wildlife protection, global warming, and safe water. They are worthy of consideration because their efforts often make possible the places and spaces in which recreational activities occur. The following are two examples:

• **Sierra Club**. Founded in 1892, the Sierra Club's purpose is to explore, enjoy, and protect the wild places of the earth; to practice and promote the responsible use of the earth's ecosystem and resources; to educate and enlist humanity to protect and restore the quality of the natural and human environment; and to use all lawful means to carry out these objectives. From grassroots campaigns to environmental law programs, the Sierra Club seeks to spread the word about the importance of protecting the planet. The Sierra Club claims more than 4.5 million members and has 64 chapters in the United States. The U.S. Sierra Club has created the Mexico Project to help support and strengthen Mexican grassroots environmental and community organizations. The Sierra Club of Canada was founded in 1963 to develop a diverse, well-trained network to protect the integrity of the global ecosystems.

• **Trust for Public Land (TPL)**. The TPL uses its more than 300 paid staff and supporting volunteers to accomplish its mission of conserving land for people to enjoy as parks, gardens, and other natural places, ensuring livable communities for generations to come. Operating in 30 offices across the United States since its inception in 1972, the TPL runs several national programs, such as the Working Lands Program (WLP) and Parks for People (PFP). The WLP protects farms, ranches, and forests that support local economies, and the PFP strives to ensure that every American enjoys close access to a park, playground, or other natural area.

Associations

The following nonprofit professional associations concern the recreation field and are resources for students and practitioners in the field:

• **Society of Health and Physical Educators.** SHAPE America supports and assists those involved

Brand X Pictures

The Trust for Public Land works to conserve land to ensure livable communities and natural places for generations to come.

in physical education, leisure, fitness, dance, health promotion, education, and all specialties related to achieving a healthy lifestyle. Founded in 1885, the association is the largest membership organization of health and physical education professionals. The organization operates through 50 state affiliates and provides leadership, professional development, and advocacy for its nearly 20,000 members at every level from preschool to graduate-level programs.

• **American Camp Association (ACA)**. The ACA is a diverse community of camp professionals dedicated to enriching the lives of children and adults through the camp experience. For nearly 100 years, the ACA has used camp programs to impart powerful lessons in community, character building, and skill development. The ACA works to preserve, promote, and improve the camp experience for 5 million campers and learners each year.

• **American Therapeutic Recreation Association (ATRA)**. With approximately 2,200 members as of 2014, the ATRA is the largest membership organization representing the interests and needs of health care providers who use recreational therapy to improve the functioning of people with illnesses or disabling conditions.

• **Canadian Association for Health, Physical Education, Recreation and Dance (CAHPERD)**. The CAHPERD is a national, charitable, voluntary-sector organization whose primary concern is to influence the healthy development of children and youth by advocating for quality, school-based physical and health education.

• **Canadian Parks and Recreation Association (CPRA)**. The CPRA is "the national voice for the parks and recreation field." It has a national network of providers that serve in over 90 percent of Canadian communities and advances its belief that parks and recreation is essential to the well-being of individual and community life. There are also provincial and territorial parks and recreation associations operating across Canada.

• **National Association of Park Foundations (NAPF)**. As one of the newest associations organized to support parks and recreation, the NAPF exists to strengthen local park foundations and other "friends of the parks" nonprofit organizations across the United States to support and enhance the local park experience.

• **National Recreation and Park Association (NRPA)**. For more than 100 years, the NRPA has advocated the importance of thriving, local park systems; the opportunity for all Americans to lead healthy, active lifestyles; and the preservation of great community places. NRPA enhances professional advancement and provides services that contribute to the development of its 18,000 members. Competency guidelines form the curricular content of NRPA-accredited colleges and universities that offer degrees in parks and recreation.

Membership or Service Clubs and Fraternal Organizations

Although we do not always think of service clubs and fraternal organizations as a part of the recreation and leisure services community, we should consider them for two reasons. First, many of these organizations support parks and recreation programs through their donations of time and money. Second, they provide personal and professional development networking opportunities for recreation professionals who become members. Two of the better-known service clubs are the following:

• **Kiwanis International**. Founded in 1915, Kiwanis International has a membership of professional business people dedicated to serving their communities. The organization has nearly 700,000 members and 115 paid staff in more than 8,300 adult clubs and nearly 8,000 youth clubs throughout the world. The organization evaluates children's issues and community needs and conducts service projects that respond to those identified needs.

• **Rotary International**. Rotary is a worldwide organization of business and professional leaders who provide humanitarian service, encourage high ethical standards in all vocations, and help build goodwill and peace in the world. The organization was founded in 1905. Members become actively involved in hands-on projects that use their vocational skills. Rotary has 1.2 million members worldwide in more than 35,000 clubs in over 200 countries who are served by 740 staff members.

Differences and Similarities Among Organizations

Organizations share differences and similarities according to several distinguishing variables (Hansmann, 1987). These variables include the beneficiaries of their services, such as youth, seniors, or animals; their function, such as service delivery or political advocacy; and their primary source of revenues, distinguishing between nonprofits that rely primarily on sales of goods or services and those that rely largely on donations. Two additional distinctions regarding service delivery are evident within nonprofit recreation organizations: whether the organization is facility based or not and the extent to which volunteers deliver services. Facility-based recreation organizations attract participants to programs that occur at specific locations. These include Boys and Girls Clubs, YMCAs, and similar organizations. Other nonprofits, such as Big Brothers Big Sisters, are not facility based and therefore rely on community-based facilities, including parks, for their program delivery. Still other nonprofits, such as Camp Fire USA, Boy Scouts, and Girl Scouts, rely in part on their own place-based facilities, such as summer camps owned by these agencies. However, for other programming they rely on community-based facilities such as schools, churches, and neighborhood centers.

Another distinction is the role of volunteers in service delivery. Volunteers provide an essential human resource to many nonprofits. In fact, in organizations such as Big Brothers Big Sisters and in Boy Scouts and Girl Scouts programs, volunteers are the delivery system. Without them, there would be no services delivered, and the mission of each organization could not be carried out. Other organizations, such as Boys and Girls Clubs, rely more on paid staff to deliver their core programs. However, in every case, volunteers serve in a variety of governance roles, such as boards of directors and task groups, and in support roles, such as fund-raising.

PROFESSIONALS IN NONPROFIT ORGANIZATIONS

In 1994, the nonprofit sector employed about 5.4 million people in the United States, representing 4.4 percent of all workers (Bureau of Labor Statistics, 2009). By 2012, however, nonprofits employed 11.4 million workers, or approximately 10.3 percent of all private-sector workers in the United States (Bureau of Labor Statistics, 2016). Career opportunities for nonprofit professionals are growing rapidly across all subsectors, including recreation and leisure services providers. In fact, employment in the U.S. nonprofit sector grew every year during the recession years in the decade beginning in 2000 through 2010 with both wages and employment outpacing business and government. Nonprofits hire people with diverse skills, just as business or government entities do, because there are as many different job functions as those found in other industries. However, many recreation and leisure nonprofits have relatively small numbers of paid staff in relation to their number of volunteers. Thus, the professional is often given broad responsibility for a variety of duties within the organization.

Given the unique nature of philanthropy in many nonprofits, staff members who demonstrate skills in raising financial resources and working with and through volunteers to accomplish organizational goals are particularly successful. In youth development nonprofits, some practitioners work directly with children. More likely, however, they are responsible for a geographic territory with responsibility for ensuring that financial and human resources are acquired and deployed within the mission of the organization.

A variety of job and career resources are available for those interested in pursuing careers in nonprofit recreation and leisure organizations. The national organization Action Without Borders is one of several entities that provides career guidance and posts job openings. Trade publications such as the *NonProfit Times* and the *Chronicle of Philanthropy* are also helpful tools.

Students pursuing degree programs in recreation who have an interest in nonprofit careers may benefit from earning national certification through the Nonprofit Leadership Alliance (NLA; formerly American Humanics, Inc.). NLA is a national alliance of colleges, universities, and nonprofit partners that prepares undergraduate students for careers in nonprofit organizations. Campus affiliates of NLA offer curricular and cocurricular offerings leading to the Certified Nonprofit Professional (CNP) credential for students pursuing nonprofit professional careers. The program was founded in 1948 and is offered in the United States at 40 colleges and universities nationwide. In 2016, an alternative pathway to the CNP credential was launched through an online certification program.

CHALLENGES AND OPPORTUNITIES FOR THE FUTURE

Based on research commissioned and released in 2009 by the James Irvine Foundation, as conducted by La Piana Consulting, several trends serve as both challenges and opportunities for the nonprofit sector. These trends include demographic shifts, technological advances, networks that enable work to be organized in new ways, rising interest in civic engagement and volunteerism, and the blurring of sector boundaries. In addition, issues of trust and accountability remain ongoing trends that require the attention of nonprofit leaders and managers.

More recently, the Independent Sector released a report in 2016 with the results of a year-long series of community conversations held across the United States that involved more than 80 organizations. The report brought together a diverse cross section of leaders from nonprofits of every size and mission and generated thousands of comments and perspectives about the challenges and opportunities for the charitable sector in the coming years. Key trends include disruption from inequality and environmental degradation, greater ethnic diversity, new generations of leadership, and technology that transforms learning, gathering, and associations. These trends, among others, suggest new models for social change will emerge along with fundamental questions that must be answered, such as the role of government in balancing competing priorities and revenue pressures, among others.

Each of these trends has direct implications for nonprofit recreation and leisure services providers. For example, as communities change and grow, many will find that most of their citizens are ethnic minorities. Sweeping demographic changes also mean that nonprofit providers must adjust to stay relevant if they want to make a broad-based impact. This trend also speaks to the need for managing staff across generations in the workplace if organizations are to be successful. Honoring their historic traditions as they change structures, processes, and programs to welcome new and diverse populations to their organizations presents both challenges and opportunities. This tension between exclusion and inclusion cuts across many demographics including race, ethnicity, culture, sexual orientation, and physical abilities. Using history as a predictor of the future, the nonprofit sector in North America will be composed of organizations that change, some that remain static, and some that are created anew.

The use of social media, online giving approaches, and other technological advances presents nonprofits with ever-evolving ways to reach stakeholders, tell their stories, and engage citizens in their efforts. The opportunity for collaboration in response to marketplace challenges addresses the need for networks that enable work to be organized in new ways. Only the rare nonprofit can afford to operate its programs without regard for other providers of similar services, be they government, nonprofit, or business providers. Issues of pricing, marketing, and consumer choice suggest that the successful nonprofit of the future must use businesslike principles without abandoning the core public service mission that earns its tax-exempt privilege. A call for greater civic engagement and volunteerism among citizens to actively participate in the process of citizenship is prevalent across many communities. It is through nonprofits that people will frequently find their place to engage by focusing their time, money, and know-how on causes they care about.

Blurring of the lines that demarcate the sectors is a trend that directly affects the recreation field. For example, during the economic downturn that was punctuated as a result of the 2007-2008 financial crisis, nonprofits were called on like never before to assume responsibilities previously provided by government. In Phoenix, Arizona, and other cities, parks and recreation departments issued proposal requests to area nonprofits interested in operating and maintaining more than a dozen city facilities that had been closed because of budget reductions. Increasingly, networks of organizations across sectors (government, business, and nonprofit) are called on to work together to provide a common good.

At least one final trend worth amplifying concerns the issue of trust and accountability. If nonprofits depend on the charitable giving of time and money to ensure their success, then such organizations must be led and managed effectively. Although other sectors also face accountability issues, the special trust held by nonprofits as stewards of philanthropy makes this issue especially important.

SUMMARY

Understanding the role of nonprofit organizations is important if recreation and leisure services are to be thoroughly understood. The nonprofit form is one way services are organized and delivered. There are enormous variations in how nonprofits are organized across North America. The extent to which the nonprofit form is used in one country compared to another is largely based on the economic, social, and political differences found among different nations.

The career field for graduates of recreation and related degree programs who seek professional opportunities is growing. A number of trends are influencing the organizations that deliver recreation services as a blurring of the lines of the three sectors (business, government, and nonprofit) occurs. Successful nonprofit managers will be those who are skillful across a range of competencies and who can span boundaries across sectors. In particular, the ability to raise philanthropic resources and to work with volunteers to achieve organizational goals are hallmarks of the successful nonprofit professional.

CHAPTER 9

For-Profit Sector: Recreation, Event, and Tourism Enterprises

Robert E. Pfister and Patrick T. Tierney

Getty Images/Blend Images/Jetta Productions

" I wanted to be an editor or a journalist. I wasn't really interested in being an entrepreneur, but I soon found I had to become an entrepreneur in order to keep my magazine going. "

Richard Branson, entrepreneur and founder of the Virgin Group

LEARNING OUTCOMES

After reading this chapter, you should be able to do the following:

> Contrast the characteristics of for-profit service providers with other service providers in the leisure and tourism industry

> Identify the range of activities undertaken by small and medium for-profit enterprises (SME) together with larger corporations in providing services in the recreation, event, and tourism (RET) industry

> Outline strategies for success in acquiring business skills central to the delivery of valued goods, services, and experiences by for-profit enterprises

> Describe trends that influence the management, marketing, and use of technology by SME owners and operators

For-profit organizations that provide recreation, special event, and tourism services are at the center of the commercial recreation sector. The term *commercial recreation* refers to any enterprise that provides recreation or leisure experiences with the intent of making a profit. The scope of a commercial enterprise's products or services may be local, national, or multinational. Such enterprises are among the many service providers that allow consumers to choose opportunities that add to quality of life and improve productivity at work. Influenced by diverse interests and expectations, we can rely on a wide array of recreation, travel, event, and tourism enterprises when it comes to our leisure choices. Consider, for example, the following scenario:

Reflecting on the past 12 months, you and your long-term partner recognize that it was a memorable year. As outdoor enthusiasts, the two of you enjoyed all your favorite outdoor activities together—downhill skiing, mountain biking, kayaking, and even an unexpected Caribbean cruise. It's December, and you are comfortably relaxed in an Aspen lodge, ready to celebrate the joy and rewards associated with a series of well-organized vacations.

You first remember the surprise Caribbean cruise coming as a rewards certificate from your favorite ski equipment retail outlet that you have been going to for over a decade. Their letter stated that they held a drawing and that you had won first prize in a customer loyalty contest. First prize was an all-expenses-paid, four-day Royal Caribbean cruise sailing from Miami.

You discovered that the vacation package was prepared by an incentive travel company that works with commercial enterprises to reward loyal customers and productive employees. The timing of the trip even allowed you to take in a professional NBA game, because the Miami Heat were playing at home before the trip departure. In late spring, you had a kayak trip on the Green River in your home state of Colorado. Then later in the summer, it was off to California for a multiday mountain bike experience put together by the Downieville Adventure Company. You had the opportunity to bike the course of one of the best-known mountain bike races in the country. Your guide urged you to stay on designated trails and demonstrated how to practice low-impact recreation. In the fall, you went back to your favorite retail outlet store to equip yourself for the upcoming ski season. So now you find yourself at Aspen, thinking about how great it was for you to do what you enjoy most with the support of a variety of key service providers.

Regardless of their services, products, or size, the commercial enterprises identified in the scenario tend to function in a similar fashion in terms of their legal status and operational practices. In addition, they share attributes that clearly distinguish the for-profit sector from the nonprofit and public sectors. Commercial business enterprises fit into a standardized statistical category under the provision of the North American Free Trade Agreement (NAFTA).

ATTRIBUTES OF FOR-PROFIT SERVICES

When you look closely at the memorable experiences in the scenario, you'll see that some were delivered by large corporate resort properties and others by small businesses. These businesses share some attributes that distinguish them from other service providers; see table 9.1 for a summary.

The pricing of services can be the same for domestic and international customers, but this is rarely the case for tax-based (e.g., public) or membership-based (e.g., nonprofit) service providers. Moreover, variable pricing, such as higher prices during peak demand times, is a marketing feature that can be designed to appeal to a targeted market and to maximize revenue.

It is common for commercial enterprises to create travel packages that appeal to certain market segments, which include specialized food, accommodation, and attractions. Packages can increase the length of stay for travelers because they offer convenience, value, and specialization, thus encouraging additional time at a destination or on vacation. These packages can serve other purposes, as in the case of incentive travel whereby companies specialize in creating specific programs that motivate and reward high-achieving company staff.

The ability to buy and sell an enterprise is particularly unique to the commercial sector. In many cases, legal ownership of a business is one of the reasons why diligent and hardworking entrepreneurs invest considerable effort in building the reputation, assets, and customer base of their businesses. This type of commitment represents value that can be appraised when selling the business.

The need to be responsive to changes in the marketplace is central to maintaining a competitive edge in the commercial sector. This attribute reflects an inherent capacity in the design of the business to respond quickly to customer preferences to remain profitable and even capture new and evolving markets. Some commercial recreation businesses may choose to operate seasonally, and this may reflect their ability to be entirely profitable on a seasonal basis or to shift their services and products in response to cyclical patterns in certain regions.

Legal Status, Business Name, and Operational Practices

The legal status of an enterprise is indicative to its choice of a name, and it is fundamental to its ability to be bought, sold, or transferred. For small and medium businesses, the most common forms of ownership are sole proprietorship and general partnership. In such cases, it is common for the venture to carry the name of those involved in the formation of the enterprise or its owners. An alternative would be for the business to carry a name that reflects its base of operation or its service territory (e.g., Downieville Adventure Company). The third legal status is to incorporate, and this form of doing business is evident in destination resorts, corporate properties, cruise ship lines, and so forth. With incorporation, companies often invest substan-

Table 9.1 Five Characteristics That Distinguish For-Profit Enterprises From Other Service Providers

	For-profit	Public	Nonprofit
Pricing of services	Single competitive price	Based on resident fees	Limited to members
Tour packaging	Commonplace	Rarely undertaken	Done for members
Business can be sold	Yes	No	No
Ability to respond quickly to changes in the market	High capability	Limited capability	Some capability
Seasonal products or programs	Outdoor operators shift between geographic regions	If facility based, programs often change	Shift based on member preferences

Reprinted, by permission, from R.E. Pfister and P. Tierney, 2009, *Recreation, event, and tourism businesses: Start-up and sustainable operations* (Champaign, IL: Human Kinetics), 11.

tially in branding and trademarks for the business because its identity is vital to name recognition in the market place. Naming conventions refer to the choices available to a business given its legal status; these are displayed in table 9.2.

For-profit service providers carry out a set of operational practices and systematic decisions to ensure that the range of goods and services they advertise are available to the people they serve. Their operational practices involve the following integrated steps:

1. Planning that goes into assessment of demand and the creation of value-added products and programs (e.g., goods and services) for the consumer
2. Marketing the products, goods, services, and programs in a well-designed communication plan
3. Delivering the goods and services in a timely manner
4. Monitoring the results of their efforts after the consumer has purchased the goods or services

All successful businesses have a vital interest in monitoring consumer satisfaction in one form or another. The services RET businesses provide must be valued by customers, and they must meet the consumers' expectations; otherwise, competitors are likely to capture the unsatisfied market. This topic of consumer satisfaction is reflected in the earlier scenario in which a retail outlet implemented a customer loyalty reward and provided a Caribbean cruise to a loyal customer. In other cases, incentives might involve discount coupons, a cash prize, air miles, or gift cards. RET businesses must also develop cash flow statements, a plan of the projected sources, and uses of cash over the year. In figure 9.1 the operational practices are displayed as a set of integrated steps performed by an enterprise, often as part of their business plan.

Table 9.2 For-Profit Legal Status and Implications for Naming Conventions

Legal status	Implications	Process
Sole proprietorship	No formalities are necessary if a person named John Gow wants to use the name John Gow Guide Service. A surname can also be used alone.	If a business name does not show the owner's surname or implies the existence of additional owners, many states require the owner to file a fictitious business name statement and publish notice. See DBA.
General partnership, joint venture, limited liability partnership	Two names generally appear in the business name.	If surnames are not used in the partnership, the owners most likely will file for a fictitious business name. See DBA.
Corporation, limited liability corporation, S corporation	When the owners create a recognized legal entity, the naming process is more involved. Laws and fees governing corporations vary from state to state. Most owners incorporate in the state in which they will conduct business. Some other considerations may be important. Nevada does not charge a state corporate income tax or personal income tax, and it allows a higher level of privacy for businesses. Business-friendly states do this to attract corporations to have offices in their jurisdiction.	Although the owners may have considerable choice for a name, guidelines for naming conventions are established by the laws of incorporation, which will vary by federal and state statute. Some words will be restricted because they are reserved for nonprofit societies or associations. More important, owners will have to research the availability of the name selected because it may not be available to be registered if an existing business has filed for it.
Doing business as (DBA)*	Owners can choose a name that simply sounds good, such as Aardvark Adventures, Dianne's Dance Studio, Frank's Fly Fishing Shop, or Bertha's Restaurant, and the owner's name does not have to be Aardvark, Dianne, Frank, or Bertha.	A business name that is not the owner's name is an assumed or fictitious name. The owner will have to complete the DBA process, which varies from one jurisdiction to another. DBA advertisements appear in the business section under DBA. Several states have online services that make the search process considerably easier.

*https://filedba.com/?r=overturead&OVRAW=Dba&OVKEY=dba&OVMTC=standard

Reprinted, by permission, from R.E. Pfister and P. Tierney, 2009, *Recreation, event, and tourism businesses: Start-up and sustainable operations* (Champaign, IL: Human Kinetics), 66.

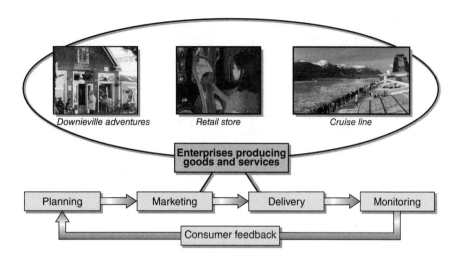

Figure 9.1 The four basic operational practices (planning, marketing, delivery, monitoring) are represented in the RET operations model.

Photos left to right: © Patrick Tierney, © Human Kinetics, and MOKreations – Fotolia

Reprinted, by permission, from R.E. Pfister and P. Tierney, 2009, *Recreation, event, and tourism businesses: Start-up and sustainable operations* (Champaign, IL: Human Kinetics), 183.

NAFTA and Recreation, Event, and Tourism Activity

The nature and attributes of the for-profit sector become even more differentiated as we look at a variety of recreation, event, and tourism enterprises in the context of their services to the consumer. The adoption of the RET label originates from a monitoring or data-collection need to standardize the coding of industry sectors for statistical purposes combined with the approach contained in NAFTA. Within NAFTA, the new **North American Industry Classification System (NAICS),** which is applicable to the United States, Canada, and Mexico, recognizes arts, entertainment, and recreation, as well as event, meeting, and convention planning sectors of the economy in a uniform way (U.S. Census Bureau, 2007). Thus, when professionals now describe RET businesses, the acronym encompasses a diverse set of businesses responsible for a wide range of commercial leisure services in urban, rural, and even remote locations that attract persons to participate in leisure or a combination of business and leisure activities and to travel to new destinations. An RET enterprise generally refers to a business that provides a set of leisure-oriented goods or services and intends to be profitable within a reasonable time.

For-profit leisure enterprises vary from those that provide indoor batting cages in East Coast urban areas to those that rent outdoor equipment in remote barrier islands off the coast. Event businesses might arrange large spectator festival events in urban venues or small family weddings in rural communities. Small tourism businesses may offer special services to large time-share resort destinations or offer dogsled trips in the Yukon Territory. Any new term seeking to capture the diversity of the aforementioned commercial activities is likely to be met with some resistance, because it is a departure from previous terminology and typologies. The following section addresses the rationale for recognizing the RET category of businesses and provides a description of how previous models or typologies chose to group types of businesses.

RET INDUSTRY MODEL

Travel is said to require a motive, information about opportunities, an affordable means of travel, destination attractions, something to do, and a place to eat and sleep. Using this idea as an organizing principle for a travel-commerce model, we can examine the primary function of each business, agency, or organization within the overall tourism industry. Synthesizing earlier theories and numerous research studies on the RET industry, we have developed the **recreation, event, and tourism (RET) industry model** shown in figure 9.2. There are three basic functional areas: (1) attractions, (2) support and facilitation, and (3) hosting functions. The model also contains two integrated functional groups that merge elements of the attraction and hosting functions.

Attractions

At the top of the pyramid, attraction businesses and public-sector facilities provide the motive and stimulation for travel and attract people to specific destinations. A basic premise is that tourism industry **attractions** provide the services and products that lead people to travel, and they power the demand for businesses in the other two functional areas by creating memorable visitor experiences. Attractions consist of three general types:

1. Tourist attractions primarily to lure nonresident tourists. They range from natural and cultural attractions to theme parks, gaming casinos, and family and friends.

2. Event experiences are short-duration activities that are not generally repeated frequently and that attract both residents and visitors. They include special events, conventions and conferences, festivals, exhibitions, and reunions.

3. Local recreation consists of facilities and activities that provide residents with frequently repeated, nearby leisure experiences. Examples of local recreation organizations

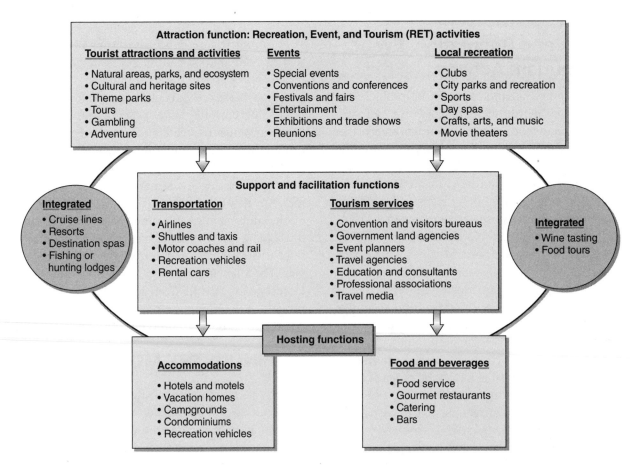

Figure 9.2   The recreation, event, and tourism (RET) model shows businesses of all sizes that represent the three functional areas of the RET industry: attractions, support and facilitation, and hosting.

Reprinted, by permission, from R.E. Pfister and P. Tierney, 2009, *Recreation, event, and tourism businesses: Start-up sustainable operations* (Champaign, IL: Human Kinetics), 15.

include clubs; city recreation departments; sport organizations; day spas; arts, craft, and music suppliers; and movie theaters.

Figure 9.2 clearly illustrates the importance of the private and public recreation and event attractions, because without them, transportation services or hospitality elements, such as accommodations and food services, would be unnecessary. The length of stay at a destination is also directly related to the number and quality of attractions. The model also shows the wide range of businesses and organizations found in the RET industry, which illustrates how vital, essential, and valuable RET is to our economy and lifestyle and the wide range of job providers within it.

Support and Facilitation Functions

The **support and facilitation function** contains two components: transportation and tourist services. Transportation providers such as airlines, taxis, railroads, recreational vehicles (RVs), and rental cars deliver tourists to the destination. Without reasonable prices and safe transportation, people would not get to the desired destination and use other elements of the system. Countless services are geared toward assisting visitors including travel facilitators (e.g., travel management agencies), convention and visitors bureaus, event planners, government land management agencies (e.g., National Park Service and Parks Canada), university tourism programs, research consultants, equipment rental firms, rental and retail businesses, and the travel media. Without these support services, other businesses would function less effectively, and people might choose another destination or be less satisfied with their experiences.

Hosting Function

The **hosting function** consists of accommodations and food and beverage services. Overnight lodging is provided to visitors by hotels and motels, vacation homes, campgrounds, RVs, bed and breakfasts, and family and friends. Lodging is a basic visitor necessity, and its quality can greatly influence the visitor's experience. A variety of accommodation options are available, some of which are free (homes of friends and relatives) or low cost (hostels and campgrounds).

MOKreations - Fotolia

A cruise ship illustrates a fully integrated RET business that offers accommodation, transportation, and attractions. Clients are attracted to buy cruise vacations because of the appealing route, activities and events on board, and often the food services.

The food and beverages functional area includes restaurants, fast food, event catering, bars, and coffee shops. Like accommodations, food and beverage services are a necessity and vary greatly in cost and quality. They can have a large effect on visitor satisfaction.

Integrated Functions

A growing number of RET businesses integrate or combine attractions and hosting functions at one site. Examples of the **integrated function** in accommodations include resorts, cruise lines, destination spas, and hunting and fishing lodges. Most integrated accommodations also provide food and beverage products.

An array of food and beverage businesses have an integrated function within RET because food and beverage service is a primary attraction for travel rather than a supporting service. Food and beverage services integrated with attractions include activities such as wine-tasting tours, food tours, catering for events, and gourmet restaurants for "foodies" or people who travel specifically to eat at a particular restaurant. A wide variety of travel packages are created around wine-tasting tours and food experiences, such as the Taste of Chicago or the San Francisco Crab Festival.

A cruise ship is a great example of a fully integrated RET business. Clients buy cruise vacations because of the activities and events on board and ashore. Passengers use a variety of tourism services, stay in cabins, and eat most meals on board while the ship transports them to new destinations.

You can use the RET model shown in figure 9.2 to identify links and understand how various types of RET businesses fit together. By doing so, you can better your understanding of the RET industry and start to envision which part of the RET businesses you might consider working in.

CONSIDERING AN RET CAREER

The pathways to a successful and rewarding RET career can be as diverse as the industry itself. Are you inclined to be in business for yourself or do you prefer to be an innovator and deliver services in a corporate setting? What are the essential education opportunities available to you that match your interest? How can you acquire the leadership skills that will be vital to a successful career? Which of the many professional associations or marketing organizations will most benefit your career development? These questions and others will offer insights to the choices you have available in the years ahead.

Entrepreneur or Intrapreneur

Preparing for a career in the business field will certainly include developing some skills that differ based on a position title and your status within an enterprise. Within the RET industry model (figure 9.2), you might choose to be a proactive, self-employed person who operates a small or medium business (e.g., **entrepreneur**), or you might choose to be a proactive, forward-thinking employee (e.g., **intrapreneur**) within a larger enterprise or corporation. The term *intrapreneur* was coined and advocated in a book by Pinchot and Pellman (1999, p. ix); they say it comes from the words *intra*corporate and entre*preneur*.

Whatever your employment status, you should have common knowledge of personal leadership skills that contribute to success. If you are employed in a corporate setting, you will need to be mindful of major changes occurring in the industry and ensure you have an innovative perspective to respond to the change. In both employment situations, knowledge about managing change will be a springboard for success, as discussed in subsequent paragraphs.

Career Preparation

Many postsecondary curriculums focus on preparing graduates to start as employees. Beginning in such a capacity offers notable benefits. Several common characteristics are found across the various RET employment opportunities. Areas of emphasis that are foundations in both entrepreneurship and intraprenueurship pertain to leadership skills and appreciating the language of business (a combination of accounting, business law, and practice related to contingency planning). Experience suggests there will be dramatic changes in the industry over time due to new markets, products, laws, and the nature of competition.

A logical first step is to identify personal opportunities that will strengthen your knowledge of leadership and its practice in the industry. Formal education combined with practical, progressive, and innovative work experiences provides a time-tested and sensible combination of activities. The content and focus of any formal or informal work experience program can occur at various points in time. If we were to reflect on Richard Branson's quote at the beginning of this chapter, we could note that his career goal to become a journalist at a young age started him on an educational journey to understand what is required to become a successful entrepreneur. His experiences are instructional.

Foremost among the leadership skills revealed in Branson's autobiography (2006) is the mind-set exhibited in dealing with a changing and challenging business environment. Many authorities stress the importance of visionary leadership qualities in business (Covey, 1992; Kotter, 1996, 1999; Nahavandi, 2009; Rickards & Clark, 2006). The authors uniformly identify the need to look at challenges with a particular perspective and to adopt skills that ensure flexibility and adaptability to a changing environment. The point is that entrepreneurial skills associated with success in a business are anchored in understanding and applying leadership practices. Moreover, these qualities and practices are portable to each of the diverse RET work environments described in figure 9.2.

The Leadership Factor

In the distinctly service-oriented RET industry covered herein, the ability to discover, adopt, and excel at acquiring basic attributes of leadership should be a priority. Covey (1992) sets out eight fundamental and notable principles in this regard. He states that a principle-centered leader is continually educated by his or her experiences and sees life as an adventure in which to chart new territory with confidence. Thus, it is not uncommon to hear principle-centered entrepreneurs say that they learned more from their mistakes than from their successes. It is a commentary on their outlook that life is an adventure and the need to see all experiences as learning opportunities.

Two other valuable principles for people who choose to work in this field are the commitment to being service oriented and belief in other people. Leadership, in Covey's view, is about service to others and recognizing the unseen potential in those with whom the leader works. These principles focus on the people skills linked to effective communication and call for each of us to build capacity to see the best in everyone.

Additional leadership principles include embracing an attitude of optimism and being productive in creative ways, which is described as being synergistic. A positive and hopeful spirit when tackling the things that need to be done lays the foundation for successful leadership. This optimism can be revealed through a sense of humor. When the need arises to negotiate win–win solutions or create change, the capacity to demonstrate synergy is invaluable. It begins with exploring options and expands into seeing new alternatives. It is an asset to every leader.

Finally, a leader needs to demonstrate a balanced lifestyle and commit to some form of regular exercise program. The balanced lifestyle is linked to seeing life as an adventure and savoring life experiences. Leaders are commonly active in many ways outside work, and they recognize the need to exercise the mind, body, and spirit.

Altogether, each of these principles for acquiring leadership qualities can be experienced in both formal and informal education programs. These are preparatory commitments that will serve those seeking to be entrepreneurs or intrapreneurs in the RET industry.

Investing in Professional Networks

Volunteering or obtaining membership in professional associations expands a person's knowledge and skills and is part of building a professional network. There will be opportunities to network with nonprofit industry organizations and specific career-related associations. Nonprofit industry associations facilitate the exchange of information, educate the travel public, and develop programs to promote professionalism within the industry. Professional and **tourism associations** have been around for a long time and exist for nearly every sector of the industry. The same can be said for **entrepreneurial associations**.

Tourism industry associations provide great opportunities for students entering the field and for established entrepreneurs to network, attend educational sessions, earn certifications, meet other professionals, and possibly find jobs or mentors. Tourism associations also conduct research on the industry. These benefits are extremely helpful for people starting out in a career. Some groups operate under the umbrella of a national organization, such as the Commercial Recreation and Tourism Section of the National Recreation and Park Association.

Numerous professional associations have been created to support young entrepreneurs. Members are challenged to address real-world businesses and economic issues in their own ventures as well as in their communities. Involvement in one or more of these associations would certainly help aspiring business-minded people obtain timely information and build valuable networks.

Destination Marketing Organizations (DMO)

Regions, states, provinces, and even countries create organizations to promote themselves as preferred tourism destinations. Because membership in these organizations often includes small and medium businesses as well as national corporations, it is instructive to observe how businesses collaborate with visitor service bureaus. It is worthwhile to investigate in a directed studies course how they work, the career options associated with them, and their influence in creating destination images. In the United States and Canada, states and provinces commit funds to tourism offices, welcome centers, visitor information centers, and their corresponding DMOs. They often provide members with opportunities for cooperative marketing by displaying company brochures in racks at visitor information centers, placing company information on the DMO website, and providing educational opportunities to attend tourism outlook meetings for the region.

Exploring websites will provide an overview of how destination marketing targets the traveler directly, the nature of the relationships with the tourism partners, and ways in which events and attractions are positioned to build a travel itinerary. Some websites have sections on how to start a business within the state or provincial jurisdiction being examined. In addition, many state and pro-vincial DMOs have regular electronic newsletters that keep subscribers up-to-date on new initiatives, changes in the programs, funding initiatives, and scheduled meetings of professional groups. Their websites tend to keep up with the latest in website technology because the marketing environment is competitive. It is worth the effort to search local websites for information; it will become apparent that the benefits of an RET career are endless.

Benefits Are Global and Diverse

When you examine for-profit RET opportunities, you will discover that you are entering an exciting array of global and diverse settings that are open to entrepreneurs or intrapreneurs of all backgrounds. The commercial sector includes a set of businesses and corporations that contribute significantly to the world economy. These businesses are ever changing and technology dependent. What do these benefits mean to a business owner? The following sections offer a partial answer.

Global Reach

For the business-minded person, the opportunity exists to explore many places around the world where your goal for a commercial enterprise might be a good fit. The World Tourism Organization (2014) reports that tourism is now the world's largest employer. Leisure travel accounts for 70 percent of all domestic and international travel spending in the United States, according to the U.S. Travel Association (2017). Domestic travel and commercial recreation have been important for a long time. Corporate, sport, and private events are held in worldwide destinations and bring together global participants such as in the Olympic Games. Although economists began talking about the emergence of a global economy about a decade ago, leisure travel, special events, and domestic tourism have been worldwide activities for more than three centuries.

At the 2014 World Tourism Day celebration, the United Nations World Travel Organization secretary-general reviewed the growth in the tourism industry. He noted that in 1950, travel involved "twenty million, in 2004 it was 760 million, in

OUTSTANDING GRADUATE

Background Information

Name: Karl Robideau

Education: Bachelor of Tourism Management from Vancouver Island University

Credentials: Effective Health and Safety certificate, Crowd and Crisis Management certificate, Leadership Development certificate, first aid and CPR training

Awards: Sales awards from Norwegian Cruise Line, Cobra Group, and Park West Gallery

Career Information

Position: Visitor Experience Manager and Head of Ticketing, Visitor Services, and Volunteer Programs

Organization: The Art Gallery of New South Wales (AGNSW) is an executive agency under the Department of Justice. It is located in Sydney, Australia, and is adjacent to the Royal Botanical Gardens and the Central Business District. The AGNSW is a world-recognized leader in the presentation of ambitious Australian and international exhibitions. The AGNSW is a center of excellence for the preservation, documentation, interpretation, and display of Australian and international art and a forum of scholarship, art education, and the exchange of ideas. Through its collections, exhibitions, programs, and research, the AGNSW aims to enrich visitors' emotional and intellectual engagement with art. Approximately 1.3 million people visit the gallery annually.

Job Description: The primary responsibility of the visitor experience manager is to facilitate an engaging experience for all visitors and support the gallery's strategic objective of connecting with existing and potential audiences more effectively. The duties include leading an integrated front-of-house team (box office, membership, gallery hosts, ticketing, and information), overseeing the gallery's volunteer committees, managing the visitor research programs to understand audience segments and visitor modes, and overseeing the coordination and communication of analytics and data reporting for gallery visitation, transactions, and front-of-house operations.

> " *Work hard, play harder, laugh loud, and love life.* "

Career path: I started my career by working and learning with the Walt Disney Corporation, Norwegian Cruise Line, and Fairmont Hotels and Resorts. In these settings, I was able to develop my passion for visitor service. These world-class organizations offered training and education that allowed me to excel in sales and business development and leadership management.

Through this professional development and via the international connections and relationships I cultivated, I was able to combine my passion for the arts and travel by working in a variety of visual arts organizations. Plymouth Auctioneering and Park West Gallery in Michigan and Florida, United States, and Mossgreen Gallery and Auctions in Melbourne, Australia, offered skills and experience that would open opportunities into a career in cultural organizations, including a professional role at the Museum of Contemporary Art Australia and membership in the New South Wales Volunteer Manager Network.

Likes and dislikes about the job: I like that my job deals with a wide range of people in a variety of settings. For example, a typical day includes engaging with local, interstate, or international visitors enjoying art and public programs in the gallery; participating in focus groups with managers and politicians for the development of the NSW Volunteer Strategy; and then finishing the day with a "pint and a pie" in a local watering hole with an artist. While I never like to dislike anything in life, it is difficult at times when we experience government cuts to funding of the arts sector. However, as a true Albertan would say, "you have to make hay while the sun shines," so it's a good thing I live in Australia.

Advice for Undergraduates

A career in tourism, recreation, and leisure opens a door to a world of possibilities and opportunities. Dedicate yourself to your passion and always allow for change and innovation in the workplace and your interests. Take advantage of the opportunities that extracurricular activities offer.

Leisure travel accounts for nearly 75 percent of all international travel, and tourism is now the world's largest employer.

UIG via Getty Images

2013 it was 1.1 billion and by 2020 it is expected that the number of international tourist arrivals will exceed 1.6 billion per year (World Tourism Organization, 2014).

Diversity

Leisure interests and tourism trends continue to expand, and new markets become evident every year. The numerous small businesses providing diverse products and services to society are vital to leisure experiences. If societal demand is present, an opportunity is available for an entrepreneur to fill it. Although no classification can reveal all the commercial enterprises that are encompassed by the leisure or tourism industry, figure 9.2 presents components of the tourism industry. Entrepreneurship is critical to tourism and travel. Gunn and Var (2002) state the case well:

> Because of the dynamics of tourism, opportunities for innovative service businesses continue to appear. . . . There needs to be a volume of business people interested in and able to see opportunity, obtain a site, gather

the financial support, plan, build and operate a new business. Small business continues to offer the greatest opportunities in spite of the many risks and obstacles. (p. 68)

Economic Impact

The economic benefits associated with commercial and tourism services are extremely important. Tourism is the fastest growing economic sector in terms of foreign exchange and job creation. This growth can stimulate public and private investment in the economy and improve local living conditions for residents. Every year, new projects are undertaken by the business council of the World Tourism Organization to strengthen public–private cooperation and partnerships. The small and medium enterprises (SMEs) that dominate the commercial sector occupy a vital role in the recreation, event, and tourism industry. Small and medium enterprises are vital to a nation's economy, and the services provided by SMEs represent 50 to 55 percent of the tourism industry within North America. The National Federation of Small Businesses found that

75 percent of all jobs in the United States are generated by small business enterprises.

Openness

The public marketplace is open to anyone who is willing to acquire the knowledge and skills necessary to participate in the leisure and tourism industry. The free enterprise system is the cornerstone of the open economy and is one of the reasons that the commercial sector thrives in the leisure and tourism field. The global trend toward privatization of public services has also opened new opportunities for RET businesses. You may have interpersonal abilities in dealing with people based on family history, personal travel experiences, language training, recreational lifestyle preferences, or even cultural heritage that will be an asset in an aspect of the industry. For example, the cultural aptitude of entrepreneurs from India may explain their inclination to dominate the SME in the U.S. lodging sector:

> Many young people immigrated to the United States from India and participated in forming the AAHOA in the late 1980's [sic] which today is the largest hotel association in the world. The association has more than 15,000 members who together own over 20,000 hotels representing more than 40 percent of all hotel properties and 50 percent of the economy lodging properties. The membership of AAHOA is individual entrepreneurs who each have a myriad of personal success stories. The market value of hotels owned by AAHOA is around $38 billion and they create at least a million jobs. (Asian American Hotel Owners Association, n.d.)

TRENDS AND CHALLENGES

Local, regional, and global trends are constantly changing and will affect recreation, event, and businesses and employment prospects in the future. The following are a few of the key current trends along with the challenges and opportunities that they present.

Increasing Requirements for Specialized Skills and Certifications

Today the RET industry demands greater professionalism and higher skill levels of workers in the field than ever before. Until recently, most professionals did not have specialized RET college degrees. Likewise, few universities offered specialized RET degree programs, and almost none offered master's degree RET specializations. In addition, managers frequently came from other industries besides RET. This situation is changing rapidly because the industry is becoming more competitive and demanding specialized skills from its workers (except for some frontline and entry-level positions). Being trained on the job for two weeks does not provide sufficient preparation to perform professional job functions. Job announcements for professional positions now have minimum degree requirements and long lists of preferred skills and experiences that are often specialized to the RET industry (e.g., hospitality accounting or legal issues in the RET field). An array of university undergraduate and graduate degrees now provide appropriate RET training and not just hotel management. In addition to obtaining a general RET degree, an increasingly common way to demonstrate competency in the field is through specialized certificates. These assure potential employers that you have met minimum skill and experience requirements. Examples of RET-related certifications include the following:

- Certified special events professional (CSEP) available through the International Special Events Society
- Certified lodging manager (CLM) available through the American Hotel and Lodging Educational Institute
- Certified recreation and park professional (CRPP) available through the National Recreation and Park Association

An RET-related degree or a certification does not guarantee a job in the field. Combined with industry experience, however, it often provides an advantage and may qualify the applicant for additional job interviews. In addition, RET graduates frequently advance more quickly than nongraduates after they are hired.

Work–Life Balance and Wellness

Along with the trend toward specialized skills and professional certifications, the push for more work hours is ubiquitous in American and Canadian societies. Work in some segments of RET is focused on nights, weekends, and holidays, which can isolate workers, affect wellness, and place extra stress on the worker's physical and mental health, family and partner relationships, and quality of life. Therefore, a new professional in the RET industry must take proactive steps to achieve a work–life balance. These moves could include selecting an employer and supervisor who do not have unrealistic work expectations and do not push salaried staff to put in large amounts of uncompensated overtime. Workers and employers must realize that staff members need time to be physically and socially active if long-term health and productivity are to be maintained.

Likewise, the RET industry is in a unique position to offer services that greatly improve the health and long-term wellness of its clients. Significant growth has been occurring in health-promoting services in the RET industry. Professionals should consider facility, food, scheduling, and activity alternatives that promote wellness. Health is a basic demand that is nearly recession proof. During the 2008 to 2010 recession, spas that focused primarily on pampering lost out to those that offered programs that fostered health as well as personal service. Professionals need to evaluate their services and products to ascertain how they can be modified or how new ones can be developed to enhance client health.

Sustainability and Stewardship

Today, growing concern about the dire environmental impacts of human activities, such as global climate change, has caused many citizens to call for significant changes in businesses' operations so they are more environmentally and socially sustainable. Federal, state or provincial, and local government agencies now require companies that permit to operate in public facilities and on public lands to have comprehensive environmental management systems and to report their performance on moving toward sustainable operations. Resorts and other businesses will need to be better stewards of natural resources and enlist their clients in these efforts. In this modern time, more than ever, the consumer is well-educated and will select a provider based not only on price, value, and quality of the services but also on the company's record of ethical behavior as well as its efforts at reducing environmental impacts and helping the local community. A recent survey of travelers found that 48 percent were willing to pay 10 percent more for services that employ green practices in the travel industry (Tierney, Hunt, & Latkova, 2011). But in the study, only 12 percent could identify a green product or service that they had recently purchased or used in the last year, and most of those were low in cost and commitment. Support for green practices is broad, but RET companies need to educate consumers about their genuine efforts toward environmental and social responsibility. Green business certification has been one way some firms have tried to distinguish themselves and verify their commitment to potential users. Companies with strong environmental and community records and certifications in these areas have competitive advantages, stronger growth, and higher profitability than firms that do not. Therefore, ethics, green practices, and sustainability are bottom-line considerations for how a business plans and operates. Workers in the RET industry who have passion as well as hard skills in delivering green practices will be in demand by employers.

Adventure and Entertainment

Large segments of the population are sedentary, and their daily routines are rather mundane. Many persons, from seniors and families to millennials, are increasingly looking toward RET activities to compensate for inactivity and boredom through adventure and excitement with safety. Others are

Courtesy of Alcatraz Cruises, LLC.

The Hornblower Hybrid, the nation's first hybrid ferry, takes visitors to Alcatraz in California.

looking to be entertained while in the care of an RET company. No longer satisfied to lie around the pool for three days, many people require resorts and other RET providers to offer active, educational alternatives and entertainment. RET providers must offer participatory alternatives despite the potentially greater initial costs, risks, and legal liability. The need is growing for highly trained recreation leaders who are technically skilled in delivery of a specific adventure or entertainment activity and also service oriented with the ability to create a quality experience for the customer.

SUMMARY

The for-profit, or commercial, sector of the tourism and travel industry encompasses a diversity of small, medium, and large enterprises largely focused on attractions, hosting, and support functions for domestic and international travelers. In addition, many SMEs also depend on serving the leisure needs of residents in the communities in which they are located. The structure and key elements of this industry are identified in the model presented in this chapter. By the nature of their financial structure, the business enterprises described in this chapter differ in a variety of ways from public and nonprofit organizations. The fact that recreation, event, and tourism business ventures can be sold, bought, and transferred from one owner to another is one distinguishing characteristic. Businesses also adopt pricing strategies best suited for their target markets that ensure profitability in the long run. One important aspect of serving the travel market is combining products and services with other commercial operations to create an all-inclusive package that appeals to customers seeking one-stop vacation shopping. Packaging products and services can be profitable because it commonly increases the length of stay for the traveler. Consumer preferences can shift quickly based on personal or economic factors and political turmoil; therefore, businesses must be responsive to unexpected changes in the marketplace. The for-profit sector must be entrepreneurial and be prepared for contingencies that arise on short notice. Seasonality of demand for products and services often dictates when attractions are in full operation and when major events are scheduled. Enterprises that rely on seasonal services must include details that address the financial implication of the seasonal nature of leisure and travel activities in their cash-flow statements.

Preparation for employment in the for-profit sector can come from work experience and formal education. Cooperative education and internship programs allow students to be placed in a work setting where they can gain valuable experience. Entrepreneurs will say that good judgment in business comes from experience, and most admit that valuable experience comes from prior bad judgment. In other words, working in a business setting allows you to learn the lessons acquired by the owner over time. In addition, knowing and applying the language of business practices (topics such as accounting, law, leadership, and contingency planning) enables a potential entrepreneur or intrapreneur to contribute to an informed business decision and, at the very least, to be an astute observer of successful practices in the industry. Working in the commercial for-profit sector of the RET industry offers numerous benefits such as travel during employment and working in the business of fun. Most important, knowledge and experience are portable across the work setting among the small, medium, and large enterprises that make up the RET industry.

CHAPTER 10

Therapeutic Recreation

Frances Stavola Daly and Robin Kunstler

Eric Isselè

> **❝** Therapeutic recreation . . . professionals assist people in various states of health to bring joy, value and meaning to their lives. **❞**
>
> Charles Sylvester, Professor Emeritus, Western Washington University

LEARNING OUTCOMES

After reading this chapter, you will be able to do the following:

> Describe therapeutic recreation and its benefits

> Explain the history of therapeutic recreation, including key legislation, and its influence on current therapeutic recreation services such as inclusion

> Comprehend the scope of therapeutic recreation services including settings, programs, interventions, and clientele

> Analyze the steps in the therapeutic recreation process

> Evaluate the components of professionalism and their significance for the therapeutic recreation profession and future professional opportunities

> Identify trends and societal changes that will affect therapeutic recreation services in the 21st century

Learning about how therapeutic recreation (TR) can help people is relevant to students and professionals working in any area of recreation and leisure services. People with disabilities and health conditions participate in recreation programs in all types of settings, and knowledge of how to support their successful participation is essential for all recreation majors. Recreation can be a powerful tool to help improve many aspects of people's lives and contribute to an optimal state of health and well-being. Recreation activities are a major vehicle to attaining this optimal state because they involve challenge, excitement, rewards, choices, concentration, and pure fun. Also, because recreation activities are pleasurable and satisfying, freely chosen, and intrinsically rewarding, people are highly motivated to engage in them. Therefore, recreation can motivate people to change, grow, and improve their health. Recreation has *re-creative* powers; in other words, people can renew, restore, and refresh themselves and develop their abilities and skills through recreation participation. People with illnesses, disabilities, or limiting conditions have the same rights to healthy and satisfying recreation participation as people without disabilities.

Approximately 50 million Americans, or one out of every six people, have at least one **disability**. The proportion of Canadians with disabilities is about the same as in the United States (Bullock, Mahon, & Killingsworth, 2010). Although only half of the people with a disability consider some aspect of their functioning to be impaired, millions of people could potentially benefit from TR services. Because conditions such as disease or disability may impose

barriers on people's ability to engage in recreation, professional assistance such as TR may be required. In fact, most of us can probably recall a situation in which our ability to participate in the things we love to do was impaired by a physical, emotional, or social condition or situation. Research on recreation experiences has found that participation provides physical, cognitive, social, and expressive benefits; promotes growth and development; and contributes to life satisfaction and well-being. For the health care system and society, successful outcomes of TR services can lead to lower health care costs and decreased demand for valuable resources (Ross & Ashton-Shaeffer, 2003).

This chapter will explain how the practice of therapeutic recreation developed; key concepts related to providing TR services; and the scope of TR settings, programs, interventions, and populations. A discussion of the TR process outlines the daily duties of a **therapeutic recreation specialist** (**TRS**). Professional issues, trends, and future challenges are examined to provide concrete information that will help you understand TR and evaluate its suitability as a career choice.

DEFINING THERAPEUTIC RECREATION

What exactly is therapeutic recreation? This question may be the hardest one that you answer when family and friends ask "What is your major?" For TR students, the answer is not simple. Many definitions of TR have been put forth over the years, each with slight variations in language and emphasis, which leads to a lively debate about the true definition of TR. However, all TR definitions include the following common components that capture the essence of TR (Negley, 2010):

- Purposeful selection of recreation activities to reach a goal or **outcome**
- Enhancement of independent **functioning** through recreation participation
- **Quality of life**, wellness, and optimal **health** as core concerns
- Focus on the individual in the context of his or her own environment, including support and resources provided by the family and community

A composite definition of TR that brings together these common components has been developed. It states that TR is "engaging individuals in planned recreation and related experiences in order to improve functioning, health and well-being, and quality of life, while focusing on the whole person and the needed changes in the optimal living environment" (Kunstler & Stavola Daly, 2010, p. 4).

The **American Therapeutic Recreation Association (ATRA)**, the national professional organization for **certified therapeutic recreation specialists (CTRSs)**, explains the relationship between key terms used in the profession:

- *Therapeutic recreation* is the field.
- *Recreational therapy* is the practice.
- *Recreational therapists* are the practitioners.
- *Certified therapeutic recreation specialists* (CTRS) are the qualified providers. (ATRA, 2016)

ATRA presents the following definition:

Recreational therapy, also known as therapeutic recreation, is a systematic process that utilizes recreation and other activity-based interventions to address the assessed needs of individuals with illnesses and/or disabling conditions, as a means to psychological and physical health, recovery and well-being. Further, "Recreational Therapy" means a treatment service designed to restore, remediate and rehabilitate a person's level of functioning and independence in life activities, to promote health and wellness as well as reduce or eliminate the activity limitations and restrictions to participation in life situations caused by an illness or disabling condition (ATRA, n.d.).

You will find that the terms therapeutic recreation, recreation therapy (RT), and recreational therapy are often used interchangeably, as shown in the previous ATRA definition. Some professionals prefer RT because it seems to emphasize the treatment aspects of the field; others prefer the broader term therapeutic recreation. For the purposes of this chapter, we will use therapeutic recreation (TR) as more all-encompassing of the range of the field.

Therapeutic recreation is provided to people of all ages, demographic characteristics, and abilities regardless of health status or level of functioning. This includes children, teenagers, adults, and older adults with physical, developmental, psychiatric, and cognitive conditions as well as those who are affected by social conditions such as homelessness, war, poverty, incarceration, natural disasters, and

Edie Layland - Fotolia

An art class is one type of intervention that a therapeutic recreation specialist might use to improve functional skills, develop a new leisure interest, or contribute to overall well-being.

risky environments. In short, any individual who can benefit from TR can be a recipient of TR services. TR has strong roots in humanistic philosophy, which asserts that people are capable of growth and change, that they strive to meet their needs and goals, and that they are autonomous (capable of making their own decisions and choices and directing their own lives) and inherently altruistic (desire to do good for others). TR is based on a system of beliefs about human nature, needs, and behaviors as well as about the meaning and purpose of recreation, leisure, and play in people's lives. Interaction with others in recreation activities is a strength of TR because it provides emotional and social support, opportunities to learn from others facing similar challenges, and a shared positive experience. For some clients, TR may be their most successful therapy because it is enjoyable and provides opportunities to make choices, set goals, and develop feelings of self-confidence, competence, and belief in their abilities.

HISTORY OF THERAPEUTIC RECREATION

Studying history can help us understand how our profession evolved to its current state and identify the trends and changes that have occurred in TR over time. Most students are fascinated to learn that although the TR profession is less than 100 years old, the benefits of participation in recreational activities for people with illnesses and disabilities were recognized thousands of years ago. The ancient Greeks, who believed in a sound mind in a sound body, built curative temples where activities such as walking, gardening, exercise, boating, and music were offered. The Egyptians created a positive environment using music and dance to treat mood disorders. In India, Charaka, a surgeon, had patients play games and drink wine while he operated on them because he knew that those activities would distract them from the pain. Nonetheless, history provides few examples of compassionate care for those with disabilities until after the Middle Ages.

In Europe, the Renaissance (1400-1600) and the Age of Enlightenment (1700s) brought a greater concern for the rights of all people. The first schools for the deaf and the blind were established in Paris in the late 18th century. In the United States in the early 19th century, hospitals were built to serve people with mental illness, and they provided recreation activities as part of more humane treatment. During the mid-19th century, Florence Nightingale, an English woman who was considered the founder of modern nursing practice, wrote that wounded soldiers should be in beautiful environments or "recreation huts," listen to music, and have visits from family and pets to comfort them and speed their recovery. During the same period, Dorothea Dix advocated for better treatment of people with disabilities and illnesses in U.S. asylums and prisons. The latter half of the 19th century brought many immigrants to North America, and this contributed to the growth of cities and social problems and led to the establishment of settlement houses, which were community centers that provided social services, education, and recreation.

The history of TR from 1889, when the first settlement house was founded, to the present day is presented in the Timeline sidebar.

Legislation

The sociopolitical movements of the latter half of the 20th century led to the passage of landmark legislation in the United States and Canada that not only broadened opportunities for people with disabilities but also reflected and promoted a societal change to more positive attitudes toward people with disabilities. Table 10.1 identifies key U.S. and Canadian laws that have significantly affected the lives of people with disabilities, their rights, and their access to recreation services, which led to the inclusion movement. Currently, Canada does not have a federal law like the Americans with Disabilities Act in the United States, although individual provinces such as Ontario and Manitoba have their own laws protecting the rights of individuals with disabilities.

Inclusion

Inclusion refers to empowering people with disabilities to become valued and active members of their communities through involvement in socially valued life activities. A key tenet of inclusion is that the community offers support, friendship, and resources to facilitate the equal participation in everyday life by all its members. Inclusion philosophy and practices evolved from the core principles and concepts identified in table 10.2. The inclusion

Timeline: History of TR 1880s-present day

1880s—Hull House, the first settlement house (opened in Chicago by Jane Addams), uses recreation to improve the lives of people with substance abuse and people living in poor circumstances.

Early 1900s—Agencies begin to provide recreation to children with disabilities living in the community.

1917-1918—The American Red Cross provides recreation to convalescing soldiers at military bases during World War I.

1920s—Recreation personnel are hired to work in military and veterans' hospitals.

Recreation services are offered in state mental hospitals.

1930s—One of the first experimental research studies is published that demonstrates the value of recreation participation in teaching social skills to children with intellectual disabilities.

Recreation is used as a treatment in psychiatry at the Menninger Clinic in Topeka, Kansas.

1940s—The Red Cross establishes a training program in basic recreation for workers during World War II.

The U.S. Veterans' Administration establishes its Recreation Service.

The first organization for wheelchair sports, the National Wheelchair Basketball Association, is founded.

1950s—Three professional organizations emerge to serve the needs of recreation practitioners working in hospitals and schools and with people with disabilities in varied settings: the National Association of Recreation Therapists (NART); the recreation therapy section of the American Alliance of Health, Physical Education and Recreation (AAHPER); and the hospital recreation section (HRS) of the American Recreation Society (ARS).

Development of standards for practice, personnel, and curricula is underway.

1960s—Special Olympics are founded.

The disability rights movement begins.

Deinstitutionalization is initiated at state and federal levels.

The National Therapeutic Recreation Society is formed from NART and HRS and established as a branch of the National Recreation and Park Association in 1966.

1970s—Landmark U.S. federal legislation is passed regarding equal access to education, provision of recreation services, and accessibility of public facilities (including recreation facilities) for individuals with disabilities.

Federal education grants fund programs, education, and research on therapeutic recreation.

1980s—The age of **accountability** in health care brings stringent documentation requirements.

The American Therapeutic Recreation Association (ATRA) is established in 1980.

The National Council for Therapeutic Recreation Certification (NCTRC) is formed in 1981.

1990s—The Americans with Disabilities Act is passed in 1990.

The inclusion movement gains momentum.

The Canadian Therapeutic Recreation Association (CTRA) is incorporated in 1996.

Evidence-based practice in health care is initiated.

2000s—CTRA and NCTRC agree that the CTRS will be the recognized credential in Canada.

Committee on Accreditation of Recreational Therapy Education (CARTE) is established as the ATRA-supported accreditation program for RT curricula.

The NCTRC establishes a specialty certification program.

The NRPA changes its organizational structures and eliminates branches including the NTRS.

Four U.S. states enact licensure for RT/TR.

RT/TR services further expand to serve people with disabilities in community settings, schools, prevention and health promotion programs, and wounded veterans.

Table 10.1 Key Laws of the United States and Canada

UNITED STATES	
Law	**Description**
PL 90-480 Architectural Barriers Act, 1968	Mandated physical accessibility and usability of buildings and facilities
Section 504 of the Rehabilitation Act, 1973	Mandated program accessibility for people with disabilities
PL 94-142 Education for All Handicapped Children Act, 1975	Stated that all handicapped children were entitled to a free and appropriate public education in the least restrictive environment and may receive recreation as a related service
PL 101-476 Individuals with Disabilities Education Act, 1990	Reauthorization of PL 94-142 that emphasized family involvement, required transition planning, and provided for assistive technology
PL 101-336 Americans with Disabilities Act (ADA), 1990	Comprehensive civil rights law intended to eliminate discrimination against people with disabilities in all aspects of American life including employment, government services, public transportation, public accommodations, and telecommunications; required that reasonable accommodation be made to facilitate participation by people with disabilities in these five areas by removing barriers and providing auxiliary aids and services as necessary
ADA Amendments Act, 2008	Expands interpretation of disability, major life activities, and major life functions to make it easier for individuals to seek protection under the ADA
CANADA	
Law	**Description**
Vocational Rehabilitation for Disabled Persons Act, 1962	Provided rehabilitation services for people with disabilities
Canadian Charter of Rights and Freedoms, 1982	Stated that all people have the right to equal protection and benefit of the law without discrimination based on mental and physical disability
In Unison: A Canadian Approach to Disability Issues (government report, not a law), 1998	Provided the basis for asserting equal rights for people with disabilities to achieve full integration and access to supports, services, employment, and income

movement has broadened the traditional view of TR from focusing solely on the person to serving the person in the context of the total environment and the settings the person inhabits throughout his or her life. The role of TRSs in facilitating inclusion is to help clients achieve their goals of living in the most inclusive environment possible through minimizing and removing barriers to inclusion.

THERAPEUTIC RECREATION SETTINGS AND SERVICES

By now you're probably wondering where you can work as a TRS and what a typical day is like for a TRS. One of the exciting aspects of the TR profession is the range of settings and populations served by TR specialists. People of all ages with all types of disabilities, health conditions, or social challenges are potential recipients of TR services,

which can include seemingly infinite types of recreation activities. Students contemplating this profession can consider many possibilities ranging from acute medical or psychiatric treatment in the hospital setting, to residential facilities for individuals with developmental disabilities or HIV/AIDS, to long-term care for people with multiple sclerosis, Huntington's disease, or dementia. TR is offered in hospice programs, physical rehabilitation centers, military bases, prisons, assisted-living facilities, adult day cares, partial hospitalization and outpatient programs, drug treatment programs, homeless shelters, group homes, schools, early intervention programs, community recreation centers, camps, and people's homes. TRSs may serve as inclusion specialists in community-based programs using their knowledge of disability, accessibility, assessment, and activity analysis to facilitate the participation of people with disabilities in these programs.

Table 10.2 Building Blocks of Inclusion

Building blocks	Definitions
Deinstitutionalization	The move away from large-scale, institution-based care to small-scale, community-based facilities; began in the late 1960s
Accessibility	Equal entry into, and participation in, physical facilities and programs by all people; accomplished through the elimination of architectural, administrative, and attitudinal barriers to create a usable environment
Normalization	Making available to people with disabilities the patterns and conditions of everyday life that are as culturally normative as possible
Integration	Physical presence and social interaction of people with and without disabilities in the same setting
Mainstreaming	Movement of people into the activities and settings of the wider community
Least-restrictive environment	The environment that imposes the fewest restrictions and barriers on a person's growth, development, and participation in a full life
Supports	Friendships, social networks, assistance, and resources that enable a person to participate in the full life of his or her community
Person-first language	Language that puts the word *person* or *people* first in the sequence of a phrase or sentence to emphasize a positive attitude toward the individual (e.g., a person with a disability rather than a disabled person)
Inclusion	Empowering people who have disabilities to be valued and active members of their communities by making choices, being supported in daily life, and having opportunities to grow and develop to their fullest potential

Job Duties and Responsibilities

The majority of TRSs spend most of their time fulfilling the TR leadership role by planning and leading group TR programs. Depending on the setting, the TRS may also provide one-to-one TR activities. To implement an appropriate TR program of activities, the TRS

- conducts individual assessments,
- develops treatment plans,
- plans a schedule of TR programming,
- motivates clients to participate in TR activities,
- observes and documents their participation and progress, and
- attends treatment team meetings (also known as *comprehensive care-planning meetings* or similar names) and in-service training.

Other duties include

- maintaining equipment and supplies,
- supervising volunteers and interns,
- providing support to family members,
- advocating for the rights of clients, and
- organizing special events and community outings.

Management responsibilities may include

- budgeting,
- risk management,
- marketing, and
- participating in strategic planning and performance improvement projects.

The TRS is recognized as a vital member of the professional health care team. The team meets regularly to develop and review the plan of care or services for the client. Depending on the setting, the other members of the team might be physicians, nurses and nursing assistants, dietitians, social workers, and physical, occupational, or speech therapists. In addition, rehabilitation counselors, mental health staff, creative arts therapists, teachers, and physical fitness trainers might be members of the team depending on the type of setting and the services offered. Each TRS should be an active participant in the team process by accurately reporting on the client's status and progress toward goals. The TRS has a significant contribution to make to the team's understanding of the client because the TRS works with the client in the most natural and relaxed setting in the service environment. The TRS can observe the client's strengths and needs during typical activities.

TR Activities and Interventions

For TR students and professionals, it is vital to understand humans and their development throughout the life span, the variations in human development and experience, the effects of these variations on lifestyle, and the potential contributions of leisure, recreation, and play to healthy human development and to have knowledge of a wide range of activities and interventions. Each of us is responsible for developing a philosophy of professional practice based on our readings, reflections, and values that will support our efforts and deepen our understanding of and commitment to our chosen field.

TRSs use a range of modalities, including traditional recreation activities such as the arts, sport, fitness and exercise, games, crafts, social activities, outdoor recreation, horticulture, aquatics, and community outings. They also use nontraditional activities such as **leisure education**, volunteering, adult education, and animal-assisted (pet) therapy. TRSs may also implement therapeutic interventions such as cognitive stimulation, sensory awareness, assertiveness training, anger management, pain management, stress management, and leisure counseling, depending on the mission and goals of the agency and the needs of the population being served. Complementary and alternative medicine (CAM) is also becoming an area for TR practice. Interventions such as relaxation, meditation, aromatherapy, yoga, and tai chi are popular.

THERAPEUTIC RECREATION PRACTICE MODELS

Depending on the setting, the TR department may follow one of the TR **practice models** that have been developed over the years. A practice model is a visual representation of the relationships between philosophy and theory and the real world and serves as a guide for practice. The benefits of providing TR services according to an appropriate practice model are that a model directs the types of programs and services offered, communicates the purposes and services of TR to other disciplines, and ensures that clients are provided the services and interven-

Fitness and exercise is just one modality a therapeutic recreation specialist may implement.

Monkey Business/fotolia.com

tions best suited to their needs and goals. Practice models often reflect the political and social realities of the period in which they were developed. In all models, TR emphasizes the abilities and strengths of the client to overcome or alleviate the limitations imposed by disability or illness. TR also stresses that people have the right to live in the optimal environment of their choice with appropriate supports. These supports may be provided by the person, his or her family and friends, community agencies, and other sectors of the environment as needed. This ecological perspective recognizes that the person's family, friends, and community are significant factors in his or her health and well-being.

The predominant TR practice models include the leisure ability model, the health protection and health promotion (HP/HP) model, and the TR service and outcomes models. Each model represents TR practice in a unique way. For example, in the leisure ability model, TR is provided along a continuum encompassing three types of services—functional intervention, leisure education, and recreation participation—to develop one's leisure lifestyle. According to the HP/HP model, the purpose of TR is to achieve optimal health in a favorable environment by using prescriptive activities, recreation, and leisure as interventions. The TR service model describes a role for TR in four areas of health care provision, including diagnosis and needs assessment, treatment and rehabilitation, education, and prevention and health promotion. In the TR outcome model, the purpose of TR is to increase quality of life by improving functioning in one or more of the behavioral domains, which should result in improved health as well.

Many of the trends over the last 25 years, such as inclusion, a shift to community-based health care, an increase in chronic conditions, people living longer with severe medical problems and disabilities, a focus on spiritual health, and strengths-based approaches to services, have led to the development of additional models. These include the self-determination and enjoyment enhancement model (Dattilo, Kleiber, & Williams, 1998) and the optimizing lifelong health through therapeutic recreation model (Wilhite, Keller, & Caldwell, 1999). More recent models reflect newer thinking regarding positive psychology, such as in the leisure and well-being model (Hood & Carruthers, 2007); the importance of the spiritual domain to well-being, such as in the leisure-spiritual coping model (Heintzman, 2008); and the strengths-based approach, such as in the flourishing through leisure model (Heyne & Anderson, 2012). The growing cultural and lifestyle diversity of North American society has also brought about a rethinking of the models in light of varying cultural beliefs and practices related to health care and individual responsibility (Deiser, 2002; Sylvester, Voelkl, & Ellis, 2001) and has led to increased focus on developing cultural competence.

In Canada, the primary model is the leisure ability model, which reflects that nation's longstanding commitment to integration of people with disabilities into all aspects of society and its recognition that recreation is a part of the vision of full citizenship for all Canadians. Practitioners in the United States also follow the leisure ability model as well as the HP/HP model, which is becoming more prevalent in clinical settings. The strengths-based approach and leisure well-being model are also becoming more widely adopted and incorporated into many aspects of the TR process in all settings. While most of the models are used in various settings, these are the ones that are currently receiving the most attention.

THERAPEUTIC RECREATION PROCESS

The NCTRC periodically conducts a job analysis to identify the job tasks of a CTRS. Most of these tasks are aspects of the TR process, which is a series of steps used to carry out TR. A handy acronym for the four steps in the TR process is APIE: assessment, planning, implementation, and evaluation. The TR process can be applied in any setting where recreation is used with therapeutic intent to help a person achieve specific outcomes. Let's examine the four steps more closely and apply them to the case of Mr. Jones, shown in the sidebar.

Assessment

The first step is **assessment**, which is a systematic process of gathering and synthesizing information about the client and his or her environment using a variety of methods, such as interviews, observation, standardized tests, and input from other disciplines and significant others, to devise an individualized

OUTSTANDING GRADUATE

Background Information

Name: Leduc Le

Education: BS in therapeutic recreation from Lehman College, Bronx, New York; AS in mental health–human services from LaGuardia Community College, Queens, New York

Credentials: Certified Therapeutic Recreation Specialist (CTRS), Certified Dementia Practitioner (CDP)

Awards: New York State Therapeutic Recreation Association (NYSTRA) 2015 Student of the Year

Affiliations: New York State Therapeutic Recreation Association (NYSTRA) professional member; president of the Lehman College Therapeutic Recreation, Recreation Education, Administration and Exercise and Sport Club, 2014-2015

Career Information

Position: Senior Certified Therapeutic Recreation Specialist

Organization: Sans Souci Rehabilitation and Nursing Center in Yonkers, New York, is part of the CareRite Centers Network. Our rehabilitation programs significantly enrich the health and well-being of our patients by delivering specialized therapies to get our patients back on their feet rapidly, which can include physical, occupational, respirational, and recreation therapy.

Organization mission: Our mission is to foster and provide unprecedented levels of genuine care and customer service for our community's rehabilitation and nursing needs in a soothing, tranquil, and state-of-the-art environment. The Sans Souci Rehabilitation and Nursing Center experience enlivens our guests' physical and emotional strength through cutting-edge technology and highly trained health care professionals.

Job description: My job responsibilities include the following:

- Plan and implement appropriate recreation activities for patients in accordance with guidelines set by the organization and the profession
- Develop programs and regularly update progress notes and care plans
- Provide therapeutic recreation intervention and maintain the physical, mental, and psychosocial well-being of each resident
- Ensure patients are oriented to recreation therapy by providing social and diversional programs as well as educating patients on community resources

Career path: I began my journey at LaGuardia Community College, where I was working toward an associate of science degree in mental health–human services. I then transferred to Lehman College, where I was planning to pursue a path to physical therapy. The director of the exercise science program asked me one question: Why physical therapy? I honestly did not know why; I did, however, tell him that I do have a passion for helping people, connecting to them in a way that will allow them to have an overall healing experience, and I wanted to do this by entering the health field. He suggested that before I make any final decision I should talk to Robin Kunstler, the head of therapeutic recreation.

Robin Kunstler ended up being one of my mentors for the next two years and would help me become the professional I am today.

Because of the love I felt for this field, I had a drive burning within to do all I could to succeed. I became the president of our recreation club and helped our department make an impression in our college community while also helping other students in our program reach our common goal of becoming true professionals. I was later recognized by the New York State Therapeutic Recreation Association (NYSTRA) as Student of the Year of 2015. Because I wanted to experience as much as I could before picking a population to focus on, I began work at Bradford Woods Outdoor Center in Indiana as the evening program coordinator of the recreation therapy summer camp program. This program serves children with physical and mental disabilities, and my job was to plan and implement large special event programs every night for groups of as many as 80 children. The time I spent there was life changing, and I was sure I would choose to work with this population; however, during my internship at New York Presbyterian Hospital, I was able to use what I had learned at Bradford Woods as well as learn new methods to add to my arsenal of TR skills. It was demanding and so different, yet completely worth the challenge. After acquiring my CTRS certification, I was hired at Sans Souci Rehabilitation and Nursing Center, where I became the recreation therapist in charge of our short-term rehabilitation unit.

Likes and disliked about the job: What I like most about working in my job is assessing my residents and creating specific programs to fit their needs. I love solving puzzles, and the best puzzle is getting to know my resident and figuring out the best way to enrich his or her life. That's a puzzle I will be more than willing to keep solving throughout my lifetime. What I dislike about my job is that there are not enough CTRSs to provide services. The more the merrier, I say.

Advice for Undergraduates

If you are a person who has a passion for helping others, this is the profession for you. Therapeutic recreation is a field unlike any other form of therapy. We have the ability to affect our patients in all aspects of their lives. This allows us to build unshakable bonds with the people we work with in a way that will also have an impact on *our* own lives. We as professionals have the power to be structured, yet so creative, allowing us to be the heart of any facility we work in. My advice for undergraduate students in therapeutic recreation is to remember that we are the future of this profession. Be involved and always strive for knowledge. When I was an undergrad—particularly when I was the president of the recreation club—I did all I could to grow as a student so I could leave an impression on my professors, my fellow students, and the TR professionals I encountered. Because of those efforts, I was able to share my love for TR with other students, which made learning that much more fun. Use your passion and continue to learn so you can better yourself and better recreation therapy. A quote from an unknown source that I live by and share with my residents is "I can do anything; I just need to be taught how to do it." Folks, we can be that teacher!

Illustration of the TR Process: The Case of Mr. Jones

As part of the TR process, the TRS might design a specific intervention that targets a client's functional limitations. For example, Mr. Jones had a stroke that resulted in muscle weakness and stiffness. The team identified his goals as strengthening his muscles and increasing his range of motion. During the TR assessment, Mr. Jones stated that he enjoyed swimming and spending time with his grandchildren and he wanted to continue to do these things. The TRS worked with the physical therapist to plan the interventions to help reach the goals. Mr. Jones agreed to participate in adapted aquatics three times a week (frequency) for 30 minutes each time (intensity) for four weeks (duration). He needed to learn how to use a flotation device to support him in the pool. The expectation was that at the end of the four weeks, he would have made predetermined improvements in his muscle strength, range of motion, and ability to use the flotation device.

The TRS can also identify and indicate in the written plan specific leadership and therapeutic approaches to use with the client. Mr. Jones might require frequent positive reinforcement, physical assistance, or a demonstration of the appropriate use of the adapted equipment to promote his progress. Mr. Jones' discharge plan might include information and scheduling about an adapted swim program for senior citizens at the local YMCA.

During the implementation phase, the TRS evaluated Mr. Jones' progress in the adapted aquatics. Formative evaluation revealed that Mr. Jones was scheduled for aquatics in the morning, but it became apparent that he was too tired at that time, so the program was moved to the afternoon. He stated he was a little fearful about entering the pool because of his muscle weakness and stiffness, and he required assistance from two staff members rather than one, as was originally planned. This change was made as soon as the need was recognized. At the end of the four weeks, the summative evaluation identified that Mr. Jones had made a 25 percent increase in his range of motion and minimal improvement in muscle strength. He also expressed feelings of relaxation because of the aquatics and a desire to invite his grandson to participate with him, thereby gaining the benefits of family recreation. Mr. Jones was successful in making measurable progress toward his functional goals and gained additional qualitative benefits from the TR experience.

treatment or service plan. The information the TRS seeks includes the client's strengths and areas that need improvement and his or her levels of physical, social, emotional, and cognitive functioning related to two areas: (1) capability to participate in different types of TR programs and (2) aspects that can be improved through TR participation. The TRS also obtains information related to the client's leisure functioning including interests, needs, perceived problems with leisure, patterns of participation, available leisure partners, planning and decision-making skills, and knowledge of and ability to use leisure resources. The client may be asked what his or her goals are to best understand motivations and develop the most appropriate plan. Obtaining input from the client, to the best of the client's ability, is an essential component of conducting an assessment so the client feels invested in the TR process.

Planning

Planning refers to the development of the client's individual treatment or program plan. By participating in the planning process with the assistance of the TRS, clients are at the center of their services. This approach increases their feelings of control over decisions affecting their care and treatment and enhances their motivation to participate, thereby maximizing the benefits of TR. TRSs also use individuals' strengths in planning to overcome their limitations and to reinforce their abilities and perceived competence, which are components of the strengths-based approach. Utilizing this approach, the TRS helps people reach their goals and aspirations through active participation in planning their services (Anderson & Heyne, 2012). Once developed, the plan is placed in the client's chart as the official record of the TR services that the client will receive. The plan generally includes an assessment summary, the client's goals and specific objectives (or steps) to reach the goals, a schedule of the client's planned participation in the TR program, and a discharge plan, if required.

Based on the assessment, the TRS specifies goals or outcomes that the client will work toward during intervention. These goals can be related to changing leisure-related behaviors, reducing health concerns, improving functional ability, and increasing quality of life. Goals are statements that provide direction for the client's services. Client goals may be identified by the professional health care team for appropriate intervention by one or more disciplines. For example, goals could be to increase range of motion, attention span, or social interaction. As a member of the treatment team, the TRS addresses team-specified goals and develops goals, with input from the client whenever possible, for client use of recreation-based interventions. In addition to addressing functional goals, the TRS can set goals related to leisure behavior. These goals could include acquiring knowledge of community resources for recreation participation or learning how to use adapted equipment to enable participation in a recreation activity. The TRS then specifies a series of behavioral objectives, also known as *measurable goals,* which are steps toward achieving the overall goal. The successful accomplishment of each behavioral objective or measurable goal in the progression will lead to meeting the overall client goals. The terms used to describe goals and objectives may differ from setting to setting. Some settings use *behavioral objectives* instead of measurable goals or *outcomes* instead of goals. The intent and purpose are the same regardless of terminology.

A major component of the planning step is the selection and scheduling of specific TR interventions or activities. Recreation activities are the primary means through which TRSs serve clients, so they need to understand which recreation activities produce which outcomes. Just as a doctor knows which medications to prescribe to treat an illness, TRSs work with their clients to select the recreation activities that offer the best chances of producing results. Understanding the benefits of participation in TR programs helps the TRS select appropriate activities to enable clients to reach their desired goals. An important TR practice is to have clients be as involved as possible in planning the TR services that they will receive. This is known as a *person-centered approach.* The TRS should work with the client to choose activities that he or she is interested and willing to participate in. Using **activity analysis**, the TRS analyzes the behaviors required to participate in an activity. The TRS can then prescribe a specific activity or a group of activities in the **individual treatment plan** or care plan. A given activity may help a client progress toward more than one goal, or several activities may address a single goal. For an older nursing home resident with dementia, playing computer games can help increase attention span, improve eye–hand coordination, stimulate cognitive functioning, and promote feelings of accomplishment. This resident may participate in a sewing group in addition to, or instead of, the computer games and be working toward the same goals.

Collaboration among disciplines at team meetings can help develop the optimal plan for the client. The TRS is often responsible for developing a weekly or monthly calendar of all TR programs and activities that are offered. To plan a feasible calendar for maximum participation, the TRS might need to coordinate with other disciplines to schedule facility use and avoid conflicts in scheduling services such as a physical or occupational therapy session, a meeting with a social worker, or a consultation with a dietitian.

Implementation

The third step in the TR process is implementation. To implement the program, the TRS puts the client's individual TR plan in action. This step involves motivating the client to participate in individual and group TR activities. Implementation considers the overall facility schedule, available space and resources, needed equipment and supplies, needs of the client, and staffing requirements of programs. Successful implementation may require adjustments to the plan to maximize the benefits to the client.

Evaluation

Evaluation is the final step in the TR process. Evaluation is both formative and summative. **Formative**

evaluation is ongoing during the implementation phase and leads to immediate changes and improvements in the treatment plan. **Summative evaluation** occurs at the completion of the program to determine whether the program helped the client reach his or her goals and whether changes are needed before implementing the program with other clients. A plan might not produce the desired results due to

- changes in the client's condition,
- use of new medications,
- lack of support from family,
- failure to obtain important information during the assessment,
- lack of skill on the part of the TRS,
- inappropriate leadership approaches, or
- inconsistency on the part of the team.

Determining the factors that may have impeded the client's progress is an important evaluation task.

The client will probably achieve the outcomes according to the treatment plan. Planned health care

Implementing a program involves motivating the client to participate in individual and group TR activities.

outcomes are generally measured in quantitative terms such as the amount of time spent in activity or improvement in the ability to perform a certain task. A client may experience some unintended benefits as well, such as feelings of relaxation or pleasure in social opportunities. These unplanned benefits may be just as significant and are often more subjective, meaning that they are unique to the participant and relate to the quality, enjoyment, and personal meaning of the experience for the client. They should not be overlooked when reporting a client's progress in TR because they can provide a fuller picture of the client's accomplishments.

Documentation

It is critical that the TRS document the client's progress. Some professionals consider this the fifth step in the TR process. TR **documentation** is the written or electronic recording of a client's participation and progress in the TR program. This information is recorded in the client's record or medical chart, which is considered a legal document, and supplies evidence of the TR services provided and the outcomes of participation for the client. The accuracy of the TRS's documentation should be above reproach. Documentation occurs at regularly scheduled intervals and is reviewed by auditors, surveyors, and regulators of accrediting bodies and governmental agencies. Every TRS must be well-informed of agency policies regarding documentation.

PROFESSIONALISM

You may now be asking yourself whether TR is right for you and what you can look forward to if you decide to become a TRS. Approximately 18,600 people are employed as recreational therapists in the United States, and this number is projected to grow by 12 percent by 2024 (Bureau of Labor Statistics, 2015). Thousands more work as recreation leaders in therapeutic settings. Most TR professionals work in hospitals (38 percent) and skilled nursing facilities (19 percent), and 80 percent work with adults and older adults (NCTRC, 2014). More jobs may also develop in community-based settings, as opposed to hospital and inpatient treatment facilities, as services develop for people in their local communities. The average salary for the 18,600 recreational therapists in the United States is $45,890 (Bureau of Labor Statistics, 2016). According to the National Council for Therapeutic Recreation Certification (2014), the average annual salary of 15,000 CTRSs in the United States was $48,417 per year. Earning potential can go as high as $100,000 per year for directors of departments who have advanced degrees and extensive experience, depending on setting and location.

Keep in mind that being a professional entails more than just carrying out your job duties and responsibilities. Being a professional in any field means

- obtaining an education,
- possessing the credentials recognized by your profession,
- being an active member of professional organizations at local and international levels,
- providing services based on professional standards of practice,
- adhering to a code of ethical behavior, and
- updating your professional knowledge through reading and research.

Education

The first step in becoming a TR professional is to obtain an education in TR, which provides a philosophical and theoretical foundation related to TR service provision and extensive knowledge in areas essential to TR practice. Knowledge areas include the nature of illness and disability, the effects of disability on functioning, the role of TR in addressing the limitations imposed by disability, and the procedures and methods used by TRSs in developing treatment plans and implementing TR services. TR curricula may be an option or specialization in a recreation degree program or its own degree program at the associate, bachelor, master, or doctoral level. College programs may apply for **accreditation**, a process by which the academic program is evaluated according to a set of standards for curriculum content. Although accreditation of curricula is not required by law, accreditation ensures that the content areas cover essential information for college students. The Council on Accreditation of Parks, Recreation, Tourism, and Related Professions (COAPRT) has developed and issued outcomes for curriculum content areas to be included in recreation degree programs that can be applied to TR. In 2010, an accreditation process exclusively for TR and RT academic programs, the Committee on Accreditation of Recreational Therapy Education (CARTE), was formally initiated with the Commission on Accreditation of Allied Health Education Programs (CAAHEP). Regardless of the accreditation status of a college program, the value of a sound education in TR cannot be overstated and is a component of requirements for obtaining appropriate professional credentials.

Credentialing

Credentialing is the process by which a profession or government certifies that a professional has met the established minimum standards of competency required for practice. Credentialing is intended to protect consumers when they receive services. The three types of credentialing programs are registration, certification, and licensure. Registration is a voluntary listing of people who practice in a profession according to established criteria. Certification also requires meeting a set of predetermined criteria and usually includes a written examination. Licensure is a process by which state governments mandate qualifications for practice and administer a licensing program. In TR, the largest credentialing program is administered by the **National Council for Therapeutic Recreation Certification (NCTRC)**. To be eligible for certification as a CTRS according to NCTRC, applicants must meet a combination of education and experience requirements and pass the certification examination. In 2010, NCTRC established a specialty certification program to recognize advanced levels of practice in five areas: physical medicine and rehabilitation, geriatrics, developmental disabilities, behavioral health, and community inclusion services. Utah,

North Carolina, New Hampshire, and Oklahoma have passed licensure laws, and several other states, including New York, are actively pursuing this legislation.

The credentialing process attests that you have met the standards to practice your profession and that your judgment and decision-making skills as a professional can be trusted. To maintain your credentials, most credentialing programs require TR professionals to participate in continuing education activities to update their knowledge and skills for practice. Workshops and conferences that cover a wide range of topics are offered by professional organizations at the local, state, regional, national, and international levels.

Professional Organizations

By becoming a member of a professional TR organization or association, you are joining your peers to promote the value of TR; participate in education, communication, and advocacy; and establish and maintain standards of professional practice and behavior. The national TR professional organizations are the ATRA in the United States and the CTRA in Canada. Almost every state and province has either a TR organization or a TR branch of the state or provincial recreation association. Examples include the New York State Therapeutic Recreation Association (NYSTRA) and Therapeutic Recreation Ontario (TRO). Local TR chapters of ATRA have also been formed, such as the New Jersey/Eastern Pennsylvania chapter. Joining professional organizations demonstrates your commitment to advancing the profession. Many TRSs agree that one of the most valued benefits of membership is the interaction with peers through networking, sharing ideas, and forging lasting friendships based on common interests and needs.

Standards of Practice

Standards of practice define the scope of services provided by TR professionals and state a minimal, acceptable level of service delivery. Adherence to these standards ensures consistent practice across service settings and helps establish the credibility of the profession. ATRA and CTRA have both developed sets of standards that cover the following core practices: assessment, treatment planning, documentation, and management. You will find that these standards are valuable guides in designing and implementing quality services and helping ensure ethical practice and behavior.

Ethics

A hallmark of a true profession is a **code of ethics**, which is a written description of the established duties and obligations of the professional to protect the human rights of recipients of services. ATRA and the provincial Canadian TR associations have codes of ethics for TR professionals. All codes cover the four major bioethical principles:

1. **Autonomy.** The client has the right to self-determination, which may conflict with what you, the family, other staff members, or the agency thinks is best for the client.
2. **Beneficence.** Only do good for your clients.
3. **Nonmalfeasance.** Use care and skill in service so you prevent and do not cause harm.
4. **Justice.** Allocate resources in a fair and equitable manner.

Other ethical concerns include confidentiality (the client has the right to control access to information about himself or herself and to know who will have access to that information), maintaining a professional relationship with clients (not overstepping boundaries into friendships or personal relationships), and cultural competence (understanding and respecting diverse beliefs and values and how they influence clients' behaviors).

Keeping Current in the Profession

The foundation of a profession is a body of knowledge derived from research. Professionals have the obligation to read and apply relevant research findings. Reading research helps practitioners become more reflective and thoughtful in their work and can enrich their practice as they apply proven techniques. TR research is published in professional journals such as the *Therapeutic Recreation Journal*, *Annual in Therapeutic Recreation*, and the *American Journal of Recreation Therapy*.

In addition to reading and applying research, professionals should actively participate in the research process to contribute to the body of knowledge in the field by writing books, chapters, and magazine articles for the TR field and for publications geared to other professions and the public. There is a need for efficacy research in TR, which is research that demonstrates that TR can produce the outcomes it claims to produce. This research leads to a refinement of TR interventions targeted to specific health care problems and goals. Many TR settings offer the opportunity to implement a research project.

Right now, you might not be interested in conducting research, but an important trend in health care, which started in Canada, uses practitioners' expertise and research findings to select the best programs and services to achieve outcomes. This approach, known as **evidence-based practice (EBP)**, enables practitioners and researchers to collaborate on systematically collecting data to provide evidence of the optimal type of care for clients. Practitioners can write up the results of their research and publish it in appropriate journals and present their findings at professional conferences. Increasing the body of knowledge of TR through research continues to be a major objective of the TR profession.

Being a professional implies a sense of calling to do more than just go to work every day and carry out assigned responsibilities and duties. Professionalism implies dedication to the beliefs and values of your chosen field, lifelong learning, and commitment to the highest standards of practice. As you explore the TR profession and meet TR practitioners, observe the demeanor and behaviors of people who demonstrate admirable qualities. Can they articulate the meaning and value of TR? Are they enthusiastic and positive about the work they do? Do they demonstrate their love of TR through professional activities outside work and keep up to date with the latest developments? To have a rewarding and fulfilling career, you may wish to emulate these professional qualities.

YOUR FUTURE IN THERAPEUTIC RECREATION

Students are often attracted to a TR major because of their interest in being part of a helping profession that works with people in health or human service settings. Sensitivity, compassion, patience, communication skills, and the desire to help people are essential to working as a TRS. Many students also are attracted to recreation as a major because of their interest in activities such as sport, fitness, outdoor pursuits, music, or art, and then they discover TR. Although no one personality type is best suited to TR, people who enter helping professions such as TR often possess certain attributes. Being self-aware, having the desire to learn new things and to communicate with people, being comfortable with taking initiative, being flexible and adaptable to change and unexpected events, and having creative ideas, energy, enthusiasm, and compassion for people are highly desirable qualities that facilitate a relationship focused on helping the client achieve his or her goals.

Whatever has led you to the TR field, essential elements to continued professional success and satisfaction are knowledge of a wide range of traditional recreation activities, the ability to implement credible programs, and the motivation to learn new activities. Although TRSs must have general knowledge of recreation opportunities, they must also be skilled in nontraditional facilitation techniques as well as the increasingly popular wellness and **health promotion** modalities described at the beginning of the chapter. These methods may include stress management, assertiveness training, sensory stimulation, and a variety of wellness and relaxation techniques. You will learn about many recreation activities as part of your TR curriculum. Attending workshops and conferences is a valuable way to gain exposure to and learn about innovative programs and techniques. Taking noncredit, continuing education, or adult education courses helps you stay up-to-date with fresh program ideas. Certifications are offered in specialty areas such as adapted aquatics, horticulture therapy, personal training, aromatherapy, and yoga. Some jobs may require a driver's license or certification in first aid, CPR, or lifeguard and water safety instruction. Obtaining specialized training and credentials will enhance your qualifications as a TRS and enrich your job performance. One of the wonderful features of TR is that your personal interests can be incorporated into professional practice. You should strive to keep your work interesting and participate with your clients with a sense of joy and fun. If *you* are bored by the programs that you lead, think about how your clients will feel!

You will benefit from learning new interventions and therapeutic methods as well as management techniques and administrative processes. Skills in budgeting, grant writing, marketing, public relations, oral and written communication, and the use of technology are essential for TRSs who wish to become supervisors and administrators of TR services. Collaboration skills are needed to work with other disciplines, departments, and agencies to improve client outcomes, maximize resources, and reduce duplication of services. **Cross-cultural competence**, which refers to the ability to understand, respect, and communicate with diverse people, is essential in the culturally diverse nations of Canada and the United States. Cross-cultural competence is essential for successful interactions with other staff members, clients, and their families.

TRENDS FOR THE 21ST CENTURY

What does the future hold for the TR profession? As you have read, TR is a broad and varied field that operates in numerous settings and with diverse people with all types of disabilities and health conditions. Changes in health care, economic pressures, social trends, demographic characteristics, and technological advances are influencing society to focus on health promotion, independent functioning, quality of life, and quality and effectiveness of services. These concerns present challenges and opportunities for growth and innovation in the TR field. Health promotion and disease prevention, particularly in the areas of obesity and stress-related illness and reducing the impacts of disability, can be achieved through participation in recreation activities such as exer-

© Jon Feingersh/Blend Images/Corbis

Attending workshops and conferences is a valuable way to gain exposure to and learn about innovative programs and techniques.

cise, dance, gardening, art, and sport. Wellness practices such as tai chi, yoga, massage, and aromatherapy are being incorporated into many TR programs. Encouraging people to take responsibility for their health can improve health status and lead to independent functioning.

The shift from the institution to the community as the primary residential setting for people with disabilities has opened the doors for TR practice in schools, day programs, group homes, community centers, military bases, schools, and individuals' homes. Emphasis in these settings is on promoting independent functioning and finding joy and meaning in life through recreation participation in the optimal living environment. TRSs have responded to these changes by offering retirement planning, early intervention, family leisure counseling, and community reintegration. The inclusion movement will continue to expand, offering opportunities for TRSs to function as community inclusion specialists, accessibility consultants, and trainers in leadership techniques and adaptations for people with disabilities. In the political arena, TR organizations have lobbied to include TR in legislation and regulations concerning health care, education, and disability. Many states are pursuing government-sponsored licensure to strengthen the value of the credentialing process for TR practitioners.

Those who enter the profession will confront several challenges. Although many professionals participate in professional organizations, obtain their credentials, keep current with the latest developments, and continually improve their programs and services, greater involvement in these professional activities is vital for the full recognition of TR as an essential service. Membership in professional organizations at every level does not reflect the number of people who identify themselves as working in TR. Many who are eligible to obtain professional credentials have chosen not to do so. Employers continue to hire people to work in TR positions who are not educated in TR. Curricula in college and university TR programs vary. Inconsistency in using the best practices of the field still exists across TR settings. These challenges need to be addressed by all professionals to ensure the most effective and meaningful services for the people we serve.

As the 21st century progresses, the following trends will continue to shape discussions about health policies and human services, including TR:

- Increasing cultural diversity in North America that represents various values and interests

- An expanding aging population of active and recreation-oriented seniors and older and frailer people who live into their 90s and beyond

- The continuing impact of both the ADA in the United States and the 1998 report of Canadian governments on the lives of people with disabilities

- Wounded veterans who return from war zones with severe and involved injuries and conditions (such as traumatic brain injury, post-traumatic stress disorder, military sexual trauma, and amputations) who will be served in Veterans Administration hospitals and facilities as well as community-based programs

- Millions of people taking personal responsibility for their health and well-being, increased use of complementary and alternative approaches, and recognition of the role of recreation and leisure in public health

- An increasing obesity crisis, declining levels of physical activity and fitness, and increases in diabetes, hypertension, and other lifestyle-associated conditions

- The spiraling cost of health care and the enormous demands placed on the health care system

- Technological innovations and increased reliance on technology in programming and as assistive devices and the high costs associated with their use

SUMMARY

This chapter described the scope and range of clients, settings, and services that make up the TR profession. The populations served by TRSs and the settings in which TRSs work will continue to multiply, and the purposes and role of TR will continue to evolve. Studying the TR definitions, models, philosophy, and benefits is essential to fulfilling a role as a TR professional. Understanding the TR process and the components of professionalism will help prepare you to make your professional choices and plan for a satisfying and meaningful career. As TR faces the challenges of the future, well-educated and credentialed practitioners will hold the key to ensuring that the benefits of therapeutic recreation are experienced by people with disabilities, health conditions, and social limitations.

CHAPTER 11

Unique Groups

Amanda Deml, Tiffany Lundy, Timothy Baghurst, Tyler Tapps, John Byl, David Kahan, Janet M. Bartnik, Jeffrey Ferguson, Ryan Cane, and Diane Blankenship

> " If bread is the first necessity of life, recreation is a close second. "
>
> Edward Bellamy,
> American author

LEARNING OUTCOMES

After reading this chapter, you should be able to do the following:

> Understand the purpose of campus recreation

> Summarize the history of campus recreation

> Describe the benefits and value of campus recreation

> Compare the programs and components associated with campus recreation

> Recognize how recreation can be implemented in the correctional system

> Understand the historical and philosophical foundations of correctional recreation

> Differentiate between different correctional recreation programs

> Understand that Christian, Jewish, and Muslim communities are interested in using recreation to enhance their communities and to bring outsiders in

> Understand there is considerable variability within Christianity, Judaism, and Islam

> Know that the three pillars of NRPA are upheld by Christianity, Judaism, and Islam, but those pillars are tempered with the larger goals of maintaining group affiliation and proselytizing

> Appreciate that many Muslims do not view their requisite behaviors (e.g., fasting during Ramadan, covering for modesty) as obstacles to recreation and that recreation professionals can provide conditions that allow for universal access to services

> Compare the definitions of community health and individual health

> Describe a step-by-step process for the development of a corporate wellness program that addresses health concerns for a business

> Describe the employer benefits of investment in employee wellness and health promotion programs

> Understand the role recreation plays in the U.S. and Canadian Armed Forces

> Compare the different programs and services offered in a military recreation setting

Campus Recreation

Amanda Deml and Tiffany Lundy

“ You can discover more about a person in an hour of play than in a year of conversation. ”

Plato, Greek philosopher

Campus recreation provides facilities and programs for campus communities to engage in recreation, sport, and wellness opportunities. Recreation services offered on a college or university campus are commonly called *campus recreation, university recreation,* or *recreational sports*. The structure and offerings of campus recreation are different based on the size of the institution, the reporting structure, and whether it is a **residential** or **commuter** **campus**. Campus recreation is unique because of the population it serves. There is regular turnover in this group, and there is an influx of new users each fall. Programming and hours of operation tend to follow the academic cycle with high participation during the academic terms and low participation during final exams and break periods.

The primary consumers for campus recreation are students and other members of the campus community, which could include faculty, staff, alumni, and sometimes the local community. Campus recreation is unique in that the main user group is traditional college-aged students ranging from 18 to 24 years old (Wallace-Carr, 2013). Another unique factor to consider is that a portion of this audience turns over every year. Colleges and universities have seen an increase in nontraditional and veteran students returning to campus, and this has diversified programming. This continual turnover requires campus recreation departments to rely heavily on marketing and communication. Often, campus recreation departments partner with student orientation programs to familiarize students with the facilities and programs during the orientation process.

HISTORY OF CAMPUS RECREATION

Campus recreation has an exciting and innovative history. Unbeknownst to most, intramural sports were the first initial form of structured, competitive sports for college students on colonial campuses in the early 19th century. Intramurals were organized for students and by students with the goal of being a diversion from the rigors of academic life (Mueller, 1971). Intramural competition was the gateway to the creation of intercollegiate athletics, which were created in the middle of the 19th century (CAS, 2015). Athletics progressed to be the dominating activity presence on campuses, and intramural sports continued to develop, change, and expand as institutions created intramural programs on their campuses.

In 1913, The Ohio State University and the University of Michigan were the first two flagship institutions to create intramural sports programs and dedicate staff members to these program areas. Additional institutions followed soon after such as Kansas State, Oregon State, the University of Illinois, and the University of Texas. The University of Michigan was the first to build a facility exclusively for the use of intramural sports in 1928. Dr. Elmer Mitchell, the first director for intramurals at the University of Michigan, is fondly considered the "father of intramural sports" (University of Michigan, n.d.).

Dr. William Wasson is another significant leader in campus recreation. In 1950, Dr. Wasson, the director of health, physical education, and recreation at Dillard University, formed an intramural institute and workshop for black colleges and universities. This was the first workshop of its kind, including 22 African American male and female intramural directors from 11 historically black institutions. This resulted in the formation of the National Intramural Association (NIA) (NIRSA, n.d.).

In 1975, the NIA was renamed the **National Intramural-Recreational Sports Association (NIRSA)** because the scope and focus of recreation were changing, and the organization was no longer exclusive to intramural programs (Wallace-Carr, 2013). The range of services and programs has expanded tremendously, and campus recreation centers now include a diverse and dynamic array of offerings including intramural sports, fitness, youth and family programs, aquatics, club sports, outdoor recreation and climbing, activity classes, adaptive recreation, and other innovative program areas. NIRSA has evolved to be a significant, holistic organization that is distinguished as a "cornerstone of students' overall collegiate education and experience" (Wilson, 2008, p. 27). In 2009, the organization name was changed again due to the scope of program and facility offerings becoming even broader and more encompassing. It is now called NIRSA, Leaders in Collegiate Recreation. The mission of NIRSA "is to advocate for the advancement of recreation, sport, and wellness by providing educational and developmental opportunities, generating and sharing knowledge, and promoting networking and growth for our members" (NIRSA, 2016). There are over 4,000 career staff, students, and businesses that make up the association. There are over 8.1 million students at colleges and universities across the United States and Canada that are participating in campus recreation programs (NIRSA, 2016).

ORGANIZATIONAL STRUCTURES

There are a wide variety of organizational structures found across campuses depending on the needs of the institution and its population, funding sources, and model. Traditionally, a department will include three areas: administration, facilities and operations, and programs.

OUTSTANDING GRADUATE

Courtesy of Kamala Ersson.

Background Information

Name: Christin Everson

Education: BA in psychology from the University of Oregon, MS in kinesiology from Indiana University

Credentials: Certified Personal Trainer, Health Coach, and Group Fitness Instructor

Awards: 2016 NIRSA Foundation Scholarship

Affiliations: Subject matter expert for American Council on Exercise (ACE)

Career Information

Position: Assistant Director of Fitness and Marketing

Organization: Seattle University (SU) is a private Jesuit institution located in the urban setting of Seattle, Washington. University Recreation (UREC) provides employment to over 120 students and is the third-largest employer of students on campus. Through sport, fitness, and outdoor programming, UREC inspires, educates, and empowers the SU community to live happier, healthier, and more successful lives. UREC serves nearly 8,000 members, made up of students, faculty, staff, alumni, and their partners and dependents.

Job description: I oversee all fitness programming and operations as well as all marketing for the department. I also have an adjunct faculty role with Seattle University in the sport and exercise science department. My specific responsibilities are to

- mentor, supervise, hire, train, and evaluate a group fitness staff of 20, a personal training staff of 10, and two part-time group fitness program managers and
- oversee all marketing operations for the university's recreation department, including four student marketing managers.

Career path: My career path is truly the result of what can happen when you have mentors who believe and invest in you. I started this path as a former competitive athlete who came to college and no longer belonged to a specific community. I found the rec center at the University of Oregon and was hooked from day one. My supervisors quickly began pushing me to challenge myself in new ways, advocating for me to attend regional and national conferences and preparing me for what a career in this field might entail. With their help, I secured a graduate assistant position at Indiana University working specifically in group exercise. As a first-generation college student, I never anticipated continuing my education past my bachelor's degree; recreation helped me achieve a goal that I didn't even know I had. Since finishing my master's degree, I have held three different professional positions in fitness. I have begun teaching for Seattle University as an adjunct faculty member, and I work with the American Council on Exercise as a subject matter expert, assisting in the creation of both the health coach and personal trainer exams.

Likes and dislikes about the job: My job is about two things: creating safe and effective programs for members to enjoy movement and reach their goals, and creating a safe and effective space for students to learn and grow. Campus recreation is the only field that combines both those items into one daily job. One drawback is the monetary value (or lack thereof) assigned to our work.

Advice for Undergraduates

Know your passion and act on it! Work hard and take every opportunity given. Each experience is useful, even when you don't think it is. Working in recreation provides so many incredible experiences, both professionally and personally. I've met some of my best friends and favorite people working in this field.

Administration

Administration is the supporting structure of the department. The functions of administration include leadership, business services, marketing and communications, budget and finance, purchasing, human resources, and information technology. Campus recreation departments most often align or report to one of the following units: **student affairs**, athletics, enrollment management, or business affairs. In most cases, building, operations, and programming costs are paid for by student fees associated with tuition. In some cases, the cost to students can be offset or reduced for departments that can sell memberships, rent spaces, and provide additional programming.

Best practices, standards, and guidelines for the administration and programming of campus recreation are established by the Council for the Advancement of Standards in Higher Education (CAS). These standards and guidelines are created by professionals working in the field of campus recreation.

Facilities and Operations

Facilities are the physical buildings, fields, and equipment used for campus recreation programs. **Operations** relates to the management of the spaces and the people in them. Campus recreation facilities are state-of-the-art, multifaceted buildings developed to meet participant needs. There is great variance in the types of facilities managed by campus recreation departments. The average facility has cardio and weight-training areas; multiuse courts for basketball, volleyball, and badminton; studio space for instruction; locker rooms; and staff offices. There are a variety of spaces that might be found in the main facility or in a separate

location often referred to as an **auxiliary facility** such as racquetball and squash courts, indoor turf fields, aquatic center, indoor and outdoor climbing and bouldering walls, ice rink, bowling center, field house, lounges, tennis center, theaters, and more.

There are dedicated staff assigned to the management of these facilities. People who work in facilities and operations positions are responsible for building and equipment maintenance, supervision of patrons and activities, scheduling, sales and services, rentals, controlled access and security, and **open recreation**.

Programs

The programs are the leagues, special events, activities, classes, and services. **Intramural sports** allow students to participate in teams they assemble and compete in organized, and often officiated, league sports, special events, and tournaments. Leagues include traditional sports such as flag football,

Intramural sports allow students to participate in teams they assemble and to compete in organized and often officiated league sports, special events, and tournaments.

basketball, volleyball, soccer, and other smaller or new and innovative sports such as Spikeball, Battleship, soccer golf, and cornhole.

Fitness programs offer students a wide variety of fitness-related activities, classes, and programs such as group fitness classes, personal training, small-group training, fitness assessments, and strength and conditioning competitions and events. For example, at the University of Oregon, innovative and trending programs include TRX, Kettlebell, Olympic lifting, playground circuits, and an affiliation with CrossFit. Group exercise programming is enhanced with unique choreographed classes such as POUND, UrbanKick, ballet strength, and top 40 dance. "Incorporating new technology in programming, such as group cycling consoles that measure and display intensity through power output, improves the user experience and increases participant success in reaching their fitness goals" (C. Russell, personal communication, June 23, 2016).

Club sports are athletic programs that are run by student leaders that compete against other universities or colleges. Many club sports are associated with regional and national governing bodies (such as USA Ultimate, USA Rugby, National Club Softball Association). Club sports often practice regularly, follow an organized schedule, and can be recreational or competitive in nature. Most often teams are allocated a budget to be able to travel, register, and purchase gear and equipment.

Outdoor and climbing programs provide exciting educational and hands-on learning opportunities for outdoor enthusiasts ranging from novice to expert levels. Programs can include climbing and bouldering walls, equipment rentals, bike and ski shops, outdoor clinics and education sessions, and guided outdoor adventure trips such as mountaineering, backpacking, rafting, ice climbing, mountain biking, and canyoneering. An exemplary program is the Adventure Leadership Institute (ALI) at Oregon State University. ALI was founded in 1947 and is the "authority in adventure leadership education, providing awe-inspiring, transformative experiences to more than 9,500 students each year." ALI spends a staggering 20,000 contact hours teaching outside the classroom each year, and it offers over 300 facilitation opportunities for students annually (Oregon State University, n.d.).

When resources are available, program areas can also include specialties such as aquatics, inclusive programs, and youth and family initiatives. Aquatics programs provide an assortment of activities and services such as formal swim lessons and classes, family swim time, lap swim, water aerobics, club sports practice (swim, diving, water polo), and open recreational swim. Many facilities have pool space dedicated to informal recreation such as diving boards, slacklining, water slides, climbing walls, lazy rivers, and other innovative elements.

Inclusive recreation programs help address the needs of individuals that feel or identify that the current programming does not meet their needs. Portland State University, for example, has inclusive recreation programs that include adaptive climbing and swimming, sitting volleyball, goalball, and wheelchair basketball. PSU also offers adaptive trips that include alpine skiing, paddling, and cycling (Portland State University, n.d.). It is important to be cognizant when implementing programs that modification, additional assistance, and support may be required to help people participate. A few factors include accessibility to facilities, modified equipment, and appropriate resources to properly relay critical information.

Youth and family programs offer a dynamic range of activities to serve the entire community in a safe, energetic environment. These programs target nontraditional students with families and are also open to the community. These programs also provide great opportunities for student employment as the instructors and camp counselors are predominantly college students. Programs can include swim, climbing, and tennis lessons; creative dance; adventure runs; day and sport camps; gymnastics; and ninja warrior training.

BENEFITS

Individual involvement in campus recreation programs and services produces three major benefits: improved overall emotional well-being, reduced stress, and improved happiness (NIRSA, 2004). Campus recreation centers are more than just facilities for physical activity; they also provide spaces where students can meet new people, hang out, study, and relax. Recreation centers are a focal point for community building and socializing.

Seventy-five percent of students report using on-campus recreation center facilities, programs, and services (Forrester, 2014). Clearly, campus recreation is a tremendous platform and has an opportunity to affect students, get them involved on campus, and provide a sense of belonging. Astin's theory of involvement (1984) states that the more a student is involved in their university, the more learning will take place. Being involved on campus directly affects student success. Astin (1993) also believes that participation in intramural sports is related to students' overall satisfaction with college.

Participating in campus recreation programs and facilities is also linked with higher academic success. A study conducted by North Carolina State University examined the relationship between exercising and graduation rates. They found that for every extra hour that students exercised, their odds of graduating (or returning the following year) increased by 50 percent (Wexler, 2016). This is supported by Ratey's (2008) findings, which state that "exercise influences learning directly, at the cellular level, improving the brain's potential to log in and process new information" (p. 35).

In addition, as demonstrated in figure 11.1, students that participate in campus recreation facilities, programs, or services report increases in

time management (75 percent), respect for others (71 percent), academic performance (68 percent), and sense of belonging (68 percent) as well as other important characteristics (Forrester, 2014).

CAREER OPPORTUNITIES

There are several career opportunities in the field of campus recreation, and there are many paths to entering this field. Many students obtain jobs in campus recreation centers as undergraduates to make money, meet new people, or gain skills; then, they realize they have a passion for working in a recreational setting and pursue it full time. Many professionals have also entered campus recreation after working in city or commercial recreation, resort or tourism, or an athletic field.

Universities vary in how they use student employees. Many employ undergraduates to work as intramural officials, facility operations staff, personal trainers, lifeguards, area attendants and supervisors, and camp counselors, to mention a few. Student employment is an excellent opportunity to expose students to the variety of career positions. Other opportunities exist after graduation, including professional internships, fellowships, workshops, certification courses, and graduate assistantships. **Graduate assistantships**

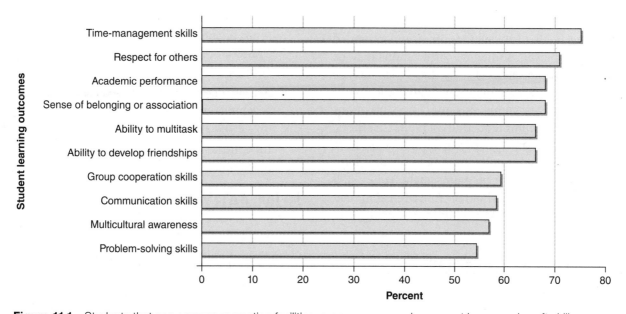

Figure 11.1   Students that use campus recreation facilities, programs, or services report increases in soft skills.

Reprinted, by permission, from S. Forrester, 2014, *The benefits of campus recreation* (Corvallis, OR: NIRSA).

are common in the field of campus recreation and are one of the best ways to move into the profession following graduation. In this type of position, full-time graduate students work part time as paraprofessionals. They are paid a stipend for their work, and the department covers their tuition. This experience is valuable to future employers who want to fill positions in their campus recreation departments (Wallace-Carr, 2013). All these professional-level experiences provide hands-on learning, mentoring, evaluation, and networking opportunities to help students reach the next level.

Organizational structures can look very different depending on the institution. Figure 11.2 illustrates a midsized university and shows the three main areas discussed previously: administration, facilities and operations, and programs. At this institution there is a multilayer hierarchy that includes a director, associate directors, assistant directors, coordinators, and graduate assistants. Additional staff can include personnel in specialty facilities (e.g., ice arenas, bowling alleys), marketing, information technology, community outreach, and public relations.

Professional certifications may be required, preferred, or recommended depending on specific areas. Commonly, CPR (cardiopulmonary resuscitation), AED (automated external defibrillator), and first aid certification are required of all personnel working in supervisory or administrative roles at a recreation facility. Blood-borne pathogen (BBP) training is also typically required and provided by the employer. Additional certifications may be required for specialized areas. Examples include lifeguard certification from StarGuard or the American Red Cross for aquatics staff. Fitness programs require or recommend that personal trainers, health coaches, and group exercise instructors have American Council on Exercise (ACE) certifications. Outdoor and climbing programs might require staff to obtain certifications from the American Mountain Guides Association (AMGA) or the Climbing Wall Association (CWA).

TRENDS IN CAMPUS RECREATION

There are many facility amenities and program offerings that have been in high demand for the past few decades. As the field of recreation progresses and the campus community evolves, so do the expectations regarding management, spaces, equipment, and programs. Departments are expected to collect and report participant statistics and also demonstrate the effects on student success. There is an increase in the demand to provide students with opportunities to learn stress management skills. Facilities and operations practices are becoming more sustainable and efficient. Recreation facilities are being built more like collegiate athletic facilities that include a wow factor and university branding. Spaces are being built such that if one activity is no longer popular, the space can be transformed for another use for minimal cost. Facilities have increased the amount of open space, high tech equipment, and natural light. Marketing has evolved to include social media.

Campus recreation programs lead and respond to trends more so than any other area of the field. These trends often require additional expertise and certifications, so program staff continually diversify and increase their levels of knowledge. Following are a few of the program trends:

- Fitness programs: functional training, Latin dance, ballet strength training, CrossFit, Olympic lifting, Pound, TRX suspension training
- Youth and family programs: break camps, different types of summer camp offerings (e.g., the University of Oregon offers four different types of summer camps: classic camp, sport camp, sport science camp, and climbing and outdoor adventure camp).
- Activity classes: lecture-based classes such as coaching, group exercise, and personal training certification
- Intramural sports: inclusive and adaptive recreation

SUMMARY

Campus recreation has become an important part of college campuses and of the student experience. Campus recreation provides opportunities for students and the campus community to stay physically and mentally healthy and to engage in play and community building. Providing recreation, fitness, and sport in the higher education field is exciting, challenging, and rewarding.

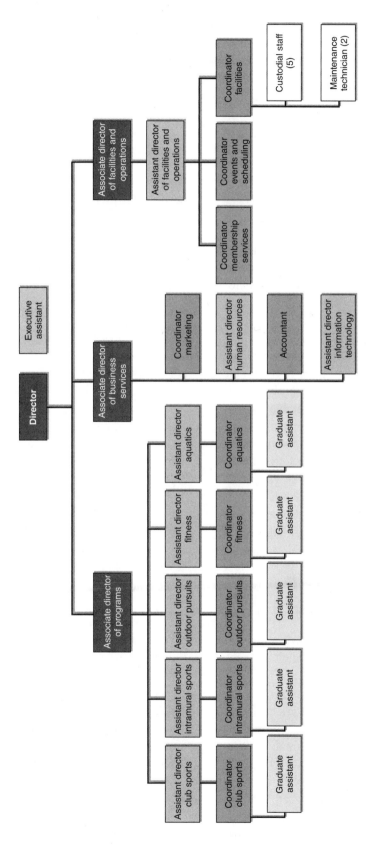

Figure 11.2 An organizational chart for a midsized university shows the three fundamental components of the campus recreation department: administration, facilities and operations, and programs.

Correctional Recreation

Timothy Baghurst and Tyler Tapps

❝ Recreation we must have, otherwise the strings of our souls, wound up to an unnatural tension, will break. **❞**

Elizabeth Prentiss, *The Mother's Journal,* edited by M. G. Clarke

Individuals that are actively **incarcerated** create a unique situation when it comes to recreation. Recreation itself represents freedom and the concept of escaping from daily life, but these individuals are restricted by their confinement. This creates an unusual challenge for staff responsible for developing standard operating procedures that address when, where, and how this segment of the population will spend their so-called free time. As the quotation suggests, some might have been incarcerated because they could not find suitable recreation, and for others it was perhaps their inability to recreate in a socially acceptable manner that led to incarceration. Recreational programs in incarceration facilities can educate and expose prisoners to socially acceptable means for spending free time, but unfortunately, much of the public does not support these activities. Therefore, this section illustrates how correctional recreation can foster and instill in prisoners appropriate outlets for expression that span the functional domains.

INTRODUCTION TO THE CORRECTIONAL SYSTEM

Both the United States and Canada have systems of facilities to house **offenders**. These include local, county, state or provincial, and federal facilities. The **correctional systems** in both countries have similar missions: to protect society and help offenders become law-abiding citizens.

According to the U.S. Federal Bureau of Prisons (n.d.), it is their mission "to protect society by confining offenders in the controlled environments of prisons and community-based facilities that are safe, humane, cost-efficient, and appropriately secure, and that provide work and other self-improvement opportunities to assist offenders in becoming law-abiding citizens." Similarly, the Correctional Services of Canada (n.d.), "as part of the criminal justice system and respecting the rule of law, contributes to public safety by actively encouraging and assisting offenders to become law-abiding citizens, while exercising reasonable, safe, secure and humane control."

Both countries have a state or provincial institutional systems. Each state or province can operate its institutions slightly differently, but the general concepts of care and control are common to all. Detention centers are located in cities, counties, or territories and are typically used as holding facilities for offenders until adjudication by the courts. Where offenders serve their time depends on the type and length of sentence they receive from the court of law. Those under the age of 18 are typically housed in secure juvenile or youth detention centers. However, some might be considered **juvenile offenders and** housed in adult facilities.

Staff members, often referred to as *probation or parole officers,* provide correctional services in settings such as halfway houses or field service units where they manage offenders serving their sentences within the community. This living situation is often part of the offender's probation, parole, or conditional-sentence orders. Residents are typically expected to obtain employment, pay room and board, and comply with specific treatment orders. The exact number of individuals under state or local supervision is hard to determine because numbers change daily.

The incarcerated population is a large group of people who could potentially be provided with recreational activities. A national program, for example, could reach a tremendous number of people.

In 2014 to 2015, there were 110,521 adult offenders either in custody or in community programs in Canada. There were 39,623 adults in custody on an average day, with 24,455 in provincial/territorial custody and 15,168 in federal custody. According to these numbers, there is 1 offender for every 724 adults. According to the U.S. Department of Justice, it is estimated that in 2014 there were 6,851,000 persons incarcerated in a total U.S. population of approximately 319,500,000 (Worldometers, n.d.). This highlights how much impact recreation in correctional facilities can have across a large population; for example, if a recreational program was mandated across the U.S. correctional system, it could potentially affect approximately 1 out of every 46 Americans.

TYPES OF CORRECTION

The nature of the correctional facility (e.g., halfway house, maximum security prison) determines how or to what extent recreation services are provided. Local facilities where those awaiting trial or sentencing are housed are unlikely to provide many recreation opportunities. In facilities that house those who have been sentenced, the nature of recreation programs is based on a variety of risk factors. Recreation is sometimes considered an approach to population management rather than a form of treatment. In facilities or units where it has been determined that offenders can be rehabilitated, recreation can have an important role in the treatment process.

The security required for people who are incarcerated or under some other category (e.g., probation) is determined by a combination of risk factors, and this is often reflected by the amount of direct staff supervision. Inmates are sentenced to a specific level of security based on the nature of their crimes and several other factors. For example, those who have committed low-level or nonviolent crimes are able to function with relatively little supervision. They are not perceived to be at risk of disrupting the institution's operations or threatening the safety of the staff, other inmates, or the public. Consequently, they can be housed in lower-security institutions that might permit a wider range of recreational activities.

People housed in formal correctional facilities have been charged with one of a wide range of crimes. Some have never been incarcerated, whereas others are repeat offenders. Those factors, in addition to the size of the facility, the staff-to-inmate ratio, and the current political climate regarding staff training and administrative expectations present the biggest challenges to providing recreation programming.

HISTORICAL AND PHILOSOPHICAL FOUNDATIONS OF CORRECTIONAL RECREATION

During the colonial period in Canada and the United States, the response to inappropriate behavior was influenced by the British practices of capital and corporal punishment (i.e., physical punishment of an offender such as flogging, mutilation, and branding). Institutionalization (placing the offender in a prison) was generally only employed to hold offenders awaiting punishment. In the colonies, the community accepted responsibility for both punishing offenders and helping to strengthen community institutions such as the family and churches as a defense against crime. As communities grew, it became more difficult to accept responsibility for the care and control of deviant people (Jennings, Higgins, Maldonado-Molina, & Khey, 2015).

During the 19th century, there was a belief that community disorder was contributing to negative behaviors, and offenders were often products of unstable community life. In response, Americans sought to establish a system of **penitentiaries** in which offenders who were removed from corrupt and unstable communities were housed and made into useful citizens (Rothman, 1971). In contrast, popular thinking in Canada at the time held that offenders were a dangerous class who posed a threat to the stability and morality of communities and therefore should be removed. Penitentiaries were built as a means of segregating these people (Beattie, 1977).

During the 1930s, interest in exploring the causes of criminal behavior emerged. One of the findings reported was that people often committed crimes because they lacked the skills to manage their free time appropriately. Prevention was considered preferable to treatment, and this became an issue for correctional officials and the recreation community. Some believed that the root problem was the community's failure to provide adequate recreation facilities and programs.

Today, the role of corrections is to provide the degree of custody necessary to contain the risk presented by an offender, to provide an environment conducive to personal reformation, and to encourage offenders to adopt acceptable behavior patterns through participation in education, social development, and work programs. Some form of recreation is typically included as a means to enhance social development and rehabilitation.

The function of correctional institutions in Canada and the United States has undergone various philosophical shifts in response to societal changes over time. The role that recreation has played within the institutions has taken various forms that are reflective of the dominant paradigms of the day. The following are philosophical approaches that have been used at various times in both Canada and the United States:

- Given the lack of activity within institutions, labor is considered to be recreation, and those most deserving are granted opportunities to work and, therefore, opportunities for recreation.

- Participation in most recreation programs is a privilege, and those who earn it have access to opportunities that will serve as incentives for positive behavior by others.

- Idle minds are susceptible to negative impulses; therefore, active engagement is required to awaken undeveloped and dormant faculties occupying the mind.

- Recreation can serve as a mechanism to control the behavior of inmates by granting or denying access to pleasurable pursuits.

- Offenders are incarcerated as their punishment and not for their punishment; therefore, access to appropriate forms of recreation should not be denied.

- The goal of incarceration is to prepare offenders for release, and because recreation is part of a normal balanced lifestyle, it must be incorporated into the institutional program.

Because offenders are completely within their care, institutions have a responsibility to work with the whole person, and that involves providing for their cognitive, physical, social, emotional, and spiritual needs. Like any philosophy, this can change as we learn more about the successes and failures of recreation in the justice system. As shown, it has changed dramatically over the past few hundred years. Although the role of recreation in corrections is still a topic of debate within the justice system today, there are more opportunities for recreation now than ever before.

RECREATION PROGRAMMING

The people incarcerated for crimes are a very diverse group of all races, backgrounds, origins, physical conditions, and age groups. With this in mind, it is the responsibility of correctional recreation professionals to provide the most effective and safe activities possible. Recreation therapists working in a correctional environment provide direct service to offenders in state or provincial facilities, federal correctional institutions and facilities, and in private treatment agencies that serve juvenile and adult offenders. Their role is most often to engage the population in recreation experiences meant to assist the offenders in developing leisure skills and attitudes that will optimize their quality of life within the institution. In addition, the recreational activities and experiences must help prepare them to use their leisure time appropriately upon rejoining the community.

Programming Goals

Many positive outcomes can be realized through recreation programs offered in correctional institutions. According to the Federal Bureau of Prisons (n.d.), correctional recreation programs are expected in large part to "help teach inmates to make constructive use of leisure time to reduce stress, improve their health and develop hobbies they enjoy. These programs keep inmates constructively occupied and contribute to positive lifestyles and self-improvement."

Correctional recreation programs are expected to keep inmates constructively occupied, reduce idleness, and enhance the physical, emotional, and social well-being of inmates.

Getty Images/Andrew Burton

The positive outcomes described are also realized when **leisure education** principles are applied. Leisure education sets out to develop the attitudes, skills, and knowledge required for optimal leisure functioning. The components of a typical program include developing the physical, cognitive, social, emotional, and spiritual skills necessary for participation in recreation activities. In addition, participants gain a knowledge of leisure opportunities and how to use the required equipment and supplies. Other components include developing an understanding of, and an appreciation for, leisure and its role in quality of life and providing opportunities to explore and experience a variety of appropriate leisure activities.

Consider these 11 goals, which can be set as part of a correctional recreation program:

1. **Develop acceptable outlets for stress**. Correctional facilities are extremely stressful environments. To cope, inmates must learn to identify and practice socially acceptable ways to relieve stress. Many people relieve stress through physical activity and exercise, but for others, cultural pursuits such as music, art, drama, and writing provide positive outlets.

2. **Identify activities that serve as alternatives to addictions**. Many people sentenced to correctional facilities have had addictions. Those who participate in treatment programs to address their addictive behaviors may find that they have significantly more free time than they used to. Therefore, pursuing recreational activities during the time previously devoted to the addiction can be an important strategy in the rehabilitation process.

3. **Foster interpersonal skills such as cooperation and teamwork**. Lack of basic skills for effective community living can cause people to engage in activities that are considered socially unacceptable. Certain forms of recreation can help participants identify and develop interpersonal skills that might provide alternatives to deviant behavior.

4. **Develop a new sense of purpose**. A person's sense of purpose is pivotal in the decision-making process; therefore, this is an important component in making a lifestyle change. Through active participation in recreation therapy, a person can explore a variety of

prosocial roles. Participants who have these opportunities can develop a clearly defined sense of purpose that will help guide their thinking and behavior.

5. **Enhance self-esteem through success**. High self-esteem is a critical component of personal accountability and respect for others, which are important goals of the correctional process. Self-esteem is also at the root of inner confidence that enables people to cope effectively with the challenges of life. Positive recreation experiences can enhance self-esteem.

6. **Increase access to new social environments**. To some extent, people are products of their environment, and they may lack the motivation to alter negative social environments. Adopting new recreation interests can serve as a catalyst to seeking new and potentially more positive social environments.

7. **Foster new interests**. Offenders often have limited experiences and lack the skills necessary to be successful at some recreational activities. This is caused in part by a negative attitude toward activities even though they have not experienced the activities firsthand (Robertson, 1993). Recreation programs can help identify the source of the negative attitudes and counter these false beliefs while helping build a more positive attitude toward a broader range of leisure pursuits.

8. **Negotiate constraints**. Many people encounter social, psychological, and structural constraints when they attempt to participate in recreation opportunities such as lack of a coparticipant, low self-esteem, and lack of skill or money. Learning how to overcome these constraints can facilitate access to a broader range of activity options.

9. **Develop awareness of personal needs and appropriate avenues to satisfy them**. Human behavior is motivated by thought, which is prompted by people's interpretations of their personal experiences and their relationships with the world around them. If delinquent behavior can become a means for satisfying real and perceived needs, recre-

ation can counter this by providing appropriate ways to satisfy specific needs.

10. **Develop decision-making and problem-solving skills**. Some offenders have not learned the skills necessary to carefully assess situations and make decisions that will not harm themselves or others. These skills can be developed and practiced in recreational settings that allow participants to experience and process the effects of their decisions.

11. **Develop new interests that could evolve into a career**. Certain offenders are highly creative and talented, but traditional approaches to education and vocational programs often fail to recognize or develop these skills. Through recreation, creative skills can be identified and channeled into pursuits such as music, writing, drama, and crafts, which could lead to meaningful employment opportunities.

Types of Programming

Recreation programs in correctional settings vary greatly depending on the nature of the institution and the resources available. When planning an activity for people who are incarcerated, the primary concern should be the safety of participants and staff. Before allowing inmates to participate, staff must carefully examine each activity to identify potential hazards. Even a board game could present a dangerous situation for inmates and staff if game pieces could be used to cause harm.

Careful supervision is required when conducting any recreational activity, and all equipment must be accounted for. Staff need to recognize that although correctional institutions are meant to serve as rehabilitation facilities, they can be aggressive and hostile settings. Recreation in a correctional setting should focus on the positive aspects of participation: teamwork, cooperation, stress management, and prosocial leadership techniques. Teaching offenders to redirect their negative energy in positive ways not only serves them while they are incarcerated, but it can also help them lead more positive, productive lives in the outside community.

Some institutions have extensive recreation facilities, whereas others have limited facilities. This often depends on the type and size of the facility as well as funds that are available and allocated to recreation activities. For example, some institutions are equipped with facilities such as a baseball field, full-length basketball court, weight room, crafts shop, and theater, whereas others may have only a small multipurpose room. It becomes the responsibility of the programmer to work with the available resources and facilities to get the best out of the situation and environment.

Active recreation programs offered in institutions include basketball, volleyball, aerobics, handball, hockey, curling, table tennis, pool, baseball, flag football, track and field, shuffleboard, soccer, in-compound orienteering, and rock climbing. Sports are popular in most institutions and have higher participation rates than passive forms of recreation. Examples of more passive forms of recreation include drawing, painting, sculpting, crafts, music, journal writing, pet therapy, board games, drama, quilting, knitting, singing, and holiday events.

Although some programs are designed with the primary goal of keeping inmates occupied during down time, others have therapeutic goals and outcomes. For example, pet therapy is an innovative recreation program offered in some locations to juveniles, men, and women at varying levels of incarceration. This type of program typically seeks to foster a sense of responsibility and nurturing toward the animal. This in turn promotes self-esteem and has the potential to provide other therapeutic benefits that can be identified and included in treatment planning for that offender. Many pet therapy programs also incorporate instruction that allows the inmate to train the animal for specialized purposes. For example, animals may be trained to assist those with a physical disability. This program has an added benefit in that it helps to promote ties to the community by providing a practical and valuable service. Although some recent research supports its effectiveness (e.g., Hemingway, Meek, & Hill, 2015), other research has questioned the lack of rigor in evaluating pet therapy programs in prisons (Mulcahy & McLaughlin, 2013).

CORRECTIONAL RECREATION PROFESSIONALS

Due to the nature and business of correctional facilities, it can be challenging to ensure that recreation programming is more than just an approach to managing the population. Diligence is needed to educate, maintain programmatic integrity, and solve problems creatively. These three points become part of the mission for recreation professionals who choose to provide services in the correctional environment.

Those who plan on becoming correctional recreation professionals can be sworn law enforcement officers or civilian personnel trained to provide services in a correctional facility. Most facilities require correctional recreation staff to hold some type of advanced degree. Having other credentials, such as certified personal trainer, therapeutic recreation specialist, or certified leisure professional, is helpful. All correctional recreation personnel should be certified in first aid and CPR and trained in, or at least familiar with, the duties of other staff working at the facility. Being fluent in a second language is also helpful. Candidates who apply for work in a correctional institution may be subject to polygraph testing, urinalysis, and background checks.

Although *correctional recreation professional* is the generic term for this position, specific job titles can vary among facilities. Examples might include recreation officer, recreation therapist, recreation specialist, program manager, or program supervisor. However, the roles of correctional recreation professionals are similar throughout North America, and irrespective of title, they all have an important role in the lives of offenders while they are incarcerated.

Those with physical education or recreation backgrounds provide valuable experiences to the populations they serve. People hired for these positions can expect to receive training related to their specific jobs and the operations of the facility. Much of the focus is geared toward safety and security, which are priorities when working in a correctional setting. You must understand that this profession carries an inherent risk because of the work environment. However, it can also hold great opportunities for learning and understanding. Being part of a correctional setting and working with offenders will help you develop a strong sense of your own personal safety and boundaries, and it will also help to develop an appreciation for human thinking and behavior.

TRENDS AND ISSUES

Although often viewed as a large and inflexible governmental machine, correctional institutions can be significantly affected by societal trends associated with its clients and administration. Because of this, they face continual change and must address challenging issues such as incarceration rates, budget cuts, philosophical shifts, aging infrastructure, and meeting the needs of the various segments of the incarcerated population based on factors such as age, sex, race, socioeconomic status, and societal norms.

A current issue in correctional recreation is how the role of recreation is viewed within correctional settings. Some correctional administrations and staff understand that participation in positive forms of recreation can be a constructive way for offenders to spend their time relieving stress, countering boredom, learning new skills, and improving health. However, some institutions are reluctant to dedicate resources to such programs because of the cost, lack of state or local administrative viewpoints, or fear of recourse from a public that supports more punitive approaches to offender treatment. In these cases, basic recreation programs are offered as a means of satisfying legal requirements, but they lack the developmental or therapeutic components that could aid in offender rehabilitation.

On a more positive note, awareness of the relationship between a lack of prosocial recreation and delinquent behavior appears to be increasing. Many people engage in criminal activity as a form of recreation; this reflects lifestyle choices they have made to satisfy their needs, both real and perceived. Research has shown that many of these people lack the knowledge, attitude, and skills to participate in personally satisfying and socially acceptable pursuits (van der Stouwe, Asscher, Hoeve, van der Laan, & Stams, 2016). Consequently, rehabilitation strategies may help them develop the appropriate knowledge and skills necessary to pursue alternatives through leisure-based programs that have strong developmental and educational components.

SUMMARY

Recreation holds the potential to assist correctional institutions, their incarcerated populations, and their staff members in achieving the goals of the correctional system. If properly administered, correctional recreation can help foster an institutional environment in which offenders can develop knowledge and skills that will enable them to live more productive lives while incarcerated and after they return to the community at large.

Faith-Based Recreation

John Byl and David Kahan

❝ The city streets will be filled with boys and girls playing there. ❞

Zechariah 8:5

People of faith often engage in recreational activities through their religious institutions. These activities are often designed to enhance internal community cohesion and to be recruiting tools to engage community outsiders (Bynum, 2003; Karlis et al., 2014; Popke, 2001). In the United States in 2014, 76.5 percent of those 18 and older identified with a religious group (Pew Research Center, 2015). Therefore, we can see why "religious organizations should be recognized as legitimate providers of recreation activities in the leisure service delivery system" (Emard, 1990, p. 146). Religious institutions play an important role in providing satisfying recreational opportunities within their communities. We examine the differences within and among faith traditions and then explore employment in faith-based recreation.

DIFFERENCES WITHIN FAITH TRADITIONS

Religious groups are not one homogeneous unit. Some of the differences are fostered because of different ways of thinking about beliefs, and some are fostered because of different ethnic roots. For example, compare two protestant Christian groups: the Christian Reformed Church (CRC), which was started by Calvinists of Dutch background, and the Canadian Mennonite Brethren (MB), which was started by Anabaptists of Germanic background. A study of the main journals for each group determined that for the CRC, "enjoying one's leisure time was highly encouraged, especially if the recreation called for a combination of active, stewardly, and playful participation in God's creation" (Byl, 1999, pp. 318-319). But they had little interest in organized church camps for evangelistic purposes. In contrast, the Mennonites valued church camps for two purposes: "One, showing young Christians how to live a Christian life, and two, leading people to Christ" (Byl, 1999, p. 320). The CRC sees recreation primarily as a way to experience God's creation, whereas the MB views recreation primarily as a teaching and evangelistic tool.

The study demonstrates that two Christian groups can hold significantly different views about the purpose of recreation and that within each denomination members hold different views (Byl, 1999). The same is true in other faith traditions. Within Judaism there is a whole range of different beliefs between liberal Jewish believers and ultra-Orthodox Jewish believers (Goldenberg, 2015). The same is true in defining Islam. Khiabany (2007, p. 61) wrote:

> Operating on the assumption of a monolithic Islamic totality suppresses the internal diversity, division and political, social, cultural and ideological rifts in a religion that encompasses one billion people from North Africa to Indonesia as well as a variety of

minority communities (increasingly under attack) throughout the Western world.

Some of the differences between religious groups relate to individual commitments and ethnic backgrounds. Some people's religious beliefs intentionally and fully shape their recreation choices, whereas others express beliefs that unintentionally and partially shape their recreation choices. Nationality also shapes unique differences between religious groups. The intersection of nationality and religious beliefs encourages some people to recreate with others with similar interests, backgrounds, religious affiliations, and languages. Being in this comfort zone within a subculture and being shaped by the subcultural values are examples of **selective acculturation** in leisure (Shaull & Gramann, 1998).

DIFFERENCES AMONG FAITH TRADITIONS

North America is home to many religious groups, but we look at the three largest faith groups to provide insight into how various traditions value and engage in recreation. We look at Christians (70.6 percent of the U.S. population in 2014), Jews (1.9 percent), and Muslims (0.9 percent) (Pew Research Center, 2015).

Christianity

The largest and most popular religion in the United States and Canada (59 to 71 percent of the Canadian population in 2012, depending on polling method used; Bibby & Grenville, 2016) is **Christianity**. Since the beginning of the Christian church, living in community with fellow believers has been valued. During the past 100 years, togetherness as a congregation has been enjoyed in church fellowship halls through coffee socials, youth clubs, annual church picnics, dances, and competitive leagues with teams from similar congregations. The purpose of this recreation is to enhance a sense of community between people of the same faith.

Typically, church programs, particularly those for kids, include a refreshment break that provides an opportunity for leaders to speak briefly about following Christian principles of living or to share personal testimonies and invite participants to accept Jesus as their savior. Special kids' programs such as KidsGames are modeled after the Olympics and take place during church summer camps during the years when the Summer Olympics and the World Cup occur. Competitions are held in various sport events, Bible knowledge, poster design, and answering essay questions. KidsGames began in Barcelona in 1985 as an evangelical Christian program in preparation for the Olympic Games in that city, and it is now used worldwide (Bynum, 2003).

Besides offering programs for kids, many Christian churches organize adult church sport leagues. These leagues generally do not permit alcohol use at games, and they include time for prayer, fellowship, and talking with others about their relationship with God. These leagues try not to overemphasize the importance of sport by limiting the number of weekly practices and games (Popke, 2001a). Many churches in the United States have built large fitness centers to serve their members and to serve and reach out to others in the community. Christian music is often played in the fitness centers, and during breaks in the activity people can share personal testimonies and pray.

Several for-profit companies have organized to fill a niche in the fitness market for Christian fitness centers that train both the body and soul. The Lord's Gym was founded in Florida in 1997 and now has more than 21 locations. Its membership is open to all people regardless of religious background, but a dress code is enforced, Christian music and television stations are played, and 10 percent of all member fees are given to charities (Popke, 2001b). Another company is Angel City Fitness, which offers classes in yoga, Pilates, KickFit, stretching, and self-defense. Other amenities include personal trainers and a cafe.

An organization that helps churches use sports and recreation programs to reach out to their communities is the Association of Church Sports and Recreation Ministers (CSRM). CSRM provides "a way for these church leaders to come together as a profession to learn from each other, to find support for their chosen ministry field, to meet others working in churches, and to share resources" (www.csrm.org). CSRM's motto is "helping churches use sport and recreation programs to reach out to their communities."

Judaism

Jews are discussed here for two reasons. First, those who identify as Jewish form the second largest religious group in the United States (Kosmin, Mayer, & Keysar, 2001). Second, although Christians and Muslims see all of life as affected by their religious commitments, Jews distinguish between sacred and secular activities, thereby providing an interesting and alternative perspective on faithful living in one's recreation.

For Jews, religion affects what happens in the synagogue and in personal and family devotional life but not what happens on the soccer pitch or in the boxing ring. But something that binds Jews together, regardless of religious affiliation, is their nation, Israel. Therefore, some recreation activities are based more on national commitments than on Jewish faith commitments. For example, the quadrennial Maccabiah Games are held in Israel the year following the Olympic Games. According to Maccabi Canada, the purpose of the Maccabiah Games is "to promote the Jewish identity and traditions through athletic, cultural, social and educational activities for both youth and adults alike and to promote a bond with the State of Israel, both domestically and abroad" (www.maccabicanada.com).

The Maccabi World Union developed the idea of holding a sort of Jewish Olympiad every four years in Israel, and the first Maccabiah Games were held in 1932. In addition, the Pan American Maccabi Games are held every four years in various South American cities. The JCC Maccabi Games, sponsored by the Jewish Community Centers, are held each summer in the United States and are the largest organized sports program in the world for Jewish teenagers (Jewish Community Centers Maccabi Games, 2017).

Another important influence on the recreation habits of Jews in the United States and Canada was the establishment of organizations to help recent immigrants adapt to their new surroundings. During the late 1800s and the early to mid-1900s, Jewish settlement houses, immigrant aid institutions, and Young Men's and Young Women's Hebrew Associations were established in cities such as Boston, New York, and Chicago. The Young

Women's Hebrew Association offered programs in calisthenics, basketball, baseball, track and field, tennis, physical culture, domestic education, aquatics, "… religious work, gymnastics, social work, and educational work to promote social and physical welfare for Jewish families" (Borish, 1999, p. 248). These centers were concerned with the Americanization of Eastern European immigrants (Borish, 1999). These organizations provided places where Jews could participate in new activities and learn about North American culture without losing their Jewish culture. These organizations merged with the Jewish Community Centers (JCC) Association of North America in 1990.

The JCC Association of North America guides the Jewish community centers across North America, serving over 1 million American Jews annually. This organization is a movement that uses community camps and community centers to promote Jewish culture and community (Jewish Community Centers Maccabi Games, 2017). These centers, like the Maccabiah Games, are concerned with "Jewish living" rather than **Judaism** as a religion.

Islam

Islam, which has its roots in present-day Saudi Arabia, was spread by the Prophet Muhammad beginning in approximately 610 AD. Over the next seven centuries it spread across North and sub-Saharan Africa, Spain, Southeast Europe, the Middle East, Central and South Asia, and as far away as the Philippines. In the Americas, Muslims lived in colonial America in the 16th century and were formally counted in Canada's initial census of 1871. Today, the Muslim populations in the United States and Canada are estimated at 2.45 million and slightly over 1 million, respectively (Pew Research Center, 2009; Statistics Canada, 2013). According to the Muslim American Survey (Pew Research Center, 2011), 78 percent of American Muslims are first-generation immigrants or second-generation Americans. Immigrants hail from 77 different countries, and most hail from Pakistan. The same survey reported that a plurality of American Muslims express a medium level of religious commitment, which considers frequency of attending mosque and daily prayer and the importance of religion in one's

Camps are a popular activity for faith-based organizations.

Getty Images/Hero Images

life. Additionally, 60 percent of women reported wearing a hijab all or most/some of the time (Pew Research Center, 2011).

The diverse cultural backgrounds and religious beliefs and attitudes of American Muslims pose unique opportunities and responsibilities for recreation researchers and practitioners. Awareness of observant Muslims' behaviors is an important step toward accommodating recreation schedules, facilities, and programs. For example, *sawm* (fasting) may be practiced daily during daylight hours during the month of Ramadan. Thus, many adherents may not be able to engage in regular recreational or leisure activities during this time, and program options that are available after sunset would be preferable. The **hijab**, which is worn for modesty and privacy in conformance with verses in the Quran (surah 24:30–31), and which was originally intended for the Prophet's wives, presents a more complex issue for recreation specialists. Given that the second caliph (Umar/Omar) specifically enjoined adherents to teach their children archery, horseback riding, and swimming as well as the many modern-day ethnic games and national sports ascribed to Muslim countries, every effort should be made to offer egalitarian access to leisure and recreation services. Keep in mind that for more observant females, gender segregated activity spaces where females cannot be seen by males may be required to allow for full participation in dance, exercise, and sport.

Much of the research conducted in Muslims' physical activity beliefs, attitudes, and behaviors has originated outside North America. Early research frequently used a deficit lens in identifying what Muslims girls could *not* do. More recent international literature is beginning to show empowered young Muslim women who are frequently supported in their physical activity habitus by parents and extended family (e.g., Knez, Macdonald, & Abbott, 2012; Miles & Benn, 2014; Palmer, 2009; Stride, 2014). These women negotiate their degree of participation by finding a balance point between their religious, cultural, and personal identities.

In the United States, Hamzeh and Oliver (2012) proposed the *hijab discourse* as a means by which Muslim girls could discover the types and circumstances of physical activity they felt comfortable participating in. Girls in their study overcame visual, spatial, and ethical hijabs when participating in swimming, basketball, and indoor rock climbing. This unveiling required them to cross religious, cultural, and self-imposed boundaries that dictated what (visual), where (spatial), and how (ethical) they could do physical activity. In light of these findings, recreation specialists should at least understand that Muslim girls want to participate in activities of their choosing, and they engage in a complex process of relativism in which they judge the ways and means by which they can be comfortable participating. In Canada, Shia Muslim young women were found to encounter and engage in similar internalized struggles while figuring out their place within and their positionality toward physical activity (Jiwani & Rail, 2010). To these women, physical activity was viewed as a way to enhance one's health and self-esteem but subservient to the importance attached to religion. They specifically recommended creating affordable and accessible activity venues within and outside the Muslim community and educating recreation providers about the needs and alternative representations of Hijabi women.

An exhaustive how-to guide for creating environments conducive to Muslim Americans' recreation needs, and specifically for the religiously observant, is beyond the scope of this section. Generally, some guidelines include surveying clients' interests and participation requirements, which may include

- alleviating time-specific conflicts associated with prayers, holidays, and fasting;
- relaxing dress codes, especially for aquatic activities;
- ensuring that changing areas offer complete privacy and that performance venues restrict physical and visual access to the same sex; and
- staffing aquatic, dance, exercise, and sport classes and sports programs with same-sex personnel (e.g., lifeguards, referees).

The following case studies show how these recommendations have been implemented:

- An independent summer day camp for Muslim youth in Irvine, California (American Camping Association, 2010)
- Various recreation providers' responses to requests by Muslim communities for swim-

ming programs that conform to Islamic propriety (Brown, 2009; Burns, 2012; Moore, Ali, Graham, & Quan, 2010)

- A basketball league for East African male teens located in metropolitan Seattle (Stutteville, 2015)
- Karate and soccer programs for Muslim girls in Columbus, Ohio (Gordon, 2014)

JUDAISM, CHRISTIANITY, AND ISLAM AND THE NATIONAL RECREATION AND PARK ASSOCIATION PILLARS

Our view of the world is shaped by what we believe in. What we say we believe in is often mixed up with our cultural norms, other significant events in our lives, and the times and place we live in. Faith traditions have distinct views on the NRPA pillars of conservation, health and wellness, and social equality. However, it is important to realize that how individuals or specific groups understand and practice these views can vary greatly.

Judaism

In terms of conservation, the Torah begins with the words that God created the "heavens and the earth" (Genesis 1:1). What God created was "very good" (Genesis 1:31), and people were instructed to work and protect the earth (Genesis 1:28). There are many examples in the Torah in which the environment was protected (not cutting down fruit trees [Deuteronomy 20:19], allowing land to lie fallow every seven years [Leviticus 25]). Related to conservation is a positive view of health and wellness. People were made in the "image of God" (Genesis 1:27), and therefore ought to care for themselves and each other. If anyone causes injury to another, helping that person heal is that person's legal responsibility (Exodus 21:19). It also follows that if all people are created in the image of God and come from the same parentage (Genesis 3:20), that all people should be viewed equally. The Torah includes instructions that when a foreign person lived among them they were to be treated as "Native-born" (Leviticus 19:34). Different cultural expectations were placed on men and women, but both are viewed as created in the image of God and therefore socially equal (Genesis 1:27).

Christianity

Christianity is also based on the Torah, but it significantly includes the lives of Jesus as Messiah and the writings found in the New Testament. The New Testament reminds its readers that "all things created, that are in heaven, and that are in earth … : all things were created by him, and for him" (Colossians 1:16), and therefore all things need to be cared for (Colossians 1:16-20). Jesus himself tells his followers to "go into all the world and preach the gospel to all creation" (Mark 16:20). Physical health was also still important, as readers are reminded in the welcome from one of the apostles: "Dear friend, I pray that you may enjoy good health and that all may go well with you" (3 John 2). Furthermore, one of the New Testament writers argues that people want to bring God a holy and pleasing worship, "offer your bodies as a living sacrifice" (Romans 12:1-2). Going beyond the Torah, in terms of social equality, the New Testament states that "there is neither Jew nor Gentile, neither slave nor free, nor is there male and female, for you are all one in Christ Jesus" (Galatians 3:28). In addition to viewing all people as one, the New Testament also encourages a respect for diversity among people (1 Corinthians 12:12).

Islam

Islam is based on the Quran, which was divinely revealed to Prophet Muhammad by the angel Gabriel in the month of Ramadan 610 AD. Muslims also follow the Sunnah, which details Prophet Muhammad's application of the Quran's principles in his daily life. Both sources provide codified guidance for a life that upholds Christian and Jewish traditions. Support for the NRPA pillars is clearly stated within these two sources. Environmental stewardship is referred to in the Quran verse 6:165 as translated by Yusuf Ali: "It is He Who hath made you (His) agents, inheritors of the earth." Muslims are enjoined to take personal responsibility for their health and wellness, which in the Quran is alluded to in verse 4:79 as translated by Muhammad Sarwar: "Whatever good you may receive is certainly from God and whatever you suffer is from yourselves. We have sent you, (Muhammad), as a Messenger to people. God is a Sufficient witness to your truthfulness." The Quran does not specifically mention physical activity, however, the Hadith (oral tradition about Prophet Muhammad's words and behavior) states that parents are to teach their children swimming, archery, and horseback riding. Regular practice of these specific activities would have resulted in military fitness, which was important at the time. In modern times, recreational pursuit of these activities would be valued as a means to emulate the Prophet. Islam's followers are most likely the most ethnically heterogeneous among the three Abrahamic religions as Islam's spread over seven centuries reached into Northern and Sub-Saharan Africa, Europe, the Middle East, Central and South Asia, and other regions. In his final sermon in 630 AD, Prophet Muhammad preordains Islam's egalitarian stance toward gender and race:

> O People, it is true that you have certain rights with regard to your women, but they also have right over you. If they abide by your right then to them belongs the right to be fed and clothed in kindness. Do treat your women well and be kind to them for they are your partners and committed helpers.

> All mankind is from Adam and Eve, an Arab has no superiority over a non-Arab nor a non-Arab has any superiority over an Arab; also a white has no superiority over a black nor a black has any superiority over white except by piety and good action. You know that every Muslim is the brother of another Muslim. Remember, one day you will appear before Allah and answer for your deeds. So beware, do not stray from the path of righteousness after I am gone.

EMPLOYMENT IN FAITH-BASED RECREATION

Professionals in faith-based recreation must meet three requirements. First, a passionate commitment to the faith is central and is the first entry point into any position. For Jewish leaders, faith is not critical, but a positive disposition to Jewish culture is important. Second, although some people with ecclesiastical training are hired, most of those hired have training in recreation and leadership. Academic training might consist of a recreation diploma from a college or a recreation, physical education, or leadership degree from a university. Third, a faith-based recreation leader must nurture the faith (or the culture, in the case of Jewish leaders) through recreation with people of various backgrounds. Although some of this nurturing involves specific spiritual instruction, the nurturing may also be primarily focused on encouraging friendships within the group.

SUMMARY

Most North Americans identify with some form of religion. Each ideology presents clear and unique ramifications on the ways followers engage in recreation. Religious institutions play important roles in advising their members on the importance of recreation and, in many cases, in providing opportunities for their members and those from the broader community to take advantage of recreational activities.

Worksite Recreation and Health Promotion

Janet M. Bartnik and Jeffrey Ferguson

" Physical fitness is not only one of the most important keys to a healthy body, it is the basis of dynamic and creative intellectual activity. "

John F. Kennedy, U.S. president, 1961-1963

In recent years, corporate wellness programming has become a billion-dollar industry. Whether operated through the company or offered to employees contractually through a separate organization that specializes in prevention work, these programs afford corporate health and wellness promotion professionals opportunities to make a difference for employers' bottom lines and employees' lives.

CORPORATE WELLNESS AND HEALTH PROMOTION

According to research compiled by the Centers for Disease Control and Prevention (CDC), about half of all adults are managing **chronic diseases** and conditions such as heart disease, risk of stroke, cancer, type 2 diabetes, arthritis, and obesity (Ward, Schiller, and Goodman, 2014). Of the top 10 causes of death in 2010, seven were chronic diseases, and heart disease and cancer accounted for nearly half of all deaths in the United States (Centers for Disease Control and Prevention, 2015). Chronic disease can be prevented or delayed through positive health behaviors.

With an earlier onset of disease and the cost of health care on the rise, individuals managing and medicating chronic diseases incur high health care costs and health insurance premiums. Employers pay a large share of these costs, and they can contain health insurance premiums by implementing corporate wellness and health promotion programs in the workplace. These programs also benefit companies through reduced sick leave and increased employee productivity.

HISTORY OF WORKSITE WELLNESS

Employers have been providing recreation and health promotion programs for more than 150 years. Two of the first documented programs were library resources and singing classes offered by the Peacedale Manufacturing Company in Rhode Island in the 1850s (MacLean, Peterson, & Martin, 1985). As the United States continued to industrialize during the late 1800s and the early decades of the 1900s, more companies began to offer employee recreation and fitness programs. In the 1860s, the YMCA became one of the first private agencies to work with business and industry to provide positive recreation alternatives to industrial workers (Cross, 1990). The YMCA built gymnasiums and offered fitness-related programs to the young men who were moving to the cities in ever larger numbers to work in the factories. The Playground and Recreation Association of America (now the National Recreation and Park Association) began assisting companies in the provision of employee recreation and wellness programs in the early 1900s. In 1941, the National Industrial Recreation Association was formed to help address concerns related to the provision and management of employee recreation services (Sessoms, Meyer, & Brightbill, 1975). In the 1930s, labor unions began to play an increased role in the provision of employee recreation and health promotion services. The growth of employer-provided recreation and health promotion services has continued since World War II. In 2000, the Employee Services Management (ESM) Association estimated that over 50,000 organizations offered on-site fitness programs (Chenoweth, 2007).

The nature of the services provided has gone through many evolutions, and services continue to evolve in the 21st century. Company-sponsored picnics, athletic teams, hobby clubs and classes, bowling leagues, aquatics programs, exercise breaks, and group vacations were typical of services offered by employers through the first 100 years of employer-sponsored recreation and health promotion programs. In the decades since World War II, many more companies have provided recreation and fitness facilities with amenities such as gymnasiums, pools, tennis courts, walking trails, golf courses, athletic fields, aerobic and strength training areas, and child care.

Today's corporate wellness and health promotion programs vary greatly in scope from social activities for employees to systematic, **evidence-based programs** focused on chronic disease prevention activities. Let's look at how a corporate health and wellness promotion professional might approach the development of systematic, evidence-based programs targeted at reducing chronic disease.

COMMUNITY HEALTH, POPULATION HEALTH, AND INDIVIDUAL HEALTH

When operating worksite wellness and health promotion programs, it is important to have a basic understanding of community health, population health, and individual health as well as the core principles related to chronic disease prevention.

The term *community health* is used to describe the health status of a defined group of people; that group might be defined by proximity, gender, race, or another common factor. The term can also include the actions taken to address health concerns for the defined group. Often used interchangeably with community health, *population health* is a relatively new term that refers to the health outcomes of a defined group of people and the distribution of such outcomes within the group. In contrast, *individual health* focuses on the health of one person.

The fitness industry has long focused on the individual. An exercise physiologist will conduct a battery of fitness tests on an individual, discuss with that person his or her fitness goals, and prescribe an exercise routine, nutritional changes, and other positive healthy behaviors to achieve specific goals. Unfortunately, this individual health focus is not always successful in the long term. In the prevention world, there is a parable of the diseased pond. A sick frog is removed from the pond, assisted in becoming healthy, and then placed back into the same diseased pond where it becomes ill again. It is thought that only when the pond itself is treated that the sick frog can become truly well. Even more, treating the pond can improve the health of all the frogs in the pond. This parable helps explain why corporate wellness and health promotion programs focus on the individual and the corporate environment to achieve the best possible outcomes for community health.

BENEFITS OF CORPORATE WELLNESS AND HEALTH PROMOTION PROGRAMS

The breadth of work necessary to improve the corporate environment (the pond) is wide. Efforts can be categorized across the wellness wheel (figure 11.3), which includes physical, social, emotional, environmental, spiritual, intellectual, and occupational wellness. These efforts work together to create a community in which health care and worker's compensation insurance costs to the employer

Figure 11.3 The wellness wheel.

are contained, use of sick leave is lessened, and employee productivity is increased.

Rapid increases in the incidence of chronic diseases combined with current economic trends in the health care industry have resulted in significant increases in health care costs, which makes a company's focus on wellness and health a priority. Benefits range from increased employee satisfaction to financial benefits to the company. Researchers have found that employees who work for companies that offer health and wellness programs are more likely to have higher levels of job satisfaction than those who work for companies without such programs (Aflac, 2012). Further, researchers (Institute for Healthcare Consumerism, 2015) compiled data from studies of 42 worksite wellness programs and found that companies that offered such programs benefited financially on four measures. On average, those companies saw a 28 percent reduction in sick leave usage, a 26 percent reduction in health costs, a 30 percent reduction in workers' compensation and disability management claims, and an average $5.93 return on a $1 investment. Another study, conducted by St. John's Health, found that companies average $5.06 in reduced absenteeism costs for each dollar invested in a wellness program (Smith, 2004).

WELLNESS AND HEALTH PROMOTION PROGRAM PLANNING AND OPERATION

In most corporations, the human resources department typically plays a lead role in the design and implementation of wellness and health promotion programs. This makes sense because human resources staff members manage a corporation's health insurance and workers' compensation insurance programs and employee benefit programs. When a corporation implements more complex wellness programs, more staff are needed to support the programs in areas such as medicine, exercise science, nutrition, counseling, and event management.

There are many private organizations designed to assist human resources managers. Hospital organizations often have the medical personnel needed to conduct **health risk appraisals (HRAs)** that assess individual and environmental needs of the population identified. These organizations often hire staff with backgrounds in nutrition, exercise

science, health promotion, and corporate wellness to manage the postassessment program implementation. Corporations of all sizes can implement corporate wellness and health promotion programs by partnering with these organizations. Facilities used for assessment can be onsite for larger corporations or offsite for smaller companies.

Corporate health professionals that use best practices will operate programs aimed at improving health risk behaviors known to be related to a higher incidence of chronic disease. The **strategic prevention framework (SPF)** is a planning process created by the Substance Abuse and Mental Health Services Administration (SAMHSA) that is used to prevent substance use and misuse (see figure 11.4). The process includes assessment of the current condition, capacity analysis, selection and planning for program and service prescriptions, implementation of those programs and services, and evaluation. Following evaluation of program outcomes, the cycle is repeated. This cycle can be adopted by the corporate wellness and health promotion professional to develop corporate wellness and health promotion programs.

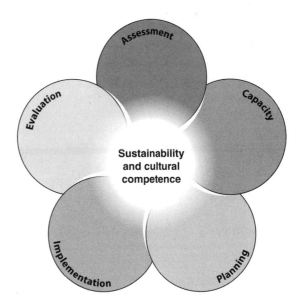

Figure 11.4 The strategic prevention framework (SPF) is a prevention model that can be used by the corporate health and wellness promotion professional to plan a corporate wellness and health promotion program.

Reprinted from Substance Abuse and Mental Health Services Administration, *Applying the strategic prevention framework (SPF)* (Rockville, MD: SAMHSA). Available: www.samhsa.gov/capt/applying-strategic-prevention-framework.

Assessment

Without an assessment of the individual and community health needs of employees, programs intended to target improvements in health and wellness are more likely to miss the mark. Programs in all areas of prevention begin with an assessment of current conditions. Assessments conducted by corporate wellness and health promotion professionals might include the following:

- Review of workplace accidents, injuries, and worker's compensation claims
- Review of health insurance premiums and employees' use of health care services, compiled in aggregate form to protect personally identifiable health information, for the organization
- Review of the use of **employee assistance program (EAP)** services in aggregate form
- Employee completion of HRAs and review of a summary of HRA results
- Review of corporate policies, programs, and services that might affect health

Following best practices, including assessing which health issues significantly affect employees, will allow the corporate health and wellness promotion professional to plan effective programs.

Identification of Resources

Once the corporate health and wellness promotion professional has reviewed the data and determined which health issues are of greatest concern for the organization and its employees, he or she should determine what resources the organization has available. Who can help from inside the organization? What partners might be available to offer assistance? What facilities can be used? Are there other companies that might be working on the same issues? Ensuring that the organization's administration understands the issues and is ready and willing to address them is a key part of this process.

Planning

Once the corporate health and wellness promotion professional has determined what resources are available, he or she will select the most-promising,

evidence-based strategies for the organization. Often these strategies are not programs. The corporate health and wellness promotion professional can look at policy changes such as vending services, on-site cafeteria offerings, and employee break policies, and company practices and culture can be targeted toward positive health behaviors. Adding facilities for physical activity can be expensive, but the return on investment is good if employees use them.

Implementation

Implementation of health and wellness programs is often the simplest step in the strategic prevention framework. An understanding of employee motivation and publicity strategies that will encourage participation is key at this stage. If only a few employees participate, the programs will not produce the desired results.

Evaluation

The final step in the process is to evaluate the success of the programs. The corporate health and wellness promotion professional should bypass reviews of employee satisfaction and instead look for changes in the aggregate health data. Programs might be well-liked but not provide a return on investment. Assessing the effects of the programs on health status will help the corporate health and wellness promotion professional adjust the programs offered to ensure they are meeting the goals of the organization.

WELLNESS AND HEALTH PROMOTION: OTHER PROGRAM TYPES

The public often considers fitness to be the sole path to leading a healthy life. However, well-rounded worksite wellness and health promotion programs target the broader spectrum of health by including recreational activities for socialization, EAPs for mental health, and other programs that address all aspects of wellness.

Recreation Programs

Athletic programs and social activities such as corporate sport challenges, lunchtime basketball games, softball teams, company picnics, and others offer opportunities to be active, interact with coworkers, build relationships, and improve morale across the company. Social and emotional wellness play a role in employee satisfaction on the job.

EAP

An EAP is a benefit program offered by a company that helps employees manage personal issues that can affect their job performance. Typical services include counseling or referral services for a wide range of mental and emotional health issues such as alcohol and substance abuse and misuse, stress, grief support, financial troubles, legal issues, and family problems.

General Wellness Programs

Corporate health and wellness promotion professionals can choose from a myriad of programs across the wellness wheel (see figure 11.3). Examples of such programs are listed in table 11.1.

IMPACTS OF RECENT LEGISLATION

The field of corporate wellness and health promotion has been affected by health care reform initiated by the passage of the Affordable Care Act in 2010. The legislation puts a stronger emphasis on disease prevention and early intervention and creates opportunities for corporate health and wellness promotion professionals to include health screenings covered by group health insurance as a part of the data collection process. More comprehensive data

collection may result in a more targeted selection of evidence-based programs for a corporate wellness and health promotion program. In addition, the Health Insurance Portability and Accountability Act of 1996 (HIPAA) includes provisions that protect people's health information. Professionals who work with medical information, even in the development of corporate wellness and health promotion activities, need to be cognizant of the privacy law and exercise due care when using and handling health information. Professionals most often use the data in aggregate form, meaning data are compiled into a single set and any references to individuals are removed.

CAREER PREPARATION

People seeking careers in worksite recreation and health promotion will need knowledge, skills, and experience in a variety of areas to remain competitive in the job market. Successful job candidates must be competent in public relations, human resource management, budget development and management, facility design and management, risk management, recreation and fitness programming, advocacy, health promotion and exercise science, and recreation sport management. Job candidates can enhance their prospects by completing a university-approved internship and obtaining professional certification through a recognized professional association.

Numerous accredited health promotion and fitness organizations offer certification programs such as the American College of Medicine's Health Fitness Instructor (HFI) or the National Commission for Health Education Credentialing's Certified

Table 11.1 Types of Wellness Programs

Physical	Social	Environmental	Occupational	Spiritual	Emotional	Intellectual
Fitness class	Company picnic	Stewardship program	Lunch and learn program	Self-esteem reflection	Employee assistance program	Book club
Back injury prevention seminar	Holiday party	Recycling program	Money management	Sabbatical program	Walking club	Tuition assistance program
Smoking cessation program	Corporate challenge participation	Safety and loss control program	Attaining work–life balance	Stewardship program	Personal financial management program	Leadership training programs

Model Program: Worksite Recreation and Health Promotion

Cerner is a health care information technology company based in Kansas City, Missouri, whose mission is to be a significant player in the health industry. Cerner offers programs designed to assist companies and communities in improving key health factors and behaviors. It isn't too surprising that a company with such a business focus would offer corporate wellness and health promotion programs and services for their own employees. This is Cerner's mission:

Together with our clients, we are creating a future where the health care system works to improve the well-being of individuals and communities. By designing leading-edge health information technology, we offer strategies that empower organizations to know, manage and engage their populations.

Cerner has embedded positive health behaviors in a pervasive company culture intended to promote positive family and company relationships, healthy lifestyles, and happy and productive employees. A few of the more unique programs are discussed here.

Healthe at Cerner

Healthe at Cerner is a set of coordinated programs and services designed around health and wellness for the employee and the employee's family. The cornerstone of the program is Cerner's Health Plan. The plan is complemented by Cerner's Healthe Living with Rewards program, which is designed to reward employees who are working toward optimal health. Cerner also offers employees access to Healthe clinics, pharmacies, and fitness centers. These components are tied together by technology created to allow employees to "stay well, manage well, and get well." Family access to wellness classes, fitness centers, and employee wellness challenges is free for the employee. Degreed exercise professionals are available to employees in the Healthe fitness centers. Cerner also sponsors individual entries for select run–walk events and the Kansas City Corporate Challenge. Cerner's cafes include healthy food options, and nutrition information is printed on labels to assist employees in their quest for optimal health.

Personal Leave of Absence Program

Cerner offers a unique sabbatical program similar to those in higher education. Employees who have been with the company for a minimum number of years and are in good standing can elect to take a personal leave of absence with pay. Employees can choose to travel, engage in mission or steward- ship opportunities, or simply enhance knowledge. The employee is required to unplug from all forms of Cerner work obligation (work e-mail, meetings, phone calls) to achieve the best benefit from the program.

Other Benefits

Some of the more traditional benefits offered to Cerner employees are the following:

- Health plan coverage that includes medical, dental, vision, and behavioral health
- CernerKids child-care facilities
- CernerKids events offered throughout the year
- Personal legal services
- Adoption services
- Travel planning services

Information from Cerner (2016).

Health Education Specialist (CHES). These organizations have various requirements that candidates must meet prior to application for certification. All these organizations require successful passage of a written exam, and some require candidates to pass a practical exam. The programs that have the highest degree of recognition among health promotion professionals also require a college undergraduate degree in exercise science, kinesiology, health education, wellness, corporate recreation and wellness, or a related field of study. The following accredited associations offer certification programs:

- American College of Sports Medicine (ACSM), www.acsm.org
- National Strength and Conditioning Association (NSCA), www.nsca-cc.org
- American Council on Exercise (ACE), www.acefitness.org
- Cooper Institute, www.cooperinstitute.org
- National Commission for Health Education Credentialing (NCHEC), www.nchec.org
- World Instructor Training Schools (WITS), www.witseducation.com
- National Exercise Trainers Association (NETA), www.netafit.org
- National Exercise and Sports Trainers Association (NESTA), www.nestacertified.com
- Aerobics and Fitness Association of America (AFAA), www.afaa.com

SUMMARY

Corporate wellness and health promotion programs vary as greatly in scope and complexity as the number and sizes of companies that offer them. Corporate health and wellness promotion professionals have an opportunity to affect employees' lives and contribute to their happiness and productivity at work. In addition, health and wellness programs have positive effects on employee absenteeism, use of worker's compensation, use of sick leave, and health care premium costs. The best-performing programs will follow a planning process that includes data collection, capacity assessment, program planning, implementation, and evaluation. Students interested in the field should have a combination of health-related and service-delivery competencies and plan on enjoying a rewarding career in a growing field.

Recreation in the Armed Forces

Ryan Cane and Diane Blankenship

❝ The Canadian Armed Forces know that physical activity, recreation, and sport are essential for promoting well-being and operational readiness at home and while deployed. Whether it be organized sports, individual activities or participation in recreational clubs, the CAF knows these types of activities provide support to our families, build capacity in our communities, and ensure our quality of life. ❞

Lieutenant-General Christine Whitecross, commander, Military Personnel Command

❝ We are dedicated to providing support and leisure services that are as outstanding as the people we serve. ❞

U.S. Army Morale, Welfare and Recreation

Recreation programs in the Canadian and the U.S. Armed Forces are based on two basic philosophies: (1) Members of the military and their families are entitled to the same quality of life that is afforded to the society they protect, and (2) quality recreation programs have a direct effect on mission readiness. Recreation programs are designed to maintain a positive quality of life that leads to a sound mind and body, a productive community, and a strong family environment. Recreation programs for the Canadian and U.S. Armed Forces have unique requirements that set them apart from other public-sector programs. These programs must support military personnel and their families at their home stations as well as in deployed environments at remote sites around the world (Canadian Armed Forces Recreation Services, 2017).

HISTORY

Recreation programs have existed in Canada and the United States for hundreds of years. In the United States, organized programs started on the battlefields of the Revolutionary War where sutlers were assigned the responsibility of providing for the personal needs of the soldiers. These itinerant merchants provided many of the services of the present-day exchange stores, and a portion of their profits were returned to the units. These unit funds were used to provide services to soldiers in the battlefield. Today, revenues generated by the profit-oriented services are still used to fund a variety of leisure activities including libraries, financial assistance programs, bands, and school projects (Canadian Army, 2017b; USA Government, 2017).

By the Civil War, sutlers had made themselves extinct by pricing themselves out of business, and their roles were assumed by canteen associations, which became essential social clubs for the units and were authorized by Congress in 1893. These had naturally become centers for command-sponsored social events and were recognized as important for promoting esprit de corps. Organized programs started on the battlefields of World War I, where the Salvation Army and Red Cross members ministered to the needs of soldiers as the forerunners of today's recreation specialists (US Army MWR, n.d.).

In 1940, at the beginning of World War II, the U.S. Morale Division, later named Special Services, was established in the U.S. Army. Between 1946 and 1955, core recreation programs were established and staffed by a combination of active-duty military personnel and civilians. Until the mid-1980s, active-duty personnel held occupational specialties in Special Services at every level of command. As those specialties were discontinued, civilians continued to operate programs with military oversight as the program requirements grew and the senior commanders came to understand the value of recreation in mission readiness (US Army MWR, n.d.).

In Canada, it has long been recognized that the success of the military depends on the physical, emotional, and spiritual well-being of the **military community**. Throughout the history of the Canadian military, **morale and welfare** programs have been available to all serving members and their families with the goal of enhancing the quality of life of the military community and contributing to the **operational readiness and effectiveness** of the armed forces. In 1996, the Canadian Forces Personnel Support Agency (which was later renamed to **Canadian Forces Morale and Welfare Services**) was created with the mission of providing the military community with morale and welfare programs and services (CFMWS, 2016).

Today, in Canada and the United States, recreation programs within the military environment are broad in scope and are evolving constantly to meet the ever-changing needs of the military community. The U.S. Armed Forces use the common acronym MWR for **morale, welfare, and recreation** to refer to those programs, whereas in Canada, the **Personnel Support (PSP) Division** of the Canadian Forces Morale and Welfare Services is the key provider of recreation services within the military environment (PSP, 2017; US Army MWR, n.d.)

MILITARY VERSUS CIVILIAN RECREATION

Military recreation departments are administered similarly to civilian recreation departments. Many of the programs, such as swimming lessons, leadership certifications, and recreation club activities are conducted in partnership with, or are modeled on the products of, civilian agencies. Like their civilian counterparts, military recreation departments employ many operational tools to more efficiently manage and profile programs and services. From recreation management software to online recreation brochures, military recreation strives to encourage participation, increase patronage, and enhance the benefits of recreation participation.

Although military recreation is modeled after civilian recreation programs, the unique environment and requirements of the military community result in several distinct differences between the two. One of the key differences is the transient nature of the client. Military families relocate frequently. Programs and services based on the expressed needs of the military community one year might be quite different the next year because the families who make up the community relocate. Recreation professionals must constantly survey the military community to be aware of the changing needs and interests of military families.

Second, many military communities are located in remote or unstable places around the world. Recreation opportunities are as important to the serving members in isolated or combat environments as they are to members and their families at the home station. Recreation professionals must be prepared and willing to provide services under difficult and sometimes dangerous conditions.

A third difference between civilian and military recreation is the scope of the recreation department. Civilian recreation departments provide services to residents and other interested users. Military recreation departments are exclusive and provide services to military members, their families, and other members of the military community such as veterans and their families. MWS and PSP often offer services to each other's primary clients when military personnel from the other country are stationed in Canada or the United States (Military Benefits, 2017).

A fourth difference is the culture that recreation programs are conducted in. Many military installations are located in foreign countries, and the recreation programs blend recreation activities and events with local, regional, and national culture of the foreign country. In many countries, joint activities and events are offered between the military and the host community. Programs such as *volksmarches* (organized walks) and *volksfests* (regional festivals) are popular activities with military families stationed in Germany (Military Benefits, 2017).

Last, volunteer management can be challenging within the military community. Volunteers are key contributors to the success of the military community recreation program. Without volunteers, many programs would be unsustainable, and with the high turnover of military families, managing volunteers is often difficult. MWR and PSP have developed viable volunteer management programs that strive to develop, support, and nurture the involvement of volunteers in recreation programs (Military Benefits, 2017).

U.S. ARMED FORCES

The **U.S. Armed Forces** provide a variety of recreation programs to maintain individual, family, and mission readiness during peacetime and in times of declared war and other contingencies. The U.S. Armed Forces consist of the U.S. Army, U.S. Marine Corps, U.S. Navy, U.S. Air Force, and U.S. Coast Guard. Although the scope of each MWR program might vary slightly, the mission is to provide quality recreation programs to U.S. fighting forces at home and abroad.

Military MWR programs are an integral part of the military benefits package, encourage positive individual values, and build healthy families and communities. They provide consistently high-quality support services that are commonly furnished by other employers or state and local governments to their employees and citizens. MWR programs promote esprit de corps and provide for physical, cultural, and social needs; general well-being; quality of life; and community support of service members and their families. Recreation programs are a vital factor in maintaining each force's ability to fight and win its nation's wars. The fighting forces need a balance of work and leisure to be ready to fight when needed, especially during frequent contingency operations. A *contingency operation* is a military operation that is either designated by the secretary of defense as a contingency operation in which members of the armed forces are or may become involved in military actions, operations, or hostilities against an enemy of the United States or against an opposing force or becomes a contingency operation as a matter of law. Families left behind during a deployment to a contingency operation must be cared for so that the service member can fight without worrying about those left at home (Military MWR, 2012).

Military mission readiness depends largely on the resilience of service members and their families. Resilience is important to the military because it helps people overcome traumatic experiences such as those encountered in contingency operations, helps family members better cope with deployments, reduces stress, and boosts energy levels. Resilience is often described as the ability to respond to and cope with difficult or stressful experiences, situations, environments, people, and setbacks common to all people in life. Although everything we do involves stress, how we respond to a particular stressor is important. Increasing the ability to handle stress and bounce back from the strains of daily life increases resilience (Military MWR, 2012).

MWR provides well-balanced recreation that normalizes behavior after a stressful experience. Participating in exercise and recreation programs reduces stress and builds mental and physical resilience. Besides building resilience, MWR enhances mission readiness. This conclusion was demonstrated by findings from the Department of Defense customer satisfaction survey conducted in 2009 and 2011 to assess MWR programs. The survey findings indicated that MWR satisfaction has the greatest effect on mission readiness. This correlation is critical to understanding the importance of MWR recreation in building resilience and influencing military mission readiness throughout the armed forces (Military MWR, 2012).

During contingency operations, MWR equipment and deployed personnel provide MWR programs and activities that build unit esprit de corps, increase morale, relieve stress, and provide greatly needed mental diversion during these operations. Internet cafes with computers are operated by MWR at no cost to service members. MWR Internet cafes also offer webcams and headsets for making videos and phone calls using voice over Internet protocol (VOIP), which costs only a few cents per minute. In addition, service members have access to all the popular social networking websites to communicate with family and friends. Portable morale satellite units provide free Internet access to remote, forward operating bases. Fitness, recreation, and social activities include cardiovascular and weight equipment, suspension training systems, sports, recreation, games, outdoor recreation equipment, large screen TVs, DVD and CD players, and up-to-date video games. Armed Forces Entertainment, in cooperation with the United Service Organizations (USO), provides much-welcomed celebrity and professional entertainment. The Department of Defense MWR online library is available through the military services library portals and offers 24/7 one-stop shopping for all library resources in print, electronic, and downloadable formats. Free downloads of thousands of e-books and audio books and free access to comprehensive databases for recreation, lifelong learning, reference, and career transition are available for all ages and all interests. In addition, monthly shipments of digital books and paperback books are provided to deployed units (Military MWR, 2012).

With an increasing number of service members returning from contingency operations with severe injuries, the MWR program provides recreation inclusion training for recreation programmers from all military services. Recognizing that recreation and sport play an important role in the recovery process, training concentrates on posttraumatic stress disorder, limb amputations, traumatic brain injury, spinal cord injuries, adaptive and specialized equipment, accessible design, age-appropriate inclusive recreation programming, and societal and cultural issues. Trained recreation programmers and recreation therapists develop or expand inclusive recreation programs at their installations, which enables wounded warriors to develop their abilities and continue their military mission (Military MWR, 2012).

The MWR program provides recreation opportunities for people of all abilities to exercise and recreate. With programs such as outdoor recreation, fitness classes, team sports, and bowling, just to name a few, MWR helps individuals and units maintain physical fitness, alleviate combat stress, and foster total family fitness. By promoting exercise and recreation, MWR enables service members and families to build physical and mental resilience to stress and affects military mission readiness. The oversight for providing recreation services in the United States is governed by specific agencies within each branch of the military (Military MWR, 2012).

• **U.S. Army**. The U.S. Army Family and Morale, Welfare and Recreation Command (FMWRC) administers the MWR program through its headquarters in San Antonio, Texas. It is a comprehensive network of quality support and leisure services that enhance the lives of soldiers, civilians, families, military retirees, and other eligible participants. MWR services and activities offer soldiers and their families opportunities to enrich their lives culturally and creatively. The programs relieve stress, build strength and resilience, and help people stay physically, mentally, and financially fit. The unique challenge to the army is the requirement to provide the same level of support to troops around the world regardless of the existence of a viable installation (location can vary from a military garrison in the United States to a tent in the desert) (Military.com, 2017).

• **U.S. Marine Corps**. The marine corps manages the MWR program through Marine Corps Community Services (MCCS) at its headquarters in Quantico, Virginia. MCCS provides fitness and recreation programs, personal services, and business activities to support individual and family readiness and retention. The vision of the marine corps MWR program is to make a difference in the lives of marines, reserves, retirees, and families by doing the right things the right way in peacetime and in war. The MWR teams strive to provide marines and their families with programs that promote optimal health, quality of life, and mission readiness (Military.com, 2017).

• **U.S. Navy**. The U.S. Navy Morale, Welfare and Recreation Division, located in Millington, Tennessee, and the Commander, Navy Installations Command, in Washington, DC, administer the MWR program to active-duty, reserve, and retired navy personnel and their families. The mission is to provide quality support and recreation services that contribute to retention and readiness and the mental, physical, and emotional well-being of sailors. The navy serves the needs of its members around the world at installations and on board ships at sea. Civilian recreation specialists carry out this mission work on installations in the United States and overseas and are assigned on board most of the navy's larger ships to manage MWR programs and services (Military.com, 2017).

• **U.S. Air Force**. The U.S. Air Force operates MWR programs through its headquarters in San Antonio, Texas, under the title of Services Agency. The mission of the air force's MWR program is to contribute to mission readiness and improve productivity through programs that promote fitness, esprit de corps, and quality of life for air force people and to provide policy and direction for the worldwide services program to help sustain the air force mission. Although not normally considered recreation programs, activities such as mortuary services and wartime feeding are included under the umbrella of MWR services, which makes its program delivery broader than those of the other service branches (Military.com, 2017).

• **U.S. Coast Guard**. The U.S. Coast Guard in the Department of Homeland Security provides recreation programs to its members worldwide. Although it is the smallest of the service branches, it offers a critical element in the quality-of-life programming for its members and their families. The mission of the Coast Guard Morale, Well-Being, and Recreation (MWR) program, operating out of Chesapeake, Virginia, is to uplift the spirits of the coast guard family and be an essential element of coast guard mission readiness and retention through customer-owned and customer-driven MWR programs and services (Military.com, 2017).

The U.S. Armed Forces have unique recreational opportunities for active duty military and their families. One such service that is mirrored throughout the armed forces is special recreation programs for single service men and women between the ages of 18 and 24. This age group represents 35 to 50 percent of military personnel. For many of these people, this is the first time they have been separated from their families, and they are stationed in communities or countries that are vastly different from their own. This creates unique needs that are different from families with children. Programs such as the Better Opportunities for Single Soldiers Program, the Single Airmen and Single Marines, Single Sailor, and Single Soldiers provide a voice to this segment to advocate for their unique needs and desires. These programs are composed of advisory councils that include a staff member and address quality of life issues such as recreation, volunteerism, and living situations in the barracks. Each council tailors their activities to the needs and unique opportunities of the local community or country (Army Study Guide, 2017).

An additional service provided by the Department of Defense is the Armed Forces Recreation Centers (AFRC). These centers are located in Garmisch, Germany; Walt Disney Resort in Florida; Seoul, Korea; and Waikiki Beach in Honolulu, Hawaii. Each of these centers is a full-service resort with an array of programs, services, tours, and recreational opportunities unique to their location. Service personnel and their families use these centers for family vacations, as areas to reunite with a family member who has been deployed and is on leave from the combat area, or as regional destinations for getaway weekends. The AFRC facilities meet various needs for recreation, relaxation, rest, and restoration from various life situations and combat (Army One Source, 2017).

CANADIAN ARMED FORCES

Canadian Armed Forces (CAF) members are proud to serve Canada by defending its values, interests, and sovereignty at home and abroad. They support freedom, democracy, the rule of law, and human rights around the world. The CAF are separate and distinct from the Department of National Defence. The CAF are headed by the chief of the defence staff (CDS), which is Canada's senior serving officer.

The CAF serve on the sea, on land, and in the air through the Royal Canadian Navy, the Canadian Army, and the Royal Canadian Air Force.

• **Royal Canadian Navy**. The Royal Canadian Navy (RCN) consists of approximately 8,300 regular force and 4,600 reserve sailors supported by about 3,700 civilian employees. The mission of the RCN is to generate combat-capable, multipurpose maritime forces that support Canada's efforts to participate in security operations anywhere in the world as part of an integrated CAF. The RCN fleet, which is divided between the Atlantic (Halifax, Nova Scotia) and Pacific (Esquimalt, British Columbia) coasts, is composed of 29 warships, submarines, and coastal defense vessels, plus many more auxiliary and support vessels. PSP recreation services are provided on both coasts and on ships while at sea (Royal Canadian Navy, 2017).

• **Canadian Army**. The Canadian Army is the land component of the CAF, and it consists of approximately 23,000 regular force and 17,000 reservists supported by about 3,000 civilian employees. The mission of the Canadian Army is to generate combat effective, multipurpose land forces to meet Canada's defense objectives. The regular force has three mechanized brigade groups composed of units stationed in Western Canada, Ontario, Quebec, and Atlantic Canada. The Army Reserve Force is organized into ten brigade groups spread across the country. PSP recreation services are an important part of the Army's mission-ready philosophy; they ensure the army community has access to programs that improve their physical, mental, and social well-being (Canadian Army, 2017a).

• **Royal Canadian Air Force.** The Royal Canadian Air Force (RCAF) includes approximately 13,000 regular force personnel and 2,400 air reserve personnel. Approximately 2,000 civilian public servants are also employed within the RCAF organization. The RCAF provides the CAF with relevant, responsive, and effective air power capabilities to meet defense challenges. The RCAF comprises 13 wings, as well as other installations, that are located across Canada. The RCAF's fleet of aircraft includes fighter jets, helicopters, and training aircraft. PSP recreation services vary wing to wing, but they are geared toward family activities. Recreation departments also participate in organizing annual wing air shows that include face painting and food concessions (Royal Canadian Air Force, 2017).

The Canadian Armed Forces Recreation Program

Canadian Forces Morale and Welfare Services (CFMWS) is responsible for administering and delivering selected morale and welfare programs, services, and activities to eligible members (table 11.2) and their families on behalf of the chief of the defence staff. CAF policy states that an officer in command of a base or unit must ensure that reasonable recreation facilities, programs, and services are organized and accessible to military personnel and their families (Statistics Canada, 2015).

Effective morale and welfare (MW) programs contribute directly and indirectly to the operational readiness and effectiveness of the CAF and encourage stability and retention. MW programs also help to mitigate some of the unwelcome consequences of military life that might otherwise disadvantage CAF members and their families compared to other Canadians. Examples of MWR programs include military fitness, sports, health promotion, and recreation (CFMWS, 2017).

Recreation programs have special value for military personnel functioning in a technically or operationally oriented force. A well-balanced program helps maintain total fitness and reduces mental fatigue tensions and frustrations that develop from everyday work. Besides the physical health benefits, a balanced recreation program that includes opportunities for participation in arts, crafts, hobbies, and cultural and special interest activities aids in maintaining high morale and work efficiency (CFMWS, 2017).

The PSP division of CFMWS is responsible for the operations of community recreation departments and activities. PSP personnel are committed to providing individuals, families, and communities with quality leisure experiences, innovative programming, and recreational facilities that meet their needs (CFMWS, 2017).

The primary responsibility of the recreation department is to provide programs and services that enhance the well-being and quality of life of participants. These programs vary but include memberships to base wing fitness facilities, swimming lessons, and dance classes. Specialty interest activities (SIAs), such as golf courses, curling rinks, and marinas, also provide unique services to Canadian military communities. Profits from SIAs are reinvested in local base funds, which allows PSP to meet additional local programming needs such as special events. Table 11.3 outlines the number of

Table 11.2 CFMWS Eligible Participants

Military community members	Approximate number of eligible participants
CAF members (regular and reserve forces)	130,500
Spouses	68,800
Family members	75,500
Surviving former members	594,500
Surviving dependents of former members	350,000
Other authorized patrons (e.g., Department of National Defence employees)	150,000
Total	**1,369,300**

Table 11.3 Canadian Armed Forces Recreation Program Numbers, 2015-2016

Total participants with gym/recreation memberships for casual facility use	50,845
Hours per week a gym is dedicated to casual recreation use	1,223
Hours per week a pool is dedicated to casual recreation use	555
Hours per week an arena is dedicated to casual recreation use	200
Facilities used for recreation use	325
Special events	282
Special event participants	100,146
Recreation clubs	228
Recreation club members	17,956
Programs	7,178
Program participants	79,697

For more information on PSP and community recreation in the Canadian Armed Forces, please visit www.CAFconnection.com.

programs and participants from the 2015 to 2016 season. Programs such as the Canadian Armed Forces Photography Contest and the Recreation Month Celebrations are run at local and national levels. Like civilian agencies, the CAF recreation program follows nationally set standards and programs such as Red Cross swimming lessons and HIGH FIVE.

Only 15 percent of the military population lives in the residential housing on bases and wings, so PSP partners with civilian agencies to ensure that their needs are met in the neighborhoods in which they live. The Canadian Forces Appreciation Program offers rate reductions and incentives that are exclusive to CAF members, particularly in the areas of family attractions, leisure, travel, and entertainment (CFMWS, 2017).

CAF Recreation Program Operations

The military recreation program is founded on seven governing principles that support numerous recreation program components. The governing principles serve to

1. provide inclusive, creative, and diversified recreation opportunities for the military community;

2. address the physical, emotional, and social characteristics, interests, and needs of all members of the military community equally and consistently;

3. operate according to the needs and interests of the military community, making optimal use of supporting resources;

4. provide opportunities for leadership development;

5. create opportunities for individual and group growth and development through responsibility, accountability, and leadership in the planning and operating of recreational activities;

6. nurture partnerships with recognized recreational agencies for the provision of high-quality, responsive recreational services; and

7. ensure that recreational services are governed in accordance with Canadian military financial, operating, and management policies.

(CFMWS, July 2017).

The importance of individual responsibility and accountability within the military community recreation program cannot be overstated. Because the CAF environment is authoritarian through necessity, it is essential that members of the military community can initiate, organize, and control their own recreation activities within the limitations imposed by the environment and existing CAF and base administrative policies. Acceptance of recreation program organization, management, and accountability is an evolving process. This process can and should be fostered through service on committees, holding offices, and working together with colleagues to meet the recreational needs of all members of the military community. Recreation staff ensure effective management of recreation personnel and volunteers, financial administration, and delivery of community recreation programs and services (CFMWS, July 2017).

Unique to the CAF recreation program are the services provided to ill and injured soldiers and those who are deployed. Soldier On is a CAF program that supports currently serving members and veterans in overcoming physical or mental illnesses or injuries through physical activity and sport. Since its inception in 2007, Soldier On has helped more than 2,200 ill and injured members obtain sporting or recreational equipment and gain access to high-level training from world-class instructors and has supported their participation in a wide range of structured activities from alpine skiing to fishing to adventure expeditions. This reintroduction to an active lifestyle provides members with opportunities to develop new skills, build confidence in their abilities, and meet peers with similar challenges. Many ill and injured members credit Soldier On with helping them adapt to their new normal and realize their full potential (CFMWS, July 2017).

Since August 2000, PSP has been deploying morale and welfare staff to manage and deliver programs for CAF personnel at overseas missions. Depending on the needs of the mission, staff members support deployed personnel by offering services such as retail operations; mess services; fitness, sports, and recreation programs; barber services; and more. Programs are often similar to the ones offered at home, although recreation professionals must be creative and flexible in their approaches to traditional offerings due to lack of facilities and challenging environments (CFMWS, July 2017).

To assist with decompression from missions, CAF provides reintegration programs for military personnel that resemble social and travel activities at the military installation. To complement the mental health services provided by CAF through the decompression activities and services, PSP organizes recreation and social activities to help members unwind and relax. During longer missions, PSP can also support rest and recreation centers in which deployed members are given a few days away from the operation. PSP at these centers organize tourist excursions and provide services similar to a hotel concierge by arranging everything from spa packages to dinner reservations (CFMWS, July 2017).

The CAF and PSP have a long tradition of providing entertainment show tours for CAF members serving overseas and at isolated locations. Typically provided at the midpoint of a six-month rotation, a Canadian Forces Show Tour brings a small piece of Canada and Canadian entertainers to deployed members wherever they may be stationed (CFMWS, July 2017).

A comprehensive, varied, and universal recreation program assures military members that their families are well cared for in their absence and provides the military family with opportunities to engage in the community while maintaining or enhancing their personal morale and welfare. Military family resource centers (MFRCs) are committed to enriching the lives of individuals and families in CAF communities through positive action, education, and support. They provide relevant programs and services that empower and encourage strong, independent individuals and families within the CAF (CFMWS, July 2017).

MFRCs encourage and facilitate the voluntary participation of CAF families, particularly spouses, in all facets of their operations from program planning and delivery to organization governance and leadership. In Canada, MFRCs are incorporated, not-for-profit, third-party organizations. They work in partnership with the local commanding officer (CO) and are governed by elected boards of directors (SPS, 2017).

MILITARY RECREATION PROGRAM AREAS

In Canada and the United States, the recreation mandate operates to serve the following MWR and PSP program offerings:

- **Sports and fitness**. At the heart of every recreation program is the sports and fitness program. Because of the need to maintain a strong and healthy force, sports and fitness programs have long been recognized by military leadership as a key to mission readiness, and they have become the centerpiece of every MWR and PSP organization. These programs offer state-of-the-art gymnasium and fitness facilities as well as organized sports competitions from intramural to competitive levels (CFMWS, July 2017; US Navy, n.d.).

- **Skill development**. A staple of the military recreation program's inventory is skill development through instructional classes. Classes are organized in response to a community's interest in skill development and leadership opportunities. The classes include specialty cardio workouts and aerobics, arts and crafts, camps, swimming lessons, weight training for youth, sport clinics, and leadership development. Programs are available for all ages and interests and are developed and implemented in consultation with members of the military community (CFMWS, July 2017; US Navy, n.d.).

- **Libraries**. Libraries remain a vital part of most MWR programs in areas that cannot provide adequate or convenient services to the military population. Libraries vary in size and offerings but generally provide standard recreation reading inventories, reading programs, educational studies, research materials, Internet and e-mail services, and support services. Library programs have become especially crucial in supporting troops in deployed locations and on ships at sea around the world where no local civilian resources are available (CFMWS, July 2017; US Navy, n.d.).

- **Outdoor recreation**. Outdoor recreation programs provide outdoor equipment and access to campgrounds, parks, beaches, and lakes as well as adventure programs and other activities that promote the care and protection of our natural resources. Because of the huge land masses placed under the care of military installations, numerous outdoor recreation opportunities are available. Military organizations are entrusted with the care and preservation of valuable natural resources, and that responsibility provides the opportunity for military personnel to develop new skills while preserving and enjoying natural resources around the world (CFMWS, July 2017; US Navy, n.d.).

- **Child and youth activities**. Child and youth programs and services are offered at all military locations where family support is offered. Programs offer various levels of support that include child development centers, youth centers, and youth activities such as skill development and sports programs. All programs are age appropriate and offer activities that focus on supporting transition, easing the stress of relocation, building and sustaining meaningful relationships, and developing a sense of belonging within the community. Activities that provide universal access to information, tools, resources, and services that support youth; activities that focus on the promotion of healthy and fulfilling life choices; and activities that encourage the development of leadership and assets in youth (40 assets developed by the Search Institute) are also central to the recreation mandate (CFMWS, July 2017; US Navy, n.d.).

- **Recreation centers**. Each military community offers a variety of drop-in opportunities for casual participation in unorganized recreation. Recreation centers are available to military members and their families and provide safe and comfortable environments for self-directed activities as well as for designed programs (CFMWS, July 2017; US Navy, n.d.).

- **Special events and entertainment**. Each military community offers a variety of annual special events to profile military community activities and accomplishments and honor the contributions of volunteers and community partners. Many services host worldwide concert series tours that provide live entertainment to troops, and others focus on local events and festivals (CFMWS, July 2017; US Navy, n.d.).

- **Business activities**. A variety of pay-as-you-go activities geared toward leisure and fitness pursuits are available at most military locations. Theaters, golf courses, special-interest clubs, restaurants, night clubs, and bowling centers are popular activities enjoyed by military families. These commercial services are generally offered when no local off-base resources are readily available. These operations provide military members with the types of services that are available in most civilian communities, and they provide a revenue source to support other morale and welfare activities (CFMWS, July 2017; US Navy, n.d.).

- **Recreation clubs and private organizations**. Recreation clubs or private organizations are self-governing and self-funded entities operated for and by specific-interest groups in accordance with established constitutions and bylaws. Recreation club constitutions and bylaws are military directives that outline club operating principles and member codes of conduct. All recreation clubs are managed by a volunteer executive council and governed by its membership. Examples of recreation club activities include specialty arts, scuba, running, woodworking, sailing, martial arts, gymnastics, swimming, figure skating, and dancing and activities for auto and motorcycle, saddle, and rod and gun enthusiasts (CFMWS, July 2017; US Navy, n.d.).

EMPLOYMENT OPPORTUNITIES

Military recreation provides vast employment opportunities because of the thousands of civilian employees around the world that make up the various MWR and PSP organizations. MWR employs more than 100,000 people in the United States and overseas. People entering employment in military recreation programs generally begin in a specialty such as outdoor recreation, club management, or child development specialist and then move into general management positions within the personnel system. The personnel system might be paid with federal tax dollars (appropriated funds) or with revenue-generating activity funds (nonappropriated funds); both systems are parallel and are considered civil service with portability between each. Careers in MWR are varied but generally start out at the entry level or through an internship with progressions to the top of the civil service ladder (PSP, 2017; Military 4 Life, 2017).

MWR assigns people to a variety of locations from the beaches of California to the sands of the Afghan desert to the icy rivers of Alaska and the high seas of the Atlantic. Variety in jobs and location means there's little opportunity for boredom in the business of providing recreation programs to the armed forces. MWR employees work hard so that others can have fun and enjoy life, and they do it seven days a week and sometimes 24 hours a day. The benefits of a career in MWR range from the great potential for upward mobility to the opportunity to travel and live abroad.

In Canada, the CFMWS is the largest employer of physical education, human kinetics, and leisure

Getty Images/Paula Bronstein

Soldiers take time out to dance at a special event. This necessary recreation helps build physical and mental resilience to stress.

study graduates. The variety of positions and the potential for mobility between Canadian military locations contribute to the attractiveness of a career in the Canadian military recreation field. Most recreation positions within the CFMWS require an undergraduate degree or college diploma plus specific qualifications, such as lifeguarding and first aid certifications or volunteer management certificates to match the position's requirements. Some senior management and director positions require postgraduate degrees and specialty knowledge and experience in the field of military morale and welfare. Furthermore, in recognition of Canada's linguistic diversity, most positions with the CFMWS require proficiency in French and English (PSP, 2017; Military 4 Life, 2017).

Each Canadian military recreation department is composed of a manager, community recreation staff, and various program-specific support staff such as an aquatics supervisor, a youth programmer, or an administration coordinator. Part-time staff, such as lifeguards, camp staff, and youth center monitors also provide programs directly to the military family. Throughout Canada, the CFMWS employs more than 6,000 staff to deliver and support morale and welfare programming.

SUMMARY

Most everyone in the profession of armed forces recreation would tell you that they feel they make a valuable contribution to the mission of the armed forces and are very proud to serve military personnel and their families. Armed forces recreation professionals work around the world and strive to improve the quality of life for soldiers, marines, sailors, airmen, and coast guardsmen and their families who are serving their countries in difficult and challenging times.

Armed forces recreation professionals are proud to support their country's military mission because they believe in the importance of what they do for the armed forces and understand the effect they have on mission readiness and, ultimately, the defense of their country. Much like their counterparts in the civilian sector, military recreation professionals must strive to ensure that the programs they provide are beneficial.

CHAPTER 12

Leisure and Recreation Across the Life Span

Tyler Tapps and Timothy Baghurst

Stewart Cohen/Digital Vision

> " There is a fountain of youth: it is your mind, your talents, the creativity you bring to your life and the lives of people you love. When you learn to tap this source, you will truly have defeated age. "
>
> Sophia Loren, Italian film actress

LEARNING OUTCOMES

After reading this chapter, you should be able to do the following:

> Describe recreation and leisure programs that effectively align with the developmental characteristics of each stage of the life span

> Identify significant milestones throughout the life span and their implications for recreation and leisure service provision

> Describe programs from the recreation industry that address developmental characteristics across the lifespan.

Recreation and leisure is one of the largest industries in the world, and it plays a role as a form of social development over the course of one's life. As the recreation and leisure industry continues to grow, a shift has occurred in the mission of recreation and leisure services. It is no longer an atmosphere of only fun and games; a new focus emphasizes the health benefits of participating in recreation and leisure activities. For example, in 2014, the National Recreation and Park Association (NRPA) announced and implemented new health and wellness and social equity aspects to their strategic plan to align with the shift in the profession. As children grow and adults age, recreation and leisure interests, activities, and definitions must also evolve and change. Therefore, changes in our recreation and leisure behavior directly reflect developmental changes.

Psychologists and other recreation and leisure researchers describe development in seven **life stages**: (1) infancy (birth-2 years), (2) early childhood (3 to 6 years), (3) middle and late childhood (7-12 years), (4) adolescence (13-19 years), (5) early adulthood (20-39 years), (6) middle adulthood (40-59 years), and (7) late adulthood (60 years and older). When recreation and leisure programmers consider how to manage the components of the recreation and leisure experience (e.g., leadership, staffing, facilities), they must line up with the developmental stage of the target audience. This increases their ability to implement successful recreation and leisure experiences and programs (Neulinger, 1974).

LEISURE FUNCTIONS ACROSS THE LIFE SPAN

If we examine the various life stages, it becomes evident that recreation and leisure fulfill different social functions. Some recreation activities are done alone, some are done with members of the same (or opposite) sex, some are done only with peers, and some are done with spouses, parents, children, or relatives. Many people choose to participate in recreation or leisure activities not because of their personal preferences but instead because they facilitate the maintenance or strengthening of social bonds with friends, neighbors, or kin (Kleiber, 1999). For example, one person might prefer a game of golf to a game of Scrabble, but the family's group decision might be to play Scrabble to be with one another, enjoy one another's company, or simply show respect to one another. The extent to which people participate in recreation and leisure activities varies throughout the life span. Among adults, particularly males, such participation is more likely to become a form of compensation or determined by perceived role. When an individual reaches old age, involvement once again is likely to become unconditional or not chosen for any other reason than because it's enjoyable (Kleiber, 1999).

INFANCY

Infancy is the time from birth until approximately 2 years old. There are many changes that occur during this period. Infants make large gains in their motor skills such as rolling, sitting, and crawling. Their memory and recognition also develop; these are often seen in an infant's reaction to seeing a parent or hearing a parent's voice. Infants start to demonstrate their personality development through their interactions with others and their toys.

Infants are often interested in the social world around them, and babies try to communicate with others (Erikson, 1950). By age 2, they exhibit signs of peer play. Infants will often show their toys to one another and offer to share their toys. This is part of their development of basic communication skills. As communication becomes more developed, they will start to show signs of cooperative play. *Cooperative play* is often defined as the organized recreation of a group of children in which activities are planned to complete a desired outcome such as place blocks in a basket.

Considerations for Programming

Infant development is rapid; infants develop **gross motor skills** and begin to recognize people, places, and objects. Recreation and leisure–based programs should foster development and prepare the infants for early childhood. It is vital that programmers develop a safe and conducive atmosphere for play. The most important aspect of play for infants is freedom. They must be permitted to make mistakes and messes. Developed play spaces that have a lot of rules, regulations, and restrictions are typically considered nonconducive to play (Kagan, 2002). Also, an environment where adults are constantly monitoring the noise levels, trying to keep clothes clean, or trying to correct play is not considered a conducive play environment. In short, it is important to let infants and toddlers discover their limits and make their own decisions about where the play-based activities should be. This is how they develop their imaginations and discover desired outcomes to activities (Kagan, 2010).

Recreation and Leisure Program Example

Parks and recreation agencies often offer programs and services for parents and their infants. These are often centered around physical movement because this is fun and helps the infants develop and master fundamental motor skills. The following is an example of a program designed for infants that is fun but also developmental.

Mommy/Daddy and Me Classes. In these classes, the activities alternate between circle time, music, songs, dance, rhythm, stories, obstacle courses, Play-Doh, and parachutes. Children at this level thrive on rapidly expanding their vocabularies, and they do so at lightning speed through songs, stories, and one-on-one and group interactions. Often, there is also exposure to outdoor recreation and the

Recreation and leisure programs for infants focus on classes with parents.

natural world, which children love to explore. These classes also include parent discussion that covers a range of child-related issues such as sleep and bedtime rituals, children's storybooks, or cultures and traditions. During the instructor-led discussion period, parents are encouraged to ask for help or ideas in specific child-rearing areas. Parents may also inspire others as they share their own experiences with the group. In interacting with other families, parents are to network and share helpful information regarding young children, siblings, and family and community events.

CHILDHOOD

When children have some independence and freedom, they are likely to play or interact with siblings and peers. Erik Erikson, a famous developmental psychologist, suggested that children's playful from being concerned with self to being more focused outward or focused on others is a way to learn to fit into the outside world. This requires children to (1) sufficiently interact with others within a social context, (2) create their own opportunities for enjoyment, and (3) show an interest in wanting to relate to others. When adults organize and structure children's free time, such skills cannot develop properly or are not tested. Also, if children become accustomed to having their free time structured, they are more likely to feel bored on the rare occasions when they are unsupervised.

The desire to be part of the wider world also moves children beyond their neighborhood friends. The latter years of childhood are devoted to establishing **relative competence**. Restrictions on free or play-based leisure at this age can lead to a sense of inferiority. In this **age of instruction**, children are attracted to groups in which they can develop skills alongside others who show the same interests. For example, the Girl Scouts, Boy Scouts, Girls and Boys Clubs, public parks and recreation sport teams, and 4-H clubs are all examples of popular organizations children often participate in. Through these activities, children find their leisure identities and begin to take their expressive abilities seriously in ways will likely define future leisure interests. It is the most likely starting place for what Stebbins (1992) refers to as **serious leisure** pursuits.

Developing Interests at School

Children usually rely on their parents and families for guidance throughout childhood. Nevertheless, most cultures have established practices and opportunity structures for moving children out of dependence on families and into preparation to be productive members of society. The ages at which children do this can vary, but when they begin school they begin the task of separation from family that will continue through adolescence. The systems of school and community coincide with a child's natural inclination to establish competence and to connect more effectively with others. Leisure activities move away from purely child-directed play and games to activities that have some connection with the wider world.

The influence of schools on the development of leisure interests and orientations is inherently problematic. The knowledge base developed in schools combined with the cognitive skills discussed previously provide a strong foundation for learning activities outside of school. However, children all too often leave such interests at the school door. Most schools use an elaborate system of extrinsic motivation, primarily in the form of grades or benchmarks, to ensure the development of the knowledge and skills necessary for continuing in school, participating in the workforce, and contributing to society. However, this process often undermines the intrinsic interests that children bring to learning in the same way that rewards and emphasis on winning sometimes take the fun out of children's games and sports. At the same time, many schools provide exposure to a wide variety of activities through art, music, physical education, recess, and extracurricular activities.

The effects of recess on leisure interests are particularly interesting. Recess has often been the focus of discussion and an often-questioned part of the school day. These breaks are only approved because they support the academic objectives of the school or curriculum. There is some evidence to suggest that recess activity might enhance classroom performance. Recess does, however, create a unique context in which play and social interaction can be shaped by the children within the constraints of a limited, timed break within the school environment. Although children might have afternoons and weekends free for self-directed activity, the defining of limits of time, space, and play groups give recess the great potential for allowing children to create their own social worlds.

Childhood can generally be broken down into two stages; (1) early and (2) middle and late. During these stages, children continue to increase their abilities to reason, and they are increasingly aware of relationships with others (e.g., they recognize gender differences). Play is still unstructured, but by the age of 5, children begin to understand competition. They continue to develop physically, mentally, and emotionally, but at a slower, steadier pace than in infancy. Through recreation and leisure activities, they can form their first close relationships outside the family. Younger children are more interested in having fun and learning skills, whereas older children are more interested in competition.

Recreation and Leisure

Children do not often use the words *recreation* and *leisure*, but they certainly understand what you mean if you say "let's play." Children also develop an understanding of recess, after-school time, vacation, and weekends. When they begin attending school, they start to experience a struggle between freedom and constraint in their time. Playtime, however, is an idea that most children learn before they start school as they come to distinguish it from activities such as cleaning up, bathing, brushing teeth, and going to bed. The youngest children tend to live in the present; they can commit themselves to the moment as if nothing else matters at that given time. Patterns of play clearly reflect changes in development that reveal the reasons for participation or intrinsic motivations as children grow. Play expresses freedom and occupies a great deal of time. Play should not be mistaken with *exploration*, which is specifically oriented to reveal the true nature of things. Play is considered a nonliteral behavior or a transformation of reality; for example, a child's doll might represent a baby, or an empty wrapping paper tube might represent a laser gun. Play shares the quality of intrinsic motivation with other forms of leisure, and because it is considered transformative, it represents the qualities that make leisure different from the realities of everyday life.

Play is considered a practice of free choice and provides a growing need to seek out motives and abilities. Thus, a child exercises whatever functions he or she can to create an effect and then make it change. Infants begin playing by putting everything into their mouths to experience it, and they repeat sounds and actions almost endlessly. The world of play at this time is considered autocosmic, or a private world within the sphere of the body. In early childhood, children enter into the microsphere when they focus their attention toward the nearest environment. This is where **pretend play** emerges and reflects the development of intelligence. Due to the increased focus on environment and intel-

ligence, children at this stage (3 to 6 years old) typically show tremendous growth in language development.

During early childhood, play is often done alone, but as children become more aware of others, their play expands from the microsphere to the macrosphere, where the world extends beyond family. Initially, children relate to others through parallel play or playing next to but not with others. However, they eventually learn to play together in *associative play* in which they share, imitate each other, and engage in pretending through the use of new social skills and physical skills. Children in early childhood have not yet learned to make decisions about the perspectives of others. It is in middle and late childhood that children engage in truly **cooperative play** and can play games with rules.

Early Childhood (3 to 6 years old)

Early childhood is the time between 3 and 6 years of age. There are many significant physical (e.g., growing taller and getting stronger) and behavioral (e.g., increasing attention span and increasing pretend play over parallel play) changes in this stage. During this period there is also significant improvement in motor skill development. Cognitively, children's attention spans increase, and they start to develop reasoning skills. They also start to think about toys or objects that are not present, which is referred to as *symbolic thinking*.

Physical Abilities

During the preschool years, boys and girls slim down and shed what is often referred to as *baby fat*, and their bodies lengthen. It is at this stage that physical gender differences related to the body become apparent. For example, girls at this stage have more fatty tissue and boys have more muscle. Brain maturation permits greater control and coordination of the arms, legs, and neck. Children in this stage show an increase in **fine motor skills**, and by the end of this period, they can construct towers out of blocks and draw pictures using multiple colors. However, due to the nervous system not being fully developed, children in this stage

During the early childhood stage, children show an increase in fine motor skills.

may have difficulty with other tasks that require fine motor skills.

Cognitive Abilities

Brain growth slows in this stage compared to the infancy stage. However, children's ability to pay attention grows during the preschool years. They can spend longer periods of time doing one activity or watching a video. Also, as they age, they can process information more quickly. Their language ability continues to evolve rapidly, and they progress from saying single sentences or repeating sounds to more complex statements that combine multiple words. For that reason, children at this age group begin to have conversations with their parents, other adults, and their peers and may show an increased interest in writing and reading.

Socioemotional Characteristics

As children age, the relationships they develop with others consume more of their time. At this stage, they can compare themselves to others and therefore can start to process and understand differences. This understanding allows them to achieve a greater understanding of who they are and where they fit in relation to their peers. Many recreation researchers have suggested that play with peers has significant results in relationship building for children in this stage (Sutton-Smith, 1971). For example, researchers have stated that play with peers releases tension, develops increased self-efficacy, increases cognitive development, increases exploration, increases comfort in an environment, promotes attachment to others, and helps children learn to cope. It also has been described as an outlet for children to learn to expel anger or learn how to deal with emotions (Larson & Verma, 1999). This stage of childhood is often described as the years of pretend or make-believe or, as most recreation researchers call it, play. At no other time in life is a person so thoroughly involved in the world of fantasy or play. Pretend play makes up approximately two-thirds of all play in this stage of childhood (Larson & Verma, 1999).

Considerations for Programming

With the increase in childhood obesity, preventative health is becoming more popular in programming for children. Obesity is a major concern during this stage of childhood; research has indicated that being overweight in preschool is likely to carry over into adolescence and adulthood. An important part of combating childhood obesity is building active play elements into recreation and leisure programs. Whether structured or unstructured, all programs should have a physically active portion that also educates participants and, if possible, parents about the benefits of being active in everyday life. The recreation professional can play a significant role in designing programs that allow for active play and educational opportunities. The NRPA website has information and resources related to the benefits of being physically active and active programming related to health and wellness.

Recreation and Leisure Program Example

Recreation programs at this stage of childhood should focus on using materials such as blocks, crayons, balls, and gym mats. Materials should be used imaginatively or in any way children think is fun.

Early childhood is a time when children enjoy new challenges to test their developing skills. Children should be active and explore. The promotion and implementation of active play activities within programs is a great way to encourage a healthy lifestyle and can result in benefits that extend to the middle childhood stage and beyond. The following is an example of a program for children in this age group.

Kids' Corner. Kids' corner is a recreation program designed for children aged 3 to 6 years. The main objective is to strengthen children's self-image and feelings of competence through physical, cognitive, and socioemotional activities. Children are encouraged to actively and creatively explore the world around them through arts and crafts, music and rhythms, field trips, storytelling, and many other learning experiences. The kids' corner activities are age appropriate and include music, stories, art, indoor and outdoor play, negotiating physical elements, and language development. Social skills are most important. Play is a child's work; therefore, children are encouraged to play.

Middle and Late Childhood (7 to 12 years old)

Children who are 7 to 12 years old are in **middle and late childhood**. The development during this stage is more complex than in previous stages because motor skills and cognitive functions become much more refined. Although children's physical development slows down, cognitive and physical changes are dramatic. School-age children can skillfully handle objects, have much longer attention spans, and think logically. The social aspect of being accepted by their peers is also important during this stage.

Physical Abilities

Physical growth is slow but consistent during this stage. Muscle mass gradually increases and muscle tone improves. Children in this stage double their strength capabilities, which allows them to run faster, jump higher, climb, and move their own weight more easily. Fine motor skills continue to improve, and by ages 10 to 12 children can demonstrate skillful handling similar to that of adults. The complex movements needed to create high-quality crafts or play music can begin to be mastered at this stage.

Cognitive Abilities

One of the most important cognitive developments of middle and late childhood is the ability to reason logically about ideas and events. Children acquire and understand principles associated with logic and learn how to apply them to specific situations. Increased thinking, knowledge, and ability to communicate clearly are significant developments in middle and late childhood. Children in this stage have thought processes that involve considering evidence, planning, thinking, and formulating guesses.

Socioemotional Characteristics

During this stage, children are interested in learning how things are made and how they work. They often struggle to master cultural values or norms of society; some research, however, suggests that increased access to technology exposes children to societal issues more quickly through more media outlets. During the middle and late childhood stage, children spend increasing amounts of time with their peers, which leads to their perceptions of how competent or smart they are compared to their peers. In this stage, children tend to be more dependent or reliant on each other for companionship and self-validation.

At this stage, personal friendships are more important than being accepted by the entire group. Increases in emotional understanding lead to the ability to control emotional responses so they are more situationally appropriate. Children can now demonstrate empathy; for example, they can have sympathy or feel sorry for a friend who is feeling down. According to research, the following are the six functions of children's friendships at this age:

1. **Companionship.** Friendships provide playmates who will spend time and interact with a child during activities.
2. **Stimulation.** Friendships provide interesting information, excitement, and amusement.
3. **Physical support.** Friends offer time, resources, and assistance.
4. **Ego support.** Friends provide encouragement and feedback, which helps the child develop and assess self-efficacy.
5. **Social comparison.** Friendships provide information about where the child stands in relation to others and whether the child is OK.

6. **Intimacy and affection.** Friendships offer warm, close relationships based on trust.

These functions are important because it has been suggested that peers play a more central role in a child's life at this stage than parents do, primarily because of the consequences of peer isolation. Children at this age are highly susceptible to bullying. Being the target of a bully can have long-term effects such as social withdrawal, depression, and anxiety. Recognizing the critical value of social interaction and friendships at this age is vital in the designing and implementing of recreation and leisure programs.

Considerations for Program Design

Children at this age usually participate in organized after-school activities. Unfortunately, many children do not participate in after-school programs that involve physical activity; instead, children engage in more sedentary activities such as watching television, playing video games, and playing cell phone games. Children should still be heavily involved in various active programs and activities, which provide physical and behavioral benefits. Recreation programmers should recognize the importance of designing and providing fun and active programs for children of this age.

Recreation and Leisure Program Example

Programs that accommodate this age group's desire to be with friends are good ways to get them involved. Recreation programs should allow for multiple social and physical opportunities. The following program is an example of one that allows for socializing, being active, and staying entertained.

Don't Get Caught with the Cookie. This recreation activity is done in a gymnasium or large outdoor space. Two children are designated as taggers, and the other participants are divided into two groups. Each student in one group receives a ball (cookie); the other group does not receive any balls. The taggers are only allowed to tag people who are holding balls. To avoid being tagged, a

Programming that emphasizes fun and physical activity is important for children at the middle childhood stage.

child with a ball can throw the ball to someone who does not have a ball, making this child a target for the tagger. If the ball is dropped while being thrown, both the thrower and the receiver must do five jumping jacks. When a child with a ball gets tagged, he or she must also do five jumping jacks. A child cannot throw a ball back to the person who threw it to them. This program is great way to promote the physical needs of children in this age group.

ADOLESCENCE

Adolescence occurs between the ages of 13 and 19. During the early part of this stage, adolescents begin to experience puberty, which has dramatic effects on their physical, cognitive, and socioemotional development. It is during this stage that adolescents begin to become more independent from their parents and form intimate friendships and romantic relationships. These are just a few factors that recreation and leisure professionals need to account for while designing and implementing appropriate programs.

Recreation and Leisure

The term *teenager* did not appear in the American vocabulary until the 1930s. It has been argued that increases in urbanization and technology have produced problems that are either exclusive to this age group or affect teens more intensely than others. Perhaps because of this, the relationships made in adolescence are more compelling than in other periods of life; friends and peer groups become all-important. This has good and bad consequences. If all a teen's friends smoke, for example, it will be difficult for the teenager to avoid smoking. Teenagers experience a great confusion of value. Although there is a strong trend toward social conformity with the peer group, teens also shift between childish and more adult-like behavior. In some ways, teenagers suffer from the same lack of clearly defined roles that the elderly do (this is discussed later in the chapter).

During the late childhood stage, teenagers often appear to withdraw into a separate society and they enjoy hanging out with one another.

Many of these situations bring teenagers closer to each other, sometimes through gangs or social groups that develop recreation and leisure patterns that are not accepted by the rest of society. High crime rates, prevalent alcohol use, and distraction-related activities such as texting while driving reflect this idea. As children enter adolescence, their independence from parents increases, and they are more affected by the influences of others their own age. Some take part-time jobs, their mobility often increases, and they begin to have greater range of recreation and leisure options.

During this period, teenagers also go through small successive shifts in status and roles that often make them uncertain about how they should behave. With increasing age and education, generally, comes increasing freedom and access to resources. Adolescents also appear to have more time for leisure and higher participation rates in leisure activities than their older counterparts. Teenagers are more likely to participate in most forms of outdoor recreation compared to those who are older, unless cars are involved. It is often suggested that at this stage of the life span, a separate "culture of youth" emerges complete with its own values, music, clothing, hairstyles, social concerns, language, attitudes, and sexual preferences. Members of such a culture are typically segregated from the rest of society, particularly in the case of males. Hanging out on street corners or in cars, arcades, social media chat rooms, and coffee shops, these teenagers often appear to withdraw into a separate society, one that typically has neither children nor adults.

Many activities are abandoned during adolescence. In the case of sports, for example, there is an enormous drop-off in participation. The peak of youth participation in sports is age 11, which can be explained through a combination of multiple factors. An overemphasis on winning, a lack of fun, an unwillingness to endure school-like discipline, the perceived lack of ability to be competitive at a high level, the lack of social interaction with a broader range of friends outside of the sport, and growing preferences for other activities are commonly discussed. However, the desire to move on and away from adult direction is part of it as well.

During this period of life, people experiment with how to relate to people of the opposite or same sex. Dating as socialization produces the opportunity for commitment between two individuals. The factors that can produce commitment to a relationship include love for the partner, the status that comes with the relationship, and the feeling of obligation to sustain the relationship. Commitment is reduced by anxiety about the relationship, the attractiveness of alternative relationships, or internal and external pressures (e.g., family or friends) to try other alternatives.

Social Development

As previously discussed, adolescents begin to form many different types of relationships, and many of their relationships will become deeply involved and more emotionally intimate. During adolescence, teens' social networks become larger and include many different types of relationships. Therefore, adolescent social development involves a more dramatic change in social relationships than in other periods of the life span.

Adolescents must learn to balance multiple relationships that compete for their time, energy, and attention. For example, as children in school they commonly had one teacher for all subjects or one coach for most sports, but as adolescents there are typically several teachers and multiple coaches that maintain their own requirements.

New communication technologies enable teens to create and to maintain social bonds in completely different ways (e.g., e-mail, text message, Snapchat, Facebook, Twitter, Skype). These technologies have dramatically expanded the size and complexity of social networks by (1) increasing the amount of time people spend staying connected with others, (2) changing the way adolescents relate to one another, and (3) redefining what it means to be a "friend." In fact, it is not unheard of to have virtual friendships without ever having face-to-face interactions.

Physical Development

Adolescence is often described as the time when teenagers transition into adults. During adolescent growth spurts, the arms and legs lengthen and eventually become proportional to the rest of the body. Teens may suddenly feel awkward and uncoordinated during this time because growth does not always occur at proportional rate, which can frustrate young teenagers.

Adolescents also experience changes in body composition (i.e., the ratio of body fat to lean muscle mass). Teen boys' lean muscle mass greatly increases during adolescence due to the rising levels of male hormones such as testosterone. In general, boys become broader at the shoulders and more tapered at the waist. Their arms and legs become more muscular and bulkier. However, factors such as heredity, nutrition, and muscle-building exercise can influence muscular development. If adolescents play sports, lift weights, or routinely work out in other ways, they are more likely to gain muscle mass. Many teen girls and boys feel self-conscious about their bodies when compared to their friends and classmates, which can lead to body image issues and other negative consequences.

Cognitive Abilities

According to Piaget, the adolescent years are remarkable because youth move beyond the limitations of concrete mental operations and develop the ability to think in a more abstract manner. Piaget used the term *formal operations* to describe this new ability. Formal operations refer to the ability to perform mental operations with abstract, intangible concepts such as justice or poverty and to be able to estimate or describe the effects of these intangible concepts. For example, formal operational stages is the answer to the question "If Christy is taller than Landon and Landon is taller than Carter, who is tallest?" This is an example of inferential reasoning, which is the ability of a child to think about things he or she has not actually experienced but can draw conclusions from.

Socioemotional Characteristics

For many parents, the adolescent period can seem like a whirlwind of rapidly changing emotions. Some earlier theories about adolescent development proposed that a period of "storm and stress" was to be expected and suggested that adolescents charac-

teristically tend to overreact to everyday situations. However, more recent research refutes that outdated notion. Developmental experts have since learned that what may appear as "storm and stress" is the natural outcome of youth learning to cope with a much larger array of new and unfamiliar situations (Larson & Ham, 1993).

In addition to navigating new and uncharted territory, teens today are subjected to increased demands on their physical, mental, and emotional resources. Social relationships outside the family have exponentially increased with the advent of social networking. Academic standards have become more stringent. Sports and other recreational pursuits are more competitive. Therefore, while teens are learning to cope with these challenges, it should be expected that they will have a diverse range of emotions that might fluctuate.

Teens must learn how to respond to new and unfamiliar situations while navigating the increased demands on their physical, mental, and emotional resources (Tapps & McKenzie, 2014). This can increase stress for teens, and the ability to cope with stress is influenced by many factors. Certain genetic factors, such as temperament, make some people more sensitive to stress. Environmental factors such as family and community, however, can help mitigate the effect of stress by enabling youth to become more resilient when faced with stressful situations.

Considerations for Program Design

Program design should follow the identified needs of adolescents. Programmers should consider a developmental approach that encourages teenagers to see themselves as resources rather than problems that need to be fixed. Historically, researchers have used a youth development model for teenagers to encourage growth in competencies. The following are the five basic competencies that should be included in programs developed for adolescents (Baltes, Lindenberger, & Staudinger, 2006):

1. **Health and physical competence.** Youth need to have appropriate knowledge, attitudes, and behaviors to ensure future health.

2. **Personal and social competence.** Youth need to have skills and traits such as self-discipline, ability to work with others, coping skills, and problem-solving.

3. **Creative competence.** Youth need to be able to participate in creative expression and develop language skills.

4. **Vocational competence.** Many degree programs focus on experiential learning and service-based learning; adolescents need to develop skills that will help them prepare for their careers and understand the value of work and leisure.

5. **Citizenship competence.** Teens need to understand community history and values and be encouraged to contribute to their communities.

Recreation and Leisure Program Example

In addition to the previous competencies, recreation and leisure programmers should incorporate the teen's own desires in their leisure choices. The following is a recreation program developed specifically for teenagers.

Swat the Fly. The objective of this recreation activity is for teams to gain the most points possible by swatting correct answers. Participants are divided into teams of about five. Each team is given one fly swatter. A participant from each team comes to the middle of the room, and participants stand back-to-back. The leader of the program asks a question about a topic such as nutrition. When the leader shouts *go*, the participants run as fast as possible to the wall or the projection on the wall to locate the correct answer. The participants must swat the correct answer with the fly swatter. The first person to hit the correct answer gets a point or prize for his or her team. This is a great activity to address competencies such as health and physical competence. The competitive aspect is often attractive to the adolescent population.

ADULTHOOD

Movement from adolescence to adulthood usually aligns with the achievement of emotional independence from the family. Young adults tend to be more accommodating than they were when they were younger, which is often associated with transition into the adult world. In U.S. culture, the assumption of roles of worker, spouse, and parent for those moving into adulthood bring dramatic changes in behavior and experience that are reflected in leisure choices.

Adulthood should be viewed as several periods with different interests and patterns of leisure. While early theories of aging assumed that adulthood was characterized by either stability or decline, more recent theories recognize the potential for age-related gains and losses in adulthood. Although adulthood has often been considered the eventual decline of skills developed in childhood, it is now thought of as a time of further skill development. The term *plasticity* is used to refer to the continuing development of skills for adults. There are many influences on adults such as psychological, biological, community-related, and historical. These influences mix together to form a path for each adult. Although plasticity can occur at any time during the life span, the potential decreases with age.

Recreation and Leisure

The adult life shapes leisure motivations, constraints, and ways of participating. Recreation and leisure also shape adult life. For example, recreation and leisure are contexts within which friendships are developed. Therefore, leisure with friends and family is highly valued throughout adulthood. Through recreation and leisure people also discover self-identity, and those in early, middle, and later adulthood gain a sense of self-determination. Specifically, recreation and leisure can be a context for self-expression, challenge, learning, credibility, recognition, and accomplishment. Recreation and leisure may also provide opportunities to disengage from everyday demands and concerns and reengage in experience that is more personally meaningful. Psychologically, there tends to be a shift from an external to a more internal sense of meaning in middle adulthood that continues into later years. Perhaps this is because of a shifting time perspective and generative concerns of middle adulthood and exclusion of older adult's productive roles. Recreation and leisure provide opportunities to step back and reengage.

The extent to which recreation and leisure experiences hold meaning for each adult vary according to their understandings of leisure and what society allows for them. The life conditions of adults vary widely in recreation and leisure resources and constraints. Some adults place a high value on leisure and construct life patterns that make a major and consistent place for recreation and leisure. Others fit recreation and leisure into their relationships. Throughout adulthood, there seem to be rhythms of leisure that rise and fall as other elements of life become the focus. New relationships, becoming a parent, caregiving, retirement, widowhood, and other conditions have effects on what is possible and what is desired. For example, the athlete might become coach of his child's baseball team and down the road may participate in senior league softball. For most of the life course, recreation and leisure are part of the balance that adults seek in expressional, relational, and productive activities.

Early Adulthood (20s and 30s)

Early adulthood is defined as comprising the years of 20 to 40. During this time, most people begin roles in employment and become intimate partners and parents. Research suggests that young adults typically establish themselves in three distinct areas: work, family, and social identity. Researchers have suggested that as youth move into early adulthood, they begin developing a dream. This dream typically has to do with career-related aspirations. For example, the dream may be to become an executive director or recreation director or to be in an administrative position within the first 10 years with a company. By their mid-30s, however, young adults often report reaching a plateau, and they become more realistic about limited opportunities that affect what it will take to realize their dreams. It is at this point that some decide to return to school to change occupations or obtain certifications or specializations in specific areas of work (Birren & Schaie, 2006).

Young adults also establish themselves in family or intimate relationships. Erikson described *intimacy* as the ability to share oneself, emotionally and sexually, to sustain a committed relationship with another person without fear of losing their own identity. He described *isolation* as the dread of getting emotionally and sexually close to another person. Intimacy is not something young adults are automatically capable of establishing. Rather, the art

Programming in early adulthood reflects the growing need for whole family programming such as concerts in the park, which appeal to both children and adults.

of dating is practice in intimacy, and through these relationships people learn how to share themselves without losing their self-identities.

Individuals in early adulthood are also seeking to establish social identities. Young adults are seeking a sense of competence and recognition for accomplishments. A lot of the expectations for success are placed upon people as social norms or what is considered the right thing to do in society (Edginton, Hudson, Dieser & Edginton, 2004). For example, one societal norm is that after college people are to get married and then buy a home. It is not a necessary event sequence, but it is common and is therefore a societal norm. Being competent as a worker, a lover or friend, and as a community member are all ways that people develop social identities in early adulthood. Competence is highly related to establishing focus on productivity in family, work, and community (Tapps, 2012).

Considerations for Program Design

The young adulthood stage often lends itself to commercial and school-based recreation and leisure experiences. As people establish families and settle down, leisure and recreation pursuits tend to become restricted due to time. Therefore, people select fewer, more specific activities that are more about the comfort of performing the leisure activity and less about the experience itself. Public recreation agencies can become important as families begin sharing leisure experiences. Therefore, programmers should focus on encouraging interaction and development of families.

Recreation and Leisure Program Example

Oftentimes, programming for parks and recreation is associated with children. However, it is important build in programs and services that are targeted to adults in the community. However, there is a specific growing need for adult programming or whole family programming due to the changes leisure and recreation desires in our society. The following program is one that young adults and families might enjoy.

Concert in the Park. Family friendly concerts in the park are common events hosted by parks and recreation departments. These evening or night events provide an entertaining social environment for families. Some places have developed theme-based concerts to target specific groups. Another great attraction is inviting local food truck vendors to provide refreshments or dinner for people who are attending the concert.

Middle Adulthood (40s and 50s)

As individuals move into **middle adulthood**, their focus shifts from employment, parenting, and intimate partner relationships to two specific themes. The first involves order, security, and stability. The second involves what Levinson (1978) describes as "making it," which includes striving to reach major goals. Many of those who fail to reach their professional goals will turn to their leisure as way to add meaning to their lives. This helps explain why hobbies might be renewed or developed at this stage.

For this group, exercise is important to maintain good health as individuals become more aware of their mortality. When people reach their 40s, they often realize their bodies will not last forever, and the need to take care of them becomes more important. This stage of adulthood lends itself toward a consumer model of leisure behavior such as buying a boat or camper, traveling on planned vacations, and going out to eat. As a result, leisure and recreation take place within the commercial rather than public sector. In other words, the focus becomes more intrinsically rewarded (Pittman, 1991).

Toward the end of the middle adulthood stage, many people experience a midlife transition. For some people, this becomes a midlife crisis, but for most it is a time when people evaluate life and make minor adjustments for the late adulthood stage. This stage of life can see a number of major life changes, such as children going to college or work, reaching a career peak, and noticing physical changes and slow recovery from physical exertion. However, there are some positive changes related to leisure as well. For example, this stage of life often comes with more free time from work and a greater financial security, which leads to a high self-expression in leisure that was not yet available in previous life stages. To this end, leisure and recreation participation has been known to serve three basic functions. First, it brings acceptance from others, which replaces the focus on achievement from young adulthood. Second, it

iStockphoto/Monika Lewandowska

The middle adulthood stage lends itself toward a consumer model of leisure behavior such as buying a boat or camper, traveling on planned vacations, and going out to eat.

helps people avoid despair or depression, which is often a major concern at this stage of life. Finally, it allows for structured time when people are starting to have more free time.

Considerations for Program Design

Although every adult is different, programs for people in this stage of life should encourage self-directed behavior (Edginton, Kowalski & Rannall, 2005). Adults in this stage are generally more self-directed than at any other times of their lives. Their leisure and recreation behaviors are more likely to be self-motivated, experientially based, related to life tasks, focused on the present, and internally motivated.

Recreation and Leisure Program Example

Programming for those in middle adulthood should focus on activities that allow people to express themselves. Programming for this age group should

address a work–life balance. During the later stages of middle adulthood, there is an increase in free time. Thus, middle adulthood is an opportunity for people to focus their interests on leisure activities for themselves as opposed to focusing on their families' needs. The following is an example of a program for people in middle adulthood.

Painting and Wine Class. These classes are designed specifically for adults who want to learn or express artistic skills. It combines an art lesson in painting with the light consumption of wine. This is a fun, social, and group setting in which an artist guides participants in replicating the night's featured painting. Typically, it is an adults-only event, and it is perfect for adults who are looking to express themselves.

Late Adulthood (60s and older)

Those in **late adulthood** are the fastest growing segment of the U.S. population. People in this stage of life are typically identified as 60 years old or older (Administration on Aging, 2014). They are also referred to as the *boomers* because most of them were born in the baby boomer generation from 1946 to 1964.

The three most common theories associated with later adulthood are disengagement theory, activity theory, and continuity theory. **Disengagement theory** suggests that people in late adulthood start to withdraw from the world on social, physical, and psychological levels. The **activity theory** suggests that successful aging occurs when people maintain the interests, activities, and social interactions they were involved in during middle adulthood. **Continuity theory** suggests that people need to maintain their desired level of involvement in society to maximize their sense of self-esteem and well-being (Baltes, 2003). Researchers have suggested that leisure is associated with well-being in later life mainly because leisure opportunities provide engagement and are meaningful (Cochran, Rothschadl, & Rudick, 2009).

Active people in later adulthood are a major market for leisure professionals. In a study conducted in 2009, leisure and recreation researchers revealed the top 10 leisure and recreation activities that people over the age of 60 enjoy participating in. Interestingly, they had recreation professionals who work with this group rank their top 10. The results are very interesting (see table 12.1), and they indicate that programmers are not really in tune with the current interests of this group (Cochran, Rothschadl, & Rudick, 2009).

Leisure and recreation programming in later life is a large market that includes senior centers, social clubs, residential communities, outreach programs, adult day-care facilities, nursing homes, and traditional leisure and recreation sites (Leitner & Leitner, 2004).

There have been numerous studies that suggest many benefits that leisure and recreation activities have on people in later adulthood. These include lowered depression (Tapps, Passmore, Lindenmeier, & Bishop, 2013), reduced risk of falls (Nied & Franklin, 2002), increased laughter, lower anxiety, higher functional independence, and higher feelings of achievement and accomplishment (Leitner & Leitner, 2004).

Retirement

Throughout our lives, very few days can cause so much joy or anxiety as the day of retirement. It signifies freedom and an opportunity to pursue lifelong dreams, but it can also represent a feeling of uselessness or cause depressive symptoms. Growing old in a world of youth can be a scary idea, but many people also find retirement to be everything they dreamed about. It is often perceived as time earned through dedicated years of employment to focus on self, family, and happiness.

It is easy to overestimate the impact of retirement on leisure and recreation behavior. Most people continue to pursue their same leisure activities, but they now have more free time to participate in them; as a consequence, some of these pursuits become

Table 12.1 Top 10 Leisure Activities Ranked for People Over 60

People who participate	Recreation professionals
1. Reading	1. Travel
2. Walking	2. Fitness
3. Gardening	3. Walking
4. Travel	4. Golf
5. Hiking	5. Social activities
6. Bicycling	6. Taking university courses/education
7. Social activities	7. Reading
8. Movies	8. Investments and finance
9. Camping	9. Music
10. Sewing/listening to music (tie)	10. Gardening

Reprinted, by permission, from L.J. Cochran, A.M. Rothschadl, and J.L. Rudick, 2009, *Leisure programming for baby boomers* (Champaign, IL: Human Kinetics), 24.

ampyang/fotolia.com

Gardening is a popular leisure pursuit during the late adulthood stage.

serious leisure pursuits (Liu, Caneday, & Tapps, 2013). In addition, older adults are often said to be "aging in place," meaning they do not move from where they resided when they were working. There is a misconception that older adults will retire, pack up, and move to a retirement community. Of those aged 65 years and older, only 1 percent move to a different state in a given year. Suburbs are becoming increasingly inhabited with older adults even though they were designed for families with children. However, older adults are discovering that these suburbs lack housing, transportation, and health care options.

The idea that people retire at age 65 is increasingly less common. In fact, the boomer generation often associates with their jobs so much that they struggle to give up that identity and work until they are in their late 60s or into their 70s (Administration on Aging, 2014). Others work past age 65 because they can't afford to retire or can't afford health care. Often it is those with a broad range of leisure and recreation skills that seem to adjust the

best to retirement; those who have limited leisure interests and skills often struggle to resurrect old leisure interests and learn new leisure skills. In the same context, those whose leisure activities are an extension of their work will have more work to do to reorient themselves to the ideas that these activities are for leisure purposes only and they are no longer associated with work or no longer spillover into work (Godbey, 2008). When work ends for these people, they often discover that many of their leisure activities are not satisfying replacements to their work. Therefore, a successful retiree must have or develop leisure skills just like they developed successful work skills.

Considerations for Program Design

Recreation and leisure service organizations should be concerned about the growth and well-being of individuals in their programs. Therefore, programs should be developed around the premise of the activity theory. Programs for people in later adulthood should include the following five things (Cochran, Rothschadl, & Rudick, 2009):

1. **Choice.** People want to pick their own activities and their own level of participation.

2. **Participant involvement.** Leisure and recreation professionals should provide opportunities for seniors to be involved in the planning process. After all, this is the group that is historically known for their leadership skills.

3. **Integration.** One common mistake is that recreation professionals believe that older adults don't want to interact with others and they want to only be with others their age. However, in today's fast-paced world, generations are starting to work together and be integrated even more. Lack of education and experience working with other groups are prevalent, but leisure can bridge those gaps.

4. **Innovation.** Older adults have spent years in the workforce and did the same job for many years. They have raised children, and many have grandchildren. They do not want the same old programs. Therefore, programmers should not be bound by traditional rules when providing activities for older adults.

Instead, traditional sports or games should be modified to facilitate senior needs.

5. **Sensitivity**. Programmers should be aware of the needs of older adults by providing user-friendly, barrier-free, and accessible facilities.

Recreation and Leisure Program Example

Older adults are a diverse population in terms of interests and abilities. Although recreation programmers might be challenged to meet the needs of such a diverse group, the idea of creating social interaction opportunities can be essential to an age group often associated and prone to disengagement. The increasing dependence of society on technology and the need for social interaction are great examples of programming needs that should be met by programmers for older adults. Facebook and other forms of social media are common and practical applications that are used today, and older adults want to learn how to use this technology. For example, a great way to enhance the ability for older adults to experience increased social interaction is through multiple forms of social media such as Facebook.

Facebook for All Ages. Facebook for all ages is a course that teaches older adults how to use the online social network on a laptop, tablet, or smartphone. The class teaches them how to connect with old classmates and friends and send messages. This technology experience can increase participant confidence. The class requires a room with a computer and overhead projector, but it is ideal if everyone has their own computer. Partnering with a local library or school is a great way to access these resources. The facilitator must know and understand Facebook. Handouts and visual instructions are also beneficial.

GENERATION EFFECT

As shown in this chapter, there is a relationship between leisure behavior and stage of life. It is important to examine the traits of each generation, because each faces different challenges. In addition, specific events from each generation can shape people's behavior. For example, one generation of older adults will behave differently from another because they had different life experiences; 60-year-olds today work more closely with other generations than 60-year-olds did in 1980.

The following are the five identified generations that are currently living together in the United States (Howe & Strauss, 1997):

1. The oldest current generation is called the *greatest generation*. It is broken into the GI generation and the silent generation. The GI generation was born between 1901 and 1924 and is a term used for Americans who fought in World War II. The silent generation was born between 1925 and 1945 and is identified as the generation born between the two world wars who were too young to join the service when World War II began.

2. The second-oldest generation in the United States is the baby boomer generation. This generation includes people born between 1946 and 1964. This period saw a 14-year increase in birthrate worldwide following World War II. Some members of this group were associated with the 1960s counterculture movement, or the hippie subculture, which began in the United States during the 1960s and was considered a worldwide phenomenon. People started their own communities, embraced the sexual revolution, and experimented with drugs that altered states of consciousness. For recreation and leisure programmers who work in assisted living, the effects of the hippie culture still show today in increased drug- and alcohol-related dementia among residents from this generation.

3. The third generation is Generation X. This generation was born between 1965 and 1985. They are commonly broken into two subgroups: baby busters and the boomerang generation. Generation X is known for being connected to pop culture of the 80s and 90s. Most people in this generation are children of the boomer generation. Baby busters are defined as the post-peak boomers due to the long slow decline of the birth rates of the boomer generation. This generation made its mark on society through festivals such as Lol-

OUTSTANDING GRADUATE

Background Information

Name: Laura Covert

Education: MS and BS in therapeutic recreation from Northwest Missouri State University

Credentials: Certified Therapeutic Recreation Specialist (CTRS)

Affiliations: American Therapeutic Recreation Association, Kansas Recreation and Parks, Kansas Recreation and Park Association Young Professionals

Career Information

Position: Assistant Professor

Organization: The health, human performance, and recreation (HHPR) department at Pittsburg State University (PSU) in Pittsburg, Kansas. There are about 7,500 students who attend PSU.

> " *Those who bring sunshine to the lives of others cannot keep it from themselves.* "
> —James Matthew Barrie

Organization mission: The mission of the Pittsburg State University HHPR department is to provide science- and field-based training in physical education, recreation, and exercise science to

- prepare graduate students for careers in K-12 education, athletic coaching, and collegiate athletic coaching; for careers as recreation and leisure professionals; or for future doctoral studies;
- prepare undergraduate physical education majors to be physical educators, athletic coaches, and exercise fitness specialists;
- prepare undergraduate recreation majors in the fields of therapeutic recreation, recreation administration, and community, corporate, and hospital wellness; and

- prepare undergraduate exercise science majors for graduate and professional schools or clinical health and wellness professions.

Job description: I teach general recreation and therapeutic recreation courses, advise recreation students, and am involved with various university committees.

Career path: I first started my therapeutic recreation career working as a personal trainer and group exercise instructor in a wellness center specifically for older adults and special populations. I then became a wellness coordinator within a retirement community. While working, I decided I wanted to become more involved with educating future therapeutic recreation specialists while pursuing my passion of studying aging and the aging population. This job is a long-term goal that I was able to achieve early on in my career.

Likes and dislikes about the job: The number of items I like about my job outweighs the number of things I dislike about the job. Top likes: interaction with students and the daily opportunity to motivate and educate students about the world of recreation and therapeutic recreation. Dislikes: all the grading.

Advice for Undergraduates

There are never-ending opportunities in the field of recreation. Find an area that you are passionate about, and pursue it as a career. Every day presents a new challenge. Have an open mind and be willing to work with others.

---

lapalooza, grunge bands such as Nirvana, and MTV (prior to the reality show movement). The boomerang generation is so named due to how often they chose to live with their parents after having lived alone. Researchers have suggested that this was due to the financial success and security afforded to them throughout their childhoods from their boomer parents (Howe & Strauss, 1997).

4. The fourth generation is Generation Y. This generation was born between 1980 and 1994. This generation is also often referred

to as *millennials*. These are children of the boomer generation and of early Generation Xers. This generation is commonly known for the culture war movement, or what is more commonly described as the publicly displayed increased argument between progressive and conservative perspectives (Howe & Strauss, 2000).

5. The fifth and final generation is Generation Z. These individuals are said to have been born between 1995 and 2001. This generation is much more difficult to identify because

researchers cannot agree on when the earliest members of Generation Z were born. This generation is known for being born into technology and the Internet. Some refer to it as the *Google generation*. Due to the prevalence of technology, research has suggested that this generation is the most obese and least physically active than any other before it. This generation spends less time outdoors, but research suggests that those who spend time outside have higher feelings of happiness and increased self-confidence (Louv, 2005; Howe & Strauss, 1997).

SUMMARY

There are many variables that affect leisure and recreation across the life span. The concept of the life span implies that life is a series of interconnected stages in which each one has an effect on the next but remains distinctive (Kelly & Godbey, 1991). Recreation and leisure service organizations play an important role in offering programs and activities to members of the public, and they must be creative in programming for people across the life span. As people change, so must programs, and recreation and leisure professionals are responsible for meeting the recreational needs of the people they serve. As researchers have pointed out, and as you have probably discovered in this chapter, leisure is not a product but rather a process that is a vital part of the life span development (Edginton, DeGraaf, Dieser, & Edginton, 2006).

PART III

Delivering Recreation and Leisure Services

.shock/fotolia.com

CHAPTER 13

Program Delivery System

Diane C. Blankenship

“ We do not remember days, we remember moments. ”

Cesare Pavese, Italian poet of the 20th century

LEARNING OUTCOMES

After reading this chapter, you should be able to do the following:

> Develop a program delivery system based on leadership
> Design a program delivery system based on program classifications
> Revise a program delivery system based on program format and skill sequencing

Recreational professionals and agencies create moments for people to remember and provide opportunities for people to meet their personal needs through the programs and services provided through the agency. The program delivery system is the comprehensive model used in developing an agency plan to meet the needs of individuals and groups within the community, provide various experiences for people with diverse skill levels and interests, and meet the agency's mission to improve or enhance the quality of life within the community. Developing a program delivery system is an art and a science that requires a creative thought process and an evaluation process. The process of developing a program delivery system requires the recreation professional to use three different yet interrelated processes: (1) leadership considerations, (2) a program classification system, and (3) a program format system. These three tools are used together while considering the mission, goals, and objectives of the organization to improve or enhance the quality of life of the people served within the community or region. This process is used across private, non-profit, commercial, and public recreation agencies to meet diverse needs based on skills, abilities, interests, and desires within the community (Rossman, J.R., & Schlatter, B., 2011).

PROGRAM DELIVERY HISTORY

The modern level of professional program delivery began as something very different and developed along with the progression of society in general from the agricultural era. During the 1800s, Canada and the United States consisted of agricultural communities and a limited number of urban centers. Within rural agricultural communities, recreation was planned and provided by either the family or the church. The isolation of families on their farms demanded that recreation be a family affair conducted at home. The church and local agricultural community planned and coordinated special gatherings around holidays and harvest festivals. These events provided an opportunity for families to socialize with others in the community. In the urban centers, recreation was focused on the family but also occurred within local park systems and involved some limited commercial entertainment. Local parks provided space for people to play on their own with little supervision. As time passed, the necessity for leadership at local playgrounds was realized. Today's process of planning programs and services began on the playgrounds within urban centers during the industrial revolution (Human Kinetics (Ed.), 2006).

The process of formalizing the planning of recreational programs and services continued to develop through the 1930s, when the process of training people for leadership positions began at colleges and universities. The process and art of planning comprehensive recreation delivery systems continued to develop along with the formalizations of community recreation departments, school recreation programs, local parks, and national destinations for vacations. The conclusion of World War II in 1945 was followed by a great expansion of wealth, roadways, and labor-saving devices. Demand grew for trained recreation professionals who could systematically and creatively develop program delivery systems to meet expanding needs, interests, and population segments such as people with disabilities, seniors, and children (Human Kinetics (Ed.), 2006).

This developmental process continued for decades and has culminated in the development of program standards that address program leadership, participant outcomes, variety and diversity of programs and services, and diverse communities and experiences. The developmental process of recreation program delivery demands that professionals look broadly across the community at the

Special events that appeal to a broad-based audience, such as mud runs like the Tough Mudder and Warrior Dash, are the newest trend in the recreation industry for program systems. Runners and walkers are looking for new events to try, and these events combine running or walking with a series of seven or more physical challenges.

needs of community members. Agencies must know how to meet those needs, provide a diverse menu of programs and services, and assess outcomes of those programs. Recreational professionals enjoy and embrace these challenges.

MISSION AND OUTCOMES

When recreation professionals face the task of developing a program delivery system, they may feel overwhelmed. The options and choices for programs and ways to deliver them are endless. The guiding light of every organization's program delivery system is the mission statement of the organization. The mission helps determine what the program delivery system should contain in areas such as fitness, health, and quality of life. The outcomes that the programs should achieve must go hand in hand with the mission. The mission focuses the program areas to address, and a list of outcomes identifies the benefits that the programs should provide to the participants. Finally, the program goals and objectives identify the specific

outcomes for participants in each program. When reviewing the outcomes within programs, you can determine whether the general outcomes for the program delivery system have been achieved and whether the organization is achieving its intended mission. The mission, outcomes, and program goals and objectives are related to one another and assist the professional in developing and evaluating the program delivery system of the organization (Moiseichik, Merry (Ed.), 2010).

Mission Statement

Every organization, whether public, private, nonprofit, or commercial, has a guiding statement such as a mission statement. The **mission statement** is broad and defines the purpose of the organization with regard to the group of people that it serves. It broadly describes why the organization exists, what it is intended to do, and whom it serves. The two mission statements noted in figure 13.1 contain the statement "quality of life" and statements concerning parks or open space. The mission statements provide choices and opportunities for the professional but also express large expectations from the people the agency serves. The reality of the profession is that the agency cannot be all things to all people. With that in mind, the agency determines the scope, boundaries, and areas for the program delivery system. After these boundaries are determined, the agency develops goals and objectives for the agency and for each program. For example, a quality of life area for Toronto and for the Maryland–National Capital Park and Planning Commission is wellness. Both agencies approach this aspect by offering a wide variety of fitness activities and requisite facilities. Both agencies have pools, fitness centers, ice-skating rinks, and a variety of classes for all ages and fitness levels. The boundaries of programs can be naturally determined by the facilities that the agencies manage and operate. An agency does not offer swimming if it does not have a pool or ice-skating if it does not have an ice-skating rink. Each program has goals and objectives that relate back to improving an element of quality of life for participants (Harenburg, V., Moiseichik, M., & van der Smissen, B. (Eds.), 2005).

Program Goals and Objectives

The program goals and objectives assess the outcomes for the participants and serve as a means for the agency to determine whether it has achieved its mission. **Goals** are broad-based intended outcomes related to the mission of the organization. These outcomes are not measurable but instead help guide the types and content of programs and services offered by the agency. **Objectives** are the steps that need to be taken to achieve agency and program goals. Objectives are observable and measureable and serve as the foundation to evaluate goals. In the case of the City of Toronto, the agency examines the collective outcomes of the programs to determine whether it is improving the quality of life for the residents of the city. All elements within the agency are interrelated and dependent on each other; therefore, the recreation professional must consider all the following elements when developing the program delivery system:

- Mission
- Resources

MISSION STATEMENTS

Toronto, Canada Parks and Recreation Mission Statement

The people in the diverse communities of Toronto will have full and equitable access to high-caliber, locally responsive recreational programs, efficiently operated facilities, and safe, clean, and beautiful parks, open space, ravines, and forest.

Services: Parks, Forestry, and Recreation is engaged in an extensive range of frontline services that contribute to the quality of life of all Torontonians and the overall health of the city's diverse communities.

www.toronto.ca/divisions/parksdiv1.htm

Maryland–National Capital Park and Planning Commission Mission Statement

Throughout 80-plus years of service, the Maryland–National Capital Park and Planning Commission has endeavored to improve the quality of life for all of the citizens of the bi-county area it serves and of the communities in which these citizens live, work and raise their families. This mission is embodied in three major program areas. These major program areas respond to the vision of our founders and are incorporated into our charter. The mission of the Maryland–National Capital Park and Planning Commission is to manage physical growth and plan communities, protect and steward natural, cultural and historic resources, and provide leisure and recreational experiences.

www.mncppc.org/About_M-NCPPC/Our_Mission.html

Figure 13.1 A mission statement helps an organization determine what the program delivery system should contain in areas such as fitness or health by keeping the organization focused on why it exists, what it is intended to do, and whom it serves.

- Goals
- Objectives

The program delivery system requires recreation professionals to create opportunities that vary in leadership interaction, program area, and format. The leadership options within the program delivery system are examined next (Harenburg, V., Moiseichik, M., & van der Smissen, B. (Eds)., 2005).

LEADERSHIP WITHIN THE PROGRAM DELIVERY SYSTEM

The leadership used within programs and services is the backbone of all **program delivery systems** within public, private, nonprofit, and commercial agencies. Leadership characteristics vary from program to program and service to service. The leadership used for a class is different from the leadership used at a public park. The leadership used affects the participants' experiences; control over the experience ranges from being highly controlled by the leader to being independent from the leader. Four options are available for leadership of programs and services: (1) general supervision leadership, (2) structured leadership, (3) facilitated leadership, and (4) indirect leadership. You should view the leadership options on a continuum from general leadership to structured leadership as shown in figure 13.2. As you move from left to right on the continuum, the involvement between the leader and participants increases and the leader assumes more control over the participants' experiences.

General Supervision Leadership

General supervision leadership focuses on providing facilities and areas in which people can recreate, play, and socialize independently. General supervision is used in facilities and spaces such as parks, trails, picnic areas, and beachfronts. These facilities and spaces provide opportunities for self-directed leisure experiences. People determine what they will do at these facilities based on their own needs, wants, desires, and personal schedules (Harenburg, V., Moiseichik, M., & van der Smissen, B. (Eds.), 2005). Think back to an experience at a park, gym, or trail and examine why you were there, what you did, and what other people were doing. For example, Brice enjoys going to the local state park and spending time at the lake beachfront enjoying the warm weather and swimming. During one of her trips to the park, she looked around to see what other people were doing. She saw a man scuba diving in the lake, families enjoying the shade trees and cooking out, people on the hiking trail, people riding bikes, people playing soccer, and others simply reading books. She was amazed at the variety of activities occurring in one location. This experience is enjoyed while under general supervision. The lifeguards were on the beach area ensuring the safety of the swimmers, and rangers came through the area regularly to ensure visitors were enjoying themselves. Both the lifeguards and rangers were providing general supervision during Brice's visit to the park (Mulvaney, M., & Hurd, A., 2010).

If you think about the region in which you live, you will likely be able to identify a wealth of facilities or open spaces that are available to the public free of charge or for a small fee. These facilities are generally owned and maintained by local, state, or regional government agencies. Facilities such as playgrounds, athletic fields, trails, and parks provide seasonal or year-round recreation opportunities. Local trails can be used by hikers, dog walkers, and runners during spring, summer, and fall. During winter, trails may be used for snowmobiling, cross-country skiing, and snowshoeing. The general supervision and maintenance of the areas permit people to use the facility or space to create their own experience based on their personal goals and objectives. This leadership

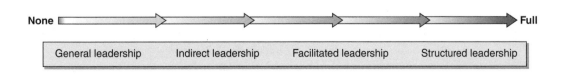

None → Full

| General leadership | Indirect leadership | Facilitated leadership | Structured leadership |

Figure 13.2 The leadership continuum shows four different leadership options available for programs and services.

option is a vital component in the program delivery system that lets people determine and control their own recreational experiences. If you review figure 13.2, you'll see that structured leadership, discussed next, is on the opposite end from general supervision.

Structured Leadership

Structured leadership is used when programs require face-to-face instruction. This approach is used in all types of classes. The participant's experience is controlled, guided, and facilitated

General supervision leadership (*a*) provides spaces for people to recreate; structured leadership (*b*) requires a leader to deliver instruction.

OUTSTANDING GRADUATE

Background Information

Name: Tom Craig

Education: BS in recreation and park management from Frostburg State University (FSU)

Credentials: Certified Wilderness Firefighter Type 2 (Arduous Fitness Level); certified in first aid, CPR, and AED use

Awards: Achieved Eagle Scout, 2007

Affiliations: FSU Recreation Society, Goshen Bears (nonprofit volunteer group), Friends of Jennings Randolph Lake, National Eagle Scout Association, Maryland Recreation and Park Association

Career Information

Position: Park Ranger

Organization: The U.S. Army Corps of Engineers Baltimore District's Jennings Randolph Lake Project (JRL). The JRL project is located on the Potomac River in Mineral County, West Virginia, and Garrett County, Maryland. The total size of the project is approximately 4,000 acres (1,619 ha), with the lake claiming 956 surface acres (387 ha) at summer pool elevation, which is 1,466 feet (447 m) above sea level. JRL receives approximately 160,000 visitors a year.

Job description: As a park ranger for the Army Corps of Engineers, my job is usually different every day. My duties include the management our volunteer program, which consists of more than 75 volunteers who help us host programs and events every weekend. Some of my other duties include trail maintenance, recreation area and lake patrolling, recreational maintenance, promotion of water

safety, and law enforcement. I currently do not have any immediate plans to move on from my position, but I aspire to be selected for the lead ranger position when it becomes available. I have often thought about becoming an operations project manager and leading a project of my own in the future. I enjoy how busy my job is and how every day is different from the next.

Career path: My career path began as a Boy Scout in Troop 457 in Rockville, Maryland, where I learned to appreciate parks and the amenities they have to offer. While I attended Frostburg State University, I worked for the National Forest Service in Montana as part of a trail maintenance crew for one summer, and I also had the opportunity to serve as a wildland firefighter. When I returned from Montana at the end of the summer, I was selected for a student position at Jennings Randolph Lake; I was selected as a full-time ranger after I graduated.

Advice for Undergraduates

My advice to undergraduate students is to utilize the tools that are available to you. For example, websites like USAJobs and other career search engines are great tools to find what positions are actually out there. Set up automatic searches, because sometimes jobs are not posted frequently or for long amounts of time. Keep searching, and don't get discouraged if a path or position doesn't work out; there's usually something bigger or better to come.

---

by the leader. Can you imagine a fitness class with no leader? Who will move the group through the warm-up, the intense exercises, and the cool-down? Programs that are instructional in any way require structured leadership from a qualified leader. For example, swimming lessons or fitness classes require a leader with the proper skills, training, and certification to conduct them. Swimming instructors and fitness instructors go through specific training and obtain necessary certifications to teach in these areas.

Structured leadership is used to assist people in moving through an experience when they lack the

knowledge to do so independently. Participants want to learn to do something, but they need help learning the skills. This type of leadership is used throughout the recreation profession within public, private, nonprofit, and commercial recreation. Each type of agency has skilled leaders and offers a variety of structured leadership programs (Harenburg, V., Moiseichik, M., & van der Smissen, B. (Eds.), 2005). For example, if a woman is looking for a fitness class in her community, she can choose from a variety of agencies such as the local recreation center, a private gym, the YMCA, or Curves. If a community lacks programs with structured leadership, this prevents people from meeting their personal needs and desires.

Facilitated Leadership

Facilitated leadership serves a different need within the community. This leadership option works with groups so they can become independent and provide programs and services for themselves. An example is working with a group so that it can become a club that independently operates out of a recreation facility (Harenburg, V., Moiseichik, M., & van der Smissen, B. (Eds.), 2005). One of the most common group types within communities is youth sport leagues such as soccer, football, hockey, lacrosse, and cheerleading. With facilitated leadership, the recreation professional within the community works with the group to set up a place for activities, a process for the league or club, and procedures for operating the group. The recreation professional and the group leadership work hand in hand to formalize the operation of the group. After the operations are established, the recreation professional is not involved with the group and the group operates independently. For example, due to limited personnel and financial resources, a local recreation department does not have the staff to coordinate and conduct a youth soccer league for the community. To meet this need, parents volunteer and formalize a board of directors that takes on the leadership role for the soccer league. This board works with the local recreation department to schedule field use and field maintenance. Beyond the use of the facilities, the board runs and coordinates the community youth soccer league to meet the need within the community.

The facilitated leadership option is a useful technique for working with groups who have special interests, manpower, and the necessary skills. These groups can conduct programs and events for the community by representing the agency, but they place few demands on the agency. You can see this in local communities particularly with sport leagues, arts councils for performing and visual arts, and recreational interests such as skiing and book clubs.

Indirect Leadership

Indirect leadership is the final leadership option that recreation professionals can use to meet the needs of the people they serve. This form of leadership falls on the continuum between general supervision and facilitated leadership. The indirect leadership option provides the agency with an opportunity to augment programs and services (Harenburg, V., Moiseichik, M., & van der Smissen, B. (Eds.), 2005). Indirect leadership focuses on providing people with equipment or services for a fee, such as equipment rental or picnic shelter rental. The only interaction between the participant and the leader occurs during the rental process. The recreation experience is determined by the participant, not the leader. Many agencies have picnic shelters for rent to accommodate people who need a place for large gatherings such as family reunions, school picnics, birthday parties, and church functions. Other centers rent bikes, canoes, and paddleboats. Indirect leadership provides ways for people to pursue activities or have group gatherings that might not otherwise occur; the recreation agency meets the diverse needs of people within the community and provides the resources for these groups to create their own experiences based on their needs.

The four leadership options within the program delivery system are generally blended together to provide a variety of programs and services to meet the needs of the people served by the agency. This mixture of leadership helps ensure that the agency meets its mission, but leadership is not the only element in the program delivery system that recreation professionals need to consider in meeting this mission. To plan the program delivery system, two other elements must be reviewed: the program classification area and the program format.

PROGRAM CLASSIFICATION

The second area of the program delivery system is the **program classification** area. This review process is both creative and challenging. The creative element involves crafting program options from those listed in table 13.1. The challenge requires looking outside of personal experiences to plan new things. The field of parks and recreation divides all programs and services into 14 classification areas. Each classification area includes hundreds of opportunities for programs and services depending on the resources of the agency. The program classifications shown in table 13.1 can be used with the leadership options to evaluate the current program delivery system and generate additional ideas for programs and services for any organization (DeGraff, D., DeGraff, K., & Jordan, D., 2010).

Let's examine the aquatics area in detail. Within the aquatics area, agencies use all the leadership options to meet a wide spectrum of needs within the community or within the group of people that the agency serves. The type of aquatic program provided helps determine the type of leadership needed for the program. For example, swim teams are common in public, nonprofit, private, and commercial agencies. Because this activity requires face-to-face leadership with swim coaches, the supervision leadership option is used to conduct a swim team program. Many recreation agencies have one or more indoor or outdoor pools of various sizes under their responsibility. These pools provide open swim or free swim times, swim team practices, pool parties, and adults-only events. Table 13.2 has a sample of activities that could be conducted in pools and the leadership options used for these programs. Recreation professionals should ask the following three questions when reviewing a list like this one:

1. Do these programs meet the mission and goals of the agency? Yes. The programs address improving the quality of life or wellness of the community.

2. Do these programs serve the various segments of the community in terms of age, gender, abilities, or ethnicity? Yes. The programs listed in table 13.2 provide opportunities for all ages with the open swim and class options. The lessons, swim team, and parties focus on children, and the master's swim

Table 13.1 Program Classifications

Classification	Description	Examples
Arts	Creative process of making items	Painting, sculpture
Performing arts	Activities or programs that focus on self-expression in music, dance, or drama	Concert in the park, community play
Crafts	Making something of decorative value	Pottery, knitting
New arts	Using technology such as digital cameras or computers	Photography class
Literary activity	Activities involving books, writing, or speeches	Book club
Self-development activity	Activities or programs that promote personal development	Stress management class, retirement seminar
Aquatics	Activities or programs done in the water	Swimming lessons, water aerobics, swim team
Outdoor activity	Activities or programs done in the outdoor environment	Hiking program, kayaking program, camping
Wellness program	Programs that focus on comprehensively improving wellness	Fitness classes, nutritional seminars, stress management seminars
Hobbies	Activities in which people collect something, create something, or educate others	Coin collecting, model railroading, garden clubs
Social recreation	Programs and services that promote social interaction	Dances, festivals, teen clubs
Volunteer services	Programs in which people provide services to others	Working the front desk, greeting customers, taking care of roadways and parks
Travel and tourism	Trips that take people to attractions	Ghost tours, biking tours, visiting casinos or national parks
Sports, games, and athletics	Activities with some rules that involve competition	Card games, soccer leagues, swim teams

Table 13.2 Aquatic Programs and Leadership Options

Leadership option	Aquatic programs
General leadership	Open swim Lap swimming Dive-in movie
Structured leadership	Swim lessons Water fitness Arthritis water fitness Swim team
Facilitated leadership	Triathlon workout club Master's swim club Water walking club
Indirect leadership	Swimming birthday parties Fins and flotation devices

program and water fitness focus on seniors, boomers, athletes, and others. The open swim can meet the needs of people of any age, group, ability, gender, or ethnic origin.

3. Do these programs serve a continuum of skill levels from introductory to advanced levels? Yes. The programs, classes, and services provide opportunities for people from the beginner level to the advanced level. Swimming lessons are the first step in learning skills. From this experience, the staff can recruit children into the swim team and introduce them to a lifetime sport that they can continue as an adult through the master's program. The current aquatic programs provide opportunities for a variety of skill levels.

As you review this list, you should recognize that a pool provides great opportunities for programs and services that use each of the leadership options to meet the agency's mission, serve a broad base of consumers, and provide activities for people of various skill levels. The process of developing a program delivery system depends on this creative planning process to generate and evaluate the programs and series within the program delivery system. One more trick of the trade can help professionals stay out of the box as they develop program delivery systems. This technique takes the planning effort from the leadership options and classification options one step further to generate different program formats within the classification areas.

PROGRAM FORMATS

Program formats, the methods through which the program is structured for participants, help the recreation professional further develop the program delivery system into a comprehensive plan. Eight program formats (listed in table 13.3) can be used within any of the classification areas and can be analyzed based on the leadership option needed for the program. This next step in developing the program delivery system helps determine the scope and variety of programs and services. This step helps the recreation professional determine whether a program should be offered only once or on a continual basis, whether the program should be leader directed or self-determined, and whether the program should have an element of competition (DeGraff, D., DeGraff, K., & Jordan, D., 2010).

Let's take a closer look at how the program format, leadership, and classification areas can be used to develop programs and program delivery systems for aquatics and soccer. What programs could be offered in aquatics and soccer using the eight formats? For many of the formats, listing a program is easy, whereas for others it is more challenging. For example, what programs could be developed for interest groups and outreach in aquatics and soccer? This task is the challenging and creative part of developing a program delivery system. Table 13.4 lists examples of various programs and services that could be offered by recreation agencies for aquatics and soccer.

Table 13.3 Program Formats

Format	Explanation	Program examples
Competition	Program that involves a competition or a contest	Indoor soccer league
Class	Instructional sessions over a series of weeks	Aerobics class
Club	Group that is self-conducted with regular meetings	Running club
Drop-in or open area	Area in the facility left for people to use freely	Open gym time
Interest group	Similar to a club but organized around an issue or program	Arts council
Outreach	Taking programs to people or reaching people not normally served by the agency	Playground day camp program, mobile arts bus
Special event	One-time large program	Arts and crafts festival
Workshop or conference	Programs that focus on learning a skill	Digital photography editing workshop

Table 13.4 Program Formats for Aquatics and Soccer

Format	Aquatics	Soccer (or other sport)
Competition	Dual swim meets	Indoor youth soccer league
Classes	Lifeguard classes	Soccer skills class
Clubs	Master's swim club	Travel team
Drop-in or open area	Open swim	Area open for practice
Interest group	Swim team advisory group	Soccer league advisory group
Outreach	Special Olympics training program	Wheelchair soccer
Special event	Pool water carnival	Soccer tournament
Workshop or conference	Stroke-and-turn judge clinic	Coaching clinic

Table 13.5 Program Formats and Leadership

Leadership type	Format	Aquatics	Soccer (or other sport)
Structured	Competition	Dual swim meets	Indoor youth soccer league
Facilitated	Class	Lifeguard classes	Soccer skills class
General	Club	Master's swim club	Travel team
Indirect	Drop-in or open area	Open swim	Area open to practice
General or structured	Interest group	Swim team advisory group	Soccer league advisory group
Indirect or general	Outreach	Special Olympics training program	Wheelchair soccer
Structured	Special event	Pool water carnival	Soccer tournament
Structured	Workshop or conference	Stroke-and-turn judge clinic	Coaching clinic

Table 13.5 pulls together the three major areas of a program delivery system: leadership, classification, and format. This table can be used to generate additional program or service options or evaluate existing programs or services. The items listed in this table comprehensively represent different leadership options for programs to provide choices for participation in leader-directed programs or self-directed activities. The activities go far beyond providing competitive formats, which are not always appealing to beginners. Finally, a review of the activities in this table shows that a logical progression of programs is available to attract new participants and keep them coming back for more programs or services at the agency. This progression provides participants with opportunities to develop their skills and use new skills in new programs. The essence of every program delivery system is

to offer diversity in programs, services, leadership, and formats to meet the varied needs and abilities of the people who are served by the organization (Rossman, J.R., & Schlatter, B., 2011).

SUMMARY

This chapter explores the program delivery system in several ways. The backbone of the program delivery system is the mission of the organization, which guides all its planning efforts. The leadership options provide a variety of participant experiences, from instructional classes to open use of facilities, for people to do what they want to do when they want to do it. The next area of consideration in developing a program delivery system is the classification of the programs and services. This step ensures that a well-balanced array of programs and services exists for the participants. The final step in developing a program delivery system involves using program format options to develop programs and services for participants. This step also ensures that one format is not overrepresented in the delivery system while others are neglected. All these considerations lead to providing a balanced menu of programs and services to participants. After the program delivery system is developed, planned, and conducted, the professional can examine the outcomes for the participants, determine whether the system is meeting the mission of the organization, and then make the necessary changes to provide quality programs and services to the community or customers.

CHAPTER 14

Recreational Sport Management

H. Joey Gray and Robert J. Barcelona

Michael Pettigrew/fotolia.com

" Sports for all means sports for all ages, all racial and ethnic groups, all ability levels, all genders, and all social strata. "

Andre Carvalho, former program manager at United Nations Development Programme

LEARNING OUTCOMES

After reading this chapter, you should be able to do the following:

> Describe the components of the foundation of recreational sport management
> List the broad scope of recreational sport activities and events
> Describe the trends affecting recreational sport management
> Analyze and evaluate the scope of participation in recreational sport
> List career opportunities in recreational sport management

Recreational sport, or sport for the masses, is a popular and appealing form of leisure and recreation to many American adults. In 2016, approximately 67 percent of Americans (213 million people) who were 6 years old or older participated in some type of sport, fitness, or outdoor activity (Physical Activity Council, 2017). More than half of 6- to 12-year-olds (56.6 percent) actively participate in team sports (The Aspen Institute, 2016). Often seen as a subset of both the sport management and recreation and leisure industries, recreational sport professionals provide sport opportunities for the masses, and their job functions and the recreational sport settings in which they work are incredibly diverse (Barcelona, Wells, & Arthur-Banning, 2016).

Sport in American society has experienced tremendous change and increased popularity over the past several decades. Today, sport and physical activity are as much a part of American culture as other institutions such as work, marriage, and the family. Sport interest and participation from all sectors of society are reaching unprecedented levels. Once considered simply a diversion from work and a tool for recreation, sport has grown to be a multibillion-dollar industry. For some people, sports such as baseball, football, and basketball are like a civil religion—what Forney (2010) calls the "holy trinity." Avid fans spend thousands of dollars on tickets, paraphernalia, fantasy camps, and the like. In 2016, the average ticket price for the Super Bowl was at an all-time high of $4,841, according to an article published in CNN Money (2016). Today, sports fans and participants alike possess unfailing devotion to sport with both their discretionary time and their money. Price (2005) further suggests that the best way to understand American sport is to take it as a "contemporary folk religion" (p. 142).

Sport has had a noteworthy influence not only in the United States but also around the globe (Kidd, 2008). Sport and physical activity have become universal phenomena (Ghafouri, Mirzaei, Hums, & Honarvar, 2009). This increased popularity and devotion to sport globally have had a significant impact on the way sport and leisure services have been delivered in the past and will continue to be delivered in the future.

On the one hand, sport has become very entertainment and spectator oriented, and record numbers of people are watching or attending professional sporting events. The explosion of social media provides sport entertainment at the fingertips of fans. Sport fans can now check scores, stats, or stream the game at any time from their phones, iPads, computers, or other electronic devices. According to Nielsen.com, in 2015 sport viewership was up 160 percent from 2005 with fans spending more than 31 billion hours watching sports on broadcast and cable TV. Professional athletes are considered folk heroes and are paid astronomical salaries. In addition, people participate in recreational sport activities by engaging in individual and team sports and fitness activities. In this regard, sport has become participant oriented, involving diverse populations in a variety of programs and activities. The growth of sport in some form in modern society cannot be questioned. Sport touches almost every facet of society, from the economy to youth development and leisure pursuits. It "is inter-connected with every major social institution in society" (Delaney & Madigan, 2015, p. 393).

EXAMINING SPORT MANAGEMENT FROM A RECREATIONAL PERSPECTIVE

The discipline that manages sports programs has been referred to by a variety of different terms and titles over the years. Although there is no consensus on the name of the field, the term *sport management* is generally the umbrella term used to identify professional careers in planning, organizing, leading, and controlling sport events, programs, personnel, and facilities (Barcelona et al., 2016). Henderson (2009) suggests that sport management covers a field of study that mainly focuses on the business side of sport. Supporting Henderson, according to the North American Society of Sport Management (n.d.), sport management addresses the application of business to the professional side of sport, which includes topics such as sport marketing, employment competencies, management competencies, event management, sport and the law, personnel management, facility management, organizational structures, and fundraising.

Professional sport management focuses on **sport performance,** and professionals often work with elite athletes (e.g., sport agents) or in the planning, promoting, or managing of professional sporting events (e.g., sport promotion, sport communication, sport equipment sales, ticketing agents). Settings include professional sport, intercollegiate athletics, sport marketing firms, and national sport governing bodies. The primary emphasis or goal in this area is to win championships with elite athletes by increasing revenue and profits for team franchise owners or stakeholders through ticket or sports equipment sales and promotion, stadium and arena facility management, and entertaining spectators.

The major defining characteristic of recreational sport management that separates it from professional sport management is its focus on **sport participation** for the masses. Recreational sport provides diverse sports programs, facilities, equipment, and services that promote and enhance greater appreciation for lifelong involvement in sport and fitness. Over the years, there has been a significant increase in the demand for broad-based recreational sports programming that meets the needs and interests of all participants regardless of age, race, gender, religion, or athletic ability. It is important to identify and understand the components of recreational sport and the role they play in the realm of sport management.

Recently, recreational sport management has begun to emphasize the leadership and management of people and resources in a variety of participatory or recreational settings. In this delivery, the key principle of active sport participation is represented by various degrees of competitive activity within many sectors. These sectors include, but are not limited to, collegiate, municipal parks and recreation, commercial, corporate, correctional, and military recreation.

From this perspective, recreational sport is a major component of people's lifestyles, either as participants in or spectators of sports during leisure (Mull, Bayless, & Jamieson, 2005). Figure 14.1 provides a leisure sport management model that illustrates the concepts of participation and spectatorship in sport programming ranging from **educational sports** at the lowest level to **professional sports** at the highest.

Many people ranging from youth to seniors actively participate in sport at the educational or instructional and recreational levels. Then, as participants progress upward in the model toward the apex, participation in the leisure experience shifts

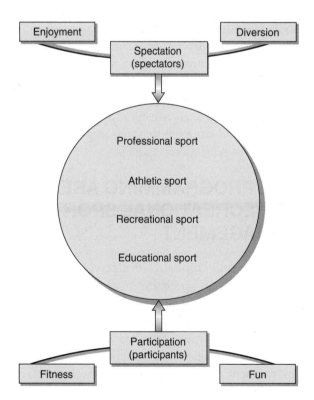

Figure 14.1 A leisure sport management model that illustrates the concepts of participation and spectatorship.

Reprinted, by permission, from R.F. Mull, K.G. Bayless, and L.M. Jamieson, 2005, *Recreational sport management*, 4th ed. (Champaign, IL: Human Kinetics), 9

from being actively involved to being a spectator. For example, at the professional level of sport, the leisure experience of most people consists of watching professional athletes perform and compete rather than being actively involved in the sport.

DEFINING RECREATIONAL SPORT

Traditionally, recreational sport has been described as intramural sport, physical recreation, physical activity, nonvarsity athletics, open recreation, intramural athletics, and so on. However, none of these accurately reflects what recreational sport is. The basis of recreational sport is the involvement during leisure time either as an active participant or as a spectator at one of the levels of the leisure sport hierarchy. The major characteristic of recreational sport management that separates it from other sport disciplines is its focus on sport participation for the masses. **Recreational sports** programs are designed to give *everyone* an active role regardless of sport interest, age, race, gender, or athletic ability. It truly is sport for all. Because recreational sports programs are participant driven, sport programmers and managers put significant effort into defining and meeting participants' wants and needs. The increasing complexity and magnitude of recreational sport management are likely a result of societal demands for more and better services that target mass participation in recreational sport.

FIVE PROGRAMMING AREAS OF RECREATIONAL SPORT MANAGEMENT

Five basic program delivery areas comprise the recreational sport spectrum: instructional sports, informal sports, intramural sports, extramural sports, and club sports. **Instructional sports** are the recreational sport activities that teach skills, rules, and strategies in a noncredit or academic environment; **informal sports** involve self-directed participation with an individualized approach focused on fun and fitness; **intramural sports** involve structured sports in the form of leagues, tournaments, and contests conducted within a particular setting; **extramural sports** consist of structured sport activities between winners of various intramural sport programs; and **club sports** are undertaken by groups of participants that organize because of a common interest in a sport.

Instructional Sport

Most traditional recreational sports programs are based on sport competition, and they appeal primarily to people who are already familiar with a sport or have some degree of skill and involvement with sport. The instructional sport program area focuses on an even larger segment of the population that needs to learn basic sport skills and how to incorporate the physical activity and fitness components of sport into daily life. This program area was developed to encourage participants to gain the core skills in various levels of sport activities and to provide a way for people to have fun and enjoy the many benefits of participating in the sport activity. The primary emphasis, then, is on participant skill development, enjoyment, and learning how to play the game.

Years ago, instructional sport was offered only through educational settings such as physical education classes and varsity athletics. But with the increased interest in and popularity of recreational sport participation, instructional sport has expanded into nonacademic settings such as YMCAs, YWCAs, Boys and Girls Clubs, municipal parks and recreation, commercial recreational sports, and the armed forces recreation sector. Practically every setting (campus, military, municipal, youth, and so on) now offers instructional sports that teach individuals or groups through classes, lessons, clinics, and workshops and usually at three instructional levels: beginning, intermediate, and advanced. Examples of instructional sports include exercise and conditioning, gymnastics, martial arts, swimming, golf, bowling, tennis, racquetball, and squash.

Informal or Self-Directed Sport

Informal sport, which is probably one of the most misunderstood and misrepresented program delivery areas in recreational sport management, is self-directed sport participation for fun and fitness. This program area is at the other end of the spectrum from structured intramural sports and possesses the least structure. Informal sport activities include backyard volleyball or softball at the family picnic, pickup basketball games at the local park, an early-morning swim or lunchtime run, or lifting weights at a fitness facility. This program area emphasizes self-directed participation. The participant designs and develops the specific personal program and goals, and the recreational sport staff facilitates the involvement or experience through appropriate and available facilities and equipment. In most sectors (municipal parks and recreation, armed forces recreation, educational recreation), informal sports involve the largest number of participants. Because informal sports are the least structured, sport takes place whenever there is an available facility or interest in the activity. For recreational sports programmers, many elements go into informal sport programming and management. Because the primary goal is to facilitate sport participation, perhaps the biggest concerns for informal sports programmers are facilities and equipment management and scheduling. Having available and accessible facilities and equipment is essential to creating a satisfying and positive experience for all participants.

Although the benefits of fitness and wellness are part of all the program delivery components, managing specific fitness and wellness programs has become a special programming area in informal sports over the past decade. Group exercise programs, such as step aerobics, trekking, indoor cycling, and mind and body activities, such as Pilates, yoga, and tai chi, are especially popular with women. These programs help participants enhance or achieve overall well-being through sport and fitness activities and play an integral role in the overall management of recreational sport.

Intramural or Structured Sports

Intramural sports involve structured participation *within* a specific setting such as leagues, tournaments, and matches. The word *intramural* is derived from the Latin words *intra* (within) and *mural* (walls). Intramural sports, then, are structured activities between teams and individuals within an agency's limits or boundaries such as the city, university campus, YMCA branch, and so on.

Intramural sports are generally limited to participation among the participants served by a particular agency and should provide opportunities for men, women, and mixed competition with a variety of rule modifications to meet the needs and interests of the participants in that setting. Intramural sports can include the following:

- **Individual sports.** Events that generally allow people to participate alone (e.g., fishing, golf, swimming, diving, trap and skeet, cycling, hunting, boxing, archery)
- **Dual sports.** Events that require at least one opponent (e.g., badminton, table tennis, tennis, squash, handball, racquetball)
- **Team sports.** Events that require a specific number of players who play as a team of either men, women, or mixed intramural divisions (e.g., baseball, basketball, softball, kickball, lacrosse, field hockey, rowing, soccer, volleyball, wallyball, water polo, flag football)
- **Meet sports.** Separate events occurring within a larger event and usually conducted over a period of one or two days (e.g., swimming, gymnastics, diving, wrestling, golf, track and field)
- **Special events.** Nontraditional activities usually not practiced regularly by the participants (e.g., Wacky Olympics, sports all-nighters and festivals, superstar competitions)

Intramural sports are typically the signature programs or mainstays of recreational sport agencies. In many instances, they provide the basic sport opportunities from which agencies build and expand their overall program offerings. This is because of the familiarity and high-profile nature of traditional sports programs, the large participation base, a well-organized and highly structured program delivery, the competitive (but wholesome) atmosphere, and the recognition and awards for participants and teams who excel.

Historically, the term *intramural sports* has been associated with recreational sports programs at colleges and universities. However, municipal and community recreation departments, churches, YMCAs, military bases, elementary and secondary schools, industries, and private clubs now offer a variety of sport events that are very similar to collegiate recreational sport but with participants that are not 18- to 22-year-old college students. These events, although not thought of as intramural sports, in fact meet the definition of sport played "within the walls" of an agency.

Extramural Sports

Extramural sports refers to structured recreational sport participation in which participants compete against those from other agencies or organizations. Competition takes place between winning teams from several programs. Extramural sports include sport programs and activities in which teams from winning programs are invited to represent their home agency and compete for an overall championship. The Little League Baseball World Series is an extramural sport event. Other examples are a navy basketball team representing its base; the Morale, Welfare and Recreation (MWR) department playing in the local municipal parks and recreation tournament; or a collegiate intramural flag football championship team from one university playing against other collegiate champions for national champion recognition. Many times, the extramural sports program fills the gap between varsity athletics and intramural sports and provides additional opportunities for many higher-skilled athletes to compete.

Club Sports

Club sports involve any group that organizes to further its interest or skill level in a specific sport activity. These interests range from very competitive club teams that travel and play in various high-level competitions to the recreational, social, and instructional clubs that conduct activities such as basic-skill instruction and tournaments among themselves.

The history of club sports is long. It is believed that club sports are the forerunners of college athletics, intramural sports, and formal physical education classes. The main purpose of a club sports program is to provide various degrees of interaction and sport participation to its members. In many instances, a club sport is formed for the social aspects that incorporate practices, informal get-togethers, and philanthropic functions. Other clubs offer instruction and skill development for beginning to advanced skill levels, and others organize for the sole purpose of competition and tournaments. Because clubs are not limited to the college setting, they can be found in the public, military, commercial, private, and correctional settings. Club sports programs have become popular because they generally operate with fewer administrative resource needs such as staffing, facilities, referees, and so on than other types of organized recreational sports programming. Many clubs are self-sufficient and generate all needed funding.

The nature of club sports allows members to direct their interests both within and outside the recreational agency. Characteristics that distinguish club sports from intramural sports, informal sports, and extramural sports include the following:

- They are self-administered and regulated to some degree with participant-developed operating policies.

- Members can conduct their club sport without substantial administrative support from the agency.

- Members seek opportunities for regular and ongoing year-round participation.

- Club sports offer a more structured design than informal sports.

- Unlike the staff-structured intramural sports program, club sport members develop, operate, and administer the club.

SCOPE OF PARTICIPATION IN RECREATIONAL SPORT

Participation in recreational sport has grown steadily over the past several decades. Millions of people around the world participate in team, individual, or dual sports in municipal parks and recreation programs, campus recreational sports programs, nonprofit agencies such as the YMCA and Boys and Girls Clubs, employee recreation programs, private clubs, commercial recreational sport facilities and sports programs, and armed forces MWR programs. The following brief descriptions of participation in recreational sports programs and sport facilities provide an overview of the scope of participation that should meet the needs of most people who want to participate in recreational sports.

Active Participation Choices

Active participation, as discussed earlier, is more integral in recreational sport management than it is in varsity **athletic sports** and professional sports. The key principles of active participation are the choice to participate in structured sports (instructional, intramural, extramural, or club) or self-directed sports (informal) and the wide variety of participation opportunities. This wide variety of recreational sport, which should be afforded to *all* people, is the distinguishing feature that differentiates it from athletic and professional sports.

Participants

It is essential for recreational sports programmers to recognize whom they provide services to so they can better meet the needs and interests of the participants. Recreational sport management is intended for the enjoyment of all age groups. These groups include children, youth, adolescents, adults, and senior citizens.

Location

Very simply, participation in recreational sport occurs in both indoor and outdoor sport facilities. Indoor recreational sport facilities include bowling centers; handball, racquetball, and squash courts; gymnasiums for volleyball, basketball, badminton, and floor hockey; billiard rooms; roller- and ice-skating rinks; aquatic centers; strength and conditioning weight rooms; and exercise rooms. Outdoor recreational sport facilities include softball and baseball diamonds; golf courses; trap and skeet ranges; fields for soccer and flag football; tennis courts; and outdoor aquatic centers. Outdoor facilities may also include natural facilities such as white-water rivers and streams, caves, lakes, and mountains.

Sport Settings

Recreational sport management is programmed in a variety of sport settings such as the following:

- Recreation departments on armed forces installations around the world
- Boys and Girls Clubs
- Churches
- City and community parks and recreation departments
- Commercial recreational facilities such as racket clubs, bowling centers, and roller- and ice-skating rinks
- Correctional institutions (city, county, state, and federal)
- Educational institutions (public and private elementary, secondary, and higher education)
- On-site industrial and corporate recreational sport facilities
- Private clubs (country clubs and fitness and health clubs)
- YMCAs and YWCAs
- Vacation resorts (hotels, motels, and cruise ships)

These settings represent thousands of employment positions in recreational sports programming and open the door to numerous job opportunities for those who want a career in this field.

Benefits

Recreational sport participation can provide one of the most important sociocultural learning environments in our society, and it provides a substantial range of benefits for participants and the community, organization, or agency that sponsors it. While active participants gain many health and physical benefits, the community or agency can also benefit from an economical or environmental perspective. By providing sport opportunities and encouraging participation, recreational sports programs can develop participant interests, knowledge, and skills to enable participation in recreational sport and fitness activities that can last a lifetime.

Personal Benefits

People who regularly participate in recreational sport activities can gain improved health, physical fitness, and self-esteem. Although physical benefits are easy to detect, active participation can also provide positive and enjoyable experiences that can decrease stress and psychological tension. Recreational sport activities provide participants the opportunity to burn excess energy and

© Bob Barcelona

Recreational sport can take place in a multitude of facilities and settings.

emotional stress not released in other aspects of their lives. These activities also create a positive social environment where people can relax and enjoy the company of others.

Competition and winning and losing help many people learn to control their emotions and express aggression in a positive way. Cooperation is fostered because people must work together to achieve a goal. By working with others, people gain interpersonal skills, learn to tolerate differences, and learn time management and goal-settings skills. People can develop integrity by establishing their own values and behavior patterns and testing them against the values and behaviors of others.

Participation in recreational sport can benefit the individual as well as the community. Individuals can boost self-esteem and decrease stress, and the community can see economic benefits from a large event as well as increase community cohesion.

Community Benefits

By providing opportunities for social interaction, recreational sports programs can help increase community cohesion and encourage community interaction by engaging different sections of the community in wholesome sporting activities regardless of age, race, ethnicity, or gender. Participation can also help deter antisocial behavior such as vandalism, gang violence, and crime. Communities can benefit economically from well-planned and well-managed sport facilities. These economic benefits include direct and indirect employment in recreational sports programs, income from sales of recreational sporting goods and services, and the revenue generated from holding local, city, state, regional, or even national recreational sports tournaments and sport events. Tourism-related activities, through the promotion of recreational sport opportunities and the quality of sporting facilities, can contribute significantly to the local economy.

Agency, Organization, or Setting Benefits

Participation in recreational sports programs can have a direct effect on the agency, organization, or setting that provides the activities. The following are examples:

- The Employee Morale and Recreation Association (EMRA) suggests that "Sports leagues and special interest clubs allow employees to express themselves as individuals. Through involvement in these activities, employees develop a broader range of skills, learn to be leaders and enjoy coming to work" (2017, para. 4). Recreational sports programs can deliver tangible benefits in terms of workplace safety and improved productivity from happier and healthier employees.

- Studies conducted by the National Intramural-Recreational Sports Association (NIRSA) report that in the collegiate setting, active engagement in recreational sports and fitness programs document the value of recreational sports programs at colleges and universities (Forrester, 2014).

- Navy MWR fleet recreational sports programs and equipment support the quality of life of more than 200,000 men and women on land and at sea on board navy ships. These mission-essential MWR programs consist of voluntary fitness and recreational sport activities conducted to promote morale and physical and mental combat readiness (Navy MWR, n.d.).

- Through the YMCA mission of "putting Christian principles into practice," recreational sport, a mainstay of the YMCA's offerings, emphasizes fun, teamwork, and friendly competition in a supportive community for all ages and skill levels (YMCA, 2017).

TRENDS IN RECREATIONAL SPORT MANAGEMENT

To be able to fully plan and make projections properly, it is essential to examine current issues and concerns. Examining current challenges and problems and forecasting their impact on the future are of great value to any profession, and recreational sport management is no exception. By identifying and studying future trends, professionals and practitioners in the field can prepare and explore many aspects of their current programs and activities. Although it is not possible to predict exactly what will occur, observing and identifying future trends might allow us to redefine the nature of what we do and how we do it.

It is also important for recreational sport managers to understand that the programs they operate and the organizations they manage operate within larger social, economic, health, educational, and political systems. Even though recreational sport participation represents a leisure activity for many people, sport is impacted and affected by larger issues and trends in society. Understanding how sport interacts with these larger socioeconomic and political trends is a key competency for recreational sport managers.

Funding

One of the top trends in administering recreational sports programs is income generation for programs and facilities. Most recreational sport administrators are not surprised by this trend because many programs have been forced to reduce budgets during the past few years because of the sluggish economy. The severe economic recession from 2007 to 2009 had a major effect on many sports programs. Because of the slower-than-normal economic recovery, there was a significant decline in recreational sport participation and sport spending. Spending on a range of sport-related purchases has been on a downward trend since 2013 (Physical Activity Council, 2017). Because of this, additional revenue and sources of income must be generated. The challenge for the recreational sport manager is to find creative ways to overcome these economic constraints.

Legal Aspects

It is imperative for recreational sport administrators to educate not only themselves in various legal aspects but also their staff and participants. Recreational sport administrators must be responsible for developing sound risk management plans and programs that reduce the likelihood of accidents and injuries that might lead to participant lawsuits against the agency. Administrators should become familiar with the laws of their state that apply to recreational sports programs and sport facilities. Effective risk management planning is essential for reducing losses and avoiding lawsuits. Well-prepared risk management plans and thorough reporting, record keeping, facility inspections, training, event supervision, and emergency procedures will help reduce the potential for lawsuits.

Sport Facilities

Facility construction is a growth area in recreational sport management. Over the past few decades, recreational sports programs in a variety of sectors have witnessed tremendous growth in the number of new sport facilities being constructed. Collegiate recreational sport is leading the way in the number of new recreational sport complexes on campuses across the country. Experts believe that participants will continue to demand larger and more specialized recreational sport facilities, which will result in even more new construction well into the 21st century. The sport industry continues to change and expand to meet the demands of current and future participants. Administrators will need to be prepared in many areas related to sport management including securing funding for existing and new sport facilities.

OUTSTANDING GRADUATE

Background Information

Name: Qi Wang

Education: BA from Central South University of Forestry and Technology, College of Tourism

Awards: Third prize in Hunan Tourism Innovation Contest

Career Information

Position: Procurement Manager

Organization: Tuniu is a leading online leisure travel company in China that offers a large selection of packaged tours, including organized and self-guided tours, as well as travel-related services for leisure travelers through its website (www.tuniu.com) and mobile platform. It has over 1,700,000 stock keeping units (SKUs) of packaged tours, covering over 140 countries worldwide and all the popular tourist attractions in China. Tuniu provides one-stop leisure travel solutions and a compelling customer experience through its online platform and offline service network, including a 24/7 call center, 180 regional service centers, and 11 international centers. There are 24 branches in China and 20 all over the world.

Job description: I design and plan outbound packaged tours for the Changsha region and coordinate the operation of different sectors.

Career path: I began as a procurement staff member and then was promoted to procurement manager. I have witnessed the ups and downs of the company and have worked at different sectors.

Likes and dislikes about the job: What I like the most are the strict rules, streamlined guidelines, and equal opportunities to move up the career ladder.

Advice for Undergraduates

Pay attention to the development of Internet technologies and online travel. Keep an eye on the general trends of the tourism industry, and know about our rivals and partners. Go to frontline sales desks to understand the supplies and demands of the market.

Technology

In the past 15 years, computing technology has significantly affected the way sport businesses and agencies deliver sports and tournament programming. Selecting appropriate technology may have the biggest effect on improving the efficiency of a sports program. Although technology is not the panacea for a quality recreational sports program, using technology, including hardware and software components, is clearly an important trend and tool that can improve the quality and speed of daily operations. Software and web-based programs make it easy for sport administrators and sports programming staff to create round-robin and single-elimination schedules for single or multisport leagues, register teams and accept payments online, and manage websites and facilities. For sport facility managers, new computer-aided facility management technologies have been designed to help them do their jobs more effectively and efficiently.

Technologically advanced exercise gadgets and equipment innovations ranging from gaming consoles and 3-D technology to sophisticated, cutting-edge fitness machines are transforming not only how participants exercise but also how they stay motivated to exercise. Once considered an enemy to physical activity among youth, motion game experiences are now engaging youth in physical activity while using technology. To that end, almost 23 percent of youth aged 5 to 16 years report that "playing a computer game is a form of exercise" (The Aspen Institute, 2016). Electronic activity trackers such as Fitbits and Apple watches are also becoming more accessible for children whose parents can afford them, and motion trackers on cell phones can provide feedback on physical activity.

Personnel

Because technology is ever changing and its use is growing, recreational sport managers must hire additional staff to maintain current computer applications to assist with registration, scheduling, facility use, and marketing efforts. The increase in the technological benefits of local area networks (LANs) and servers owned by recreational sport agencies will cause an increase in the number of part-time computer generalists and full-time LAN and network administrators on the traditional recreational sports programming staff. In addition, because of the popularity of the web, individuals who are knowledgeable in web programming will be critical to sports programs. Last, because of the power of social media (e.g., Facebook, LinkedIn, and Twitter) to reach the masses, sport agencies will use these platforms to advertise and monitor programs, and to communicate with their participants (Evans, 2012). Specialists will be needed to create and maintain this presence.

Marketing has become a core activity for recreational sport management due to the diversity and rapid expansion of programs and facilities to meet the growing needs of participants. Recreational sport staffing now includes marketing specialists with the skills, experience, and dedicated time to plan and implement marketing strategies to support the sports programs and services. These staff members have a significant effect on the success of the agency because marketing can have a direct effect on participation, revenue, and program expenditures (Barcelona et al., 2016).

Parental Concerns

The leading cause of injury in adolescents is participation in sport (Emery, Roy, Hagel, Macpherson, & Nettel-Aguirre, 2016). In recent years, an alarming number of head injuries and related concussion issues have occurred primarily in professional football but also in other sports and at the youth and collegiate levels. Parents and sport administrators are concerned. Many parents have chosen not to let their children participate in football, basketball, or other contact sports because of the increased risk of these types of head injuries. Sport administrators from the NFL down to the neighborhood youth sport association are now reviewing and updating sports rules, regulations, and standards for sports equipment, especially helmets used in football. Emery et al. (2016) says "there is an increasing body of rigorous scientific evidence to inform best practice and policy in injury prevention in youth sport" (p. 220). Thus, sport administrators must ensure best practices and policy are established, communicated, and followed.

Paramount to recreational sport is staff education and the use of background checks among youth sports programs. Recreational sport agencies must ensure that all staff and volunteers are properly trained by providing educational sessions such as workshops, certification opportunities, educational materials, and routine supervision. In addition, screening staff and volunteers is no longer an option; yearly criminal **background checks** should be mandatory for all coaches and volunteers for youth sport agencies (Gould, 2016).

Costs for background checks can be a concern for youth sport agencies. Ways to offset these costs are to require the staff member or volunteer to pay for the background check, have the agency pay part of the fee, use free sources (web, local, and state agencies), or seek grants or private funding to assist with costs. Regardless, each youth sport agency must ensure the safety of its participants by requiring background checks.

Programming

Recreational sports and fitness programs are immensely popular and usually attract large numbers of participants. Millions of Americans partake in a variety of recreational sport and outdoor recreation activities throughout the year. *Sports, Fitness and Recreation Participation—Overview Report* (Physical Activity Council, 2017) summarizes data related to physical activity and sport participation and spending in the United States for people ages 6 and older. Among the many facts listed in the report are the following:

- Overall participation in sports, fitness, and related physical activities increased slightly between 2011 and 2016.

- Participation at a healthy level, which is defined as participating in high-calorie-burning activity at least 151 times during the year, has declined by approximately 0.6 percent per year between 2011 and 2016.

- In 2016, approximately 62.7 percent of people over age 6 participated in fitness sports such as aerobics, dance, step, Pilates, and running or jogging, and 48.6 percent participated in outdoor sports such as canoeing, snowboarding, stand-up paddleboarding, kayaking, and bicycling.

- Participation in individual sports such as triathlons, martial arts, bowling, skateboarding, and archery has declined by an average of 1 percent each year since 2011.

serguacom/iStock/Getty Images

Participation in outdoor sports such as stand-up paddleboarding is increasing.

- Millennials (49 percent) and Generation X (48 percent) are the most active generations, and boomers had the highest percentage of inactive people (33.7 percent).

The economy and the economic recession from 2007 to 2009 had a major effect on spending in sport, fitness, and recreation and continued to affect spending in 2015.

School physical education programs continue to be the key pathway to regular participation among youth during their school years as well as when they reach adulthood. Adults who reported having physical education are more likely to be active as adults compared to those who did not have physical education in school (80.3 percent versus 60.9 percent) (Physical Activity Council, 2017).

From a programming perspective, recreational sports programmers must be aware of these trends when planning and developing sport activities for their agencies. Knowing and understanding participant trends can provide a better understanding of participant needs and interests, which can enable

Table 14.1 Participation Rates by Activity Category

Rank	Category	Participant rate
1	Fitness sports	62.7 percent
2	Outdoor sports	48.6 percent
3	Individual sports	34.6 percent
4	Team sports	23.6 percent
5	Water sports	13.8 percent
6	Racquet sports	13.7 percent
7	Winter sports	7.6 percent

Physical Activity Council 2017

agencies to better plan, design, and implement comprehensive recreational sports programs. Table 14.1 provides the estimated number of participants in several recreational sport activities. Fitness sports and outdoor sport activities hold a commanding lead for the top active recreational sport trends in the United States. The Physical Activity Council (2017) reports trends by activity. Notably, spectator sport participation is the top passive recreational sport activity for both men and women (The Physical Activity Council, 2017). Most sources indicate that the most popular spectator sport is professional football followed by professional baseball, college football, and auto racing (Shannon-Missal, 2016).

INTERNATIONAL PARTICIPATION IN RECREATIONAL SPORT

Although participation in recreational sport is immensely popular in the United States, it is just as popular in some other countries. In 2014, approximately 60 percent of Canadian children aged 3 to 17 years participated in organized sports (Solutions Research Group Consultants Inc., 2014). Over 11.1 million Australians aged 15 years and older (60 percent) participated in recreational sports during 2013 and 2014. As was the case in the United States, walking was the most commonly reported activity among Australians (Australian Bureau of Statistics, 2015). In England, almost 16 million people 16 years and older participated in sports at least once per week in 2016, an increase of 1.75 million over the past decade (Sport England, 2016). According to the Global Matrix 2.0 on Physical Activity, of the 38 counties surveyed, Denmark scored the highest on organized sport participation (81 percent or more); this score is notable considering the average score was 40 to 59 percent (Tremblay et al., 2016). Increasing recreational sport participation continues to be a priority for these countries and others. Many have made sport and active recreation a key policy priority in order to improve national concerns such as fitness, health, economic development, community cohesion, and social equity.

CAREER OPPORTUNITIES

Although a general core of sport management competencies is required to work in the sport management profession, the various career settings and venues will dictate specific competency areas (Barcelona & Ross, 2005). Those interested in working in professional sport management will need advanced knowledge of business and marketing principles and techniques, whereas recreational sport professionals will need more knowledge in sports programming, including tournament scheduling, personnel management (e.g., officials, supervisors, lifeguards), training and scheduling, and facility management. Regardless of the career path chosen, the growing popularity of sports programs will create significant demand for competent professionals, both full and part time, who can deliver and oversee sport management programs and services in diverse employment settings. The number of positions and specific job responsibilities will vary depending on the sport setting.

Five Sectors of Recreational Sport Organizations

With the growth and interest in recreational sports programs, there have been increased opportunities for employment ranging from leadership positions working face to face with participants to top administrative positions. The following five general levels of personnel (figure 14.2) are commonly found in settings that provide recreational sport management (Barcelona et al., 2016):

- **Upper-level administration.** The administrative staff personnel are the ultimate authorities and provide the overall direction and leadership for the entire recreational sports program and its resources including staff, budget, facilities, and equipment. Specific duties of the administrator are to determine the nature, scope, and direction of the program; evaluate overall program efficiency in terms of goals and standards; provide guidelines, establish priorities, and determine schedules for the acquisition and construction of recreational sport facilities; and explain policy and major program changes to staff and the public. Typical job titles at this level are administrator, director, or executive director. Because of the wide range of recreational sports programs and the need for experience in decision making, top administrators usually hold a master's degree and have a minimum of 10 years of experience.

- **Middle management.** Middle management are full-time professionals who support upper-level administration. They also help formulate and administer policies, guidelines, and resources while

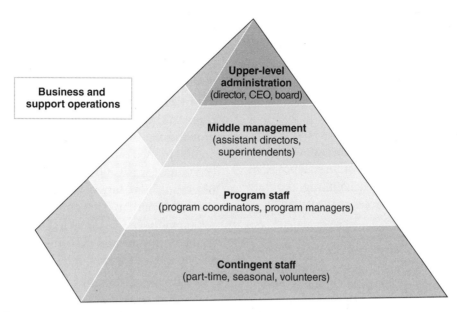

Figure 14.2 Five sectors of recreational sport organizations.

Reprinted, by permission, from R. Barcelona, 2016, *Recreational sport: Program design, delivery, and management* (Champaign, IL: Human Kinetics), 152.

monitoring programs, facilities, and program staff. People in this role serve as liaisons between the top administrator and the program staff in day-to-day decision making. Job titles are often specific to the sport setting, but general titles at this level include associate director, program director, fitness director, public relations director, operations director, facility manager, and sport coordinator or director. People in these positions usually hold bachelor's degrees and many hold master's degrees in recreation, sport management, or a related field and have a minimum of five years of programming-related experience.

• **Program staff.** This refers to many entry-level positions within an organization. Work responsibilities require specialized skills and training in organizing and conducting various sports programs. People in this role may initiate publicity and promotion, purchase and inventory equipment, and implement policies for safety, participant control, and governance. The program staff is also responsible for recruiting, hiring, training, and scheduling support staff, including sport officials, lifeguards, and supervisors. Typical job titles are assistant director, marketing assistant, coordinator, building manager, personal trainer, pool operator, leader, and activity specialist. Many of these positions require

a bachelor's degree, but many employers prefer candidates with master's degrees.

• **Contingent staff.** The contingent staff are part-time, hourly, or volunteer positions that engage in face-to-face contact with the program participants. The contingent staff primarily consists of seasonal or part-time positions such as officials, scorekeepers, supervisors, aerobics and group exercise leaders, equipment room attendants, aquatics instructors, fitness consultants, facility entry attendants, lifeguards, maintenance crews, and youth sport coaches. Although this is the level at which many program staff members gain experience, people seeking employment at this level usually do not have degrees but might have some type of specialized sport credential or certification such as first aid, water safety instructor, CPR, sport official, or youth sport coach.

• **Business and support operations.** Business and support operations provide technical assistance to the other four sectors to help the recreational sport organization achieve its core mission. Support staff provide administrative assistance, perform maintenance duties, coordinate transportation, or handle hospitality and business services such as vending or merchandising. Additional support could also come in the areas of marketing, accounting, purchasing, or human resources management depending on the size and scope of the recreational sport organization. Most recreational sport organizations will use business and support operations staff in some capacity, although the exact positions will differ depending on organization and setting. Some of the job functions of business and support operations may be embedded in other staff positions such as marketing, financial accounting, program evaluation, or human resources management.

Job Outlook

Finding a career in recreational sport management is a promising prospect for those willing to pursue it. There are various levels of recreational sport management positions in thousands of for-profit and nonprofit institutions throughout the United States. These institutions support recreational sports programs that serve millions of people of all ages. In many settings, the demand for qualified recreational sport management specialists far exceeds the supply, which provides great job opportunities for students interested in this field. According to the Bureau of Labor Statistics (2017), employment of recreation workers is projected to grow 10 percent from 2014 to 2024, faster than the average for all occupations. Employment opportunities in recreational sport management include the following:

• The Amateur Athletics Union (AAU), founded in 1888, has a philosophy of "sports for all, forever" that is shared by nearly 700,000 participants and more than 150,000 volunteers in the United States. The AAU is divided into 56 distinct associations that annually sanction more than 34 sports programs, 250 national championships, and over 30,000 age-division events across the country. These activities and events provide employment opportunities involving sport facilities, programming, and operations (Amateur Athletics Union, 2017).

• Armed forces recreation supports a full range of sport and recreation services provided for military service personnel and their families in all branches of the U.S. military. Sport programmers and sport directors run programs and manage facilities on military bases and installations in the United States and throughout the world. The Personnel Support Division of the Canadian Forces Personnel Support Agency is the key provider of recreational services within the Canadian military environment.

• Boys and Girls Clubs of America serves more than 4.2 million youth in more than 4,000 chartered clubs in the United States. It is one of the fastest growing youth services agencies and has nearly 56,000 trained full-time professional staff members (Boys and Girls Clubs of America, 2017). The 102 Boys and Girls Clubs of Canada serve 210,000 children and youth in 650 community-based locations nationwide. The organization has more than 5,100 trained full-time and part-time staff (102 Boys and Girls Clubs of Canada, 2017).

• The Association of Church Sports and Recreation Ministers (CSRM) serves a network of church recreation and sport ministry professionals.

• The Canadian government funds the National Sport Organizations (NSOs), which oversees 58 sports programs in Canada. Alpine skinning alone has over 50,000 volunteers and 200,000 supporting members (Government of Canada, 2017).

• Collegiate and campus settings offer a variety of recreational sport career opportunities across the United States.

• Commercial sports offer thousands of job opportunities in country clubs, bowling centers, theme parks, health and fitness spas, racket clubs, tennis centers, ski resorts, golf courses, aquatic centers, hotels, and natural settings for boating, rafting, and fishing.

• Correctional recreation programs are staffed by practitioners at the federal, state, and local levels who work in juvenile, medical, and community-based facilities. A growing emphasis in this specialty is on promoting inmate health and fitness and providing sport opportunities.

• Employee recreational sports provide career opportunities for sport programmers in business, commercial, and industrial employee recreational sports programs.

• In 2015, there were an estimated 55.3 million people who belonged to 36,180 health clubs in the United States. Fitness is a $25.8 billion industry in the United States alone. The International Health, Racquet and Sportsclub Association is a global trade association that represents more than 10,000 health and fitness facilities in 75 countries (International Health, Racquet & Sportsclub Association, 2017).

• Municipal parks and recreation departments provide recreational sports and physical activity programming for children, youth, adults, and seniors in towns and cities throughout the United States and Canada. It has been estimated that up to 80% of municipal recreation programs are related to sport or physical activity (Barcelona, et al., 2016).

• State games festivals are organized by the State Games of America, a property of the National Congress of State Games (NCSG), which is a membership organization composed of 30 summer state games and 10 winter state games organizations. The NCSG is a community-based member of the U.S. Olympic Committee. Nearly 200,000 athletes of all ages, backgrounds, and skill levels participate nationwide (National Congress of State Games, 2017). Job opportunities are available at the national and state levels for full-time sport directors and event management coordinators as well as thousands of volunteers needed to conduct these large, multisport events across the United States.

• The 2,700 YMCAs and 302 YWCAs in the United States (now known as *the Y*) employ approximately 20,000 full-time professionals. Of these positions, 4,000 are related to recreational sports. The Y serves more than 45 million participants in 119 countries (YMCA, 2017). YMCA Canada is a federation of all 53 YMCAs and YMCA–YWCAs in Canada and serves 2.1 million members and hosts 51,000 staff and volunteers. Each of the 47 clubs is independent, hires its own staff, and recruits its own volunteers (YMCA Canada, 2017).

• In the past 10 years, Big Brothers Big Sisters of America served more than 2 million children ages 6 through 18 with over 300 affiliates around the country providing after-school sports programs and other recreational activities (Big Brothers Big Sisters of America, 2017). Big Brothers Big Sisters of Canada is the leading child- and youth-serving organization in Canada and has more than 117 local agencies in over 1,000 communities and serves more than 42,000 children (Big Brothers Big Sisters of Canada, 2017).

Professional Associations and Organizations

Sport management professionals need to remain current in theoretical and practical concerns in the field. Many sport practitioners hold active memberships in a variety of professional associations and organizations that sponsor a wide range of continuing education courses, institutes, workshops, regional and national conferences, and other in-service training for people working in this field. Professional associations and organizations provide practitioners and students with opportunities for conferences, workshops, seminars, and management schools that help them stay abreast of trends and practices and their implications for program delivery in the rapidly changing sport management field.

SUMMARY

The role of recreational sport as an integral part of human enjoyment and vitality is well established and recognized. Participation in sport for fun and fitness is a very popular leisure-time pursuit among Americans and Canadians. Active participation in recreational sports is an important part of day-to-day existence for many people and involves an individual's choice of participating in structured sports (instructional, intramural, extramural, club) or self-directed sports (informal) in a multitude of sport settings. These settings, which range from municipal parks and recreation, campus recreation, YMCA, and military installations to youth service organizations, offer recreational sports programs and events that provide mental, physical, social, and emotional benefits to all participants.

With the increasing interest in recreational sport participation and fitness activity for all age groups, there is a need for broad-based recreational sports programming that reflects these needs and interests. This will continue to spur the growth of recreational sport management and provide a variety of exciting and fulfilling job opportunities in diverse settings.

CHAPTER 15

Health, Wellness, and Quality of Life

Matthew Symonds, Rhonda Cross Beemer, and Terrance Robertson

pressmaster - Fotolia

“ The first wealth is health. ”

Ralph Waldo Emerson,
American poet, lecturer,
and essayist, 1803-1882

LEARNING OUTCOMES

After reading this chapter, you should be able to do the following:

> Describe at least three current trends in health

> Share the four factors that affect health

> Explain the interconnectedness of the dimensions of wellness

> Discuss at least three roles that parks, recreation, and allied professions play in developing and maintaining healthy lifestyles

As one of three pillars of the National Recreation and Park Association, health and wellness promotion plays a critical part in the daily activities of effective parks and recreation professionals. This role facilitates the development of healthier communities, healthier citizens, and improved quality of life. This chapter provides a broad overview of three areas where parks and recreation professionals have widespread influence: health, wellness, and quality of life. The personal and professional growth opportunities in these areas are limitless for future parks and recreation professionals who are committed, motivated, academically prepared, and appropriately credentialed. Although people generally appreciate the benefits of good health, many take it for granted until it is gone. Health experts have long advocated for the implementation of diverse behaviors to prevent disease and disability, a view that importantly goes beyond clinical treatment of signs and symptoms of illness. As long ago as 1946, the World Health Organization (WHO) adopted the following definition of **health**: a "state of complete physical, mental, and social well-being and not merely the absence of disease and infirmity" (Grad, 2002). While for many populations education has improved, income levels have risen, and life expectancies have increased, societal, technological, and behavioral changes have led to increasing incidence of lifestyle-related diseases such as obesity and diabetes. In North America, a significant portion of the population remains overweight or obese (CDC, n.d.). This singular health concern presents many challenges and opportunities for people entering parks and recreation and related professions. As you learn more about health, wellness, and quality of life in this chapter, think about the important foundational information you can gather and use as a future parks and recreation professional.

PERSONAL HEALTH

Individual or **personal health** is a specialized discipline. Those interested in this area professionally can find careers in the health sciences such as a primary care physician, physical therapist, athletic trainer, health educator, dietitian, and many other career paths. The options are broad and often specialized, which requires professional education preparation.

Personal health and wellness are often assessed using a standard set of indicators and **anthropometric measurements** including blood pressure, body mass index, amount of physical activity, diet, alcohol and tobacco use, and access to health care. Ultimately, a person's health affects both **community health** and **population health**.

Current State of Health in the United States and Canada

People in many locations are living longer than previous generations. According to data from 2013, the U.S. Centers for Disease Control and Prevention (CDC) noted a record life expectancy at birth of nearly 78.8 years in the United States. In addition, age-adjusted death rates for 2013 were at a record low (Xu, Kochanek, Murphy, & Tejada-Vera, 2016). In contrast, the life expectancy in 1940 was 62.9 years, meaning life expectancy has increased nearly 16 years in about seven decades. Similarly, Canada is experiencing changes in its population. In 2015, there were more people in Canada 65 years of age or older (16.1%) than there are under age 15 (16%). Those aged 65 years and older in Canada are expected to increase to 20.1% of the population by the year 2024 (Statistics Canada, 2015).

The health status of the youngest members of society also provides a picture of overall health. U.S. infant mortality rates have shrunk to historic lows of just under six deaths per 1,000 live births (Xu et al., 2016). Infant mortality rates in Canada are also decreasing with trends indicating that the major decrease in infant mortality is occurring after the first month of life (Statistics Canada, 2015). According to the WHO (n.d.-b), global infant mortality rates have declined from 65 deaths per 1,000 live births in 1990 to 31 deaths per 1,000 live births in 2016. Generally, lower infant and child mortality rates equate to healthier communities.

According to the 2013 Youth Risk Behavior Survey, many U.S. high school students engage in behaviors that can lead to compromised health, and some of these behaviors can have health implications that last into adulthood. Such risky behaviors include not wearing a seat belt, texting and driving, riding in a car with a driver who has been drinking, using marijuana and alcohol, having unprotected sexual intercourse, and smoking cigarettes (CDC, 2014). In addition, many violence and safety issues exist for this segment of the population.

High school students' nutrition and physical activity practices continue to be of concern. These poor eating habits and low physical activity levels are associated with obesity, type 2 diabetes, and heart disease, all of which are increasing in children and young adults in the United States. Data indicate that obesity is common and contributes to four of the top 10 leading causes of death (heart disease, cancer, stroke, and diabetes) (CDC, 2016). Childhood obesity concerns are associated with low socioeconomic status and education level, which provides additional insight into health literacy issues for parts of the population.

The potential economic impact of obesity is staggering. In 2008, the annual medical costs related to obesity in the United States were $147 billion (CDC, 2016). In fact, a large portion of the nation's total health care costs is incurred by treating lifestyle-related chronic diseases. Despite the current dialogue and public attention, lifestyle-related health concerns remain a pressing issue. These health-related issues result in many opportunities for parks and recreation professionals.

Poor eating habits and low physical activity levels are associated with obesity, type 2 diabetes, and heart disease.

World Leisure and Health Promotion and Disease Prevention

Issues of health, wellness, and quality of life are of interest to professionals, educators, and people at community, national, and global levels. Health assessment and surveillance have taken place for many years throughout the world. Similarly, parks and recreation professionals around the world are interested in analyzing health status and implementing health promotion and disease prevention strategies. In August 2010, the World Leisure Organization formed a commission on health promotion and disease prevention that developed and adopted a global vision, an approximate timeline for work focused on health promotion and disease prevention, and the following seven essential tenets (World Leisure Organization, 2012):

1. Leisure is an essential element of the human experience.
2. Participation in leisure pursuits contributes to a person's health capacity.
3. Leisure engagement contributes to the health capacity of a community.
4. A lack of access to or participation in health-based leisure adversely affects a person's long-term health capacity.
5. A variety of factors influence the provision of leisure-related resources and opportunities for engagement.
6. The environment and human experiences are inextricably linked and significantly affect leisure experiences.

7. Governments, nongovernmental organizations, and private-sector entities must be engaged in the process of planning for, monitoring, and advancing the roles of leisure, recreation, and play as deterrents to lifestyle-related illnesses and disease.

Using these tenets, the commission's work will continue to focus on the factors that affect health and well-being, including the physical, intellectual, social, emotional, environmental, and spiritual components of wellness.

Factors That Affect Health

The four major categories that affect health are (1) genetic and personal factors, (2) health behaviors, (3) health care factors, and (4) environmental factors. Although it is not an exhaustive list, table 15.1 outlines several important items in each of these categories.

Positive changes in health behaviors are important for developing a healthy population and economy. Research has demonstrated that even moderate changes in health behaviors, such as decreased smoking, increased fruit and vegetable consumption and physical activity, and decreased alcohol consumption, can have significant health benefits that can lead to improved **morbidity**, even if **mortality** is not impacted (Irvin & Kaplan, 2016).

A Global Perspective

Many indicators of health are monitored globally by experts who look for triangulation of causes or indicators. Individual indicators are direct or leading indicators, whereas others are considered

Table 15.1 Selected Factors That Affect Health

Genetic and personal factors	Health behaviors	Health care factors	Environmental factors
Age	Alcohol consumption	Access to health care	Access to fitness facilities
Body mass index	Fruit and vegetable consumption	Regular physical examinations	Access to healthy food sources
Body type	Hours of sleep	Blood pressure	Access to parks and trails
Gender	Physical activity	Blood glucose levels	Access to public transportation
Height	Seatbelt use	Preventative age- and gender-specific screenings	Living environment
Race and ethnicity	Stress management	Total cholesterol (HDL & LDL)	Working environment
Weight	Tobacco use		Air and water quality

secondary or contributing indicators or factors. Examples of leading indicators include low birth weight and genetic risk factors. For example, as seen in figure 15.1, **body mass index (BMI)**, which is a secondary indicator of obesity, is mapped by the WHO (2010) and shared globally. The global obesity rate more than doubled between 1980 and 2014. In 2014, 1.9 billion adults were overweight, and of those, 6 million were obese. In addition, over 42 million children under the age of 5 were overweight or obese in 2013 (WHO, 2016).

Leading causes of death are another common way to monitor health. Leading causes of death often vary by geographic region and income level. However, lifestyle-related disease continues to account for many premature deaths regardless of income level (WHO, n.d.-a). These deaths are independent of genetic predisposition, aging-related causes, and acquired illnesses. A comparison of the leading causes of death between 2000 and 2012 is shown in figure 15.2.

Health can be illustrated from multifaceted perspectives. One example of a multifaceted model includes personal factors, environmental factors, and situational factors; this PES model attempts to address the previously mentioned major factors that affect health: genetic and personal factors, health behaviors, health care factors, and environmental factors (see figure 15.3). There are also communication and health logic models and complex plotting and factoring models to understand factors such as relationships, timelines, causation, and so on. Ideally, model development would allow the prescription of services (assessment, monitoring, treatment, and so on) and implementation of potential interventions to decrease morbidity and mortality. Parks and recreation professionals should approach the

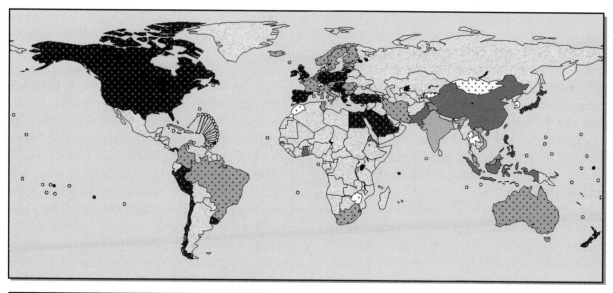

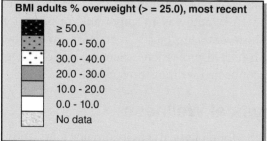

BMI adults % overweight (> = 25.0), most recent

- ≥ 50.0
- 40.0 - 50.0
- 30.0 - 40.0
- 20.0 - 30.0
- 10.0 - 20.0
- 0.0 - 10.0
- No data

Figure 15.1 Global estimates of body mass index (BMI).

Reprinted from *Global database on body mass index*, World Health Organization, copyright 2012. Available: http://apps.who.int/bmi/index.jsp

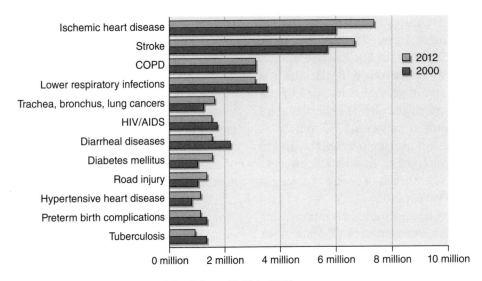

Figure 15.2 Changes in leading causes of death from 2000 to 2012.

Adapted *The top 10 causes of death*. Fact sheet No. 310, World Health Organization. Copyright 2017. Available: http://www.who.int/mediacentre/factsheets/fs310/en/

development of health promotion programs from a multifaceted perspective.

Traditionally, the United States has focused on diagnosis and treatment of disease. Only recently has it moved to adopting a health promotion or prevention perspective that includes a more holistic wellness approach. Other countries (including Canada) adopted the prevention or wellness model long ago. Regardless of the treatment or prevention activity, service providers usually focus their activities on people within prescribed geographic areas, eventually expanding based on patterns of individuals or diseases.

Assessment and monitoring of disease and the use of evidence-based diagnosis and treatment are collaborative global efforts. The WHO is generally considered responsible for collection and dissemination of these data on a global level. In the United States, the CDC is the primary national collection and dissemination agency. Data collected from local public health departments are sent to respective individual state health departments, and from there they are sent to the CDC and then to the WHO.

THE WELLNESS PERSPECTIVE

In thinking about the WHO's early definition of health, the current state of health, and the factors that affect health, we begin to see that achieving optimal health is a multidimensional endeavor. This whole-person approach can be referred to as **wellness**. The wellness perspective includes examining health across several interrelated components or dimensions, including physical, intellectual, emotional, social, environmental, occupational, and spiritual wellness. This holistic approach helps us make a connection between our health, wellness, and quality of life. This holistic approach to health also demonstrates a clear role for parks and recreation professionals in the health promotion process for individuals and communities at large.

Even though a great deal of information is available at our fingertips, not all consumers have the same level of health literacy. **Health literacy** can be defined as the degree to which people have the capacity to obtain, process, and understand basic health information and services needed to make appropriate health decisions. The degree of health literacy affects every dimension of wellness (see figure 15.4), and it is an important consideration for those entering parks, recreation, and other health-related professions. Here we explore these interconnected wellness dimensions.

Physical Wellness

Nutrition and physical activity provide foundations for overall wellness. People control several components of physical wellness such as eating and activity habits. Let's explore some accepted guidelines as

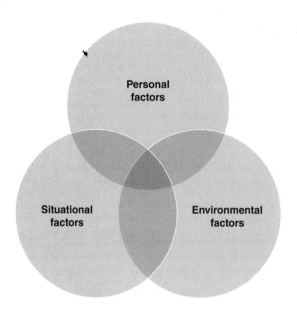

Figure 15.3 In the PES model, health can be viewed as interaction of personal factors, environmental factors, and situational factors.

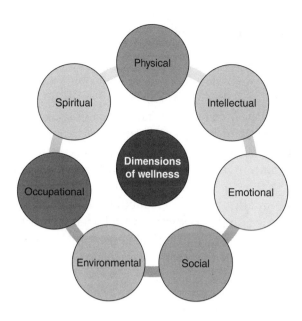

Figure 15.4 The seven dimensions of wellness.

well as the roles that parks and recreation might play in physical wellness.

Proper nutrition has many health benefits, such as decreasing the likelihood that a person will become overweight or obese and decreasing the risks for some chronic diseases such as high blood pressure, type 2 diabetes, and some cancers. The amount and types of food people eat greatly affect health. For example, a child will have different calorie and nutritional needs compared to an adult. If calorie guidelines are met but there is poor nutrition, detrimental health impacts are still likely. In addition, calorie requirements vary based on other factors such as physical activity levels.

Commonly accepted dietary practices recommend a healthy diet that emphasizes fruits, vegetables, whole grains, and low-fat or fat-free dairy; includes lean meats, poultry, fish, beans, eggs, and nuts; and is low in certain fats, cholesterol, sodium, and added sugar. Although people might understand the importance of proper nutrition, many do not meet recommended dietary guidelines. You can learn more about proper nutrition, develop an individual nutrition plan, and track your progress at www.choosemyplate.gov.

Being physically active is not an all-or-nothing proposition. Health benefits can be derived even from low levels of physical activity. According to

the WHO (2016), physical inactivity is among the 10 leading risk factors for death worldwide, and more than 80 percent of the world's adolescent population is insufficiently active. How much physical activity is enough? People aged 5 to 17 years should participate in moderate to vigorous physical activity for 60 minutes per day and should include strength training three times per week. People aged 18 to 64 years should perform moderate physical activity for at least 150 minutes per week (or vigorous activity for at least 75 minutes per week) and should include strength training at least two times per week (WHO, 2016).

People are living longer, which creates the need and opportunity for physical activity programs for adults over age 65. It is recommended that these people also complete 150 minutes of moderate or 75 minutes of vigorous activity throughout the week. Because people aged 65 and older can have mobility problems, the physical activity might need to be more specialized, such as incorporating a fall prevention program (WHO, 2017).

Physical activity requirements present several opportunities for parks and recreation programs. Efforts must be made to create community programs for youth that instill a healthy mind-set for the future. Separate programming for aging populations should also be in included. Combining physical activity and nutritional programs will further enhance people's health.

There are many benefits to leading a physically active lifestyle such as controlling weight; decreasing the risk of cardiovascular disease, type 2 diabetes, metabolic syndrome, and some cancers; strengthening bones and muscles; improving mental health and abilities to complete activities of daily living; and increasing life expectancy (CDC, n.d.). Other benefits include improving the quality of sleep, reducing falls and other injuries, and improving overall quality of life. Improving the physical dimension of wellness can assist in improving many other dimensions as well.

Physical activity and nutrition and weight management programs are commonplace in all sectors of the parks and recreation profession such as worksite wellness programs, health clubs, public parks, hiking and biking trails, and aquatic facilities. Programs and facilities managed by parks and recreation professionals provide outlets for physical activity for individuals, families, and communities. Physical activity and nutrition trends point toward a continued focus on these programs and services for parks and recreation professionals. People will continue to visit spas, national parks, and other destinations to improve personal health.

Intellectual Wellness

One of the many benefits of physical activity is improved cognitive function. Intellectual wellness focuses on learning throughout life. We live in a dynamic, changing, fast-paced world; to adapt, we need to continue to read, think, and reflect throughout our lives. Our minds require frequent stimulation. The adage "use it or lose it" applies to our bodies and our minds.

Although parks and recreation professionals may not consider intellectual development their primary goal, there are many programming and service opportunities for intellectual wellness development. A book club during which people discuss books while walking on a community trail contributes to physical and intellectual wellness. Creating a scavenger hunt in which children learn the various plants and animals that can be seen in a park and then identify them on a map while exploring the

environment is another example that incorporates learning and physical activity.

Using educational manipulatives will also enhance understanding and problem-solving. For example, a recreational professional can compile a list of items that can be seen while hiking on a nature trail. The professional can show learners a maple leaf, and they can touch it and ask questions about, draw it, and identify which tree it belongs to. Once all items are found and discussed, the learners can see how many items they can identify on the next hike.

Adding a reflective portion to any parks and recreation activity will enhance learning. Professionals can embrace facilities as centers for lifelong learning where individuals, families, and communities gather to learn new skills and apply their knowledge and skills in recreation settings. The possibilities are limitless.

Emotional Wellness

Mental health issues and mood disorders are on the rise and can be directly linked to emotional well-being. Nearly one-fourth of Americans have experienced a mental illness during the previous year, and as many as half will develop a mental illness at some point (CDC, 2011). Over the course of a lifetime, a person will encounter many challenges. The National Institute for Health (2015) notes that people who are emotionally well have fewer negative emotions and can bounce back from these challenges. The wellness perspective includes a component that encourages people to develop a skill set that will allow them to effectively handle these emotional encounters. New friendships, relationships, job challenges and opportunities, and the death of friends and family members are examples of events that present emotional challenges. Parks and recreation programs can offer outlets that can foster emotional development with many of these challenges.

Abundant research supports the link between emotional health and overall health. Stress has been linked to the six leading causes of death. Moreover, positive emotional health has been shown to increase longevity and increase productivity at work (American Psychological Association, 2011). Emotional health and the ability to cope with stress

OUTSTANDING GRADUATE

Background Information

Name: Molly Patience

Education: BS in psychology from San Diego State University, MS in recreation administration from California State University at Long Beach

Awards: California Parks and Recreation Society (CPRS) District 10 Hall of Fame

Affiliations: California Parks and Recreation Society (CPRS) Aging Services and Activities Section Board Region 5 Representative

Career Information

Position: Recreation Supervisor

Organization: City of Newport Beach Recreation and Senior Services Department

Organization mission: Our mission is to enhance quality of life by providing diverse opportunities in safe and well-maintained facilities and parks. We pledge to respond to community needs by creating quality educational, recreational, cultural, and social programs for people of all ages. With a combination of over 100 full- and part-time staff members, we serve over 80,000 residents, with an additional 40,000 during peak seasons.

> " *Every mountain top is within reach if you just keep climbing.* "

Job description: I am responsible for youth and adult sports programs. This includes adult sports leagues, sports-related contractors, seasonal youth sports organization field allocations, and park rentals.

Career path: I began as a recreation leader in youth programming at the age of 15, working my way up through five different organizations to become a sports coordinator before securing my current position. In this capacity, I sometimes struggle with having less direct contact with the community, but I thrive on being able to mentor my staff to connect and innovate. An exciting thing about recreation is that there will always be opportunities for both lateral and promotional opportunities that relate to different aspects of the field, meaning there is consistently something new to learn.

Advice for Undergraduates

Don't wait until you graduate to start networking, get involved in CPRS, or begin working in the field. Recreation is a profession that rewards people who are hardworking, compassionate, and not afraid to challenge themselves.

---

are important parts of a healthy life. People can deal with emotional situations in many ways that reinforce the interconnectedness of health and wellness such as learning stress management or meditation techniques, participating in physical activity such as a running program or yoga class, eating a healthy diet, developing a support system of friends and family, or relying on religion or spiritual growth.

Although an improved outlook and attitude may not seem like a primary goal of many parks and recreation programs, because of the interrelated nature of the wellness perspective, emotional benefits are oftentimes a secondary outcome of many programs. Because exercise, diet, relationships, and stress management affect mental and emotional well-being, we can easily see the influences that parks and recreation can have on this important component of wellness.

Social Wellness

Humans are, by nature, social creatures. Social interaction is an important part of leading a well-rounded, healthy lifestyle. Social wellness represents a person's ability to interact and participate effectively in a variety of environments and includes communication skills, meeting new people and building relationships, showing respect for self and others, and developing a supportive network of family and friends. Social wellness is also important in allowing people to participate effectively in the workplace, in communities, and in society.

Often, the concepts of compassion, volunteerism, fairness, inclusivity, and justice are viewed as parts of social wellness; and as part of social wellness, all aforementioned concepts can exist in parks and recreation programs. As leisure professionals, we frequently use volunteers in our programs. In addition, fairness and programming for everyone are fundamental to our efforts. Finally, we provide many opportunities for people to interact with one another while being active in leisure pursuits. Incorporating buddy systems, team challenges, and social ice breakers are just a few examples of these interactive opportunities. Parks and recreation professionals and programs provide social wellness opportunities across the life span.

Environmental Wellness

Environmental wellness has received increased attention over the past several years. As communities focus on green initiatives, the impact that the environment has on health has become more evident. Ranging from access to parks, trails, and community fitness and recreation facilities to the products that we buy and the services that we use, everyone makes measurable contributions to the state of the environment. Conversely, environmental factors have an important effect on the wellness of people, communities, and regions. For example, consider two instances of obesity rates in the United States: The natural environment in a state like Colorado may influence or lead to lower rates of

obesity due to lifestyle activities, nutritional practices, type of career, and even cultural influences when compared to the environmental conditions in a major metropolitan area like New York City. In Colorado, many people are active in the natural environment, whereas in New York City (or other urban areas), individuals may need to attend a fitness center or exercise on sidewalks to be physically active, or travel to other locations to be active in the natural environment. In other words, built and natural environments affect multiple dimensions of wellness.

In many cases, parks and recreation professionals develop activities in natural and manmade environments all the time. Whether a built environment is used for developing parks and trails, campaigning for a bond issue to build new facilities, or renovating existing parks and swimming pools, the built environment is often used to improve access to and use of public areas for physical activities. Clearly, these purposeful contributions are important to developing an environment that can promote wellness. In addition, developing environmentally friendly building and energy practices and providing prosocial opportunities, such as recycling programs or go-paperless programs, within parks and recreation

One aspect of environmental wellness is access to community fitness and recreation facilities.

Tomasz Trojanowski/fotolia.com

sectors can instill a sense of purpose, fulfillment, and accomplishment for participants. This will also affect emotional wellness.

The Robertson and Robertson (R&R) model is helpful in understanding the relationships between a person's (or organization's) behavior, the environment, and the resources available (see figure 15.5). The figure illustrates that a person who has high regard for her or his environment and resources will interact with the environment and thus exhibit healthier behavior. A person who has low regard for her or his environment and resources will be inactive and thus exhibit behaviors that are less healthy. Of course, a person could have high regard for the environment and low regard for available resources and thus be reactive in exhibiting healthy behaviors. Finally, a person could have high regard for her or his resources and low regard for the environment, in which case the person would be proactive in exhib-

iting healthy behaviors. To help someone move from one area to another (e.g., move from being inactive to proactive), a service provider would need to help the person increase her or his regard for resources or help improve or increase available resources. To help someone move from reactive to interactive, a service provider would need to help the person increase or improve available resources (real or perceived).

Occupational Wellness

Occupational wellness is interconnected with many of the other dimensions of wellness. A person's occupation, as well as how that person performs in the occupation, is important and can directly affect physical health and emotional well-being. If a person is unable to balance his or her work activities with leisure time, then workplace stress

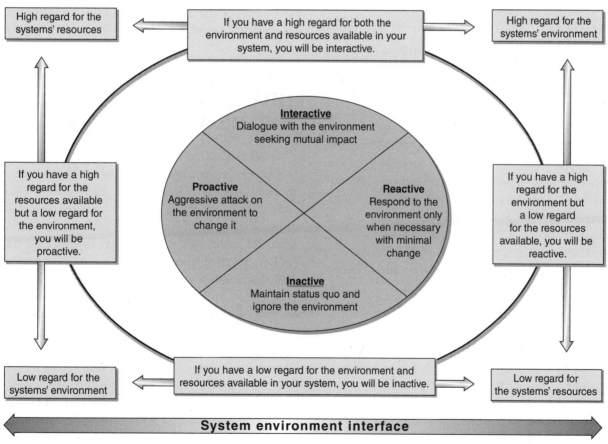

Figure 15.5 The R&R model of interaction between the environment and resources.

© Terry Robertson and Clifford Robertson.

can occur. Work performance can decrease and dissatisfaction in the workplace can increase, and this can also lead to an increase in illness. Health can decline due to poor occupational habits such as improper or risky techniques (causing physical injury), sedentary behavior, and poor dietary decisions during the workday. If a person is completely dissatisfied with the job, then emotional well-being is hindered.

What role can parks and recreation professionals play in improving occupational wellness? Programming can offer an outlet for employees before, during, or after work. Communicating programming efforts and teaming up with constituents in the area will improve the health and well-being of employees and will foster healthy relationships. By incorporating the physical dimension of wellness in the job (such as teaching and encouraging employees to be physically active and eat proper nutritional portions), the occupational well-being of workers and their production may also improve.

Parks and recreation professionals can team up with others in the community to promote healthy activities throughout the workday such as stress management, physical activity, and nutritional programming and education. Not all occupations and personnel will incur the same work-related health problems; therefore, it is important to have many programs available that allow for healthy activities and awareness throughout the workday. The health promotion activities can also directly relate to improvement of **health risk assessments (HRAs)**. Activities implemented by a parks and recreational professional might include exercises that can be done at the office, fitness challenges, or education on the importance of nutrition and hydration with an accompanying water or nutritional challenge. The programming is limitless, but it must address the specific needs of a community.

Spiritual Wellness

The spiritual wellness component is different for everyone because it involves values, ideals, beliefs, and purpose in life. Often, spiritual wellness is viewed as the concept of balance between what we need as individuals and our interactions with the world in which we live. According to the National Wellness Institute (2011), "you'll know you're becoming spiritually well when your actions become more consistent with your beliefs and values, resulting in a 'world view.'" Spiritual wellness follows these tenets:

- It is better to ponder the meaning of life for ourselves and to be tolerant of the beliefs of others than to close our minds and become intolerant.
- It is better to live each day in a way that is consistent with our values and beliefs than to do otherwise and feel untrue to ourselves. (National Wellness Institute, 2011)

Each person can follow a different route to spiritual wellness. It may involve prayer, meditation, or other practices that support the person's progress toward a spiritual place or connection. The roles of parks and recreation professionals in spiritual wellness promotion may be more passive than their roles in other areas. Although they may actively offer yoga or meditation classes, a sanctuary of escape, or travel, their roles in the development of spiritual wellness may be more about providing safe and positive places for people to practice their spirituality at their own pace and in their own way.

QUALITY OF LIFE, HEALTH, AND HEALTHY COMMUNITIES

The term *quality of life* is often used, but it is sometimes overused or abused. Similarly, the term *healthy community* is familiar to many and can also be overused or abused. Combining these two terms when speaking of health (think about the definition of health previously provided) can further confuse issues, purpose, and intent, so each topic is briefly discussed here.

Quality of life (QOL) is often considered the degree of well-being felt by a person or group of people. Unlike a standard of living (SOL) approach that primarily uses socioeconomic measures to determine relative health or **health status**, QOL examines broader conceptual and theoretical constructs to describe it. As such, QOL is not a physically tangible concept, so it cannot be measured directly. Instead of using a single, direct type of measure (say economic status), an examination of QOL uses indicators that represent various aspects

Measuring Health-Related Quality of Life

A growing field of research is concerned with developing, evaluating, and applying quality of life measures within health-related research (e.g., randomized controlled trials) and especially health services research. Many of these investigations focus on the measurement of health-related quality of life (HRQOL) rather than a more global conceptualization of quality of life. They also focus on measuring HRQOL from the perspective of the patient or person and thus take the form of self-completed questionnaires. The International Society for Quality of Life (www.isoqol.org) was founded in response to this research and is a useful source of information on the topic.

Many groups and agencies around the world, including the United Nations and the WHO, have tried to develop ways of assessing quality of life. In addition, many disciplines and individual researchers have studied or are currently studying quality of life, but few are studying this for people who have disabilities. Why do you think this is?

of health and wellness. QOL generally consists of two components: physical and psychological. The physical aspect includes items such as health, diet, physical activity (frequency, intensity, and time), and protection against pain and disease. The psychological aspect includes stress, worry, pleasure, and other positive or negative emotional states. Environmental QOL indicators often include air, water, and soil quality; diet and nutrition; access or lack of access to fresh foods; built or natural environments; and diseases caused by environmental exposure. Holistic wellness, health, and health status are conceptually linked to QOL, and they have similar measures. Although these are all related, they are different in some key ways.

Another method for measuring differences in QOL is to examine differences in the standard of living (SOL) between individuals or groups based primarily on economic indicators. For example, income would be an indicator of health and a predictor of health status; therefore, the more a person earns, the better his or her health and health status should be. Further, according to the technical application of health status, people in rural areas and small towns, who generally have lower income levels, might be reluctant to move to larger urban areas even if doing so would mean a substantial increase in their standard of living (income). Conversely, some people living in urban areas might prefer a higher SOL in exchange for a lower QOL. Thus, the QOL experienced by living in a rural area may or may not be of enough value to offset a lower standard of living. Similarly, people are sometimes paid more to accept jobs that would lower their QOL. Night jobs, jobs that require extensive travel, or jobs that are potentially hazardous might pay more, so the difference in salaries can also be a measure of the value of QOL.

QOL, SOL, and wellness are integrally related. The measures or indicators can be similar or the same. In each of these areas, an ecological or holistic approach is preferred. Professionals and participants (individuals, patients, people with disabilities, seniors, organizations, cities, and so on) are interested in and concerned about affecting at least three things in order to make positive sustained changes or improvements: the person (or organization), the environment, and any leading or causal situations (PES). The R&R model (figure 15.5) is an informal model that a person or organization can use for self-examination in relation to resources, environment, and interactions with each.

Predicting the QOL of a specific person is virtually impossible because the combination of attributes that leads one person to be content is rarely the same for another. But we can presume with some confidence that better-than-average diets, shelter, safety, freedoms, and rights in a general population will result in a better overall QOL. As mentioned before, health literacy is the one of the primary predictors of health status, and both health status and its predictors can be measured directly. Further, those who teach or provide health and recreation or wellness services are not the only ones who are interested in it. For instance, the magazine *International Living,* which focuses on retirees, uses a variety of sources to create its QOL index. According to its website, nine categories are analyzed: cost of living, culture and leisure, economy, environment, freedom, health, infrastructure, safety and risk, and climate (International Living, 2016). Other examples of QOL indexes also exist, applying a variety of methodologies including things like job security, the political environment, individual freedom, education, and the environment to determine an overall index. These indexes illustrate that there may be more to overall quality of life than thought of at first glance.

Economist Robert Putnam's seminal work *Bowling Alone* (2000) looks at the economic and civic effects of changing trends within communities. In the book, Putnam presents evidence from more than 500,000 interviews on how we have become increasingly disconnected from family, friends, neighbors, and our democratic structures. The issue of social capital (who we know) is also a major element of this book. Putnam warns that our stock of social capital has plummeted, impoverishing our lives and communities. As evidence, Putnam says that as a society we sign fewer petitions, belong to fewer organizations that meet face to face, don't know our neighbors as well, meet with friends less frequently, and even socialize with our families less often. His evidence also indicates that we are bowling alone: Although more Americans are bowling than ever before, they are not bowling in leagues. Changes in work, family structure, age, suburban life, television, computers, women's roles, and other factors have contributed to this decline in social capital. Clearly, each of these factors is related to QOL. Given that civic engagement is a major part of the original thought behind the healthy communities movement, it is logical to surmise that those interested in civic engagement could also have interest in QOL.

More than having an interest in civic engagement, those interested in healthy communities are interested in health—the health of each person, the health of specific groups, the health of the community, and, of course, the health of the general population. So, what is a healthy community? A healthy community is one in which people (volunteers or paid personnel) come together to make their community (a place where they live, work, or play) better for themselves, their families, their friends, their neighbors, and others today and in the future. It is a community where citizens purposefully work together to create a healthier, more livable, and more sustainable environment. Creating such an environment takes time and commitment. A healthy community creates open and ongoing dialogue, generates leadership opportunities for all, embraces diversity, connects people of all ages and backgrounds, and fosters a sense of community. More important, it shapes its future through a shared vision, shared work, and shared learning. Healthy communities are self-developed, self-guided, and self-directed. Most use common language and concepts, whereas others try to create unique terminology to help establish a specific identity or to brand themselves and their work.

Parks and recreation professionals should recognize that a healthy community is about more than physical activity; clean, safe, and nurturing programs, services, and environments are also essential. As a professional, you need to consider how your programs, services, and environments can contribute to the health of your community and its citizenry. Further, you should look at how you can do more than offer passive support. Instead, try to build the promotion of health and well-being into your place of work, the place where you live, and the leisure that you enjoy. Be a role model. Assess yourself, your family, and your environments and identify opportunities to make a difference within the lives of others now and in the future.

HISTORY IN THE MAKING: HEALTHY COMMUNITIES

The term *healthy communities* owes its origins to a conference in Toronto, Ontario, held in 1984 and organized by Trevor Hancock. The conference, called Beyond Health Care, had one day set aside for discussion of the health of cities that developed into the concept of healthy cities. The healthy cities concept proposed the use of a comprehensive, community-based approach to improving public health. More specifically, a healthy city was defined as "one that is continually creating and improving those physical and social environments and strengthening those community resources which

Easily accessible playgrounds can increase the quality of life within a community.

enable people to mutually support each other in performing all the functions of life and achieving their maximum potential" (Hancock & Duhl, 1988). As a result, a healthy cities network began in Europe. Subsequently, the U.S. Public Health Service facilitated a comprehensive nationwide examination for ways to improve the health of communities. The result was the start of the U.S. healthy communities movement.

From 1987 to 1997, two primary groups of actors were active within the movement: (1) hospitals and health care providers and (2) related professionals and community problem-solvers (volunteers, civic leaders, investors, entrepreneurs, and so on). In the early to mid-1990s, there was a bit of fragmentation between medical and civic groups. Today this split has widened and has spread into many areas of life. Businesses, governments, educational institutions, and organizations of all types have adopted the healthy communities terminology and approach, sometimes as part of their approach to quality or customer service standards and other times as part of human resources or training efforts. The

growth of the healthy communities movement may result from the fact that living or working in a healthy community is surely more desirable than living or working in an unhealthy community. This movement became a more integral part of the U.S. agenda via the CDC, which funded 331 communities and 52 state and territorial health departments through its Healthy Communities Programs (HPS) from 2008 to 2012. More recently, HPS efforts have been refined to three primary program areas: (1) partnerships to improve community health (PICH), (2) national implementation and dissemination for chronic disease prevention, and (3) racial and ethnic approaches to community health (REACH).

CAREER OPPORTUNITIES

Career opportunities, continuing education opportunities, and research opportunities within the health and wellness area are too extensive to comprehensively cover here. A list of potential careers related to the six components of wellness appears in table 15.2. Within an area of interest, you can

Table 15.2 Career Opportunities Categorized by Wellness Component

Wellness area	Potential employers	Possible position titles
Physical	Municipalities, community centers, health clubs, Boys and Girls Clubs, YMCAs and YWCAs, health departments, schools, universities, private companies	Fitness instructor, group exercise leader, personal trainer, nutritionist, massage therapist, athletic trainer, researcher, community health professional
Intellectual	Schools, colleges, universities, federal governments, state and local governments, private companies, nonprofit organizations, web design firms, public relations firms, professional associations	Teacher, leader, researcher, writer, consultant, graphic designer, musician
Emotional	Home health agencies, hospitals, community health care organizations, municipalities, nonprofit organizations, religious organizations, churches, synagogues	Therapist, counselor, religious worker, hospice worker, researcher, community worker, advocate
Social	Private companies, not-for-profit organizations, cruise ship lines, travel organizations, tourism bureaus, hotels, municipalities, country clubs, amusement parks, specialty camps	Special event manager, tournament director, researcher, game designer, manufacturer, social media developer, public relations specialist, social justice advocate, cruise ship director, activity director
Environmental	Health departments, federal governments, state and local governments, parks, developers, private organizations, schools, universities	Emergency management officer, community health professional, public health professional, researcher, environmental health professional, resource manager, health officer, solid waste manager
Spiritual	Churches, synagogues, hospitals, nonprofit organizations, private companies, military branches	Church or religious worker, life coach, personal advisor, pastor, youth leader, 12-step program director, motivational speaker, product developer, landscape architect, funeral service provider
Occupational	Businesses and industries, hospitals, universities, governments, military branches, schools, national parks	Health promotor, wellness director, health educator, safety coordinator

investigate opportunities that are specific to individual wellness component areas. The potential employment opportunities are diverse in terms of role expectations, potential political and fiscal support, mobility, and longevity.

These opportunities are just starting points. As in every viable profession, the dynamic nature of the area combined with increased knowledge, changes in technology, population trends, and evolving public policy creates constant change in the science and application of the profession. Continuing education, training, and research are essential. Opportunities will come and go, although not as quickly as in less robust and diverse professions.

SUMMARY

This chapter introduced a variety of concepts related to health, wellness, and quality of life. An understanding of the factors that affect health, the current health status and risks in communities, the components of wellness, and other quality of life issues provides a basis for many parks and recreation programs and activities. Professionals have many opportunities to study, apply, or create new ways to contribute to the health and well-being of their communities. The time is right and the key elements are in place, so the opportunities to explore, contribute, and provide services are wide open. They are available only to those who are motivated to pursue a common vision: a healthy, sustainable, accessible, and livable community.

CHAPTER 16

Outdoor and Adventure Recreation

Bruce Martin, Garrett Hutson, and Marni Goldenberg

falkjohann/fotolia.com

" Those who contemplate the beauty of the earth find resources of strength that will endure as long as life lasts. **"**

Rachel Carson, American conservationist and author of *Silent Spring*

LEARNING OUTCOMES

After reading this chapter, you should be able to do the following:

> Provide an overview of outdoor and adventure recreation in the United States and Canada

> Summarize the history of outdoor and adventure recreation in the United States and Canada

> Describe outdoor and adventure recreation in various settings

> Outline career opportunities in outdoor and adventure recreation

> Identify and discuss contemporary trends and issues related to outdoor and adventure recreation in the United States and Canada

What comes to mind when you think about time spent outdoors that has shaped your life in positive ways? What made those experiences fun, impactful, educational, or even therapeutic? Was it time spent alone by a quiet lake at dawn with the smell of pine trees in the air? Was it an activity, such as skiing or snowboarding, that required intense focus as cold snow hit your warm face? Was it a person that you became friends with by sharing a canoe during a university outdoor orientation program? Perhaps you learned about resilience while being temporarily lost on a hiking trip with friends. Or maybe meaningful outdoor experiences in your life combine themes from some of the scenarios mentioned. This chapter will encourage you to think further about these questions by providing an overview of outdoor and adventure recreation (OAR) in the United States and Canada.

Broadly speaking, participation in OAR activities is on the rise in Canada and the United States, and it profoundly affects the leisure landscapes of both countries. In 2014 and 2015, Parks Canada reported nearly 22 million person visits to Canadian national parks and national historic sites. In 2015, nearly half of all Americans (142.4 million participants, 11.7 billion outings) participated in outdoor recreation in some way (Outdoor Industry Foundation, 2016). Outdoor recreation was responsible for helping to create 6.1 million jobs and $646 billion in consumer spending in the United States in 2015 (Outdoor Industry Foundation, 2016). The U.S. Congress recognized the growing significance of outdoor recreation to the U.S. economy through the passage of the Outdoor Recreation Jobs and Economic Impact Act in November 2016. The act was signed into law by President Obama in December 2016. Due to this law, the outdoor recreation economy is now taken into account as part of the national gross domestic product of the United States. Needless to say, the current economic outdoor recreation climate means opportunities for businesses big and small. To support this trend, a new master's of business administration degree in the outdoors industry is scheduled to launch at a college in Colorado in 2018; this program will be the first of its kind (Gear Junkie, 2017).

Not only is outdoor recreation good for the economy, but it is also good for our health. The health benefits of participating in OAR activities and programs continue to be uncovered by researchers. These benefits include enhanced psychological well-being and social functioning; increased self-esteem, self-respect, and self-confidence; the development of pro-environmental behaviors; and the promotion of active lifestyles (Dustin, Bricker, & Schwab, 2010; Duvall & Kaplan, 2014; Goldenberg & Soule, 2014; Halpenny, 2010).

OAR influences American and Canadian societies in powerful and positive ways that are clearly aligned with the three pillars of the National Recreation and Park Association: conservation, health and wellness, and promoting social equity (NRPA, n.d.). The purpose of this chapter is to explore why and how this happens through a discussion of OAR definitions, values and benefits, history, settings and delivery systems, and trends within various contexts. We start by offering a definition of terms.

DEFINITIONS OF OUTDOOR AND ADVENTURE RECREATION TERMS

There are many terms associated with the outdoor industry. The title of this chapter encompasses two of these terms: *outdoor recreation* and *adventure recreation.* Other commonly used terms include *experiential education, adventure education, outdoor education, environmental education,* and *environmental interpretation.* How do we define each of these terms? How do they relate to one another? The following discussion offers definitions of these different terms and considers how they relate to one another. We focus primarily on the terms outdoor recreation and adventure recreation because these terms represent the focus of this chapter.

Outdoor Recreation

Outdoor recreation is a sub-phenomenon of leisure and recreation (Cordes & Hutson, 2015). It is commonly defined as participating in intrinsically motivating outdoor activities during free time that depend on human–nature interaction and an appreciation of the natural world (Curtis, 1979; Ford, 1981; Ibrahim & Cordes, 1993; Plummer, 2009; Sessoms, 1984). The natural elements involved (mountains, rivers, forests, canyons, etc.) are the defining features that outdoor recreation depends on. For example, sea kayaking is outdoor recreation because it depends on the rhythms of the ocean, wind conditions, and tides that are affected by the position of the moon in relation to the earth. Skiing and snowboarding are forms of outdoor recreation because they rely on mountains, winter weather patterns, precipitation rates, and the moisture content of the snowpack. Rock climbing is outdoor recreation because it depends on millions of years of geologic history that produced unique formations of limestone, sandstone, and granite cliff lines. All these examples are tied to nature, which is the key ingredient of the outdoor recreation experience. Therefore, conservation (wise use) of the natural environment is another important aspect of outdoor recreation that will be discussed later in this chapter.

Adventure Recreation

To adventure means to dare, to take a chance, and to be bold. **Adventure recreation** may or may not occur outdoors. Adventure recreation is commonly defined as "a variety of self-initiated activities often utilizing an interaction with the natural environment that contains elements of real or apparent danger in which the outcome, while uncertain, can be influenced by the participant and circumstance" (Ewert, 1989, p. 6). Danger connotes risk and

Adventure recreation involves an interaction with the natural environment that contains elements of real or apparent danger.

Human Kinetics/Mark Anderman/The Wild Studio

uncertainty and is commonly discussed within the context of objective and subjective dangers (Ewert & Vernon, 2013). Objective dangers are observable, measurable, and generally agreed upon by those familiar with certain environments and activities. Weather, river levels, the height and age of a ropes course element, avalanche conditions, and the time the sun sets are all objective dangers. Subjective dangers relate more to human dimensions and perceptions of risk. For example, those new to canoeing may perceive a high subjective danger or risk of drowning, but under appropriate supervision and instruction of a trained outdoor leader, the actual chances of drowning are very small. For the novice canoeist, being on the water for the first time might feel like quite the adventure. The seasoned paddler, however, likely does not experience it this way; for him or her, a day on the water might simply be casual outdoor recreation with friends (Ewert & Vernon, 2013).

Whether a participant experiences a sense of adventure during recreation is largely in the eye of the beholder. Uncertainty, fear, a realistic understanding of competence, and perceptions of risk are all necessary parts of the adventure recreation experience. In fact, many people "enjoy the emotions that are tied up in setting their own abilities against such activities" (Bunyan, 2011, p. 10) and are intentionally seeking the ideal balance between competence and danger. Priest (1990) called this optimal balance *peak adventure,* and for many, it is the major thrust to continued participation in adventure recreation activities.

Related Concepts and Definitions Within OAR

There are other important concepts related to OAR. Some of these concepts will be covered later in the chapter and are introduced here to provide common understandings and distinctions between concepts.

Experiential education is defined by the Association for Experiential Education as "a philosophy that informs many methodologies in which educators purposefully engage with learners in direct experience and focused reflection in order to increase knowledge, develop skills, clarify values, and develop people's capacity to contribute to their communities" (AEE, n.d.).

OAR activities may or may not be considered experiential education. An example of when OAR activities are used as experiential education is during adventure education. Adventure education is typically delivered through structured programs intended "to facilitate opportunities for personal and interpersonal growth through adventure experience as traditionally conceived" (Martin, Breunig, Wagstaff, & Goldenberg, 2017, p. 26). For example, an adventure education program might use focused reflection in a discussion about increasing trust following the use of a challenge ropes course or might facilitate communication and conflict resolution skill-building by processing challenges faced during a wilderness experience (Martin et al., 2017).

Outdoor education is historically defined in two distinct ways: (1) as an educational method and (2) as educational subject matter. Characterizing outdoor education as an educational method, Julian Smith wrote: "Outdoor education is a means of curriculum enhancement through experiences in the outdoors" (1963, p. 21, as cited in Ewert & Garvey, 2007). Characterizing outdoor education as subject matter, Donaldson and Donaldson wrote that outdoor education is "education in, for, and about the outdoors" (1958, p. 17). As these varying views show, outdoor education means different things to different people. Likewise, outdoor education is practiced in a variety of ways depending on what one is aiming to accomplish. Examples of outdoor education include YMCA camps in Canada and the United States, Outward Bound programs and the many extended wilderness expeditions they organize around the world, and agricultural education programs such as 4-H, which was originally intended to teach young people across rural America about new developments in agricultural sciences. Today, 4-H programs challenge young people to address a wide variety of issues from global climate change and sustainable energy to childhood obesity and food security.

Environmental education, also often referred to as *education for sustainability,* specifically involves curriculum that teaches about entire ecosystems and the ways people affect the natural world along with strategies to minimize those effects (Martin et al., 2017). Environmental education centers in Canada and the United States often align environmental curricula with K-12 curricula for field trip school visits. **Environmental interpretation** is historically associated with park visitor centers and uses various strategies to translate the meaning of cultural and natural resources found in parks through exhibits, signage, electronic media, and educational talks and tours, all with an aim of inspiring visitor appreciation and curiosity about the site. **Place-based education** involves local curricula and programs that emphasize learning about specific places and their histories to reenvision the roles of local community members to improve social and environmental quality of life (Gruenwald & Smith, 2008; Sobel, 2004).

Tourism is generally understood as "voluntary travel to a destination which is more novel than the place from which one traveled" (Godbey, 1999, p. 217). **Outdoor and adventure tourism** is characterized by travelers who intentionally seek personal challenge in remote outdoor locations with high levels of activity and excitement (Loverseed, 1997). Outdoor and adventure tourism has also been described in terms of tourism products that travelers seek to purchase, such as a guided mountaineering trip to Nepal or a treetop trekking experience in the province of Ontario (Swarbrooke, Beard, Leckie, & Pomfret, 2003). **Ecotourism** relies on travelers' desires to visit ecosystems that have rare, fragile, and unique ecological characteristics and may provide outdoor recreation opportunities not found elsewhere (Plummer, 2009). The International Ecotourism Society defines ecotourism as "responsible travel to natural areas that conserves the environment, sustains the well-being of the local people, and involves interpretation and education" (International Ecotourism Society, 2015). Costa Rica is a popular ecotourism destination for many North Americans who want to explore the country's active volcanoes, biodiverse landscapes, pristine rivers, and hidden beaches.

All these OAR concepts often involve some form of OAR activity, and many of them are interrelated in theory and practice. These concepts can be thought of as the details that tell the story of OAR as it is currently understood. Finally, these concepts represent an introduction to the various pathways into the OAR professions that will be covered in greater detail later in the chapter.

HISTORY OF OUTDOOR AND ADVENTURE RECREATION IN CANADA AND THE UNITED STATES

The history of OAR in Canada and the United States is rich, complex, and intertwined. This section begins with an overview of indigenous people of North America and the ways they shaped and created the foundations of OAR. It then addresses the romantic origins of the conservation movement in the United States and Canada and the way in which the romantic era framed more modern notions of the value of OAR activities and spaces and why these spaces are worth protecting. It then addresses the emergence of the camping movement in the United States and Canada. Finally, it highlights how railroads, automobiles, and air travel expanded opportunities for OAR in North America and around the world and helped OAR become mainstream within the tourism sector.

Indigenous People of North America

Many OAR pursuits common in North America today are rooted in the indigenous traditions of the American Indians, First Nations, Métis, and Inuit (among others) of North America. It has been theorized that the first people of North America traveled over a land bridge between present-day Russia to Alaska and then throughout the continent between 14,000 and 20,000 years ago. The values, traditions, rituals, and spiritual beliefs of the first people of North America influence the ethics often associated with OAR today.

For example, many indigenous beliefs rely on the concept of interdependence or that all things within the natural world depend on one another without any one thing being considered more important than the other. Indigenous ceremonies, celebrations, and rituals brought the concept of interdependence to life by coinciding with harvests, hunting patterns, the changing of seasons, and rites of passage involving survival in outdoor environments. What we might consider outdoor recreation activities today often overlapped with everyday life patterns of indigenous people because no real division between work and play necessarily existed (McClean & Hurd, 2011).

The use of the canoe by indigenous people of North America has shaped the outdoor recreation identity of Canada and the United States to some degree, especially given that other modes of travel during those times were out of the question due to the challenging landscape and climate. In fact, the French word *voyageur,* or traveler, was used to identify French Canadians who traveled great distances by canoes during the fur trade era. The ethos of the Canadian voyageur explorer lives on today in part due to indigenous and early European use of the canoe (Cordes & Hutson, 2015).

Romantic Origins

Views of the natural world from visionaries of the 19th century American romantic era shaped modern thinking about why nature should be thought of as sacred, special, and spiritual (Cordes & Hutson, 2015). Most well-known among these visionaries were Ralph Waldo Emerson and Henry David Thoreau, who fueled the transcendentalist movement that began in the northeastern United States. Transcendentalism relies on the notion that universal truths can be accessed through experiences in nature with strong emphasis on intuition and individual experience. These ideas were contrary to the prominent religious beliefs of the time. Perhaps the most famous of all American transcendentalist writing was Thoreau's book *Walden*, which chronicled his two years living in a cabin near a Massachusetts' pond on Emerson's land. Thoreau's purpose for living near Walden Pond was to practice self-reflection and simple living and to develop a broader understanding of the world. These beliefs about the value and benefits of nature-based experiences were novel and rare for the time and contributed to the conservation movement of Canada and the United States that followed (Plummer, 2009). Literary figures such as Emerson and Thoreau gave voice to the aesthetic and spiritual values that draw so many of us to wilderness environments and natural areas to engage in OAR pursuits. With the rise of industrialism and urbanization, traditional views of nature as forbidding and dangerous spaces were flipped, and nature became viewed as a place for

Oleg Kozlov/fotolia.com

The romantic origins of outdoor and adventure recreation are still seen today where participants view nature as a place for spiritual renewal and a place where one's character can be tested.

spiritual renewal and a place where one's character could be tested and forged. Nature became a place that inspired a sense of adventure and provided opportunities to test one's abilities and challenge one's limitations.

The Emergence of the Conservation Movement

The conservation movement in the United States and Canada was the result of shifting philosophical beliefs and attitudes toward nature such as those reflected within the transcendentalist movement led by Emerson and Thoreau. The conservation movement was also a result of natural science advancements such as Charles Darwin's theory of evolution and Alexander von Humboldt's well-documented observations of interconnected life systems. Perhaps most important, the conservation movement in Canada and the United States was due to the observation of ostentatious destruction of natural resources, especially as the American and Canadian frontiers came to a close. Clearcutting of forests, abandoned mines, observable loss of species such as the passenger pigeon, and catastrophic fires all contributed to shifting mind-sets about the relationship between people and nature (Dennis, 2012).

City planners, landscape architects, and others began to recognize the value and necessity of green space within rapidly expanding cities. Frederick Law Olmsted (considered by some to be the father of the American park) and Calvert Vaux designed New York City's Central Park, which was established in 1857. Toronto's largest park within city limits, High Park, was officially opened in 1876. Perhaps the world's most famous conservationist, John Muir, had the foresight to recognize what would be lost if large expanses of wilderness in the western United States were not protected. Muir played a major role in helping protect Yosemite Valley, California, through legislation passed in 1864; this legislation later helped Yellowstone in Wyoming become the world's first national park in 1872 (Nash, 1982). Muir also helped form the Sierra Club in 1892, which has a history of protecting wilderness in the American west. Canada's first national park, Banff National Park, was established in 1887 near hot springs that were discovered in Alberta four years prior (Campbell, 2011). Parks Canada was estab-

lished in 1911 as the world's first federally managed park service, and the U.S. National Parks Service was established in 1916 (Ewert & Vernon, 2013). Overall, these major events signaled the beginning of a movement based on wise use and protection of outdoor environments that continues to shape how Americans and Canadians think about places where OAR takes place today.

The Emergence of the Camping Movement

Somewhat concurrently with the conservation movement, the camping movement gained momentum as a way to positively affect youth development beginning in the late 1800s and continuing throughout the industrial revolution. Historically, children in U.S. schools had summers off to help with the family farm. As populations in North American cities increased, many suggest that camping helped reconnect children to nature and teach valuable life lessons that no longer occurred on the family farm during the summer. Furthermore, camp programs were increasingly viewed by social reformers as useful to counteract society's shortcomings and were considered part of the progressive education era (Ozier, 2012). William Frederick Gunn of Connecticut's Gunnery School is often credited with starting the first summer camp for boys in 1861. Records show that the Brooklyn, New York, YMCA took 30 boys camping in 1881 (Turner, 1985). Between 1900 and 1915, well-known youth-serving organizations such as the American Camp Association, Boy Scouts, Girl Scouts, 4-H, Campfire Girls, and Boys Club emerged. The Canadian Camping Association was founded in 1936. In the United States, there were 106 camps by 1910, 1,248 by 1924, and 3,485 by 1933, and most were located in the northeastern United States (Bernard, 1999; DeMerritte, 1999).

The Emergence of Outdoor and Adventure Tourism

The emergence of outdoor and adventure tourism is directly related to access to transportation. The expansion of railroads across the United States and Canada increased opportunities for recreation. The first transcontinental railroads opened in the United

States in 1869 and in Canada in 1886. In fact, it was Canadian Pacific Railway workers who originally discovered hot springs near Banff, Alberta, and the Canadian government realized they could use the same railway to profit from transporting Canadians to Banff National Park for outdoor recreation tourism. However, it was transportation by automobile that was the greatest influence on outdoor and adventure tourism growth in the United States and Canada. Automobiles began to become more widely available and affordable to the masses beginning in the early 1900s. Although city parks provide much-needed green space within densely populated urban centers, outdoor recreation facilities such as ski resorts and state, provincial, and national parks all required travel outside of cities either by railroad or car. By 1920, more Americans had visited national parks by car than by train (Virden, 2006). Travel by airplane became commercialized during World War I and opened further opportunities for outdoor and adventure tourism on a global scale. Air travel shaped the development of outdoor adventure tourism activities such as snow skiing, high altitude mountaineering, and surfing by giving a greater number of people access to such activities. Transcontinental highway systems in the United States and Canada combined with the continued growth of parks in both countries from 1920 forward created further opportunities for outdoor and adventure tourism (Virden, 2006).

SETTINGS AND DELIVERY SYSTEMS

OAR incorporates many different settings and delivery systems. Settings range from park systems to commercial ski resorts, from retail shops to summer camps, and from wild rivers to open spaces used for rock climbing. This section introduces the various OAR settings, delivery systems, and career opportunities in the various settings and participation trends in these settings.

Parks and Protected Areas

Most of the OAR field operates in parks and protected areas. An understanding of parks and protected areas is essential for anyone interested in working in the OAR field. Parks and protected areas are often run by government agencies such as the U.S. National Park Service, the U.S. Forest Service, the U.S. Bureau of Land Management, or Parks Canada. These organizations operate differently but all have the goal of maintaining natural land and open spaces. Many countries have their own systems to protect and preserve natural areas. There are several organizations within the U.S. federal government that manage and facilitate the use of public land for preservation and conservation purposes. Many countries have passed laws and acts that protect and preserve natural spaces for future generations. In the United States, for example, the Wilderness Act of 1964 sets aside land in remote roadless areas to be preserved as wilderness areas. Parks and protected areas are also managed by local and state agencies such as municipalities, counties, states, or regions. Managing agencies and the legal frameworks under which they operate determine the purpose and uses of the public lands and other natural resources. Some public land is set aside for multiuse purposes, whereas other land is strictly set aside for preservation. As a user of the land, it is essential to know the regulations and rules that the managing agency uses to govern the land. Protection of cultural and natural resources is an integral part of maintaining parks and protected areas.

Various career opportunities in parks and protected areas include park rangers, interpreters, land managers, government agents, biologists, researchers, or law enforcement agents. Some careers require certain education and training, and others might be more open, such as a seasonal park aide. Various park ranger academies exist that offer training needed for the various jobs. If a person loves and appreciates the natural areas, working in parks and protected areas may be a very rewarding career option. The various government agencies have webpages that provide career information (e.g., www.fs.fed.us for the U.S. Forest Service, www.nsp.gov for the National Park Service).

Resorts

Commercial resorts are for-profit enterprises that focus on the economic potential of an area. Resorts centered around OAR can be focused on any outdoor activity such as skiing, river running, or fishing. Commercial resorts can be either public

OUTSTANDING GRADUATE

©Kay Tufts

Background Information

Name: Kay Tufts

Education: MS in recreation and sport sciences from Ohio University; BS in recreation, parks, and tourism from Radford University

Credentials: Certified Therapeutic Recreation Specialist (CTRS), American Canoe Association (ACA) Level 3 River Safety and Rescue, ACA Level 3 River Kayaking Instructor, SOLO Wilderness First Responder, Leave No Trace training

Career Information

Position: Assistant Director of Outdoor Programs

Organization: Known as Base Camp Cullowhee (BCC), the outdoor program in the department of campus recreation and wellness at Western Carolina University (WCU) aims to provide outdoor trips, experiential education opportunities, and gear rentals to the 9,000 members of the WCU community.

> " *I believe that there is a subtle magnetism in Nature, which, if we unconsciously yield to it, will direct us aright.* "
> —Henry David Thoreau

Job description: My job responsibilities include planning and implementing adventure activities, with a focus on water-based outdoor trips; supervising student workers; implementing and assessing outdoor programs; overseeing the climbing wall; overseeing the university's trails system; and coordinating the Tuck River cleanup initiative.

Career path: I completed my undergraduate degree in recreation, parks, and tourism at Radford University and completed my master's degree in recreation and sport sciences at Ohio University. I served as a graduate teaching assistant at Ohio University, teaching courses in wilderness living skills, wilderness navigation, caving, canoeing, and whitewater kayaking to undergraduate students at the university. I also assisted in teaching two sections of a nearly month-long outdoor leadership course for students majoring in outdoor recreation and education.

After completing my graduate degree, I jumped into the field of commercial recreation as a seasonal worker to further develop my technical skills. I worked as a commercial raft guide for Wildwater Limited on the Nantahala, Ocoee, and Chattooga rivers in the southeastern United States for several years. I also worked as an instructor for Adventure Treks, leading adolescents on weeklong adventure trips in western North Carolina, with activities such as backpacking, rock climbing, and whitewater rafting. After several years of seasonal work, I began to look for new opportunities and found myself being pulled back into the field of higher education. I feel fortunate to have been offered the position of assistant director of outdoor programs at WCU because of the deeper connections that I can develop with the community I am serving through my current position. I am especially interested in promoting the development of students with whom I am working over the course of their participation in my programs.

Advice for Undergraduates

My advice to undergraduate students is to not be afraid of hard work. Having a willingness to put yourself out there, learn, work hard, and demonstrate humility will most likely be rewarded. I feel excited at the start of every work day and satisfied at the end. I am passionate about sharing the outdoors with others, and I could not imagine working in any other field.

---

or private. Public commercial resorts are typically operated through concession programs within public parks and protected areas systems. They are often based on a pay-to-play system and can include commercially managed rivers or ski resorts. An example of a public commercial ski resort is Mammoth Mountain ski resort in California. Mammoth Mountain offers skiing during the winter and is considered the "premier bike park in the U.S." during the summer, offering terrain for all levels of bikers, lessons and clinics, MTB events, rentals and demos, lift tickets, and more (Mammoth Mountain Ski Area, n.d.). They also offer a kids' adventure park and gondola rides. Private commercial resorts are typically operated on privately owned land. Many private commercial resorts, such as country clubs, hunting clubs, and other club resorts, require a membership. Martis Camp in Lake Tahoe, California, is considered "possibly the best four-season private community in the U.S." (Olmsted, 2013). This resort offers golf as well as a real, full-sized ski mountain, lakes, 16 miles of hiking and cross-country ski trails, and various other outdoor amenities. Career opportunities in commercial resorts can include resort manager, instructor, marketing expert, and many others.

Guide Services

Many outdoor adventure activities require specialized equipment or training. For example, whitewater rafting uses equipment such as rafts, PFDs, paddles, wet suits, and so on. In addition, specific knowledge of rivers in general, knowledge of the specific river they are running, water safety skills, and group dynamics skills are all needed. To make various outdoor activities accessible to the public, guides are available to enable participants to experience the activity. One example of a guiding company is Alaska Mountain Guides and Climbing School Inc. (AMGCSI), which guides expeditions throughout the world including in Alaska, Mexico, Nepal, Indonesia, and Kenya. AMGCSI takes groups on expeditions to go mountaineering, ice climbing, whitewater paddling, trekking, and other outdoor activities. Another example of a guiding company is the Wildland Trekking Company, which markets itself as providing unforgettable hiking vacations in locations such as the Grand Canyon, Zion, Yellowstone, and Yosemite National Parks. Various types of hiking trips are offered, such as backpacking trips, stock and porter trips, inn-based trips, and photography tours.

People in the outdoor adventure guiding industry work long hours to take participants through an outdoor experience and are responsible for safety, education, and providing a meaningful experience. Guides typically have expertise in an area and a passion for sharing that expertise with others. Guides can provide introductory experiences, such as rock climbing or surfing for a few hours to a day, as well as multiday experiences for a group on a long expedition.

Summer Camps

Summer camps range in location, price, availability, and numbers of days. Some are day camps and

Ski resorts provide a classic example of outdoor adventure recreation opportunities for a fee.

Denis Pepin/fotolia.com

others are overnight camps. Some camps cater to a specific population, such as adults with specific religious affiliations, whereas other camps are open to anyone. Many of us grew up attending some sort of camp experience such as an overnight experience in a different state or city or in a local area. This first exposure to a camp setting could be why you are interested in the field of recreation, parks, and tourism. Some camps operate year-round, even if they are primarily summer camps. Year-round operations could include a challenge course, retreat center, or lodging facility. Rancho El Chorro Outdoor School on the Central Coast of California is an example of an environmental center that operates year-round to provide environmental education to youth. Many visit environmental education centers as part of their curriculum in elementary school. Careers in summer camps can start with your first summer as a camp counselor, and you can work up to a director or programmer. Some career paths in summer camp settings are seasonal, but others might be longer.

The American Camp Association (ACA), one of the largest nonprofit organizations for camps, serves over 9,000 members in providing a community for camp professionals to share knowledge and ensure quality programs through setting standards and accreditation. The mission of ACA is to enrich "the lives of children, youth and adults through the camp experience" (American Camp Association, n.d.). Many camps inside and outside the United States run under the ACA standards. Camp Mardela in Denton, Maryland, is an accredited member of ACA that offers various camps such as camps for those with little camping experience, camps for those who wish to learn about equestrian safety and riding, and camps that focus on outdoor adventure activities.

Outdoor Adventure Programs

National Outdoor Leadership School (NOLS) and Outward Bound are two of the leading outdoor organizations that provide instructors for groups to have a shared learning experience in the outdoor context. NOLS, a nonprofit organization that focuses on outdoor leadership development, is based out of Lander, Wyoming, but offers courses throughout the world including in locations such as New Zealand, Patagonia, and the Yukon. Skills learned on courses can range from backpacking, caving, Leave No Trace, and sea kayaking. NOLS's mission is to "be the leading source and teacher of wilderness skills and leadership that serve people and the environment" (NOLS, n.d.). Outward Bound has many bases in over 30 countries and collectively serves around "a quarter of a million people a year" (Outward Bound, n.d.). Outward Bound teaches similar skills as NOLS but their focus is on changing lives through discovery. Many other programs exist, such as the Wilderness Education Association, the International Wilderness Leadership School, or Alaska Mountain Guides, and programs vary by country.

In outdoor adventure programs, the outdoors is used as the classroom environment to teach technical and interpersonal skills to individuals and groups. The emphasis in these programs is on providing educational experiences and maximizing learning for the participants. Some groups are predetermined and know each other in advance, whereas other group members may be from a variety of backgrounds and locations. These programs focus on the educational component of the experience, which may include cooking, working with a group, leading a group, preparing a campsite, experiencing navigation, or a variety of other outdoor skills. Often programs will vary in terms of length, location, and skill development. Among the many desired outcomes are development of leadership skills, personal reflection and development, and positive group development.

Career opportunities in the outdoor adventure programming field include directors and managers, course instructors and educators, and logistical operators. Some organizations, such as NOLS and Outward Bound, offer instructor training programs and courses that provide students the opportunity to learn skills needed for the organization while also assessing whether the individual would be a good fit as an instructor.

The Retail Industry

The retail industry is an integral part of the outdoor and adventure field and includes apparel and equipment needed to operate a program or activity. Several retail stores are available in cities and on the web for purchasing equipment. There are small local companies that design and sell equipment, and there are also national retail chain stores that serve the industry. Career opportunities in the retail industry can include equipment designers and testers, store owners and managers, or working as a representative or sales manager. Many companies now have sales, marketing, special events, and design teams. Many students get their start in the retail industry by working for a company as an intern running their special events or assisting with marketing.

Military Recreation

Morale, welfare, and recreation (MWR) offers activities on most U.S. military bases throughout the world. MWR includes opportunities for outdoor and adventure recreation through participation in activities (if you are in the military) or careers in MWR. Adventure activities include offering military personnel and their families opportunities to participate in camping, backpacking, fishing, or other activities available in the local environment. At the naval base in Annapolis, Maryland, MWR rents various outdoor equipment, whereas the U.S. Army MWR offers new skills, guided tours, and gear to military personnel. MWR in Italy offers escorted and guided cultural trips, high adventure activities, skiing and snowboarding, water sports, and hiking and biking (U.S. Army MWR, n.d.). Traditionally these activities are offered at discounted rates and are there to encourage military personnel and their families to have well-balanced lives. Careers in MWR are available for civilians and military personnel. Internships, entry-level positions, and director positions are available. A desire to see the world, work with people, and provide recreational opportunities are musts for these positions.

Ecotourism and Adventure Travel

OAR includes the areas of ecotourism and adventure travel. Ecotourism is a form of nature-based tourism focused on learning about and developing an appreciation for ecosystems that have rare, fragile, and unique ecological characteristics. A popular ecotourism destination for North Americans is

Costa Rica, which has protected approximately 25 percent of its lands through a system of parks and protected areas intended to draw tourists to the country. There are numerous companies in Costa Rica that promote ecotourism opportunities throughout the country, and there are a variety of professional opportunities within the industry, including working for guide services, eco-lodges, national parks, and so on.

Adventure travel is a travel experience in which risk is a central component of the experience. Whitewater rafting on the Colorado River through the Grand Canyon is an example of adventure travel. OARS is an example of a company that offers rafting trips on the Colorado River and around the world. Mountain climbing in places such as the Pacific Northwest is another example of adventure travel. There are numerous companies in both Canada and the United States that specialize in guiding clients to the mountain summits throughout North America and around the world.

CONTEMPORARY TRENDS AND ISSUES IN OUTDOOR AND ADVENTURE RECREATION

Societies around the world have evolved dramatically since the outdoor and adventure recreation industry first began to emerge in the 18th and 19th centuries. With these changes have come changes to the outdoor industry itself. With the rapid expansion of nature-based tourism in the 1950s and 1960s, the natural spaces that served as venues for outdoor and adventure recreation pursuits began to be negatively affected by overuse. Many parks and protected areas began to experience a "tragedy of the commons" (Manning, 2007). As the modern environmental movement emerged in the 1960s, so too did an expression that characterized our new relationship with natural areas: We were loving them to death. One of the key reasons for the negative impacts of OAR pursuits at the time is that many visitors to parks and protected areas operated on the principles of the woodcraft movement (Turner, 2002). The woodcraft movement represented a traditional approach to camping that entailed cooking over open fires, building lean-tos and other natural shelters, hunting and foraging for food, and so forth. The carrying capacity of a given area tends to be low when visitors engage in these practices while visiting.

To address the dilemmas posed by the woodcraft movement, a new outdoor ethic began to emerge that emphasized wilderness living and travel techniques that resulted in minimal environmental impacts. This movement ultimately culminated in the establishment of the Leave No Trace Center for Outdoor Ethics, an organization devoted to protecting the outdoors by educating the public to use natural and open spaces in environmentally responsible ways. The emergence of Leave No Trace represented a shift from an environmental ethic that prevailed during the late 19th and early 20th centuries that emphasized the virtue of living off the land to an ethic that emphasizes minimizing our impact on recreation resources and preserving them for successive generations of users. This new ethic, embodied in the seven principles of Leave No Trace (figure 16.1), has prevailed since. However, scholars and practitioners in the field of OAR have begun to question the efficacy of this approach in the face of new environmental dilemmas resulting from global climate change. They are beginning to ask about the effects that we have on the recreation resources that serve as venues for OAR pursuits and question the effects of the retail industry that supports this minimal-impact approach to outdoor and adventure recreation (Alagona & Simon, 2009, 2012; Andre, 2012).

Just as the transition from a predominantly rural and agrarian economy to a predominantly industrial and urban economy resulted in dramatic societal changes during the late 19th and early 20th centuries, new economic and technological developments are yielding equally dramatic changes in society. The development of new technologies, the globalization of trade and commerce, and global climate change will continue to perpetuate changes that will redefine the ways we engage in OAR pursuits. The following explores some of these trends.

The Challenge of Global Climate Change to the Outdoor Industry

A phenomenon that has emerged in the tourism industry in recent years is last-chance tourism (Lemelin, Dawson & Stewart, 2012). Tourism destinations threatened by global climate change have become destinations for tourists who hope to experience their unique environmental and cultural attributes before they disappear or are drastically altered as a result of climate change. Examples of last-chance tourism opportunities include polar bear viewing in the Hudson Bay region of Canada, glacier viewing in the Waterton-Glacier International Peace Park along the U.S. and Canadian border in northern Montana and southern Alberta, and skiing in certain alpine areas in the United States and Canada. In many cases, entire ecosystems are at risk of being drastically altered or disappearing altogether. Coastal wetlands are a prime example of this. Sea levels are projected to rise by as much as six feet over the next 100 years. Freshwater wetlands in coastal areas around the world stand

---

FIGURE 16.1 THE SEVEN PRINCIPLES OF LEAVE NO TRACE

- Plan ahead and prepare.
- Travel and camp on durable surfaces.
- Dispose of waste properly.
- Leave what you find.
- Minimize campfire impacts.
- Respect wildlife.
- Be considerate of other visitors.

For more information on the Leave No Trace Center for Outdoor Ethics, visit www.lnt.org.

to be inundated by rising sea levels. With the loss of these freshwater wetlands will come the loss of tourism opportunities associated with them. The Florida Everglades, for example, is a popular destination for wildlife viewing, canoeing and kayaking, and other types of OAR tourism. Many coastal resort communities along the Outer Banks of North Carolina on the east coast of the United States will be inundated by the Atlantic Ocean from the east and the Albemarle and Pamlico Sounds to the west. As the area is inundated by rising waters, much of the tourism industry that currently flourishes on the Outer Banks will disappear.

There are many dire consequences that are likely to result from global climate change, and perhaps the implications of these consequences for the tourism industry should be the least of our worries. However, the reality of global climate change raises important questions for those professionally engaged in the outdoor industry and for citizens who participate in outdoor and adventure recreation activities and tourism opportunities. In what ways does our participation in these activities contribute to global climate change? And, short of foregoing participation in these activities altogether, what can we do to help mitigate the problem of global climate change in the outdoor and adventure recreation field?

Alagona and Simon (2009, 2012) have highlighted an uncomfortable paradox in the adoption of Leave No Trace as an approach to mitigating the environmental impacts of natural resource recreation and tourism activities. They argue that Leave No Trace has been effective in mitigating direct effects of users of these resources. However, in doing so, Leave No Trace has merely displaced these effects, which helps perpetuate a consumerist outdoor retail culture focused on supplying equipment and goods needed to participate in OAR activities without negatively impacting the land. Tents and other forms of synthetic shelter have taken the place of lean-tos built from natural materials found on the land. Camp stoves have eliminated the need for campfires in the camp kitchen. Visit any REI store in the United States or Mountain Equipment Co-op store in Canada and you will find a plethora of equipment and clothing produced by manufactures such as Patagonia, Sierra Designs, Marmot, and others that is intended to help you experience the outdoors in an enjoyable and comfortable fashion while minimizing your impact on the land. Yet, all these consumer goods are produced through

Brand X Pictures

While Leave No Trace has been effective in mitigating environmental impacts, it has contributed to a consumerist outdoor retail culture.

manufacturing processes that inevitably contribute to broader environmental problems that are a result of the consumer-oriented economy of which they are a part. There are numerous issues related to environmental and social justice that arise because of the roles that Leave No Trace and the outdoor retail industry play in contributing to environmental degradation around the globe.

Few would advocate returning to the woodcraft movement to which Leave No Trace was a response. Leave No Trace has been successful in fulfilling its mission of protecting outdoor recreation resources from the direct effects of their users. However, the question becomes, what can we do to mitigate the broader environmental effects that have resulted from outdoor industry over the past half century or more? Although we have mitigated direct local effects to our parks and protected areas through adherence to the principles of Leave No Trace, we are now facing indirect environmental effects to these areas that threaten the existence of the very environmental and cultural attributes that make them unique. To address this shortcoming of Leave No Trace, Alagona and Simon (2012) proposed adding an eighth Leave No Trace principle: Leave No Trace starts at home. They suggest extending the ethos embodied in the Leave No Trace principles to our daily lives. Indeed, although not embedded in its list of principles, Leave No Trace has promoted this idea over the years with the mantra "from our backcountry to your backyard." Perhaps it is time to formalize this idea by including it as an explicit Leave No Trace principle, as Alagona and Simon (2012) suggest. In any case, we must all begin to consider participating in OAR activities in ways that minimize our contributions to the broader environmental effects of the industry.

The Influence of New Technologies on the Nature of OAR Experiences

New technologies developed over the past century have redefined and will continue to redefine the ways and the extent to which humans experience nature. Prior to the development of modern modes of communication (e.g., radio communication, satellite phones), explorers and adventurers were on their own when venturing into the wild. Explorers and adventurers would step into uncharted territory with no means of communication with the outside world. The success of an expedition was unknown until the explorers returned (or failed to return). George Mallory and Sandy Irvine, for example, disappeared while attempting a first ascent of Mt. Everest in 1924. Their fate was shrouded in mystery for 75 years until Mallory's frozen and mummified body was found at the base of the Northeast Ridge of the mountain. They had ventured into a remote and harsh environment without any means of communication with the outside world, without the ability to communicate distress, and without any hope of rescue from an outside party should they suffer a mishap. Edmund Hillary and Tenzing Norgay made the first successful climb of Mt. Everest in 1953, and, since that time, over 4,000 climbers have reached the summit. The mountain is no less dangerous than it was when Mallory and Irvine attempted to summit it in 1924. Gardener (2016) reports that 265 people have died on Everest between 1922 and 2014. However, the development of new technologies has revolutionized how climbers experience the mountain. These new technologies have increased the safety of climbers on the mountain and have made the mountain more accessible to expert and amateur climbers alike. The influence of new technologies on OAR experiences is not unique to mountaineering. The same is true for nearly every OAR pursuit from whitewater kayaking to sailing to adventure trekking.

Howard T. Welser (2012) argues that the development of new technologies has diminished the quality of OAR experiences and threatens to end wilderness experience as we traditionally conceive it. He argues that new information technologies have created a ubiquitous bridge to civilization and consequently "reduce our opportunity to experience the self-reliance, isolation, adventure, exposure to the wild, and natural consequences that define the wilderness experience for recreationists" (p. 153). These technologies tend to inhibit our ability to disconnect with the modern realities that define our lives and consequently diminish the restorative value of the environments into which we venture to participate in OAR pursuits. Welser (2012) also argues that modern communication technologies have resulted in increased awareness of remote and exotic recreation areas, thus promoting the popularity and overuse of these areas.

SUMMARY

This chapter introduced you to the field of outdoor and adventure recreation and offered definitions of outdoor and adventure recreation and various terms associated with the field. The chapter illustrated ways in which the practice of OAR in the United States and Canada can be used to promote the three pillars of the National Recreation and Park Association: conservation, health and wellness, and social equity (NRPA, n.d.). The chapter provided an overview of the history of the field as well as an introduction to various sites and settings through which OAR goods and services are delivered. In doing so, we presented many career opportunities associated with the field. Finally, the chapter presented a discussion of contemporary trends and issues that have significantly affected OAR over the past half century and will continue to affect the field for generations to come.

At the start of this chapter, we posed a series of questions and challenged you to consider these questions as you progressed through the chapter. We hope that this chapter has offered you an opportunity to revisit some of these experiences and to consider them in a new light and continue to draw lessons from them. We also hope that you will find inspiration and meaning in future OAR experiences, whether as an outdoor professional or as an OAR enthusiast.

CHAPTER 17

Arts and Culture

Julie Voelker-Morris

“ Since parks are the democratic spaces of a city, where communities can come together to express their identities, the marriage of parks and the arts makes perfect sense. Parks can be a vital place for the cultural expression of a community and a city. ”

City Parks Forum

LEARNING OUTCOMES

After reading this chapter, you should be able to do the following:

> Demonstrate an understanding and awareness of arts and cultural experiences
> Explain the importance of providing arts and cultural experiences in North America
> Identify components of arts and cultural programming
> Describe the meanings and benefits realized by organizations, individuals, and communities through arts and cultural experiences and programs
> Compare the amount, type, and breadth of arts and cultural experiences available

The provision for arts and cultural experiences has a long tradition in recreation and leisure settings. More than 60 years ago, Meyer and Brightbill (1956) advocated that arts and crafts, dancing, dramatics, literary activities, and music activities be standard in comprehensive recreation programs and settings. Arts and cultural opportunities have been valued as means of improving peoples' lives, livelihoods, and neighborhoods via connection to others through cultural experiences, positive economic contributions, and development of skills as a result of lifelong arts offerings (Americans for the Arts, 2017; Arnold, 1976; Carpenter, 2008; World Tourism Organization, 2013; National Endowment for the Arts, 2013; National Governors Association, n.d.; Powell Hanna, 2016). Healthy communities are built when recreation specialists build relationships between artists and diverse members of a specific community. **Arts and cultural activities** in recreation settings engage and honor a variety of skill levels while emphasizing health and wellness through psychomotor, cognitive, and affective skills development.

Arts and cultural recreation opportunities to support and enliven communities continue to be part of public agencies' responsibilities to their citizens and viable offerings in self-support programs. This chapter discusses the importance of providing arts and cultural experiences to broad publics as part of life in a democratic society. Benefits of arts and cultural programming for individuals, organizations, and communities are explored. Contemporary arts and cultural programs, with a focus on the United States and Canada, are highlighted throughout the chapter to show the broad range of organizations and types of programs, provide context for historical and contemporary participation, and show trends in the field. Select constraints are included when the

benefits of such programming are discussed. Each example seeks to build social equity or contribute to health and wellness of residents, tourists, and others in the communities.

TYPES OF ARTS AND CULTURAL EXPERIENCES IN RECREATION AND LEISURE

Leisure is sometimes considered a nonactivity—the time in which one rests, relaxes, steps out of the rest of life. However, leisure is also the experience that brings about activities and experiences of engagement found in recreation services (Carpenter, 2008). Such engagement and participation can and should include arts and cultural experiences within community settings.

The **arts and cultural sector** in North America is a large, heterogeneous set of individuals, entrepreneurs, and nonprofit, private, and unincorporated organizations engaged in creation, production, presentation, distribution, preservation, and education about aesthetic, heritage, and entertainment activities, products, and artifacts (Wyszomirski, 2002). Organizational contexts such as parks and recreation, leisure education, and tourism are all viewed as part of the arts and culture sector in North America. Leisure behaviors (e.g., collecting, cuisine) and pursuits (e.g., gaming, sports) are other components in the sector. In 2012, the National Endowment for the Arts (2013), in partnership with the U.S. Census Bureau, completed the most recent iteration of the Survey of Public Participation in the Arts (SPPA). The SPPA has been conducted about every five years since 1985 and examines how adults engage with the arts. The study has covered the multiple ways that people participate in leisure activities around the arts such as consumption of the arts through electronic and digital media (music, dance, critiques of art, interviews with artists, etc.) and at discipline-specific venues (cinemas, galleries, performing arts centers); voluntary reading and art making; art sharing via social media, blogging, or websites; and arts production and learning through individual or group performances, exhibitions, classes, and workshops in a specific instrument, dance style, theatrical performance, creative writing, photography, and the like. This study confirmed much of Chartrand's (2000) well-regarded mapping of arts and cultural industries that included parks and recreation, leisure, education, tourism, antiques and collectables, cosmetics, cuisine, funeral practices, furniture and fixtures, gaming, multiculturalism, native cultures, languages, physiotherapy and psychotherapy, sports, and religion (see figure 17.1).

As such, a wide variety of leisure organizations, activities, and behaviors are considered part of the contemporary arts and culture sector.

McCarthy and Jinnett (2001) remind us that defining what we mean by the arts can be challenging because many make a distinction between the *classic arts* (opera, ballet, dance, theater, classical music, painting, sculpture, literature), the more *popular arts* (rock and roll, hip-hop, graffiti murals), and *entertainment enterprises* (film, radio, television, computers). Given what we know from the SPPA study, it seems reasonable to conclude that the arts include notions associated with auditory, visual, movement, and experiential factors and might also include ethnic activities, religious ceremonies, specific types of athletics, crafts and culinary arts, and horticultural practices (Arnold, 1976). Popular arts, which was a term suggested by Arnold (1978) to

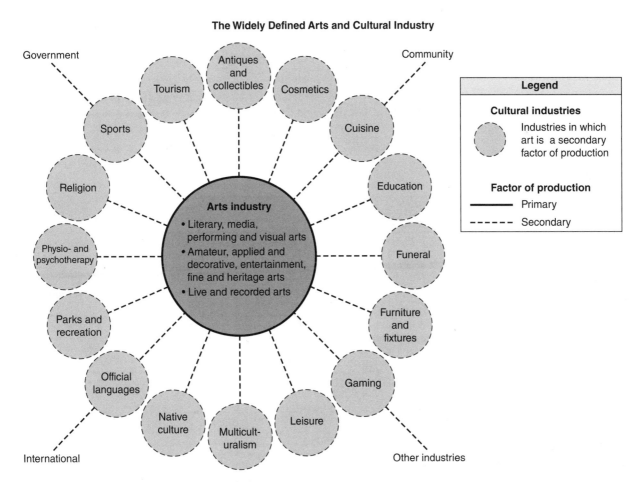

Figure 17.1 Chartrand's art and cultural industry map.

Adapted, by permission, from H. H. Chartrand, 2000, *Toward an American arts industry.* In *The public life of the arts in America,* edited by J.M. Cherbo & M.J. Wyszomirski (New Brunswick, NJ: Rutgers University Press), 22-49.

categorize arts experiences, includes 10 content areas. As depicted in table 17.1, the arts have often been defined by activity descriptors. Arnold's categories were the first definitions of the various popular arts experiences found in parks and recreation programs. Over the years, Arnold's categories have proven useful to recreation professionals.

TYPES OF ORGANIZATIONS AND ROLES AVAILABLE

Traditions for supporting popular arts and cultural experiences in leisure and recreation are numerous (Meyer & Brightbill, 1956). Such traditions include ways that such programs have been organized, managed, and administered. Most arts and cultural organizations are nonprofit, public, or quasi-public organizations that have their own missions and resources for meeting their goals (American Assembly, 1997). Such organizations include community arts centers and recreation centers, art museums and performing arts organizations, art commissions and councils, historic sites and folklore associations, museums and reenactments, libraries and literary organizations, arts and cultural festivals, and youth and senior citizen organizations that offer special arts and cultural programs.

Arts organizations often have a mix of paid staff, governing boards, and one-time project-based volunteers in addition to temporary and permanent employees. Before training and education in specific arts and cultural activities were available, people had to learn on the job. Table 17.2 lists jobs that were recently acquired by graduates of the University of Oregon's arts and administration master's degree program. Positions are categorized by type (i.e., museums and visual arts, performing arts, **community arts**, media, education and public programs). Most of these positions are in arts and cultural organizations rather than parks and recreation agencies. These professionals work in performing arts centers, community arts organizations, government-affiliated sites, for-profit production companies, and museums and galleries. The positions depicted are typical of options available to graduates of master's programs that emphasize **arts, culture**, and **community**. The table indicates the increasing degree requirements in the field. Arts and cultural organizations often have many types of employees who work with professional and amateur performers, artists, crafters, teachers, and facilitators to offer arts and cultural experiences. Many of these organizations partner with public and unincorporated groups to provide arts and culture

Table 17.1 Categories for Popular Arts

Category	Description
Horticulture arts	Parks, gardens, houseplants, growing scenes, topiary
Craft and culinary arts	Weaving, crafts, cooking, fabrics, decorating, interior and food design
Athletic arts	Art gallery exhibitions of artworks by athletes or about athletics, competitions or specific exhibitions of athletic arts such as martial arts, gymnastics, fencing
Folk arts	Fairs, festivals, circuses, instrument making, basket and net weaving, fisher and cowboy poetry
Cultural and ethnic arts	Arts participation by a particular culture, cultural dance or singing by ethnic-specific performing groups, design and build skill-based workshops around ethnic or culturally specific styles of art and craft such as pottery, textiles, or musical instruments
Fine arts	Painting, sculpting, photography, architecture
Performing arts	Ballet, opera, theater, and symphonies performed on stage or other settings in public spaces
Communication arts	Theater arts for television, radio, speech, some modern dance, children's theater, extemporaneous theater, improvisational theater
Sensual arts	Arts experiences that provide exploratory use of the senses
Child art	Initial mark making, painting or drawing before reading and writing skills develop, children's representations of and experimentations with life in visual forms or performances, sidewalk chalk

Adapted from N.D. Arnold, 1978, "Pop art: The human footprint in infinity," *Journal of Physical Education, Recreation and Dance* 49(8): 56-57.

Table 17.2 Examples of Professional Positions in Arts and Cultural Organizations

Museums and visual arts	Performing arts	Community arts	Media	Education and public programs
Memberships and visitor services, University of New Mexico Art Museum	Marketing coordinator, Portland'5 Centers for the Arts, Oregon	Community engagement manager, Portland'5 Centers for the Arts, Oregon	Content marketing specialist, Gallery Systems, international locations	Museum educator, Midway Village Museum, Rockford, Illinois
Collections manager, Pratt Museum, Homer, Alaska	Events coordinator, Lied Center, Lawrence, Kansas	Youth programs manager, Santa Cruz Museum of Art and History, California	Studio producer, Swift Agency, Portland, Oregon	Public programs and marketing assistant, Isabella Stewart Gardner Museum, Boston, Massachusetts
Curator, National Mining Hall of Fame & Museum, Leadville, Colorado	Director of annual fund, Baltimore Symphony Orchestra, Maryland	Director of programs, The Art of the Rural, Kentucky & Minnesota	Assistant manager, digital communication, Hammer Museum, Los Angeles, California	Education outreach coordinator, Metro Arts Alliance, Des Moines, Iowa
Collections & exhibits coordinator, Albany Regional Museum, Oregon	Associate producer, Oregon Contemporary Theatre, Eugene	Project manager, Art in Public Places at Washington State Arts Commission, Olympia	Manager & web developer, University of Oregon-Eugene	Project assistant, Imagination International, Inc., Eugene, Oregon
Development manager, Boise Art Museum, Idaho	Lease relations & events manager, Gallo Center for the Arts, Modesto, California	Community arts coordinator, Utah Department of Heritage and Arts, Salt Lake City	Web development & graphic designer, Backcountry Gear, Eugene, Oregon	Public programs coordinator, Hollywood Theatre, Portland, Oregon
Gallery assistant, Cultural Arts Council of Estes Park, Colorado	General manager, Hopkins Symphony Orchestra, Baltimore, Maryland; Executive director, Mid-Atlantic Symphony, Ocean Pines, Maryland	Development associate, Portland Art Museum, Oregon	Software trainer, Making Everlasting Memories, Cincinnati, Ohio	Director of marketing & music education, Eugene Concert Choir, Oregon

activities in recreation and leisure settings. The diversity of positions further illustrates the growth that is taking place in arts and culture programming. Part of this growth stems from changes in participation in arts and cultural activities that we touch on next.

PARTICIPATION IN ARTS AND CULTURE ACTIVITIES

Arts and culture recreation opportunities are increasingly sought after by contemporary individuals, families, and groups who want to connect with a variety of people in their communities. Many activities compete for people's time: sports, concerts, birthday parties, meetings, community picnics, hikes in the woods, cultural celebrations, religious commemorations. Why is interest in arts and cultural events increasing? Reasons cited include the number and variety of experiences available, organizational initiatives, arts education, inviting venues, and participant expectations (Carpenter, 2013). Participation in arts and culture must also be viewed outside organizational or agency contexts. From knitting to bicycle repair to individually created modifications for Minecraft and other forms of maker and do-it-yourself (DIY) culture in digital and physical spaces, people are participating directly in group and individual activities of creative expression. Quantification of this change in venues and definitions for arts participation was first identified in a report by the National Endowment for the Arts (2011b). For almost 30 years, this report has tracked the numbers of public participants in the arts. The report was previously based on art forms such as opera, theater, and ballet, but in 2008, participation criteria was revised to include access to the arts via the Internet and digital tools as well as creating arts and crafts. After this revision, the data indicated that that at least 75 percent of Americans participate in the arts. Contemporary participatory culture and **participatory arts,** in which the public assists in contributing to or making the art, are often perceived as welcoming because there are relatively few barriers to artistic expression and civic engagement.

As interest in arts and cultural participation has proliferated, ideas regarding who provides arts and cultural experiences and where such experiences are encountered have expanded (Americans for the Arts, 2017; Arts Midwest & Metropolitan Group, 2015; Carpenter, 2008, National Endowment for the Arts, 2011b). Communities are now reclaiming public squares, plazas, gardens, and more as democratic spaces where conversations and performances occur and diverse members of society mingle (Project for Public Spaces, 2017). Individuals and their related social groups interested in arts and cultural activities are moving away from nights spent reading on their tablets, playing Xbox at home, or examining others' lives on reality television. Unique festivals, maker spaces hosted in libraries or community centers, or performances held outside of as well as within traditional arts settings and digital sites bring audiences, artists, and administrators together. As Rosewall (2014) reflected, "Arts participation has moved out of arts-specific venues like concert halls and museums and into bookstores, community centers, homes, and city streets" (p. 3). People are seeking arts experiences in their everyday lives within their local neighborhoods, outdoor settings, or otherwise easily accessible locations. Recreation professionals are essential to providing these arts and cultural activities within specific neighborhoods or regions for all audiences. For example, the Oregon Arts in the Parks program features up to five Oregon artists making presentations about the historical and cultural significance of their crafts at state parks across Oregon. Arts in the Parks was developed by the Oregon Folklife Network (OFN) in collaboration with the Oregon Parks and Recreation Department (OPRD), the Oregon Arts Commission, and the Oregon Cultural Trust. These programs showcase

Photo courtesy of Oregon Folklife Network.

Fiber artist Pat Courtney Gold during the Oregon Arts in the Parks program called Artistry Traditions of the Wasco and Klamath Cultures. Gold demonstrates how she makes traditional Wasco Sally Bags, which are functional and decorative art objects made with local grasses or fibers, and explains the significance of motifs in Wasco and Klamath weaving. In this example, we see participants learning directly from an artist in a scenic setting of Collier Memorial State Park.

cultural traditions such as folk music, fly-tying, basket-weaving, and storytelling in Oregon while bringing people together to enjoy and learn about state parks. Such opportunities allow residents and visitors to converge in egalitarian settings of parks and other public spaces to share arts and cultural experiences. Parks and open spaces are enhanced and more fully treasured by neighborhoods, community members, and tourists when artists and cultural leaders perform or lead events that show the benefits and opportunities of community engagement within the natural space.

Arts and cultural programs have become more visible because of administrative initiatives to provide arts and cultural experiences and because arts programmers have been responsive to the desires of people for more choices of things to do during their discretionary time. Though still constrained by funding parameters, outlets for marketing, and limited staffing, successful efforts to build arts participation have resulted from restructuring efforts undertaken by small nonprofit and community-based arts organizations as well as large nonprofit and commercial arts institutions (Friedenwald-Fishman & Fraher, 2016; McCarthy & Jinnett, 2001). Such practices show ways that the arts and culture sector contributes to and benefits a healthy economy and diverse and healthy society.

BENEFITS OF ARTS AND CULTURAL RECREATION OPPORTUNITIES

Arts and cultural activities may initially appear to be in competition with social service providers and programs. However, individual and group-based arts and cultural activities provide benefits in their own right and offer additional support for health and human service programs and the social needs of mental, physical, and occupational support by providing skill development and social connection. Studies have shown multiple benefits associated with personal, social, economic, and environmental leisure (Arts Midwest & Metropolitan Group, 2015; Canadian Parks Council, 2011; Ontario Ministry of Tourism & Recreation, 1992). For individuals, such rewards may be the personal pleasure of the immediate experience, individual growth, social connection, or skill building through involvement in focused learning. For communities, we find increases in economic strength, social identity, and shared values.

Individual Benefits of Arts and Culture

Examining how people in a democratic society choose to spend their discretionary time has been of interest to recreation professionals and arts managers whose jobs are to develop and produce arts and cultural programs. It is important to understand the expected benefits that people realize during leisure engagement. Feelings of individual freedom and choice characterize leisure and are central to the nature of creative activity (Carpenter, 2013; Kelly

& Freysinger, 2000). Further, the arts add excitement and joy to life, and arts-related experiences can create an understanding and appreciation of the arts throughout one's life (Orend, 1989). By offering programs in crafts and culinary arts, music and dance, poetry and weaving, hiking and tree climbing, parks and recreation professionals provide people with the best opportunities for enjoyment through creative endeavors, quiet contemplation, and adventuring.

Benefits realized from arts and cultural participation vary by individual and type of experience (Carpenter, 2013). Further, repeat participation in certain leisure activities is due, in part, to the unique benefits people receive from participation. Though many people might participate in the same experience, such as playing in a community jazz band, it produces different benefits for different people. One person might relish the music while another might delight in the friendships that jamming with others facilitates.

An example of joy in arts participation is *cosplay* (costume play), which can be seen at Comic-Cons (comic conventions), Harry Potter book releases, Star Wars nights at sport events, or live symphony performances of a film score while the film plays. Though anyone can cosplay anywhere, such specific events invite artists, fans, academics, and other interested participants to engage with contemporary and historic impacts of popular culture and related art forms (Comic-Con International: San Diego, 2016). Cosplayers design, create, and present their costumes because they enjoy it just as other individuals enjoy leisure activities such as sports, hobbies, or needlework. Events such as Comic-Con also host audiences who will very likely appreciate the skill, time, and attention taken to create such costumes and who will celebrate individual interests.

Social Benefits of Arts and Culture

Together with individual benefits of arts and culture in leisure settings, research shows us that there are important **social benefits**. For example, Driver and Burns (1999) suggested that social benefits of involvement in arts and cultural experiences include cultural and historical awareness and appreciation; social support; understanding

Photo courtesy of Michelle McKeon.

Dr. Who cosplay fans. This family participated in a regionally sponsored cosplay contest. They designed and built the costumes and props because of their personal interest and fan practices around the televised series and character, *Dr. Who*. The intensive creative process and cleverness of the final products were rewarded through recognition on social media sites and at a special event. Most important, they were individually satisfied with the labor, time, and skill they applied in development of this work.

and tolerance of others; community integration; social bonding, cohesion, and cooperation; and reciprocity and sharing. Additional social benefits that contribute to community building include reduction of alienation or antisocial behaviors for youth and adults, promotion of ethnic and cultural harmony, bonding for families and neighbors who participate in recreation together, community pride in the quality of the local leisure programs and facilities, and opportunities to increase civic engagement and shared management and ownership of local resources (Ontario Ministry of Tourism & Recreation 1992). Next, we discuss some ways that these social benefits are offered through organizations, groups, and communities.

Group Benefits of Arts and Culture

Professionals in recreation and leisure have recognized individuals' desires to participate in arts and cultural activities and other recreation and leisure activities with friends, family, and other community networks (Arnold, 1978). This notion has been further corroborated by national U.S. data suggesting that 73 percent of study participants identified the opportunity to "socialize with friends or family" as the top motivator for attending arts events and activities (National Endowment for the Arts, 2015, p. 10). Beyond attendance and participation with friends and family, volunteering in arts and cultural activities provides direct group benefits.

Volunteering is a serious leisure pursuit that has gained increased importance in arts and cultural agencies (Stebbins, 1992; Stebbins & Graham, 2004). Stebbins (1992) found that **serious leisure** is the systematic and determined pursuit of an activity by an individual or group of amateurs, hobbyists, or volunteers. Volunteering affects arts and cultural organizations and participants because volunteers donate hours and expertise to advance an organization's mission and programs and volunteering serves as a leisure experience for the individual and for groups who volunteer together around a purpose or cause (Carpenter, 2013). In particular, Stebbins (2005) explored the concept of **project-based leisure** contributing an understanding of group behavior and benefits. Group project-based serious leisure provides clear purpose, drive, and social connections; an example of this can be found at Lotus World Music Festival in Bloomington, Indiana, which hosts more than 600 volunteers. The connections and sense of contribution to the larger Bloomington community maintain cohesive group behavior that then generates successful outcomes for the volunteers and for the festival. Without the support of these annually consistent project-based volunteers, Lotus would not hold the same strong national and international reputation or local and regional educational and economic collateral.

Community Benefits of Arts and Culture

Arts and cultural recreation experiences are socially significant beyond the friend, family, or volunteer group benefits previously described. Shared recreational pursuits are based on kinship, friendship, special interests, work, and neighborhood contexts (Gray, 1984) in which people build a sense of community with others. Community benefits of arts and culture in recreation and leisure abound. For example, researchers in Philadelphia found that local cultural activity has a dramatic influence on neighborhoods (Stern & Seifert, 2002). Their findings showed that cultural activity creates positive social environments and results in greater civic participation and gradual residency growth; reduction of neighborhood, ethnic, and class divisions; and lower truancy, delinquency, and poverty rates. Stern and Seifert (2015) further found that sense of community values and connection, school effectiveness, and greater safety can arise with arts and cultural offerings in public settings. This can be seen when arts, recreation, and community come together around **creative placemaking**, which is when public, private, not-for-profit, and unincorporated community sector entities strategically partner and plan to shape the economic, physical, and social character of a neighborhood, town, city, or region around arts and cultural activities (Markusen & Gadwa, 2010).

A unique example that highlights the social and economic community benefits of creative placemaking is the Arts Foundation for Tucson and Southern Arizona (Arts Found Tucson), formerly known as the Tucson Pima Arts Council. This area in southern Arizona has a wide range of ethnic groups and is near the border with Mexico. Since 2008, Arts Found Tucson's people, land, arts, culture, and engagement (PLACE) initiative has sought to enhance the region's historical and contemporary assets as well as systemic problems of imbalanced cultural groups and geographic landscapes through creative expression opportunities, increased arts education, economic development in the creative sector, and changes in public cultural policy. This focus has ultimately built a strong identity and sense of place for the community (Stern & Seifert, 2009; Tucson Pima Arts Council, 2013b). Collaborating with artists and arts organizations, parks and recreation programs, government entities, private foundations and businesses, volunteers, and citizens in specific neighborhoods, PLACE has facilitated social cohesion, belonging, and distinct cultural and community identity based in a Mexican–American borderland and desert territory (Tucson-Pima Arts Council, 2013a, 2013b) that is continually shifting. The PLACE initiative has led to successful

Photo courtesy of Youth Art Exchange.

Children and adults interact with a pop-up chalk wall, which is a temporary interactive creative space for sharing ideas and artwork that was created by Youth Art Exchange members to inspire conversation with and creation by passersby and neighbors on a street corner in San Francisco.

outcomes for employment and tourism, increased civic engagement, high rates of arts-related businesses and spending on arts and cultural endeavors, improved property values and public safety, and other positive economic effects for the region.

Festivals are another form of creative placemaking. Festivals bring a temporary sense of social connection, identity, and value to a specific geographic location or cultural group. Arts managers and parks and recreation agencies often produce large-scale public festivals, and many hold art fairs and festivals as part of significant promotional and fundraising efforts. Participants' beliefs about the social benefits of a festival may include an enhanced image of the community, a sense of community well-being, or the ability to have a variety of cultural experiences. These positive effects can be weighed against social costs such as reduced local community privacy, overcrowding, and increased noise levels during the festival (Delamere, 2001; Delamere & Rollins, 2008; United Nations Environment Programme, n.d.). Whether at large-scale festivals such as Coachella or Burning Man or art fairs in local parks, socially responsible tourism must be practiced when developing festivals. The local host community's identity and values, economic operations and benefits, and social services must also be recognized and supported (International Labor Organization, 2013). Building relationships between festivals and their host communities brings health and well-being for individuals, the environment, and communities.

Educational Benefits of Arts and Culture in Recreation

Historically, general knowledge of arts and culture and appreciation for and aptitudes in the many forms of artistic and cultural expression were developed in school, craft workshop, or family settings. Research shows that early exposure to recreation and arts experiences, arts learning, growth in a skill set, and the valuing of the arts and recreation by family members and peers leads toward continuing participation in adulthood (Iso-Ahola, 1980; Kleiber, 1999; Orend, 1989; Powell Hanna, 2016; Zakaras & Lowell, 2008). Further, knowing oneself and how to understand, participate in, critique, solve problems, and seek change in the varied cultural values and orientations in democratic civic

life are benefits of education in arts and culture activities in leisure settings (Chapman, 1978, 2003; Darts, 2004; Freedman & Stuhr, 2004; Kelly, 1996; Lanier, 1969; McFee, 1961, 1978; Tavin, 2003). Arts education in public schools dates back to the late 1800s and typically included drawing, painting, music, dance, and theater at the elementary and secondary levels. Recently, the value of arts education and teacher training programs has waxed and waned dependent upon political priorities. Shifts in teaching practices and educational goals as well as budget constraints in school districts show that American public schools are no longer adequately preparing students to participate in artistically and culturally rich lives (National Endowment for the Arts, 2011a; Wallace Foundation, n.d.; Zakaras & Lowell, 2008). As these cycles have evolved, partners outside of school settings have emerged to advocate for, support, stimulate, or restore the loss of school arts programs (Webster, 2003). This has resulted in an expansion of arts education programs offered in community arts centers, professional artist residencies in schools, and after-school classes offered by recreation and nonprofit organizations. Those working in schools, community centers, or after-school programs might be trained as arts education specialists, education generalists, or professional or amateur artists or interpreters of art (Webster, 2003).

For example, Youth Art Exchange in San Francisco (2016) provides free classes, field trips, and events in fashion design, architecture, photography, dance, music, and other art forms to low-income high school students. Participants learn from local professional artists about ways of thinking, creating, and leading through creative practice. Through opportunities for expressive activity, participants apply their creative abilities and further their potential (Sternberg, Grigorenko, & Singer, 2004; Sternberg, Kaufman, & Pretz, 2002), and ultimately, they begin to think like studio artists. This allows students to acquire and apply specific techniques; persist in sustained work even when it is challenging; visualize new ideas, forms, or practice; express personal voice and ideas; observe and critique; and better understand art, themselves, and the world by trying new things, taking risks, and engaging and persisting to build on mistakes (Csikszentmihalyi, 1990; Hetland, Winner, Veenema, & Sheridan,

2007). Students also have the opportunity to host public exhibits and performances of their creative work, participate in youth arts summits, and work with neighborhoods throughout San Francisco on public art and architecture projects such as the ART/LIT Living Innovation Zone on Fulton Street, the Excelsior Neighborhood Art Cart, the Persia Triangle Kiosk, and the Bayview Asian Garden. In addition, through events and pop-up exhibits on street corners, in parks, and other public and private spaces, these students are able to democratically "speak back" to the community about locally needed social change to support low-income and racially disadvantaged teenage youth within a city that is almost 80 percent white and Asian and only 16 percent of the population is under the age of 18 (MTC-ABAG Library, n.d.). As Vincent Lanier (1969), an influential 20th century art educator, stated, "Art education must engage the 'guts and hopes' of youngsters [and] give the art class a share of the process of exploring social relationships" (p. 314). This combination of opportunities provides students who would otherwise be unable to access these resources with time, space, and tools to build individual skills in an art form, learn how to self-critique and reflect, collaborate with others toward end goals, experience real-world practice, and network with local institutions.

Economic Benefits of Arts and Culture Recreation Opportunities

A recent study by the National Recreation and Park Association (2015) showed the important economic effects of local and regional park agencies. Information generated by various studies shows that when community leaders invest in the arts and parks, they also invest in the economic health, tourism, and livability of their local communities (Bourdieu, 1986; City Parks Forum, 2008; Coleman, 1988; Edin & Kefalas, 2011; Portes, 1998; Putnam, 2000; Stack, 1975). Cultural activities attract tourists and spur the creation of ancillary facilities such as restaurants and hotels and the services needed to support them. Cultural facilities and events enhance property values, tax values, tax resources, and overall profitability for communities. In this way, the arts are direct contributors to urban and rural revitalization (Americans for the Arts, 2017; Conference Board of Canada, 2008; National Governors Association, n.d.). Further, arts and culture and park activities not only offer individual and social health and wellness, but they also attract companies and educated workers to geographic regions. This results in greater economic health and wellness for communities, local governments, and business enterprises (Americans for the Arts, 2017; City Parks Forum, 2008; Florida, 2002).

The following examples describe some aspects of the **economic impact** of arts and cultural and parks participation in the United States and Canada:

- The total economic activity in the nonprofit arts industry in the United States was $166.3 billion during 2015 (the latest data sets available). $27.5 billion in revenue for local, state, and federal governments was generated, 4.6 million jobs supported, $63.8 billion spent by arts and cultural organizations, and an additional $102.5 billion spent in event-related expenditures by nonprofit arts audiences (Americans for the Arts, 2017).

- As of 2013, 76 percent of all leisure travelers (129.6 million total leisure travelers) in the United States have been defined as cultural or heritage travelers, which means they have participated in cultural, arts, heritage, or historic activities or events on their most recent trip or within the past three years (Mandala Research, LLC, 2013). Cultural tourists spend more and stay longer than other types of U.S. tourists. Further, nonlocal U.S. arts patrons who attend performances, festivals, and other events spend almost twice as much as local attendees do.

- Statistics Canada (2016) estimated that the direct economic impact of culture industries (arts, cultural, library and archives, media and film, and heritage) was $61.7 billion in 2014, or 3.3% of the country's gross domestic product, which is higher than either agricultural or sports-affiliated economic impacts.

- The Canadian Tourism Commission routinely gathers data that describe the demographics, market size, and cultural activities of festival tourism participants. These participants, referred to as *festival tourism enthusiasts,* exhibit sustained interest in festivals when they travel.

- In 2013, local and regional public park agencies in the United States generated almost $140 billion in total economic activity (National Recreation and Park Association, 2015).
- As of 2009, C$5.2 billion in spending was attributed to Canada's national, provincial, and territorial parks (Canadian Parks Council, 2011).

As these examples show, arts and cultural activities and parks make significant contributions to the economic health of communities, regions, and countries.

CONTEMPORARY TRENDS FOR RECREATION PROFESSIONALS WHO IMPLEMENT ARTS AND CULTURE ACTIVITIES

Contemporary strategies enhance participation and the planning and implementation of arts and cultural activities. Such practices include recognizing changing generational values and lifestyles, offering connections in a variety of digital and physical public spaces, and addressing access and opportunity as well as concerns of equity, inclusion, and diversity. To gain a clearer picture of current trends in arts and cultural programming, this portion of the chapter looks at roles played by parks and recreation, festivals, artists, government and foundations, and private enterprises. The last portion of the chapter examines several contemporary strategies in providing arts and cultural experiences.

Managing Arts and Culture in Parks and Recreation

Parks and recreation agencies have traditionally provided a number and variety of arts and cultural opportunities for people of all ages. Arts and cultural activities have been part of comprehensive recreation programs and training offered to the public at community, state and provincial, regional, and national levels since the beginnings of arts-related

recreation programs at Hull House in Chicago and the playground movement in Boston (Carpenter, 2013). Programming in public recreation settings requires planning and design, administration and management, and leadership and creativity whether focused on arts and culturally integrated environmental activities, sports and games, volunteering, and social recreation or typical categories such as art, crafts, dance, drama, and music (Corbin and Williams, 1987; Farrell & Lundegren, 1978, 1983, 1991; Kraus, 1966, 1979, 1985). No matter the type of programming, the programmer's task is facilitating individual and group engagement in leisure based on their understanding of how leisure is experienced (Rossman, 1995; Rossman & Schlatter, 2008).

To be most successful, arts and cultural activities—whether festivals, historical reenactments, musical or theater performances, or culinary events—must emphasize procedures associated with cultural patterning. Such patterning is based on structured needs assessments, program development, implementation, evaluation, and modification (Carpenter & Howe, 1985). One successful cultural pattern example is found in Cumberland Trail State Park (CTSP). Bobby Fulcher, park manager for CTSP (personal communication, May 10, 2016), notes that extensive fieldwork completed over the past 35 years via the Tennessee State Parks Folklife Project (Tennessee State Library and Archives, n.d.) has been highly influential on continuing opportunities for arts and cultural engagement throughout the park system in Tennessee. Modifications in programming based on findings of this fieldwork have led to opportunities for individuals and groups to engage with permanent and temporary exhibitions, online and physical archives, publications, recordings, 27 folklife festivals (some of which have operated for 20-30 years), 21 oral history projects, and 14 regular park-sponsored jam sessions (B. Fulcher, personal communication, May 10, 2016). Cumberland Trail State Park offers a unique arts and culture program that extends well beyond the geographic boundaries of the park: the world's only known active recording label connected with a park. Along with the recording label, the park is the only known state or national park with a consistent weekly, lengthy, interpretive broadcast that features local and regional musicians who play bluegrass, gospel, rockabilly, ballads, vintage country, western swing, blues, and other unique music styles specific to the location of this park system (WDVX, n.d.). For the past 15 years, this weekly radio program has been broadcast on local airwaves and available via webcast. This broadcast and the recording label, along with the live performances, were put into place based on cultural patterning information that showed desire for a regular outlet and celebration of Appalachian and bluegrass music in regional parks and leisure settings. As Fulcher noted, "I've considered it [the recording, broadcast, preservation, and broad reach of our arts programs] fundamental work for responsible management of state park resources" (personal communication, May 10, 2016).

Arts and Cultural Festivals in Parks and Recreation Settings

The social and economic benefits of community festivals highlight the importance of individual, group, organizational, and community engagement in arts and culture (Delamere, Wankel, & Hinch,

2001). Urban and city parks have been important settings for arts and cultural programs. In the late 19th century, parks commonly hosted parades, festivals, cultural celebrations, and musical events. By the beginning of the 20th century, dance, theater, and the new medium of film began to be represented in parks programming (City Parks Forum, 2008).

Festivals and other gatherings throughout North America have shown the rich diversity of cultures, landscapes, and interests in topics that range from mushrooms, to wool, to fisher and cowboy poetry, to world music, to local heritage. Congdon and Blandy (2003) found that participating in the culture of everyday life through art—broadly conceived of as *folklife*—is something all of us do. The authors describe a direct relationship between arts and culture and everyday life that includes the myriad ways in which people assemble, work, and act together for a variety of political, aesthetic, economic, familial, religious, and educational purposes. Within this context, the inclination to make and appreciate art is so ordinary that its extraordinary contributions to commonplace activities such as cooking, fishing, keeping house, gardening, computing, and the many other endeavors of daily life is often

Jules Abbott, University of Oregon Museum of Natural & Cultural History.

The art of fly-tying as shown by fly fisher and fly-tier Sherry Steele. Fly-tying is an example of a folklife practice that is also an arts and cultural activity often shared in park settings.

overlooked. Such folklife practices are honored at cultural events such as the National Folklife Festival and the Smithsonian Folklife Festival in the United States that are well-known internationally. The Niagara Folk Arts Festival (NFAF) in St. Catharines, Ontario, is billed as "Canada's oldest continually-running Heritage Festival" celebrating the "blend of the cultures and people that make Canada a nation to be envied" (NFAF, n.d., para. 1). Diverse culinary arts, music, dancing, visual arts, balls, tours of historic sites, parades, costuming, and other forms of entertainment from the variety of ethnicities and cultural backgrounds are on display in parks and other recreational settings throughout the month of May each year. Further, the festival hosts a Canadian citizenship ceremony for those members of the region newly recognized as formal Canadian citizens. This is a celebration of rich cultural diversity and immigration in the largest city of the Niagara Falls region.

Artists in Parks and Recreation

Beyond festivals, direct sponsorships of artists and art practices have long-held traditions from historical commissions by nobles of kingdoms and the Catholic Church to current commissions by corporations, foundations, or government entities. The U.S. National Endowment for the Arts sponsors the Traditional Arts Apprenticeship grant programs (TAAP) in several states to support preservation and passing down of traditional practices from skilled crafters and artists to those who are apprentices in the art or craft. For example, by hosting specific events at parks and reservoir sites to celebrate and showcase specific artists, Traditional Arts Indiana (n.d.) expands public awareness of traditions and cultural values in Indiana's traditional arts practices through interviews, audio or video recordings, photographs, archives and publications, webinars, exhibits, and other public programming. Based on the success that Traditional Arts Indiana has had in parks, the Indiana Arts Commission began a new $300,000 Arts in the Parks initiative in 2015 that encourages public participation in state parks and forest systems through arts activities such as artist residencies, performing arts events, exhibitions, creative hands-on activities, and educational residencies (Indiana Arts Commission, n.d.). As the examples of the Niagara Folk Festival and Traditional Arts Indiana show, engagement in diverse arts experiences around everyday leisure is desired throughout North America.

Photo courtesy of Irene Lupham and Alex Llumiquiger Perez.

Alex Llumiquinga Perez shows his skills at Andean Charango and Quena Instrument Making, a traditional Andean practice supported by Oregon's Traditional Arts Apprenticeship Program.

Government-Sponsored Arts and Culture in Public Spaces

Government agencies are offering community members more opportunities to engage in arts in public spaces. For example, 28 states and territories in the United States and Canada have Percent for Art programs that designate a certain percentage of funds toward public art when building or remodeling new public structures or related activities (National Assembly of State Art Agencies, 2013). In addition, public art can assist in building attractive, livable, interesting communities and neighborhoods, particularly if residents are involved in decision-making and claim ownership of public art in their regions (Knight Foundation, n.d.; Project for Public Spaces, 2017).

Public art support in local communities includes the long-standing traditions of murals and other visual public arts design, submission, and placement programs in metropolises such as Los Angeles and Philadelphia. Since the 1970s, for example, Philadelphia, Pennsylvania, has operated the Mural Arts program (2017). Originally started as an anti-graffiti movement under Wilson Goode, the first African American mayor of Philadelphia, the program has expanded exponentially to almost 3,000 murals created by local, national, and international artists based on specific neighborhood goals and identities. Public art installations assist in engaging the public in democratic process and activity, encouraging discussion and debate about public policy or site-based work, and developing a space as dynamic, exciting, and inviting for neighbors to meet with one another in public spaces (Blandy, 2008).

Private Enterprise and Foundations in Arts and Culture

Private enterprises can take risks to pursue new markets and new arts and cultural experiences whose outcomes are sometimes too uncertain for nonprofit organizations or public entities. Because of this ability to take calculated chances, businesses and industries add to the number and variety of arts and cultural opportunities for people of all ages. Entrepreneurs in particular have created mul-

tiple ways for people to spend their discretionary income during their leisure time. Corporate and small entrepreneurial endeavors exist everywhere, from Nashville, Tennessee to Vancouver, British Colombia, and from Disneyland to Las Vegas to Toronto. Individuals, families, and social groups support local businesses that combine carousels, pizza parlors, and music for birthday parties; buy early access tickets to a favorite touring Broadway production; experience a talented impression artist's performance at the local casino; or watch the Metropolitan Opera at the local cinema. Each of these activities is a form of engagement with arts and cultural programming that is provided by private businesses.

Private-sector enterprises also support public and nonprofit organizations through sponsorships and

Photo courtesy of Julie Voelker-Morris

The Tuskegee Airmen were a group of African American military pilots who fought in World War II in the 332nd Fighter Group and the 477th Bombardment Group of the United States Army Air. This mural is on the side of the building above a corner parking lot in Philadelphia. It commemorates notable individuals from the community, provides a sense of history, and invokes civic pride.

grants. Through advertising sponsorships, general fund sponsorships, or grant funding, businesses provide money to organizations that helps provide arts or cultural offerings. Sponsorships are a way for businesses to advertise themselves and their roles in international, national, or local communities by aligning themselves with respected arts organizations or cultural initiatives. Arts and recreation managers, as well as public school professionals, have become very skilled in securing sponsorships that allow for planning and implementing a wider variety of arts experiences for general and specific publics. Businesses have learned that it is good for business to contribute to their communities in this way. U.S. Bank (n.d.), for example, offers a robust network of arts and culture partnership opportunities that support low- and moderate-income adults and children in playing and creating. The company notes that they want to support areas in which populations are potentially underserved or have less access to museums, aquariums, visual and performing arts centers, and other cultural activities. In addition, U.S. Bank is piloting a program in conjunction with the Minnesota Vikings that seeks to improve the quality, safety, and accessibility of a variety of trails, athletic facilities, playgrounds, and parks (para. 4). Support by private enterprises such as U.S. Bank lowers entry costs for certain types of leisure experiences. As more arts and culture–related leisure experiences become accessible to more people, the choices and opportunities increase; this, in turn, increases the number of people who are able to participate in more, although not necessarily the same, experiences.

Addressing Lifestyle and Value Trends

Recognition of current lifestyle and value shifts is necessary and important to recreational arts and culture leisure programmers. The wide range of audiences for whom programs are planned and implemented is significant. Though defining generations can be challenging, they can generally be described as individuals of an approximately similar age who have experienced specific political changes, economic shifts, or other historical events that may influence their worldviews. Given this definition, recreation professionals must think about different generations and their expectations for programming and how well-being, access, and opportunity factor into each generation's arts interests and needs. Aspects of these expectations are described next.

Millennials, for example, are younger adults who are often single, seek novelty, and might be living at home during questionable financial times (Fromm & Garton, 2013). Arts and cultural activities that are inviting to this generation encourage groups to socialize, are high energy, are of short duration, low cost, digitally marketed, and easily accessible. Following an entrepreneurial model to which many millennials may gravitate, the Back Room Shakespeare project in Chicago, Illinois, presents works that are rehearsed only once and are performed in bars (i.e., back rooms) for a single performance. The locations provide little to no overhead costs to performers or audiences, and they encourage groups to attend together, maintain a high energy and engage audience attention in spaces where other events and activities are happening, and are accessible to most adult audience members because they must comply with physical accessibility laws.

Generation Xers are in the middle of their careers and are often tugged in a variety of directions by children and aging parents (New Strategist Publications, 2004). These individuals seek programs that accommodate families, teach skills and knowledge to children, and provide them with entertainment and enjoyment during their designated leisure time. This can also include time in unexpected leisure opportunities such as in an airport. In partnership with the San Francisco Arts Commission and SFO Museum, San Francisco International Airport (SFO) offers programmed leisure engagement through permanent public art, specifically selected interior design pieces for comfort and aesthetics, rotating exhibitions through the airport terminals, and an aviation library and museum in the SFO International Terminal. Audiences (primarily airline passengers and airport staff) self-select the amount of time and energy to devote to such opportunities. No matter the amount of time available, families, couples, and individuals can be entertained and educated about topics such as arts and disabilities in the Bay Area, histories of airline attire, art disciplines such as prints or pottery, or art movements (see www.flysfo.com/museum for more).

It is important to acknowledge the large number of baby boomers, many of whom are retiring. They are seeking opportunities for their expendable energy, time, and money (Harris & Edelman, 2006). Studies have shown that older people who have consistently participated in a core of leisure activities throughout their lives display positive attitudes toward their leisure over time and lead a more balanced life (Kelly, 1996; Kleiber, 1999). Leisure programming for adults has been a regular activity for over a century and included the Lyceum and Chautauqua movements, among others, of the late 19th and 20th centuries. Lifelong learning for seniors is contemporarily supported by organizations such as the Geezer Gallery (Geezer Gallery, 2016), whose motto is "a whole new old." Geezer Gallery is a not-for-profit organization that spotlights talented senior artists and their creative works. It further offers dedicated studio space for the senior community to create art, participate in workshops, socialize, and exhibit and sell their work. In collaborating with other regional and national organizations, Geezer Gallery builds intergenerational connections by partnering elders of the Siletz Tribe to share art and craft skills with youth from the tribe. Such interactions contribute to studies of therapeutic arts programs and their effects on quality of life and cognitive functioning in the elderly. Geezer Gallery and similar leisure organizations focused on this generation of participants to build on the notion of "being creative in using life experiences to invent new ways of living . . . to be generative and to contribute to one's own life and the lives of those across generations" (Powell Hanna, 2016).

Personal Touch with Multiple Connections

Shared experiences are a common ingredient of many recreation events (Gray, 1984), and they often bring people together who might not share other interests or relationships. Not only do recreation organizations assist in educating the public about leisure options in the arts and culture sector, but they also play a key role in defining and perhaps establishing social values and addressing social inequalities that reinforce the idea that creative opportunities and pleasure for all is a good thing

(Van Deursen & Van Dijk, 2014). Shared live and digital activities that involve others can be beneficial in forming and validating friendships and relationships that revolve around shared passions for arts and cultural experiences.

For example, to reach a wide audience from many walks of life and regions, the Washington National Opera, a program of the Kennedy Center in Washington, DC, partners with the Washington Nationals baseball stadium to simulcast select performances. Through partnerships with the M&M corporation and other generous donors, audience members attend for free and can sit in the outfield lawn (normally for members of the baseball team), enjoy a picnic, and watch the opera on the stadium's jumbotron. This allows a diverse group of people to experience the same musical performance at the same time in the same location. For individuals who are unable to access the baseball stadium, online digital access to productions is available via live streaming. These events also increase access to an art form that can sometimes appear staid, incomprehensible, or less desirable than current popular forms. Having broad exposure to a lesser known art form can increase people's desire for more engagement with the art form, and can therefore increase ticket sales for other opera productions, spread word-of-mouth praise for the performance or the organization, and provide other tangible and intangible benefits to the organization. In addition, it brings audience goodwill and desire to return to the baseball stadium for future leisure events. Organizations such as the Washington National Opera engage audiences where and how they live in contemporary society through multimodal access points—from traditional physical gathering spaces featuring live performances to digital gathering spaces such as live-streaming sites, Second Life, or Instagram.

Access and Opportunity

A wide array of arts and culture programs increases opportunities for diverse members of a community to participate in recreation and leisure settings. Arts and cultural programming that represents specific cultural groups within a region can encourage members of such groups to both produce and consume specific types of art. Encouraging participants from

OUTSTANDING GRADUATE

Background Information

Name: Sarah Turner

Education: BA in American history (with minors in museum studies and gender studies) from Lynchburg College; MS in arts management (emphasis in community arts) from University of Oregon

Awards: 2012 Award for Outstanding Achievement in Museum Studies; 2013 Laurel Award in Curatorial Studies from Jordan Schnitzer Museum of Art; Graduate Teaching Fellowship; Jordan Schnitzer Museum of Art Student Council President, 2013-2014; 2014 Award for Arts and Advocacy for the Lesbian Community from University of Oregon; Emerging Leaders in the Arts Network, 2013-2014

Career Information

Position: Program Coordinator

Organization: Houseguest is a residency program hosted at Pioneer Courthouse Square (PCS), the largest and most accessible public plaza in Portland, Oregon. PCS hosts over 800,000 visitors per month. Houseguest is an experiment in site specificity, collaboration, and participatory public art. The purpose of this project is to provide space, time, and resources for regional artists to install or perform contemporary innovative works while simultaneously training PCS staff to program contemporary art in a public space. In 2016, Houseguest hosted four artists who each receive a stipend of $20,000 and access to PCS over the course of a three-day weekend to implement their project and engage the public around relevant contemporary issues.

Job description: As program coordinator, I work with applicants and selected artists, curators who select the projects, PCS staff who program the space, and the public and other community organizations through outreach and marketing. My administrative duties include running the application platform, generating contracts, and facilitating programming around artists' installations. Nina Simon sums up my practice well: "Risk-takers need 'space-makers' to provide them with the support, the creative license, and the encouragement to try new things, fail, and get up again." I carve out space both physically (in the plaza for artists to display their work to a general, accessible audience) and conceptually (with PCS staff, board, and Portland City Park officials).

Career path: Houseguest aligns with my career goals to develop skills in artistic programming, space-making, community outreach, relationship-based projects, and social practice. This builds on my graduate student work in place-making and community building around the arts.

Advice for Undergraduates

I've learned this: Programming does not equal partying. There is authenticity in people gathering to create and to support creativity that may catalyze social or civic change.

---

a variety of cultural groups expands the diversity of who interacts in these activities, increases opportunities for equitable representation, and encourages greater social health through intercultural communication and participation. Providing access to spaces and activities that might otherwise be inaccessible due to finances, time, location, or opportunity is a goal of the Prince George County Department of Parks and Recreation Arts (PG Parks) division in Riverdale, Maryland (a suburb of Washington, DC). Their mission is to "celebrate the arts and embrace the cultural diversity of Prince George's County and value the contributions of the artists and arts organizations who make this an electrifying and inspiring place to live" (Prince George County Department of Arts and Recreation, n.d.,

para. 1). As part of this nationally award-winning programming, the types of arts and cultural experiences offered by the division range from traditional performing arts and visual arts venues with exhibits, performances, workshops, camps, and classes to an equestrian center and a local radio station. Opportunities abound to attend free concerts, plays, and festivals in parks, community centers, historic sites, museums, and nature centers. PG Parks also features unique programs such as Arts on a Roll, which brings visual and performing arts to groups who want to create and engage in their own creative expression but may not have access to transportation to participate in other locations; Café Groove, which provides monthly opportunities for teens to share their own creative works and meet with a professional artist; and Art on the Trails, which asks "local artists [to] re-purpose materials found along nature trails to create sculptures, totem poles, and other park fixtures that reflect the wildlife and environment of the trail" (Prince George County Department of Arts and Recreation, 2014, para. 2). PG Parks has strategically planted desire in participants for sharing arts experiences, ideas, dialogue, and connections with others. The breadth of rich program offerings aids in addressing continuing calls for cultural equity and the rights of audiences as producers and consumers of culture and the arts in this region (Mauldin, Laramee Kidd, Ruskin & Agustin, 2016).

Equity, Diversity, and Inclusion

Current access to and opportunity for arts participation in public spaces is a social and cultural equity issue that is greater than ever (Mauldin et al., 2016). Organizations, managers, programmers, and educators who provide arts and cultural activities have a legal, moral, and social obligation to serve the public as a whole (Cuyler 2007, 2013; Stein, 2000). Citing examples such as Jim Crow Laws, which prohibited the integration of arts audiences, Cuyler (2013) reminds us that we need to "anticipate and understand the financial, historical, individual, psychological, and social barriers that prevent underrepresented students from pursuing degrees in arts management" (p. 103). In addition, we need to understand that diversity is related to educational background, economic class, country of origin, first language, sexual orientation, physical ability, employment history, gender identity, ethnicity, and many more aspects that make up intersectional human identity (Loden Associates, Inc., 2010). For arts and cultural programming to be equitable, diverse, and inclusive of many in our communities, we need to read literature on these topics; thoughtfully speak with and hear from community members; and reexamine our own policies, practices, and procedures. Such activities can then lead to changes in our organizations, programs, marketing, and education for specific and general audiences (Friedenwald-Fishman & Fraher, 2016; Mauldin et al., 2016).

For example, Know Your City (2016), a nonprofit organization in Portland, Oregon, offers varied series of events and programming to encourage community members to better know and respond to their neighbors by using physical public art and concepts of social justice and creative community development as catalysts. Their board and staff members are diverse in class, race, gender, ability, and other identities. They seek to examine such identities and histories through programming. A series of walking and biking tours tells stories from laborers' histories (loggers, fishers, black pioneers, and Chinese immigrants), specific neighborhoods or districts (Albina, Halprin, Jade) in the city, and specific types of communities (LGBTQIA, food justice, music genres). Publications, lectures, comics workshops, youth-targeted courses, and specific portable and digital art and history projects round out the organization's overarching goals to expand and connect cultural studies, history of place, and contemporary community needs. Originally, this was a small unincorporated group interested in these topics and needs in the Portland region. Demand increased to such an extent that incorporation was necessary for managing its operations and overall desired outcomes. Know Your City's programming through arts and cultural events and projects clearly allows residents and visitors to Portland to better understand themselves, details of Portland's past and public art within local blocks, and their relationship within the larger community historically and contemporarily.

SUMMARY

As we have seen in this chapter, informal groups, nonprofit organizations, private companies, municipalities, and state and national sites across North America are offering more arts and cultural activities in parks, forests, gardens, libraries, sidewalks, and other public settings. Audiences are seeking and requesting more democratic events and activities in public and digital spaces rather than in formal or difficult-to-erect and maintain buildings. Pop-up and mobile arts and culture events and programs are highly popular because they are inexpensive and readily accessible and offer a quick sampling of experiences that provide a sense of innovation, quality, and novelty.

This chapter provided evidence of the importance of arts and cultural activities throughout historical and contemporary experiences of leisure in parks and recreation. People have enjoyed arts through recreation and parks programming for a lifetime of engagement, learning, individual health, and social networking. Programmers of arts and cultural recreation throughout North America need to remain open to alternative ways of bringing experiences to traditional and new audiences in unanticipated or previously unimagined ways. Recreation professionals with interest in providing arts and cultural experiences need to keep abreast of current trends in the field and find multiple partners for funding and programming that provide individual, group, and community benefits. Arts and cultural experiences continue to communicate and critique our social values, help us understand contemporary and historical life, and be vital to our individual and social well-being.

CHAPTER 18

The Nature of Recreation and Leisure as a Profession

Denise M. Anderson and Tracy L. Mainieri

Brand X Pictures

> " We don't build bridges; we build the people who build bridges. "
>
> Fran McGuire, professor, Clemson University

LEARNING OUTCOMES

After reading this chapter, you should be able to do the following:

> ❯ Describe the benefits of the recreation and leisure profession for society and the practitioner
> ❯ Outline the six criteria of a profession
> ❯ Define what is meant by a *human services profession*
> ❯ Explain career planning and the nine steps of career positioning
> ❯ List six current trends in the recreation and leisure services profession

Let's be honest. How often have you had a conversation with your parents, aunts and uncles, or roommate about your career choice in recreation and leisure services only to have them say, "Well, that sounds like fun"? Or have you ever tried to explain to your grandmother what recreation and leisure service management is only to have her stare at you blankly and ask why you aren't studying something meaningful like medicine or engineering? Although these comments may be well intentioned, they shed a great deal of light on the misperceptions associated with the recreation and leisure services profession. This chapter provides you with the answers to your friends' and family members' questions and a framework with which to move toward a successful career in the recreation and leisure services profession.

VALUE OF THE PROFESSION AND BENEFITS TO THE PROFESSIONAL

Recreation and leisure services have long provided many benefits to all sectors of society. Because it contributes to the quality of life and enhances communities, the field is identified as a core value within the United States, Canada, and other countries. Those who work in the field enjoy a career with numerous benefits.

Working within a profession that can provide an array of benefits to society can undoubtedly provide a great deal of satisfaction to the professional. But the benefits to the professional go beyond self-satisfaction. For many, the desire to work in the field stems from a love of recreation and leisure. Those professionals have chosen a career path that allows them to combine their passion with their paycheck. For the park ranger, a love of being outside and spending time in some of the most beautiful places on earth lends itself to working to protect those

areas. A student with a passion for travel may end up using that knowledge and interest to help ensure that others develop the same passion. Whatever branch of the profession you choose to enter, you will have the opportunity to live your passion. Certainly, the workplace itself can be a benefit. State and national parks, sport arenas, cruise ships, golf courses, and other leisure spaces are settings that can be beautiful, exhilarating, and just plain fun.

Professionals in the field of parks and leisure services also find themselves drawn to the profession by their love of working with the public. When you are working with the public, no two days are the same. Boredom tends to be nonexistent because a job in the field provides constant challenges and opportunities for growth as well as interaction with a diverse set of people.

CHARACTERISTICS OF THE RECREATION AND LEISURE SERVICES PROFESSION

Remember that conversation you had with your parents or grandparents about your chosen career path? Part of their concern may have stemmed from the all-too-common confusion about working as a professional in the field. But a strong case can be made that recreation and leisure services is indeed a noble profession. The following six commonly accepted markers explain what makes a job not just a job but a profession, and recreation and leisure services appears to measure up (McLean & Hurd, 2012).

Social Value and Purpose

The first criterion recognizes that a profession must have a social value and purpose. That is, the field in question must contribute to the greater good of society. With its emphasis on health, wellness, youth development, quality of life, community and economic development, the environment, and sustainability, recreation and leisure services easily meets this requirement (McLean & Hurd, 2012).

Public Recognition

The second standard is that the field has public recognition. That is, the public acknowledges the importance of recreation and leisure and, perhaps more important, is willing to pay for it. Certainly, the acknowledgment differs among the various sectors of the field. Spending patterns related to travel and tourism and other forms of commercial recreation differ from those of government-sponsored (or public) recreation. Of course, the means of funding for each are also different. The private sector, or commercial recreation, depends entirely on the willingness of people to choose one product over another (e.g., Disney World versus Six Flags), whereas public-sector organizations such as local parks and recreation agencies get at least a portion of their funding through appropriated government funding such as property and hospitality taxes (McLean & Hurd, 2012).

Specialized Professional Preparation

The third necessary component of a profession is specialized professional preparation, which refers to the degree to which the profession has requirements that those working in the field must meet before they can practice or the degree of professional authority that a practitioner must possess. In recreation and leisure services, three areas are related to this criterion: professional preparation in recreation and parks, a specialized body of knowledge, and **accreditation** in higher education (McLean, Hurd, & Rogers, 2008).

Professional preparation refers to the college and university curricula that have been developed including two-year associate degrees, four-year bachelor's degrees, and master's and doctoral degrees. The four-year bachelor's degree is the most common requirement for entry into a full-time position within the field, although the degree specifications can vary from program to program depending on a student's specific area of interest.

For example, in many recreation and leisure service university programs, students have a choice of concentration areas that might include community recreation management, sport management, camp management, travel and tourism, therapeutic recreation, recreation resource management, and professional golf management. Therefore, although most programs develop their core curricula around accreditation standards, which are discussed next, course requirements following completion of the core delve more specifically into the concentration area requirements.

The specialized body of knowledge refers to whether the field has a unique knowledge base that a practitioner must have to be effective. A cursory look at any recreation and leisure services curriculum might suggest that the field has simply absconded and claimed as its own knowledge from a variety of areas, including communications, management, marketing, and finance, and added a parks and recreation spin on the content. On closer look, however, it becomes apparent that this spin, as well as an increasingly specialized research base that contributes to the overall body of knowledge in the field, has assisted the recreation and leisure services field in developing its own specialized body of knowledge. In fact, an examination of our growing base of literature, exemplified by books about recreation and leisure services and journals focused on the field of leisure research, illustrates the advancements that have been made in understanding how the field is unique. Further enhancing this body of knowledge are practical, defined internship experiences that are required of recreation and leisure services students. These internships allow students to put this knowledge into action. This hands-on experience combined with our growing understanding of the nature of recreation and leisure services as a human services profession provides students and practitioners with the confidence to identify recreation and leisure services as a profession that has a specialized body of knowledge.

Finally, this specialized professional preparation is enhanced through a commitment to accreditation in higher education. Accreditation requires academic programs to meet standards set by a governing body that has identified the critical skills and knowledge needed to work in a profession. Although not all recreation and leisure programs are accredited, those that are have demonstrated to the governing body that their curriculum is designed to teach those skills and has also been successful in doing so, as verified by outcome measurement. Recreation and leisure services enhanced its standing as a legitimate area of scholarship concern through the development and approval of standards by the Council on Postsecondary Accreditation in 1982. Today, the Council on Accreditation of Parks, Recreation, Tourism and Related Professions (COAPRT) is the accrediting body for recreation and leisure services curricula and is recognized by the Council for Higher Education Accreditation (CHEA), which provides oversight to COAPRT.

Existence of a Professional Culture

The existence of a professional culture and related professional associations is the fourth indication that a field is recognized as a profession (McLean & Hurd, 2012). Professional associations are membership organizations that provide a variety of services related to the development and advancement of the field. Professional associations can serve as advocates for the goals of the profession and provide opportunities for networking and con-

tinuing education of their members to advance the profession. For instance, the National Recreation and Park Association (NRPA) has identified three pillars of focus: conservation, health and wellness, and social equity. NRPA serves as an advocate nationally and internationally through interaction with government officials and partnerships with public- and private-sector agencies. Eight primary activities of professional associations have been identified (Edginton, DeGraaf, Dieser, & Edginton, 2006):

1. Advocacy for the profession's ideals
2. Educational opportunities for members
3. Written and electronic communication among members
4. Face-to-face and electronic networking opportunities
5. Promotion of standards of practice
6. Recognition of best practices and exemplary performance by individuals and agencies
7. Research and fact finding that will advance the profession
8. Provision of liability, health, or retirement benefits

All these activities contribute to the growth of individual members and the profession as a whole. See

Students who major in recreation and leisure services often get a large amount of hands-on learning in skills such as programming.

Christopher Futcher/iStock/Getty Images

the web study guide for a partial list of professional associations in the field.

Credentialing and Standards

Fifth, true professions will recognize credentialing, certification, and agency accreditation as key indicators of quality within the field. *Credentialing* refers to qualifications that professionals must meet before they can practice in a field. Although recreation and leisure services, as a diverse field, has no unified credentialing system, various arms of the field have certification processes designed to set standards for practice. Numerous certifications exist for a variety of specific areas ranging from tourism (e.g., event planning) to sport management (e.g., coaching certifications) to park services (e.g., interpretive guides). Two of the most well-known certifications are the certified park and recreation professional (CPRP) and the certified therapeutic recreation specialist (CTRS). Certification ensures that a practitioner in the field has attained a certain level of skill and knowledge as measured by a standardized exam. Practitioners must meet certain education or experience guidelines to sit for the certification exam and, upon successful completion of the exam, earn a predetermined number of continuing education units over a specified time to retain certification, thereby ensuring that their knowledge remains current. Detailed information on the certification processes can be found for the CPRP at www.nrpa.org/cprp and for the CTRS at www.nctrc.org. Like academic programs, public parks and recreation agencies can also undergo an accreditation process through the Commission for Accreditation of Parks and Recreation Agencies (CAPRA) to ensure that they are practicing at a high level with respect to the services they offer. This type of accreditation process also ensures higher levels of professionalism in the recreation and leisure services field (McLean & Hurd, 2012).

Code of Ethical Practice

The final criterion for a profession is that it has developed a **code of ethical practice**. This code outlines the responsibilities of the field to the public and the ways professionals will carry out services in the field. Although the recreation and leisure services profession does not have an overarching code

of ethical practice such as that found in the medical field, individual agencies typically develop their own codes, or, more commonly, professional associations for the various sectors of the field develop codes of ethical practice that agencies then follow (McLean & Hurd, 2012). For instance, the Code of Ethics for the America Therapeutic Recreation Association addresses issues such as autonomy, justice, fairness, and confidentiality (www.atra-online.com). Figure 18.1 illustrates the code of ethics for Greenville County Parks, Recreation, and Tourism.

NATURE OF THE PROFESSION

The recreation and leisure services field is associated with enhancing the quality of life for participants. The goals and outcomes associated with programs, facilities, and services are designed to improve individuals' lives and enhance communities in a variety of ways. For these reasons, a career in recreation and leisure services is a career in a **human services profession**.

Human Services Profession

The human services field has the objective of meeting human needs through an interdisciplinary knowledge base by focusing on prevention and remediation of problems and maintaining a commitment to improving the overall quality of life of those they serve. Human services professions also promote improved service delivery systems not only by addressing the quality of direct services but also by seeking to improve accessibility, accountability, and coordination among professionals and agencies in service delivery (National Organization for Human Services, n.d.). Recreation and leisure services agencies certainly fit this profile. Whether the service population is interested in youth programs, a cruise around the world, a game of tennis, camping, or rehabilitation services, our field is about improving people's lives through recreation and leisure. So, what does that mean for you?

Recreation and leisure services professionals provide numerous services to the public in a variety of ways. Professionals can be direct service providers, information providers, or advocates, or they may take on facilitator or educator roles in the provision of services (Henderson, 2014). A **direct service provider** is a professional who is

---

GREENVILLE COUNTY PARKS, RECREATION, AND TOURISM CODE OF ETHICS

The proper operation of democratic government requires that actions of public officials and employees be impartial; that the government decisions and policy be made within the proper channels of the government structure; that public office not be used for personal gains; and that the public have confidence in the integrity of its government. Recognition of the goals establishes a Code of Ethics for all officials and employees appointed and employed by Greenville County Parks, Recreation, and Tourism.

Code of Ethics:

1. No employee shall use their official position for personal gain; nor shall engage in any business or transaction, nor shall have a financial or other interest, direct or indirect, which is in conflict with the proper discharge of their official duties.

2. No employees shall, without proper legal authorization, disclose confidential information concerning the property, government or affairs of the Department. Nor shall they use such information to advance the financial or other private interest of themselves or others.

3. No employee shall accept any gift valued at more than $25.00, whether in the form of service, loan, item or promise from any person, firm or corporation which is interested directly or indirectly in any manner whatsoever in business dealing with the Department; nor shall employees accept any gift, favor or item of value that may tend to influence an employee in the discharge of their duties, nor grant in the discharge of their duties any improper favor, service or item of value.

4. No employee will accept from any contractor or supplier doing business with the Department any materials or service for the private use of the employee.

5. No employee shall represent private interests against the interest of the Department in any action or proceedings of which the Department is part.

6. No employee shall engage in or accept private employment or render services for private interests when such employment or service is incompatible with the proper discharge of their official duties or would tend to impair their independent judgment or action in the performance of their official duties.

7. Violations of this Code of Ethics may constitute a cause for suspension, removal from employment or other disciplinary action. Ethics violators are subject to criminal prosecution and penalties which include fines and incarceration; violations may be reviewed by the South Carolina Ethics Commission and/or related agencies.

Fiugre 18.1 A well-defined code of ethics will facilitate the adherence to professional standards by organizational staff.

Reprinted, by permission, from Greenville South Carolina.

---

responsible for a program from start to finish and leads the participants through the program. In other words, the direct provider controls the program, and participants are responsible for little more than participating in the program. An example would be a youth soccer league.

A professional who is serving as an **information provider** focuses on facilitating engagement in recreation by serving as a conduit through which information about opportunities available in the community can flow. In addition, this service delivery method may include making direct referrals to specific programs or people so the agency can meet the recreational and other needs of community members. No single person or agency can provide everything that a community wants in terms of recreation. Therefore, an agency that is committed to providing information about other services not provided by its own staff is providing a needed service to the community, although it is not engaged in direct service provision.

A third way that professionals serve the public is by becoming advocates. An **advocate** is a professional who recognizes an injustice that prevents community members from engaging in recreation and leisure services. For example, advocating for people with disabilities is just one role that professionals in recreation and leisure might play. Although the information referral approach would provide people with disabilities with information about activities available to them, it may not recognize the significant barriers to participation beyond lack of knowledge about available opportunities. The advocate would work to gain a better understanding of these barriers and try to help that group overcome the barriers. Therefore, if the barrier to participation in a wheelchair sport was the cost of a wheelchair sport chair, an advocate might work with local agencies or funders to provide those chairs for people with disabilities to increase their participation in recreation and leisure programs.

The final type of service provision is that of a **facilitator** or educator. This type of professional facilitates participants' engagement in leisure such that they are responsible for many of their own leisure experiences. The provision of leisure education is an excellent example of this type of service delivery. A practitioner who can improve the public's attitudes, knowledge, skills, and awareness toward leisure provides the necessary components for community members to meet their leisure needs on their own outside the context of programs offered by direct service providers (Henderson, 2014).

All four of these types of services can be found in the numerous sectors of service provision in the recreation and leisure services profession. From travel and tourism to outdoor recreation to therapeutic recreation, all recreation agencies will likely incorporate direct service provision, information referral, advocacy, and enabling services (Murphy, Niepoth, Jamieson, & Williams, 1991). For example, the nonprofit sector of the field, which includes agencies like the YMCA, is well-known for its direct service provision in which professionals such as after-school program directors and youth sports coordinators work directly with participants. But the same sports coordinator might also serve as an information provider if someone is looking for a youth swim team and the agency does not offer one. The sports coordinator might be able to provide parents with information about the swim team that the parks and recreation department offers down the road. The result is the same

whether the YMCA or the parks and recreation agency offers a swim team: the child gets to swim. The role played by the professional, however, differs based on circumstances. Likewise, a front-desk manager at a hotel may serve the role of information referral provider when she or he directs guests to restaurants in town. On the other hand, a hotel staff member may play the role of an advocate if she or he, after learning from guests that a local attraction is not easily accessible for people in wheelchairs, tries to persuade the attraction to make changes. Making the necessary changes would likely be in the best interest of the attraction and would provide increased leisure opportunities for people who use wheelchairs. There are many various employment opportunities available in the recreation and leisure services profession. Regardless of the type of position a new professional is interested in, he or she should be prepared to serve the public in many ways to provide leisure and recreation opportunities.

A Day in the Life of a Human Services Professional

There is no typical day for a human services professional. The two critical words are *human services*. Professionals who deal with people are in many ways engaged in professions that never sleep. Don't worry—I didn't say *professionals* who never sleep. But dealing with the public, a public that is often passionate about its recreation and leisure pursuits, is indeed a full-time job. The profession works to facilitate the public's quality of life. See the sidebar to look at one day in the life of a professional in the field: a day camp director. With myriad responsibilities from providing a fun, enriching environment for young children while keeping them safe to managing parent expectations and supervising numerous staff, day camp directors have to be on top of their game each and every day.

CAREER PLANNING

Many professionals' first glimpse of the option to work in recreation and leisure services did not occur until they were in college. Others, after working as lifeguards, attending camps as children, or serving as volunteers for special events, knew that providing

A Day in the Life of a Day Camp Director

Working at a day camp with hundreds of children can be highly rewarding, but no two days are the same. The following is an example of the type of work that a professional in this type of position may encounter in one day's time.

7:15 a.m.: Arrive on site. The director unlocks and walks through all activity areas and bathrooms and checks for any setup, maintenance, or safety concerns.

7:30 a.m.: Early shift camp staff arrive. The director sets up the office for the day including daily sign in and sign out sheets, financial forms, parent communications, daily schedule, cleaning list, and other daily needs.

9:30 a.m.: Late shift camp staff arrive. Daily briefing with all staff to make any announcements, schedule changes, or daily notes. Once everyone is ready, the camp whistle is blown and planned activities start.

9:30-10:00 a.m.: All camp "round tree" meeting. The director stays in the camp office to record daily payments received during check in and to sign in late-arriving campers. Assistant director and head counselor make announcements and lead morning songs and activities for the whole camp.

10:00 a.m.: Morning snack. Due to the significant number of food allergies among campers, the director, assistant director, and head counselor each go to a designated eating area to provide additional staff in the event of a food-related emergency. (This also occurs during lunch and afternoon snack.)

10:30 a.m.-12:00 p.m.: Morning activities. While campers are in planned morning activity times, the director works on the schedule and registration list for the following week. Field trips, swim days, and transportation are confirmed for the following week along with any guests coming into camp. Additional camp-wide activities are planned for the following week that relate to the theme. Once the schedule is made, counselors are assigned to groups and given their rosters and schedules to begin planning.

12:00 p.m.: Lunch.

12:45-3:00 p.m.: Afternoon activity rotations. Depending on the day, the director, assistant director, and head counselor rotate through activity areas to address any needs of the campers or counselors, handle any behavior issues that may occur, attend to first aid needs as needed, or participate in activities with campers if time allows. Three days per week, campers swim at an offsite location. The director, assistant director, or head counselor will go to the pool ahead of the campers to help transition the group in and out as well as act as extra eyes in the pool. On field trip days, the director and assistant director will go ahead to the site to pay admission fees and find designated bus parking and the best area for the campers to gather once busses have been unloaded.

3:00-5:30 p.m.: Afternoon pickup. The director catches up on office work and prepares for the next day.

5:00-5:30 p.m.: Daily afternoon cleaning duties and camp lock up. The director signs out afternoon staff once cleaning duties are completed and locks all exterior doors. Once all campers have been signed out, a final check of all areas is conducted, the alarm is set, and staff is finished for the day.

leisure for others was the career path for them. For many, the opportunity to work in recreation and leisure services seems almost too good to be true. People can be paid for providing fun? A major in recreation and leisure services, regardless of area of interest, is often seen as a discovery major. But discovery of the field as a profession is just the first step. Planning for a career in the profession requires taking some specific steps to ensure success. Important steps to making a successful transition to a full-time career are outlined next, and a student benchmark checklist (figure 18.2) is provided that

---

STUDENT BENCHMARK CHECKLIST

This checklist provides suggestions for activities beyond required course work that will make a student more successful and competitive when entering the job market.

☐ Volunteer 50 hours each semester with at least two recreation agencies.

☐ Create and maintain a professional LinkedIn profile.

☐ Find a part-time job in a sector that aligns with your career goals.

☐ Attend one regional professional conference.

☐ Visit the campus career center once a semester for seminars and mock interviews.

☐ Join a professional association and become active in it.

☐ Contact agencies you are interested in working with and familiarize them with your name.

☐ Review your personal social media presence to ensure information is professional.

☐ Complete a 10-week internship (more than one internship is recommended by graduation).

☐ Obtain at least one job in a recreation field.

☐ Job shadow for at least two recreation sectors.

☐ Establish at least one professional mentor in a career field of interest.

☐ Get to know your professors via office hours.

☐ Meet with three different faculty members to discuss career options in your chosen field.

☐ Develop your career portfolio throughout your time as a student (resume, work samples, transcripts and degrees, awards and honors, letters of reference).

Figure 18.2   Students who were intentional in their professional development will be more competitive in the workforce upon graduation.

Created by Tracy Mainieri.

outlines an array of activities that can help a student stand out after graduation.

Education

Education is critical because it's the beginning of your path to success. You may choose to begin with a two-year degree, but a four-year degree is often preferred. Management positions sometimes require a graduate degree, particularly when you are working in higher education such as campus recreation. Employers usually look for degrees from accredited programs in recreation and leisure services. The accreditation process, described earlier in this chapter, helps to ensure that students in a specific academic program are gaining the necessary education to be competent professionals in the field. Program requirements include the education level of faculty members, available facilities such as library and technological resources, and administrative requirements. Accreditation is the hallmark of a

quality degree program that has been vetted by an objective outside group.

Networking and Mentoring

Beyond education, networking can be crucial to getting your foot in the door. **Networking** is the process of developing a list of professional contacts who can assist with your career development. Networking can take place formally or informally. Formal networking may occur through a professional conference where, perhaps with the help of a faculty member, you can gain opportunities to meet professionals in the field whose contact information may be helpful when you start looking for an internship or job. Even if those you meet do not have positions available, they may know other professionals in the field who are hiring. Informal networking is less structured but may be less intimidating and more productive. At a professional conference, job seekers often inundate practitioners, so you may get lost in the crowd. Informal networking opportunities may be a good way to build your list of contacts. Informal networking opportunities can include introducing yourself to staff members at a recreation event that you are attending or volunteering with or talking with a guest speaker outside of class if the opportunity presents itself. Today, popular career networking sites such as LinkedIn can provide job seekers with access to an even broader network of professionals. Regardless of the situation, presenting yourself professionally through your words and actions will go a long way in enhancing your network.

Mentoring is another way to advance your career, and it too can be formal or informal and done early in your career or late in your career. In a formal mentoring program, an agency assigns you to an experienced person who can help you navigate the hiring process (e.g., a graduate of an academic program, a faculty member). The same type of mentoring can take place informally when you identify someone you feel comfortable going to with questions and who can help provide insight into the hiring process. Formal and informal mentoring is more common in the workplace after you are hired. Professional mentoring focuses on how to navigate the process of career advancement, especially the politics of career advancement. Because mentoring can enhance employee satisfaction and commitment, agencies sometimes develop a formal mentoring program. Research has shown, however, that informal mentoring in which the mentor and the mentee are involved in the selection process can be more effective because the parties have a higher comfort level. Either way, a mentor can be an invaluable tool at all stages of your career.

Getting Your Feet Wet

In the field of recreation and leisure services, gaining experience is the most effective way to further your career. The recreation and leisure services field is incredibly hands on. Without that hands-on experience, you will not have success navigating the hiring process. In fact, the hands-on nature of the field is the rationale behind the internship requirement in academic programs. The fact that a typical internship is a 10-week, 40-hours-per-week experience suggests how important it is. Beyond the internship, other ways to gain experience include part-time work and volunteering. Both are excellent ways to increase your experience and make additional contacts in the field. Faculty members recognize how important this hands-on experience is and typically want students to do more than meet the internship requirement, so they build a variety of volunteer experiences into the curriculum. Any future employer will want to see commitment to the profession in the form of related work experience that goes beyond the internship. Although paying your way through school is admirable, doing it in a position that is relevant to the field is both admirable and smart.

Professional Certifications and Continuing Education

As mentioned earlier, one hallmark of a profession is the availability of certifications and continuing education. Certifications are a good way to indicate to a potential employer that you have the skills and knowledge base needed to be an effective employee. The certified parks and recreation professional (CPRP) is one of the most widely known professional certifications in the field and recent research has found a positive link between the CPRP credential and perceptions of job performance capabilities among public park and recreation professionals (Mulvaney, Beggs, Elkins, & Hurd, 2015). Beyond this relationship, additional benefits exist for individuals, agencies, and the profession when staff are certified, including serving as a career kick-starter, career advancement, improved agency performance, and increased legitimacy for the profession (Mulvaney, 2015).

See the sidebar Routes to Eligibility for Sitting for the Certified Parks and Recreation Professionals (CPRP) Examination for more information.

Membership in Professional Associations

Membership in professional associations can be an effective way to address all the points made previously. For this reason, you should begin their membership while still in school. Professional associations are committed to engaging future professionals early, so they often offer significantly

Routes to Eligibility for Sitting for the Certified Parks and Recreation Professionals (CPRP) Examination

To qualify to take the CPRP examination, applicants must

- have just received, or be about to receive, a bachelor's degree from a program accredited by the Council on Accreditation; or
- have a bachelor's degree from an institution in recreation, park resources, or leisure services and have no less than one year of full-time experience in the field; or
- have a bachelor's degree or higher in a major other than recreation, park resources, or lei-

sure services and have no less than three years of full-time experience in the field; or

- have an associate's degree and have four years of full-time experience in the field; or
- have a high school degree or equivalent and have five years of full-time experience in the field.

For purposes of measuring years of experience, one year of part-time work experience in the field (20 or more hours per week) is equivalent to six months of full-time work experience in the field (NRPA, 2016).

Attendance at professional conferences can help practitioners learn about the latest trends in the field as well as provide networking opportunities with other professional association members.

reduced membership fees to students. Professional associations offer numerous opportunities for networking as well as continuing education through their sponsorship of annual meetings, schools, and conferences designed to bring together professionals with common interests. For example, the International Festivals and Events Association offers an annual convention where practitio-

ners from around the world meet to share ideas related to careers in festival and event planning. Another example is the National Association for Interpretation, whose annual workshop brings together more than 600 interpreters to train, network, share ideas, and enjoy a different part of the country as the conference moves from region to region.

CAREER POSITIONING: A NINE-STEP PROCESS

Although planning is an important first step in the road to a career in the field of recreation and leisure services, you may need a systematic plan known as *career positioning* to put yourself in the best launch point for the specific career path that you hope to embark on. Kauffman (2010) outlined nine steps that students can take to position themselves for a career in the recreation and leisure services profession.

Seeking Proximity

First, proximity is everything. You need to determine a career path and locate yourself in various ways to secure that career path. Proximity does not always mean physical proximity; it is an alignment that puts you close to a position. Four main types of proximity are relevant to developing a career. The first type of proximity concerns people. Identifying the people who can help you find a position you want can be key to your success. These people can include faculty members, mentors, and internship and volunteer supervisors. The second type of proximity variable is place. You need to figure out where you want to work. This preference can be influenced by many factors including significant others, family, and desire. You might want a job that will require a move, or you may have to move for other reasons before looking for a job. If you don't restrict your job search by location (and you are not forced to by extenuating circumstances), you will have the most success finding an appealing job because more options are available. A third issue is proximity by organization. You might be interested in working for a specific organization. Your willingness to gain experience with that organization through part-time or volunteer experience may allow greater access to a full-time job because you will have a foot in the door. Finally, you should consider proximity by knowledge, skills, abilities, and other characteristics (KSAOCs) that you possess. A student with a strong set of KSAOCs will often be at the top of the applicant pool if the KSAOCs align with what the agency needs. The applicant is close to the ideal candidate. Therefore, you should identify areas of career interest, examine how your current KSAOCs line up with a desired position, and work to gain additional experience in areas in which you are deficient.

Being Proactive

The second step involves beings proactive rather than reactive. People who wait for jobs to come to them typically find themselves without jobs. Whether by seeking additional credentials, identifying new career opportunities, or doing whatever it takes to advance her or his career, a proactive person will be in a stronger position to meet career goals.

Thinking Evaluation

The third step in positioning yourself for a successful career is thinking evaluation. In other words, ask yourself "Why should they hire me?" This self-evaluation can help you determine your strengths and weaknesses and position yourself for the job you are interested in. If you have identified a specific job of interest, you can compare the KSAOCs you currently have with those outlined in job announcements for the type of position you are interested in. A table can provide a visual representation of where you stand in relation to what employers are seeking. For instance, if you are interested in a position involving youth sport and every job announcement lists a requirement for first aid and CPR training, then you would want to obtain those certifications. After examining the completed table, you can start to identify which KSAOCs you need to start working on to position yourself for the type of position that you desire.

Bridging

The fourth step involves **bridging**, which is preparing for the job you seek. Vertical bridging involves acquiring the KSAOCs that you need to move up in an organization or advance your career. Horizontal bridging entails obtaining the KSAOCs necessary to make a lateral move into a new discipline or career. Academic preparation is one form of bridging. You need to consider a number of variables to determine whether a program will provide the necessary bridge to your desired career. One variable is the academic content of a program or department and whether it is accredited. A second variable is the networking ability of faculty. Is the faculty able and willing to help you make connections with practitioners in the field who can facilitate your career development? Another area to look at is the availability of service learning opportunities within the department. Do class projects or other academic opportunities help you get real-world, hands-on experience that will build your resume? Academic opportunities such as internships, practica, volunteer experiences, and continuing education can help with vertical and horizontal bridging. Other nonacademic experiences such as part-time jobs, volunteer experiences outside of class requirements, and other professional development opportunities can also go a long way whether you are trying to advance your career or change career paths.

Professional Networking

Professional networking, the fifth step to positioning your career, is similar to seeking proximity. Professional networking is all about meeting the people who will either hire you or introduce you to other professionals who will hire you. Networking can take many forms, and some more effective than others. Asking faculty, mentors, or other practitioners which avenues can be the most effective for networking is a good starting point. Attending networking events such as professional conferences, professional meetings, and job fairs can provide the right environment for meeting a wide variety of professionals. In addition, activities such as volunteering will not only build your skill set but also introduce you to professionals who are running the event or program. Kauffman (2010) recommends developing a professional family. A professional family will grow over time as your career grows. If you nurture the family, it can provide you with a wide-ranging net of potential opportunities.

Casing the Joint

The sixth step, casing the joint, sounds less than professional. Casing the joint forces you to examine what you know about a job that you are seeking or the organization for which you want to work. You can use a number of approaches to find out more about jobs in general and specific positions you are interested in. Casing the joint may start with casing the field, which involves identifying trends

and major issues in the field. Gathering this type of information can help you determine growth and hiring trends and give you a better picture of necessary KSAOCs for working in the field both now and in the future. Other ways to learn more about the big picture of the field include becoming a member of a professional organization, reviewing major publications in the field to familiarize yourself with current research and trends, attending conferences and other educational sessions, and identifying major players in the field.

Casing an organization is more specific. In this case, you work to gain a thorough understanding of the purpose of the organization, its structure, and the organizational chain of command. If possible, you may want to try to get a feel for the corporate culture and discern the strengths and weaknesses of the organization. This type of information can help you gain perspective on whether you really want to work for that organization. You also want to find out more about the specific type of position that you are looking for. Obviously, the first step is identifying the position. The next step is to determine the career track of the position and evaluate the match between your KSAOCs and those required of the position.

Finally, you should case the people. Identify the people who will hire for the position. Researching key people can give you insight into the type of people who work for the agency and whether you would want to work for them.

One-on-One Interviewing

The seventh step is the one-on-one interview, which is a positioning technique used to convince an organization that they need you when they have not announced any job openings. Start by identifying the person in the organization you are interested in working for and who might hire you. Kauffman (2010) recommends a seven-step sales model to position yourself for a job in the organization:

1. Identify the organization that you want to work for (your prospect).
2. Engage the decision-maker (the person who will do the hiring).
3. Survey the organization to see how you might fit in.

4. Design a job description and job announcement to use in convincing the person that you would be a good fit for the agency.

5. The employer agrees that the agency needs someone for the job that you are seeking and offers you the position.

6. Negotiate and accept the position.

7. If you are not hired, send a thank-you note or an open-ended note. A note along the lines of "even if you can't hire me now, please remember me" can go a long way in leaving a positive impression.

Formal Interviewing

The formal interview, the eighth step, is a necessary step in response to a posted job announcement. The formal interview can give you the opportunity to move beyond your application or resume. Talking to your strengths and turning weaknesses into strengths as you position yourself as the strongest candidate for a job allows an organization to see how you might fit beyond what they see on your resume. Your resume can get you in the door, and the formal interview might allow you to shut that door on all other applicants.

Developing Communication Tools

Finally, developing communication tools is a vital piece of positioning. If you are not able to communicate with the people whom you hope to work for or with, all other aspects of positioning become irrelevant. Communication tools include resumes, portfolios, cover letters, phone skills, and electronic tools such as e-mail. In addition, social media presence through platforms such as Twitter and Facebook can also be an effective way to communicate. These communication skills will be invaluable when it comes to preparing for the job search, entering the job search, and securing and retaining the position. Good verbal skills in networking can go a long way toward impressing a decision-maker and securing yourself a good contact (at worst) or a foot in the door for a job (at best). These same skills, along with a well-written resume and cover letter, will be instrumental in a one-on-one interview for a specific position. If you are unable to communicate your fit for a position, you are not likely to secure one. Basic skills such as how to answer a phone, speak on the phone professionally, and make appropriate use of technology such as e-mail need to be refined if you expect to be seen as a worthy job candidate and employee. On-campus resources, such as career centers or contacts that you have made in the field including volunteer and internship supervisors, can provide constructive feedback on communication tools such as your resume and cover letter.

Students (and professionals) should keep a few points in mind with respect to e-mail and social networking sites like Facebook. Many students have personal e-mail accounts outside their university accounts on which they have less-than-professional user names. A potential internship supervisor or employer will not react kindly to a resume or e-mail note from someone with a user name like cutiepatootie or studmeister. Although social networking sites are a great way to connect with friends, remember that what ends up on the Internet is forever. Future employers will often run background checks on applicants by simply searching a person's name online. Incriminating pictures or stories can cause a lot of damage to your professional reputation. Therefore, students and professionals alike, regardless of the type of communication tools they use, need to be sensitive to the messages that they convey.

CHANGES IN THE FIELD: RESPONDING TO AN EVER-CHANGING WORLD

As you get ready to embark on a career path in recreation and leisure services, a working knowledge of current trends in the field is instrumental to having a broad perspective of where the field is and where it is heading. Professionals in the field are working in numerous areas to increase the relevance of recreation and leisure services at all levels. All the trends are centered on the profession's overarching mission of increasing happiness and quality of life for all. From the individual micro level to the community and global macro levels, recreation and leisure services improve lives.

Staying on Top of Trends

In the coming sections, you will read about six current trends that are capturing the attention of recreation and leisure services professionals; however, the trends that affect the field at any given time will change. You should develop some skills in identifying trends as they arise. Many of the strategies you just read about for planning and positioning yourself for a career in recreation and leisure services will allow you to stay on top of the trends that affect your profession because they will keep you engaged in the professional conversations taking place in your field. Professionals who regularly attend conferences, visit other agencies to see what they're doing, talk with other professionals, and read professional publications are the ones who have their fingers on the pulse of the field. By regularly engaging in these activities, you will be able to pick up on patterns in what professionals are talking about. For example, by subscribing to and reading your national professional organization's listserv or daily e-mail digest, you may see the same topic come up time and time again; usually, that can point you to a trend you should learn more about. Also, if you're reading the professional publications for the sectors, segments of population, and services you're interested in, you're likely to run across articles and other resources that will identify trends for you. For example, *Recreation Management* magazine releases a state of the industry report each year that provides insight into the trends that affect facility construction, programming, operations, and so on based on a survey it conducts each year with recreation and leisure services professionals (Tipping, 2015).

Environmental Sustainability and Stewardship

One trend in the field is focusing on environmental sustainability and stewardship. Sustainability refers to meeting our current needs for resources, such as food and water, without compromising the ability of future generations to meet those same needs. Environmental stewardship refers to cooperative planning and management that protect environmental resources. Although these topics are not unique to recreation and leisure services, the profession must prioritize the focus on this trend. Many big cities in the United States, including Seattle, Portland, San Francisco, Chicago, and Sacramento, are taking steps to increase their sustainability, but agencies of all sizes can make intentional efforts to be more environmentally sustainable in their practices by considering things like the size of their carbon footprint, the amount of chemicals entering the water system at their facilities, how much waste they produce, and the types of materials they use and by controlling the lighting and temperatures in buildings. For example, City of Boulder Parks and Recreation incorporates a variety of sustainable practices such as native plant management, sustainable golf course management, staff vehicle mileage reduction, alternative fuel vehicle purchases, storm water pollution prevention, and zero waste facilities.

Eugene's Parks and Open Space Department exemplifies the concept of going green. Park workers eschew the use of motorized vehicles and instead ride bicycles with trailers behind them as they work on trails and landscape beds. In addition, Eugene uses no chemical pesticides in six neighborhood parks and has plans to use herds of goats to control invasive plants in park spaces in the summer. Other examples of going green include using vegetable oil rather than diesel fuel in chainsaws and planting trees that shed fewer leaves in the fall to reduce leaf blowing (Lyman, 2009).

Environmental stewardship is critical to sustainability and conservation. Partnerships, often between public and private agencies, go a long way in assisting the conservation and preservation of resources. Examples such as the North Cumberlands Conservation Acquisition initiative illustrate how partners can work together to protect open space for years to come. Without the cooperation of the state of Tennessee, the Nature Conservancy, and two timber companies, Conservation Forestry and Lyme Timber, it would have been difficult if not impossible to protect 127,000 acres (51,000 ha) of land that had been identified as among the most important temperate hardwoods in the world and that served as home to countless unique species (Fyke, 2009).

Also tied to sustainability and environmental stewardship is the trend of ecotourism. The International Ecotourism Society (n.d.) defines

OUTSTANDING GRADUATE

Courtesy of Chela Cervantes.

Background Information

Name: Delores Balogun

Education: BS in recreation and park administration from Illinois State University

Awards: Rejuvenate's 2016 list of 40 Under 40

Affiliations: Professional Convention Management Association

Career Information

Position: National Advanced Associate (Event Planner)

Organization: Contracted by the White House for First Lady Michelle Obama

Job description: I was responsible for planning large-scale events, ranging in attendance from 75 to over 10,000 guests, on behalf of Michelle Obama. My responsibilities included the following:

- Designing and implementing sites and coordinating local and national press and crowd logistics for events
- Developing plans for press coverage, contacts, and logistics as well as overall event production
- Facilitating event management by recognizing difficulties and determining effective solutions
- Engaging, inspiring, and managing volunteers on-site at events
- Facilitating principal movements and communications through briefings, scheduling, and feedback regarding local issues of importance
- Implementing plans for each site to successfully train and engage volunteers in event management duties while developing a plan with state and federal agents to ensure secure, effective events

Career path: I was afforded the opportunity to obtain this position through my work for another organization. While employed by National PTA, I planned a large-scale event for which First Lady Michelle Obama was the guest speaker. In working directly with the first lady and her staff for this event, I was contacted by the White House and offered the position of National Advanced Associate for First Lady Michelle Obama.

While some would believe that the most rewarding part of this job is the ability to work in the White House, the location of this position is a minor point. In reality, one of the most enjoyable parts of this position is my ability to grow *while* working with the first lady of the United States. While I have always been atten-tive to detail and committed to creating unforgettable events, working for First Lady Michelle Obama has afforded me the opportunity to glean from her the expectation and execution of excellence for every event planned. Furthermore it allows me to fulfill one of my dreams: consistently creating memorable events that bring people together.

While I greatly enjoy the opportunity, working as the National Advanced Associate for First Lady Michelle Obama is but an intermediate stop on my career ladder. My favorite quote by Brian Tracy states, "Successful people are always looking for opportunities to help others. Unsuccessful people are always asking, 'What's in it for me?'" And while I feel that working in the recreation and leisure field provides excellent opportunities for growth and demonstration of skill, working in the recreation and leisure field for *yourself* provides *others* with excellent opportunities for growth and demonstration of skill. So while working in this role I have launched a 501(c)(3) organization called iGlow Mentoring; its mission is to empower young women by promoting success, reinforcing positive choices, and inspiring girls to lead our world. Through this mentoring organization, I have continued to execute events of White House caliber, raising thousands of dollars through grants and fundraising, creating events with world-renowned keynote speakers, and ensuring that every event was memorable and executed with excellence—and most important, having an impact on the lives of thousands of Chicagoland girls.

Advice for Undergraduates

If I had to leave a word of advice to undergraduates pursuing careers in recreation and leisure studies, I would encourage the following: While your work will always speak for you, it is up to you to be sure that your name is known well enough to be spoken of. In other words, be intentional about your professional networking. Sharpen your professional skills, keep your business cards handy, and always be *positively* memorable. My work ethic spoke louder than my physical voice ever could, and because of the extra steps I'd taken to be a part of professional development associations, I've been exposed to and assisted by others who were far more advanced in the field than myself and whom I could emulate.

Health in All Policies Connects Sectors to Address Public Health

With the increasing complexity of public health issues, efforts are being made to formalize connections between the various sectors that can affect public health. One example of such efforts is Health in All Policies (HiAP). The Public Health Institute, the California Department of Public Health, and the American Public Health Association have created a 169-page guide for state and local governments who want to employ "a collaborative approach to improving the health of all people by incorporating health considerations into decision-making across sectors and policy areas" (Rudolph, Caplan, Ben-Moshe, & Dillon, 2013, p. 6). Parks and recreation agencies are among the key community stakeholders highlighted in HiAP as potential collaborators in policies and projects related to public health. For example, the HiAP guide names promoting physical activity, contributing to livable communities via green space, and supporting social networking as three ways through which parks and recreation agencies can advance public health efforts in a community. HiAP provides one clear indication that parks and recreation agencies will play a key role in effective public health strategies moving forward.

ecotourism as "responsible tourism to natural areas that conserves the environment and improves the well-being of local people." With a focus on both introducing tourists to remote sections of the world and providing opportunities for native peoples to enhance their standing through tourism, ecotourism is seen by many as a responsible form of tourism. But ecotourism providers must meet certain guidelines to ensure that ecotourism is a positive experience for both sides. National Geographic has identified Brazil, Dubai, Canada, Belize, and Kenya as the current top five destinations for ecotourism.

Leisure and Public Health

Professionals both inside and outside the recreation and leisure services field are increasingly recognizing parks and recreation agencies' roles in the larger public health efforts of their communities. As communities become more complex, have fewer resources, and encounter more dynamic problems, more sectors will need to collaborate to effect change, and parks and recreation agencies' roles in public health will continue to increase. Dee Merriam (2016), with the National Center for Environmental Health's Healthy Community Design Initiative at the Centers for Disease Control, recently said that "public health and parks and recreation departments have many synergistic goals that could be leveraged to make both more effective." Since parks and recreation agencies are in frequent contact with the public, they are in a unique position to be part of the solution to public health issues such as obesity and lack of physical activity, healthy community design, and disease prevention. In fact, approaches such as the Health in All Policies initiative is a perfect example of interagency collaboration (see sidebar).

Today's obesity crisis has agencies scrambling to find new (and hopefully more successful) ways of helping people get on a better path to health and longevity at all ages. The National Physical Activity Plan in the United States is an excellent example of efforts being taken by representatives from all sectors of society including health care, education, business, media, government, and nonprofits to encourage physical activity. In fact, the overarching goal of the plan is that one day all Americans will be physically active and will live, work, and play in environments that facilitate physical activity. Parks, recreation, fitness, and sport is one of eight sectors identified as playing fundamental roles in the plan. Within this sector, the plan outlines multiple strategies for improving levels of physical activity, which include improving existing programs and facilities and adding new ones, recruiting proactive leaders who will advocate for physical activity, securing sustainable funding for relevant services, and enhancing evaluation to document the effectiveness of efforts.

To address physical inactivity, traffic issues, air quality concerns, and a range of other public health issues, communities are turning their attention to becoming more walkable and bikeable. Parks and recreation departments are lending their own knowledge of recreation, physical activity, park design, and multiuse surfaces to these efforts. They can also collaborate on crucial programming initiatives to increase walking and biking as modes of transportation such as commuting challenges, walking programs, and walking school bus days. These initiatives affect the individual, environmental, and social health of a community. The U.S. surgeon general released a call to action that details five strategic goals to enhance the walkability of American communities and to increase walking activities (U.S. Department of Health and Human Services, 2015). Parks and recreational facilities are among the nine key community sectors named as integral to the success of the strategies.

A final area of public health that may become increasingly important for recreation and leisure agencies to consider is preventing the spread of diseases. Professionals in the tourism industry have been considering strategies to mitigate the spread of infectious diseases and invasive species across international borders. Park professionals have been working to curb the spread of mosquito-carried viruses (e.g., Zika) or tick-related diseases (e.g., Lyme disease) by educating visitors and community citizens about insect control best practices and employing those practices themselves.

Aging and Generational Shifts

Today's seniors look significantly different from those 50 years ago, and leisure opportunities need to reflect this difference. People are living longer than ever before. In the United States, there were more people aged 65 years and older in the 2010 census than any census done before. In fact, this age group grew at a faster rate than the total U.S. population between the 2000 and 2010 censuses (Werner, 2011). The most rapid growth of this population occurred in the West region, and the South had the largest number of people in this age group (Werner, 2011). Because women have longer life expectancies than men, more female seniors find themselves single.

Today's senior population is more educated than ever before, and advancements in medicine

have improved their health. Because they have an increasingly better understanding of this population (and its size), recreation professionals can embrace the notion of "Ulyssean living," a philosophy held by seniors who are seeking new adventures and opportunities in later life, much as Ulysses did. These activities can be designed to increase health, such as the Senior Games. Seniors are looking for activities that challenge them and help them further develop their mental and physical skills. Volunteering and participating in hobbies are two ways that seniors stay involved (McGuire, Boyd, & Tedrick, 2009).

Generational changes are also important to consider in recreation and leisure services workplaces. People now work longer, and workplaces are becoming increasingly multigenerational. In the United States, the workplace is nearly equally distributed between members of the baby boomer, Generation X, and millennial generations. This unique multigenerational workplace will persist for the near future and requires intentional efforts by professionals to overcome the possible conflicts and leverage the potential strengths of a multigenerational workplace. Workers must overcome the urge to stereotype coworkers from other generations and to strive to get to know the motivations and communication needs of others. On an organizational level, agencies are incorporating cross-generational mentorships and work groups, employee training about cross-generational communication, flexible benefit and recognition systems to tap into generational differences, and manager training to ensure that the multigenerational workplace remains a celebrated asset.

Mobile Technology and Social Media

The use of technology, and particularly mobile technology, is of paramount importance to recreation and leisure services. Mobile technology and social media are tools that recreation professionals cannot ignore. In 2015, reports indicated that 64 percent of Americans and 68 percent of Canadians owned smartphones. Mobile and personal technology affects a variety of sectors and services in the recreation and leisure field. Personal technology tools such as activity trackers and phone apps have changed the way participants engage with and track

Seniors are living longer and healthier lives due to advancements in medicine. Programming such as Senior Games can further develop physical skills.

their activities, and fitness professionals are looking for ways to integrate these new technologies into fitness programming and equipment. Recreation and leisure services agencies are also continually evaluating the use of apps for internal operations and participant outreach. Youth sport professionals are using apps to schedule and manage their sport leagues, event planners are using apps to plan and facilitate their events, parks are using apps to provide interpretations and information to their visitors, and the list goes on. For example, the Central Park Conservancy offers an app for visitors to Central Park that includes an interactive map, event listings, celebrity tours of popular locations in the park, an extensive list of things to see in the park, social media feeds for the park, and a souvenir shop. Professionals are tapping into mobile technologies in sport and arena management to enhance the fan experience at professional sport events. For example, the San Francisco 49ers have an official in-stadium app that features in-stadium food delivery and ordering, instant replays, e-ticketing, and live game statistics.

Recreation and leisure services agencies also need to consider the use of social media in their operations and services. Talk to a current professional in the recreation and leisure services field and they will tell you that the most successful agencies have employees who understand how to use social media to professionally market their programs, engage participants, connect staff members, and advocate for what they do. Sport teams have been particularly keen to use social media to increase fan engagement with their teams; for example, they use Google Hangouts during games, maintain active YouTube channels, and use Snapchat to give fans an inside look into team practices. Public parks and recreation agencies are increasingly devising intentional strategy plans so that they can engage with and lead the conversations about their agencies via Twitter. Many times these strategies include notices about event registration, seasonal facility hours, giveaways, emergency procedures, and positive comments from users. No matter what sector or segment you're interested in, it's clear that being able to use and apply mobile technology and social media in a professional manner will be part of your future as a young professional.

Injuries in Youth Sport

Though we can agree on the many benefits that participation in sport can bring to youth, there are growing concerns about injury in youth sport, particularly related to sport specialization and concussions.

Increasingly, youth are choosing to specialize in a single sport at earlier ages, which typically involves year-round play and intensive training. Early sport specialization might increase the risk of overuse injuries, and there is a concern that such injuries are on the rise (DiFiori et al., 2014). To prevent overuse injuries, youth sport professionals need to devise creative ways to collaborate with schools, parents, and sports medicine experts to encourage youth to participate in multiple sports, decrease repetitive movements, monitor schedules for overuse, and provide proper training to ensure youth are participating in their chosen sports safely.

Another area of concern is concussions. From lawsuits and conversations happening in the National Football League to concerns for the safety of youth sport participants, concussions have received considerable attention in the national media. A recent study reported that of the 1.35 million children seen in emergency departments with sport-related injuries in 2012, nearly 164,000 were seen for concussions; a child is seen in an emergency department for a sport-related concussion every three minutes (Ferguson, Green, & Hansen, 2013). With recent evidence that concussions can result in long-term health concerns, a variety of initiatives and strategies have been developed to decrease the occurrence and the negative impact of concussions such as equipment and helmet modifications, early concussion identification protocols, and ready-to-play guidelines that dictate when an athlete is ready to return to a sport after a concussion. Legislation is being considered in almost every state that formalizes ready-to-play guidelines and other strategies to decrease the negative impacts of sport-related concussions. The White House also hosted a Healthy Kids and Safe Sports Concussion Summit to address the issue.

To provide safer youth sport experiences, the CDC developed Heads Up, an initiative focused on educating parents, coaches, schools, sport clinicians, officials, and athletes about concussions. This program includes free online training to learn about, recognize, and respond to concussions as well as other resources such as tool kits, scripts for public service announcements, and fact sheets. You can access these materials at www.cdc.gov/HeadsUp.

Welcoming the LGBTQ Community

Inclusive services are necessary given today's diverse population. In some cases that diversity is easily identified, but in others the diversity is less marked. People are becoming more willing to share their diversities, and they expect programs and services that are sensitive to religious beliefs, sexual orientation, and gender identity.

One diverse population that must be considered is the LGBTQ community. People who do not identify as heterosexual encounter discrimination based on their sexual identity, and this can affect their willingness and ability to access recreation and leisure services. Recreation and leisure services agencies are increasingly embracing their responsibility to ensure that such barriers are broken through policies, staff education and training, and marketing materials that indicate a welcoming environment for all people regardless of sexual identity.

Recreation and leisure services agencies also need to consider how they can successfully reduce barriers for people along all areas of the gender spectrum. Traditionally structured facilities (e.g., bathrooms, locker rooms), programming (male and female sports), and marketing materials can pose significant barriers to transsexual or gender nonconforming people who want to participate in recreational and leisure services. Because these are new and unfamiliar topics for many professionals and agencies, forward-thinking agencies are forming coalitions or work groups that consist of a variety of stakeholders and issue experts to research these issues and formulate strategies that will be successful and inclusive. The Vancouver Board of Parks and Recreation created the Trans and Gender-Variant Inclusion Working Group. After nearly a year of input gathering, community engagement, and research, this group released a final report with specific recommendations to support the needs of the trans and gender-variant community through all levels of service such as facilities, programming, human resources, and literature (Taylor, 2014).

SUMMARY

The field of recreation and leisure services provides exciting opportunities for those who choose to make it their career path. The field offers economic, physical, psychological, social, and many other benefits to individuals and communities. Professionals also benefit because they enjoy fulfilling careers. Those employed in recreation and leisure services work long hours, but they gain a great deal of personal satisfaction and have fun providing services that improve participants' quality of life.

Working in recreation and leisure services means that you are working in a field replete with possibilities, and you have the opportunity to enhance the profession through your service. Recreation and leisure services has proved its worth as a human services profession dedicated to the betterment of people. As a human services profession, the field is constantly changing. Demands for services, changing interests, enhancements in technology, and generational shifts have all contributed to the evolution of the field. To reach their full potential, the profession and the practitioners working in it need to constantly challenge themselves to meet the changing needs of society. Becoming part of this dynamic profession will take hard work and perseverance. Clear career planning and positioning, as described in this chapter, will go a long way in setting the stage for an illustrious career in the field. From networking to improving communication skills, the best and brightest students and professionals set their course for success early in their careers. It's never too early to make a good impression.

This chapter started with the quote "We don't build bridges; we build the people who build bridges." Certainly, building bridges is important; getting to certain places would be tough without the engineers who are responsible for those bridges. The bridges are tangible representations of the hard work of engineering professionals, and the public respects that. An engineering major never has to justify his or her choice of profession. But what does the recreation and leisure services professional build? She or he builds people—happier, healthier, more confident people. Those people are likely to be engineers, teachers, doctors—the list could go on. Seeing what recreation and leisure services professionals build is difficult. What the recreation and leisure services professional does is ensure that all those people are better because of what our field does to build them.

CHAPTER 19

International Perspectives on Recreation and Leisure

Richard R. Jurin, Diane Gaede, Arianne C. Reis, Alcyane Marinho, Jinyang Deng, Huimei Liu, Franz U. Atare, and Felicia S. Ekpu

Elenathewise/fotolia.com

" The bow cannot always stand bent, nor can human frailty subsist without some lawful recreation. "

Miguel de Cervantes, Spanish novelist, poet, and playwright

LEARNING OUTCOMES

After reading this chapter, you should be able to do the following:

> Understand the basis of sustainability as a concept for better living globally

> Understand how cultural interactions between more-developed countries and less-developed countries, through the former's tourism, nature travel, and leisure activities, can encourage sustainable systems in both

> Recognize how tourism, nature travel, and leisure activities are becoming increasingly global sustainability activities

> Understand the effects of social and economic issues on leisure pursuits

> Value the different ways individuals and communities socialize and enjoy leisure time in different societies

> Appreciate the similarities and differences between developed and developing countries' leisure pursuits

> Recognize how historical events, whether political, cultural, economic, or social, contribute to current leisure practices

> Describe the scope and importance of recreation and leisure in China

> Identify the characteristics of recreation and leisure pursuits among people of different walks of life

> Explain the influence of modernization and globalization on the pursuits of leisure and recreation of Chinese people

> Describe how traditional games influence leisure and recreation in Nigeria

> Explain how topography and geographical locations influence leisure preferences in Nigeria

> Characterize the effects of urbanization, economy, and social media on leisure service use

International Perspectives: Sustainability and Ecotourism

Richard R. Jurin and Diane Gaede

66 Recreational development is a job not of building roads into the lovely country, but of building receptivity into the still unlovely human mind. . . . A thing is right when it tends to preserve the integrity, stability and beauty of the biotic community. It is wrong when it tends otherwise. 99

Aldo Leopold, American author, philosopher, forester, and conservationist

As people become more aware of the concept of sustainability, the opportunity to see how it takes shape with decreasing consumerism, increased community resilience, and improved positive human connections to the natural world arises. At home, and especially abroad, this new worldview has spawned new niches that the recreation, tourism, and leisure industry are now addressing. Rather than just recreate in any setting, there is a drive to be out in natural settings, where people are beginning to see and feel a deeper connection to natural areas. This inevitably leads to experiences where many visitors are eager to see how human and natural systems can coexist for mutual benefit. In many places worldwide, this transition to sustainability can be seen where natural ecological systems are now viewed as having more value when designated as biosphere reserves, and also where agricultural and living practices are more aligned with healthy natural systems.

SUSTAINABILITY

Sustainability is a word that is often used but is poorly understood. Too often it is simply used as a synonym for *being green* or *advanced environmentalism*. In fact, it is a new vision of how we live within the world and how we connect with the natural world. A simple, yet all encompassing, definition is to live within the limits of nature's ecosystem services and to live together in communities that are equitable, regenerative, resilient, and adaptive. To do that, we must live mindfully and consciously and think systemically—that is, about the whole system. The other major misnomer about sustainability is that it is somehow about giving things up or, worse, about sacrificing lifestyle. In fact, it is about enhancing our lives to make us happier, healthier, and more prosperous and improving our overall well-being through rebuilding community and using resources from our ecosystems that are renewable and in harmony with the natural world. It is a positive vision, but it is one we have to consciously choose. By not actively choosing this new vision, you complacently choose to accept the current, increasingly detrimental, business-as-usual model (Jurin, 2012). Sustainability means changing our worldview about ourselves and how we fit within the natural world.

The term *nature-deficit disorder* (NDD) was coined as a way of describing the apparent disconnect of modern thinking from the natural world (Louv, 2008). While it is true that natural systems are not front and center in most people's thinking, it is probably more accurate to say we are highly distracted by modern technology and lifestyles. To emphasize how people are really connected to the natural world, consider some of the obvious indications. If you find yourself stopped in a line of cars within a national park, it is inevitably because some large elk, moose, bison, or bears are close to the road, and people cannot help but stop to admire

Teaching children about nature will provide them with lifelong benefits.

Image Source/Digital Vision/Getty Images

these magnificent animals. If you find a parking area with a spectacular view, it will inevitably be full of people who want to take in the grandeur from a perfectly situated, people-only viewing spot. This seems true worldwide. As renowned biologist E.O. Wilson points out in his book *Biophilia* (1984), people have an innate love of living things and a natural affinity with nature. Whenever we consider nature and scenic environments, we inevitably find that our feelings and emotions are much deeper than mere curiosity. We often use the words *awe* and *reverence* for what we are observing. This spiritual component is inherent in much of our interactions with the natural world, and it doesn't necessarily have to do with religion. When we are in a location in which we feel a deep connection (often referred to as a *sense of place*), research shows that things outside straight knowledge drive the feeling of being in place. The components that guide our responses to a sense of place in a location are attachment (emotion-related), aesthetics (senses-related), and ethics (mind-related). **Spirituality** (soul-related) is now accepted as an essential fourth component to the idea of being in place (Porteous, 1991). Notably, sense of place is often linked to communities where we grew up, places we have lived, or anywhere that we have had profound experiences that indicate that the place is special and even sacred—these prior experiences of place are transferable to new locations.

For most of human history, humans are reputed to have lived with a profound reverence and sense of place to those areas they inhabited. Jared Diamond (2012) comments on how tribal societies that have not yet been changed by modern living offer insights into how people can live together in relative peace and harmony with one another and the natural world. He contrasts that with modern technological systems of living, and he says that both have good and bad traits. He ultimately concludes that the way humans used to live coupled with some of the modern attributes of globalized living and traveling offer us a way to live for the future. It is when we understand the global system as both a human system and a natural system that we can begin to understand how a sustainable human future can exist harmoniously with the natural world (Jurin, 2012).

In many **less-developed countries (LDCs)**, community social and cultural systems are still relatively intact. In **more-developed countries (MDCs)**, technological development has exceeded the ecosystem's limits with high amounts of pollution. In addition, community living has been decimated by a hyper-individualized consumer mind-set that simply treats nature as a commodity to be used. The good news is that LDCs can find balance as they raise their standard of living while still living harmoniously within nature. Meanwhile, MDCs are finding out about different ways of living (often through travel) that are appealing (especially holistic community), and they are becoming aware of how the consumer mentality is eroding the joy of living. Typical of this is a growing understanding of the immense benefits of organic farming, small-scale agriculture, and slow food compared to the detrimental fast food system and its accompanying industrialized agriculture.

In many European countries, sustainability is being slowly implemented in terms of greener technology and also a return to family-based gardens. This is creating a shift in community-based living where the food is now a responsibility of the whole community and not just farmers. In Switzerland, many homeowners grow food in their gardens and maintain some animals. Homeowners will then barter with others to obtain various foods. Todmorden, England, has created an Incredible Edible project in which the whole **community** grows food all over the village to boost healthy eating and community building and to educate others about how urban gardening should be the way of the future. Tourists come from far and wide to see how this has transformed this quiet town nestled within the Pennine hills of Britain. In northeastern Scotland, Findhorn Ecovillage, with its renewable energy generation and world-class food gardens, is a destination for people from all over the world who come to see a sustainable community project come to life in which the human **built environment** is as close to harmonious with the natural world as can be at this time, yet the inhabitants enjoy a modern, community-based lifestyle. Almost weekly, people from all over the world come to Findhorn Ecovillage to attend various conferences and to explore the uniqueness of this intentional community.

There is now increased interest in Cuba as a tourist destination. When the Soviet Union dissolved and Cuba found itself embargoed and without any outside support, the people were immediately forced into finding ways to be self-sufficient and sustainable. Cuba is also home to the Caribbean's largest and best-preserved wetland area, the Cienaga de Zapata Biosphere Reserve, and overall its protected natural areas have grown more than 43 percent since 1986.

Projects do not have to be big to attract people. Everywhere in the world there are agricultural and ecosystem-sensitive projects that have spawned whole industries with a responsible travel ethic: ecotourism, **agricultural tourism**, and **natural tourism and travel**.

Recreation, tourism, and leisure (RTL) is big business in the global economy, and it is continuously expanding. One of the fastest growing sectors of tourism is that of sustainable tourism and nature-based tourism specifically. It was in 1995 that the United Nations World Tourism Organization and the World Travel and Tourism Council joined forces with the Earth Council to promote an action plan to improve the environment and make the tourism industry more sustainable. Then, 20 years later, in September 2015, 154 heads of state gathered at the United Nations Sustainable Development Summit to formally adopt the 2030 Agenda for Sustainable Development (United Nations, n.d.) along with 17 sustainable development goals (SDGs). The tourism industry was included in the plan for the first time as a means to end extreme poverty, fight inequality and injustice, and tackle climate change. The definition of *sustainable tourism* that we use is "achieving growth in a manner that does not deplete the natural and built environment and preserves the culture, history, heritage, and the arts of the local community" (Edgell, 2006, pg. 4). The relationship between tourists, the host community, local businesses and recreational activities, and the environment is interactive, complex, and very interdependent. As mentioned earlier, maintaining sustainable systems now attracts tourists' worldwide. Communities that are using sustainable food systems are now destinations in themselves whether they are in exotic locations or simply in tourists' own backyards. A future with localized sustainable systems of food and energy production is now becoming a focus for people hopeful about new ways of living sustainably (Jurin, 2012).

INTERNATIONAL OVERVIEW

In communities around the world, including yours, RTL is undergoing a significant transformation. Technological developments as well as economic and social priorities have changed how RTL is now viewed. During the last quarter century, three aspects have accelerated changes in the RTL field. First, the growth of the Internet has had a revolutionary impact on nearly all areas of life such as information sharing and policy production and management, and transparency is more notable; consider how social media is transforming the world. Second, RTL is changing how governments at all levels are prioritizing community **quality of life.** Third, youth participation in decision-making is emerging as a key priority area in many fields, including RTL (Donohoe, 2013).

INTERNATIONAL ORGANIZATIONS

The World Leisure Organization, founded in 1952, is a worldwide, nongovernmental association dedicated to fostering conditions that allow RTL to serve as a force for human growth, development, and well-being (World Leisure Organization, n.d.). Access to meaningful RTL experiences is as important as the need for shelter, education, employment, and fundamental health care. This occurs deliberately and organically when policy makers include all stakeholders in decision-making (Donohoe, 2013). Internationally, world RTL research and evaluation creates essential knowledge and information about the personal and social potentialities of RTL experiences for increased benefit to human and natural systems. This collection of research and evaluation is disseminated through various print, verbal, and online formats. In addition, the organization offers scholarships to promote learning, training, and engagement. The Future Leaders Program, for example, cooperates with leading educational institutions, governmental agencies, and the United Nations to offer informed **advocacy** by promoting conditions that optimize RTL experiences: legislation, infrastructure, leadership, and programming.

There are several groups that regularly report on sustainable tourism developments and trends and regularly discuss current issues (e.g., www.sustainabletourism.net, http://sustainabletravel.org). For example, the founders and staff at Sustainable Travel International believe that "people's inherent wanderlust, their desire for new experiences and concern for the places they care for most can inspire the protection of the world's natural and cultural bounty and generate economic opportunity in destinations that rely on visitors" (Sustainable Travel, n.d.). Since 2002, the organization has been charting a new course for travel and tourism that hopefully will lead to a healthier environment, greater economic opportunities and social justice, and the protection of natural and cultural resources. Like other business sectors, the tourism and hospitality industry must incorporate sustainable planning and management into their business model, because the effects of global climate change are very apparent in the tourism world (e.g., rising sea levels affect beaches, less snow at ski resorts). Tourists themselves are demanding that sustainable operating practices be acknowledged and followed. Destinations must be clean, healthy, and have protected natural and cultural resources to be attractive to visitors and to compete for the tourist dollar. Whether tourists are lying on a beach, hiking in the mountains, biking, boating, or otherwise enjoying outdoor recreational activities, it is the experience and the enjoyment of it that are marketed by the tourism industry. The tourism industry is tremendously reliant on the local environment and what the locale offers in terms of a unique tourist experience.

In the last decade, the hospitality industry has made costlier investments in their built environment including not using toxic bleaches or dyes in furniture fabric; using paint, wallpaper, carpeting, and draperies that do not have toxic chemicals; and using furniture made with wood harvested from sustainably managed forests (Edgell, 2006). In their effort to save water and electricity, hotels are inviting guests to reuse towels and not have bedding changed daily. The United Nations World Tourism Organization (UNWTO, n.d.) tracks nature-based tourism and estimates that ecotourism and all nature-related forms of tourism account for approximately 20 percent of total inbound travel (visits to a country by nonresidents) (Commission for Environmental Cooperation, 2000). Nature-based travel has grown so significantly in the past 30 years that the United Nations designated 2002 as the year of ecotourism (Edgell, 2006). As sustainable tourism has evolved over time, ecotourism has also gone through a kind of metamorphosis and is viewed as a travel philosophy that is based on a set of principles. These principles were outlined in the United Nations World Tourism Organization Global Code of Ethics for Tourism (n.d.):

1. It includes all nature-based forms of tourism in which the main motivation of the tourists is the observation and appreciation of nature as well as the traditional cultures that prevail in natural areas.

2. It contains educational and interpretation features.

3. It is generally, but not exclusively, organized by specialized tour operators for small groups. Service provider partners at the destinations tend to be small, locally owned businesses.

4. It minimizes negative effects on the natural and sociocultural environments.

5. It supports the maintenance of natural areas that are used as ecotourism attractions by
   - generating economic benefits for host communities, organizations, and authorities that manage natural areas with conservation purposes;
   - providing alternative employment and income opportunities for local communities; and
   - increasing awareness of the conservation of natural and cultural assets among locals and tourists.

ECOTOURISM AND NATURE TRAVEL

Ecotourism and nature travel should not be viewed as the same thing. A river-rafting trip through the jungle might be fun and educational and provide a great family vacation, but only if the trip directly promotes the protection of nature and tangibly contributes to the well-being of local people does it become ecotourism. For many purists, ecotourism is provided by Nongovernmental Organizations (NGOs) and governmental organizations that are dedicated to protected area land management such as those in Ecuador and the Galapagos Islands. But the temptation to create mass island tourism by simply purchasing a boat and offering tours is constantly present. A regulated system is required, and bona fide organizations maintain expected levels of compliance to protect natural and cultural sites as well as the local people. Of the 745 World Heritage sites, 582 are cultural (e.g., the Taj Mahal). The remaining 172 sites contain natural (149) and mixed natural and cultural (23) sites. These 172 sites comprise more than 500 protected areas, of which the Great Barrier Reef and the Serengeti of Tanzania are the most well-known. Tourism's performance in those sites is rather mixed, because it is a challenge to replace timber extraction as a basis for regional economy, correct unsustainable visitor management practices, and transfer millions of tourist dollars for the benefit of local people (Buckley, 2004).

Often, destinations seek to convert mass tourism to ecotourism because of the strong marketing advantage that is perceived. But there has been a continuous growth of a more literate and educated public interested in knowing more about nature, biodiversity, wildlife, and local cultures and willing to pay for the conservation and protection of an area. With the growth (since 2005) of a wealthier and more educated mobile public that is curious about natural and cultural histories of places and people, there are increasing numbers of ecotourists eager to see and learn about them. Conservationists and the industry are seeing the need to invest more time, effort, and resources into educational experiences, which will ensure that the market for ecotourism will grow continuously. Ecotourism companies must re-create an interest and curiosity about nature, wildlife, and cultures through different approaches and techniques in outdoor education to continue to expand the repertoire of natural and cultural heritage that can fascinate and inspire the visitor (Buckley, 2004).

Ecotourism and its management is not without its major problems, however. In a simple interactive online ecotourism game (Educational Web Adventures, n.d.), the user goes through some of the more crucial decisions of a small Amazon population attempting to cater to ecotourists while also trying to maintain the **natural environment** that defines their culture. Worldwide, within developing countries especially, small sleepy hamlets that draw tourists because of their uniqueness struggle with how to manage everything and still keep their cultural and natural commons intact. It can be a fine line between giving visitors a unique and selective experience and losing one's soul in becoming a mega resort. The latter have their place, but decisions on what to do must address the local people and their best interests and the best interests of the local environment; adopting a corrupting bottom-line mentality must be avoided.

RECREATION, TOURISM, AND LEISURE DEVELOPMENT AND ADVOCACY

The availability of the Internet and the knowledge sharing that it enables has transformed the way that RTL is planned and managed. Best practices can often be found by turning to the Internet and finding experts and communities that have applicable situations. The translation features of Google and other search engines now make it possible to access information in other languages in countries where RTL may be conceived and practiced in different ways. This sharing of information across geographical and cultural borders is enriching the way that RTL is evolving globally. The spatial reach and the **Internet penetration rate** continue to grow in developing countries where 1 to 2 billion new users are located. This has immense and widespread sociocultural and economic implications. Many countries, including Estonia, Finland, and Spain, have declared access to the Internet a legal right for citizens (Donohoe, 2013).

Technological developments are changing political, economic, and social conditions, and RTL policy has also undergone transformation. Worldwide, RTL is a major income generator that acts as a stimulus to other forms of economic, social, and sustainable development. Governments are now seeing this as a continuing rationale for becoming more involved. This is also seen as the impetus for more **commodification** of RTL programs, products, and services by private businesses. This joint influence is rapidly changing the global RTL landscape. Consequently, RTL policy and practice, which had changed subtly over time, are now changing significantly. For example, China gained an economic presence in world markets after hosting the Olympics in 2008. International sporting events can raise the international profile of the host country, attracting tourists and foreign investment, and can leave an RTL legacy for the host communities (e.g., new RTL facilities). Consequently, as a result of hosting international events, many countries have made political commitments to begin enhancing the quality of life of their own citizens and their environments (Donohoe, 2013).

Advocacy plays a critical role in the way that RTL is being shaped for today and tomorrow. International organizations work tirelessly to ensure that RTL is a priority in communities around the world and that sustainable development is a central focus. As we move forward in the 21st century, the RTL fields will require a new generation of strong leaders and skilled professionals. As future leaders, students (typically aged 15 to 24 years) have a critical role to play in their own communities and on the world stage as advocates for sustainability, ecotourism, and agricultural tourism as well as how people perceive RTL. Every year on August 12, International Youth Day is celebrated and youth everywhere are encouraged to use the activist framework to work with their own communities (United Nations, 2010). Similarly, the United Nations Educational, Scientific, and Cultural Organization (UNESCO) encourages the participation of young men and women by fostering partnerships with youth networks and organizations (UNESCO, 2010, 2017). These collaborations are meant to integrate their views and priorities into the development of projects and programs in a variety of areas including sustainable development and RTL (Donohoe, 2013).

SUMMARY

People from MDCs are now traveling more to experience different cultures and unique natural settings and to feel a sense of connection with places different from their own. This is much more than simple recreation and leisure. More important, they are doing this in ways that minimize impact on the places they are visiting. The concepts and principles of sustainability are becoming important as tourists learn that the ideas they see in LDCs can be transplanted to their own communities. Likewise, ecologically conscious travelers support resources for their travels that are sustainable and benefit the communities they visit.

Recreation and Leisure in Brazil

Arianne C. Reis and Alcyane Marinho

  ❝ All persons have a need to celebrate and share our diversity in leisure. **❞**

São Paulo Declaration, World Leisure Association

Brazil is an exciting and diverse country. Most people have heard of at least one of these Brazilian trademarks: *carnaval*, **samba**, the **Amazon**, "The Girl From Ipanema," **bossa nova**, and *caipirinha*. But these are far from what this country is all about. A nation as large and as populous as Brazil cannot possibly be summarized in a few words. This chapter intends to briefly present the **cultural diversity**, contrasting worlds, and rich history of Brazil that might be better understood if experienced firsthand. Therefore, the chapter provides only a glimpse of what Brazil is and what its people do to have fun, relax, enjoy their friends and family, and seize the day. In summary, it describes what they do for leisure and recreation.

With a total area of 8,514,877 square kilometers (about 3.2 million square miles), Brazil is the fifth largest country in the world and the largest in the Southern Hemisphere. It is also the fifth most populous country, containing more than 190 million people within its borders (IBGE, 2011). Brazil is too large to display a uniform pattern of leisure and recreation. Brazil has a colonial history that created the ideal environment for the development of regions as *silos*, which enabled cultural developments that were distinct from each other in several ways. As discussed in previous chapters, culture plays a vital role in producing leisure patterns and behaviors. Therefore, Brazil has distinct leisure practices in different parts of the country, although a few commonalities are seen across the nation. In the following sections, these leisure patterns and behaviors will be explored in more detail. Before that, however, we provide general information about the country to build a better understanding of leisure practices and traditions in Brazil.

Brazil has an extensive coastline, which is also where most of its development has occurred since the early days of colonialism. Approximately 90 percent of its territory sits between the equator and the Tropic of Capricorn (IBGE, 2011). From this we can conclude a few things that have a considerable influence on some general aspects of Brazilian leisure choices:

- Brazil has a significant beach culture on large white sandy beaches blessed with tropical weather.

- Because most of its population resides along the coast, free coastal recreation pursuits are in high demand by tourists and locals.

- The warm weather is conducive to a variety of outdoor cultural experiences and activities all year long. In Brazil these are dominated by **folklore festivals**, popular parties (religious and pagan), and unregulated sport and physical activities (**football** played on the beach or in any open area, walking and jogging, *capoeira*, skateboarding, and so on).

Brazil's colonial history contributes significantly to its diversity. For more than 300 years, the labor force in Brazil was composed almost entirely of African slaves, particularly along the eastern coastline and hinterland, where sugar cane and coffee plantations predominated. This region was therefore significantly exposed to African culture, and today African cultural expressions are still predominant in music, religion, dance, and food along the coastline. In the Amazon region, where colonialism was not so present, indigenous people left a stronger mark on the local culture, and leisure practices have been significantly influenced by their customs.

After slavery was abolished in 1888, the Brazilian government encouraged European immigration to the country. Germans, Italians, Japanese, Turkish, and others were attracted to various regions of the country and particularly to the southern regions. Therefore, in the southeastern and southern regions of Brazil, visitors will feel the European and Asian influences in food, dance, festivities, and general customs.

Other major aspects that affect leisure and recreation practices are the social and economic conditions of a given population. Those without financial resources will obviously have limited access to some forms of paid leisure opportunities such as cinemas, theme parks, theater, and concerts. Also, some recreation practices require the purchase of specific equipment, such as climbing gear, sailboats, and kayaks, or entrance to private spaces such as golf clubs and gyms. In addition, some leisure and recreation practices are in part determined by the local physical environment, such as easy access to green parks, open public spaces, and bars and restaurants, among others. Brazil has great differences in its social class structure and economic distribution of wealth, and these disparities help determine the leisure and recreation patterns of its diverse population (Mascarenhas, 2003).

For the past 30 years, Brazil has consistently been among the 15 most powerful economies in the world. In more recent years, it has climbed to the top 10, and in 2014, it was classified as the seventh-strongest global economy (World Bank, 2016). But Brazil is ranked 75th in the United Nations **Human Development Index** (HDI) (UNDP, 2015), which indicates that a rich country can exhibit extreme inequality and exclude many of its inhabitants from access to their most basic needs, including leisure opportunities.

In the last 15 years, consumer power has generally increased (Beghin, 2008; Cetelem, 2011; Neri,

2011), but approximately 25 percent of the population, or more than 40 million people, still live in poverty. In contrast, 25 percent of the population has a standard of living that is similar to that in the developed nations of North America and Europe. This contrast is apparent in leisure choices and behaviors, as we will discuss later. There is a clear difference between the leisure choices and opportunities of those who have economic power and those who do not and between those who live in the exclusive neighborhoods and those who live in the shantytowns or *favelas*.

HISTORICAL DEVELOPMENT OF RECREATION AND LEISURE IN BRAZIL

Brazilian modern history is commonly divided into three main periods: colonial (1500-1824), imperial (1824-1888), and republican (1889-present). Highlighting some significant aspects of these historical moments in Brazilian life can help you understand how some leisure practices and traditions have evolved.

The colonial and imperial periods were characterized by slave labor and colonial regions that were independent from each other. The Catholic Church played a significant role in Brazil's cultural development because it was a colony of Portugal, which was a conservative European Catholic power at the time. This context fostered the suppression of expansive manifestations of leisure; in addition to Catholics' negative views on leisure participation in general, physical recreation was associated with slave labor and was therefore avoided by all free residents (De Jesus, 1999). Moreover, any joyful activity engaged in by slaves, such as dancing, singing, and playing, were immediately suppressed by landowners who viewed these activities as distractions from work (Gebara, 1997). Slave leisure practices were therefore clandestine, but fortunately they have survived and are expressed today by the hugely popular martial art *capoeira*; by the *congado*, an annual sacred and pagan festivity; by the extensive use of African drums in music (*batucadas*); and many other forms.

The republican era, which started in the last decade of the 19th century, has been divided into various periods. In the first half of the 20th century, Brazil became a predominantly urban society, and the government pushed for industrialization and economic development. This context favored the creation of social clubs that heavily promoted the practice of sport, which was a late phenomenon compared with the European context (De Jesus, 1999). The explanation for this was the aforementioned rejection of any physical activity by the Brazilian elite until some decades after the abolishment of slavery in the country. The general feeling was one of optimism and civic pride, which translated into value being given to unique expressions of Brazilian culture in music, dance, theater, and other arts and access to these being extended to the working class through the public presentation of arts and the construction of open leisure spaces in the urban environment (Almeida & Gutierrez, 2005; Melo, 2003).

In 1964, a military coup changed the cultural environment of the country again and consequently changed its leisure practices. Repression and censorship curtailed spontaneity, and fear led people to spend more of their free time at home. Mass communication networks developed during this period, and television became one of the most important forms of leisure in the country, which continues today (Mascarenhas, 2003). Soap operas were used for political propaganda and therefore were highly supported by the government. Nevertheless, they became increasingly popular. The dictatorial government also dramatically reduced the accessibility of artistic expression to the working class, which in turn increased the significance of television as a pastime for this group. The elite, on the other hand, were starting to go to the cinemas, new shopping centers, and their second homes; these phenomena increased substantially during this period. Because of the economic development experienced during this time, the Brazilian elite also started to travel more, particularly to overseas destinations, and their leisure choices became increasingly more influenced by the international trends in recreation and leisure (Almeida & Gutierrez, 2005).

The rapid development of the cities along with a political regime that repressed most forms of leisure and recreation practices led to a decrease in public open spaces where the working class, who were increasingly marginalized economically, could freely recreate. Traditional folklore phenomena began to fade away, and sport became the major form of recreational pursuit. In fact, sport practices were encouraged by the government, which used them as political propaganda (Almeida, Gutierrez, & Marques, 2013), as did several other dictatorial regimes across the world (e.g., see Brady, 2009; Lee & Bairner, 2009; Van Steen, 2010).

With the fall of military power in the mid- to late 1980s, Brazil rapidly opened up to the international market. But because of the historical contingencies mentioned earlier, urban areas became extremely crowded because open spaces were not appropriately planned and developed. With the rise of poverty, violence became a problem in most urban centers, which caused people to curtail their exploration of streets, parks, and other open areas of the city. Therefore, visits to shopping centers, concerts in closed spaces, parties, restaurants, cinema, and television started to rank higher among choices of leisure activities. The poor and working class, who could not afford to go to the same places as the elite, improvised and created their own parties, such as the **baile funk** in Rio de Janeiro, or they went to bars in their neighborhoods where problem drinking and illegal gambling were constantly present

(Mascarenhas, 2003). This scenario is still a reality today (Caldeira, 2014).

This historical background helps contextualize the contemporary leisure and recreation programs and services provided by various agencies in Brazil today and is, therefore, crucial to a better understanding of the current leisure practices of its citizens. In the following section, we further explore the common activities, programs, and services that are available and popular across the nation.

TYPES OF SECTORS, SEGMENTS, AND SERVICES

As in developed nations, the growth of leisure services in Brazil has been concentrated in metropolitan areas and some tourist areas. The larger cities contain the largest public recreational facilities such as the main facilities of the Serviço Social do Comércio (Social Service for Commerce, SESC), which is one of the most significant providers for leisure and recreation in the country; sports clubs with the best infrastructure; the main concert venues; the major hotel chains; and modern shopping malls.

Capoeira is a Brazilian martial art that combines dance and music that was developed as part of slave leisure practices.

Getty Images/golero

SESC, a public–private institution whose main aim is to provide quality of life to the working class, was established in 1946 and is present in all Brazilian state capitals as well as in several midsized cities and small towns. SESC owns and operates several activity centers with large facilities and extensive infrastructure including hotels, theaters, sport complexes, cinemas, spas, schools, and environmental protection areas. SESC policies follow Dumazedier's (1980) understanding of leisure practices as divided into five main realms: artistic, intellectual, sportive or physical, manual, and social. Programs therefore range from permanent sports programs with weekly classes to theater groups, open cinema showings, technical courses in hospitality, camping trips, and nature walks.

More broadly, the framework proposed by Dumazedier to classify leisure pursuits has been influential and has been interpreted as a set of strategies to be implemented in programs and projects for leisure at the national level in government initiatives.

Private clubs in contemporary Brazil play an important role as recreation providers, particularly with their holiday camps. The holiday camps target school-aged children and youth and are open to all members of a particular club or community. YMCAs across the country were influential in developing holiday camps as alternative leisure activities for children during their holidays and are particularly common in the southeast region of the country (Stoppa, 1999).

Sports programs are also commonly associated with clubs in Brazil, and sports such as volleyball, gymnastics, futsal, tennis, swimming, handball, and basketball are among the most popular in clubs and among youth. The most popular organized sport in Brazil is undoubtedly football (called soccer in North America). Although it is popular in clubs, football is played, usually informally, by everyone anywhere there is a small area of dirt, grass, or pavement. Poles for the goals are made with anything available such as cans filled with small rocks, coconuts, bricks, or stones. Every kid has a football, even if it is made old socks. Going to football games, whether in big stadia in the major cities or in open grass areas with iron stands in rural areas, is an important form of leisure in Brazil. Watching games on television at home, in a bar, or in a restaurant, or just listening to the radio broadcast, is popular in every corner of the country by rich and poor alike.

The hotel industry is also active in the provision of leisure opportunities in Brazil. Active leisure providers in the hotel industry are usually **farm-stays**, hotel spas (particularly in thermal spring areas), resorts, and **ecolodges** (Ribeiro, 2004). In the early 1970s, Club Mediterranée on Itaparica Island, Bahia, was the first resort to implement organized leisure activities for its clients. It was run by so-called gentle organizers—trained staff whose main job was to entertain guests by providing various leisure and recreation activities. Leisure-focused hotels can be found across the country. Luxury resorts are usually found along the coast, and farm-stays are located in the hinterlands and mountain regions.

As in North America and elsewhere around the world, shopping malls in Brazil are significant spaces of leisure that provide many entertainment options such as shops, cinemas, theaters, amusement parks, skating rinks, and go-carting. The highest concentration of shopping malls is in São Paulo. Shopping malls have grown to become part of the urban fabric for Brazilian urban dwellers. Middle-class families have exchanged traditional places of recreation, such as public squares and parks, for the alleys of the malls, increasingly because of the security and convenience offered by these spaces (Ferreira, 2004). In Rio de Janeiro, a city surrounded by free leisure opportunities (e.g., forest parks and beaches), the proliferation of malls is oddly intense. Barra da Tijuca, a large middle-class neighborhood in the city, has the most malls per square mile in the country. Some argue that the building of malls is a result of the violence and criminality found in large Brazilian urban centers and is a means of separating the lower and poor classes, who are confined to the few open and free leisure spaces of the city, from the middle and upper classes, who increasingly "hide" in private and paid leisure spaces.

In one place, however, worlds collide harmoniously: the beach. As mentioned earlier, Brazil has a significant beach culture. Along the long coast of Brazil, the beach is one of the central spaces for leisure and recreation. From north to south, the poor and the rich share this space, and several recreation practices were born and have thrived on sandy Brazilian beaches. *Futvôlei* (an interesting mix of soccer and volleyball played on the sand) and *frescobol* (a beach paddleball game) were created on Brazilian beaches and now have been exported to beaches across the world from California to Australia. Surfing and body boarding are also extensively practiced along the Brazilian coast. Poorer children might start their adventures in the ocean with only a wooden board and later gain worldwide recognition.

Another popular leisure practice in Brazil is the engagement in folk festivals as active participants or spectators. These festivals range from large folkloric parties and festivities (some of national and international reach) to small, local, traditional festivals in small towns and *vilarejos*. What they hold in common is their significance to a community's identity and history.

One of the main folkloric festivities in Brazil is the *Boi-Bumbá*, a performance influenced by the country's Portuguese culture blended with African traditions. The performance is a play in which an ox dances, dies, and is resurrected to the sound of drums and singing by all participants. The title and interpretation of the colorful play vary across the country (e.g., *Bumba-meu-boi*, *Boi-calemba*, *Bumba-de-reis*, *Reis-de-boi*, *Boi-pintadinho*, and *Boi-de-mamão*; Cavalcanti, 2006), but it is always

dramatic and spectacular and involves hundreds of people in the main public squares of small towns and large cities.

Another important Brazilian folk festival is the *Festa Junina*. These festivals, which are among the most significant Catholic festivals in the country, take place in June in honor of St. Peter, St. Anthony, and St. John. Dances around big bonfires, crafting, the launching of colorful hot air balloons, sales of typical foods in rustic stalls, and the staging of a forced-marriage play are central aspects of these festivities. Music is a main theme, and the genres played are genuinely Brazilian, such as the *forró*, *xaxado*, and *baião*, and are played with violas, accordions, triangles, and traditional instruments.

The most popular Brazilian festival, however, is certainly the *carnaval*, a blend of European traditions adapted to a tropical country with a large population that is of African descent. *Carnaval* is eagerly awaited by most of the population, rich and poor, all year round, and it is certainly part of the country's international imagery as well as its local identity. *Carnaval* parties in clubs developed from the European masked balls of years past. Parades

Football is the most popular organized sport in Brazil, and it is also played informally anywhere there is space and a ball.

Getty Images/Vetta/RichVintage

of floats (*escolas de samba*) are based on similar European traditions, and street music with lots of drums and percussion hails from the African influence. *Carnaval* is celebrated annually 46 days before Easter. It is officially celebrated for four days (national public holidays), but it usually goes on for an entire week. It is present in various forms in every town of the country. The cheerful and lively atmosphere is the commonality between all celebrations.

TRENDS, DEMAND, AND FUTURE GROWTH

Besides the examples already mentioned, another expanding recreation segment in Brazil is adventure activities in parks, wilderness areas, and built environments. The diversity of natural resources in all Brazilian regions facilitates outdoor pursuits, and activities such as climbing, rafting, caving, diving, and paragliding have become popular in some parts of the country. Adventure and ecotourism are among the fastest growing leisure pursuits in recent years, and numerous agencies and businesses have emerged (Oliveira & Rossetto, 2013). Following this trend, large urban centers also are catering to the adventure market by establishing skate parks for skateboarding, in-line skating, and scooters and indoor climbing gyms for sport climbing. These innovative approaches to recreation follow international trends, represent the social dynamics of the area, and enable participants to take on new behaviors and create new lifestyles (Marinho, 2005). These activities are still enjoyed primarily by the middle and upper classes because the gear required can be too expensive for the less affluent.

Outdoor education has become increasingly popular in schools, and adventure activities in the natural environment are commonly used as part of an educational program that aims to teach children about nature issues and help them develop leadership and teamwork skills. This approach is also increasingly popular in large businesses. Employees might spend a day in the outdoors experiencing challenges that can be drawn on later in the competitive working environment. The success of these programs shows how adventure and nature-based leisure and recreation activities are becoming more popular in Brazil.

As discussed earlier, Brazil is a fast-growing economy and the demographics of its population are changing rapidly (IBGE, 2011). Because of the increase in consumer power in the last 15 years and the likelihood that the trend will continue, more Brazilians will start enjoying the benefits of disposable income to be spent on leisure activities. In addition, because levels of education are also increasing, what are currently considered pastimes of the intellectual elite, such as visit to museums, outings to the theater or to arts exhibitions, and attendance at classical music concerts or ballets, might be more widely enjoyed. According to Mascarenhas (2003), 46 percent of the population has never been to a theater play, 52 percent has never been to a museum, 88 percent has never been to a ballet, and, surprisingly, 49 percent has never gone to a football stadium to watch Brazil's number-one game live. These statistics are likely to change in the next few years.

The rapid demographic change in Brazil is also reflected in the increase of the urban population. Towns that were previously considered small or medium-sized have moved to city status, and with this change have come associated problems of space. Urban planning has never been a strong focus of Brazilian urban development, and less open land is available for the public. In this context, virtual reality games, participation in social networks on the Internet, and general Internet surfing have experienced exponential growth. According to a study by the Fundação Getúlio Vargas, one of the largest research institutes in the country, Brazil has 1.2 mobile devices per inhabitant (Meirelles, 2016). In the last 25 years, the number of computers in the country has doubled every four years, and monthly Brazilian Facebook users reached 45 percent of the total population in 2015 (Facebook Business, 2015). This trend in behavior directly affects how people spend their free time. The use of electronic games, electronic devices, and social media are becoming important leisure experiences in Brazil and in more developed nations.

SUMMARY

The Brazilian elite today enjoy the leisure opportunities and practices that are available in any developed country in the world, and they engage in similar pursuits. The working class and the poor, however, have had their leisure options increasingly restricted by the unplanned and unsustainable development of the cities. These options include limited public open spaces, such as beaches and urban parks, which are usually underfunded and not always suitable for some leisure practices. Along the coast, however, beaches are enjoyed by all groups of society, and citizens value them highly. As poverty rates decrease and purchasing power increases, leisure disparities are changing. We hope that the creativity expressed by marginalized groups in overcoming barriers throughout the years will remain and that along with this we will witness a fairer distribution of leisure and recreation opportunities across all segments of society.

Recreation and Leisure in China

Jinyang Deng and Huimei Liu

66 Play is one of the essential needs for people. We need to have the culture of play, do academic research in play, and master skills in and develop the arts for play. 99

Guangyuan Yu, renowned economist and contributor to leisure development in China

Although leisure, recreation, and tourism are conceptually different, they are inherently interdisciplinary and practically interrelated (Smith & Godbey, 1991). A recreationist and a leisure pursuer often share the same resources, use the same facilities, and generate similar social and psychological outcomes (McKercher, 1996). Thus, as far as the scope of leisure, recreation, and tourism is concerned, drawing a distinct line between the three is difficult. In fact, recreation and leisure are usually discussed under the rubric of leisure in Western literature. This line of thought has also been followed by most Chinese tourism and leisure researchers and scholars. That is, all leisurely activities or anything meant to be enjoyed (i.e., entertainment, recreation, tourism) during free time falls into the category of the leisure industry. This understanding and classification of the leisure industry is reflected by the two most authoritative publications on China's leisure industry: the *Annual Report on China's Leisure Development*, also known as the *Green Book of China's Leisure*, which has been complied annually since 2010 by the Tourism Research Center at the Chinese Academy of Social Science (TRC CASS), and the *Annual Report of China Leisure Development*, which has been complied annually since 2011 by the China Tourism Academy.

The development of recreation and leisure as an industry and particularly as an academic field in China is a recent phenomenon, although the Chinese words for leisure, 休闲 (*xiu xian*), can be traced back at least three millennia (Liu, Yeh, Chick, & Zinn, 2008). Leisure has been pursued in many forms (e.g., tai chi, mahjong) by people of different walks of life for thousands of years in China.

Although a consensus on what constitutes leisure has been achieved internationally and domestically, no common understanding of what constitutes the leisure industry has been reached among Chinese researchers and scholars. For example, Qing (2007) considers the leisure industry to be made up of three types of industries: the primary leisure industry (e.g., leisure agriculture, leisure forestry, leisure husbandry, and leisure fishery sectors), the secondary leisure industry (e.g., leisure food and beverage processing and manufacturing sector, leisure appliances and equipment manufacturing sector, and leisure construction sector), and the tertiary leisure industry (e.g., tourism leisure sector, fitness and cosmetics sector, culture and entertainment sector, hospitality sector, and others). You and Zhen (2007) argue that the contemporary leisure industry in China can be classified into the following 11 categories:

1. Entertainment leisure (singing halls, dance halls, discotheques, concert halls, tea houses, cafes, chess houses, bars, cinemas, theaters, resorts, performing arts centers, karaoke bars, KTVs)

2. Sporting leisure (all kinds of sports and adventurous outdoor activities)

3. Health leisure (springs, forest recuperation, flower recuperation, water therapy, mud therapy, salt therapy, spas, baths, sun baths, beauty, hairdressing, massage, oxygen bars, and so on)

4. Tourism leisure (natural and historical sites, theme parks, zoos and botanical gardens, and urban scenic spots and belts)

5. Rural leisure (happy farmer inns, happy fisher inns, happy ranch inns, folk villages, and rural historical towns)

6. Educational leisure (libraries, memorial halls, galleries, all types of museums, martyr cemeteries, religious temples, college campuses, industrial parks, bookstores, and so on)

7. Food leisure (restaurants, hotels, guesthouses, flavor snack bars, and food courts)

8. Shopping leisure (shopping malls, exhibitions, wholesale markets, pedestrian streets, specialty shops, auctions, pawn shops, and so on)

9. Hobby leisure (pets, image design, gardening, stamp collecting, collecting of antiques and other items, sculpture, calligraphy, painting, knitting, flower arranging, pubs, making ceramics for fun, and phone bars)

10. Social leisure (charity, volunteering, social media and Internet cafes, festivals and events, making friends, cell phone messages, parties, and so on)

11. Leisure products manufacturing (leisure foods and beverages, leisure clothing, leisure health care, leisure books and materials, leisure equipment, and leisure facilities)

Similar to Qing's (2007) classification, Wei (2009) states that the leisure industry should consist of three subindustries: the leisure foundation industry (e.g., tourism sector, sporting leisure sector, and cultural leisure sector), the leisure extension industry (e.g., leisure agriculture sector, leisure commerce sector, which primarily includes business recreation areas, pedestrian streets and special shopping stores, and leisure real estates), and the leisure support industry (e.g., leisure manufacturing sector, leisure information technology sector, and leisure brokerage sector). More recently, TRC CASS (2015) proposed the concept of "leisure and related industries," which involves the tourism leisure sector, the cultural leisure sector, the sports leisure sector, and other sectors (e.g., food and beverage).

The aforementioned classification (Qing, 2007; You & Zhen, 2007; TRC CASS, 2015) of China's leisure industry demonstrates that China's leisure industry encompasses a wide range of sectors, many of which have emerged in the past two decades or so because of the influence of modernization and globalization. These sectors have begun to play an increasingly important role in the country's economic growth and "the construction of a harmonious society," which was a national goal proposed by the former President Jintao Hu in 2004 when he suggested, in an address to a high-level seminar at the Party School of the Central Committee of the Communist Party of China, that a high priority be placed on social harmony. This came at a time when the country was confronted with a series of social problems, such as disparity in development and distribution, inequality, injustice, and corruption, despite rapid economic growth.

In recent years, the leisure industry in China has played an important role in generating revenue and jobs. In 2014, domestic visits reached 3.6 billion and generated a domestic tourism revenue of 3.0 trillion RMB (approximately US$496.7 billion), an increase of 10.7 percent and 15.4 percent, respectively, over 2013 (National Tourism Administration of China, 2016). In the same year, 27.8 million people were directly and 50.9 million people were indirectly employed in the tourism industry, which accounted for 10.2 percent of the total employment of the country. In addition, the total gross domestic product (GDP) from tourism was estimated at 6.6 trillion RMD (or approximately US$1,082 billion) in the same year, which accounted for 10.4 percent of the national GDP. According to the most recent *Annual Report on China's Leisure Development* (TRC CASS, 2015), the total GDP from the leisure industry (domestic tourism leisure sector, cultural leisure sector, sports leisure sector, and others) was estimated at 3.6 trillion RMD (approximately US$590.2 billion), which accounted for 5.7 percent of the national GDP. This is a conservative estimate because estimates for other leisure sectors were not included.

Currently, China's leisure industry is concentrated in urban areas, particularly in large and mid-sized cities where the leisure industry has grown quickly on a large scale and has generated considerable benefits. For example, Hangzhou, dubbed the Oriental capital of leisure, has seen a rapid development and growth of tourism and leisure in the past decade. In 2014, the total tourism and leisure revenue (both domestic and international) reached 188.6 billion RMB (approximately US$30.9 billion), which accounted for 6.8 percent of the total GDP of the city (TRC CASS, 2015). In addition to the urban tourism that has been well-developed in the city, rural tourism has also become increasingly popular among urban residents in the suburban areas of Hangzhou and in many other large and mid-sized cities in the country. For example, in 2014, there were 2.3 million rural tourists in the metropolitan area of Hangzhou, which is an increase of 63.3 percent over the previous year. Rural tourism brought in a total revenue of 2.7 billion RMB (approximately US$442.6 million), which is an increase of 157 percent over 2013.

Parallel to the rapid development of the leisure industry in China is the continuing growth of tourism and leisure education at various levels. For example, in 2014, there were 2,055 tourism education institutions (including 1,122 higher education institutions) that enrolled 753,300 students, including 435,200 undergraduates. In addition, 18 forestry and agriculture universities offer outdoor recreation education. The first forest recreation department was established in 1993 at the Central South University of Forestry and Technology in Hunan Province. Recently, because *leisure* has become a buzzword among the public, 14 sport universities or schools and several other universities with tourism programs have begun to offer four-year undergraduate degrees in leisure studies. Furthermore, a doctoral degree program in leisure studies, the first and the only one in China, was approved in 2007 for Zhejiang University. Finally, several leisure research centers have been established since 2003, when the Center for Leisure Culture Study, the first leisure research center in China, was created by the Chinese Academy of Arts.

Photo courtesy of Ling Ping.

Tai chi is a traditional healthy exercise that has been practiced by people of different walks of life for thousands of years in China.

A BRIEF HISTORY OF CHINA'S LEISURE DEVELOPMENT

Contemporary recreation and leisure began to emerge as an important sector in China in the early 1980s when China began to adopt an open-door policy and make major economic reforms, which resulted in impressive economic development in the following decades. As in advanced economies, the increase of discretionary income and free time has stimulated increasing demand for leisure pursuits in China. The central government played an important role in formulating national policies for leisure industry development. For example, in 1995, China adopted a 40-hour week, and in 1999, the State Council approved three **golden weeks** (i.e., the Spring Festival Golden Week, the National Day Golden Week, and the Labor Day Golden Week) as national holidays. (Note, the Labor Day Golden Week was abolished on November 17, 2007.) Along with the two-day weekends and other holidays, the golden weeks increased the free time of the country's working class to 115 days per year. In addition, the 11th **Five-Year Plan** placed higher priority on industry structure transformation by focusing on the tertiary sectors, or the service industry. The 12th Five-Year Plan has implemented national tourism and leisure strategies that aim to increase awareness of leisure among the public and promote leisure industry development to a higher level. Furthermore, the *Guidelines for National Tourism and Leisure (2013-2020)* promulgated by the State Council in 2013 set up goals and laid a foundation for the development of tourism and leisure.

Leisure and recreation has been an important research topic since 1993, when the first recreation research center, the Center for Forest Recreation, was established at the Central South Forestry University. Since then, many research centers on leisure and recreation have been established across the country. Table 19.1 lists the research centers that, to the best of our knowledge, are among the most academically influential. These research centers, along with many others that are not listed, have made significant contributions to leisure and recreation research in China. In addition, in 2009, topics on leisure research were included in the application guidelines of the National Social Science Fund for the first time.

Several key people have played an essential role in promoting leisure development and leisure studies and education in the country. Among the most important is the late leader Xiaoping Deng, who pointed out on many occasions that more emphasis should be placed on tourism development to increase national income. Other important

Table 19.1   Selected Centers for Leisure and Recreation Research in China

Name	Year established	Affiliation
Center for Forest Recreation Research	1993	Central South University of Forestry and Technology, Hunan
Center for Leisure Studies	2000	Chinese National Academy of Arts, Beijing
China Leisure Economic Research Center	2004	Renmin University of China, Beijing
Asia-Pacific Center for the Study and Training of Leisure	2004	Zhejiang University, Zhejiang
Research Center on Convention/Exhibition and Leisure Culture	2006	Hunan Normal University, Hunan
China Center for Leisure and Tourism Research	2008	Sichuan University, Sichuan
Research Center on Culture and Leisure Industry	2008	University of International Business and Economics, Beijing
Research Center for Leisure Sports Development	2012	Hubei University, Hubei
Sichuan Landscape and Recreation Research Center	2012	Chengdu University, Sichuan
Central China Research Center on Leisure Culture	2013	Hubei Polytechnic University, Hubei

Note: All tourism research centers in the country, including some of the most prestigious ones, such as China Tourism Academy established in 2008 (affiliated China National Tourism Administration) and the Tourism Research Center established in 1999 (affiliated with Chinese Academy of Social Science), are not listed in the table because the words *leisure* and *recreation* are not part of the title of the research agency.

figures include Professors Guangyuan Yu and Huidi Ma, who have made great contributions to leisure development and leisure education and research in the country. Besides their own writings and talks on leisure, they also translated and published five books written by renowned leisure scholars in North America. Other key people include Professor Chucai Wu, who was proclaimed a national-level expert by the State Council and who, along with Professor Zhangwen Wu, founded the country's first four-year outdoor recreation program in 1993 in Central South Forestry College (later renamed Central South University of Forestry and Technology). In addition, Professor Xuequan Pang, director of the Asian Pacific Centre for the Education and Study of Leisure, Zhejiang University, has played an essential role in promoting leisure studies within and beyond the university.

In recent years, China has organized several international leisure conferences (e.g., an annual international leisure development forum held in Hangzhou since 2003, the Ninth World Leisure Congress and 2006 World Leisure Expo, the 2009 International Sociological Association Research Committee on Leisure Study [RC 13] Mid-Term Conference, the 2015 International Forum on Metropolitan Leisure and Tourism) and national leisure forums (e.g., 2007, 2008, 2009, and 2010 National Leisure Industry Economics Forums and the Annual Conference on Leisure Studies) that have increased public awareness of leisure and facilitated collaboration and cooperation between Chinese leisure scholars and their international counterparts.

RECREATION OPPORTUNITIES IN CHINA

China has abundant natural and cultural resources that offer great opportunities for leisure and outdoor recreation pursuits. This section introduces the settings, organizations, and structures as they relate to the provision of leisure and recreation opportunities in the country. A brief description of popular recreation and leisure activities pursued by the public follows.

Settings, Organizations, and Structures

The most popular outdoor recreation settings in China are scenic areas, nature reserves, and **forest parks**. As of 2015, China had 3,234 forest parks, including 826 at the national level, that covered

Forest parks such as Zhangjiajie National Forest Park (which was the original model for Hallelujah Mountain in the movie *Avatar*) are popular outdoor recreation settings in China.

©Jinyang Deng

44.5 million acres (18.02 million ha) (China State Forestry Administration, 2016) and 2,740 nature reserves, including 450 national ones, comprising 363.2 million acres (147 million ha). As of 2012, China had established 962 scenic areas, including 225 at the national level, with a total area of 47.9 million acres (19.37 million ha). In addition, numerous urban parks, farmlands, and forest areas provide outdoor recreation opportunities for urban dwellers. Chinese people also enjoy leisure activities in indoor settings such as tea houses, mahjong houses, spas, foot massage houses, and bars of all kinds, among other places.

Most outdoor recreational opportunities are provided by public agencies, including

- the State Forestry Administration, which manages all forest parks at all levels;
- the Ministry of Housing and Urban–Rural Development, which manages all scenic areas at all levels;
- the Ministry of Agriculture, the State Marine Bureau, the Geological and Mineral Bureau, the Ministry of Environmental Protection, and the Ministry of Water Resources, which, along with the previous two agencies, manage nature reserves across the country; and
- the Ministry of Culture, which manages world heritage sites and thousands of cultural and historical sites across the country.

Popular Recreation and Leisure Pursuits

China is made up of 56 ethnic nationalities that are distinctively different from one another, culturally and historically, resulting in distinct patterns of leisure pursuits from group to group. Obviously, the scope of this chapter precludes detailed description of the leisure patterns of every nationality. Because the Han nationality accounts for 98 percent of the country's population and represents the mainstream culture of the country, the following discussion of recreation and leisure pursuits of Chinese people refers primarily to the Han nationality.

In comparison with North Americans, Chinese people tend to prefer quiet or passive leisure pursuits. For example, a comparative cross-cultural study (Jackson & Walker, 2006) found that the most frequent or most enjoyable leisure activities were passive for 84 percent of Mainland Chinese university students versus 64 percent for Canadian students, who reported that their most frequent or most enjoyable leisure activities were active. This finding was endorsed by a survey study on leisure activities pursued by urban residents in China, which found that watching TV, reading books or newspapers, listening to the radio, playing mahjong, and chatting with family members were the most popular leisure activities (Yin, 2005). Playing golf was the least popular because of its high cost, and tennis, billiards, ice-skating, fishing, hunting, and playing bridge were also less popular (Yin, 2005). Another study (Jim & Chen, 2009) about leisure activity patterns in Zhuhai, a newly developed city situated on the south coast of Guangdong province on the banks of the Pearl River estuary and close to Macau and Hong Kong, found that residents in the city reported participating in activities in the home more frequently than in activities outside the home. Moreover, they were more likely to participate in passive activities than active ones. In-home physical exercise and sport games outside the home accounted for 10 percent of all reported leisure participation. More recently, Wei, Huang, Stodolska, and Yu (2015), in examining a nationwide survey on leisure, found that "passive leisure activities (e.g., watching TV, surfing on the Internet) are related to happiness, [and] active leisure activities (e.g., exercising, socializing, shopping) do not seem to contribute to happiness in China" (p. 571).

Leisure is so highly related to culture that culture is often viewed as a synonym of leisure in the country (Ma, 1999). Leisure in China is closely related to "philosophy, aesthetics, literature and the arts, and practices of health and wellness" (Gong, 1998, as cited in Wang & Stringer, 2000, p. 35). Pursuit of such leisure activities is justified by Confucianism, which encourages a scholar or student to excel at playing the harp and chess and doing painting and calligraphy. In this way, leisure pursuits involving learning and culture could be regarded as high leisure, whereas leisure pursuits such as mahjong can be viewed as popular leisure.

China is at a crossroads of social, economic, and political transformation. During this transformation, the traditional Chinese cultural values formed in a traditional agrarian society could be

OUTSTANDING GRADUATE

Background Information

Name: Wenhua Huang

Education: BA from Central South University of Forestry and Technology, College of Tourism

Credentials: Intermediate Engineer in Forests

Awards: First prize in the 2007 Hunan Province University Undergraduate Tourism Forum Paper Contest

Career Information

Position: Deputy Director

Organization: Badaling National Forest Park in Yanqing County, Beijing, China, is under the jurisdiction of Beijing Municipal Bureau of Landscape and Forestry. It is located near Juyongguan and Badaling Great Wall, with an area of 7,265 acres (2,940 ha) and a forest coverage of 96 percent. Its highest peak is 4,062 feet (1,238 m) above sea level. Badaling National Forest Park is known as "the green gem by the bottom of the Great Wall" and is home to 539 varieties of plants and 158 varieties of animals. It is the first ecological public welfare forest area in China that is certified by the Forest Stewardship Council (FSC). The forest park mainly consists of Red Leaves Scenic Area, Qinglonggu Scenic Area, Lilac Valley Scenic Area, and Shixia Scenic Area. The park is abundant in negative oxygen ions and is famous for the most gorgeous red leaves in the autumn. The park is an AAA Tourism Scenic Area and serves as the Beijing Eco-Moral Education Base for Juveniles, the Beijing Popular Science Education Base, the National Forestry Science Education Base, and the Research, Teaching, and Internship Base for Beijing Forestry University. The park has been developed as a sustainable park that involves nature experience, environmental education, and ecotourism.

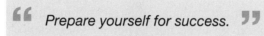

Prepare yourself for success.

Organization mission: The park is responsible for the protection of park resources and the ecological environment, maintenance of its natural appearance and human-cultural landscapes, and appropriate use of the forest resources; the overall plan and site designs of the park and associated submission, approval, and implementation; the development of tourism products, infrastructure construction, and the operation of forest tourism; and the construction of eco-civilization and natural experience and environmental education, among others.

Job description: Daily operation and management of the park, organization and arrangement of forest recreation activities.

Career path: I worked in different offices (e.g., park infrastructure construction office, planning and strategic office, and operation office) for four years before being promoted to deputy director of the park.

Likes and dislikes about the job: What I like the most is that I can always be close to nature.

Advice for Undergraduates

Be passionate and inquisitive. Enjoy experiencing nature and learn more about the demands of different visitor groups.

---

changed in the process of modernization. Economic globalization could accelerate this change. In fact, globalization has already had great influence on the daily life of Chinese people. For instance, attitudes toward beauty pageants, fashion shows, sexual behavior, consumption behavior, dress, hairstyles, celebration of Western festivals, and leisure have largely changed in the past two decades because of modernization and globalization. In recent years, Western leisure pursuits and sports that are active and adventurous have been introduced to China (e.g., rock climbing, mountaineering, camping, picnicking and barbecuing, using recreational vehicles, water rafting, playing tennis, golfing). These activities are becoming increasingly popular among Chi-

nese people, especially the youth. Another example is that cultural leisure pursuits among Chinese people have been fundamentally influenced. For instance, American movies are much more popular than local movies. Watching American movies and playing board games are rated as top leisure activities by current college students. Another cultural leisure pursuit that has been greatly influenced by globalization is the celebration of Western festivals and holidays, which have become more popular than Chinese ones, especially among the youth. For instance, many people celebrate the Western style of Valentine's Day; *qi xi*, the traditional Chinese version of this holiday, is almost unknown among most Chinese people. Christmas is another holiday celebrated with great passion by Chinese people. A survey study of leisure pursuits of the Chinese middle class found that the leisure patterns pursued by the youth fall into one of four leisure types: tag (fashion followers) (Zhou, 2008), entertainment and relaxation, function (utilitarianism), and free.

Of the numerous leisure activities pursued by Chinese people, tai chi and mahjong are arguably the favorite traditional ones, particularly among middle-aged and older people. Tai chi is taught to college students in physical education classes, but because of its slow tempo, few young people like it. When people grow older, however, they realize the importance of being healthy, and they learn to practice tai chi. Although the Chinese government has favored tai chi as a healthy exercise, mahjong was once banned as a gambling activity and is not endorsed by the government today, although people of all classes, occupations, and ages are obsessed with the table game.

Another leisure activity that has recently become popular among residents in almost every city in China is public dance, or **square dance**, in which dozens to hundreds of people dance together for several hours, usually in the evening, in an urban open space (public square or plaza). Most of these dancers spontaneously stand in formation and follow one or two dancers in front who lead the dance, which has simple moves and a relatively slow tempo. A survey study conducted in Chongqing, a northwest city, found that 45 percent of the city's residents reported having participated in this group activity (Li, Zhou, & Chen, 2009). The significance of public square dance has also attracted the attention of researchers (Peng, 2010).

CHALLENGES AND TRENDS FOR THE FUTURE

Although the leisure industry in China has experienced rapid growth in recent years, there is no sign that this growth will stop if the country's economy continues to grow. However, the leisure industry faces a number of challenges.

First, attitudes toward leisure among Chinese people are generally negative (Wei et al., 2015). As recently as the 1970s, leisure (*xiu xian*) was a bad word and a symbol of pursuing the lifestyle of capitalist societies. Wang and Stringer (2000) observed

that Chinese people are less likely to view leisure as an important component of their lives compared with North Americans because Chinese, in general, tend to have a stronger work ethic (see also Ap, 2002; Xiao, 1997). Potentially, this view of leisure reflects the traditional values that Chinese place on hard work and achievement. But this negative attitude toward leisure has changed considerably in recent years due to rapid economic development, increasing living standards in mainland China, and the influence of globalization (Wei, 2009). In recognition of the global trends in leisure and its importance to enhancing the quality of life of Chinese people, many scholars have recently called for devoting more attention to leisure and leisure research in China, which, we contend, has led to greater awareness of leisure among the public. That said, many Chinese people still consider leisure as similar to being lazy.

Second, leisure education is lacking among Chinese. Chinese education is fundamentally examination and score oriented, which deprives students of time for leisure. The education system is extremely competitive, which put students under heavy pressure. As a result, leisure awareness is not well nurtured among Chinese (Deng, 2002; Liu, 2007).

Third, China is experiencing rapid urbanization. Open spaces are shrinking, and limited facilities are available for leisure. For example, a survey (Lu & Yu, 2005) found that 37 percent of residential areas in Beijing had no sport and fitness facilities. In addition, Beijing had only 1.96 community sport and fitness centers per 10,000 people in 2003, whereas Germany had 9.08 centers per 10,000 people in 1976 (Lu & Yu, 2005). To address this issue, community sport and fitness centers are designated in most cities to provide opportunities for residents to exercise and socialize. For example, beginning in 2013, Beijing started adding outdoor fitness facilities to 97 deteriorating districts and neighborhoods. These facilities provide a variety of fitness opportunities for residents of all ages including chess and poker areas, rehabilitation areas, playgrounds, trails, tai chi areas, areas for walking with caged birds, and so on. It is estimated that more than 1,000 residents use these fitness areas every day (Beijing Youth Daily, 2016).

Finally, there is inequality in leisure pursuits. Although China has experienced rapid economic development in the past two decades and has become the world's second-largest economy after the United States, the country is confronted by a number of issues, including unequal economic development across regions and a growing income gap between the wealthy and the poor, resulting in unequal leisure opportunities for the public. For example, in 2010, China had an estimated 230 million migrant workers who emigrated from the countryside to cities looking for better-paying work in construction sites and factories. Most of these migrant workers do not pursue leisure activities because their pay is low and they have to work long hours.

Even some middle-class people do not have time for leisure because they are busy with work and cannot fully relax. A recent study showed that Chinese leisure time has decreased in recent years. Specifically, urban and rural residents had an average of 1,774 hours and 1,766 hours for leisure in 2012 as opposed to 1,351 hours and 1,502 hours in 2015, respectively (China Tourism Academy, 2016). According to another study (Zhou, 2008), 58.6 percent of Chinese participants were not satisfied with their leisure, and only 5 percent reported being very satisfied. The survey also showed that over 65 percent of the middle class had less than 20 hours per week of leisure time, 80 percent reported that their leisure was constrained by work, 80 percent felt heavy work pressure, and 28 percent believed that their work pressure had reached an intolerable point. Their salaries are lower than expected given the high pressure that they are under, which further affects their leisure quality.

Although China's leisure industry faces significant challenges, it will likely continue to grow due to several trends. First, although domestic travel continues to increase, more Chinese can afford to travel to other countries. In 2009, the ratios of domestic, inbound, and outbound tours were 90.8 to 6.5 to 2.7 (Liu, Gao & Song, 2010, p. 13). It is safe to say that most Chinese will enjoy travel as a leisure activity in their lives. Second, unlike traditional package tours arranged by a tour operator or travel agent, various kinds of independent tours that are planned by individuals are thriving because of the rapid development of highway and railway systems and the increasing ownership of cars. For example, of the 4 billion domestic visits in 2015, 3.2 billion (80 percent) are independent visits made by individuals without the assistance of a travel agent (National Tourism Administration of China, 2016). Third, technological developments make it possible to accomplish many more things online. More leisure activities, such as online reading and gaming, will be accomplished through Internet use. In addition, online selling and purchasing of leisure services will increase tremendously in every sector of the leisure industry. Finally, with increasing globalization and modernization, Western culture will continue to affect the leisure pursuits of Chinese people, which may cause the loss of local cultural traits. In other words, Chinese people's worldviews and behaviors may change over time through the pursuits of leisure activities with Western characteristics due to increasing Americanization or globalization.

SUMMARY

Traditionally, Chinese people placed less value on leisure and instead emphasized hard work and education. Although this view of leisure is still prevalent in the current Chinese society, it has gradually changed in recent years due to modernization and globalization. More people have come to realize that leisure is an essential part of daily life. As a result, the leisure industry has seen steady growth over the past two decades, which has caused tremendous economic and social changes in the country. The central government has played an essential role in promoting and guiding leisure pursuits of Chinese people. In addition, leisure attitudes and behaviors have been shaped by leisure researchers, particularly those who have actively promoted public leisure participation through conferences, forums, mass media, magazines, and academic publications.

Although many public agencies provide an array of outdoor recreational opportunities for the public, Chinese people tend to enjoy indoor passive leisure activities more than they do outdoor activities. Some of those indoor passive leisure activities are deeply rooted in traditional Chinese culture and are found to be significantly related to happiness.

The leisure pursuits of Chinese people, particularly the youth, have been considerably influenced by Western culture because of globalization. Leisure pursuits in China have traditionally been different from those in Western society. But cultural distance and distinctive leisure pursuits between China and Western society have diminished under the pressure of cultural diffusion resulting from economic and cultural globalization. Although cultural diffusion may bring with it some negative impacts, the concept of harmony, which is strongly rooted in Chinese culture, plays an essential role in the absorption of elements of other cultures. Moreover, the proactive policies of the Chinese government help maintain traditional Chinese culture. Thus, the negative influence of globalization on the leisure pursuits of Chinese people may be cushioned by the compatible nature of Chinese culture and the preemptive measures taken by the Chinese government.

Recreation in Nigeria

Franz U. Atare and Felicia S. Ekpu

> " The minute you lose consciousness of the need to recreate you start de-creating. "
>
> Yomi Awosika, professor emeritus, University of Ibadan

Nigeria comprises 36 states and its Federal Capital Territory. Nigeria is located in West Africa and shares land borders with the Republic of Benin (west), Chad and Cameroon (east), and Niger (north); its coast to the south lies on the Gulf of Guinea in the Atlantic Ocean. Present-day Nigeria has been the site of numerous kingdoms and tribal states spanning more than 1,000 years. Nigeria is often referred to as the "giant of Africa" due to its large population and economy. With approximately 174 million inhabitants, Nigeria is the most populous country in Africa and the seventh most populous country in the world. Nigeria also has one of the largest populations of youth in the world. The country is inhabited by 500 ethnic groups, each of which has its own unique forms of recreation and leisure activities.

The country has a varied landscape. The far south is defined by its tropical rainforest climate, and annual rainfall is 60 to 80 inches (152.4 to 203.2 cm). The country has interesting natural resources that shape the recreation and leisure behavior of the inhabitants such as the Obudu plateau in Cross River, the coastal plains in Lagos, the mangrove forests in Delta and Bayelsa, the highland hills and mountains that form the Marbella plateau in Taraba (the highest in Nigeria), and Shere Hills in Jos. The topography and climate conditions largely influence the types of recreation and leisure available in a given location. For example, swimming is popular in Lagos, Bayelsa, Delta, and Rivers due to their proximity to the Atlantic coast (Morakinyo & Atare, 2005).

Another issue that defines recreational interests is religion. Nigeria is roughly divided in half between Christians, who live mostly in the southern and central parts of the country, and Muslims, who are concentrated mostly in the northern and southwestern regions. Muslims tend to frown on the forms of recreation that come from Europe and the United States and perceive them as ploys to derail the faith and religious attitudes of their adherents. Christians are more receptive to Western forms of recreation. This division between Christians and Muslims is eliminated in **competitive sports**, especially in football.

In 2014, Nigeria's gross domestic product became the largest in Africa at more than $500 billion, and it surpassed South Africa to become the world's 21st largest economy. It is also listed among the next 11 economies set to become the biggest in the world. This is not reflected in the population, however. The poverty gap continues to widen, and most citizens live on less than $1 per day. The implication to leisure service use is that most people cannot afford recreation pursuits that are not free. This further explains why, despite its vast natural tourism potential, recreation and tourism apart from Nollywood (the Nigeria film industry) did not account for the gross domestic product. Most Nigerians continue to spend their leisure hours seeking additional sources of livelihood at the expense of leisure and recreation endeavors.

The population distribution is 51.7 percent rural and 48.3 percent urban, and the population density is 167.5 people per square kilometer. Modern infrastructure for recreation is located in urban areas. There is a steady increase in rural to urban migration, and this gradually leads to a loss of **cultural heritage** and recreation options in rural areas. Due to the population increase in major cities and high rates of unemployment, the cities have attracted criminal and gang activity, thus raising security concerns. Public recreation centers and parks are often neglected due to fear of being robbed or kidnapped.

At the same time, there is a rapid expansion in the entertainment industry. Most people capitalize on this by staying at home and watching movies. This contributes to the growth of the filmmaking industry. Nollywood is the second largest producer of movies in the world. Nigerian cinema is Africa's largest movie industry in terms of value and number of movies produced per year.

HISTORICAL DEVELOPMENT OF RECREATION AND LEISURE IN NIGERIA

Sports, games, and dances in Nigeria, as indeed in most African states, dates back as far as the origin of Africans. Starting from the desire to meet basic needs such as the provision of food and defense against hostile environments, sporting activities like hunting, wrestling, and bow shooting served as sports and recreation. In the traditional African setting, survival demanded the profitable use of available free time to do things that contributed to comfort in people's lives. Children learned to dress hides, weave clothes, shoot weapons, and play during all adult life activities. When the adults were not stalking game, they were mending weapons, and when they were not tilling the soil, they were repairing implements. These activities are mimicked by children as their own form of recreation and they derived fun and satisfaction for doing so. In pastoral societies, storytelling, songs, and dances were important features of recreation. In pre-colonial Nigeria, no organized program of

recreation was deemed necessary. Very little leisure time was available, and it was not put to a worthy use by the exigencies of the culture. When time permitted, the tribes created recreation through songs, stories, and dance.

Recreation is not new to any community in Nigeria. Each has its own modes of recreation and various times or occasions for participation. The traditional lives of many Nigerians have always provided for worthy use of leisure hours. In modern times, young people and adults in all regions in Nigeria engage in recreational activities that are indigenous to their region (with the exception of team sports, which were introduced from Europe) that are often referred to as *games*. During the early post-independence era, Nigeria was divided into four distinct regions (North, East, West, and Midwest). These regions had different languages and cultural patterns that influenced the types of games played based on their environment. Those games served recreational, leisure, cultural, and religious functions. The games formed the basis of their everyday and cultural life (Amuchie, 2003)

Although bastardized by colonial influences, many of these games are still practiced today. Recreational activities vary between states, communities, and ethnic groups, but some are shared. Activities include traditional boxing (*dambe*), archery, canoeing (boat regatta), and dancing (*atilogwu, egwuamara, ekpe, eyo, fuji, afrojuju, awigiri, ikenike, ekong, uta, ebre, abang*, etc.). Climbing, which is recreational and used in fruit harvesting, helps develop the muscles of the trunk, arms, and legs. Hunting is done individually or communally on certain market days. In the early 1900s, very successful hunters were traditionally honored because hunting served as an occupation and a hobby. Wrestling was one of the earliest leisure activities in Nigeria, and it is practiced in all parts of the country. **Abula** and *langa* are the most popular forms to date; they are taught in schools, and there are wrestling competitions during national sport festivals.

Horse racing is a common recreational activity in the northern regions, especially Kaduna and Borno states, where it is at its peak. Good horse riders jump obstacles and use horses to play a game called *polo* that resembles hockey. Horse riding is also a popular pastime among the elite Hausas and Fulanis ethnic groups that dominate the northern region. Owning and maintaining a horse is an expensive form of recreation not open to those of low economic means.

Moonlight games are recreational games with little organization that are used as a form of relaxation after a strenuous day's work and night meals. They vary in structure, but their common feature is that they usually need no equipment and are played during the full moon. Common moonlight games include touch and run, cock fight, hide and seek, dance, storytelling, frog jump, and others. Moonlight games offer youth the opportunity to socialize, recreate, and develop mentally, physically, and emotionally, thus satisfying the World Health Organization's concept of health as a state of complete physical, mental, and social well-being, and not merely the absence of diseases or infirmity. The games are popular in all states of Nigeria, especially in the rural areas, and they are sometimes featured on national television.

The introduction of formal education into the country, especially physical education, changed recreation to reflect modern sports taught in schools. The British colonial masters fostered outdoor activities for recreation. Athletics, horse riding, fishing, hunting, swimming, tennis, skating, golf, football, archery, and hockey were common features of English life, and these were passed down to colonies including Nigeria. Most other foreign sports, such as gymnastics and volleyball, have common features with Nigerian traditional sports.

Before the incursion of the British colonialists in Nigeria, women were traditionally involved in several physical activities for fun and recreation even while they were performing domestic chores and agricultural duties. Dancing was a prominent recreational activity that was featured during festivals, ceremonies, and celebrations. Examples are New Yam and Argungu Fishing festivals. Ceremonies include naming, wedding, initiation, and burial. Celebrations included birthdays; housewarming; good health or recovery from illness; escape from accident, death, or robbery; safe delivery; traveling hazard; chieftaincy installation or coronation; and anniversaries (Ikulayo, 2003).

To date, dancing is highly cherished as a means of traditional and cultural recreation. It produces joy, fun, happiness, and fulfillment and is a strong means of self-expression, even among men.

Ayo is one of the oldest seed and board games in Nigeria. It has been given different names by different language groups, such as *mancala, oware, bao, onweso, oko, enkeshin, nsa,* or *isip isong*. It is played with seed and a board with 12 holes or with 12 holes dug in the ground. Each hole has four seeds. It can be played by two to four people. Today it is included in the basic school curriculum as a recreational activity for all school children (Udomiaye & Umar, 2010).

Since independence in 1960, football has been the most popular form of recreation. It is regarded as a national obsession and is popular with male and female citizens of all ages. Watching live football matches from the English Premier League (EPL), Spanish League (*Laliga*), and German League (*Bundus liga*) is a popular pastime.

Apart from football and basketball, in which Nigeria has made a mark on the international scene, sports do not attract large crowds except during national sport festivals. As in Brazil and other football-loving nations, youth use any available space to play football, such as roads, sand banks, and beaches. Many young people have sacrificed education for a career in football; examples include international soccer stars such as Kanu Nwankwo, Austin Okocha, Mikel Obi, and Sunday Oliseh, all of whom started their football careers in the street but now play in major leagues.

Market days, which are a social and economic feature prevalent among agriculturally based groups, are held on different days in all parts of Nigeria and in many other West African countries. Traditionally, the farmers and most other craftsmen and women rest on important market days, some Sundays, and other special days. These special days are dedicated to local deities, and some dances and sacrifices are featured in these ceremonies. These resting days are also set aside for burial ceremonies and marriages. Apart from these resting days, some ceremonial activities also take place when farmers and the traders return from their farms and markets. On market days rural traders have increased leisure hours that are used for recreational purposes such as storytelling, riddles, and jokes, as other strenuous daily activities are prohibited. In some communities market day is held either weekly or fortnightly. Some youth engage in wrestling and other physical displays. Girls and small children participate in moonlight games, dances, songs, and jokes. It is an important day in the life of most communities, as visitors from nearby communities exchange visits and cultural displays.

Each cultural group, village, or town and families or group of families are noted for some particular occupation and other cultural activities. In some cases, individuals that are gifted with some special cultural talents contribute to the recreation needs of the community. These activities help solidify families and ethnic groups.

Cinema halls and viewing centers, shopping malls, and comedy performances are also prominent leisure activities in major cities across Nigeria.

SETTINGS, ORGANIZATION, AND STRUCTURES

Agencies are responsible for recreational activities and programs, but they are also supervised by the government. An agency is a government department, business, or private organization that provides a specific service. In Nigeria, there are four types of agencies: public, private, commercial, or voluntary. Recreation areas handled by commercial agencies exist for financial profit that accrues from the provision of recreation services. Voluntary agencies seek enrichment of individual and community life. According to Atare (2003), the structure of recreation organizations in Nigeria can be classified into five agencies based on the provision of recreation facilities, activities, and programs:

1. **Individual and home**: Recreation requires individual engagement and involvement. Many forms of recreation such as walking, artwork, hobbies, and caring for pets are essentially individual. They are, however, more enjoyable when engaged in with a group. Modern homes devote much space to recreational use. In the backyard, pets, gardening, and toys play an important role in the lives of many families. Much of indoor play takes place at home in different forms such as games, reading, playing with toys, playing musical instruments, or having parties. The most common forms of home recreation for young people are watching videos, listening to music, and tending gardens. Home activi-

ties tend to occupy more leisure hours than recreation provided by outside agencies.

2. **Private agencies.** These agencies usually restrict their recreational programs to members. The use of facilities might be extended to family members and close associates. These agencies do not depend on community support; rather members' payment of dues and fees help to administer programs and build and maintain the facilities. These clubs exist in every major city (e.g., Uyo Club, founded in 1935) in Nigeria and on all university campuses (e.g., senior staff club). Some industries also have recreational clubs for their workers (e.g., Shell Petroleum Development Company, Chevron Nigeria Unlimited).

3. **Voluntary agencies.** Voluntary agencies in Nigeria provide services for varying age groups and many require membership. Facilities and programs are usually funded through contributions from individuals, united funds, sponsorships, and membership fees. These agencies can be grouped into those that restrict participation to members and those who permit nonmembers to participate.

4. **Commercial agencies.** Commercial recreation agencies capitalize on the natural demand for recreation and the avoidance of boredom by people of different classes. The influx of commercial agencies in the provision of recreation programs reflects the inability of other agencies to meet the demand to provide adequately for recreation. Although commercial agencies are profit-oriented, many of them sometimes offer free and discounted services in a way to encourage those who enjoy passive forms of recreation The most popular forms of commercial recreation are amusement parks and entertainment, travel and tourism, and athletics and sports.

5. **Governmental agencies.** An increasing number of government departments and bureaus (e.g., National Park Service, Forest Service, Fish and Wildlife Service, Bureau of Reclamation, Ministry of Youth and Sports) provide recreation services to the general public in cooperation with other agencies. The Nigerian government has shown remarkable

concern in matters relating to recreation and sports since the end of the Nigerian civil war in 1970. Large sums of money have been allocated and spent on sports and recreation programs.

DIVERSE POPULATIONS AND THEIR INTERESTS

One of the cardinal principles of recreation is to provide ample opportunity for everyone irrespective of age, religion, sex, or social belief. Other opportunities still available for recreation are as follows:

Recreation for Those in School. Recreation in most cases is treated as a function of the family, but it is also that of the school. The schools provide programs and facilities that help children develop recreation leadership skills that will eventually be translated to adult life. Recreation facilities are not prominent in government-owned primary and secondary schools as compared to private schools. The situation is different in tertiary institutions (all states have at least four tertiary institutions) with facilities for recreation and sport. The quantity in terms of facilities and program offered varies from institution to institution according to need and scope of program offered. Conventional universities have more recreational and sporting facilities than specialized institutions (Atare & Ekpu, 2014b). In all institutions of higher learning, there are no classes after noon on Wednesday to facilitate participation in recreational opportunities. It also serves as a selection process for students who will represent the institution in the Nigeria University Games Association (NUGA), the Nigeria Polytechnic Games Association (NIPOGA), and the Nigeria Colleges of Education Games Association (NICEGA) games. The curriculum of basic education includes dance, computer games, *ludo,* chess, draught, Scrabble, music, novel reading, table tennis, swimming, bow and arrow, *langa*, and *abula* and is designed to prepare youth to develop recreation consciousness that they will transfer to adult life.

Recreation for the Family During Holidays. A more recent trend in the industry is carnivals. In Nigeria carnivals are held in streets and they are prevalent during national holidays. These carnivals are similar to those held in Brazil in terms of dressing, number of participants, duration, age groupings, and tourist draw, and they provide families ample time away from home solely for recreation and amusement. Carnivals draw many

Getty Images/Lonely Planet Images/Jane Sweeney

Recreation for families takes place at the many carnivals and festivals that take place throughout Nigeria, such as the Durbar Festival.

visitors, and children and youth in particular enjoy them. Prominent among them are the Eyo Festival in Lagos, Calabar Carnival, Uyo Carnival, Durbar Festival, Kaduna, August Meeting in Owerri (among the Ibo-speaking women, August is a time when all the women return home to take part in this carnival that has many opportunities for the leisure service and hospitality industries), Argungu Fishing Festival, Boat Regatta in Warri and Lagos, and Abuja Carnival.

Recreation for Industrial Workers. Big industrial companies (e.g., Shell Petroleum Development Company, Chevron Nigeria, First Bank of Nigeria, Delta Steel Company) also provide recreation. These corporate bodies understand the integration between business and recreation and thus are expending personnel, space, and financial resources to promote recreation activities for their workers.

Recreation for Religious Adherents. Many religious groups in Nigeria are now aware of the importance of recreation in the life of their followers; hence members are encouraged to participate in wholesome recreation activities as they contribute to the spiritual well-being of the individual. Some Christian religious organizations provide school break camps for children, retreats, annual conventions, overnight vigils, and other programs during holidays such as Christmas, especially in the southern part of the country that is dominated by Christians. Some have provided standard recreational facilities such as a football pitch, volleyball courts, swimming pools, and aerobic halls in the same premises as worship. Muslims encourage members to spend time with their families and friends in parks during holiday seasons such as *Id el Fitr* and *Id el Kabir*.

Recreation for Adults. Among adult men, draught (a highly intellectual 40 seed game played on a square board of 100 smaller square boxes, where each player has 20 seeds evenly distributed within the first 40 boxes on each side), pet keeping, reading newspapers, and watching television are popular pastimes, especially for those who are no longer regularly employed (e.g., pensioners and retirees). For adult women, domestic chores, religious activities, and gardening rank high among pastimes. A popular leisure activity for middle-aged women is participation in social clubs and associations that meet weekly in the homes of members.

Meetings are characterized by dancing, singing, and merriment, especially when humanitarian assistance is offered to members in times of need. These meetings can last three to six hours depending on the size of the group.

CHALLENGES, ISSUES, AND TRENDS

Outdoor recreation is not popular due to the country's climate. There are two seasons in Nigeria: rainy and *harmattan* (the tropical continental airmass). November to February is the harmattan season, when the northeast trade wind blows across the Atlantic Ocean and causes dryness. The rainy (the tropical maritime airmass) season has heavy downpours and lasts from March to October with annual rainfall ranging from 79 inches (2,000 mm) to 185 inches (4,700 mm) with its highest peak in July. Those who engage in outdoor activities do so for economic reasons rather than for recreational interest.

Although Nigeria has a high GDP, the per capita income is low, which means many citizens live below the poverty line. As a result, expensive forms of recreation are not within reach for those in the low income groups.

Comedy shows have become increasingly popular. Ali Baba, Basket Mouth, Ay, Gordons, I Go Die, Teju Baby Face, and others have made comedy a very important form of recreation. Some individuals prefer to buy the videos and watch them at home rather than visiting theaters, museums, and play houses to watch them live. In general, the increasing demand for home video entertainment has led to a drastic decline in physical recreation activities. Most elite people prefer to visit a gym for physical activity than to engage in brisk walking or jogging; this trend is also related to security concerns. The few individuals who engage in physical recreation do so for health (e.g., prevention of obesity or diabetes), fitness, and sport competition reasons (Atare, 2014).

The number of Nigerians that visit stadiums to watch international football matches continues to increase, but the reverse is true for **local club sides,** or Nigerian football clubs. Between 1990 and 2005, Nigerian local clubs enjoyed a great following: Fans traveled long distances to watch live matches and tickets were bought in advance.

Now, most clubs play in nearly empty stadiums. The situation is different with international matches: In the 2019 African Cup of Nations qualifiers held on June 10, 2017 at the Godswill Akpabio International Stadium in Uyo between Super Eagles of Nigeria and Bafana Bafana of South Africa, the stadium was filled to capacity (30,000 people). In that same stadium one week later, Akwa United football club played Katsina United football club and the attendance was less than 2,000. A September 2012 survey conducted by NOIPolls reported that 89 percent of Nigerians interviewed are supporters of foreign football clubs and 52 percent said they do not follow Nigerian club sides (NOIPolls, 2014).

Technology growth has also greatly influenced leisure behavior, and it seriously threatens active leisure. Many people, especially children and women, spend increasing amounts of time on their mobile devices playing games or using social media programs such as 2go, Facebook, WhatsApp, Badoo, BBM, and Twitter.

Despite the growth in the leisure service industry, few institutions of higher learning offer degree programs in leisure and recreation. In almost all degree-awarding institutions, recreation is taught only as a course in the department of physical and health education. A few Nigerian universities offer degree programs in recreation (University of Ibadan, University of Benin, and University of Nigeria). Many universities offer programs in hospitality management and tourism.

Recreation and leisure services are now an integral part of everyday living and creating a balanced life. The number of fitness and recreational clubs, gyms, spas, stadiums, and carnivals are increasing. Apart from health concerns that have attracted many to avail themselves to recreation, consciousness of recreational activities is great among the average Nigerian. There is also a high demand for recreational goods and products. The Nigerian market is open for manufacturers of recreational goods and products that combine traditional and modern games. This growth is likely to increase with the introduction of recreation in the secondary school curriculum and easy access to popular forms of recreation shown on television such as merry-go-rounds, computer games, rope skipping, tug-of-war, and cartoon movies.

Most rural areas are quickly evolving into urban towns due to rapid growth in settlement areas and increasing building developments. There is a concern that these new towns lack space provisions for parks or recreation centers. If this trend is sustained, people who seek recreation will have to travel long distances to participate.

SUMMARY

This section examined the historical development of recreation in Nigeria and how the geopolitical distribution of the country affects recreational service delivery. Passive forms of recreation appear to be more popular than physical recreation due to security and economic concerns. Recreation is administered through five agencies that meet the recreation needs of those in school, families, industrial workers, sports enthusiasts, and adults. Nigerians enjoy many forms of recreation; we hope that in the near future abundant natural and human resources that promote recreation will be properly developed and will make Nigeria a recreation, holiday, and tourist destination of choice.

References

CHAPTER 1

Active Living Research. (2015). *Active education: Growing evidence on physical activity and academic performance.* Retrieved from http://activelivingresearch.org/sites/default/files/ALR_Brief_ActiveEducation_Jan2015.pdf

Association for Psychological Science. (2014). *Creative hobbies linked with job performance.* Retrieved from http://www.psychologicalscience.org/index.php/news/minds-business/creative-hobbies-linked-with-job-performance.html

Barton, J., Griffin, M., & Pretty, J. (2011). Exercise-, nature- and socially interactive-based initiatives improve mood and self-esteem in the clinical population. *Perspectives in Public Health, 132*(2), 89-96. doi:10.1177/1757913910393862

Buchholz, A.C., Ginis Martin, K.A., Bray, S.R., Craven, C., Hicks, A. L., Hayes, K. C., … Wolfe, D. L. (2009). Greater daily leisure time physical activity is associated with lower chronic disease risk in adults with spinal cord injury. *Applied Physiology Nutrition & Metabolism, 34,* 640-647.

Corwin, M.R. (2001). Guess who I am? *Parks & Recreation, 168.*

Csikszentmihalyi, M. (1991). *Flow: The psychology of the optimal experience.* New York, NY: Harper Perennial.

Driver, B. (1998). The benefits are endless . . . but why? *Parks & Recreation, 26.*

Helliwell, J., Layard, R., & Sachs, J. (2016). *World happiness report 2016, update (Vol. I).* New York, NY: Sustainable Development Solutions Network. Retrieved from http://worldhappiness.report/ed/2016/

Ibsen, M., & Bump, T. (2015). *The economic impact of the bicycle industry in Portland.* Portland, OR: Bureau of Planning and Sustainability. Retrieved from http://www.portlandoregon.gov/bps/article/555482

Kardan, O., Gozdyra, P., Misic, B., Moola, F., Palmer, L.J., & Berman, M.G. (2015). Neighborhood greenspace and health in a large urban center. *Scientific Reports, 9.* Retrieved from http://www.nature.com/articles/srep11610

The Nature Conservancy. (n.d.). *Why is our water in trouble? Threats to freshwater ecosystems.* Retrieved from http://www.nature.org/ourinitiatives/habitats/riverslakes/threatsimpacts/

Potwarka, L.R., Kaczynski, A.T., & Flack, A.L. (2008). Places to play: Association of park space and facilities with healthy weight status among children. *Journal of Community Health, 33*(5), 344-350.

Saint Louis University Medical Center. (2014). *Older adults feel less hip, knee pain when moving to the groove.* Retrieved from https://www.sciencedaily.com/releases/2014/06/140612174449.htm

Texas Parks and Wildlife Department. (2014). *Texas A&M study trumpets Texas State Parks' economic benefit [Media release].* Retrieved from https://tpwd.texas.gov/newsmedia/releases/?req=20141106c

Tourisme Montréal. (2014). *Annual report.* Retrieved from http://documents.tourisme-montreal.org/Montreal-Tourism/R-and-D/Statistics/EN/ra-2014-en.pdf

United States Environmental Protection Agency. (n.d.). *Smart growth and preservation of existing historic buildings.* Retrieved from https://www.epa.gov/smartgrowth/smart-growth-and-preservation-existing-and-historic-buildings

CHAPTER 2

American Alliance for Health, Physical Education, Recreation and Dance (AAHPERD). (n.d.). *About.* Retrieved from http://www.aahperd.org/about/

Canadian Parks and Recreation Association (CPRA). (2015). *A framework for recreation in Canada: Pathways to well-being.* Retrieved from https://www.cpra.ca/about-the-framework/

Canadian Parks and Recreation Association (CPRA). (n.d.). *What is CPRA.* Retrieved from https://www.cpra.ca/what-is-cpra/

Cross, G. (1990). *A social history of leisure since 1600.* State College, PA: Venture.

Dare, B., Welton, G., & Coe, W. (1987). *Concepts of leisure in Western thought: A critical and historical analysis.* Dubuque, IA: Kendall/Hunt.

DeGraff, J., Wann, D., & Naylor, T.H. (2001). *Affluenza: The all-consuming epidemic.* San Francisco, CA: Berrett-Koehler.

Edgington, C., Jordan, D., DeGraff, D., & Edgington, S. (1998). *Leisure and life satisfaction: Foundational perspectives.* Boston, MA: WCB/McGraw Hill.

Francis, R.D., Jones, R., & Smith, D. (1988). *Origins: Canadian history to confederation.* Toronto, ON: Holt, Rinehart and Winston of Canada.

Goodale, T., & Godbey, G. (1988). *The evolution of leisure.* State College, PA: Venture.

Harrington, M. (1996). Women's leisure and the family in Canada. In N. Samuel (Ed.), *Women, leisure and the family in contemporary society: A multinational perspective* (pp. 35-48). Wellingford, UK: CAB International.

Horna, J. (1994). *The study of leisure: An introduction.* Toronto, ON: Oxford University Press.

Ibrahim, H. (1979). Leisure in the ancient world. In H. Ibrahim & J. Shivers (Eds.), *Leisure: emergence and expansion* (pp. 45-78). Los Alamitos, CA: Hwong.

Ibrahim, H. (1991). *Leisure and society: A comparative approach.* Dubuque, IA: Brown.

Illinois State Museum. (n.d.). *The Illinois: Society, recreation.* Retrieved from http://www.museum.state.il.us/muslink/nat_amer/post/htmls/soc_rec.html

Interprovincial Sport and Recreation Council (ISRC). (1987). *National recreation statement.* Retrieved from http://www.lin.ca/resource/html/statemen.htm

Karlis, G. (2004). *Leisure and recreation in Canadian society: An introduction.* Toronto, ON: Thompson.

Karlis, G. (2016). *Leisure and recreation in Canadian Society: An introduction* (3rd ed.). Toronto, ON: Thompson.

Kim, J., & Van Puymbroecke, M. (2011). Providing culturally competent therapeutic recreation for East Asian immigrant clients. *Annual in Therapeutic Recreation, 19,* 114-124.

Kim, K., Compton, D.M., & McCormick, B. (2013). The relationship among motivational environment, autonomous self-regulation and personal variables in refugee youth: Implications for mental health and youth leadership. *Journal of Leisure Research, 16*(3), 230-251.

Kraus, R. (1971). *Recreation and leisure in modern society.* Glenview, IL: Scott Foresman.

Kraus, R. (1990). *Recreation and leisure in modern society* (4th ed.). Glenview, IL: Scott Foresman.

Kraus, R. (2001). *Recreation and leisure in modern society* (6th ed.). Sudbury, MA: Jones and Bartlett.

LaPierre, L. (1992). *Canada, my Canada: What happened?* Toronto, ON: McLelland & Stewart.

MacNeil, R., & Gould, D.L. (2012). Global perspectives on leisure and aging. In H. Gibson & J. Singleton (Eds.), *Leisure and aging: Theory and practice* (pp. 3-26). Champaign, IL: Human Kinetics.

Markham, S. (1992). Our leaders speak up. *Recreation Canada, 50*(2), 15-19.

Markham, S. (1995). The early years: 1944 to 1951. *Recreation Canada, 53*(3), 6-16.

McFarland, E.M. (1970). *The development of public recreation in Canada.* Ottawa, ON: Canadian Parks and Recreation Association.

McLean, A.D., Hurd, A.R., & Rogers, N.B. (2005). *Kraus' recreation and leisure in modern society.* Sudbury, MA: Jones and Bartlett.

Mendelsohn, D. (2004, August). What Olympic ideal? *New York Times Magazine,* 11-13.

Missouri State Parks and Historic Sites. (n.d.). *The history of Missouri's state park system.* Retrieved from http://mostateparks.com/page/59044/history-missouris-state-park-system

National Alliance for Youth Sports (NAYS). (n.d.). *Mission and history.* Retrieved from https://www.nays.org/about/about-nays/mission/

National Recreation and Park Association (NRPA). (n.d.). *About.* Retrieved from http://www.nrpa.org/About-National-Recreation-and-Park-Association/

Parks and Recreation Ontario (PRO). (n.d.). *Who we are.* Retrieved from http://www.prontario.org/index.php?ci_id=3669

Parks Canada. (n.d.). *The Parks Canada mandate and charter.* Retrieved from http://www.pc.gc.ca/en/agence-agency/mandat-mandate

ParticipACTION. (n.d.). *About: Leading Canada towards sitting less and moving more.* Retrieved from https://www.participaction.com/en-ca/about

The ParticipACTION Archive Project. (n.d.-a). *The early years: TV, radio and print media.* Retrieved from http://scaa.sk.ca/gallery/participaction/english/motivate/theearlyyears.html

The ParticipACTION Archive Project. (n.d.-b). *Historic timeline.* Retrieved from http://scaa.sk.ca/gallery/participaction/english/structure/timeline.html

PHE Canada. (n.d.-a). *Our history.* Retrieved from http://www.phecanada.ca/about-us

PHE Canada. (n.d.-b). *Our vision and mission.* Retrieved from http://www.phecanada.ca/about-us/vision/mission

Poliakoff, M. (1993). Stadium and arena: Reflections on Greek, Roman and contemporary social history. *Olympika: The International Journal of Olympic Studies, 2,* 67-78.

Pruchno, R. (2012). Not your mother's old age: Baby boomers at 65. *The Gerontologist, 52*(2), 149-152.

Rainwater, C. (1992). *The play movement in the United States.* Chicago, IL: University of Chicago Press.

Recreation Nova Scotia. (n.d.). *Discover RNS.* Retrieved from http://www.recreationns.ns.ca/discover-rns/

Saskatchewan Parks and Recreation Association (SPRA). (n.d.). *About.* Retrieved from http://www.spra.sk.ca/spra/

Searle, M., & Brayley, R. (1993). *Leisure services in Canada: An introduction.* State College, PA: Venture.

SHAPE America. (n.d.). *About SHAPE America.* Retrieved from http://www.shapeamerica.org/about/

Shivers, J., & deLisle, L. (1997). *The story of leisure: Context, concepts and current controversy.* Champaign, IL: Human Kinetics.

Sperazza, L., & Bannerjee, P. (2010). Baby boomers and seniors: Understanding their leisure values enhances programs. *Activities, Adaptation, and Aging, 34*(3), 196-215.

United Nations. (2015). *Population facts: Trends in international migration, 2015.* Retrieved from http://www.un.org/en/development/desa/population/migration/publications/populationfacts/docs/MigrationPopFacts20154.pdf

Vennum, T., Jr. (n.d.). *The history of lacrosse.* Retrieved from https://www.uslacrosse.org/about-the-sport/history

Virginia State Parks. (n.d.). *History of Virginia state parks.* Retrieved from http://www.dcr.virginia.gov/state-parks/history

Westland, C. (1979). *Fitness and amateur sport in Canada—government's programme: An historical perspective.* Ottawa, ON: Canadian Parks/Recreation Association.

Wetherell, D.G., & Kmet, I. (1990). *Useful pleasures: The shaping of Alberta 1896-1945.* Regina, SK: Canadian Plains Research Centre.

Wright, J.R. (1983). *Urban parks in Ontario, part I: Origins to 1860.* Toronto, ON: Ministry of Tourism and Recreation.

CHAPTER 3

Alexander, E., & Alexander, M. (2008). *Museums in motion: An introduction to the history and functions of museums.* Plymouth, UK: AltaMira Press.

Borgmann, A. (1984). *Technology and the character of contemporary life: A philosophical inquiry.* Chicago, IL: University of Chicago Press.

Cross, G. (1990). *A social history of leisure since 1600.* State College, PA: Venture Publishing.

Cuno, J. (2004). The object of art museums. In J. Cuno (Ed.), *Whose muse? Art museums and the public trust.* Princeton, NJ: Princeton University Press; Cambridge, MA: Harvard University Art Museums.

de Grazia, S. (1963). *Of time, work and leisure.* Garden City, NJ: Doubleday.

Falk, J., & Dierking, L. (2000). *Learning from museums: Visitor experiences and the making of meaning.* Plymouth, UK: AltaMira Press.

Featherstone, M. (1991). *Consumer culture & postmodernism.* London: Sage Publications.

Gerbner, G. (1999). The stories we tell. *Peace Review, 11*(1), 9-15.

Groarke, L. (2017). Informal logic. In E.N. Zalta (Ed.), *Stanford encyclopedia of philosophy* Retrieved from https://plato.stanford.edu/entries/logic-informal/

Haughwout, A., Lee, D., Scally, J., & van der Klaauw, W. (2017). *Household borrowing in historical perspective.* Retrieved from http://libertystreeteconomics.newyorkfed.org/2017/05/household-borrowing-in-historical-perspective.html

Hein, G. (1998). *Learning in the museum.* Oxon, UK: Routledge.

Hemingway, J. (1988). Leisure and civility: Reflections on a Greek ideal. *Leisure Sciences, 10,* 179-191.

Hemingway, J. (1996). Emancipating leisure: The recovery of freedom in leisure. *Journal of Leisure Research, 28*(1), 27-43.

Hunnicutt, B. (1990). Leisure and play in Plato's teaching and philosophy of learning. *Leisure Sciences, 12,* 211-227.

Jackson, A., Fawcett, G., Milan, A., Roberts, P., Schetagne, S., Scott, K., & Tsoukalas, S. (2000). *Social cohesion in Canada: Possible indicators—highlights.* Ottawa, ON: Canadian Council on Social Development.

Johnson, R., & McLean, D. (1994). Leisure and the development of ethical character: Changing views of the North American ideal. *Journal of Applied Recreation Research, 19*(2), 117-130.

Kubey, R., & Csikzentmihalyi, M. (1990). *Television and the quality of life: How viewing shapes everyday experience.* Hillsdale, NJ: Lawrence Erlbaum.

Nash, R. (1982). *Wilderness and the American mind* (3rd ed.). New Haven, CT: Yale University Press.

Neulinger, J. (1974). *The psychology of leisure: Research approaches to the study of leisure.* Springfield, IL: Charles C Thomas.

Pieper, J. (1998). *Leisure: The basis of culture* [R. Scruton, Trans.]. South Bend, IN: St. Augustine's Press.

Putnam, R. (2000). *Bowling alone.* New York, NY: Simon & Schuster.

Rojek, C. (1995). *Decentering leisure: Rethinking leisure theory.* London, UK: Sage Publications.

Rojek, C. (2010). *The labour of leisure.* London, UK: Sage Publications.

Russell, B. (1960). *In praise of idleness: And other essays.* London, UK: George Allen & Unwin.

Schor, J. (1998). *The overspent American.* New York, NY: Basic Books.

Sylvester, C. (1991). Recovering a good idea for the sake of goodness: An interpretive critique of subjective leisure. In T.L. Goodale and P.A. Witt (Eds.), *Recreation and leisure: Issues in an era of change* (pp. 441-454). State College, PA: Venture.

Veblen, T. (1998). *The theory of the leisure class.* Amherst, NY: Prometheus Books. (Original work published 1899)

Weber, M. (1958). *The Protestant ethic and the spirit of capitalism* [T. Parson, Trans.]. New York, NY: Scribner's. (Original work published 1930)

CHAPTER 4

Beaubier, D. (2004). Athletic gender equity policy in Canadian universities: Issues and possibilities. *Canadian Journal of Educational Administration and Policy, 34,* 49-59.

Beauregard, A. (1996). *Running feet.* Retrieved from http://www.lehigh.edu/~dmd1/art.html

Bell, C.M., & Hurd, A.R. (2006). Research update: Recreation across ethnicity: People of different races often seek contrasting recreation opportunities. *Parks & Recreation, 41*(10), 27-36.

Byrne, J.A. (2007). *The role of race in configuring park use: A political ecology perspective (Doctoral dissertation).* University of Southern California, Los Angeles.

Central Intelligence Agency. (2013). *World factbook.* Retrieved from https://www.cia.gov/library/publications/the-world-factbook/rankorder/2172rank.html#us

Clark, W. (2008). Kids' sports. *Canadian Social Trends, 85*(3), 54-61.

Clinton, W. J. (2013). *Howard University commencement address.* Retrieved from https://www.c-span.org/video/?312699-1/howard-university-commencement-address

Countries and Their Cultures. (n.d.). *Pakistan.* Retrieved from http://www.everyculture.com/No-Sa/Pakistan.html

Crawford, D., Jackson E., & Godbey, G. (1991). A hierarchical model of leisure constraints. *Leisure Sciences, 9,* 119-127.

Curtis, J. (1979). *Recreation: Theory and practice.* St. Louis, MO: Mosby.

Edwards, H. (1973). *Sociology of sport.* Homewood, IL: Dorsey Press.

Eshleman, J., Cashion, B., & Basirico, L. (1993). *Sociology: An introduction* (4th ed.). New York, NY: Harper Collins College.

Floyd, M. (1998). Getting beyond marginality and ethnicity: The challenge for race and ethnic studies in leisure research. *Journal of Leisure Research, 30*(1), 3-22.

Fredriksen-Goldsen, K.I., Kim, H.J., Shiu, C., Goldsen, J., & Emlet, C.A. (2015). Successful aging among LGBT older adults: Physical and mental health-related quality of life by age group. *The Gerontologist, 55*(1), 154-168.

Gruneau, R. (1999). *Class, sports, and social development.* Champaign, IL: Human Kinetics.

Henderson, K. (1997). A critique of constraints theory: A response. *Journal of Leisure Research, 29*(4), 453-458.

Henderson, K. (2010). Leisure studies in the 21st century: The sky is falling? *Leisure Sciences, 32*(4), 391-400.

Henslin, J.M. (1993). *Sociology: A down-to-earth approach.* Boston, MA: Allyn & Bacon.

Kelly, J.R. (1987). *Freedom to be: A new sociology of leisure.* New York, NY: Macmillan.

Kelly, J.R. (2012). *Leisure* (4th ed.). Urbana, IL: Sagamore.

Kivel, B.D., & Kleiber, D.A. (2000). Leisure in the identity formation of lesbian/gay youth: Personal, but not social. *Leisure Sciences, 22,* 215-232.

Lenski, G., & Lenski, J. (1987). *Human societies: An introduction to macrosociology* (5th ed.). New York, NY: McGraw-Hill.

Lenski, G., Nolan, P., & Lenski, J. (1995). *Human societies: An introduction to macrosociology* (7th ed.). New York, NY: McGraw-Hill.

McChesney, J., Gerken, M., & McDonald, K. (2005). Reaching out to Hispanics. *Parks & Recreation, 40*(3), 74-78.

Mill, R. (1986). Tourist characteristics and trends. *Literature review: The President's Commission on Americans Outdoors.* Washington, DC: Government Printing Office.

Nash, J. (1953). *Philosophy of recreation and leisure.* Dubuque, IA: Brown.

National Federation of State High School Associations. (2011). *High school athletic participation survey.* Indianapolis, IN: Author.

NCAA. (2006). *NCAA gender-equity survey results 2005-2006.* Retrieved from http://files.eric.ed.gov/fulltext/ED503212.pdf

Newman, D. (1999). *Sociology of families.* Thousand Oaks, CA: Pine Forge Press.

Phillip, S. (2000). Race and the pursuit of happiness. *Journal of Leisure Research, 32*(1), 121-124.

Prebish, C. (1993). *Religion and sport: The meeting of sacred and profane.* Westport, CT: Greenwood Press.

Roberts, K. (2010). *Sociology of leisure.* Sociopedia.isa. doi: 0.1177/205684601371

Robinson, J.P., & Godbey, G. (1997). *Time for life: The surprising ways Americans use their time.* University Park, PA: Penn State University Press.

Russell, R.V. (2002). *Pastimes: The context of contemporary culture* (2nd ed.). Champaign, IL: Sagamore.

Shinew, K.J., Floyd, M.E., & Parry, D. (2004). Understanding the relationship between race and leisure activities and constraints: Exploring an alternative framework. *Leisure Sciences, 26,* 181-199.

U.S. Census Bureau. (2010). *United States census 2010.* Retrieved from https://www.census.gov/2010census/

U.S. Department of Labor. (2010). *Women's employment during the recovery.* Retrieved from http://www.dol.gov/_sec/media/reports/femalelaborforce/

Veblen, T. (1998). *The theory of the leisure class.* Amherst, NY: Prometheus Books. (Original work published 1899)

CHAPTER 5

Advisory Commission on Intergovernmental Relations. (1964). *The problem with special districts in America.* Washington, DC: U.S. Government Printing Office.

Babcock, R.F., & Larsen, W.U. (1990). *Special districts: The ultimate in neighborhood zoning.* Cambridge, MA: Lincoln Institute of Land Policy.

Bannon, J., & McKinney, W. (1980). *White paper: A study and analysis of Illinois park districts.* Champaign: University of Illinois Press.

Barlow, E. (1977). *Frederick Law Olmsted's New York.* New York, NY: Praeger.

Blinn, S.R. (1977). *The professional preparation of municipal recreation and park executives.* Boston, MA: Boston University.

Bollens, J.C. (1957). *Special districts in the United States.* Berkeley: University of California Press.

Bollens, J.C., & Schmandt, H.J. (1975). *The metropolis: Its people, politics and economics.* New York, NY: Harper & Row.

Botkin, R., & Kanters, M.A. (1990). *Benefits of Illinois park district leisure services.* Macomb: Western Illinois University Printing.

Brinberg, D., & McGrath, J.E. (1997). *Validity and the research process.* Beverly Hills, CA: Sage.

Bromage, A.W. (1962). *Political representation in metropolitan agencies.* Ann Arbor: Institute of Public Administration, University of Michigan.

Brown, D. (1980). *A presentation of the oral testimony received at hearings of the special district subcommittee.* Springfield, IL: League of Women Voters.

Bureau of Labor Statistics. (2017). *Leisure and hospitality.* Retrieved from https://www.bls.gov/iag/tgs/iag70.htm

Burton, T.L. (1971). *Experiments in recreation research.* Totowa, NJ: Rowman & Littlefield.

Butler, G.D. (1976). *Introduction to community recreation.* New York, NY: McGraw-Hill.

Cairns, M. (1997). The history of Illinois park districts. *Illinois Parks and Recreation, July/August,* 23-27.

Cape, W.H., Graves, L.B., & Michaels, B.M. (1969). *Government by special districts.* Manhattan, KS: Government Research Center Press.

Chadwick, B.A., Bahr, H., & Albrecht, S. (1984). *Social science research methods.* Englewood Cliffs, NJ: Prentice Hall.

Collins, M.F., & Cooper, I.S. (1998). *Leisure management issues and application.* London, UK: Wallingford.

Cook, C. (1972). *A description of the New York Central Park.* New York, NY: Blom.

Dickason, J.G. (1983). The origin of the playground: The role of the Boston Women's Clubs, 1885-1890. *Leisure Sciences, 6,* 83-98.

Dickinson, M.M. (1978). *The history of the Illinois Association of Park Districts, May 1928-October, 1978.* Springfield: Illinois Association of Park Districts.

Driver, B.L., Brown, P.J., & Peterson, G.L. (1991). *Benefits of leisure.* State College, PA: Venture.

Edginton, C.R., Jordan, D.J., DeGraaf, D.G., & Edginton, S.R. (2002). *Leisure and life satisfaction.* Boston, MA: McGraw-Hill.

Edginton, C.R., & Williams, J.G. (1978). *Productive management of leisure service organizations.* New York, NY: Wiley.

Elazar, D.J. (1970). *Cities of the prairie.* New York, NY: Basic Books.

Emanuelson, D.N. (2002). *A comparative analysis of Illinois Park Districts and Illinois Municipal Parks and Recreation Departments.* DeKalb: Northern Illinois University.

Fahrion, K.A. (1984). *Development and powers of Illinois park districts.* Springfield: Illinois Legislative Council.

Finkler, S.A. (2009). *Financial management for public, health, and not-for-profit organizations* (3rd ed.). Upper Saddle River, NJ: Prentice Hall.

Flickinger, T.B., & Murphy, P. (2004). *The park district code.* Springfield: Illinois Association of Park Districts.

Foster, K.A. (1997). *The political economy of special purpose government.* Washington, DC: Georgetown University Press.

Halsey, E. (1940). *The development of public recreation in metropolitan Chicago.* Chicago, IL: Chicago Recreation Commission.

Hendon, W.S. (1981). *Evaluating urban parks and recreation.* New York, NY: Praeger.

Henry, N. (2001). *Public administration and public affairs.* Upper Saddle River, NJ: Prentice Hall.

Howard, D.R., & Crompton, J.L. (1980). *Financing, managing and marketing recreation and park resources.* Dubuque, IA: Brown.

Human Kinetics (Ed.). (2006). *Introduction to recreation and leisure.* Champaign, IL: Author.

Hurd, A.R., Barcelona, R.J., & Meldrum, J.T. (2008). *Leisure services management.* Champaign, IL: Human Kinetics.

Ibrahim, H. (1991). *Leisure and society: A comparative approach.* Dubuque, IA: Brown.

Illinois Association of Park Districts. (2001). *The park district advantage.* Springfield: Illinois Association of Park Districts.

Illinois Municipal League. (2000). *Illinois municipal directory.* Springfield: Illinois Municipal League.

IRS. *Charitable purposes.* (n.d.). Retrieved from https://www.irs.gov/charities-non-profits/charitable-purposes

Kaszak, N.L. (1993). *Handbook of Illinois park district law.* Springfield: Illinois Association of Park Districts.

Lutzin, S.G. (1979). *Managing municipal leisure services.* Washington, DC: ICMA Press.

Milakovich, M.E., & Gordon, G.J. (2004). *Public administration in America.* Belmont, CA: Wadsworth.

Mitchell, J. (1999). *The American experiment with government corporations.* Armonk, NJ: Sharpe.

Mobley, T.A., & Newport, D. (1996). *Parks and recreation in the 21st century.* Myrtle Beach, SC: Springs.

Nalbandian, J. (1991). *Professionalism in local government.* San Francisco, CA: Jossey-Bass.

National Recreation and Park Association. (1997). *The legends of parks and recreation administration* [video]. Arlington, VA: Author.

Olmsted, F.L., & Kimball, T. (1973). *Frederick Law Olmsted: Landscape architect.* New York, NY: Blom.

Rainwater, C.E. (1922). *The play movement in the United States.* Chicago, IL: University of Chicago Press.

Riess, S.A. (1996). *City games: The evolution of American urban society and the rise of sports.* Champaign: University of Illinois Press.

Rosenweig, R., & Blackmar, E. (1992). *The park and the people: A history of Central Park.* Ithaca, NY: Cornell University Press.

Searle, G.A.C. (1975). *Recreation economics and analysis.* New York, NY: Longman.

Sessoms, H.D. (1993). *Eight decades of leadership development.* Arlington, VA: National Recreation and Park Association.

Shivers, J.S. (1967). *Principles and practices of recreational service.* New York, NY: Macmillan.

Shivers, J.S., & Halper, J.W. (1981). *The crisis in urban recreation.* East Brunswick, NJ: Associated University Press.

Smith, S. (1975). Similarities between urban recreation systems. *Journal of Leisure Research, July,* 270-281.

Stetzer, D.F. (1975). *Special districts in Cook County.* Chicago, IL: University of Chicago.

Sullivan, A., & Sheffrin, S.M. (2003). *Economics: Principles in action.* Upper Saddle River, NJ: Pearson Prentice Hall.

van der Smissen, B., Moiseichik, M., Hartenburg, V.J., & Twardzik, L.F. (2000). *Management of park and recreation agencies.* Ashburn, VA: National Recreation and Park Association.

CHAPTER 6

Adirondack State Park Agency. (n.d.). *About the Adirondack Park.* Retrieved from http://www.apa.state.ny.us/about_park/index.html

American Planning Association. (2007). *How cities use parks to help children learn.* Retrieved from http://www.planning.org/cityparks/briefingpapers/helpchildrenlearn.htm

America's State Parks. (n.d.). *State park facts.* Retrieved from http://www.stateparks.org/about-us/state-park-facts/

Balmford, A., Beresford, J., Green, J., Naidoo, R., Walpole, M., & Manica, A. (2009). *A global perspective on trends in nature-based tourism.* PLoS Biology, 7(6): e1000144. doi:10.1371/journal.pbio.1000144

Belasco, W.J. (1979). *Americans on the road: From autocamp to motel 1910-1945.* Baltimore, MD: Johns Hopkins Press.

Brown, D. (1970). *Bury my heart at Wounded Knee: An Indian history of the American West.* New York, NY: Henry Holt.

Bureau of Land Management. (n.d.-a). *About the BLM.* Retrieved from https://www.blm.gov/about. (n.d.-b). *The Bureau of Land Management's outdoor recreation and visitor services accomplishments report 2006-2008.* Retrieved from http://www.blm.gov/wo/st/en/prog/Recreation.html

Bureau of Reclamation. (n.d.). *About us—fact sheet. Retrieved from https://www.usbr.gov/main/about/fact.html*

Canada Council on Ecological Areas (CCEA). (2016). Report on protected area in Canada. Retrieved from http://www.ccea.org/carts-reports/

Cavallo, D. (1981). *Muscles and morals: Organized playgrounds and urban reform, 1880–1920.* Philadelphia: University of Pennsylvania Press.

Chape, S., Blyth, S., Fish, L., Fox, P., & Spalding, M. (Compilers). (2003). *2003 United Nations list of protected areas.* Gland, Switzerland, and Cambridge, UK: IUCN; Cambridge, UK: UNEP-WCMC.

Chavez, D.J. (2002). Adaptive management in outdoor recreation: Serving Hispanics in southern California. *Western Journal of Applied Forestry, 17*(3), 129-133.

Cordell, H.K., Betz, C.J., Green, G., & Owens, M. (2005). *Off-highway vehicle recreation in the United States, regions and states: A national report from the national survey on recreation and the environment (NSRE).* U.S. Forest Service Southern Research Station. Retrieved from http://www.fs.fed.us/recreation/programs/ohv/OHV_final_report.pdf

Eagles, P.F.J. (2014). Fiscal implications of moving to tourism finance for parks: Ontario Provincial Parks. *Managing Leisure, 19*(1), 1-17.

Eagles, P.F J., McLean, D., & Stabler, M.J. (2000). Estimating the tourism volume and value in parks and protected areas in Canada and the USA. *George Wright Forum, 17*(3), 62-76.

Ehrlich, G. (2000). *John Muir: Nature's visionary.* Washington, DC: National Geographic.

Environment and Climate Change Canada. (n.d.). *National wildlife areas across Canada.* Retrieved from https://ec.gc.ca/ap-pa/default.asp?lang=En&n=2BD71B33-1

Foster, J. (1978). *Working for wildlife: The beginning of preservation in Canada.* Toronto, ON: University of Toronto Press.

Glendening, J. (1997). *The high road: Romantic tourism, Scotland, and literature, 1720-1820.* New York, NY: St. Martin's Press.

Harnick, P. (2000). *Inside city parks.* Washington, DC: Urban Land Institute.

Hudson, B.J. (2001). *Wild ways and paths of pleasure: Access to British waterfalls, 1500-2000. Landscape Research, 26*(4), 285-303.

Johnson, C.Y., Bowker, J.M., English, D.B.K., & Worthen, D. (1997). *Theoretical perspectives of ethnicity and outdoor recreation: A review and synthesis of African-American and European-American participation.* General Technical Report SRS-11. Asheville, NC: USDA Forest Service, Southern Research Station.

Jones, K.R., & J. Wills. (2005). *The invention of the park.* Cambridge, UK: Polity Press.

Keene, A. (1994). *Earthkeepers: Observers and protectors of nature.* New York, NY: Oxford University Press.

Kentucky State Parks. (n.d.). *Lake Barkley.* Retrieved from http://parks.ky.gov/parks/resortparks/lake-barkley/default.aspx

Killan, G. (1993). *Protected places: A history of Ontario's provincial park system.* Toronto, ON: Dundurn Press.

Landrum, N.C. (2004). *The state park movement in America: A critical review.* Columbia, MO: University of Columbia Press.

Leduc, J. (2009). *The Canadian Heritage Rivers System.* Hull, PQ: Canadian Heritage Rivers Board.

Lovgren, S. (2004). *U.S. national parks told to quietly cut services.* Retrieved from http://news.nationalgeographic.com/news/2004/03/0319_040319_parks.html

Lysenko, I., Besançon, C., & Savy, C. (2007). *2007 UNEP-WCMC global list of transboundary protected areas.* Retrieved from http://www.tbpa.net/docs/78_Transboundary_PAs_database_2007_WCMC_tbpa.net.pdf

Manning, R. (2007). *Parks and carrying capacity: Commons without tragedy.* Washington, DC: Island Press.

Manning, R., Lawson, S., Newman, P., Hallo, J., Monz, C., & Barber, J. (forthcoming). *Natural quiet and natural darkness: Managing the "new" resources of the national parks.* Lebanon, NH: University Press of New England.

Marty, S. (1984). *A grand and fabulous notion: The first century of Canada's parks.* Toronto, ON: NC Press.

McFarland, E. (1982). The beginning of municipal park systems. In G. Wall & J. Marsh (Eds.), *Recreational land use: Perspectives on its evolution in Canada.* Ottawa, ON: Carleton University Press.

McWilliam, W., Eagles, P., Seasons, M., & Brown, R. (2010). Assessing the degradation effects of local residents on urban forests in Ontario, Canada. *Journal of Arboriculture and Urban Forestry, 36*(6), 253-260.

Miller, C. (2004). *Gifford Pinchot and the making of modern environmentalism.* Washington, DC: Island Press.

Nash, R. (1982). *Wilderness and the American mind* (3rd ed.). New Haven, CT: Yale University Press.

National Park Service. (2003). *A brief history of the National Park Service: National Park Service created.* Retrieved from https://www.nps.gov/parkhistory/online_books/kieley/

National Park Service. (n.d.-a). *How many areas are in the National Park System?* Retrieved from https://www.nps.gov/aboutus/faqs.htm

National Park Service. (n.d.-b). *National Park Service visitor use statistics.* Retrieved https://irma.nps.gov/Stats

National Park Service. (n.d.-c). *Protecting lands and giving back to communities.* Retrieved from https://www.nps.gov/subjects/lwcf/index.htm

National Park Service. (n.d.-d). *Work with us.* Retrieved from https://www.nps.gov/aboutus/workwithus.htm

National Wild and Scenic Rivers System. (n.d.). *About the WSR Act.* Retrieved from https://www.rivers.gov/wsr-act.php

Nebraska Game and Parks Commission. (n.d.). *Eugene T. Mahoney State Park.* Retrieved from http://nebraskastateparks.reserveamerica.com/campgroundDetails.do?topTableIndex=CampingSpot&contractCode=ne&parkCode=0273

Parks Canada. (2017). *World Heritage sites in Canada.* Retrieved from https://www.pc.gc.ca/en/culture/spm-whs

Parks Canada. (2017). *National Parks List.* Retrieved from https://www.pc.gc.ca/en/pn-np/recherche-parcs-parks-search

Parks Canada. (n.d.). *Parks Canada attendance 2011-12 to 2015-16.* Retrieved from http://www.pc.gc.ca/eng/docs/pc/attend/index.aspx

Pergams, O.R.W., Czech, B., Haney, J.C., & Nyberg, D. (2004). Linkage of conservation activity to trends in the U.S. economy. *Conservation Biology, 18*(6), 1617-1623.

Pergams, O.R.W., & Zaradic, P.A. (2006). Is love of nature in the US becoming love of electronic media? 16-year downtrend in national park visits explained by watching movies, playing video games, Internet use, and oil prices. *Journal of Environmental Management, 80,* 387-393.

Ramsar. (2017). *Wetlands: Our natural safeguard against disasters.* Retrieved from http://www.ramsar.org/sites/default/files/documents/library/wwd2017_presentation_e.pdf

Ritvo, H. (2003). Fighting for Thirlmere: The roots of environmentalism. *Science, 300*(5625), 1510-1511.

Runte, A. (2010). *National parks: The American experience* (4th ed.). Lincoln: University of Nebraska Press.

Rybczynski, W. (1999). *A clearing in the distance: Frederick Law Olmsted and America in the nineteenth century.* New York, NY: Scribner.

Saunders, A. (1998). *Algonquin story* (3rd ed.). Whitney, ON: Friends of Algonquin Park.

Sears, J. (1980). *Sacred places: American tourist attractions in the nineteenth century.* Amherst: University of Massachusetts Press.

Seibel, G.A. (1995). *Ontario's Niagara parks, Niagara Falls.* Niagara Falls, ON: Niagara Parks Commission.

Sellars, R.W. (1999). *Preserving nature in the national parks.* New Haven, CT: Yale University Press.

Shaffer, M.S. (2001). *See America first: Tourism and national identity, 1880-1940.* Washington, DC: Smithsonian Institution Press.

Sheail, J. (2010). *Nature's spectacle: The world's first national parks and protected areas.* London, UK: Earthscan.

Smith, C. & M. Greshko. (2017). *UN Announces 23 New Nature Reserves while US removes 17. National Geographic.* Retrieved from http://news.nationalgeographic.com/2017/06/unesco-new-biosphere-reserves-us-withdraws-reserves/

Tate, A. (2001). *Great city parks.* New York, NY: Routledge.

Taylor, A.F., Kuo, F.E., & Sullivan, W.C. (2001). Views of nature and self-discipline: Evidence from inner city children. *Journal of Environmental Psychology, 22,* 49-63.

Tennessee Valley Authority. (n.d.). *Recreation.* Retrieved from http://www.tva.gov/river/recreation/index.htm

Trans Canada Trail. (2017). *The Great Rail.* Retrieved from https://thegreattrail.ca/

Trudeau, J., & Obama, B. (2016). *U.S.-Canada joint statement on climate, energy, and Arctic leadership.* Retrieved from http://pm.gc.ca/eng/news/2016/03/10/us-canada-joint-statement-climate-energy-and-arctic-leadership

UNEP-WCMC (2017). *Protected area profile for Canada.* Retrieved from: https://www.protectedplanet.net/country/CAN

UNESCO. (2017a). *Biosphere reserves in Canada.* Retrieved from http://unesco.ca/home-accueil/biosphere%20new/biosphere%20reserves%20in%20canada-%20reserves%20de%20la%20biosphere%20au%20canada

UNESCO. (2017a) *Biosphere reserves in the USA.* Retrieved from http://www.unesco.org/mabdb/br/brdir/europe-n/USAmap.htm

UNESCO. (2017c.) *Biosphere reserves – learning sites for sustainable development.* Retrieved from http://www.unesco.org/new/en/natural-sciences/environment/ecological-sciences/biosphere-reserves/

UNESCO. (n.d.). *World Heritage list.* Retrieved from http://whc.unesco.org/en/list

U.S. Army Corps of Engineers. (n.d.). *Recreation overview.* Retrieved from http://www.usace.army.mil/Missions/Civil-Works/Recreation/

USDA Forest Service. (2016). *National Visitor Use Monitoring Survey Results U.S. Forest Service National Summary Report - FY 2011 through FY 2015.* Retrieved from https://www.fs.fed.us/recreation/programs/nvum/pdf/5082015NationalSummaryReport-Final062316.pdf

USDA Forest Service. (2017). *By the Numbers.* Retrieved from https://www.fs.fed.us/about-agency/newsroom/by-the-numbers

U.S. Department of the Interior. (n.d.). *Bureau of Indian Affairs.* Retrieved from http://www.bia.gov

U.S. Fish and Wildlife Service. (2013). *National Wildlife Refuge System overview.* Retrieved from http://www.fws.gov/refuges/about/pdfs/NWRSOverviewFactSheetApr2013revNov032013.pdf

Virden, R.J., & Walker, C.J. (1999). Ethnic/racial and gender variations among meanings given to, and preferences for, the natural environment. *Leisure Sciences, 21*(3), 219-239.

Wals, A.E.J. (1994). Nobody planted it, it just grew! Young adolescents' perceptions and experiences of nature in the context of urban environmental education. *Childrens Environment, 11*(3), 1-27.

Wetlands International. (2005). *Introduction to Ramsar Sites Information Service.* Retrieved from http://archive.ramsar.org/cda/en/ramsar-activities-rsis/main/ramsar/1-63-97_4000_0__

Young, T. (2004). *Building San Francisco's parks, 1850–1930.* Baltimore, MD: Johns Hopkins University Press.

Zaslowsky, D., & Watkins, T.H. (1994). *These American lands: Parks, wilderness and the public lands.* Washington, DC: Island Press.

Zinser, C.I. (1995). *Outdoor recreation: United States national parks, forests and public lands.* New York, NY: Wiley.

CHAPTER 7

Americans With Disabilities Act of 1990, Public Law No. 101-336, 104 Stat. 328 (1990).

Broadway Neighbourhood Centre. (n.d.). *About.* Retrieved from http://www.thebnc.ca/about/

Burton, T.L., & Glover, T.D. (1999). Back to the future: Leisure services and the reemergence of the enabling authority of the state. In E.L. Jackson & T.L. Burton (Eds.), *Leisure studies: Prospects for the twenty-first century.* State College, PA: Venture Publishing.

Canadian Heritage. (n.d.). *Mandate.* Retrieved from http://canada.pch.gc.ca/eng/1461064135424/1461064244449

Canadian Parks and Recreation Association. (2017). *What is CPRA: CPRA Vision.* Retrieved from https://www.cpra.ca/what-is-cpra

Constitution Act, Statutes of Canada (1982). Retrieved from http://laws-lois.justice.gc.ca/eng/const/page-15.html#h-38

Davis, R. (2010). Inclusive sports. In Human Kinetics (Ed.), *Inclusive recreation* (pp. 193-207). Champaign, IL: Human Kinetics.

Hironaka-Juteau, J.H., & Crawford, T. (2010). Introduction to inclusion. In Human Kinetics (Ed.), *Inclusive recreation* (pp. 3-18). Champaign, IL: Human Kinetics.

Indigenous and Northern Affairs Canada. (2016). *Urban indigenous peoples.* Retrieved from https://www.aadnc-aandc.gc.ca/eng/1100100014265/1369225120949

Interprovincial Sport and Recreation Council (ISRC). (1987). *National recreation statement.* Retrieved from http://lin.ca/resource-details/4467

Justice Canada.(2017). *Table of public statutes and responsible ministers.* Retrieved from http://laws-lois.justice.gc.ca/eng/TablePublicStatutes/index.html

MacIntosh, D., Bedecki, T., & Franks, C.E.S. (1988). *Sport and politics in Canada: Federal government involvement since 1961.* Kingston, ON: McGill-Queen's University Press.

McFarland, E.M. (1970). *The development of public recreation in Canada.* Ottawa, ON: Canadian Parks and Recreation Association.

The National Physical Fitness Act., Statutes of Canada (1943, c. 29). Ottawa, ON: King's Printer.

NCHPAD. (n.d.). *Park and recreation departments.* Retrieved from http://www.nchpad.org/277/1758/What~to~Know~Before~You~Go~~The~Big~Questions~to~Ask~Before~Arriving~at~Your~~Accessible~~Recreation~Destination

Parks and Recreation Association of Canada. (1947). *Charter.* Toronto, ON: Author.

Peters, M. (1913). Annual report of the committee on vacation schools and supervised playgrounds. In National Council of Women of Canada (Ed.), *The yearbook containing the report of the twentieth annual meeting of the National Council of Women of Canada* (pp. 43-48). Toronto, ON: National Council of Women of Canada.

Physical Activity and Sport Act, Statutes of Canada. (2003, c.2). Retrieved from http://laws-lois.justice.gc.ca/eng/acts/P-13.4/FullText.html

Rutherford, P. (Ed.). (1974). *Saving the Canadian city: The first phase, 1880-1920.* Toronto, ON: University of Toronto Press.

Schrodt, B. (1979). *A history of Pro-Rec: The British Columbia provincial recreation programme: 1934-1953* (Unpublished dissertation). University of Alberta, Edmonton.

Social Planning Toronto. (2016). *Newcomer youth access to recreation in Toronto: Relationships, resources, and relevance.* Retrieved from https://d3n8a8pro7vhmx.cloudfront.net/socialplanningtoronto/pages/419/attachments/original/1472010169/Newcomer-Youth-Recreation-FINAL.pdf?1472010169

Stanton, T., Markham-Starr, S., & Hodgkinson, J. (2013). Public recreation. In Human Kinetics (Ed.) *Introduction to recreation and leisure* (pp. 109-142). Champaign, IL: Human Kinetics.

Statistics Canada. (2013a). *Aboriginal peoples in Canada: First nations people, Metis and Inuit, national household survey, 2011*. Retrieved from http://www12.statcan.gc.ca/nhs-enm/2011/as-sa/99-011-x/99-011-x2011001-eng.pdf

Statistics Canada. (20013b). *Immigration and ethnocultural diversity in Canada, national household survey, 2011*. Retrieved from http://www12.statcan.gc.ca/nhs-enm/2011/as-sa/99-010-x/99-010-x2011001-eng.pdf

Statistics Canada. (2017, February 8). *The Daily - Population size and growth in Canada: Key results from the 2016 Census*. Retrieved from http://www.statcan.gc.ca/daily-quotidien/170208/dq170208a-eng.pdf

Statistics Canada. (2017, May 3). *The Daily – Age and sex, and type of dwelling data: Key results from the 2016 Census*. Retrieved from http://www.statcan.gc.ca/daily-quotidien/170503/dq170503a-eng.pdf

Strong-Boag, V.J. (1976). *The parliament of women of Canada, 1893-1929*. Ottawa, ON: National Museums of Canada.

Sunset Community Association. (2016). *2016 Annual general report*. Retrieved from http://www.mysunset.net/wp-content/uploads/Sunset-Community-Association-AGM-Report-2016.pdf

Vancouver (n.d.) *Sunset census data* Retrieved from http://vancouver.ca/files/cov/Sunset-census-data.pdf

Westland, (1979). *Fitness and amateur sport in Canada: The federal government's programme: An historical perspective*. Ottawa, ON: Canadian Parks and Recreation Association.

CHAPTER 8

American Automobile Association. (n.d.). *AAA fact sheet*. Retrieved from http://newsroom.aaa.com/about-aaa/aaa-fact-sheet/

ASAE Foundation. (2012). *Association FAQ*. Retrieved from www.thepowerofa.org/wp-content/uploads/2012/03/Associations-Matter-FINAL.pdf

Bureau of Labor Statistics. (2009). *U.S. Department of Labor, wages in the nonprofit sector: Management, professional, and administrative support occupations*. Retrieved from https://www.bls.gov/opub/mlr/cwc/wages-in-the-nonprofit-sector-management-professional-and-administrative-support-occupations.pdf

Bureau of Labor Statistics. (2016). *Nonprofits in America: new research data on employment, wages, and establishments*. Retrieved from https://www.bls.gov/opub/mlr/2016/article/nonprofits-in-america.htm

Center for Association Leadership. (2015). *The power of associations: An objectives snapshot of the U.S. association company*. Retrieved from http://www.thepowerofa.org/wp-content/uploads/2012/03/PowerofAssociations-2015.pdf

Corporation for National and Community Service. (2015). *Volunteering and civic life in America*. Retrieved from http://www.volunteeringinamerica.gov/vcla

Giving USA 2017: The Annual Report on Philanthropy for the Year 2016, a publication of Giving USA Foundation, 2017, researched and written by the Indiana University Lilly Family School of Philanthropy. Retrieved from http://www.givingusa.org

Hall, M., & Banting, K.G. (2000). *The nonprofit sector in Canada: An introduction*. Kingston, ON: McGill-Queen's University Press.

Hall, M.H., de Wit, M.L., Lasby, D., McIver, D., Evers, T., Johnston, C., . . . Murray, V. (2005). *Cornerstones of community: Highlights of the National Survey of Nonprofit and Voluntary Organizations*. Ottawa, ON: Statistics Canada. Retrieved from http://www.imaginecanada.ca/sites/default/files/www/en/library/nsnvo/nsnvo_report_english.pdf

Hansmann, H. (1987). Economic theories of non-profit organizations. In W.W. Powell (Ed.), *The nonprofit sector: A research handbook*. London, UK: Yale University Press.

Independent Sector (2016). *Threads: Insights from the charitable community*. Retrieved from: https://www.independentsector.org/resource/threads/

Mason, D. (1999). Address on accepting ARNOVA's Award for Distinguished Lifetime Achievement. Speech presented to the Association for Research on Nonprofit Organizations and Voluntary Action, Washington, DC.

Nanus, B., & Dobbs, S.M. (1999). *Leaders who make a difference: Essential strategies for meeting the nonprofit challenge*. San Francisco, CA: Jossey-Bass.

National Center for Charitable Statistics. (2010). *Number of nonprofit organizations in the United States, 1999-2009*. Retrieved from http://nccsdataweb.urban.org/PubApps/profile1.php

National Center for Charitable Statistics. (2015). *The Nonprofit Sector in Brief 2015: Public Charities, Giving and Volunteering*. Retrieved from http://www.urban.org/research/publication/nonprofit-sector-brief-2015-public-charities-giving-and-volunteering

O'Neill, M. (2002). *Nonprofit nation: A new look at the third America*. San Francisco, CA: Jossey-Bass.

Payton, R.L. (1988). *Philanthropy: Voluntary action for the public good*. New York, NY: American Council on Education and Macmillan.

Revenue Canada. (2001). *Definition of a nonprofit organization*. Retrieved from http://www.cra-arc.gc.ca/E/pub/tp/it496r/it496r-e.html

Salamon, L. (1999). *America's nonprofit sector* (2nd ed.). New York, NY: Foundation Center.

Salamon, L.M., & Anheier, H.K. (1996). The international classification of nonprofit organizations: ICNPO-revision 1. *Working Papers of the Johns Hopkins Comparative Nonprofit*

Sector Project (Vol. 19). Baltimore, MD: Johns Hopkins Institute for Policy Studies.

Statistics Canada. (2013). *Highlights from the 2013 Canada survey on volunteering and charitable giving.* Retrieved from http://www.statcan.gc.ca/pub/89-652-x/89-652-x2015001-eng.pdf

YMCA. (n.d.). *Facts & figures.* Retrieved from http://www.ymca.net/organizational-profile/

CHAPTER 9

Asian American Hotel Owners Association. (n.d.). *About AAHOA.* Retrieved from https://www.aahoa.com/about-AAHOA

Branson, R. (2006). *Screw it, let's do it: Lessons in life.* London, UK: Virgin Books.

Covey, S.R. (1992). *Principle-centered leadership.* New York, NY: Simon and Schuster.

Gunn, C.A., & Var, T. (2002). *Tourism planning: Basics, concepts, cases* (4th ed.). London, UK: Routledge.

Kotter, J.P. (1996). *Leading change.* Boston, MA: Harvard Business School Press.

Kotter, J.P. (1999). *What leaders really do.* Boston, MA: Harvard Business School Press.

Nahavandi, A. (2009). *The art and science of leadership.* Upper Saddle River, NJ: Pearson.

Pinchot, G., & Pellman, R. (1999). *Intrapreneuring in action: A handbook for business innovation.* San Francisco, CA: Berrett-Koehler.

Rickards, T., & Clark, M. (2006). *Dilemmas of leadership.* London, UK: Routledge.

Tierney, P., Hunt, M., & Latkova, P. (2011). Do travelers support green practices and sustainable development? *Journal of Tourism Insights, 2*(2), 1-2.

U.S. Census Bureau. (2007). *North American Industry Classification System.* Retrieved from http://www.census.gov/eos/www/naics/

U.S. Travel Association. (2017). *U.S. travel answer sheet.* Retrieved from https://www.ustravel.org/answersheet. July 10, 2017.

World Tourism Organization. (2014). Facts and figures edition page. Retrieved from http://www2.unwto.org/facts/eng/highlights.htm

CHAPTER 10

American Therapeutic Recreation Association (ATRA). (n.d.). *What is RT/TR?* Retrieved from http://www.atra-online.com/what/FAQ

Anderson, L. & Heyne, L. (2012). Flourishing through leisure: An ecological extension of the leisure and well-being model in therapeutic recreation strengths-based practice. *Therapeutic Recreation Journal, 46*(2), 129-152.

Bullock, C., Mahon, M., & Killingsworth, C. (2010). *Introduction to recreation services for people with disabilities: A person-centered approach* (3rd ed.). Champaign, IL: Sagamore.

Bureau of Labor Statistics. (2015). *Occupational outlook handbook: Recreational therapists.* Retrieved from https://www.bls.gov/ooh/healthcare/recreational-therapists.htm

Bureau of Labor Statistics. (2016). *Occupational employment statistics.* Retrieved from http://www.bls.gov/oes/current/oes291125.htm#nat

Dattilo, J., Kleiber, D., & Williams, R. (1998). Self-determination and enjoyment enhancement: A psychologically-based service delivery model for therapeutic recreation. *Therapeutic Recreation Journal, 32*(4), 258-271.

Dieser, R. (2002). A cross-cultural critique of newer therapeutic recreation practice models: The self-determination and enjoyment enhancement, Aristotelian good life model, and the optimizing lifelong health through therapeutic recreation. *Therapeutic Recreation Journal, 36*(4), 352-368.

Heintzman, P. (2008). Leisure-spiritual coping: A model for therapeutic recreation and leisure services. *Therapeutic Recreation Journal, 42*(1), 56-73.

Heyne, L., & Anderson, L. (2012). *Therapeutic recreation practice: A strengths approach.* State College, PA: Venture.

Hood, C., & Carruthers, C. (2007). Enhancing leisure experience and developing resources: The leisure and well-being model, part II. *Therapeutic Recreation Journal, 41*(4), 298-325.

Kunstler, R., & Stavola Daly, F. (2010). *Therapeutic recreation leadership and programming.* Champaign, IL: Human Kinetics.

National Council for Therapeutic Recreation Certification (NCTRC). (2014). *CTRS professional profile.* New City, NY: Author.

Negley, S. (2010). Therapeutic recreation. In C. Bullock, M. Mahon, & C. Killingsworth (Eds.), *Introduction to recreation services for people with disabilities: A person-centered approach* (3rd ed., pp. 335-377). Champaign, IL: Sagamore.

Ross, J., & Ashton-Shaeffer, C. (2003). Selecting and designing intervention programs for outcomes. In N. Stumbo (Ed.), *Client outcomes in therapeutic recreation services* (pp. 127-148). State College, PA: Venture.

Sylvester, C., Voelkl, J., & Ellis, G. (2001). *Therapeutic recreation: Theory and practice.* State College, PA: Venture.

Wilhite, B., Keller, M.J., & Caldwell, L. (1999). Optimizing lifelong health and well-being: A health enhancing model of therapeutic recreation. *Therapeutic Recreation Journal, 33*(2), 98-108.

CHAPTER 11

Aflac. (2012). *Aflac workforces report.* Retrieved from https://www.aflac.com/docs/awr/pdf/archive/2012_awr_executive_summary.pdf

American Camping Association. (2010). Serving diverse populations: A profile of three camps. *Camping Magazine, 83*(6), 58-63.

Army One Source. (2017). *Armed forces recreation centers.* Retrieved from http://www.myarmyonesource.com/RecreationTravelandBOSS/ArmedForcesRecreationCenters/Default.aspx

Army Study Guide. (2017). *Better opportunities for single soldiers.* Retrieved from http://www.armystudyguide.com/content/army_board_study_guide_topics/army_programs/about-better-opportunitie.shtml

Astin, A.W. (1984). Student involvement: A developmental theory for higher education. *Journal of College Student Personnel, 25,* 297-308.

Astin, A.W. (1993). *What matters in college: Four critical years revisited.* San Francisco, CA: Jossey-Bass.

Beattie, J.M. (1977). *Attitudes toward crime and punishment in upper Canada, 1830-1850: A documentary study.* Toronto, ON: Centre of Criminology, University of Toronto Press.

Bibby, R.W., & Grenville, A. (2016). What the polls do show: Toward enhanced survey readings of religion in Canada. *Canadian Review of Sociology, 53*(1), 123-136.

Borish, L. (1999, Summer). Athletic activities of various kinds: Physical health and sports programs for Jewish American women. *Journal of Sport History, 26*(2), 240-270.

Brown, N. (2009). Accommodating the recreation needs of Muslims is especially challenging to public aquatics providers. *Athletic Business, 33*(4), 86-88.

Burns, M., (2012). *YMCA offers women-only swim hours for Muslim women.* Retrieved from http://www.kpbs.org/news/2012/jun/26/ymca-offers-women-only-swim-hours-muslim-women-and/

Byl, J. (1999). Calvinist and Mennonites: A pilot study on SHEPHERDing Christianity and sport in Canada. In J. Byl & T. Visker, (Eds.), *Physical Education, Sport, and Wellness* (pp. 311-326). Dordt College Press: Sioux Center.

Bynum, M. (2003). The little flock: Church rec ministries connect with youths through an innovative sports-based day camp. *Athletic Business, 27*(5), 36-40.

Canadian Army. (2017a). *About the army.* Retrieved from http://www.army-armee.forces.gc.ca/en/about-army/organization.page

Canadian Army. (2017b). *History and heritage.* Retrieved from http://www.army-armee.forces.gc.ca/en/about-army/history.page

Centers for Disease Control and Prevention. (2015) *Leading causes of death and numbers of deaths, by sex, race, and Hispanic origin: United States, 1980 and 2014 (Table 19).* Health, United States. Retrieved from https://www.cdc.gov/nchs/data/hus/hus15.pdf#019

Cerner. (2016). *2016 Unites States benefits.* Retrieved from http://www.cerner.com/uploadedFiles/Content/About_Cerner/Careers/2016 United States Cerner Benefits Brochure.pdf

CFMWS. (2016). *CFMWS celebrates its 20th anniversary.* Retrieved from https://www.cfmws.com/en/AboutUs/Library/MediaCentre/Archive/Pages/CFMWS-20th-Anniversary-.aspx

CFMWS. (2017). *CFMWS annual report 2016-2017.* Retrieved from http://cfmws-ar-2016-2017.strikingly.com/

CFMWS. (July 2017). *About CFMWS.* Retrieved from https://www.cfmws.com/en/AboutUs/CFPFSS/Pages/default.aspx

Chenoweth, D.H. (2007). *Worksite health promotion* (2nd ed.). Champaign, IL: Human Kinetics.

Correctional Services of Canada. (n.d.). *About us.* Retrieved from http://www.csc-scc.gc.ca/about-us/index-eng.shtml

Council for the Advancement of Standards in Higher Education. (2015). *CAS professional standards for higher education* (9th ed.). Washington, DC: Author.

Cross, G. (1990). *A social history of leisure since 1600.* State College, PA: Venture.

Emard, M. (1990). Religion and leisure: A case study of the role of the church as a provider of recreation in small Ontario communities. Unpublished master's thesis. University of Waterloo.

Federal Bureau of Prisons. (n.d.). *About our agency.* Retrieved from https://www.bop.gov/about/agency/agency_pillars.jsp

Forrester, S. (2014). *The benefits of campus recreation.* Corvallis, OR: NIRSA.

Gordon, K. (2014, September 30). Hilliard sisters build confidence in Muslim girls through karate, soccer. *The Columbus Dispatch.* Retrieved from http://www.dispatch.com/content/stories/life_and_entertainment/2014/09/30/goal-tenders.html

Hamzeh, M., & Oliver, K. L. (2012). "Because I am Muslim I cannot wear a swimsuit:" Muslim girls negotiate participation opportunities for physical activity. *Research Quarterly for Exercise and Sport, 83,* 330-339.

Hemingway, A., Meek, R., & Hill, C. E. (2015). An exploration of an equine-facilitated learning intervention with young offenders. *Society & Animals, 23*(8), 544-568. doi:10.1163/15685306-12341382

Institute for Healthcare Consumerism. (2015) *Do workplace wellness programs work?* Retrieved from https://www1.marathon-health.com/blog/do-workplace-wellness-programs-work

Jennings, W.G., Higgins, G.E., Maldonado-Molina, M.M., & Khey, D.N. (2015). *The encyclopedia of crime and punishment.* New York, NY: John Wiley & Sons.

Jewish Community Center Maccabi Games. (n.d.). *About.* Retrieved from http://www.jccmaccabigames.org/about/

Jiwani, N., & Rail, G. (2010). Islam, hijab and young Shia Muslim Canadian women's discursive constructions of physical activity. *Sociology of Sport Journal, 27,* 251-267.

Karlis, G., Karadakis, K., & Makrodimitris, P. (2014). Recreation and Christian youth ministries: The Ottawa chapter of the Greek Orthodox Youth of America. *International Journal of Sport Management Recreation & Tourism, 14,* 21-37.

Khiabany, G. (2007). Is there an Islamic communication? The persistence of "tradition" and the lure of modernity. *Critical Arts, 21*(1), 61, 106-124.

Knez, K., Macdonald, D., & Abbott, R. (2012). Challenging stereotypes: Muslim girls talk about physical activity, physical education and sport. *Asia-Pacific Journal of Health, Sport and Physical Education, 3*, 109-122.

Kosmin, B., Mayer, E., & Keysar, A. (2001). *American religious identification survey.* New York: The Graduate Center of CUNY.

MacLean, J., Peterson, J., & Martin, W.D. (1985). *Recreation and leisure: The changing scene* (4th ed.). New York, NY: Macmillan.

Miles, C., & Benn, T. (2014). A case study on the experiences of university-based Muslim women in physical activity during their studies at one UK higher education institution. *Sport, Education and Society.* Advance online publication. doi:10.1080/13573322.2014.942623

Military Benefits. (2017). *Morale, welfare, and recreation (MWR) benefits.* Retrieved from http://militarybenefits.info/morale-welfare-and-recreation-mwr-benefits/

Military 4 Life. (2017). *Military MWR.* Retrieved from http://www.military4life.com/military-mwr-morale-welfare-recreation-list-of-mwr-facilities-worldwide/

Military.com. (2017). *U.S. armed forces overview.* Retrieved from http://www.military.com/join-armed-forces/us-military-overview.html

Moore, E., Ali, M., Graham, E., & Quan, L. (2010). Responding to a request: Gender-exclusive swims in a Somali community. *Public Health Reports, 125*, 137-140.

Mueller, P. (1971). *Intramurals: Programming and administration* (4th ed.). New York, NY: Ronald Press.

Mulcahy, C., & McLaughlin, D. (2013). Is the tail wagging the dog? A review of the evidence for prison animal programs. *Australian Psychologist, 48*(5), 370-378. doi:10.1111/ap.12021

NIRSA: Leaders in Collegiate Recreation. (2004). *The value of recreational sports in higher education: Impact on student enrollment, success, and buying power.* Champaign, IL: Human Kinetics.

NIRSA: Leaders in Collegiate Recreation. (n.d.) *NIRSA history.* Retrieved from https://nirsa.net/nirsa/about/history/

NIRSA: Leaders in Collegiate Recreation. (2016) *NIRSA About.* Retrieved from https://nirsa.net/nirsa/about/

Oregon State University. (n.d.). *What is the Adventure Leadership Institute (ALI)?* Retrieved from http://recsports.oregonstate.edu/ali/what-is-ali

Palmer, C. (2009). Soccer and the politics of identify for young Muslim refugee women in South Australia. *Soccer & Society, 10*, 27-38.

Pew Research Center. (2009). *Mapping the global Muslim population: A report on the size and distribution of the world's Muslim population.* Washington, DC: Author.

Pew Research Center. (2011). *Muslim Americans: No signs of growth in alienation or support for extremism.* Retrieved from http://www.people-press.org/2011/08/30/muslim-americans-no-signs-of-growth-in-alienation-or-support-for-extremism/

Pew Research Center. (2015). *America's changing religious landscape.* Retrieved from http://www.pewforum.org/2015/05/12/americas-changing-religious-landscape/

Popke, M. (2001a). Spread the word: Sports ministry programs—from church-run sports leagues to full-fledged fitness centers—are taking athletics and recreation in a whole new direction. *Athletic Business, 25*(10), 55-61.

Popke, M. (2001b). Spiritual profit. *Athletic Business, 25*(10), 58.

Portland State University. (n.d.). *Inclusive rec.* Retrieved from https://www.pdx.edu/recreation/inclusive-rec

PSP. (2017). *Recreation.* Retrieved from https://www.cfmws.com/en/AboutUs/PSP/recreation/Pages/default.aspx

Ratey, J. (2008). *Spark: The revolutionary new science of exercise and the brain.* New York, NY: Little, Brown and Company.

Robertson, B.J. (1993). The roots of at risk behaviour. *Recreation Canada, 41*(4), 21-27.

Rothman, D. J. (1971). *The discovery of the asylum.* Toronto, ON: Little, Brown.

Royal Canadian Air Force. (2017). *Welcome to the Royal CANADIAN Air Force.* http://www.rcaf-arc.forces.gc.ca/en/index.page

Royal Canadian Navy. (2017). *Welcome to the Royal Canadian Navy.* Retrieved from http://www.navy-marine.forces.gc.ca/en/index.page

Sessoms, H.D., Meyer, H., & Brightbill, C.K. (1975). *Leisure services: The organized recreation and park system* (5th ed.). Englewood Cliffs, NJ: Prentice Hall.

Shaull, S., Gramann, J. (1998). The effect of cultural assimilation on the importance of family-related and nature-related recreation among Hispanic Americans. *Journal of Leisure Research, 30*(1), 47-63.

Smith, S. (2004). *Study finds employee wellness plans increase productivity.* Retrieved from http://ehstoday.com/news/ehs_imp_37035

Statistics Canada. (2013). *Immigration and ethnocultural diversity in Canada: National Household Survey, 2011* (Catalogue No. 99-010-X2011001). Ottawa, ON: Minister of Industry.

Stride, A. (2014). Let US tell YOU! South Asian, Muslim girls tell tales about physical education. *Physical Education and Sport Pedagogy, 19*, 398-417.

Stutteville, S. (2015, March 20). B-ball unites, uplifts a new generation of East Africans. *The Seattle Times,* pp. B1, B7.

Substance Abuse and Mental Health Services Administration. (n.d.) *Applying the strategic prevention framework (SPF).* Retrieved from http://www.samhsa.gov/capt/applying-strategic-prevention-framework

University of Michigan. (n.d.). *History of recreational sports.* Retrieved from https://recunionrenovations.umich.edu/article/history-recreational-sports-0

USA Government. (2017). *Military history and museums.* Retrieved from https://www.usa.gov/history#skiptarget

US Army MWR. (n.d.). *History.* Retrieved from https://www.armymwr.com/about-us/history

US Navy. (n.d.). *Serving the fleet, fighter and family*. Retrieved from http://www.navymwr.org/programs/

van der Stouwe, T., Asscher, J.J., Hoeve, M., van der Laan, & Stams, G. (2016). Social skills training for juvenile delinquents: Post-treatment Changes. *Journal of Experimental Criminology, 12*, 515-536. doi:10.1007/s11292-016-9262-2

Wallace-Carr, J. (2013). Campus recreation. In *Introduction to Recreation and Leisure* (2nd ed., pp. 218-223). Champaign, IL: Human Kinetics.

Ward, BW, Schiller, JS, & Goodman, RA. (2014). Multiple chronic conditions among US adults: a 2012 update. *Prev Chronic Dis*. 2014;11:E62.

Wexler, E. (2016). *No pain, no gain*. Retrieved from https://www.insidehighered.com/news/2016/05/04/study-recreational-physical-activities-increase-odds-academic-success

Wilson, P.E. (2008). History and evolution of campus recreation. In NIRSA (Ed.), *Campus recreation: Essentials for the professional*. Champaign, IL: Human Kinetics.

Worldometers. (n.d.). *U.S. population*. Retrieved from http://www.worldometers.info/world-population/us-population/

CHAPTER 12

Administration on Aging. (2014). *A profile of older Americans*. Washington, DC: U.S. Department of Health and Human Services.

Baltes, P.B., Lindenberger, U., & Staudinger, U. (2006). Life span theory in developmental psychology. In W. Damon & R. Lerner (Eds.), *Handbook of child psychology* (6th ed.). New York, NY: Wiley.

Birren, J.E., & Schaie, K.W. (2006). *Handbook of the psychology of aging*. San Francisco, CA: Academic Press.

Cochran, L.J., Rothschadl, A.M., & Rudick, J.L. (2009). *Leisure programming for baby boomers*. Champaign, IL: Human Kinetics.

Edginton, C.R., DeGraaf, D.G., Dieser, R.B., & Edginton, S.R. (2006). *Leisure and life satisfaction: Foundational perspectives*. New York, NY: McGraw-Hill.

Edginton, C.R., Hudson, S.R., Dieser, R.B., & Edginton, S.R. (2004). *Leisure programming: A service-centered and benefits approach* (4th ed.). Boston, MA: McGraw-Hill.

Edginton, C.R., Kowalski, C.L., & Ranall, S.W. (2005). *Youth work: Emerging perspectives in youth development*. Champaign, IL: Sagamore.

Erikson, E.H. (1950). *Childhood and society*. New York, NY: Norton.

Godbey, G. (2008). *Leisure in your life: New perspectives*. State College, PA: Venture Publishing.

Howe, N., & Strauss, B. (1997). *The fourth turning: What the cycles of history tell us about America's next rendezvous with destiny*. New York, NY: Broadway Books.

Howe, N., & Strauss, B. (2000). *Millennials rising*. New York, NY: Vintage Books.

Kagan, J. (2002). Behavioral inhibition as a temperamental category. In R.J. Davidson, K.R. Scherer, & H.H. Goldsmith (Eds.), *Handbook of affective sciences*. New York, NY: Oxford University Press.

Kagan, J. (2010). Emotions and temperament. In M.H. Burnstein (Ed.), *Handbook of cultural developmental science*. New York, NY: Psychology Press.

Kelly, J.R., & Godbey, G. (1991). *The sociology of leisure*. State College, PA: Venture Publishing.

Kleiber, D. (1999). *Leisure experience and human development*. New York, NY: Basic Books.

Larson, R.W., & Ham, M. (1993). Stress and storm and stress in early adolescence: the relationship of negative events with dysphoric affect. *Developmental Psychology, 29*, 130-140.

Larson, R.W., & Verma, S. (1999). How children and adolescents spend their time across the world: Work, play and developmental opportunities. *Psychological Bulletin, 125*, 701-736.

Leitner, M.J., & Leitner, S.F. (2004). *Leisure in later life* (3rd ed.). New York, NY: Haworth Press.

Levinson, D. (1978). *The seasons of man's life*. New York, NY: Alfred A. Knopf.

Louv, R. (2005). *Last child in the woods: Saving our children from nature-deficit disorder*. Chapel Hill, NC: Algonquin Books.

Liu, S., Caneday, L., & Tapps, T.N. (2013). The relationship between lifestyle and serious leisure of amateur volleyball players in a rural community. *The Journal of Applied Leisure and Recreation Research, 16*(4), 23-36.

Neulinger, J. (1974). *The psychology of leisure*. Springfield, IL: Charles C. Thomas.

Nied, R., & Franklin, B. (2002). Promoting and prescribing exercise for the elderly. *American Academy of Family Physician, 65*(3), 419-426.

Pittman, K.J. (1991). *Promoting youth development: Strengthening the role of youth serving community organizations*. New York, NY: Center for Youth Development and Policy Research.

Stebbins, R.A., (1992). *Amateurs, professional and serious leisure*. Montreal, QC: McGill-Queen's University Press.

Sutton-Smith, B. (1971). Children at play. *Natural History, 80*(1), 55.

Tapps, T.N. (2012). *Diversity and the college experience: Workbook*. Dubuque, IA: Kendall Hunt.

Tapps, T.N., & McKenzie, E. (2014, October). The importance of young professional's involvement with community organizations. *Parks and Recreation Magazine, 49*(10), 44-45.

Tapps, T.N., Passmore, T., Lindenmeier, D., & Bishop, A. (2013). An investigation into the effects of resistance physical activity participation on depression of older adults in a long-term care facility. *Annual in Therapeutic Recreation, 21*(1), 63-72.

CHAPTER 13

DeGraff, D., DeGraff, K., & Jordan, D. (2010). *Programming for parks and leisure services: A servant leadership approach* (3rd ed.). State College, PA: Venture.

Harenburg, V., Moiseichik, M., & van der Smissen, B. (Eds.). (2005). *Management of parks and recreation agencies*. Ashburn, VA: National Recreation and Park Association.

Human Kinetics (Ed.). (2006). *Introduction to recreation and leisure*. Champaign, IL: Human Kinetics.

Moiseichik, Merry (Ed.). (2010). *Management of park and recreation agencies* (3rd ed.). Urbana, IL: Sagamore.

Mulvaney, M., & Hurd, A. (2010). *Official study guide for the certified park and recreation professional* (4th ed.). Urbana, IL: Sagamore.

Rossman, J.R., & Schlatter, B. (2011). *Recreation programming* (6th ed.). Urbana, IL: Sagamore.

CHAPTER 14

102 Boys and Girls Clubs of Canada. (2017). *Facts*. Retrieved from https://www.bgccan.com/en/AboutUs/FactsStats/Pages/default.aspx

Amateur Athletic Association. (2017). *About AAU*. Lake Buena Vista FL. Retrieved from: http://aausports.org

Australian Bureau of Statistics. (2015). *Participation in Sport and Physical Recreation, Australia, 2013-14*. Retrieved from http://www.abs.gov.au/ausstats/abs@.nsf/0/9FD67668EE42A738CA2568A9001393AC?Opendocument

Barcelona, R., Wells, M., & Arthur-Banning, S. (2016). *Recreational sport: Program design, delivery and management*. Champaign, IL: Human Kinetics.

Barcelona, R.J., & Ross, C.M. (2005). An analysis of the perceived competencies of recreational sport administrators. *Journal of Park and Recreation Administration, 22*(4), 25-42.

Big Brothers Big Sisters of America. (2017). *National office*. Retrieved from http://www.bbbs.org/national-office

Big Brothers and Big Sisters of Canada. (2017). *Company overview*. Retrieved from https://www.facebook.com/pg/bigbrothersbigsistersofcanada/about/?ref=page_internal

Blumenthal, K.J. (2009). Collegiate recreational sports: Pivotal players in student success. *Planning for Higher Education, 37*(2), 52-62.

Boys and Girls Clubs of America. (2017). *About us: Careers*. Retrieved from https://www.bgca.org/about-us/careers

Bureau of Labor Statistics. (2017). *Recreation workers: Job outlook*. Retrieved from https://www.bls.gov/ooh/personal-care-and-service/recreation-workers.htm

Delaney, T. & Madigan, T. (2015) *The sociology of sports: An introduction,* (2nd ed). Jefferson, NC: McFarland & Company, Inc.

Emery, C., Roy, T.O., Hagel, B., Macpherson, A., & Nettel-Aguirre, A. (2016). Injury prevention in youth sport. In Caine, D., Purcell, L. (Eds.), *Injury in pediatric and adolescent sports* (pp. 205-229). Cham, Switzerland: Springer International Publishing.

Employee Morale and Recreation Association. (2017). *Employee morale & recreation programs*. Retrieved from http://esmassociation.roundtablelive.org/page-372979

Evans, D. (2012). *Social media marketing: An hour a day* (2nd ed.). Indianapolis, IN: Wiley.

Forrester, S. (2014). *The benefits of campus recreation*. Corvallis, OR: NIRSA.

Forney, C. A. (2010). *The holy trinity of American sports: Civil religion in football, baseball, and basketball*. Macon, GA: Mercer University Press.

Ghafouri, F., Mirzaei, B., Hums, M.A., & Honarvar, A. (2009). Effects of globalization on sport strategies. *Brazilian Journal of Biomotricity, 3*(3), 261-270.

Gould, D. (2016). Quality coaching counts. *Phi Delta Kappan, 97*(8), 13-18.

Government of Canada. (2017). *Sport organizations*. Retrieved from http://canada.pch.gc.ca/eng/1414085745696

Henderson, K.A. (2009). A paradox of sport management and physical activity interventions. *Sport Management Review, 12*, 57-65.

International Health, Racquet & Sportsclub Association (2017). *About IHRSA*. Retrieved from http://www.ihrsa.org/about/

Isidore, C. (February 7, 2016). Super Bowl 50 tickets the most expensive in U.S. sports history. *CNN Money*. Retrieved from http://money.cnn.com/2016/02/03/news/super-bowl-tickets-price/index.html

Kidd, B. (2008). A new social movement: Sport for development and peace. *Sport in Society, 11*(4), 370-380.

Mull, R.F., Bayless, K.G., & Jamieson, L.M. (2005). *Recreational sport management* (4th ed.). Champaign, IL: Human Kinetics.

National Congress of State Games. (2017). *About*. Retrieved from http://stategames.org/about

Navy MWR. (n.d.). *Navy MWR fleet recreation*. Retrieved from http://www.navymwr.org/

Nielsen.com. (2016). *The year in sports media report: 2015*. Retrieved from http://www.nielsen.com/us/en/insights/reports/2016/the-year-in-sports-media-report-2015.html

North American Society of Sport Management. (n.d.). *NASSM home*. Retrieved from http://www.nassm.com

Physical Activity Council. (2017). *2017 participation report*. Retrieved from http://www.physicalactivitycouncil.com/pdfs/current.pdf

Price, J.L. (2005). *From season to season: Sports as American religion*. Macon, GA: Mercer University Press.

Shannon-Missal, L. (Ed.). (2016). *The Harris poll*. Retrieved from http://www.theharrispoll.com/sports/Americas_Fav_Sport_2016.html

Solutions Research Group Inc. (2014). *Massive competition in pursuit of the $5.7 billion Canadian youth sports market*. Retrieved from http://www.srgnet.com/2014/06/10/massive-competition-in-pursuit-of-the-5-7-billion-canadian-youth-sports-market/

Sport England. (2016). *Active lives survey*. London: England. Retrieved from https://www.sportengland.org/media/11498/active-lives-survey-yr-1-report.pdf

The Aspen Institute: Project Play. (2016). *State of play: Trends and developments*. Aspen, CO: The Aspen Institute.

Tremblay, M. S., Barnes, J. D., González, S. A., Katzmarzyk, P. T., Onywera, V. O., Reilly, J. J., & Global Matrix 2.0 Research Team. (2016). Global Matrix 2.0: report card grades on the physical activity of children and youth comparing 38 countries. *Journal of Physical Activity and Health*, 13(11 Suppl 2), S343-S366.

YMCA. (2017). *About us: Organizational profile*. Retrieved fromhttp://www.ymca.net/organizational-profile/

YMCA Canada. (2017). *Who we are: Organizational structure*. Retrieved from http://ymca.ca/Who-We-Are/Organizational-Structure

CHAPTER 15

American Psychological Association. (2011). *Mind/body health: Did you know?* Retrieved from http://www.apa.org/helpcenter/mind-body.aspx

Centers for Disease Control and Prevention (CDC). (2011). Mental illness surveillance among adults in the United States. *Morbidity and Mortality Weekly Report*, 60, 1-32.

Centers for Disease Control and Prevention (CDC). (n.d.). *Physical activity and health*. Retrieved from https://www.cdc.gov/physicalactivity/basics/pa-health/

Centers for Disease Control and Prevention (CDC). (2014). Youth risk behavior surveillance – United States, 2013. *Morbidity and Mortality Weekly Report*, 63, 4.

Centers for Disease Control and Prevention (CDC). (2016). *Adult obesity causes and consequences*. Retrieved from https://www.cdc.gov/obesity/adult/causes.html

Grad, F.P. (2002). *The preamble of the constitution of the World Health Organization*. 80(12): 982. Retrieved from http://www.who.int/bulletin/archives/80(12)981.pdf

Hancock, T., & Duhl, L. (1988). *Promoting health in the urban context*. WHO Healthy Cities Pap. No1. Copenhagen: FADL. 54 pp.

International Living. (2016). *Quality of life index*.Retrieved from https://internationalliving.com/?s=quality+of+life+index

Irvin, V. L., & Kaplan, R. M. (2016). Effect sizes and primary outcomes in large-budget cardiovascular-related behavioral randomized controlled trials funded by NIH since 1980. *Annals of Behavioral Medicine*, 50(1), 130-146. Doi: 10/1007/s12160-015-9739-7.

National Institute of Health. (2015). *Positive emotions and your health, developing a brighter outlook*. News in Health. Retrieved from https://newsinhealth.nih.gov/issue/aug2015/feature1

National Wellness Institute. (2011). *A definition of spiritual wellness*. Retrieved from http://www.nationalwellness.org/general.php?id_tier=2%20&%20id=684

Statistics Canada. (2015). *Mortality overview*. Retrieved from http://www.statcan.gc.ca/pub/91-209-x/2013001/article/11867-eng.htm

Statistics Canada. (2015). *Canada's population estimates: Age and sex, July 1, 2015*. Ottawa, ON: Author.

World Health Organization (WHO). (2010). *WHO global infobase: Data for saving lives*. Retrieved from https://apps.who.int/infobase/

World Health Organization (WHO). (n.d.-a). *Burden of disease attributable to the modifiable environment, 2002*. Retrieved from http://www.who.int/quantifying_ehimpacts/national/countryprofile/mapenv/en/index.html

World Health Organization (WHO). (n.d.-b). *Infant mortality*. Retrieved from www.who.int/gho/child_health/mortality/neonatal_infant_text/en/

World Health Organization (WHO). (2016). *Obesity and overweight*. Retrieved from http://www.who.int/mediacentre/factsheets/fs311/en/

World Health Organization (WHO). (2017). *Physical activity fact sheet*. Retrieved from http://www.who.int/mediacentre/factsheets/fs385/en/

World Leisure Organization. (2012). *Commission on health prevention and disease prevention*. Retrieved from http://worldleisure.org/template.php?id=144&Health+Prevention+and+Disease+Prevention

Xu, J., Kochanek, K.D., Murphy, S.L., & Tejada-Vera, B. (2010). Deaths: Final data for 2007. *National Vital Statistics Reports*, 58, 1-72.

CHAPTER 16

Alagona, P.S., & Simon, G.L. (2009). Beyond Leave No Trace. *Ethics, Place & Environment: A Journal of Philosophy & Geography*, 12(1), 17-34.

Alagona, P.S., & Simon, G.L. (2012). Leave No Trace starts at home: A response to critics and vision for the future. *Ethics, Policy and Environment*, 15(1), 119-124.

American Camp Association. (n.d.). *Mission and vision*. Retrieved from http://www.acacamps.org/about/who-we-are/mission-and-vision

Andre, E. (2012). Is it time for a global ethic, not just local etiquette. In B. Martin & M. Wagstaff (Eds.), *Controversial issues in adventure programming (pp. 248-253)*. Champaign, IL: Human Kinetics.

Association for Experiential Education (AEE). (n.d.). *What is experiential education?* Retrieved from http://www.aee.org/what-is-ee

Bernard, M. (1999). The camping movement takes shape. *Camping Magazine*, 72(6), 20.

Bunyan, P. (2011). Models and milestones in adventure education. In M. Berry & C. Hodgson (Eds.), *Adventure education: An introduction (pp. 5-23)*. London, UK: Routledge.

Campbell, C.E. (2011). Governing a kingdom: Parks Canada, 1911-2011. In C.E. Campbell (Ed.), *A century of Parks Canada 1911-2011* (pp. 1-19). Calgary, AL: University of Calgary Press.

Cordes, K., & Hutson, G. (2015). *Outdoor recreation: Enrichment for a lifetime* (4th ed.). Champaign, IL: Sagamore.

Curtis, J. (1979). *Recreation: Theory and practice*. London, UK: C.V. Mosby Company.

DeMerritte, E. (1999). The emergence of the camping movement. *Camping Magazine, 72*(6), 18-19.

Dennis, S. (2012). *Natural resources and the informed citizen*. Champaign, IL: Sagamore.

Donaldson, G., & Donaldson, L. (1958). Outdoor education: A definition. *Journal of Physical Education, Recreation & Dance, 29*(17), 17.

Dustin, D., Bricker, K., & Schwab, K. (2010). People and nature: Toward an ecological model of health promotion. *Leisure Sciences, 32*(1), 3-14.

Duvall, J., & Kaplan, R. (2014). Enhancing the well-being of veterans using extended group-based nature recreation experiences. *Journal of Rehabilitation Research and Development, 51*(5), 685–696.

Ewert, A. W. (1989). *Outdoor adventure pursuits: Foundations, models, and theories*. Scottsdale, AZ: Publishing Horizons.

Ewert, A. W., & Garvey, D. (2007). Philosophy and theory of adventure education. In D. Prouty, J. Panicucci, & R. Collinson (Eds.), *Adventure education: Theory and applications* (pp. 19-32). Champaign, IL: Human Kinetics.

Ewert, A. W., & Vernon, F. (2013). Outdoor and adventure recreation. In *Introduction to Recreation and Leisure* (2nd ed., pp. 321-339) Champaign, IL: Human Kinetics.

Ford, P. (1981). *Principles and practices of outdoor/environmental education*. New York, NY: Wiley.

Gardener, T. (2016). *Everest: Facts and figures*. Retrieved from https://www.thebmc.co.uk/everest-facts-and-figures

Gear Junkie.. (2017). *Colo. university to offer "outdoors MBA."* Retrieved from https://gearjunkie.com/western-state-co-university-outdoors-mba

Godbey, G. (1999). *Leisure in your life: An exploration* (5th. ed.). State College, PA: Venture Publishing.

Goldenberg, M., & Soule, K. (2014). A four-year follow-up of means-end outcomes from outdoor adventure programs. *Journal of Adventure Education and Outdoor Learning, 15*(4), 1-12.

Gruenwald, D., & Smith, G. (2008). Making room for the local. In D. Gruenwald and G. Smith (Eds.), *Place-based education in the global age* (pp. xii-xxiii). New York, NY: Lawrence Erlbaum.

Halpenny, E. (2010). Pro-environmental behaviour and park visitors: The effect of place attachment. *Journal of Environmental Psychology, 30*(4), 409-421.

Ibrahim, H., & Cordes, K. (1993). *Outdoor recreation*. Boston, MA: WCB McGraw-Hill.

International Ecotourism Society. (2015). *What is ecotourism?* Retrieved from http://www.ecotoruism.org/what-is-ecotourism.

Lemelin, R. H., Dawson, J., & Stewart, E. J. (Eds.). (2012). *Last chance tourism: Adapting tourism opportunities in a changing world*. New York, NY: Routledge.

Loverseed, H. (1997). The adventure and travel industry in North America. *Travel and Tourism Analyst, 6*(1), 87-104.

Mammoth Mountain Ski Area. (n.d.). *Mammoth Bike Park*. Retrieved from http://www.mammothmountain.com/summer/bike-park-overview/bike-park

Manning, R.E. (2007). *Parks and carrying capacity: Commons without tragedy* (2nd ed.). Washington, DC: Island Press.

Martin, B., Cashel, C., Wagstaff, M., & Breunig, M. (2017). *Outdoor leadership: Theory and practice* (2nd ed.). Champaign, IL: Human Kinetics.

McClean, D., & Hurd, A. (2011). *Kraus' recreation and leisure in modern society*. Burlington, MA: Jones & Bartlett Learning.

Nash, R. (1982). *Wilderness and the American mind* (3rd ed.). New Haven, CT: Yale University Press.

National Outdoor Leadership School (NOLS). (n.d.). *About NOLS*. Retrieved from https://www.nols.edu/en/about/

National Recreation and Park Association (NRPA). (n.d.). *About NRPA*. Retrieved from http://www.nrpa.org/About-National-Recreation-and-Park-Association/

Olmsted, L. (2013, October). Martis Camp: Possibly the best four-season private community in the U.S. *Forbes*. Retrieved from https://www.forbes.com/sites/larryolmsted/2013/10/02/the-best-four-season-private-community-in-the-us/#363f547f7f1d

Outdoor Industry Foundation. (2016). *2016 outdoor recreation topline report*. Retrieved from http://www.outdoorfoundation.org/research.participation.2016.topline.html

Outward Bound. (n.d.). *In the world*. Retrieved from http://www.outwardbound.org/about-outward-bound/outward-bound-today/in-the-world/

Ozier, L. (2012). *Camp as educator: A study of summer residential camp as a landscape for learning and living* (Doctoral dissertation). Teachers College, Columbia University, New York.

Plummer, R. (2009). *Outdoor recreation: An introduction*. New York, NY: Routledge.

Priest, S. (1990). The semantics of adventure education. In J. Miles & S. Priest (Eds.), *Adventure Education* (pp. 111-114). State College, PA: Venture Publishing.

Sessoms, H. (1984). *Leisure services* (6th ed.). Englewood Cliffs, NJ: Prentice Hall.

Sobel, D. (2004). *Place-based education: Connecting classrooms and communities*. Great Barrington, MA: Orion Society.

Swarbrooke, J., Beard, C., Leckie, S., & Pomfret, G. (2011). *Adventure tourism: The new frontier*. New York, NY: Taylor and Francis.

Turner, E. (1985). *100 years of YMCA camping*. Chicago, IL: YMCA of the USA.

Turner, J.M. (2002). From woodcraft to "Leave No Trace": Wilderness, consumerism, and environmentalism in twentieth-century America. *Environmental History, 7*(3), 462-484.

U.S. Army MWR. (n.d.). *Outdoor recreation.* Retrieved from http://italy.armymwr.com/europe/italy/programs/outdoor-recreation

Virden, R. (2006). Outdoor and adventure recreation. In *Introduction to recreation and leisure* (pp. 307-332). Champaign, IL: Human Kinetics.

Welser, H.T. (2012). The growth of technology and the end of wilderness experience. In B. Martin and M. Wagstaff (Eds.), *Controversial issues in adventure programming* (pp. 147-155). Champaign, IL: Human Kinetics.

CHAPTER 17

American Assembly. (1997). *The arts and the public purpose.* Retrieved from http://americanassembly.org/publications/arts-and-public-purpose

Americans for the Arts. (2017). *Arts and economic prosperity 5: The economic impact of nonprofit arts and culture organizations and their audiences.* Retrieved from http://www.americansforthearts.org/by-program/reports-and-data/research-studies-publications/arts-economic-prosperity-5

Arnold, N.D. (1976). *The interrelated arts in leisure: Perceiving and creating.* Saint Louis, MO: C.V. Mosby Company.

Arnold, N.D. (1978). Pop art: The human footprint in infinity. *Journal of Physical Education, Recreation and Dance, 49*(8), 56-57.

Arts Midwest & Metropolitan Group. (2015). *Creating connection: Research findings and proposed message framework to build public will for arts and culture.* Retrieved from http://www.creatingconnection.org/research

Blandy, D. (2008). Cultural programming. In G. Carpenter & D. Blandy (Eds.), *Arts and cultural programming: A leisure perspective* (pp. 173-184). Champaign, IL: Human Kinetics.

Bourdieu, P. (1986). The forms of capital. In J. Richardson (Ed.), *Handbook of theory and research for the sociology of education* (pp. 241-258). New York, NY: Greenwood.

Canada Review Agency. (1991). *Festivals and the promotion of tourism: Policy statement.* Retrieved from http://www.cra-arc.gc.ca/chrts-gvng/chrts/plcy/cps/cps-005-eng.html

Canadian Parks Council. (2011). *The economic impact of Canada's national, provincial and territorial parks in 2009.* Retrieved from http://www.parks-parcs.ca/english/pdf/econ_impact_2009_part1.pdf

Carpenter, G. (2008). Overview of arts and cultural programming. In G. Carpenter & D. Blandy (Eds.), *Arts and cultural programming: A leisure perspective* (pp. 3-23). Champaign, IL: Human Kinetics.

Carpenter, G. (2013). Arts & culture. In *Introduction to recreation and leisure* (2nd ed.). Champaign, IL: Human Kinetics.

Carpenter, G. & Howe, C. Z. (1985). *Programming leisure experiences.* Englewood Cliff, N.J.: Prentice-Hall.

Chapman, L.H. (1978). *Approaches to art in education.* New York, NY: Harcourt Brace Jovanovich.

Chapman, L.H. (2003). Studies of the mass arts. *Studies in Art Education, 44*(3), 230-245.

Chartrand, H.H. (2000). Toward an American arts industry. In J.M. Cherbo & M.J. Wyszormirski (Eds.), *The public life of the arts in America* (pp. 22-49). New Brunswick, NJ: Rutgers University Press.

City Parks Forum. (2008). *How cities use parks for arts and cultural programming.* Chicago, IL: American Planning Association. Retrieved from https://www.planning.org/cityparks/briefingpapers/arts.htm

Coleman, J.S. (1988). Social capital in the creation of human capital. *American Journal of Sociology, 94,* 95-120.

Comic-Con International: San Diego 2016. (2016). *About Comic-Con International.* Retrieved from https://secure.comic-con.org/about

Conference Board of Canada. (2008). *Valuing culture: Measuring and understanding Canada's creative economy.* Retrieved from http://www.conferenceboard.ca/e-library/abstract.aspx?DID=2671

Congdon, K.G., & Blandy, D. (2003). Administering the culture of everyday life: Imagining the future of arts sector administration. In V.B. Morris & D.B. Pankratz (Eds.), *The arts in a new millennium* (pp. 177-188). Westport, CT: Praeger.

Corbin, H.D., & Williams, E. (1987). *Recreation: Programming and leadership* (4th ed.). Englewood Cliffs, NJ: Prentice Hall.

Csikszentmihalyi, M. (1990). *Flow: The psychology of optimal experience.* New York, NY: Harper & Row.

Cuyler, A. (2007). The career paths of non-European American opera administrators in the United States. *Dissertation Abstracts International, 68*(5).

Cuyler, A. (2013). Affirmative action and diversity: Implications for arts management. *The Journal of Arts Management, Law, and Society, 43,* 98-105.

Darts, D. (2004). Visual culture jam: Art, pedagogy, and creative resistance. *Studies in Art Education, 45*(4), 313-327.

Delamere, T. A. (2001). Development of a scale to measure resident attitudes toward the social impacts of community festivals, part II: Verification of the scale event management. *Annals of Tourism Research, 7* (1), 25-38.

Delamere, T.A. & Rollins, R. (2007). Measuring the social impact of festivals. *Annals of Tourism Research, 34*(3), 805-808.

Delamere, T.A., Wankel, L.M., & Hinch, T.D. (2001). Measuring resident attitudes toward the social impact of community festivals. Pretesting and purification of the scale. *Festival Management and Event Tourism, 7*(1), 11-24.

Driver, B.L., & Burns, D.H. (1999). Concepts and uses of the benefits approach to leisure. In E.L. Jackson & T.L. Burton

(Eds.), *Leisure studies: Prospects for the twenty-first century* (pp. 349-369). State College, PA: Venture Publishing.

Edin, K., & Kefalas, M. (2011). *Promises I can keep: Why poor women put motherhood before marriage.* Berkeley: University of California Press.

Farrell, P., & Lundegren, H. (1978). *The process of recreation programming: Theory and technique.* New York, NY: Wiley.

Farrell, P., & Lundegren, H. (1983). *The process of recreation programming: Theory and technique* (2nd ed.). New York, NY: Wiley.

Farrell, P., & Lundegren, H. (1991). *The process of recreation programming: Theory and technique* (3rd ed.). New York, NY: Wiley.

Florida, R. (2002). *The rise of the creative class.* New York, NY: Basic Books.

Freedman, K., & Stuhr, P. (2004). Curriculum changes for the 21st century: Visual culture in art education. In E. Eisner & M. Day (Eds.), *Handbook of research and policy in art education* (pp. 815-828). Reston, VA: National Art Education Association.

Friedenwald-Fishman, E., & Fraher, D. (2016). Creating connection through creative expression. *CultureWork: A Periodic Broadside for Arts & Culture Workers, 20*(2). Retrieved from https://culturework.uoregon.edu/2016/04/12/april-2016-vol-20-no-2-creating-connection-through-creative-expression-eric-friedenwald-fishman-and-david-fraher/

Fromm, J., & Garton, C. (2013). *Marketing to millennials: Reach the largest and most influential generation of consumers ever.* New York, NY: AMACOM.

Geezer Gallery. (2016). *Mission.* Retrieved from https://geezer-gallery.com/mission/

Gray, D. (1984, April). *The great simplicities.* J.B. Nash Scholar Lecture, Anaheim, CA.

Harris, L.M., & Edelman, M. (2006). *After sixty: Marketing to baby boomers reaching their big transition years.* Ithaca, NY: Paramount Market Publications.

Hetland, L., Winner, E., Veenema, S., & Sheridan, K. (2007). *Studio thinking: The real benefits of arts education.* New York, NY: Teachers College Press.

Indiana Arts Commission. (n.d.). *Arts in the parks and historic sites.* Retrieved from https://in.gov/arts/2905.htm

Iso-Ahola, S.E. (1980). *The social psychology of leisure and recreation.* Dubuque, IA: Brown.

Kelly, J.R. (1996). *Leisure* (3rd ed.) Boston, MA: Allyn and Bacon.

Kelly, J.R., & Freysinger, V.J. (2000). *Twentieth century leisure: Current issues.* Boston, MA: Allyn and Bacon.

Kleiber, D.A. (1999). *Leisure experience and human development.* New York, NY: Basic Books.

Knight Foundation. (n.d.). *About Knight soul of the community.* Retrieved from http://www.knightfoundation.org/sotc/about-knight-soul-community/

Know Your City. (2016). *Programs.* Retrieved from http://knowyourcity.org/

Kraus, R. (1966). *Recreation today: Program planning and leadership.* New York: NY: Appleton-Century-Crofts.

Kraus, R. (1979). *Social recreation: A group dynamics approach.* St. Louis, MO: Mosby.

Kraus, R. (1985). *Recreation program planning today.* Glenview, IL: Scott Foresman.

Lanier, V. (1969). The teaching of art as social revolution. *Phi Delta Kappa, 50*(G), 314-319.

Loden Associates, Inc. (2010). *Primary and secondary dimensions of diversity.* Retrieved from http://www.loden.com/Site/Dimensions.html

Mandala Research, LLC. (2013). *The cultural traveler.* Retrieved from https://theculturaltraveler.com/

Markusen, A., & Gadwa, A. (2010). *Creative placemaking.* Retrieved from https://www.arts.gov/sites/default/files/CreativePlacemaking-Paper.pdf

Mauldin, B., Laramee Kidd, S., Ruskin, J., & Agustin, M. (2016). *Executive summary: Los Angeles County Arts Commission cultural equity and inclusion initiative literature review.* Los Angeles, CA: Los Angeles County Arts Commission. Retrieved from http://artsequityla.com/

McCarthy, K.F., & Jinnett, K. (2001). *A new framework for building participation in the arts.* Santa Monica, CA: Rand.

McFee, J.K. (1961). *Preparation for art.* San Francisco, CA: Wadsworth Publishing Company.

McFee, J.K. (1978). Art abilities in environmental reform. *Art Education, 31*(4), 9-12.

Meyer, H.D., & Brightbill, C.K. (1956). *Community recreation: A guide to its organization.* Englewood Cliffs, NJ: Prentice-Hall.

MTC-ABAG Library. (n.d.). *Bay Area census: San Francisco city and county.* Retrieved from http://www.bayareacensus.ca.gov/counties/SanFranciscoCounty.htm

Mural Arts Philadelphia. (2017). *About.* Retrieved from https://www.muralarts.org/about/

National Assembly of State Art Agencies. (2013). *Percent for art policy brief.* Retrieved from http://www.nasaa-arts.org/Research/Key-Topics/Public-Art/State-Percent-for-Art-Programs.php

National Endowment for the Arts. (2011a). *Arts education in America: What the declines mean for arts participation.* Retrieved from https://www.arts.gov/sites/default/files/2008-SPPA-ArtsLearning.pdf

National Endowment for the Arts. (2011b). *Beyond attendance: A multi-modal understanding of arts participation.* Retrieved from https://www.arts.gov/sites/default/files/2008-SPPA-BeyondAttendance.pdf

National Endowment for the Arts. (2013). *How a nation engages with art: Highlights from the 2012 survey of public participation in the arts.* Retrieved from https://www.arts.gov/sites/default/files/highlights-from-2012-sppa-revised-oct-2015.pdf

National Endowment for the Arts. (2015). *When the going gets tough: Barriers and motivations affecting arts attendance.* Retrieved from https://www.arts.gov/sites/default/files/when-going-gets-tough-revised2.pdf

National Governors Association. (n.d.). *Arts and the economy: Using arts and culture to stimulate state economic development.* Retrieved from http://www.nga.org/files/live/sites/NGA/files/pdf/0901ARTSANDECONOMY.PDF

National Recreation and Park Association. (2015). *The economic impact of local parks: An examination of the economic impacts of operations and capital spending on the United States economy.* Retrieved from http://www.nrpa.org/uploadedFiles/nrpa.org/Publications_and_Research/Research/Papers/Economic-Impact-Study-Summary.pdf

New Strategist Publications (Eds.). (2004). *Generation X: Americans born 1965 to 1976.* Ithaca, NY: New Strategist Publications.

Niagara Folk Arts Festival (NFAF). (n.d.). *Welcome.* Retrieved from http://folk-arts.ca/festival/

Ontario Ministry of Tourism & Recreation/Parks and Recreation Federation of Ontario. (1992). *The benefits of parks and recreation: A catalogue.* Gloucester, ON: Canadian Parks/Recreation Association.

Orend, R.J. (1989). *Socialization and participating in the arts.* Princeton, NJ: Princeton University Press.

Portes, A. (1998). Social capital: Its origins and applications in modern sociology. *Annual Review Sociology, 24*, 1-24.

Powell Hanna, G. (2016). Arts, health and aging. In P. Dewey Lambert (Ed.), *Managing arts programs in healthcare* (pp. 189-201). London, UK: Routledge.

Prince George County Department of Arts and Recreation. (2014). *Innovate parks and rec.* http://pgplanning.org/315/Innovate-Parks-Recreation

Prince George County Department of Arts and Recreation. (n.d.). *About us.* Retrieved from http://arts.pgparks.com/About_Us.htm

Project for Public Spaces. (2017). *What is placemaking?* Retrieved https://www.pps.org/reference/what_is_placemaking/

Putnam, R.D. (2000). *Bowling alone: The collapse and revival of American community.* New York, NY: Simon & Schuster.

Rosewall, E. (2014). *Arts management: Uniting arts and audiences in the 21st century.* New York, NY: Oxford University Press.

Rossman, J.R. (1995). *Recreation programming: Designing leisure experiences.* Champaign, IL: Sagamore.

Rossman, J. R., & Schlatter, B. E. (2008). *Recreation programming: Designing leisure experiences* (5th ed.). Champaign, IL: Sagamore.

Stack, C.B. (1975). *All our kin: Strategies for survival in a black community.* New York, NY: Basic Books.

Statistics Canada. (2016). *Income and expenditure accounts technical series: Provincial and territorial culture indicators, 2010 to 2014.* Retrieved from http://www.statcan.gc.ca/pub/13-604-m/13-604-m2016081-eng.htm

Stebbins, R.A. (1992). *Amateurs, professionals, and serious leisure.* Montreal, QC: MC-Gill-Queen's University Press.

Stebbins, R.A. (2005). Project-based learners: Theoretical neglect of a common use of free time. *Leisure Studies, 24*(1), 1-11.

Stebbins, R.A., & Graham, M. (2004). *Volunteering as leisure/leisure as volunteering: An international assessment.* Cambridge, MA: CABI.

Stein, T. (2000). Creating opportunities for people of color in performing arts management. *Journal of Arts Management, Law, and Society 29*, 304-318.

Stern, M.J., & Seifert, S. (2002). *Culture builds community evaluation summary report.* Philadelphia, PA: University of Pennsylvania School of Social Work.

Stern, M.J., & Seifert, S. (2009). *Documenting civic engagement: A plan for the Tucson Pima Arts Council.* Retrieved from http://repository.upenn.edu/siap_civic_engagement/3/

Stern, M.J., & Seifert, S. (2014). *Communities, culture, and capabilities: Preliminary results of a four-city study.* Retrieved from http://repository.upenn.edu/cgi/viewcontent.cgi?article=1000&context=siap_ccc

Sternberg, R.J., Grigorenko, E.L., & Singer, J.L. (Eds.). (2004). *Creativity: From potential to realization.* Washington, DC: American Psychological Association.

Sternberg, R.J., Kaufman, J.C., & Pretz, J.E. (2002). *The creativity conundrum.* New York, NY: Psychology Press.

Tavin, K. (2003). Wrestling with angels, searching for ghosts: Toward a critical pedagogy of visual culture. *Studies in Art Education, 44*(3), 197-213.

Tennessee State Library and Archives. (n.d.). *Tennessee State Parks folklife project.* Retrieved from http://sos.tn.gov/products/tsla/tennessee-state-parks-folklife-project

Traditional Arts Indiana. (n.d.). *What is Traditional Arts Indiana?* Retrieved from http://www.traditionalartsindiana.org/about/what-is-traditional-arts-indiana/

Tucson-Pima Arts Council. (2013b). *Creating prosperity: How the arts improve our economy and our community value.* Tucson, Arizona: Tucson-Pima Arts Council.

Tucson-Pima Arts Council. (2013b). *People, land, arts, and engagement: Taking stock of the PLACE initiative.* Tucson, Arizona: Tucson-Pima Arts Council.

United Nations Environment Programme. (n.d.). *Negative socio-cultural impacts from tourism change or loss of indigenous identity and values.* Retrieved from http://drustage.unep.org/resourceefficiency/impacts-tourism

U.S. Bank. (n.d.). *Community possible grant program—play.* Retrieved from https://www.usbank.com/community/community-possible-grant-program-play.aspx

Van Deursen, A.J., & Van Dijk, J.A. (2014). The digital divide shifts to differences in usage. *New Media & Society, 16*(3), 507-526.

Wallace Foundation. (n.d.). *Knowledge center: Arts education.* Retrieved from http://www.wallacefoundation.org/knowledge-center/arts-education/Pages/default.aspx

Webster, M. (2003). Arts education: Defining, developing, and implementing a successful program. In C. Dreezen (Ed.), *Fundamentals of arts management.* Amherst, MA: Arts Extension Service.

WDVX. (n.d.). *Cumberland trail.* Retrieved from http://wdvx.com/program/the-cumberland-trail/

World Tourism Organization. (2013). *Sustainable tourism for development guidebook.* Retrieved from http://cf.cdn.unwto.org/sites/all/files/docpdf/devcoengfinal.pdf

Wyszomirski, M.J. (2002). Arts and culture. In L.M. Salamon (Ed.), *The state of nonprofit America* (pp. 187-218). Washington, DC: Brookings Institution Press.

Youth Art Exchange. (2016). *About: What.* Retrieved from https://youthartexchange.org/about/what

Zakaras, L. & Lowell, J.F. (2008). *Cultivating demand for the arts: Arts learning, arts engagement, and state arts policy.* Santa Monica, CA: Rand.

CHAPTER 18

DiFiori, J.P., Benjamin, H.J., Brenner, J.S., Gregory, A., Jayanthi, N., Landry, G.L., & Luke, A. (2014). Overuse injuries and burnout in youth sports: A position statement from the American Medical Society for Sports Medicine. *Clinical Journal of Sport Medicine, 24,* 3-20.

Edginton, C.R., DeGraaf, D.G., Dieser, R.B., & Edgington, S.R. (2006). *Leisure and life satisfaction* (4th ed.). Boston, MA: McGraw-Hill.

Ferguson, R.W., Green, A., & Hansen, L.M. (2013). *Game changers: Stats, stories and what communities are doing to protect athletes.* Washington, DC: Safe Kids Worldwide.

Fyke, J. (2009). Connecting the Cumberlands: A public lands success story in Tennessee reveals the benefits of cooperative partnering. *Parks & Recreation. 44*(2).

Greenville County Parks, Recreation, & Tourism. (2014). *Code of ethics policy.* Retrieved from http://greenvillerec.com/wp-content/uploads/2014/03/4.1.1.a-Code-of-Ethics-Policy.pdf

Henderson, K.A. (2014). *Introduction to recreation services: Sustainability for a changing world.* State College, PA: Venture Publishing.

International Ecotourism Society. (n.d.). *What is ecotourism?* Retrieved from http://www.ecotourism.org/what-is-ecotourism

Kauffman, R.B. (2010). *Career development in recreation, parks, and tourism.* Champaign, IL: Human Kinetics.

Lyman, F. (2009). Parks unplugged: Getting greener by the day. *Parks & Recreation 44*(20), 42-45.

McGuire, F.A., Boyd, R.K., & Tedrick, R.E. (2009). *Leisure and aging: Ulyssean living in later life* (4th ed.). Champaign, IL: Sagamore.

McLean, D.D., & Hurd, A.R. (2012). *Recreation and leisure in modern society* (9th ed.). Sudbury, MA: Jones & Bartlett Learning.

McLean, D.D., Hurd, A.R., & Rogers, N.B. (2008). *Kraus' recreation and leisure in modern society* (8th ed.). Boston, MA: Jones and Bartlett.

Merriam, D. (2016). Parks: An opportunity to leverage environmental health. *Journal of Environmental Health, 78*(6), 112-114.

Mulvaney, M. A. (2015). Living up to the hype: The certified park and recreation professional certification. *Parks and Recreation Magazine 50*(9), 64.

Mulvaney, M. A., Beggs, B. A., Elkins, D. J., & Hurd, A. R. (2015). Professional certifications and job self-efficacy of public park and recreation professionals. *Journal of Park and Recreation Administration 33*(1), 93-111.

Murphy, J.F., Niepoth, E.W., Jamieson, L.M., & Williams, J.G. (1991). *Leisure systems: Critical concepts and applications.* Champaign, IL: Sagamore.

National Organization for Human Services. (n.d.). *What is human services?* Retrieved from http://www.nationalhumanservices.org/what-is-human-services

National Recreation and Park Association (NRPA). (2016). *Certification programs.* Retrieved from http://www.nrpa.org/certification/

Rudolph, L., Caplan, J., Ben-Moshe, K., & Dillon, L. (2013). *Health in all policies: A guide for state and local governments.* Retrieved from http://www.phi.org/uploads/files/Health_in_All_Policies-A_Guide_for_State_and_Local_Governments.pdf

Taylor, D. (2014). Park for all: Parks in Vancouver seek to welcome and serve people all along the gender spectrum. *Parks & Recreation, 49*(7), 34-35.

Tipping, E. (2015). *State of the industry: A look at what's happening in recreation, sports and fitness facilities.* Retrieved from http://recmanagement.com/state-of-the-industry/

U.S. Department of Health and Human Services. (2015). *Step it up! The surgeon general's call to action to promote walking and walkable communities.* Washington, DC: Author. Retrieved from https://www.surgeongeneral.gov/library/calls/walking-and-walkable-communities/call-to-action-walking-and-walkable-communites.pdf

Werner, C. A. (2011). *The older population: 2010: 2010 census briefs.* Retrieved from https://www.census.gov/content/dam/Census/library/publications/2011/dec/c2010br-09.pdf

CHAPTER 19

Almeida, M.A.B., & Gutierrez, G.L. (2005). O lazer no Brasil: Do nacional-desenvolvimentismo à globalização. *Conexões, 3*(1), 36-57.

Almeida, M.A.B., Gutierrez, G.L., & Marques, R.F.R. (2013). Leisure in Brazil: The transformations during the military period (1964-1984). *Revista Brasileira de Educação Física e Esporte, 27*(1), 101-115.

Amuchie, F.A. (2003). Pre-colonial sports in Nigeria: Their influence on contemporary sports development in Nigeria. In L.O. Amusa & A.L. Toriola (Eds.), *Sports in contemporary African Society: An anthology* (pp. 47-64). Technikon Pretoria: Africa Association for Health, Physical Education Recreation Sports and Dance.

Ap, J. (2002, April). *Inter-cultural behavior: Some glimpses of leisure from an Asian perspective.* Paper presented at the Leisure Futures Conference, Innsbruck, Austria.

Atare, F.U. (2003). *Introduction to recreation and leisure education.* Warri, Nigeria: COEWA.

Atare, F.U. (2014). The health benefit of walking: A Nigerian reflection. *World Leisure Journal, 56*(2), 164-167. doi:10.10 80/16078055.2014.903731

Atare, F. U. & Ekpu, F. S. (2014b). Status of recreation facilities in health promoting tertiary institutions in Akwa Ibom state – Nigeria. *International Journal of Humanities Social Sciences and Education. 1*(4), 69-74.

Beghin, N. (2008). Notes on inequality and poverty in Brazil: Current situation and challenges. In Oxfam (Ed.), *From poverty to power: How active citizens and effective states can change the world.* Retrieved from http://policy-practice. oxfam.org.uk/publications/notes-on-inequality-and-poverty-in-brazil-current-situation-and-challenges-112516

Beijing Youth Daily. (2016). *Forty-four old and deteriorating neighborhoods started renovating fitness facilities.* Retrieved from http://beijing.qianlong.com/2016/1215/1214539.shtml

Brady, A.-M. (2009). The Beijing Olympics as a campaign of mass distraction. *The China Quarterly, 197,* 1-24.

Buckley, R. (2004). *Environmental impacts of ecotourism.* Wallingford, Oxfordshire: CABI Publishing.

Caldeira, T.P.R. (2014). Qual a novidade dos rolezinhos? *Novos Estudos, 98,* 13-20.

Cavalcanti, M.L.V.C. (2006). Tema e variantes do mito: Sobre a morte e a ressureição do boi. *Mana, 12*(1), 69-104.

Cetelem. (n.d.). *O observador.* Retrieved from http://www.cetelem.com.br

China State Forestry Administration. (2016). *China forest parks in 2015.* Retrieved from http://zgslgy.forestry.gov.cn/portal/slgy/s/2452/content-862765.html

China Tourism Academy. (2016). *Annual report of China leisure development (2015-2016).* Beijing, China: Tourism Education Press.

Commission for Environmental Cooperation. (2000). *2000 annual report.* Retrieved from http://www.cec.org/about-us/annual-reports/2000-annual-report

De Jesus, G.M. (1999). Do espaço colonial ao espaço da modernidade: Os esportes na vida urbana do Rio de Janeiro. *Scripta Nova, 45*(7). Retrieved from http://www.ub.edu/geocrit/sn-45-7.htm

Deng, R. (2002). Leisure education and the strategy of Chinese higher education. *Studies in Dialectics in Nature, 18*(6), 46-48.

Diamond, J. (2012). *The world until yesterday: What can we learn from traditional societies?* New York, NY: Viking.

Donohoe, H. (2013). *Introduction to recreation and leisure* (2nd ed.). Champaign, IL: Human Kinetics.

Dumazedier, J. (1980). *Valores e conteúdos culturais do lazer.* São Paulo, Brazil: SESC.

Facebook Business. (2015). *45% da população brasileira acessa o Facebook mensalmente.* Retrieved from https://www.facebook.com/business/news/BR-45-da-populacao-brasileira-acessa-o-Facebook-pelo-menos-uma-vez-ao-mes

Edgell, D.L. (2006). *Managing sustainable tourism: A legacy for the future.* New York, NY: Haworth Hospitality Press.

Educational Web Adventures. (n.d.). *Amazon interactive: The ecotourism game.* Retrieved from http://www.eduweb.com/ecotourism/eco1.html

Ferreira, R.F. (2004). Shopping center. In C.L. Gomes (Ed.), *Dicionário crítico do lazer* (pp. 211-213). Belo Horizonte, Brazil: Autêntica.

Gebara, A. (1997). Considerações para a história do lazer no Brasil. In H.T. Bruhns (Ed.), *Introdução aos estudos do lazer* (pp. 61-81). Campinas, Brazil: Unicamp.

IBGE. (2011). *Sinopse do censo demográfico 2010.* Rio de Janeiro, Brazil: Author.

Godbey, G., & Shim, J. (2008). The development of leisure studies in North America: Implications for China. *Journal of Zhejiang University (Humanities and Social Science), 38*(4), 21-29.

Ikulayo, P.B. (2003). Women in sports: An historical perspective. In L.O. Amusa & A.L. Toriola (Eds.), *Sports in contemporary African Society: An anthology* (pp. 67-87). Technikon Pretoria: Africa Association for Health, Physical Education Recreation Sports and Dance.

Jackson, E.L., & Walker, G.J. (2006). *A cross cultural comparison of leisure styles and constraints experienced by Chinese and Canadian university students.* Abstracts of the 9th World Leisure Congress, Hangzhou, China.

Jim, C.Y., & Chen, W.Y. (2009). Leisure participation pattern of residents in a new Chinese city. *Annals of the Association of American Geographers, 99*(4), 657-673.

Jurin, R.R. (2012). *Principles of sustainable living: A new vision of health, happiness, and prosperity.* Champaign, IL: Human Kinetics.

Lee, J.W., & Bairner, A. (2009). The difficult dialogue: Communism, nationalism, and political propaganda in North Korean sport. *Journal of Sport & Social Issues, 33*(4), 390-410.

Li, S., Zhou, Z., & Chen, Y. (2009). The functions, problems and strategies of group dance in squares in the establishment of community culture. *Science & Technology Information, 19,* 491.

Liu, D., Gao, X., & Song, R. (2010). *Song green book of China's leisure no. 1.* Beijing, China: Social Sciences Academic Press.

Liu, H. (2007). The education of leisure loses the position, the dislocation and turns over to the position. *Studies in Dialectics in Nature, 23*(4), 67-70. (*Note:* This is the original title of the paper, but it is not a good translation; it should be "the losing position, dislocation, and relocation of leisure education.")

Liu, H., Yeh, C.K., Chick, G.E., & Zinn, H.C. (2008). An exploration of meanings of leisure: A Chinese perspective. *Leisure Sciences, 30*(5), 482-488.

Louv, R. (2008). *Last child in the woods: Saving our children from nature-deficit disorder.* Chapel Hill, NC: Algonquin Books.

Lu, Y., & Yu, Y. (2005). Investigation on sport facilities in Beijing residential areas. *Sport Science Research, 26*(5), 20-24.

Ma, H. (1999). *Call for leisure studies in China.* Retrieved from http://www.chineseleisure.org/onatheory.htm

Marinho, A. (2005). Atividades de aventura em ambientes artificiais. In R.R. Uvinha (Ed.), *Turismo de aventura: Reflexões e tendências* (pp. 247-268). São Paulo, Brazil: Aleph.

Mascarenhas, F. (2003). O pedaço sitiado: Cidade, cultura e lazer em tempos de globalização. *Revista Brasileira de Ciências do Esporte, 24*(3), 121-143.

McKercher, B. (1996). Differences between tourism and recreation in parks. *Annals of Tourism Research, 23*(3), 563-575.

Meirelles, F.S. (2016). *Tecnologia de informação.* Retrieved from http://eaesp.fgvsp.br/sites/eaesp.fgvsp.br/files/pesti2016gvciappt.pdf

Melo, V.A. (2003). Lazer e educação física: Problemas historicamente contruídos, saídas possíveis—um enfoque na questão da formação. In C.L.G. Werneck & H.F. Isayama (Eds.), *Lazer, recreação e educação física* (pp. 57-80). Belo Horizonte, Brazil: Autêntica.

Morakinyo, E.O., & Atare, F.U. (2005). Ecological constraints of outdoor recreation participation among municipal workers in Delta state, Nigeria. *Journal of the International Council for Physical, Health Education, Recreation, Sports and Dance, 41*(3), 51-54.

National Tourism Administration of China. (2016). *China tourism in 2015.* Retrieved from http://news.china.com.cn/2016-01/05/content_37457113.htm

Neri, M.C. (2011). *Desigualdade de renda na década.* Rio de Janeiro, Brazil: FGV/CPS.

Oliveira, M.A.S., & Rossetto, A.M. (2013). Políticas públicas para o turismo sustentável no Brasil: Evolução e perspectivas de crescimento para o setor. *Revista Turismo: Visão e Ação, 15*(3), 322-339.

NOIPolls. (2014). *Reforming the Nigerian premier league.* Retrieved from http://www.noi-polls.com/root/index.php?pid=143&ptid=1&parentid=14

Peng, W. (2010). Square leisure culture and the construction of a harmonious, healthy and civilized lifestyle. *Proceedings of the 11th World Leisure Congress, Chuncheon, Korea,* 189-190.

Porteous, J.D. (1991). Transcendental experience in wilderness sacred space. *National Geographical Journal of India, 37,* 99-107.

Qing, Q. (2007). Leisure industry: Concepts, scopes and statistical issues. *Tourism Tribune, 22*(8), 82-85.

Ribeiro, O.C.F. (2004). Hotéis de lazer. In C.L. Gomes (Ed.), *Dicionário crítico do lazer* (pp.107-112). Belo Horizonte, Brazil: Autêntica.

Smith, S.L.J., & Godbey, G.C. (1991). Leisure, recreation, and tourism. *Annals of Tourism Research, 18*(1), 85-100.

Stoppa, E.A. (1999). *Acampamentos de férias.* Campinas, Brazil: Papirus.

Sustainable Travel. (n.d.). *About us.* Retrieved from http://sustainabletravel.org/

Tourism Research Center of the Chinese Academy of Social Sciences (TRC CASS). (2015). *Annual report on China's leisure development (2013-2015).* Beijing, China: Social Sciences Academic Press.

Udomiaye, M., & Umar, Z. (2010). *Understanding physical and health education for junior secondary school.* Benin City, Nigeria: Waka Fast Publishers.

United Nations. (2010). *International year of youth.* Retrieved from http://www.un.org/esa/socdev/unyin/documents/iyy/guide.pdf

United Nations. (n.d.). *Sustainable development knowledge platform: Sustainable development goals.* Retrieved from https://sustainabledevelopment.un.org/sdgs

United Nations Development Programme (UNDP). (2015). *Human development report 2015.* Retrieved from http://hdr.undp.org/sites/default/files/2015_human_development_report.pdf

United Nations Educational, Scientific, and Cultural Organization (UNESCO). (n.d.). *Youth program.* Retrieved from http://www.unesco.org/new/en/social-and-human-sciences/themes/youth/

United Nations World Tourism Organization (UNWTO). (n.d.). *Who we are.* Retrieved from http://www2.unwto.org/content/who-we-are-0

United Nations World Tourism Organization (UNWTO). (n.d.). *Ethics and social responsibility.* Retrieved from http://ethics.unwto.org/en/content/global-code-ethics-tourism

Van Steen, G. (2010). Rallying the nation: Sport and spectacle serving the Greek dictatorships. *International Journal of the History of Sport, 27*(12), 2121-2154.

Wang, J., & Stringer, L. A. (2000). The impact of Taoism on Chinese leisure. *World Leisure, 42*(3), 33-41.

Wei, X. (2009). *China leisure industry: Review and prospect.* Retrieved from http://weixiaoan.blog.sohu.com/144349753.html

Wei, X., Huang, S., Stodolska, M., & Yu, Y. (2015). Leisure time, leisure activities, and happiness in China. *Journal of Leisure Research, 47*(5), 556-576.

Wilson, E.O. (1984). *Biophilia*. Cambridge, MA: Harvard University Press.

World Bank. (2016). *GDP ranking*. Retrieved from http://data.worldbank.org/data-catalog/GDP-ranking-table

World Leisure Organization. (n.d.). *Description*. Retrieved from https://www.worldleisure.org/about/

Xiao, H. (1997). Tourism and leisure in China: A tale of two cities. *Annals of Tourism Research, 24*(2), 357-370.

Yin, X. (2005). New trends of leisure consumption in China. *Journal of Family and Economic Issues, 26*(1), 175-182.

You, B., & Zhen, X. (2007). *On the leisure society and the leisure industry of China*. Retrieved from http://www.gogoplay.cn/html/xiuxianlilun/200711/20071110164526733.html

Zhou, X. (2008). *Survey of Chinese middle class*. Beijing, China: Social Science Academic Press.

Glossary

A

abula—A ball and bat game played in a rectangular court by a team of eight players with four players on the court and the other four on the bench as substitutes. The ball is played over the net and a rally is initiated until there is a default by one team. It is similar to volleyball but played with a bat.

accessibility—The extent to which a facility or activity space allows a person to navigate and engage with the surrounding environment and all its elements.

accommodation—The removal of barriers that otherwise might prevent successful participation in an activity.

accountability—Providing services that produce results as efficiently and effectively as possible.

accreditation—Assurance that a program, institution, or agency has met essential requirements or standards as set by a governing body.

activity analysis—A systematic procedure to identify the behaviors required to participate in an activity.

activity theory—Suggests that successful aging occurs when people maintain the interests, activities, and social interactions they were involved with during middle adulthood.

adaptation—Modification of equipment, rules, or the surrounding environment directly associated with an activity to allow for successful participation.

adapted sport—Sports program that allows rule adaptations to adjust the level of challenge and competition to meet the abilities of participants.

adolescence—One of the seven life stages; from 13 to 19 years old.

adventure recreation—A recreation experience in which risk, whether real or perceived, is a central component of the experience.

advocacy—The act of supporting a specific cause, policy, or idea.

advocate—A recreation and leisure services professional who recognizes an injustice that prevents community members from engaging in recreation and leisure services and works to resolve the injustice.

aesthetics—The branch of philosophy that deals with questions of the nature of beauty, particularly in relation to the natural environment and human-made art objects. In terms of provision of leisure services, aesthetics is an important managerial consideration for enhancing the experience of leisure in built and natural environments.

age of instruction—The period in which most learning is through basic instructions.

agricultural tourism—Any agricultural activity that draws tourists to visit, stay, or work.

Amazon—The largest rainforest in the world, covering more than 1 billion acres (400 million ha) of land in South America; it encompasses land in nine South American countries, and 60 percent of it is in Brazil.

American Therapeutic Recreation Association (ATRA)—The national professional organization for certified therapeutic recreation specialists (CTRSs).

amusement—A pleasure-seeking activity that Aristotle judged to be inferior to leisure.

anthropometric measurements—Quantitative techniques used to measure the human body such as size, shape, and composition.

arm's-length provider—One of the five roles that governments can take in delivering public services; the government creates a special-purpose agency, such as a museum, that operates outside the regular apparatus of government.

arts—Arts include material objects as well as experiences that originate in the mind or body and manifest in forms of expression such as opera, dance, theater, music, painting, sculpture, literature, graffiti, film, radio, television, and digital media.

arts and cultural activities—The activities that make up the arts and cultural sector. These include art and craft making; consumption of arts digitally, through live performance, or through books; learning through public programs, classes, or workshops; art sharing through digital environments; and producing or sponsoring programs.

arts and cultural sector—The individuals, entrepreneurs, and formal and informal organizations (nonprofit, private, public, and unincorporated) that create, produce, present, distribute, preserve, educate about, fund, and advocate for aesthetic, heritage, and entertainment activities, products, and artifacts.

assessment—A systematic process of gathering and synthesizing information about the client and his or her environment using a variety of methods, such as interviews, observation, standardized tests, and input from other disciplines and significant others, to devise an individualized treatment or service plan.

Athenian ideal—An ideal combination of soldier, athlete, artist, statesmen, and philosopher that was valued in ancient Greece.

athletic sports—Participation in sport to achieve excellence through advanced skill and strategy.

attraction—A feature, facility, program, event, or natural phenomena that has the capability to attract, lure, or entice an individual to travel.

auxiliary facility—A supplementary and separate building or space that is used and managed by campus recreation but is not part of the main facility.

B

backcountry—The areas in a park or protected area that are not accessible by roads and are characterized by low use levels.

background check—A process that provides data about an individual's criminal, commercial, and financial records.

baile funk—Large dance party in a favela that plays mostly Brazilian rap, hip-hop, and electro-funk music; it originated in Rio de Janeiro, but today the concept is widespread across the country and has reached middle- and upper-class circles, although it is still mostly staged in low-income communities.

biosphere reserves—A designated geographic area where people exemplify various ways to sustain local economies and use resources while also conserving the biodiversity found in different kinds of ecosystems. As of July 2017, there were 669 biosphere reserves in 120 countries.

body mass index (BMI)—A measurement of weight divided by height that is used as a health indicator.

bossa nova—A music style developed in Brazil in the mid-1950s that became famous worldwide in the beginning of the 1960s; it evolved from samba but has a mood similar to jazz. "The Girl from Ipanema" is one of bossa nova's most famous songs, and it illustrates this style well.

bread and circuses—An ancient Roman concept that was meant to pacify unrest through pleasurable experiences that included free food and entertainment.

bridging—Acquiring the necessary knowledge, skills, abilities, and other characteristics or making professional contacts that can help a person move from one career to a new one or from one level of management to a higher level.

built environment—Human-constructed surroundings such as buildings, designed parks, or transportation systems.

businesses—Organizations that provide a service or product and charge a price that is higher than the cost of production. The difference between the cost and the price is the profit.

C

caipirinha—A Brazilian cocktail that is popular around the world, particularly in Europe; it is made with cachaça (a traditional Brazilian spirit made of sugar cane), sugar, ice, and lime.

campus recreation—A department that provides facilities and programs for campus communities to engage in recreation, sport, and wellness opportunities that contribute to the physical, social, and emotional well-being of students and the campus community.

Canadian Armed Forces (CAF)—Collectively, the Royal Canadian Navy, the Canadian Army, and the Royal Canadian Air Force.

Canadian Forces Morale and Welfare Services (CFMWS)—An organization that manages morale and welfare programs for the Canadian military community.

capoeira—The most elaborate martial art of the African diaspora. It is a spectacular combination of dance, acrobatic kicks, evasive maneuvers, slow martial arts sparring, and improvised musical performance, and it is widely practiced in Brazil as a true cultural expression.

carnaval—The most popular and famous Brazilian celebration. It is held 46 days before Easter and officially lasts for four days; it is celebrated across the country and involves music, costumes, and parades of various colors, types, and styles.

carrying capacity—The amount and type of use that an area or resource can accommodate without being unacceptably damaged.

caste system—A system of classification in which social position is ascribed at birth.

certified therapeutic recreation specialist (CTRS)—An individual who, through knowledge and experience, has met the National Council for Therapeutic Recreation Certification's CTRS certification standards.

charities—The most readily identifiable form of nonprofit that represent diverse organizations that often serve the most vulnerable populations for free or for reduced fees. Charities in the United States are organized under Section 501(c)(3) of the IRS code.

Christianity—A religious faith that follows the teachings of Jesus as laid out in the Bible.

chronic disease—A disease that persists for a long period of time such as diabetes, heart disease, chronic obstructive pulmonary disease (COPD), and others.

class system—A system of classification in which social position is earned by wealth, power, and status.

club sports—Sport activities organized by individuals because of a common appeal or interest in a sport. Teams practice regularly, follow an organized schedule, and can be recreational or competitive; many are associated with regional and national governing bodies.

code of ethical practice—Statements outlining the ethics that an agency or organization deems critical to fulfilling its duties.

code of ethics—A written description of the established duties and obligations of the professional to protect the human rights of service recipients.

commercial recreation—Any enterprise that provides recreation or leisure experiences and has the intent of making a profit.

community—Those who are physically in a specific geographic location or region or political district or boundary; a group of people who have common interests such as social causes, gaming, or academic fields; or a group of people who hold similar identities based on affiliation, appearance, or lifestyle.

community arts—Participatory arts that can be distinguished by their nature as critical, exploratory, experimental, innovative, challenging, or even radical commentaries on society in a given moment, time, place, or cultural juncture.

community education—A concept, philosophy, and practice that focuses on community participation in planning, developing, and offering activities and programs that strengthen and benefit individuals, families, and communities.

community health—The health status of a defined group of people (e.g., grouped by proximity, gender, race, or other common factor).

commuter campus—A college or university in which students live off campus and travel to the school for class.

competitive sports—Sports competitions designed for a true champion to emerge. They can be individual or team events.

consequence-based ethics—An ethical theory that determines what is good or bad based on outcomes. It typically aims to maximize the greatest good for the greatest number of people.

conservation—Using natural resources such as trees, water, or rangeland in a wise, regulated, or planned manner so that it is not destroyed and can be used and renewed indefinitely.

constitutional monarchy—The part of the British Commonwealth with allegiance to the queen of England. In Canada, the Crown is the foundation of the executive and judicial branches of government.

constitutional republic—A form of government in which the executive branch is elected and the judicial branch is appointed by the chief executive, as in the United States.

contemplation—The highest form of leisure in ancient Greece; it involved the pursuit of truth and understanding.

continuity theory—Suggests that people need to maintain their desired levels of involvement in society to maximize their sense of self-esteem and well-being.

cooperative play—Form of play in which children work together to achieve a common goal.

correctional system—A program of treatment and rehabilitation for offenders through penal custody, parole, and probation.

creative placemaking—The process of identifying, supporting, and mobilizing local arts and culture toward community betterment.

credentialing—The process by which a profession or government certifies that a professional has met the established minimum standards of competency required for practice.

critical thinking—The application of the rules and principles of informal logic in evaluating arguments and inferences to distinguish good reasoning from fallacious reasoning.

cross-cultural competence—The ability to understand, respect, and communicate with diverse people.

cultural diversity—The heterogeneity encountered in the values and knowledge of various peoples, societies, or groups that share a common background.

cultural heritage—The way of life of a people that is transferred from generation to generation.

culture—The rich variety of ways that human work, thoughts, attitudes, and values of a certain time and place are communicated through practices, beliefs, behaviors, religions, institutions, and the creative arts.

D

direct provider—One of the five roles that governments can take in delivering public services; the government develops and maintains leisure facilities, operates programs, and delivers services using public funds and public employees.

direct service provider—A recreation and leisure services professional who has responsibility for a program or service from start to finish.

disability—Any restriction or lack of ability to perform an activity in the manner or within the range that is considered normal.

disability sport—Sports program designed for people with disabilities that provides participants with a continuum of competition levels from beginner to elite that adhere to traditional rules and regulations of the sport rather than allowing individualized adaptations.

disengagement theory—Suggests that people in late adulthood start to withdraw from the world on social, physical, and psychological levels.

documentation—The written or electronic recording of a client's participation and progress in therapeutic recreation.

dual sports—Sport events that require at least one opponent (e.g., badminton, table tennis, tennis, squash, handball, racquetball).

duty-based ethics—An ethical theory that determines what is right and wrong based on what obligations must be satisfied.

E

early adulthood—One of the seven life stages; people in this stage are 20 to 39 years old.

early childhood—One of the seven life stages; people in this stage are 3 to 6 years old.

ecolodges—Commercial accommodations that are usually certified for providing environmentally sustainable facilities and services. These lodges are most often small and located in areas of great natural beauty.

economic impact—The influence that an industry or sector has on a given economy; this is measurable in any industry or organization that spends money or has audiences spending money.

ecotourism—Travel to visit ecosystems that have rare, fragile, and unique ecological characteristics that might provide outdoor recreation opportunities not found elsewhere.

educational sports—The act of teaching or learning sport skills for the purposes of education and improvement.

emotional intelligence—The capacity to accurately perceive and understand one's own emotions and the emotions of others and to successfully manage one's emotions.

emotional labor—The ability to manage one's emotional responses when confronting work situations that are emotionally challenging, such as maintaining an appropriately professional demeanor with a rude, agitated customer.

empiricist—People who believe the philosophical thesis that knowledge is derived from observations and sensory experiences.

employee assistance program (EAP)—A work-based intervention program designed to assist employees in resolving personal problems that might adversely affect their performance.

enabler and coordinator—One of the five roles that governments can take in delivering public services; the government identifies organizations and agencies that produce leisure services and helps coordinate their efforts, resources, and activities.

entrepreneur—An individual who organizes and runs a small or medium-sized business and accepts all the financial risks and rewards of the business venture.

entrepreneurial associations—Well-established regional, national, and global organizations that focus on advancing the interests of their entrepreneurial membership.

environmental education—A curriculum that teaches about entire ecosystems and the ways people affect the natural world as well as strategies to minimize those effects; also referred to as *education for sustainability.*

environmental interpretation—Uses various strategies to translate the meaning of cultural and natural resources found in parks through exhibits, signage, electronic media, and educational talks and tours with an aim of inspiring visitor appreciation and curiosity about the site.

epistemology—The branch of philosophy that examines the sources of our knowledge, the methods we use in gaining knowledge, the kinds of knowledge that are possible for us to obtain, and how certain we can be of our knowledge. Epistemology poses the philosophical question of how we really know what we think we know.

ethical dilemma—A situation in which a basic moral choice must be made but neither option appears desirable.

ethics—The philosophical study of morality and moral justification.

ethnicity—Distinctive cultural characteristics.

evidence-based practice (EBP)—The combined use of practitioners' expertise and research findings to select the best programs and services to achieve outcomes.

evidence-based program—A program that demonstrates reliable and consistent positive changes in important health-related measures.

experiential education—Experiential education has been characterized as a philosophy that informs a variety of methodologies intended to engage students in experiential learning activities and focused reflection that can promote the growth and development of the learner.

extramural sports—Structured sport activities between winners of various intramural sports programs.

F

facilitated leadership—This type of leadership works with groups so they can become independent and provide programs and services for themselves.

facilitator—A recreation and leisure services professional who facilitates participants' engagement in leisure in such a way that they are responsible for many of their own leisure experiences.

farm-stays—Commercial accommodations provided in farm houses; an increasingly popular form of bed and breakfast in the countryside that serves as a second source of income for farm owners.

favelas—The Brazilian term for shantytowns.

fine motor skills—Movements of the small muscles of the body that are used for activities such as writing, cutting, and picking up small objects.

fitness programs—Instructor-led activities and classes focusing on strength, mobility, endurance, and cardiovascular health.

Five-Year Plans—A series of social and economic development strategies proposed every five years by the Chinese central government.

flow—A state of being in which a person is fully engaged in an activity that results in feelings of energy, focus, and success that often turn out to be the optimal life experiences for that person.

folklife—The ways that people assemble, work, and act together through commonplace activities for a variety of political, aesthetic, economic, familial, religious, and educational purposes.

folklore festivals—Festivals of dance, music, or any other art or cultural form that involve traditional practices of a particular cultural group or a mix of various groups.

football—The most popular team sport in the world; it is played with a ball and 11 players on each team (called *soccer* in North America).

formal operations—The ability to perform mental operations with abstract concepts, such as justice or poverty, and estimate the effect of these concepts.

formative evaluation—Evaluation that is ongoing during the implementation phase and leads to immediate changes and improvements in the treatment plan.

foundations—Nonprofits that amass resources and provide grants or direct programs for the public good. There are private foundations, operating foundations, and community foundations, among examples of such nonprofits.

front country—The parts of a park or protected area that are developed, accessed by roads, and contain primary visitor use locations.

functioning—The ability to perform specific functions in each of the five domains of health: cognitive or mental, physical, psychological or emotional, social, and spiritual.

G

gender—A social category that includes attitudes, expectations, and expressions of masculinity and femininity.

general supervision leadership—Leadership that focuses on providing facilities and areas in which people can recreate, play, and socialize independently. The participants create and control their own experiences.

goals—Broad-based intended outcomes related to the mission of the organization that help guide the types and content of programs and services offered by the agency.

golden weeks—A week-long national holiday in China (e.g., the Spring Festival Golden Week, the National Day Golden Week, and the Labor Day Golden Week).

governmental unit—A generic term that describes a government group at any level: national, state, county, or city. It can be used to refer to one large unit (e.g., the state) or subdivisions within the unit (e.g., departments).

graduate assistantships—Positions in which full-time graduate students work part time as paraprofessionals; they are paid a stipend for their work and the department covers their tuition.

gross domestic national product—The sum of total goods and services manufactured or provided by all businesses, nonprofits, and government entities in a country.

gross motor skills—Movements of the large muscles of the body that are used for activities such as throwing, walking, crawling, and sitting up.

H

health—A state of complete physical, mental, and social well-being and not merely the absence of disease or infirmity, according to the World Health Organization.

health literacy—The degree to which people have the capacity to obtain, process, and understand basic health information and services needed to make appropriate health decisions.

health promotion—Engaging in healthy lifestyle practices to promote health and wellness.

health risk appraisal (HRA)—A group of screening tools used as a first step in assessing the health status of an individual or a group.

health risk assessments (HRAs)—A type of health questionnaire developed to evaluate a person's quality of life and health risks.

health status—The existence or absence of illness or disease.

hedonism—A philosophy that focuses on pleasure as the ultimate goal.

hijab—To cover, screen, or veil; the hijab is a garment (e.g., headscarf, cloak) worn by some Muslim women to cover their heads and neck to signify modesty and Muslim identity.

hosting functions—Agencies and businesses that offer accommodations and food and beverage services.

Human Development Index—A United Nations initiative that assesses and ranks nations as high, medium, or low according to their level of human development by measuring dimensions such as life expectancy, literacy, access to sewage, and clean water.

human services profession—A profession that has the objective of meeting human needs through an interdisciplinary knowledge base, focusing on prevention and remediation of problems, and maintaining a commitment to improving the overall quality of life of those they serve.

I

incarcerate—To put in prison and subject to confinement.

inclusive recreation programs—The modification or adaptation of activities addressing needs of individuals that feel or identify the current programming does not meet their needs.

indirect leadership—A leadership option that provides the agency with an opportunity to augment programs and services for the community. It focuses on providing people with equipment or services for a fee; the only interaction between the participant and the leader occurs during the rental process.

individual health—The health status of one person.

individual sports—Events that generally allow participants to engage in the sport alone (e.g., fishing, golf, swimming, diving, trap and skeet, cycling, hunting, boxing, archery).

individual treatment plan—A written course of action to be taken by, for, and with the client based on assessment; this is part of a client's record.

infancy—One of seven life stages; people in this stage are 2 years old and younger.

informal sports—Self-directed, nonstructured participation in sport that is focused on fun and fitness.

information provider—A recreation and leisure services professional who focuses on facilitating engagement in recreation by providing information about opportunities that are available in the community.

instructional sports—Sport activity that emphasizes the learning of skills, rules, and strategies in a nonacademic credit environment.

integrated function—A combined, coordinated set of services or activities that links one or more of the key hosting, support and facilitation activities, or attractions functions of the recreation, event, and tourism system.

International Union for Conservation of Nature and Natural Resources (IUCN)—An international body that coordinates conservation and sustainable development activities worldwide.

intramural sports—Structured sport activity in the form of leagues, tournaments, and contests conducted within the boundaries or walls of a particular setting.

intrapreneur—A person in a large corporation who takes direct responsibility for turning an idea into a profitable finished product. This corporate management style integrates risk-taking and innovation approaches with the reward and motivational techniques that are commonly associated with entrepreneurship.

Islam—A religious faith that follows the teachings of Muhammad as laid out in the Quran and Hadith.

J

Judaism—A religious faith that follows the teaching of God as laid out in the Torah.

juvenile offender—A minor who is convicted of an offense.

L

land taxes—The taxes that landowners pay, which are calculated according to the value and uses of the land and the mill rate assigned by the municipality. This is also known as a *real-estate tax*.

langa—The Hausa name for a one-legged hop game. Known by various names in other parts of Nigeria such as *kokoye, sapasapasingiri, lanka-lanka,* and *wogidija.* The game has three variations (ruwa, tureshi and kawoshi), all played in a rectangular area with two concentric circles.

late adulthood—One of the seven life stages; people in this stage are 60 years old and older.

legislator and regulator—One of the five roles that governments can take in delivering public services; the government passes laws that leisure services providers and consumers must abide by.

leisure—Originally defined by the ancient Greeks as the most worthy activity that humans could engage in. For Plato and Aristotle, leisure consisted of philosophical contemplation. Modern definitions of leisure emphasize time outside of work and other duties and the perceived freedom to engage in intrinsically motivated activities.

leisure education—The process by which people explore their own attitudes toward leisure and recreation, understand the influence of leisure on society and in their own lives, and develop the skills to participate in the recreation activities of their choice.

less-developed country (LDC)—An underdeveloped or less industrialized nation; often called the *third world.*

life stages—The stages of growth and maturation across the life span.

local club sides—Football clubs that play in the Nigerian Premier league, such as Enyimba FC, Akwa United FC, Warri Wolves FC, and Kano Pillars FC.

logic—The branch of philosophy that examines the structure and rules of reasoning and sound argumentation. Logic is important not only for the methods of leisure research but also for the decision-making process of leisure services practitioners.

M

market days—Dedicated buying and selling days held weekly or fortnightly in Nigeria.

marketing approach—An approach in which businesses focus on the customer because the transaction between the business and the customer provides the business its lifeblood.

meet sports—Separate sport events that occur within a larger sport event and are usually conducted over a period of one or two days (e.g., swimming, gymnastics, diving, wrestling, golf, track and field).

mentoring—A professional relationship between an experienced recreation and leisure services professional and one with less experience that focuses on career advancement and how to navigate that process, including the politics of career advancement.

metaphysics—The branch of philosophy that deals with the study of what really exists and the ultimate nature of reality. In the leisure research literature, the most prominent metaphysical issue concerns whether leisure is a state of mind (if you think an experience is leisurely, then it really is leisure) or a state of being (the circumstances of your life need to satisfy certain conditions for you really to be at leisure).

middle adulthood—One of the seven life stages; people in this stage are 40 to 59 years old.

middle and late childhood—One of the seven life stages; people in this stage are 7 to 12 years old.

military community—Military service members, their families, and supporting partners that sustain the military environment.

mission statement—A broad statement that defines the purpose of the organization with regard to the group of people that it serves.

morale and welfare—Within a military community context, this refers to the quality of life and operational ability of military service members individually and globally.

morale, welfare, and recreation (MWR)—The key provider of recreational, fitness, family, and community services to U.S. military members and their families.

morbidity—The incidence or prevalence of a disease.

more-developed country (MDC)—A highly industrialized, economically developed country; often called the *first world*.

mortality—The number of deaths due to a specific cause.

multiple-use management—Managing natural areas for a variety of uses concurrently such as outdoor recreation, range grazing, timber production, watershed protection to control pollution and erosion and allocate water uses, and wildlife and fish habitat.

N

National Council for Therapeutic Recreation Certification (NCTRC)—A nonprofit, international organization that administers the largest credentialing program in therapeutic recreation.

national forest park—An area that has spectacular forest scenery as well as historical and heritage sites with scientific and cultural values. It is located in a region with proper tourism accommodations and services, and is renowned regionwide, nationwide, or internationally.

national park—A protected area managed mainly for ecosystem protection and recreation. It is a natural area of land or sea designated to protect the ecological integrity of one or more ecosystems for present and future generations; exclude inappropriate exploitation or occupation of the area; and provide a foundation for spiritual, scientific, educational, recreational, and visitor opportunities, all of which must be environmentally and culturally compatible.

natural environment—All the natural living and nonliving things that are not part of the built environment.

natural tourism and travel—Responsible travel to areas of natural attraction that conserves the environment and improves the welfare of local people.

nature-deficit disorder (NDD)—The consequences of the divorce between human and natural habitats.

networking—The process of developing a list of professional contacts that can assist with a person's career development.

Nigeria Colleges of Education Games Association (NICEGA)—The body that organizes sports competition among Nigerian Colleges of Education biannually.

Nigeria Polytechnic Games Association (NIPOGA)—The highest body vested to organize sports competition among Nigerian polytechnics biannually.

Nigeria University Games Association (NUGA)—The highest body vested to organize sports competition among Nigerian universities and select players that will represent Nigeria in World University Games.

NIRSA, Leaders in Collegiate Recreation—A professional organization that supports and is composed of leaders in collegiate recreation. Its mission is "to advocate for the advancement of recreation, sport, and wellness by providing educational and developmental opportunities, generating and sharing knowledge."

nonprofit organization—An organization with tax-exempt status under the U.S. Internal Revenue Service code or by Revenue Canada. Contributions to them are tax deductible. A nonprofit is governed by a volunteer board of directors and is operated for public benefit, and its business is not conducted for profit.

Organizations of this type are said to belong to the nonprofit sector.

nonprofit sector—The segment of society composed of organizations that are private and nongovernmental and seek to serve the public good without the motivation of profit.

North American Industry Classification System (NAICS)—A classification system employed by census agencies in Canada, the United States, and Mexico to ensure that the enumeration of businesses is collected and codified in the same way.

O

objectives—The steps that need to be taken to achieve agency and program goals. Objectives are observable and measureable and serve as the foundation to evaluate goals.

off-highway vehicle (OHV)—Vehicles such as all-terrain vehicles (ATVs), dune buggies, jeeps, motorcycles, four-wheel-drive vehicles, dirt bikes, and snowmobiles whose drivers engage in activities such as mudslinging, trail rides, rallies, hill climbs, and rock crawls.

offender—A person who is convicted of an offense.

open recreation—Unstructured use of activity spaces by drop-in users.

operational readiness and effectiveness—The mental, physical, emotional, and social conduct of military service members that steers their ability to be prepared for and perform in combat, peacekeeping, and military operational settings.

operations—The oversight, management, and maintenance of facilities and fields and the people in them; includes managing entrance and exiting processes, equipment check out, supervision and policy enforcement, and emergency response.

outcome—A measurable short- or long-term change in a client's health status or well-being as a result of receiving therapeutic recreation services.

outdoor and adventure tourism—An experience that blends outdoor adventure and tourism and is characterized by travelers who intentionally seek personal challenge in remote outdoor locations with high levels of activity and excitement.

outdoor and climbing programs—Hands-on learning opportunities for outdoor enthusiasts such as climbing and bouldering walls, outdoor clinics and education sessions, and guided outdoor adventure trips such as mountaineering, backpacking, rafting, ice climbing, mountain biking, and canyoneering.

outdoor education—As an educational method, outdoor education is intended to enhance the curriculum through the delivery of educational experiences in the outdoors. As educational subject matter, outdoor education is intended to teach students about the natural environment.

outdoor recreation—Participation in intrinsically motivating outdoor activities that depend on human–nature interaction and an appreciation of the natural world; a subphenomenon of leisure and recreation.

P

participatory arts—Art, artists, events, and organizations that involve the public in making art.

paternalism—Performing an act you believe is in the best interest of another person without that person's consent.

penitentiary—A public institution in which offenders against the law are confined for detention or punishment; a state or federal prison in the United States.

person visit—One person entering a park once.

personal health—The health status of a specific person.

Personnel Support (PSP) Division—A division of the Canadian Forces Personnel and Family Support Services that delivers recreational, fitness, family, and community services to Canadian military personnel and their families.

philanthropy—Voluntary action for the public good through acts of giving (time, money, and know-how) by individuals and organizations to causes that they care about.

philosophy—Literally, lover of wisdom. In ancient times philosophy referred to all scholarly inquiry, including the natural sciences. However, in present-day scholarship the scope of the discipline of philosophy has been reduced to five sub-fields: metaphysics, epistemology, logic, ethics, and aesthetics.

place-based education—Locally based curricula and programs that stress learning about specific places and their histories to reenvision the roles of local community members to improve social and environmental quality of life.

plasticity—The ability to continue to develop skills in adulthood.

play—A pleasurable, spontaneous, creative activity that is associated with recreation, games, music, and theater in which the rewards are intrinsic.

playground movement—A movement in the late 1800s aimed at improving quality of life through recreation and leisure.

population health—The health status of a defined group of people and the distribution of health outcomes within the group.

postmodern—Refers to both a time period (postmodernity) and a state of mind and associated values (postmodernism). As a period of time, postmodernity follows the recent modern era and is marked by a number of characteristics including the dissolving of boundaries between elite and mass forms of culture and the mixing of leisure and work. Though related to postmodernity, postmodernism is a skeptical outlook that questions generally accepted ideas and values of the modern era, such as the belief that scientific inquiry results in the advancement of knowledge and the improvement of the human condition.

practice model—A visual representation of the relationships between philosophy and theory and the real world that serves as a guide for practice.

preservation—Protecting a natural area, wildlife, and ecosystem in a relatively undisturbed natural state (different from conservation in that the focus is on protection rather than use).

pretend play—Form of play that incorporates conventional imaginative play (e.g., play with toys such as dolls or trucks) and symbolic play (e.g., play with unstructured objects or inanimate objects).

primary group—A group based on intimate, long-term associations such as family and close friends.

professional and trade associations—Nonprofits organized to promote the business interests of a community, industry, or profession. They generally qualify for tax exemption under Section 501(c)(6) of the IRS tax code.

professional organizations—Formal groups that provide support, education, and resources to members who are professionals in a specific field.

professional sports—Sport events played by elite athletes that emphasize winning, entertainment, and generating money.

program classification—The designation of a program into one of 14 areas (e.g., hobby, sport, outdoor activity). Each classification area includes hundreds of opportunities for programs and services depending on the resources of the agency.

program delivery system—The system used to provide programs, services, and opportunities to a community. The system takes into consideration leadership, program classification, program format, development sequences, and characteristics of participants (e.g., age, ethnicity). The content of the program delivery system is guided by the agency's mission, goals, and objectives.

program formats—Eight program types (e.g., competition, class, outreach program) that help the recreation professional develop the program delivery system into a comprehensive plan.

project-based leisure—Clearly defined, somewhat complicated, and creative but usually short-duration activities that can be carried out in free time for a specific purpose and often as part of a group.

Protestant work ethic—The idea that work (rather than leisure) is the foundation of a worthy life and that one should diligently pursue one's calling in life.

provincial park—Parks designated and managed by a province in Canada that usually contain diverse landscapes and outdoor recreation activities. They are often classified as national parks according to the IUCN categories of national parks and protected areas.

public recreation center—A gym owned and managed by governmental agencies and funded through taxes.

purple leisure—Questionable activities that bring pleasure to participants but may harm society.

Q

qi xi—A traditional romantic festival in China similar to Valentine's Day in Western society. It is also called the Double Seventh Festival because it takes places on the seventh day of the seventh lunar month.

quality of life—A person's perception of satisfaction with life or feelings of general well-being based on self-assessment of one's ability to function in everyday life, relationships, mood, access to resources, and other personal and environmental factors.

quasi-public entity—A nonprofit organization that is organized privately to promote public ideals.

R

race—Inherited biological characteristics that distinguish groups.

Ramsar Convention—An international agreement and convention monitored by UNESCO to protect wetlands designated as internationally important under the Convention on Wetlands (1971). These wetlands are commonly known as Ramsar sites. Globally, in 2017, there were 169 contracting parties to the convention and 2,243 wetland sites, totaling 535 million acres (216,338,080 ha) designated for inclusion in the Ramsar List of Wetlands of International Importance.

rational recreation movement—A 19th century movement composed of leisure reformers who were concerned with the proper use of leisure in the rapidly expanding industrial cities of England and America and who advocated for expanding the opportunities of the working classes to engage in what were perceived as ennobling, middle-class leisure activities such as visiting cultural institutions, public gardens, and urban parks.

rationalist—People who believe the philosophical thesis that knowledge is derived from the thought processes of our minds.

recreation—A leisure activity that is often characterized as pleasurable and intrinsically motivated. Refers to activity undertaken for amusement, enjoyment, distraction, or restoration. In Western culture, recreation has been valued as a way to refresh oneself from the burdens of work.

recreation, event, and tourism (RET) industry model—A complex and integrated model that describes the linkages between service providers, the sectors that they represent, and the primary roles that each component provides in transporting, hosting, feeding, and entertaining the consumer in recreation, event, and tourism opportunities.

recreational sports—Sport activities for the sake of fun, fitness, and participation.

relative competence—The ability to do something successfully and efficiently.

religion—Beliefs and practices that separate the profane from the sacred and develop a community of believers.

residential campus—A college or university in which most students live on campus in housing facilities that include dining services and social spaces.

S

samba—A Brazilian musical genre and dance style that has its origin in African religious traditions practiced by Brazilian slaves during colonial times; it is Brazil's most famous rhythm and is extremely popular across the country. It is characterized by the use of percussion and string instruments, such as the *cavaquinho*.

schole—Having peace and quiet, having time for oneself, and being engaged in an activity for its own sake.

secondary group—Compared with a primary group, a larger, more formal, and impersonal group based on a shared interest.

Section 501(c)(3)—A U.S. Internal Revenue Service classification for qualifying nonprofits that gives such organizations tax-exempt status to operate for purposes of the public good. Most U.S.-based nonprofits operate under this tax-exempt category.

selective acculturation—A process by which one chooses to form relationships with people with similar interests, backgrounds, religious affiliations, and languages and allows this subculture to shape his or her values.

serious leisure—The systematic pursuit of an amateur, hobbyist, or volunteer activity that is highly substantial, interesting, and fulfilling; typically, participants find careers in acquiring and expressing a combination of its special skills, knowledge, and experience.

sex—The biological characteristics that distinguish males and females.

sexual identity discrimination—Treatment or consideration of a person in any area (e.g., work, leisure, education) based on prejudices regarding sexual orientation.

social benefits—The entirety of benefits to society from producing or consuming a good or service or participating in civic or other activities that have positive effects that extend beyond the individual to other people, groups, and organizations or a community, culture, or environment more broadly.

social capital—The network of social contacts that people develop to support them in times of difficulty and enhance the quality of their lives.

social inclusion—Shared activities and experiences that allow for mutually beneficial and respectful relationships to develop and persist regardless of disability.

social welfare organizations—Nonprofits involved in advocacy, lobbying, and political campaign activities under the U.S. 501(c)(4) IRS code.

society—People who share a culture and a territory.

solitary leisure—Activities undertaken without the physical presence of another person.

special events—Nontraditional activities that are usually not practiced regularly by the participants (e.g., Wacky Olympics, sports all-nighters and festivals, superstar competitions).

spirituality—The paths and practices that people take in their efforts to find, conserve, and transform the sacred in their lives; the quality of being concerned with the human spirit.

sport participation—Individual physical involvement in recreational sport activities.

sport performance—The evaluation of skill in sport; also includes spectator participation in elite or professional sports.

square dance—A form of group dancing performed to popular music in public squares, plazas, or parks across China.

standards of practice—Standards that define the scope of services provided by TR professionals and state a minimal acceptable level of service delivery.

state park—A park that is designated and managed by the host state in the United States that usually showcases an area of historical importance or a representative natural environment for that state (e.g., prairie in Illinois, beaches in Florida).

strategic prevention framework (SPF)—A planning process created by the Substance Abuse and Mental Health Services Administration (SAMHSA) that is used to prevent substance use and misuse.

structured leadership—Leadership that is used when a program requires face-to-face instruction. This approach is used in all types of classes, and the participant's experience is controlled, guided, and facilitated by the leader.

student affairs—A department or division within the university or college structure that provides students with support outside of their academic pursuits.

summative evaluation—Evaluation that occurs at the completion of a program to determine whether it was effective in helping the client reach his or her goals and whether changes in the program are needed before implementing it in the future.

support and facilitation functions—Diverse key business activities that support the ability of a person or group to travel to desired destinations or that provide the knowledge, information, and contacts that allow travelers to make informed decisions.

supporter and patron—One of the five roles that governments can take in delivering public services; the government provides support to existing organizations that produce public leisure services.

sustainability—Living within the limits of nature's ecosystem services and living together in communities that are equitable, regenerative, resilient, and adaptive.

T

tai chi—The widest practiced fitness exercise in China; it is a combination of yielding, softness, and balance.

team sports—Events that require a specific number of players who play as a team of either men, women, or mixed intramural or extramural sport divisions (e.g., baseball, basketball, softball, kickball, lacrosse, field hockey, rowing, soccer, volleyball, wallyball, water polo, flag football).

therapeutic recreation specialist—A person with the appropriate education and experience to carry out the duties and responsibilities of therapeutic recreation practice.

three-sector model—Nonprofits (the social sector), businesses (the economic/market sector), and government (the public, political sector) are ways in which individuals and organizations are organized to provide services and products in society. Recreation organizations are found in all three sectors.

Title IX—Legislation enacted in the United States in 1972 that directed educational institutions to develop parity for men's and women's sports.

tourism—Travel to a destination for recreation, education, or other types of experiences.

tourism association—A nonprofit group of professionals within the travel and tourism industry, or a specialized subsection of it, whose mission is to educate its members and advocate for the industry.

traditional sports—Sports and games that originated in a locality and are organized and played by a group of people within that locality.

traditions—The conventions, values, norms, and attitudes perpetuated in any community.

transparency—Being clear and open with information.

trend—A change that is general in nature and has overriding implications.

U

U.S. Armed Forces—Collectively, the U.S. Army, U.S. Marine Corps, U.S. Navy, U.S. Air Force, and U.S. Coast Guard.

V

virtue-based ethics—An ethical theory that focuses on the character of the individual rather than on moral rules or principles.

visitor day—One day of recreation for one person.

visitor studies—A field of study and professional practice that examines and evaluates the leisure motivations, behaviors, and informal learning experiences of attendees at cultural venues.

W

wellness—The subjective perception of a person's relative holistic health status and fitness level across all domains (social, emotional, physical, intellectual, occupational, and spiritual) and the absence or management of disease.

wilderness—Large areas left in an entirely natural condition, usually without roads or motorized vehicles, with no buildings or utilities. This is also a formal designation of land use and protection in the United States.

wildlife refuge—Lands, wetlands, and waters that are primarily managed as wildlife or fish habitats or protected areas (although some allow regulated hunting and fishing) by fish and wildlife agencies, usually at the state or federal level. Limited recreational use compatible with wildlife management is permitted in most refuges.

wise-use philosophy—A philosophy that holds that the earth's resources were meant to be exploited for human gain and profit, typically with more of a short-term focus. Wise use tends to be promoted by the extractive industries such as mining and lumber companies who lobby politicians to influence multiple-use agencies such as the Forest Service and the Bureau of Land Management toward a so-called wise-use orientation.

work—A productive, purposeful activity that was disliked by the ancient Greeks but that has great importance in modern societies.

World Heritage site—A specific site (such as a forest, mountain range, lake, desert, building, complex, or city) that has been designated within the international World Heritage Convention administered by UNESCO. The World Heritage list in 2017 included 1,073 properties that the World Heritage Committee considered as having outstanding universal value. These include 832 cultural sites, 206 natural sites, and 35 mixed properties in 167 countries.

Y

youth and family programs—Activities that serve the entire family and foster development in a safe and energetic campus environment.

Index

About the Editors

Tyler Tapps, PhD, is an assistant professor at Northwest Missouri State University. He received his PhD in health, leisure, and human performance from Oklahoma State University in 2009. In 2015, he was certified as a park and recreation professional by the National Recreation and Park Association, from which he also received the Robert W. Crawford Young Professional Award. He also was awarded the Charles Adam Esslinger Outdoor Recreation Fellowship.

Tapps is a military veteran with recreation programming experience in the military. He is a member of the Academy of Leisure Sciences board and is the president of the Leisure Educators section of Missouri Park and Recreation Association. He is also the chair of the Academy of Leisure Science's Future Scholars program. Tapps enjoys running, working out, boating, and spending time with his wife and two sons.

Photo courtesy of Northwest Missouri State University.

Mary Sara Wells, PhD, is an associate professor in the University of Utah's department of parks, recreation, and tourism. She teaches courses in youth development, community recreation, and sport management.

Since 2004, Wells has researched sportsmanship issues in youth sport. She has published her research in numerous journals, presented at several national and international conferences, and conducted trainings and evaluations for multiple municipal youth sport agencies across the country.

©Mary Sara Wells

About the Contributors

Denise M. Anderson, PhD, is a professor in parks, recreation, and tourism management and associate dean for undergraduate studies in the College of Behavioral, Social, and Health Sciences at Clemson University. Anderson has been a faculty member in the area of community recreation for 16 years, working closely with both undergraduate and graduate students. In addition, she maintains close connections to the field through community-based research projects such as needs assessments and program evaluation. Anderson's professional experience includes working in campus recreation and as a program coordinator for the Champaign Park District in Champaign, Illinois. Her research interests include community recreation management, youth development, gender equity, and student development through leisure. Anderson teaches courses in evaluation, finance, programming, and management and she is a core instructor in Clemson University's innovative PRTM immersion semester experience, EDGE (Engaging in Diverse, Guided Experiences).

Robert F. Ashcraft, PhD, is the executive director of the Lodestar Center for Philanthropy and Nonprofit Innovation and Saguaro Professor of Civic Enterprise in the School of Community Resources and Development at Arizona State University. He has over 30 years of experience working in nonprofit leadership and management roles and teaching students the theory and practice behind that work. Ashcraft served for 10 years on the national board of the YMCA of the USA and served as the youngest executive director of a local chapter of the American Red Cross. Ashcraft served as Chair of the Board of Directors of the National Recreation and Park Association (NRPA), among other leadership roles, and is past president of the Nonprofit Academic Centers Council. He serves on the board of the National Association of Park Foundations and has served as director and in many other capacities for the Nonprofit Leadership Alliance, an undergraduate nonprofit management education program based in Kansas City.

Franz U. Atare, PhD, is an assistant professor in the department of physical and health education at the University of Uyo in Nigeria. Since 2014, he has served as the director of sports and recreation. Atare has a doctorate in leisure and recreational sports management and has taught hundreds of students over the course of 16 years. He is the author of nearly 40 papers in national and international journals. His most prominent publication, "The Health Benefit of Walking: A Nigerian Reflection," appeared in the *World Leisure Journal*. Atare is a member of the World Leisure Organization and the World Recreation Education Association.

Timothy Baghurst, PhD, RFSA, is an associate professor at Oklahoma State University, teaching within the health and human performance program area. He serves as the coordinator of the physical education and coaching science programs. Baghurst has four graduate degrees across various kinesiology disciplines, which have enabled him to teach a variety of classes across the health and wellness spectrum. Baghurst has published multiple textbooks and over 90 peer-reviewed articles across many different fields including physical activity, fitness, and personal health. One of his primary foci is investigating the importance of modeling health and wellness in health and wellness professions. He also researches male body image and muscle dysmorphia, and the efficacy of requiring skill or fitness tests in kinesiology-based collegiate programs. Much of his recent grant work has been focused on developing and evaluating the benefits of physical activity programming within the community and after school. Baghurst is a board member of the Oklahoma Association of Health, Physical Education, Recreation, and Dance and the Oklahoma National Strength and Conditioning Association. He is also a member of the Society of Health and Physical Educators, which recently awarded him with Research Fellow status for his contributions to the field.

Robert Barcelona, PhD, is an associate professor and chair of the department of recreation management and policy at the University of New Hampshire. He teaches courses in recreational sport management, youth development, and organizational administration and leadership for both undergraduate and graduate students. Since 1995, Barcelona has worked with numerous recreation and sport organizations in both programming and research efforts. Barcelona's research examines issues regarding access and barriers to active recreation and sport opportunities and focuses on the ways that recreation and sport organizations build healthy and sustainable programs and communities. His research has been published in numerous national and international peer-reviewed publications, and he has authored several books and multiple book chapters on recreation and sport management.

Janet Bartnik, MS, CPRP, is the director of parks and recreation in Liberty, Missouri, where she has engaged community partners in a project to study and strategically plan how to address childhood obesity in Liberty. She is currently implementing a corporate wellness program at the Liberty Community Center to address obesity and chronic disease. These projects reflect her belief that an ideal corporate program goes beyond a membership program to an evidence-based, date-driven wellness program. Bartnik has previously served as an indoor facility supervisor, a fitness coordinator, and a health instructor. She is a member of the National Recreation and Park Association and the American Academy for Park and Recreation Administration.

Rhonda Cross Beemer, PhD, ATC, is an assistant professor of health science and wellness at Northwest Missouri State University and is a certified athletic trainer. Beemer's primary teaching responsibilities are in health promotion, nutrition, and physical activity courses within the School of Health Science and Wellness where she also advises applied health science students. Previously, Beemer has had park and recreational experiences serving children in the southern United States, was a former director of experiential education at a Midwest university where she received a Rising Leader award from the National Society for Experiential Education, and had a previous career in athletic training at the recreational, high school, and collegiate levels. Her research interests revolve around health, wellness, and physical activity.

Diane C. Blankenship, EdD, is a professor at Frostburg State University in Frostburg, Maryland. She has 35 years of programming and special event management experience crossing several areas of the recreation industry from residential camps as a recreation therapist, as a recreation specialist for the department of the army in Germany and the United States, and as a faculty member at Frostburg State University working with people ranging in age from 2 to 80 years old. Blankenship is the author of *Evaluation and Research Methods in Park and Recreation* (Human Kinetics). She is a member of the Maryland Recreation and Parks Association (MRPA) and has served numerous times on the conference committee to assist with the program development and mentor program for students. In addition, she serves as a site visitor for the Commission for Accreditation of Park and Recreation Agencies (CAPRA) and is a member of two CAPRA certification committees for the National Recreation and Park Association.

Brooke N. Burk, PhD, is an assistant professor at Minnesota State University, Mankato. She is the author of the ancillaries for this book. She has served as the Young Professional Network chair for the National Recreation and Park Association as well as a member of the board of directors for The Academy of Leisure Sciences. Burk has taught several courses in the recreation field including introductory, administrative, and program planning courses. Her research interests include examining the health and well-being of underserved populations and how recreation plays a role in improving the whole person.

John Byl, PhD, is a professor emeritus of physical education at Redeemer University College in Ancaster, Ontario, Canada, where he taught wellness courses. Byl is president of CIRA Ontario, which promotes fun active participation for all through intramurals and recreation programs. Byl has been a professor since 1986 and has edited, authored, or coauthored more than 30 books, including *101 Fun Warm-Up and Cool-Down Games*, as well as *Christian Paths to Health and Wellness*. He is a recipient of the Christian Society for Kinesiology and Leisure Studies' Presidential Award, which recognizes those who have displayed actions compatible with the mission of the CSKLS. In 2013, Byl was awarded the Queen Elizabeth II Diamond Jubilee Medal for his significant contribution to making physical activity a priority in his community and in the country.

Ryan Cane is the senior manager of the Canadian Forces' recreation and social wellness programs. He has been deployed overseas four times with the Canadian Forces Operations. He has worked for the Canadian Armed Forces for 12 years and has 20 years of experience in the field of recreation and community development. While working for the Canadian Forces, Cane served as project director for the selection and national implementation of a new content management system and the convergence of two organizations' websites into www.CAFconnection.ca, which better serves military families. Cane is editor in chief of the magazine Play, which published his interview with the host of *The Amazing Race Canada* in 2017. He is a member of Parks and Recreation Ontario and the Lifesaving Society.

Frances Stavola Daly, EdD, CTRS, CPRP, is a professor and the recreation administration program coordinator in the department of physical education, recreation, and health at Kean University in New Jersey. She is coauthor of the text *Therapeutic Recreation Leadership and Programming*. She has over 40 years of experience in the recreation field as both a practitioner and a professor and as a consultant to numerous agencies and is a frequent speaker at state, regional, and national conferences. Stavola Daly has served as the president of the National Therapeutic Recreation Society (NTRS) and as a member of the board of trustees of the National Recreation and Park Association (NRPA). She is a recipient of the Presidential Citation from the NTRS in 2007 and the Lifetime Achievement Award from the New York State Therapeutic Recreation Association in 2004. In 2010, she received the Presidential Distinguished Service Award from Kean University.

Amanda Deml, MS, is the assistant director for Intramural Sports at the University of Oregon. She served as the tournament director for the Region VI National Intramural-Recreational Sports Association (NIRSA) Regional Basketball Tournament in 2016 and created the first multisport youth summer camp for Colorado State University-Pueblo Student Recreation Center. Deml holds professional membership in NIRSA. She graduated with a master of science in education-athletic administration from Northwest Missouri State University, where her graduate research paper, "Imagery Use and Sport-Related Injury Rehabilitation," was published in *The Sport Journal* in May 2015.

Jinyang Deng, PhD, is an associate professor in the recreation, parks, and tourism resources program at West Virginia University. He received his PhD in recreation and leisure studies from the University of Alberta, Canada. Deng's current research interests focus on ecotourism, tourism planning, rural tourism, and urban forests. He explores subjects such as environmental attitudes and behaviors among ecotourists, GIS applications in recreation and tourism, stakeholders' attitudes toward rural tourism, and scenic beauty and recreational benefits associated with urban forests. Deng's research has been funded by the USDA, the Appalachian Regional Commission, the Department of Commerce of West Virginia, and the Claude Worthington Benedum Foundation. His research has been published in *Annals of Tourism Research, Tourism Management, Journal of Sustainable Tourism, Journal of Travel Research, Leisure Sciences, Journal of Leisure Research, Journal of Environmental Management, Environment and Behavior, Urban Forestry and Urban Greening,* and other outlets. Deng has served on the editorial board of *EurAsian Journal of BioSciences* since 2009 and of *Journal of Hospitality Management and Tourism* from 2012 to 2013. He was also invited as guest associate editor for *Journal of Park and Recreation Administration* in 2012.

Paul F.J. Eagles, PhD, is a professor at the University of Waterloo in Canada. Eagles has worked as an employee, consultant, and researcher in parks and protected areas in over 30 countries. He has extensive experience in Canadian parks at all levels. He has been the chair of the tourism task force of the World Commission on Protected Areas for 15 years and is also a consultant to the World Bank, United Nations Environment Programme, World Conservation Union, World Tourism Organization, Forestry and Agricultural Organization, United Nations Environment, Scientific and Cultural Organization, World Resources Institute, and the U.S. Environmental Protected Agency. He has undertaken work in nature-based tourism in more than 25 countries. Eagles has authored more than 350 publications in tourism, planning, management, and related areas. He coauthored the book *Sustainable Tourism in Protected Areas: Guidelines for Planning and Management* (2003).

David N. Emanuelson, PhD, served as president and CEO of Impact Planning and as a partner at Public Research Group. Impact Planning provides planning and financial analysis to parks and recreation agencies, and Public Research Group conducts community needs assessment surveys, studies, and political polls to help parks and recreation agencies provide better services. He has served as a parks and recreation professional for over 30 years. He received his PhD in political science from Northern Illinois University. Emanuelson also served seven years as an assistant professor in recreation administration at George Williams College of Aurora University in Williams Bay, Wisconsin. He has received the Gold Medal Award for Excellence in Park and Recreation Management, nine Certificates of Achievement for Financial Reporting, three literary awards from *Illinois Parks and Recreation Magazine* and one from *Wisconsin Park and Recreation Magazine*, and the Distinguished Scholar and Distinguished Manuscript awards from Northern Illinois University.

Felicia Ekpu, PhD, is a professor in the department of physical and health education at the University of Uyo in Nigeria, where she has taught for more than 18 years. She has more than 50 articles published in national and international journals, and she serves as the publications officer for the Akwa Ibom State Chapter of the Nigeria Association for Physical and Health Education, Recreation, Sports and Dance. Ekpu is an executive member of the Nigeria School Health Association and a member of the International Council for Health, Physical Education, Recreation, Sport and Dance.

Jeffrey Ferguson, EdD, is a professor emeritus of Northwest Missouri State University, where he created the corporate recreation/wellness degree program in 1989. While there, he developed field experience and internship requirements for undergraduate and graduate students, and he assisted in the advancement of student, faculty, and staff wellness programs. He also helped establish a wellness section in the Missouri Parks and Recreation Association. Ferguson is a member of the Missouri Parks and Recreation Association and the American Association of Worksite Health Promotion.

Diane Gaede, PhD, is a professor emeritus at the University of Northern Colorado where she was an associate professor of recreation, tourism, and hospitality for 18 years. For 14 of those years, she taught a module on ecotourism as part of the Introduction to Commercial Recreation and Tourism course. Gaede is a member of the National Association for Interpretation and a Certified Heritage Interpreter. In 2010, her article "Nature-Based Tourism Businesses in Colorado: Interpreting Environmental Ethics and Responsible Behavior" was published in the *Journal of Tourism Insights*.

M. Rebecca Genoe, PhD, is an associate professor in the faculty of kinesiology and health studies at the University of Regina, where she teaches in the therapeutic recreation program. Genoe completed her PhD at the University of Waterloo in recreation and leisure studies with a specialization in aging, health, and well-being. She is a member of the Canadian Association of Leisure Studies and the Canadian Therapeutic Recreation Association. Her research focuses on the meaning and experience of leisure among older adults.

Marni Goldenberg, PhD, is a professor in the department of experience industry management at California Polytechnic State University, San Luis Obispo. She teaches courses in recreation, parks, and tourism administration with a focus on outdoor and adventure leadership. She has instructed courses for the Wilderness Education Association (WEA) and North Carolina Outward Bound School, and she has worked as a ropes course facilitator for more than 25 years. Her research focuses on outcomes and benefits associated with participating in recreation and outdoor experiences. She has received several awards for her teaching, research, and service at California Polytechnic and has several publications and presentations on various outdoor and adventure topics.

H. Joey Gray, PhD, is an associate professor in the department of health and human performance and program director of leisure, sport, and tourism studies at Middle Tennessee State University. She has received several prestigious teaching awards, including Teacher of the Year in 2016, and has published several articles related to pedagogy in recreation. Gray has many years of professional experience in sport management and special-event planning both in the public and private sectors. She has also served as the athletic director of the National Youth Sports Program. Gray has given presentations at the local, state, and national levels in recreational sport management and pedagogical aspects of recreation.

Jeffrey C. Hallo, PhD, is an associate professor in the department of parks, recreation, and tourism management at Clemson University. Hallo's research and teaching are focused on understanding, planning for, and managing visitor use in parks, forests, and other protected areas. He has completed carrying capacity and visitor use management-related projects at Delaware Water Gap National Recreation Area and Denali National Parks. Both of these projects have directly informed long-range planning for these parks. He has authored or coauthored over 50 peer-reviewed scientific journal articles, books, or book chapters on these topics. In 2011 he taught a course on visitor/tourist management at the Maasai Mara National Reserve in Kenya. In 2012, Hallo received an award for Excellence in Research from Clemson University, and in 2013 he was listed as an "Up and Coming Recreation Researcher" by the National Recreation and Park Association. In 2016, Hallo released his first children's book titled *Rosy Ralph Visits His National Parks*. This book represents one of Hallo's most important publications because it is intended to inspire the next generation of park advocates and stewards.

Tristan Hopper, MA, is a PhD student at the University of Alberta and is a member of The Academy of Leisure Science and the Canadian Association of Leisure Studies.

Garrett Hutson, PhD, is an associate professor of recreation and leisure studies at Brock University in St. Catharines, Ontario, Canada. He has done considerable work exploring the topics of outdoor recreation management, outdoor leadership, and person–place relationships. His current research projects explore how human dimensions of place can inform sustainable outdoor recreation practices. Hutson currently helps to facilitate sustainability initiatives and research between the Ontario Ministry of Natural Resources and Forestry, the Niagara Parks Commission, and the Ontario Climbing Access Coalition. Hutson also serves as co-editor of the peer-reviewed journal, *Research in Outdoor Education*. Prior to academic life, Hutson worked full time as a ski patroller helping to launch one of the first ski areas to operate on U.S. Bureau of Land Management lands in Southwest Colorado. Additionally, Hutson worked as a NOLS instructor in Wyoming, Alaska, and the Yukon Territory and as a climbing guide for organizations accredited by the American Mountain Guides Association in both Oregon and Colorado. Hutson currently enjoys outdoor leadership fieldwork with undergraduate students and finds it a privilege to explore Ontario landscapes with Canada's future outdoor leaders.

Richard R. Jurin, PhD, is a professor emeritus at the University of Northern Colorado where he created and directed the environmental and sustainability studies program for 16 years. Jurin received the University of Northern Colorado Academic Leadership Excellence Award for 2010-2011. He is a board member for the North American Association of Environmental Education and an officer for the College and University Academics section of the National Association for Interpretation. The author of three textbooks and three children's books, Jurin is particularly interested in environmental and sustainability issues that promote critical thinking to worldwide audiences. His most prominent publication, *Text on Principles of Sustainable Living*, reveals the lifestyle choices that lead to modern problems of environmental degradation and then promotes different paradigms that resolve these problems for the benefit of both human society and the natural world. Jurin has also published interdisciplinary research on economic-ecological thinking and tourism.

David Kahan, PhD, is a professor in the School of Exercise and Nutritional Sciences at San Diego State University. Kahan holds life membership in SHAPE America, has fellowship status in the Research Consortium, and serves as an associate editor for *Research Quarterly for Exercise and Sport*. An author of over 50 peer-reviewed publications, Kahan is particularly interested in researching the relationships between religion, cultural identity, and physical activity and has completed descriptive and intervention studies among Catholic, Jewish, and Muslim youth. An avid outdoorsman, in his spare time, Kahan runs, bikes, and swims. When not exercising, Kahan enjoys solving crossword puzzles, going out for ethnic food, and discovering the many and varied activities that San Diego offers.

Douglas A. Kennedy, EdD, CPRP, is professor and chair of the department of recreation and leisure studies at Virginia Wesleyan University. Kennedy received a BS from the University of Delaware, MSEd from Southern Illinois University, and an EdD from Temple University. He is a three-time recipient of the College's Samuel Nelson Gray Distinguished Teaching Award. He has also received the Fellows Award from the Virginia Recreation and Park Society, as well as the Outstanding Alumnus award from Southern Illinois University. His professional service has included serving as president of the Virginia Recreation and Park Society, chair of the National Council on Accreditation, leadership of two educational delegations to Uzbekistan, and more than 100 presentations at conferences and symposia. A sought-after speaker and consultant, he regularly works with public agencies and for-profit corporations in the areas of team-building and high performance management.

Robin Kunstler, ReD, CTRS, is a professor in the department of health sciences and the director of the recreation education and therapeutic recreation programs at Lehman College of the City University of New York. She is coauthor of the text *Therapeutic Recreation Leadership and Programming*. With over 40 years of experience in the field of therapeutic recreation as both a practitioner and a professor, she has presented at many state and national conferences, authored numerous articles and book chapters on therapeutic recreation, and served as editor and reviewer for the leading journals in the field. A member of numerous committees and boards of national and state professional organizations, she is a recipient of the Lifetime Achievement Award from the New York State Therapeutic Recreation Association and the New York State Recreation and Park Society Literary and Research Awards.

Huimei Liu, PhD, is a professor in the School of International Studies at Zhejiang University in China. She is also a researcher in the Asia Pacific Centre for the Education and Study of Leisure at Zhejiang University. She earned her BA and MA in English in 1993 and 1996 from Xiangtan Normal University (now named Hunan University of Science and Technology) and Changsha Railway University (now named Central South University), respectively. She earned her PhD in 2008 from Zhejiang University. She spent a year (2007-2008) at Pennsylvania State University on a Fulbright Scholarship for a U.S.-Sino joint PhD program. She was also a visiting scholar to the University of Alberta in 2012-2014 and 2016. Her research interests are cross-cultural studies of leisure, leisure policy, and cultural heritage. She currently teaches a leisure and culture course.

Terry Long, PhD, is the director of the School of Health Science and Wellness at Northwest Missouri State University. He has worked in the realm of inclusive recreation for 20 years as an educator, research, author, and consultant. He has worked with the National Center for Physical Activity and Disability to field test several instruments for measuring the accessibility of parks, recreation centers, and fitness center and coordinated the Missouri Park and Recreation Association's response to proposed ADA codes for park and recreation facilities. He has served on the board of directors for Midland Empire Resources for Independent Living and was able to regularly advocate for inclusion in the NW Missouri Region in regard to recreation and other areas. He is a member of NRPA and ATRA.

Tiffany Lundy, MS, is the associate director of facilities and operations at the University of Oregon. She has worked as a professional in the campus recreation field for 12 years. Lundy is a member of the National Intramural-Recreational Sports Association and has served as its Region VI Conference Program Chair and a Nominations and Appointment Committee member, among other positions. At the University of Oregon, she designed and implemented an undergraduate internships program and assisted in the design, construction, and completion of a $50 million facilities expansion project.

Tracy Mainieri, PhD, is an assistant professor in the recreation and park administration program in the School of Kinesiology and Recreation. She received her BA in anthropology from Furman University and both her MS and PhD in parks, recreation, and tourism management from Clemson University. Mainieri joined the Illinois State University faculty in the fall of 2013. Since then she has taught in both the undergraduate RPA program and the graduate recreation administration master's program, teaching leadership, management, and trends courses. Mainieri's professional background and research is in summer camp so she strives to bring what she's learned at camp about fun, facilitation, and experiential learning into the classroom. Mainieri has experience as a camp counselor, camp administrator, and camp researcher. Her research interests include camp evaluation, implementation evaluation, and the scholarship of teaching and learning.

Alcyane Marinho, PhD, is a lecturer in the physical education department at Santa Catarina State University (Udesc) in Brazil. She completed her bachelor's degree in physical education at Sao Paulo State University (Unesp) in 1995 and her master's degree in 2001 and PhD in 2006 at Campinas State University (Unicamp) in Brazil. Her research interests include leisure and tourism, adventure tourism, and outdoor education. Some of her more recent publications (in Portuguese) are *Leisure, Sport, Tourism and Adventure: Nature in Focus* (2009), *Travels, Leisure and Sport: The Space of Nature* (2006), and *Tourism, Leisure and Nature* (2003).

Susan Markham-Starr, PhD, is professor emerita at Acadia University in Wolfville, Nova Scotia. She has taught history of recreation and parks and history of leisure courses for over 30 years and is a practitioner and consultant in recreation and parks planning. Markham-Starr is one of the leading Canadian experts regarding the history of recreation and parks systems and volunteer organizations. She is the former president of the Canadian Association for Leisure Studies (CALS) and served as chair for the Canadian Parks and Recreation Association (CPRA) Editorial Committee and Integrated Research Dissemination Project, and the Wolfville Recreation Commission. Markham-Starr wrote the CPRA research policy and coedited its 50th-anniversary publication. She was a board member of the Leisure Information Network; and the first managing editor of *PHEnex*, an online open access journal. She contributed to the background papers of the Canadian Recreation Summit in 2011 and to the advisory committee of the Canadian Parks Summit in 2016 and the Canadian Parks Conference in 2017. She also wrote the first City of Halifax recreation master plan and is a member of CALS.

Bruce Martin, PhD, is an associate professor and department chair in the department of recreation and sport pedagogy at Ohio University in Athens, Ohio. He has been in higher education since 1998, and he has significant and varied experience as an outdoor leader and instructor. He has worked as a camp counselor, professional river guide, and Outward Bound instructor. Martin has been associated with and served in varying capacities for professional organizations such as the Association for Experiential Education, the Wilderness Education Association, the Leave No Trace Center for Outdoor Ethics, the American Canoe Association, and the Association for Outdoor Recreation and Education. His current teaching and research interests are focused on the practice of outdoor leadership and adventure programming. At Ohio University, he regularly teaches both theoretically oriented and practically based courses related to outdoor leadership, adventure programming, and experiential education. Martin is also author of numerous publications related to outdoor leadership and adventure programming.

Juan Tortosa Martínez, PhD, is an associate professor in physical activity and sport science at the University of Alicante, Spain. He earned his undergraduate degree from the University of Valencia. He lived for several years in Illinois, where he earned a master's degree in recreation, park, and tourism administration at Western Illinois University. During this time, Tortosa worked in various recreation settings from the small rural community of Virginia, Illinois, to the city of Elgin, Illinois. He has been interested in comparing the leisure and recreation fields in the United States and Spain, publishing three papers about the topic in Spain and teaching an international seminar in the University of Alicante with students from Western Illinois University and students from the University of Alicante about leisure and recreation in Spain and United States. His research has been shifting to leisure, physical activity and aging, as well as physical activity and recreation for special populations. He currently runs various therapeutic physical activity and recreation programs for people with mental health problems and people with mild cognitive impairment and Alzheimer's disease.

Donald J. McLean, PhD, is a professor and coordinator in the department of recreation, park, and tourism administration at Western Illinois University–Quad Cities in Moline, Illinois. He holds advanced degrees in both philosophy and recreation and leisure studies. He coauthored *Issues in Recreation and Leisure: Ethical Decision Making* (2005) with Daniel Yoder for Human Kinetics. He is also a certified interpretive trainer as well as a member of the National Association for Interpretation and the Visitor Studies Association. In his leisure time, he enjoys downhill skiing, walking, and golfing (which, as Samuel Clemens says, simply "is a good walk spoiled").

Ellen O'Sullivan, PhD, serves as principal for Leisure Lifestyle Consulting. She is the author of two marketing books for the field as well as two of the original benefit-based publications for NRPA. In her roles as camper, camp counselor, community recreation director, college professor, and consultant, O'Sullivan has witnessed firsthand the power of play, parks, and recreation for people and society. She is an NRPA National Distinguished Professional and received the William Sutherland Award from the American Academy of Parks and Recreation for Outstanding Practice. She also served as lead trainer for Hearts N' Parks, a project that she helped develop in North Carolina that led to a nationwide program for the National Institutes of Health that established the groundwork for further initiatives into health and wellness by the park and recreation movement. She created the initial benefits program for NRPA that addressed the four essential benefit categories for parks and recreation: individual, community, environmental, and economic.

Robert E. Pfister, PhD, is a retired professor with the department of recreation and tourism management at Vancouver Island University (VIU) in Nanaimo, British Columbia, Canada, where he currently serves as an adjunct faculty member. For over 35 years, Pfister instructed courses in entrepreneurial recreation and tourism to students in the United States and Canada. He held full-time tenured faculty appointments at California State University at Pomona, University of Northern British Columbia, and East Carolina University (ECU). In 2010, the ECU College of Health and Human Performance bestowed on Pfister the meritorious and emeritus service award for his contribution during his time there. In 2011, he was recognized at the VIU commencement ceremony for his teaching, scholarship, and leadership in creating a new graduate program focused on sustainability in recreation and tourism. Pfister is a member of the Association of American Geographers and served as chairperson of the recreation, tourism, and sports specialty group. He is a member of the Society of Park and Recreation Educators, the Canadian Council for Small Business and Entrepreneurship, and the World Leisure Organization. He served on the editorial board of *Tourism Geographies* and on the board of directors for Tourism Vancouver Island and Tourism Prince George, both regional tourism destination marketing organizations.

Arianne C. Reis, PhD, is a senior lecturer in leisure and recreation studies at Western Sydney University. Reis is originally from Brazil, where she completed her undergraduate and master's studies in physical education. Before completing her PhD work at the University of Otago, New Zealand, Reis worked for several years for public and private institutions in Brazil in the fields of nature-based recreation and sport management. Her research interests have developed from these professional experiences and have focused on outdoor recreation and the sustainability issues of sport events. Reis has presented her work in local, national, and international conferences, and her research has been published in sport, tourism, and recreation journals and books over the past decade. She is a member of the International Academy for the Development of Tourism Research in Brazil and was the executive board member of the Australian and New Zealand Association for Leisure Studies (ANZALS) from 2013 to 2016.

Terry Robertson, PhD, is the interim associate dean at California State University Long Beach. Formerly, he was professor and chair of the department of health, physical education, recreation, and dance at Northwest Missouri State University. Robertson worked in various areas of health for several years (i.e., director of special services for Clark County Parks and Recreation Department in Las Vegas, Nevada, consultant to long-term care and managed care organizations, substance abuse counselor, case manager, and assistant director of rehab services for a small hospital). As an educator, Robertson has continued his contact with the field through consulting and through special university-related programs and research projects. Current research projects are focused on at-risk and adjudicated youth as well as the development of regional health care cooperatives. He has consulted for a variety of municipalities, including the cities of Las Vegas, Reno, and San Jose; the North Suburban Special Recreation District; the Nevada and Florida Developmental Disabilities Councils; and a host of not-for-profit agencies and health care agencies. He is a past president of the National Therapeutic Recreation Society and of the Midland Empire Independent Living Center Board of Directors (currently serving nine counties).

Jerome F. Singleton, PhD, CTRS, is a professor in the recreation and leisure studies department in the School of Health and Human Performance at Dalhousie University. He is also cross-appointed to the school of nursing, the sociology and anthropology departments, and faculty of management at Dalhousie. Singleton's research is focused on leisure and aging. He graduated from the University of Waterloo with a bachelor's degree in recreation with honors, completed his master of science degree in recreation at Pennsylvania State University, and received his PhD in leisure studies at the University of Maryland. He also completed the academic requirements for a doctorate certificate in gerontology at the University of Maryland. Currently Singleton teaches courses in therapeutic recreation and aging, therapeutic recreation techniques, and introduction to recreation and leisure and aging at Dalhousie University. He was made a fellow of the World Demographic Association in 2006 and was named Professional of the Year by the Canadian Therapeutic Recreation Association in 2007. He was recognized by the recreation and leisure studies program at the University of Waterloo as a distinguished alumni in 2008 and is the founding member of the Leisure and Aging Research Group, which was established in 2008. Singleton received the Dr. Gonzaga da Gama Memorial Award from the Canadian Therapeutic Recreation Association in 2011 and was made a fellow of the Academy of Leisure Science by the Society of Park and Recreation Educators in 2011. Singleton is currently a research associate with the Dalhousie European Center of Excellence. He has advised 25 graduate students who have investigated questions related to leisure and aging and has published over 80 journal articles during his career and made local, national, and international presentations related to the area of leisure and aging. He has served on the editorial boards for *Therapeutic Recreation Journal*, *American Therapeutic Recreation Annual*, *Topics in Geriatric Rehabilitation*, and *Recreation and Society in Africa, Asia, and Latin America*. He has reviewed articles for *Loisir*, *Leisure Science*, and *Topics in Geriatric Rehabilitation*.

Jill R. Sturts, PhD, is an assistant professor in the department of recreation and leisure studies at Virginia Wesleyan University, where she teaches in the recreation management concentration. She completed a BA at Baldwin Wallace University, a MEd at Bowling Green State University, and a PhD at Indiana University. Her professional experience is in campus recreation and recreational programming. She is a member of NIRSA: Leaders in Collegiate Recreation and The Academy of Leisure Sciences, an editorial board member for the Recreational Sports Journal, and a faculty member for the NIRSA School of Collegiate Recreation. She has delivered multiple presentations at the local, state, national, and international levels on issues related to recreational sport management, physical activity, and pedagogy.

Matthew Symonds, EdD, is an associate professor in the School of Health Science and Wellness at Northwest Missouri State University. Symonds also coordinated the university's faculty and staff wellness program for eight years. His primary teaching responsibilities are in the applied health and sport science area and his research interests are in physical activity and sport behavior. Symonds has served as board president and is in his fifth term on the Maryville Parks and Recreation Board of Directors. Symonds is also a past president and former health division chair of the Missouri Association for Health, Physical Education, Recreation, and Dance.

Patrick T. Tierney, PhD, is a professor in the department of recreation, parks, and tourism at San Francisco State University. He received a PhD in recreation resources management and a master's in recreation resources from Colorado State University. Tierney is the author of numerous research projects, such as an economic impact study of the California ski industry, and co-author of the textbook *Recreation, Event and Tourism Businesses: Startup and Sustainable Operations*. For 25 years, Tierney was co-owner/operator of Adrift Adventures, a touring and experiential education business, with a seasonal staff of 27, offering summer whitewater rafting and adventure learning programs in Colorado, Utah, and Alaska. His roles were manager of operations and finance and he was the primary National Park Service contract liaison. The company was nominated for the Conde Nast Traveler Magazine International Ecotourism Award.

Julie Voelker-Morris, MS, is a senior instructor in arts and cultural programming at the University of Oregon. She is the editor of *CultureWork: A Periodic Broadside for Arts & Culture Workers*, an electronic publication of the University of Oregon Center for Community Arts and Cultural Policy. She has served in various positions for theater companies across multiple states, including the general manager for Lord Leebrick Theatre Company in Eugene, Oregon. Voelker-Morris is a member of the Association of Arts Administration Educators and the National Art Education Association. She is a recipient of the Rippey Innovative Teaching Award.

Daniel G. Yoder, PhD, is a professor and chair in the recreation, park, and tourism department at Western Illinois University in Macomb. His research and teaching are focused on leisure and sociology. In his position as a parks and recreation director in Colorado, he observed and organized activities for a diverse group of people and faced practical leisure and sociological issues on a daily basis. He coauthored *Issues in Recreation and Leisure: Ethical Decision Making* (2005) with Don McLean for Human Kinetics. Yoder is a member of the Academy of Leisure Sciences and the Illinois Park and Recreation Association, having served in a number of positions with the IPRA. He is also involved in a variety of nonprofit organizations dealing with recreation and youth in his community. Yoder has served on various university committees and boards. Besides his teaching and community involvement, he is a husband, father, part-time farmer, full-time conservationist, and avid beekeeper. Because optimal experiences have profoundly affected Yoder's life, he is committed to the exploration of this life-enriching phenomenon for himself and others.